Elders Of Edens

"CAT 6 - 2033"

Dear Reader,

As I embarked on the journey of crafting this novel, music became my constant companion, much like it does for one of the central characters. The melodies helped shape the vibrant and evocative scenes you are about to experience. I invite you to immerse yourself in this world with a similar harmony.

*To enhance your reading experience, I've curated a playlist titled **"Elders of Edens CAT6"** on your preferred music platform currently on Spotify. Each time you encounter the word **"Song"** in the text, I encourage you to play that popular track from the playlist. Should you lose your place, fret not; simply let the music flow as you continue reading, trusting that the symphony will guide you. Some may be cut short, but that's part of the plan.*

Go to eldersofedens.com for more information.

*Start the first **"Song"** now!....*

With best regards,

R. H. Burton

Prologue:

Start the first **"Song"** now. *Child in Time*

The alarm blared, shattering the tense silence. Relief swept through the room as the deafening sound abruptly ceased. V scanned the faces around her, heart pounding. Fair sat on the cold floor, prompting the others to follow her lead. V realized her tablet was back in her room and reached for Alex's instead.

"Tap the sun icon at the bottom left of your tablets," Fair instructed, her voice strained but steady. "You'll see the countdown. The power might flicker when the shockwave hits. Turn off your tablets a minute before and turn them back on a minute afterward."

V, sitting close to Alex, glanced at his tablet. Four minutes remained.

"Where are Candido and Tonari? Are we all going to die?" Prezzy's voice trembled with fear.

"They bolted when the alarm went off," V replied, tense. "Kahput went after them. He'll bring them back safely."

Fair, attempting to steady herself, spoke again, "We're not going to die. I've been through this before. We're inside the moon. We're safe."

Prezzy's voice wavered. "What was it like last time?"

Fair's calm facade cracked. "There's a shockwave coming. The lights might go out, and static electricity could surge. Things might get thrown around. We weren't ready for this one, so it won't be pretty. But next time, we'll be prepared." She checked her tablet. "Three minutes left."

V's gaze swept the room. Fear etched every face. Even Rugrog and Fair, veterans of this experience, remained glued to their tablets, anxiously watching the countdown.

She glanced at Alex, who met her eyes with a reassuring smile, his arm wrapped protectively around her. The timer read two minutes. She shivered, trying to suppress the rising dread.

"Get ready to turn off your tablets," Rugrog's voice rang out.

Just then, Kahput burst through the door, Tonari and Candido in tow. Relief and anxiety intermingled as everyone shouted their names. Kahput urged them to sit and stay calm. Tonari sobbed while Candido, pale and petrified, clung to her, his wide eyes fixed on the ceiling.

Kahput and Rugrog exchanged grim looks. The university was unprepared. They had all seen images of the sun's explosive solar flares in class.

V glanced at Alex's tablet as it dimmed. She searched his face for reassurance but found only mirrored uncertainty. Her thoughts raced. I should have stayed with the Intelligence Bureau. At least I would have lived. What was I thinking? No one's thinking about the main catastrophe. We're just hoping to survive this Pulse Reversal, whatever that is.

In the vault, Tonari's sobs grew louder. Candido clung to her, trembling. Declan held Miko close, their eyes shut tight. Lin huddled with Lev in the corner, his gaze unblinking. Prezzy, tears streaming, nestled under Swaraj's protective arm, stared at the ceiling, hopeless.

V closed her eyes, mentally counting down. Fifteen people are in this vault, buried inside the moon. No one will find us. This is the end.

SNAP! The lights went out. Her eyes flew open. In the hallway, emergency lights flickered weakly.

"Here we go! Hold on!" Kahput's voice cut through the darkness.

How much longer? Are we going to die? No, they've survived this before. The Creator, my grandmother's warnings... It's happening sooner than predicted. Believe what you see. The Creator wouldn't have warned us if we weren't meant to survive. We will make it, she thought desperately.

She turned to Alex to speak, but then it hit. CRASH! The university shook violently. The noise was deafening. She squeezed her eyes shut. No, no, stop. This can't be happening. She felt herself sliding across the cold floor, back and forth, as the room lurched. The shockwave seemed endless. Seconds later, a surge of electricity filled the room.

Blinding flashes of light burst through the door. Please stop, she pleaded silently as the cacophony of noise reverberated through the university. Safety deposit boxes flung open, doors slammed against walls, and crashes echoed down the hallway.

Alex held her tightly, offering what little comfort he could. She opened her eyes just as darkness enveloped them again, punctuated only by intermittent flashes from the open door. When will it stop? Are we going to die? This is no longer just a university, she thought, panic rising.

Static electricity prickled her skin, making her hair stand on end. She felt the cold floor beneath her as the relentless sliding finally ceased. Moments later, the flashing lights and deafening noises faded, leaving behind only the sound of sobbing and whimpering. Tonari and Maria were especially distraught.

"I think it's over. Everyone okay?" Kahput's voice was cautious.

"Yeah, we're okay," Lev responded after a deep, shaky breath.

Declan let out a nervous chuckle. "We made it."

"Everyone, stay put," Rugrog advised. "Wait a minute, then turn on your flashlights. It'll take a while to restore power, but everything's going to be okay." V watched as he stood up, peered out the door, and then returned to his spot. "Let's wait just a little longer," he said, his breathing heavy.

I'm never leaving my tablet behind again. At least we made it. Why didn't I tell them about the messenger right away? V's thoughts were a whirlwind of regret as she began to tear up.

Fair took a deep breath, her voice shaky but trying to sound reassuring. "That wasn't too bad. I wish we'd known in advance. Next time, we'll be better prepared. Sorry about that."

"It wasn't supposed to happen to you all for a couple of years. Now I see why Alex and V are receiving these extraordinary Gifts so soon. It makes sense now."

V clung to Alex, tears streaming down her cheeks. *I should've told them about the Creator's message. Why didn't I speak up right away? This information is too critical. I see that now.*

She began to shake Alex, her voice barely a whisper. "Why didn't we tell them? What's wrong with us?" Alex, still shaken by the ordeal, struggled to find the right words.

Seeing V in tears, Alex felt helpless but tried to console her. "It's going to be okay. We'll tell them when they get back," he whispered.

But V couldn't wait any longer. She whispered urgently, "I need to tell Fair now, Alex! Now!" Alex, sensing her distress, held her even tighter, offering silent support.

Barely able to speak through her tears, V turned to Fair. "Fair, Alex and I have more to tell you and the other Elders about Friday night."

Fair chuckled softly. "We knew there was more. There's no way an Eagle Transfer can happen without a prayer or some interaction from the Creator."

"You saw something, didn't you? We all felt it. Something happened Friday night, didn't it? We just didn't know what it was. Let's discuss it in the common room in an hour. How does that sound?"

V, almost blubbering now, nodded, resting her head on Alex. "Okay. I'm not sure why we didn't tell you right away."

"It's okay, you're telling us now," Fair reassured her with a gentle smile.

Kahput's tablet illuminated the room as everyone began to stand. V shielded her eyes in shame as they all rose.

Alex helped her to her feet. "We'll figure it out together," he said, his voice full of determination.

"Go ahead and turn on your tablets and lights; it's safe now," Kahput confirmed.

As the room filled with light, a few hesitant smiles appeared as they all started to leave the vault of doom.

V felt the tightness in her chest and the congestion from crying begin to ease as they walked down the hallway toward the dining area and the common room of the university.

Table of Contents

I

While listening to the third **"Song,"** *Your Lullaby,* he felt the sun's high-energy photons penetrating his skin, coursing through his arms and face, stirring a warmth within. Their journey from the depths of space to the surface of his being invited contemplation. Some were absorbed, others ricocheted, while a few ventured off into the ether. Tilting his head back, he absorbed the spectacle, his gaze capturing every nuance of the landscape, until a solitary magpie, straying from his brothers and sisters' V formation, seized his attention. In that moment, he felt an inexplicable bond with the lone bird, a connection deeper than mere observation.

A dreamer and a thinker, he had engaged in a spirited six-hour discussion with friends the previous day, dissecting the mysteries surrounding Göbekli Tepe, Puma Punku, and the Pyramids of Giza.

Music served as his constant companion, fueling his thoughts and guiding his reflections. Each note was a thread weaving through the tapestry of his mind, stitching together fragments of memory and emotion.

Whether with one earbud or two, he reveled in the symphony of sound, a backdrop to his journey through the Northern Territory, where he traversed dusty roads on his desert racer, immersed in the rhythm of creation.

Alexander Cooper Katz, a descendant of the unknown Cooper Maximilian Katz—a German from the Rhine River imprisoned over two centuries ago for impersonating an Egyptian valuator and assayer—sensed the winds of change stirring in his bones.

As the sun dipped below the horizon, casting a fiery glow upon the land, memories of yesterday's meeting soured his mood.

A part of his conversation had dealt with political intrigue—a tangled web of deceit and ambition that tainted the serenity of the moment. Observing the magpies as they reunited in formation, he marveled at their innate understanding of life's rhythms. *They know their purpose, their place in the world, while humanity stumbles blindly forward, shackled by its own folly.*

1

Gazing upon the sandy soil beneath his feet, he contemplated humanity's legacy of conflict and strife.

It's a legacy I long to transcend, to forge a path toward a brighter future.

With a sense of urgency, he plucked a Larapinta flower from its home in the sandy soil, its fragile beauty a stark contrast to the harsh realities of the world. Perpetual wars and power-hungry leaders—these were the chains that bound humanity to its past. Yet, in the shadows of ancient monuments, he glimpsed the possibility of redemption.

The Pyramids of Giza Puma Punku—all bore witness to a time when humanity stood united, its collective will harnessed for a higher purpose.

As he scrolled through images on his phone, questions swirled in his mind. *How were they built? Who built them?*

It was a puzzle he was determined to solve, a mystery that held the key to humanity's salvation. For in the silence of the desert, amidst the whispers of forgotten civilizations, Alexander knew in his bones that change was coming—if not to the world, then to him.

The **"Song"** changed. *Nessun Dorma*

Skip exclaimed, "They're coming! Mate, they're coming!"

Alex turned and saw a 20-foot dust wake approaching. Raising his hands toward his uncle to confirm that he heard him, he then sprinted back to the makeshift pit area.

Alex and his family raced the Finke for fun and for advertising purposes for the family business. They knew they weren't going to win this time—it was a family tradition. It was day two, and they were 100 kilometers from Alice Springs. Just a quick pit stop before the end of the race. Earlier that day, Skip and Alex had spent some time exploring near the track.

Filled with adrenaline, Alex and Skip Katz sprang into action. The Katz family desert racer dubbed the "There and Back," roared towards them with one thousand horsepower.

The vehicle, sporting a Monarch Orange body, Screaming Green Rhino rims, and Maxxis forty-inch Trepador tires, drifted over the red sand at over two hundred kilometers an hour before skidding to a halt.

They swiftly added fuel to the vehicle, checked the tires, and hastily cleaned the forward and rear camera lenses.

Skip removed the mesh netting on the passenger side door window to check on Alex's sister, Audrey, while Alex hurried to talk to his dad, Max.

"How's it going?" Alex asked as Max adjusted his helmet to speak.

"Everything is running smoothly. The whoops are vicious. My kidneys hurt. Better than last time. Much drier. We could have a chance this year." He chuckled. "See you back at camp."

Max, with a mischievous grin, replied. Although Alex couldn't see it, he could tell by the squint in his eyes.

Alex said, "Okay. Great, Dad. Good luck. See you then." He waved his hands forward, signaling his father to proceed down the track. Max hit the accelerator. Even with earbuds in, the noise was unbearable, and Alex's face was pelted with sand and small rocks as the racer sped off down the dirt road.

Alex and Skip leaped into the air, celebrating like two linebackers after a quarterback sack, exchanging an enthusiastic high five.

"That was fun. I'm glad Audrey got a chance to ride this year," Skip exclaimed to Alex as they gathered their tools. After tapping some dirt off his boots, Skip grabbed the checkered flag shop towel and placed it in the tool cart while Alex took hold of the lift gate handle.

With a somber expression, Alex turned to Skip. "By the time everyone gets home from the race, I'll only have half a day before I have to fly off. It just seems like time flew by so fast. I hope I can get back before the four years are up for another race."

His uncle, an engineer like his father, stood six feet five inches tall, dark-skinned from the desert sun, and bald. Skip grabbed his hat, slapped it on his knee a couple of times, and then reached for a couple of beers. "Full scholarship, everything paid? I didn't even know you were thinking about another four years of university."

As the tool cart rolled into the truck, Alex replied, "I wasn't, but it seemed like such an incredible opportunity. I couldn't say no."

Skip nodded. "Great, let's finish loading the truck."

As they drove through the bush outback, Alex grabbed his phone, picked out some music, and looked over to Skip. "Check out this **"Song"** *Deutschland* I found last week." He put his phone down and drummed his hands on the dashboard. Skip, half-listening turned down the radio.

I'm not sure why that Harvey guy had me do a physical. Why did he need a blood sample and retinal scan? That part was weird. Alex gazed into the distance, pondering.

He glanced over to Skip, expecting a response to the music or even a smile, while their bodies jiggled vigorously in the big U.S.-made M-35 truck, historically called the "Deuce and a Half."

Looking out the windshield as the sunset dimmed, Alex remarked, "It's going to be a beautiful night back at camp." There was a five-knot wind, and the temperature was around 16 degrees Celsius. It was the King's birthday weekend celebration. A big bush party would be happening around Alice Springs.

Skip shook his head and asked, "Who is this 'Harvey guy'—your recruiter? Harvey Goldmen? Isn't he originally from the U.S.? What's your major for your master's, anyhow?"

Alex perked up, turned in his seat, and waved his hands as he explained, "I want to be a design engineer. I want to learn how to build the ultimate desert racer with the ultimate engine and fuel—maybe even more advanced than a Formula One-type engine."

Skip glanced over at Alex and said, "In five to six years, maybe it will be your design. Maybe your buggy, with your engine. Maybe you'll be the one to break the record at Finke. Right!"

Alex leaned forward in his seat. "I wanted to follow in my dad's and your footsteps in Design Engineering."

Skip smiled, raising his eyebrows. "How you came up with the design of the injectors on that Cadillac engine, I'll never know."

"And you get to go to the U.S. You'll be the first Katz to be out of the country for a couple of generations. That's saying something."

Alex started thinking about leaving again and what Harvey had told him about school. He had never been outside Australia before. *What will it be like in the United States?*

A minute later, his expression went blank, his face still. Something stirred in his mind, a feeling he had never experienced before. He suddenly yelled, "Stop the truck!" The **"Song"** changed. *Tantrum*

Skip slammed on the brakes, and the truck skidded to an abrupt stop on the sandy road.

Alex and Skip looked up into the distance as around twenty kangaroos emerged from the bush—some fast, some slow. A couple stopped in the middle of the road and seemed to look right at them as if to say hello.

Skip, gripping the steering wheel, glanced quickly at Alex, who was still in a daze, then back at the road. "What the hell, son?"

The truck rolled forward slowly, nearing the lingering kangaroos. Skip took a deep breath. "Did you see them coming? How did you know?"

Alex said nothing. Then he smiled as he took in the view of the country and the sunset. He put his fingers up to cover his nostrils and down to his chin, scratching at his unshaven jaw, deep in thought. Finally, he turned to his uncle with complete confidence, raising a finger.

"Have you ever thought about how it all started? This world? Us? Our consciousness? After millions of years, how did the planet become like this?"

Skip released his grip on the wheel, taking an even bigger breath, and looked further down the road. "You okay? What the hell are you talking about?"

Alex sat up, turned in his seat, and excitedly looked straight at him. "Trillions of planets, trillions of stars, galaxies—how many are like this? None. *What a world this is!*"

He turned back to the road. "It's all too perfect. The way the cycles are. The patterns. Just look at them. Those roos. Not a care in the world. *How is it all like this? Why are we the way we are? Tell me that.*"

"Look at these pyramids," Alex held up his phone. "How did they build them? Who built them? I'm going to try and figure it all out."

The sun had now dipped below the horizon, and the remaining kangaroo left the road.

"It's like *a world beyond worlds.* How?" Alex looked off into the distance in awe.

Skip laughed, hit the gas, and the truck sped down the dirt road. He looked over at Alex, smirked, paused, and said, "You are a strange bird, Alexander Cooper Katz. One of a kind. Maybe you're from a different world? Aye. I love yah, mate."

An hour or so later, darkness enveloped the surroundings as Alex and Skip arrived at the Katz family campsite.

The **"Song"** changed. *Spirit of Capricorn.*

In the midst of this lively scene, Max, Alex's father, approached the group, his face smudged with dust from his quad racing adventures just moments before, resembling a raccoon. A well-built, handsome man, Max bore the signs of the sun on his red-tanned skin.

The glow from the makeshift firepit and tiki torches lent an ethereal quality to the campsite, highlighting the camaraderie of the Katz family.

As Max's gaze flickered between the flames and his family, he addressed them, his face alight with the fire's glow. "Another successful race, though we didn't clinch the win this time. But here's to next year—aiming for victory!" He chuckled. "However, we must acknowledge that my son Alex won't be here next year to aid our preparations." He pointed to Alex.

"Yet, I trust he'll return in time for race day. So, Skip, Audrey, and my dear wife, who keeps us fed and warm during the race, will need to fill Alex's shoes."

Ella, his wife, shot Max a curious, somewhat incredulous glance, silently questioning his timing.

"Alex is off to university, embarking on a journey filled with learning, abundant opportunities—and possibly love." He chuckled again. "Here's to all of us!"

Max raised his beer, taking a hearty swig, his face radiant with pride.

"Cheers!" echoed around the camp as everyone lifted their drinks in unison.

Amidst the festivities, Alex's sister, with a playful grin, initiated some lively dancing, sparking laughter among the family. Ella rose from her seat to embrace Alex, her affectionate gesture barely audible over the din. "We're going to miss you! Please be careful."

The party continued well into the night.

The following day, Alex, Max, Ella, and Audrey gathered at Gate 9 of Darwin International Airport, poised for Alex's departure to Boston, Massachusetts.

As they rose to board, Audrey, with a mischievous grin and a warm hug, quipped, "Good luck at MIT. Watch out for those blondes in the U.S.!"

Alex, with a raised eyebrow, gently pushed her away. "Sure thing, love you too." Then, with a whisper, he added, "You know you're blonde." He chuckled.

Max, towering over Alex by only a few inches, extended a firm handshake, his grin akin to the Cheshire cat's. "Make us proud, Alex. Not that we have any doubt. Love you, mate."

Ella, a striking blonde exuding a sense of quiet strength, wrapped her arms around Alex, her touch conveying a mix of pride and maternal concern. "Alex," she murmured, holding him close, "I love you, son. Whatever you need, just let us know." After a lingering embrace, she reluctantly released him, her eyes shimmering with unshed tears.

"Final boarding, Gate 9," echoed over the loudspeakers as Max imparted some final words of advice to his son, his expression suddenly serious. "I know what you did for the family and for your brother. I'm proud of you. But I don't want you to take risks like that again. Losing a few fingers was lucky compared to what could've happened."

Alex, taken aback by his father's unexpected admonition, straightened his posture, meeting his father's gaze squarely. "Yes, sir," he replied, his mind racing with questions. *He knows. I wonder, does my mother? And what happened to Melissa? Where has she been since my brother's death?*

As his family bid him farewell with waves and words of encouragement, Alex's thoughts were consumed by the unknown journey ahead.

Walking down the expansive airport corridor, Alex pivots right, trailing the gate signs, his mind swirling with anticipation. *This is it. America. Which tune should I play? Which playlist should I start for the long flight?* Lost in thought, he barely notices the security guard's interruption.

"Are you Alex Katz?" the guard inquires.

Alex, his brow furrowing in confusion, nods. "Yeah, that's me."

With a nod, the guard ushers Alex toward a door, swiftly punching in a security code before guiding him through.

"Here you go, sir," the guard offers.

"Mr. Goldmen?" Alex queries, curiosity piqued. "I wasn't aware I was meeting you here."

Harvey, standing just under six feet with wavy brown hair cascading over his collar, possesses a tan complexion hinting at Middle Eastern heritage. His West Coast American accent is evident. Clad in grey slacks and a faded plaid jacket sans tie, he extends a warm smile.

"Alex, it's wonderful to see you. I'd like to chat before we depart. It concerns the next four years and what lies ahead. Shall we find an airport restaurant and talk for a few minutes?"

Alex, still puzzled, responds, "Certainly, no problem. But what about my luggage?"

Motioning for Alex to follow, Harvey reassures him, "I've taken care of your luggage. I'll fill you in on everything over a snack. Are you more excited about leaving home, or is the prospect of traveling and school piquing your interest?"

Alex replies, "I'm thrilled about returning to school and exploring new places. There's so much to look forward to."

As they stroll, Alex contemplates. *Why is Harvey here? This seems excessive for MIT. What's going on?* They turn the corner and see the restaurant.

Harvey draws a deep breath. Now sitting at the table, he fixes his gaze on Alex. "So, have you been curious about the extent of the tests and evaluations we put you through to gain entry to the university?"

Alex reflects. "I found the retinal scan and blood draw puzzling, not to mention the lengthy written exams. It felt rather military-like."

Harvey grins knowingly. "Indeed, there's much you're unaware of. Keep an open mind as I explain." With a reassuring smile, Harvey continues, "There are twelve individuals globally, much like you, with unique genetics and AB Neutral blood type. They emerge once every four thousand years, and you're among them."

Alex leans in, intrigued but questioning. "What are you talking about?"

The table is silent as the waiter brings the chips and beers.

Harvey leans back, taking a long swig of his beer. "We're redirecting you to a special institution, the Eternal University, for four years. Your cohort, including yourself, holds a specific responsibility for humanity. I don't want to tell you too much now. You will start to learn all about it tomorrow at the university."

As Alex absorbs this revelation, Harvey adds, "You're part of a lineage tasked with preserving knowledge and guiding civilization, akin to the stewards of bygone civilizations—ones not yet known by our modern society."

Alex, astounded, hesitates before responding, "Is this some sort of elaborate prank?" He looks around the room, searching for signs that others might be in on it.

Harvey meets his gaze squarely. "You're all remarkably intelligent, pursuing advanced degrees. There are twelve of you—six females, six males—each possessing extraordinary potential. Do you believe in a higher power?"

Harvey pauses, scanning the restaurant before continuing, looking around as if someone is watching. "The Creator, as referred to in our historical past, has bestowed special Gifts upon the Elders like you throughout history. There is a cataclysm that hits the planet every forty-four hundred years."

"The people it happened to last time are going to teach you what to do. Gig and Fem—you will meet them tonight. They are the Master Elders. Do you believe in a Creator?" He places both hands on the table, waiting for a response.

Alex, grappling with the enormity of this revelation, exhales slowly. "I don't know. It's a topic I've thought about once in a while." He leans back in his seat. "The intricacies of our world suggest a higher design for sure. I've thought about this often. But all of this—it's overwhelming. I don't see how it happened all on its own. My family… do they know about any of this? And what's an Elder?"

Harvey interjects, "Your accomplishments are staggering. You've set speed records for patented innovations—all at just twenty-one. You're uniquely qualified for what awaits. You were chosen, actually."

Alex, still processing, mutters, "Shit, Harvey. No MIT. Can I say no?"

Harvey pauses, scanning the restaurant again. "Look, this is going to be far better than anything MIT has to offer. Since I've known you, Alex, I've seen that you're searching for something. You're going to find many of the answers you've been looking for. If you say yes, your questions will be answered, I assure you. And you will eventually be able to help humanity in the process. I mean, really help."

"For a long time. These people have been around for thousands and thousands of years. We've talked about such things."

Alex, adjusting in his seat, suggests he might be giving in. He sees a Lear-type jet taking off through the window and thinks, *I can always come back. Right?* He pauses… "Alright, let's do this. I don't know what this is, but I'm willing to give it a try."

With a final handshake, Harvey reassures Alex, "You're embarking on an extraordinary journey. Trust me."

As they exit the restaurant, Alex's mind races. *What have I gotten myself into now?*

Alex walked briskly down the corridor, thoughts swirling in his mind. *I went with Uncle Skip to Tasmania, to Boyd Island—just the two of us—for a two-week survival challenge. I have a feeling this is going to be a hundred times more extreme. And how did Harvey know about that trip?*

After about three minutes of navigating various corridors and hallways, they arrived at two unusually large double doors.

A keypad adorned the wall next to the giant door. It was accompanied by a sign reading:

"Alva Global Industrial" "10100101 Mont-Blanc Terrace"

"Mont-Blanc, Geneva" "Switzerland"

"Emergency, Please Contact"

"Rev or Mod @agi.com"011-41-22-555-2151" "Code in, AGI Australia"

"Instructions will be given"

Alex speculates. *We must be at the far end of the airport. What's going to happen in the next four years? What the hell have I gotten myself into now?*

Harvey pointed to the keypad. "Put your eye up to the keypad. You can enter or exit this building at any time, day or night."

"Alva Global is the corporation we all use. If you need anything—anything on or off the planet—use this contact information. Buildings to enter, secure video calls anytime from anywhere. Your contact email is ack@agi.com

Alex thought, *What does he mean 'on or off the planet'?*

Harvey continued, "Rev and Mod are your main contacts on Terraenti. You are a very important person now, Alex."

What the hell is Terraenti? Alex wondered silently.

Harvey smiled. "Send them an email, and they'll contact you through the tablet you'll get tomorrow. Memorize this information."

Alex nodded. "Alright, I'll memorize the info."

Harvey gestured for Alex to put his eye up to the pad. The red light turned green. "Now, type in your email address," Harvey instructed. "You can use either to enter."

Alex complied, and after a metallic clunk, the doors opened automatically.

Inside, the room featured tiled floors, a family-style area with couches and a flat-screen, and a sleek kitchen. Two black custom Subaru SUVs stood on the right, while another smaller door with a keypad occupied the opposite wall. A ceiling boom suggested heavy lifting capabilities. "Make yourself comfortable."

"We'll be leaving in the next half hour," Harvey said, heading to the kitchen. "The flight takes around three hours; you should use the head. There's one on the ship, but it's not very comfortable or private."

"The head?" Alex queried.

Harvey chuckled. "The toilet. It's through there."

Alex made his way through an archway, noting a storage area on the right filled with safety gear, guns, water, tools, and a plethora of canned and freeze-dried food—reminiscent of a prepper's stash. The bathrooms were to the left. After finishing in the bathroom, Alex returned.

Harvey called out, "You're an aggressive, focused person, right?"

Alex approached the kitchen. "Yeah, I guess so."

"In the next four years, you must focus. Double your efforts. Stay out of trouble, and if possible, avoid relationships. Total commitment to what you're learning. Understand?"

"I get it. Focus," Alex replied, still taking in the surroundings.

The double doors opened again, their presence a constant reminder of the new path unfolding before him. Two women burst into the building, locked in a heated argument.

One, a tan and attractive blonde, wore short cutoff jeans and a T-shirt under a hoodie that looked like it belonged at the beach. She was clearly upset. "I told you I'd go, but I'm not happy about it. I've been planning my trip to Santa Barbara for years now."

The older woman had an enigmatic beauty. Her skin was darker, her large, alien-like blue eyes striking against her chestnut hair. She was fit and stood at the same height as Harvey, dressed in a green and blue pantsuit adorned with an array of jewelry. She tried to calm the younger woman. "Trust me, this experience will be far beyond anything you could have imagined."

As they approached the kitchen, Harvey greeted them with a smile. "Hello, this is Alex Katz. Alex, meet Prezzy Bondi and Beauta. And, of course, I'm Harvey." Alex smiled and nodded at Prezzy, who returned the gesture.

Harvey then turned to Beauta, chuckling as he offered a big hug. "Long time no see! How are you? What's it been, three days?"

Beauta smiled back and hugged him. "Yes, good to see you, Harvey. Did you visit your family?"

"Yes," Harvey replied. "Did you check the ship?"

"Yesterday. Everything is great," Beauta confirmed.

Harvey glanced at the clock on the wall. "Alright, it's time. We need to head out."

They walked to a smaller door where Harvey pointed to four sets of odd-looking coveralls hanging on hooks. The gray suits were unattractive, equipped with two small hose connections and numerous buckles.

"Put these on over your clothes," he instructed. "You don't have anything pointy in your pockets, like pens or pencils, do you? These suits will put a lot of pressure on your body, and I don't want you to get hurt."

Prezzy and Alex shook their heads, indicating they understood.

"Alright, Alex, another keypad. Type or say to the retinal scan, 'Elders of Edens.' Both of you, remember that."

Alex thought to himself, *Elders of Edens? What the hell is this? Where are we going? Alright, calm down. Just breathe. I think I trust Harvey.*

Harvey and Beauta helped put on their jumpsuits, and Alex placed his eye up to the pad. He said, "Elders of Edens." The light turned green, and the door's pins disengaged.

Harvey grunted, "Alright, guys, help me with this door; it's a heavy one." Alex and Prezzy assisted in opening the door.

They entered what looked like a regular hangar, housing a unique plane. It resembled a small jet but was thicker and flat black in color. The rear appeared normal, with typical jet engines near the tail fin, but below them were two longer, rectangular engines, four in total. A small panel on the side of the plane was barely visible until Harvey placed his hand on it, causing the door to lower with a built-in staircase. As the door opened, the main viewer screen automatically descended inside the plane and turned on, beeping softly.

The cabin featured four large, full-back black leather bucket seats with neon green vertical stripes, arranged two by two—two in the front and two in the back.

There was a small luggage area in the rear. The interior looked like a modern aircraft but with fewer instruments, some of which seemed to be mere façades.

Beauta directed, "You two in the front. Harvey and I will sit in the back this time. The suits have two disconnects on your right side for the hoses. There's only one way to connect them. Let me know if you need help. For the buckles, secure the ones near your ankles, then your waist, and finally your shoulders."

Alex and Prezzy nodded, taking their seats and fastening their suits as instructed.

Beauta leaned forward as everyone got situated. "Place your hands around the armrests. On your right is a button to engage your personal monitor. Press it again to disengage it."

Alex didn't hesitate and started operating his personal monitor.

Harvey leaned forward, motioning to the two of them. "When all your buckles and hoses are secure, the red button between your legs will turn green. Make sure that the button is always green during acceleration and deceleration. The overalls you're wearing are actually G-suits. They will fill with fluid to lock you in during the flight's acceleration and deceleration."

Excitedly, Beauta leaned forward again. "These are just four-seaters, but we have two-seaters, a couple of eight-seaters, and some thirty-seaters too. Several large cargo ships, and we're starting on two galactic battl—"

Harvey cut her off, pulling her back. "Nope, just transport ships. We don't do anything with battleships."

He whispers something in Beauta's ear, and Alex hears her softly say, "Sorry."

With a shocked look, Prezzy asks, "Wait! What? What do you mean by galactic? With these ships, we can travel outside our solar system?"

"Yes, of course," Harvey replies. "But today, just to the moon. That's where the EU—The Eternal University—is. Your new university."

This revelation hits Alex hard, like the first time he saw a thousand-horsepower engine. Excited, his mind floods with questions. Trying to turn in his seat but unable to because his suit is buckled, he exclaims, "Get out of here! What? We're going to the moon? This is awesome! Harvey, you said it takes three hours. Didn't it take over three days last time? How does that work? I want to know everything."

"Alright, calm down," Harvey responds. "It's noon, and we need to take off right now."

"We have a schedule to meet. We want to meet up with the others at the same time. Just relax; it's like a normal jet at first. Alright, let's go."

He pulls up his display and starts tapping the touchscreen on his monitor. The big doors roll to the sides as Harvey communicates with ground control, and the ship makes its way to the runway.

Alex, lost in thought, barely notices what Harvey is doing. He's trying to wrap his mind around how they can reach the moon in such a short time. He hears Harvey talking to Darwin Tower as the ship takes off like a typical small jet. As they ascend, Alex gazes out over the ocean, smiling at Prezzy. He feels he should say something.

"This is some crazy stuff, huh?"

Prezzy responds nervously, "Not sure about all this. I don't know what the hell I've gotten myself into. She told me that I'm special somehow." She slightly smiles at Alex, then looks forward toward the clouds coming into the distance. "And how does it fly out of the galaxy?"

She shakes her head, takes out her ear pods and phone, and starts listening to something. Looking back at Alex, she adds, "I don't feel special."

Alex smiles and chuckles, placing a comforting hand on her arm. She pulls away sharply, signaling, "Don't touch me!"

Alex thinks to himself, *She'll be okay; we are going to the freaking moon! This is freaking awesome!* He looks down at the clouds as they start to feel weightless.

II

When she looked down, the clouds below appeared as a solid layer of divine, majestic blankets of white crafted by her God. They were patterned, candid, and inflated—a sight she had never experienced at this altitude. *Cotton balls,* she thought.

As the ship ascended to weightlessness, she thought of her sister, who affectionately called her V. Her arms lifted from the armrests, a mix of anticipation and anxiety coursing through her. She glanced at her personal monitor, which displayed the flight path from Biju Patnaik International Airport to the moon. Amazingly, the countdown clock indicated they would arrive in just under four hours.

The regular engines hummed at maximum capacity. The moon appeared on the horizon as the ship adjusted its course. Unlike Alex's, this ship, 3,800 miles away from his, was eerily silent.

She sat quietly, contemplating her decision to attend the secret Eternal University. Her thoughts raced. *This is incredible. What's next? What have I gotten myself into now? Should I have stayed and taken the position at the Bureau? Freida is telling me nothing. Why? I already knew I was special, smart, and determined.*

Sanjay cleared his throat. "Okay, everyone, this is where it gets a little uncomfortable."

V heard him tapping his touchscreen. She watched as the main monitor displayed the ship finding the Thread.

"Once we find the Thread, we will accelerate. Your suits will be injected with a colloidal semisolid mass called Jella. Breathe in through your nose and exhale through your mouth," Sanjay instructed.

Freida added, "Once the ship finds the Thread, we can travel at a high speed."

The screen displayed *Stepped Leader Thread found,* and the computerized voice announced over the speakers, "Step leader found."

Sanjay braced everyone. "Here we go. Hold on. Remember to breathe."

The computerized voice continued, "Thread T-31C found. Initiating the Jella in 3, 2, 1."

V heard a hissing sound and felt pressure enveloping her body. At first, it was bearable, even pleasant, as warmth spread throughout her body—like soaking in a hot tub.

This is nice, she thought.

The computer then announced, "Accelerating in 5, 4, 3, 2, 1."

V gripped the armrests firmly as the ship accelerated with a SNAP! CRACK! BOOM! SWOOSH! Flashes of light filled the windows.

The ship vibrated intensely. V felt immense pressure on her body, teeth, and eyes, pushing her back into her seat. Her whole body was being crushed. *Breathe. Help me!* she thought, the previous comfort now a distant memory. Her body felt tight and compressed.

"Aakhir kya baat hai? Yah kya badatameezee hai? Bhagavaan meree madad kar! What the hell is this? Please make it stop. God help me."

She heard only cursing and grunts in the cabin. "How long will this last?" She tried to speak out.

She closed her eyes, gripping the armrests tighter, counting.

One, one thousand. Two, one thousand. Three, one thousand.

She reached forty-one thousand when the computer beeped. "Max acceleration achieved. Releasing the Jella in 3, 2, 1." As the Jella retracted, everyone breathed heavily.

Thank God! Never again. I'm out! This is not good. Why did I say yes to this? V thought, now able to breathe again.

She turned her head back to Freida. "What the hell, Freida? What was that? That wasn't fun. How many times do we need to do that?"

Freida, taking deep breaths, smiled at V. "One more time when we decelerate. Believe me, it's going to be worth it. Look!" V looked up to see the moon coming into clearer view. "You can unbuckle now. You two are very special. The next four years, the next few weeks, and months will be life-changing. You'll see."

V stared at the screen showing the ship's speed: over one hundred thirty thousand KMPH, with an arrival time of just under three and a half hours.

"I can't believe we're going that fast," she said.

Swaraj, the other student from India, turned to her. "I can't believe it either. It must be possible. We're doing it, right?"

Struggling to turn in his seat, Swaraj saw Steward Sanjay lean forward. "Let me help you," he said, unbuckling his shoulder straps. "You both can unbuckle now until we decelerate. I know it's not a fun experience. We will go through it one more time." Sanjay tapped his monitor. "There. Now you can see the planet on the main screen."

V watched as the planet grew smaller and smaller.

"Amazing," Swaraj said.

V, eyes wide open, looked out the window again. "This is incredible. We thought we were going to a regular university on Earth, but we're headed to the moon. To a completely different kind of university."

A university inside the moon. That's crazy. What will that be like? What about the other ten? Where are they from? Are there only twelve in our class? This is all so crazy.

Swaraj activated his monitor and began exploring the touchscreen. Freida closed her eyes. Mr. Babu reached to the left seat locker and pulled out a book. V and Swaraj released the rest of their buckles on their uncomfortable G-suits.

Vibrean had earlier remarked in Hindi that her parents would have a field day analyzing her if they ever found out she was on a ship to a university on the moon. She gazed out to her left, watching the stars and the moon get closer, wondering what the future might hold. After a few minutes, she looked back at the main monitor, seeing the Earth shrink further and further away.

How long until I see her again? Until she sees me? Without me there, my parents would surely use the same tactics on Saanvi that they used on me, she thought. Saanvi, her sister, would now bear the brunt of their parents' psychological manipulations. Both of V's parents were psychologists working for India's Intelligence Bureau, and growing up with them had made it difficult for V to have a normal life.

Her parents seemed indifferent, self-absorbed, and uncaring. She couldn't remember the last time she received a hug from either of them.

V struggled with leaving Saanvi in their parents' care. The guilt was overwhelming. As she stared out the window into the stars, she contemplated how to help her sister.

When I get there, maybe Saanvi can stay with Aunt Anaya. She was always a more positive role model for me. I'll call Anaya and make sure she checks in on her.

This is what I can do for now. I don't have a choice. I must decide. Something big is coming, and unfortunately, Saanvi is not part of it. She will have to wait; all the family stuff will have to be put at the back of my mind for now. It's not what I want, but what is necessary.

V looked back into the darkness of space and closed her eyes. She had made her decision; she was on her way to a new adventure.

Hours later, the main cabin display beeped, and the ship's computer announced,

"Disengaging from the thread in three minutes."

As everyone looked up simultaneously, the moon grew closer and closer, filling the entire view from the thick composite glass.

They all buckled back up, their expressions a mix of awe and anticipation.

Swaraj looked at V with a big smile, then back at the moon, exclaiming, "Avishwasneey." *Unbelievable.*

The main display showed the ship's path. The computer's voice continued, "Jella initiated. In 3. 2. 1."

V grabbed the armrest as warmth filled her jumpsuit. She glanced at Swaraj, who had his eyes closed.

The ship's voice said, "Disconnecting from the thread in 5. 4. 3. 2. 1."

SWOOSH! BOOM! CRACK! SNAP!

They all winced in pain as the Jella applied pressure to their bodies.

She felt herself pulled forward fiercely, unable to move, her body wracked by the force. Flashes of light appeared outside the window, and her eyes hurt from the intensity. The static electricity in the cabin made her hair stand on end. She noticed it on her arm and saw the hair on her head lifting in all directions from the reflection in the glass. She pinched her eyes closed further, thinking, *When will it end? Please, God. This is too much.*

After a few more seconds, it was over. Deceleration took just under a minute. Everyone in the cabin breathed deeply as the computer beeped. The Jella retracted from their jumpsuits. With a collective sigh of relief, they all smiled, glad that part was over.

Freida excitedly announced, "Yes! From here on out, we are on nuclear fusion and battery-powered thrusters. Another fifteen minutes, and we'll be in the tunnels."

V smiled and, in her Indian accent, said, "Look, another ship."

Swaraj, looking to the right, pointed and said, "A ship on this side as well."

Sanjay added, "There are three more behind us. As we said, there are twelve of you and twelve of us altogether. And the other Elders at the university as well."

Swaraj questioned, "Other Elders?"

Freida replied, "There are Master Elders and Elders. You will see."

As the ships approached the surface, they saw a low-profile building in a dark area of a small crater on the southwest side of the Sea of Tranquility. As all the ships rotated to land with their thrusters, several landing pads lit up with an array of soft sky-blue lights.

Like Olympic synchronized swimmers, the ships maneuvered together, landing on their respective pads, probably controlled by computer. Six long, thin grapples emerged from the moon's surface, magnetically securing each ship. Slowly, it placed each ship onto illuminated tracks. All at once, six large round doors opened on the crater wall, and the ships entered the tunnels. The tunnels appeared to have been carved out by enormous boring machines.

Mr. Babu said, "A little advice for both of you: stay as focused as possible—from this point forward. Focus on your studies. You two and the ten others are Earth's history keepers, its defenders. Try to keep to yourselves as much as possible."

As V's ship descended vertically, then moved horizontally through the tunnel, it passed through a final large round door alongside the other ships now on one track. It felt like a slow roller coaster ride.

They entered a colossal cavern. Buildings upon buildings stacked like layers of clamshells or eggshells filled the space, with floor after floor featuring arches for doors and windows. V tried to count the floors before noticing the cavern's sides were pure white, illuminated walls. To the left of the massive structure, two large waterfalls cascaded down. One flowed directly into the main building, with two smaller falls flowing out back into a small lake below. Beneath the building lay a clear ice formation, possibly a glacier. A small lake, a kilometer below, sparkled. She got to six levels before getting distracted.

Swaraj looked over at Freida and asked, "How long has this been here?"

Smiling in her sweet Indian accent, she replied, "We know of five CAT cycles, each around forty-four hundred years. We believe it's been here since humankind emerged from the Ice Age. Before that, we are not sure."

Swaraj looked forward as the ships docked towards the bottom of the main building. He asked, "What do you mean by CAT cycles?"

Freida explained, "CAT stands for Catastrophe. It's what happens to our solar system every forty-four hundred years. Our sun goes through a cycle that severely affects Terraenti. You'll learn more about it in your History and Future of CATs classes starting tomorrow."

Struggling to turn due to the jumpsuit, V questioned, "Terraenti?"

Freida responded, "That's what other planets call Earth."

In shock, Swaraj unbuckled his G-suit, asking, "Other planets?"

V thought, *Other planets? A university on the moon? Am I losing my mind?*

The door opened, and Vibrean Padame' Aboli got up and moved to the door. Following her beliefs in Hinduism, she smiled. *Here we go. Let's conquer this shit. But do it the right way. Let's be patient. I am in command.* She took a deep breath of the cavern air. It was pleasant, the humidity soothing on her skin. Something about it felt different, almost tropical. The lighting was strange, with the walls illuminated in a way that lit the massive dock structure pleasingly.

V looked around and saw the other ten students and their Stewards getting out of their ships and removing their G-suits. Large archways connected the rooms, while two large round doors bore massive seals. She noticed two larger ships—one without side windows—and two smaller ones, likely two-person ships. Large tanks lined one wall, along with various big machines, cranes or lifts mounted to the ceiling, and other mechanical pumps and pipes. She had no idea what they were for.

The group gathered on the floor as Harvey announced, "Okay, a lot is going to happen in the next few days. First, you'll meet everyone at dinner tonight. Then we'll get you settled into your rooms. Classes start first thing tomorrow morning. Leave your luggage; we'll take care of it."

V looked at the other students; half seemed excited, the other half terrified, ready to flee.

As they began to walk through the door, V glanced back and caught sight of two little people grabbing the bags and placing them on a cart. Then she noticed two very large, tall people approaching and talking to them.

Little people, giants? What kind of place is this? Are these the people from the previous CATs? The Elders they mentioned—are they from Earth's past?

From the docks, they ascended past a control room and other areas, up a long ramp through another large archway into a dining area.

Harvey stopped the group and announced, "Through this room is our main dining area, where we'll have all our big meetings and dinners."

"This room here is where you will have your regular meals."

Above the archway, possibly made from whalebone, V noticed a hand-carved sign that read *Terraenti Hall.*

As they entered the magnificent hall, they saw huge tapestries depicting various times and peoples from the past five CAT cycles. The tapestries showed portraits, buildings, farms, and iconic religious structures from different eras but nothing from the last four thousand years.

V thought, *The amount of knowledge, the victories, the failures of humanity over so many thousands of years. Unbelievable. If this is all true, I could be in a dream.*

In the middle of the room stood a massive single-piece hand-carved wood table, likely made from a large Sequoia tree that had sat in the ocean for a while. It looked to seat over fifty.

Above it, a ceiling fixture resembling a large Ammonite shell hung, with hundreds of smaller illuminated shells of the same type dangling from it. Near one wall, a buffet table offered a variety of cultural foods, with plates and cups made of wood, metal, ceramic, and glass. There was even a small modern soda fountain, like those in charging or fuel stations. Large vases with intricate artwork adorned the sides of the tables and the archways. The walls of the hall were illuminated in changing tones, just like in the dock. On the opposite side, a slow-flowing waterfall, like a pane of glass, flowed through to the floor below.

The group looked around curiously. Harvey, having a quiet chat with Freida, stopped and suggested, "Everyone, get some food and sit down. This is your home now."

V smiled at Freida and headed to the buffet table. She overheard someone say, "There's a pool below." She looked over to see a very tall couple sitting at the head of the table, quietly conversing and politely observing the new arrivals. The man had long blondish-brown hair, darkish skin, and gray eyes like a wolf. The woman, almost as tall, had long blonde hair down to her waist and crystal gray eyes—almost wolf-like, similar to his.

Their skin was hairier than that of modern humans. As everyone made their plates, the Stewards sat closer to the head of the table near the giant couple while the students sat down towards the end.

V started to eat and overheard the guy next to Swaraj say, "Well, I'm Declan. This is Lin, we're Brits."

Declan spoke with a quick Scottish accent. He was thin but muscular, with wavy reddish-brown hair half in his face. He had a slight shadowy beard. He smiled and resumed eating.

V noticed the student next to him looking disturbed. V could hear her say, "What the hell are you doing? Why are you introducing me? You don't even know me."

Declan scoffed, possibly flirting, "I could, you know, get to know you?"

Prezzy, sitting next to Alex and across from V and Swaraj, quietly announced, "Prezzy from Australia," while raising her hand slightly above the table.

V saw Alex, glowing and somewhat mesmerized, looking straight at her. He said, "Alex, I'm from Darwin."

V looked over at the most elegant, petite, and attractive girl of the group, who confidently said, "I'm Toni, and this is Candido. We are from Brazil."

V then looked at a petite Asian girl who seemed shy or scared. She nervously announced, "I'm Miko." Then she returned to eating.

Next to her, a young man said, "I'm Kyoryk. Miko and I, we're from Japan."

With everyone looking at them and after a long pause, another girl said, "I'm Maria, and this is Lev. We're from Saint Petersburg." Lev, with a mouth full of food, blinked a couple of times and raised his fork.

Lin said, "I'm Lin. I came with this knucklehead."

Declan retorted, "Hey, you don't even know me."

Lin gave him that look again.

Swaraj said, "I'm Swaraj."

V interrupted, saying, "I'm V."

She leaned forward and questioned, "Who are those two at the head of the table? They're like giants."

Lin excitedly exclaimed, "What the hell are these? They're spectacular. They're like baby, barbecue Brussels sprouts or something?"

Swaraj turned his head to V and questioned, "Yeah, who are they?"

Alex interrupted Swaraj, saying, "Those two are the Master Elders. They're from CAT 5."

Declan, looking at Alex, smiled and asked, "What happened to your hand?"

Alex had a metal and composite three-finger prosthetic on his right hand.

Lin punched him again, pointing out, "That's rude."

Declan argued, "What?" He raised his hand almost as if to back off.

Alex, with furrowed brows and a deeper Aussie accent than normal, responded, raising his hand again with the missing fingers and the metal replacements, "Oh, this? Got bit by a gator."

V thought to herself, *This guy is making shit up.*

She gave Alex a disdainful look.

Alex, seeing her look, reconsidered and admitted, "No, it was a machine shop accident." He joked, smiling at her, then to Declan, "If I ever need a hand, I'll let you know."

Declan laughed, and Lin confirmed, "See." V smiled back at Alex.

Alex leaned forward to them all near him and stated, "This place has been here since before CAT 2. That's over seventeen thousand years ago. The little people are from CAT 1. This place is amazing, isn't it?"

Alex looked right at V. Determined and always in command of her situation, V glanced at the other students and the Stewards at the other end of the table, thinking to herself, *I'm going to figure all this shit out. Who is this guy, Alex, and why does he keep smiling at me? How does he have all this information already?*

"How do you know all this already?" V asked.

"I got into the tablet on the ship and typed in some key words," Alex admitted with a smile.

As she finished her dinner, she noticed the three-meter man smoking a pipe. His wrinkled face and deer-hide clothing, which looked soft and expensive, shimmered from the light above. He began to stand, his enormous chair grinding on the floor, took a big slurping drink from his wooden mug, grabbed a hand-sized crystal rock from the table, and slammed it down like a gavel.

In a low, rustling voice, he declared, "Welcome to Eternal University. I'm Gig, and this is Fem'. We are the Master Elders from CAT 5."

V looked over at Alex. He smiled. She looked back at Gig as he slammed the rock again, and a virtual image appeared above the table, spinning just below the massive chandelier.

The students were amazed as the three-dimensional video of Terraenti and all its natural wonders spun around the room.

V looked at Alex, who was trying to figure out how the screen worked, looking under the table. The image showed the planet and its spectacular natural areas.

Gig continued, "From what we know, modern humanity has lived on this planet for over twenty-two thousand years. Some think even longer." He took another big swig from his drink and a huge puff from his pipe, blowing out an impressive amount of smoke.

He said, "We are the guardians, the watchers from above. The guardians of all history. We record and keep track of all the history of Terraenti. We represent our planet to the other planets."

"In the coming months and years, you will learn about the past and the truth about the present."

He paused and said, "You are its future. You will be the future Elders. Two of you will become the Master Elders, keeping records of over nine billion individuals." He took another hit from his pipe and slammed the rock on the table again.

The screen changed, showing a series of other solar systems in the galaxy. Gig took a drink, spilling a little as he set the mug down. He said, "Five other planets in our galaxy have different cultures and technologies. The Creator gave consciousness to six different planets, but he doesn't want us to interfere with their or our populations; those are the Laws and Directives set down by him."

V shook her head, thinking, *Who is this guy? Is he drunk or high or both? This is crazy. There are five planets with people on them. What are they like? I need to get the hell out of here. This shit is crazy.*

Gig continued, "Open your minds. Our solar system and the six others. Fem' and I now live in the seventh system where the planet Amotaious is." The screen displayed the seventh system.

Prezzy, with a cringed expression, asked openly, "Is he drunk?"

Alex replied, "Maybe, or maybe it's something in that pipe he's smoking."

Gig continued, "From the Gifts you will receive to the knowledge you will gain at the university, you will have all the tools you need to keep all this running. Endless possibilities await your future. In the next four years, you will learn about all this, how to keep the records, and how to use your Gifts."

V looked across the table and saw Alex's face focused on Gig, but she could see one eye was still on her. She thought *This guy is still looking at me. What's his deal? Did Gig just say that God gave consciousness to five other planets? And what are these Gifts he's talking about? How special are the twelve of us? Have I just landed in some kind of fantasy novel or something?*

Fem' looked at Gig, disturbed, pulling on him to sit down. Gig smiled at her, then sat down and finished his sentence, "Okay, well, welcome, everybody, to your first night at Eternal University." Looking at his wife, he reluctantly sat down.

Fem' stood, her gown glistening in the light as she rose. "Thank you, Gig. I'm Fem'." She smiled warmly at everyone and waved her hand slowly around the room. With watery eyes, she reiterated, "Welcome to Eternal University. Gig and I have been here a long time. We are the Master Elders."

V looked at Prezzy, who remarked, "I think she's tipsy too."

Prezzy and Alex laughed quietly. Fem' grabbed a green crystal stone from the table, placed it in one hand, and laid her other hand on top of it.

Standing upright, she looked down the long table at the students, smiled, and said, "We have a lot to accomplish in the next four years."

"On this special night, like some, we start off with a prayer, then we will celebrate."

Declan sat up in his seat, "Celebrate? I like the sound of that."

"We pray to our Creator, Raba Rashi."

Everyone in the room who knew said, "Raba Rashi," quietly and with reverence, bowing their heads, some clasping their hands.

Fem smiled again, looking down at the table at the students. "Just relax, take it all in."

V whispered to Swaraj, "The Creator's name is Raba Rashi?"

Fem' cleared her throat. "We've been waiting for your arrival for a very long time." She looked down at Gig and gave him a loving smile. She stood even more pronounced. Gig sat forward and slammed the rock gavel down again on the table. The screen disappeared. The room seemed to shudder slightly. The stone in her hand started to do something—it glowed faintly.

Fem began to chant, "Oh! Raba Rashi! Naash! Oh, Raba Rashi! Cama See La Ruh! Terraenti, Pupa, Comensi Luna! Shanka, Fem'a Da Giga! Universisheni, Creata Di Elders! Di Pat!"

V thought, *This is some Harry Potter shit or something; what the hell?*

The lights in the room dimmed, the stone in Fem's hands glowed even brighter, and the room grew warmer. The air swirled around, the tapestries fluttered, and V heard low-toned heavenly thunder echoing through the cavern.

She felt something happening to her body.

Gig slammed the rock gavel down again.

The stone in Fem's hand glowed even brighter once again, and a blue sapphire lightning bolt arrow of light emerged, swirling around the room. All the students followed it with their eyes.

Declan yelled out, "Holy shit!"

Gig, looking at the group, slammed the rock again, and the arrow split into three, gently passing through all the students, Stewards, and then the Master Elders.

V looked at Alex, who seemed just as bewildered as she was.

Everyone's bodies felt warm and tingly, almost like the moment before a climax or something. Their eyes shut, heads tilted back, arms stretched out on the table, feeling as though they were being electrocuted with three phases of alternating current.

V's body locked, still, unconscious-like.

All of this happened without her consent.

She opened her eyes.

As unexpectedly as it all started, it ended.

V looked at Alex, who also seemed confused.

V thought, *What the hell was that? Should I run? Okay, I'll remain calm. What does this attractive, silly guy across the table think?*

I've never met an Australian before. I wonder what kind of body he has. Maybe I'll talk to him later. I feel really good right now. Did they just drug me? What was that arrow or light thing?

A feeling of warmth and joy spread over everyone. The Student Elders looked at each other across the table. V saw the Stewards get up, hug, smile, and laugh—she noticed they were more like a family. Then, some started to exit the archway towards the louder waterfalls.

Then she noticed Alex smiling at her like the impossible had just become possible.

He tried to say something but couldn't quite get out any words.

A minute later, V saw Alex looking at Harvey as if to say, *What the hell, man!* and shook his head. Harvey looked back, shrugged his shoulders, and smiled.

V questioned Alex, "You okay?"

With a deep breath, Alex replied, "Yeah, I think so."

V saw Alex feeling his neck.

He put his hand there and reiterated, "It feels like a burn?" He noticed a similar mark on V's neck and said, "You have the same mark."

He looked at Prezzy, and V saw the same thing on her neck. Puzzled, they all questioned what had just happened.

Gig's chair ground on the floor again as he slowly stood, raising his big mug. With everyone back in their seats, his face crumpled up in a big grin, like he had been waiting for this moment for a million years. "Welcome, Eternal Guardians. You are now Elders, Student Elders," he announced, looking at the students with a possible tear in his eye.

He then looked at Fem', and pulled her up by the hand to help her stand. "We have waited a long time for your arrival."

"Your lifespan has just been extended."

"You're going to live a very long time. We are very happy you all are here. Come join Fem, me, and the other Elders in celebration. The future awaits you all."

The two of them looked at the group as if everything in their world had changed and walked towards the archway behind them. They went through it and stopped at the balcony.

V, not knowing what to think, looked at the other Students, hoping to get some answers. They looked as puzzled as she felt. Music started to echo through the archway.

Declan excitedly said, "I'm beginning to like this place. I like Gig and Fem' already."

V smiled at Alex as they all made their way through the archway. All the Students were chatting about the experience, the prayer, and the eagle marks as they walked to gather by the balcony with Fem and Gig.

The music grew louder as they reached the balcony rail, looking down at a very large deck below. Alex, his mouth wide open in awe, stood frozen. V now saw the incredible view of the falls and the lake below.

The deck was another story. It held around fifty people standing and sitting near the stage. She recognized a few from when they passed through the dining area. The deck had many tiered balconies overlooking the lake. The glacier-cavern walls glistened, making the view even more spectacular. Gig and Fem stopped talking once all the Students were present. He raised his hands to silence the music below.

Prezzy, on her toes, blurted out, "Oh my God!"

Declan reached the railing. "Unbelievable," he said, looking at Alex. "Can you believe this?"

The music stopped, and the large crowd below looked up at Gig and the new attendees. He announced, "May I introduce the Elders of CAT six! Join me in welcoming them."

The crowd burst into cheers, chanting, "CAT six! CAT six! Elders of CAT six!" The band started playing again. V and the other Students were surprised, looking at the view, the deck, and all the people waiting for them two to three stories below.

She couldn't believe it all. A new "**Song**" started—an orchestral version of a popular tune. *Vogue.*

The unusual people, the mist of the falls rising to the top of the building, the grays and blues of the jagged rocks from the ceiling down to the waterfalls, and a solid blue glacier all the way at the bottom. Could it be a glacier or solid rock? Possibly a glacier that sustained the university with water and oxygen? One waterfall flowed directly into the university, while the other cascaded into the lake, misting and creating a tropical humidity in the air. The deck area had more plants than V had seen anywhere else since she'd arrived.

The far wall across the lake was smooth and seemed illuminated, like most of the other walls at the university.

The whole area was dynamic and enchanting—something never read about because it had never existed before. Gig and Fem tried to give out handshakes and hugs to the new Elders as they all descended to the deck.

Walking next to Alex, V heard him mention to Harvey, "Damn, Harvey, you weren't kidding this morning. This is something. I'm trying to comprehend it all. This place is extraordinary, to put it mildly. It's going to be a whole different reality from now on—for me, you, for all of us."

Harvey chuckled. "Yes, it's new for me too, kid. It's new for all of us; you got that right. I've only been here a year, and I still can't get over the enormity of it all."

Alex said, "Not quite sure if I should thank you yet. Give me a couple of days."

Harvey, with a look of concern, replied, "Remember what I said about focusing. Have fun tonight; tomorrow, you have class."

Alex saluted Harvey. "Roger that."

V could already tell that Alex was attracted to her. She thought to herself, *I've got this Alex guy all figured out. He doesn't hesitate to speak his mind or be shy in any way. And for the rest of them, I'll figure them out.*

She worked her way around the deck, where most were drinking and dancing now. The view of the cavern from the deck was unbelievable. The crowd consisted of previous Elders from the last twenty or so thousand years, some of the university crew—who could mostly be described as little people. I'm not sure what culture or time they were from; Alex had said CAT1, but everyone seemed to be having a great time.

V, wearing a dark green dress open through the middle with a tight-fitting leotard underneath and open-toed shoes, most notably had majestic light green eyes—rare for an Indian woman. Or so she thought. But when she smiled at you, it was like she knew what you were thinking. *At least, I think so. Maybe that's from some of my previous training at the Bureau.*

Alex approached V.

V asked, "How is your neck?"

Alex replied, "It's better. I'm not sure what the hell happened up there, but I'm going to find out. I have a lot of questions. Yours looks kind of like an eagle."

V asked, "You're from Australia, right? Where about?"

Alex replied, "Yeah, Darwin."

V questioned, "Is it nice there?"

Alex replied, "Warm and humid in the winter, it's not bad. We do a lot of racing. My family owns an engineering design company. Where are you from?"

V replied, "A city called Bhubaneswar. I was supposed to be going to the Institute of Science."

Alex said, "Really? I was going to MIT. I can't believe all this, and what was with that prayer? How did it make you feel? I feel kind of different."

V grabbed Alex's hand and pulled him out to the dance floor. "You dance?" she asked.

Alex said, "I can, I guess."

V thought to herself, *If I try to run, how could I get away? I'm probably a couple of miles inside the moon. Take it slow; let's try to figure this place out. I'll talk to Freida in the morning. Let's see what tomorrow brings.*

This Alex guy seems okay. V looked at Alex while dancing and thought, *Not a very good dancer, oh well.*

V and Alex took in a couple more dances. All the Students started to get acquainted. She couldn't believe the day she had, but after a couple of glasses of wine, she felt more comfortable and put her worries off till the next day.

The Students were then shown to their rooms by Keira and Hugh from England.

III

He opened his door to the hallway.

"Showers are down that way," Maria from Russia said as she walked by, her robe hanging over her shoulder, exposing her naked form.

Alex smiled, nodded, and replied, "Thanks." Excitedly, he added, "First day of class!"

He mentally berated himself, thinking, *What an idiot. That was a stupid thing to say. Well, she's not shy. She has a nice body and looks like she works out. I wonder if everyone's going to walk around naked. I need to chill.*

Alex continued down the hallway, hearing Maria's flip-flops snap as she entered her room. He turned to the facilities at the end of all the Students' rooms to the left, observing the setup: showers on the right, toilets on the left. Or could he call them showers? They were more like waterfalls. Eight areas were divided by thin smoked glass, the rest was all in marbled stone.

Water flowed down a horizontal trough and out through eight marble rounds with slots in them, creating the shower heads. The brilliant white and maroon, red marble walls contrasted with the red sandstone-colored floor. It all just flowed as he walked in; an old "Song" *Close To You* from the '70s played on the speakers. He heard Declan singing along as he stepped under the water.

Alex soaped up.

Declan noticed Alex and exclaimed, "Hey Alex, isn't this shower awesome?" Alex responded with a nod.

Miko, Lin, and Kyoryk exited the showers, Lin suggesting they enjoyed the tune she had left playing.

Declan, drying off with an arrogant look, glanced back at Alex. "V was just finishing up when I got here. Sorry, you missed her. The first night, we spent drinking and partying with our teachers. This is a unique university for sure."

Confident and sure-footed, Alex, slightly bigger than Declan, replied, "No worries, mate. Yeah, it should be interesting."

Alex thought to himself, *People are so quick to judge. I only danced with her a couple of times. I hope she didn't think I was too forward or clingy.*

As Declan left through the archway, he said, "See you in class."

Alex continued singing where Declan had left off. Realizing he was alone, Alex sang louder.

He took another look to ensure he was still alone but heard some girls giggling in the distance.

Later, in the theater-type classroom, Alex took his seat next to Prezzy. The room was furnished with plush leather recliner seats, contrasting with the fifteenth-century décor. Everyone seemed relaxed and comfortable. Alex scanned the room for V and saw her sitting next to Declan a row up.

There were four seats in the front, four in the middle row, and six in the back row, each with a table stowed to the right and a satchel containing books and a personal tablet. As Alex settled in, the two Stewards who had shown them to their rooms entered the room.

"Today, we're going over the CATs, their periods in time, their people, and a little summary about their cultures. Declan, if you could swap with Swaraj, that would be great. We'd like to keep you all paired up for now, thanks if you could all look in your tablets under History and click on *Chronicle Terraenti*. Your tables are on the left side of your chair in your satchel. Please pull your tables to the upright position; thanks."

"I'm Keira Clarke, and this is Hugh Hardy." Declan scoffed but reluctantly changed seats with Swaraj. Keira and Hugh waited while the group found their tablets and moved the tables to the upright positions.

Keira continued, "The first chapter is a summary of Terraenti's Cataclysm history."

"I know you have a load of questions. If we could answer a few at the end of class, that would be brilliant. Thanks. These tablets are yours. They contain all the information we'll cover, plus everything about you and your ongoing performance. Many questions you have will be answered by looking into these tablets."

"The reason for the performance ratings is to put you in the best possible positions after you finish here at the university. Okay, brilliant. Let's get to the task at hand."

Alex clicked on *History* and *Terraenti*, still trying to get that tune out of his head, and thinking about V, saw:

History, CAT 1 Through CAT 5

Every 4,400 years, a catastrophe strikes Terraenti. Before the CAT, Eternal Elders and Stewards are selected by the Creator. They are then brought to *Luna / Eternal University* to train and to be educated, becoming the history takers of the planet. Finding you wasn't easy. You have special genetic markers. There are 24 individuals from your current time: 12 Students and 12 Stewards. You are here to train at the University.

Currently, *Amotaious*, the seventh planet, is the base of operations for all Eternal Elders from all six planets from all previous CATs. After your training here, when you become True Elders, you will live on Amotaious with all other previous Elders from Terraenti and the other planets. Yes, you will be able to have a residence on Terraenti.

- **Terraenti** – Earth and the Eternal University, the one-mooned planet.

- **Vattan** – The two-mooned planet, mainly an ocean.

- **Regnolnm** – A three-mooned planet with a very tropical environment, mostly landmass.

- **Vindor** – Surrounded by four moons, it experiences big storms and strong winds. Its people used to be able to fly.

- **Kall** – Five-mooned in a perpetual ice age.

- **Elducan** – The hottest planet, desert-like, has six moons.

- **Amotaious** – Seven moons, the biggest planet with the smallest population, all of Elders.

All six planets go through catastrophes from their suns, ranging in cycles from four thousand to fifteen thousand years. The first catastrophe on Terraenti, where humans with consciousness lived, that we know of, occurred 22,000 years ago. It was before CAT 1 that the moon base was created. This culture started the moon base, but it didn't become a university until after CAT 1 because of space flight. Amotaious was found by Terraenti between CAT 2 and CAT 3 after the Thread was discovered, enabling high-speed space flight. Amotaious has been around long before that.

CAT 1

22,000 years ago.

People who finished building the Eternal University. Average height: 1.1 meters. Lived: Underground. Average lifespan: 100 years. Development/Progress/Technology: Thermal, like Terraenti's AI. Currency: None. Governments: Self. Religion: One. Population: Over one billion.

CAT 2

17,600 years ago.

Average height: 1.5 meters. Lived: Underground/Land. Average lifespan: 50 years. Development/Progress/Technology: No Electricity, Mechanical Clock. Currency: Coin/Barter. Governments: 3. Religion: 5. Population: Over three billion.

CAT 3

13,200 years ago.

People who found the Sun-to-Sun Thread, enabling high-speed travel on the Thread. Average height: 1.9 meters. Lived: Ocean. Average lifespan: 150-200 years. Development / Progress / Technology: Nuclear, Beyond Transhumanism. Currency: Paper/Coin/Barter. Governments: 70. Religion: 150. Population: Over 10 billion.

CAT 4

8,800 years ago.

Average height: 2.1 meters. Lived: Land and Ocean. Average lifespan: 100 years. Development/Progress/Technology: Thermal/Wind/Water, Industrial. Currency: Coin. Governments: 2. Religion: 100+. Population: Less than eight hundred thousand due to a technology collapse.

CAT 5

4,400 years ago.

Average height: 2.8 meters. Lived: Land and Ocean. Average lifespan: 100 years. Development/Progress/Technology: Thermal/Wind/Water, Industrial. Currency: Barter/Family trade. Governments: 1. Religion: 500+. Population: Over four billion.

CAT 6

Present time.

Average height: 1.8 meters. Lived: Land and Ocean. Average lifespan: 80 years. Development/Progress/Technology: Thermal/Wind/Water, Pre-Transhumanism. Currency: Paper/Barter-Coin. Governments: Hundreds. Religion: Thousands. Population: Currently nine billion.

Alex looked up to see Mr. Hardy working the control console, displaying a virtual screen with graphics showing the years, average height, living locations, lifespan, development / progress / technology, currency, governments—everything he had just been reviewing on his tablet.

Alex, looking back at his tablet, tapped *Knowing Your Role*, which listed *Non-Disclosure, 12 Habits of Elders, Relationships,* and *Who Are You.*

He clicked on *Who Are You?*

It read:

You have 25% more genes, 26 pairs of chromosomes, IQ above 180, Gifts TBD, blood type AB Neutral, and your birthdate is December 12, 2012. Because of your genetic makeup, you are less receptive to cosmic rays and less likely to have problems in 0-G. Your SpO2 level is above 110%, and you adapt well to stressful situations.

You think before you act. You're sensitive. Open-minded.

Alex thought to himself, *How do they know all this? Oh, that's what all the tests were for. This is insane. My body can handle 0-Gs? What the hell? Is this before or after our Gifts and the Common Mind?*

Alex jolted as Mr. Hardy, a tall, dark-haired man with a military crew cut, began speaking again. With a distinctive British accent, Mr. Hardy commanded, "Alright folks, make sure you read this chapter about the previous catastrophe."

"If I ask you a question in a couple of days, you'd better know the answer. These classes are a brief outline. It's up to you all to delve deeper into the information. You can find it all on your tablets or in the library."

Declan, now sitting in the back, turned to Lin and whispered, "What's he going to do, make us do KP Duty?"

Lin responded with a hard punch to Declan's arm. Unfortunately, it caught Mr. Hardy's attention.

He addressed them sternly, "Lin, Combat is tomorrow. And Declan, there are some shite jobs even here at the University."

"Listen up, everyone," Mr. Hardy continued. "Until now, you've only been responsible for yourselves. Now, you're responsible for many, many people. You'll understand the importance of all this in the weeks and months to come." He paused, scanning the room before adding, "Read the material."

He nodded to Miss Clarke, signaling her to take over. She asked, "Alright, any questions?"

Lev from Russia spoke up, "What kind of combat class is it?"

Mr. Hardy replied, "Art of self-defense, from multiple disciplines. We'll test your mind and body in numerous ways, and you'll receive a workup on potential improvements. We may even see one or two of your special abilities come to light—your Gifts. They should all come about in the next month or so."

Kyoryk asked, "What is the thread, and how did we travel on it?"

Miss Clarke straightened her posture and explained, "Think of it as an electric cord in space, connecting one sun to another. They are scattered throughout space, near all the planets."

"Once the ship finds the electric cord—the Thread—we can travel on it with our specially designed engines, like a high-voltage current, either a negative or positive charge, similar to a lightning bolt but faster than the speed of light."

"You'll learn more about it in this class later. It was first used and developed before CAT 3. They were beyond AI in terms of Transhumanism. You will eventually meet a few of the Elders from that time."

"In the time of Atlantis and a city called Mammotaious," Miss Clarke continued.

Miko interrupted, "When can we visit home?"

As soon as she said *Atlantis*, Alex's mind flashed back to the discussion he had with his friends the other day. *That's it! Harvey told me. And what's this city called Mammotaious? Where was that? What's going to happen to all our cities of today? This is all insane. How can they all just sit up here and do nothing?*

Keira smiled, and Hugh laughed, replying, "Miko, already homesick? We have you scheduled to return to the planet a day or two before your birthday and come back after New Year's. But there may be other trips back, possibly to Amotaious as well. Lots of adventure awaits you all in the years to come. Keep an open mind."

"Focus on your studies, and I assure you, you're going to have a great time. This is not an ordinary school. Lots of things are going to happen. Any other questions right now?"

Without waiting for a response, he looked at Keira and said, "Right, let's break for lunch."

Alex surveyed the small dining room, teeming with people. The walls were adorned with tapestries depicting ancient animals, varied agricultural methods, and diverse architectural styles. Dominating the center of the room was a large fireplace with a vent extending to the ceiling. A waterfall cascaded down the wall, over the back of the buffet area, and disappeared into the floor. The buffet offered burgers, fresh vegetables, fries, onion rings, and an assortment of juices and energy drinks.

In her crisp British accent, Lin marveled, "It's fascinating that they can communicate so quickly using the Thread. And use it to fly through space faster than, what did she say? The speed of light. That's incredible."

Alex nodded, adding, "The fact that there are other planets to communicate with is the bizarre part. I can't wait to meet some of those people." He scanned the room again, his gaze settling on Lin. She had reddish-auburn hair and an alluring, mysterious aura like a fortune teller.

Last night, she had told V about her parents moving to an off-grid farm, living a hippie lifestyle. Alex glanced around the table, thinking of home, then back at Lin, wondering what she was thinking. Then he saw V. *She's perfect. Her eyes. It's like that tune Lin was playing in the bathroom, except her eyes are green.* He smiled at her again, still thinking. "If I can only get to know her better." He was seated with V, Declan, Prezzy, Lin, and Swaraj.

V asked, "What did she mean by going home before Miko's birthday?" Alex gave V a puzzled look. "When is your birthday?"

"December 12, 2012," V replied.

Declan almost jumped out of his seat, nearly spitting out his food. "That's my birthday."

Everyone at the table exchanged astonished glances.

Alex exclaimed, "Mine too."

Lin and Prezzy echoed, "Mine too."

"All twelve of us?" Prezzy questioned, bewildered.

V stood up and approached the other Students over at the other table, asking about their birthdays. They confirmed, "December 12, 2012." Everyone looked at her in amazement as she returned to the table.

"What the hell? Were we all born in a Petri dish? Knowing my parents, maybe," V said, sitting down in disgust.

Alex was surprised at how quickly V was becoming comfortable with the group. He said, "Out of nine billion people, it's possible."

Declan, looking at the ceiling, said, "Wasn't there a movie about December 12, 2012? About the Mayan calendar or something?"

V motioned for Alex to look at the Stewards. He noticed them laughing, amused that the Students had just discovered they shared the same birthday.

V remarked, "They think it's funny that we just found out. I want to know more about this Creator."

Swaraj looked at Lin and said, "I don't think you fly in space." He smiled flirtatiously. "Just saying."

Lin moved her seat closer. "Then what is it called, smarty pants?"

Swaraj's expression turned smug. "There's no air in space, so you can't fly like a plane. You understand?" Lin shook her head. "No, not really."

Declan interrupted, "What's next?" Some looked at him confusedly. He clarified, "What class is next?" Lin responded, "Future. Hopefully, they'll tell us about the other CATs and Earth's future."

V, looking disturbed, asked, "Great, when is that?" Declan replied, "Do you mean Armageddon or the next class? The next class is in forty minutes."

Lin stood up. "I'm going to check out the library. Does anyone want to join me?" She raised her hand, addressing Swaraj, "You say there is no air in space, so you can't fly? How do you travel then?"

V and Prezzy got up and confirmed, "Yep." V said, "Sounds good." Lin looked at the guys. "Are you coming?"

Alex stood up. "You push and pull in space, like using a vacuum or thrust. There's no gravity. Not in the way you think, anyhow. Don't we have any physics majors here?" He exhaled sharply, almost whistling. *That's what it is. The Thread. I have no idea what that is.*

Swaraj raised a finger, smiling at Lin. "That's what I'm saying." Lin smiled back at him.

The group stood and headed down a long, sloped hallway, then descended a wide, three-story spiral staircase.

The walls were adorned with paintings and pictures of what Alex assumed were great authors and scientists from various societies and cultures throughout history.

Alex glanced back and saw Kyoryk and Miko following them. V and Alex stopped to wait for them. V greeted, "Hey, Miko." Miko responded, "You're V, right?"

"Yeah, it's short for Vibrean." Miko smiled. "That's a pretty name."

"Thanks. What university were you going to?" "Cambridge. For Environmental Sciences. I almost made it to the Olympics, but my parents wanted me to go to Cambridge." Declan, overhearing, interjected, "The Olympics?"

Miko nodded. "Yeah, I am a gymnast."

Declan grinned. "That's my favorite in the Olympics, that and diving."

Lin spoke up. "Why is that Declan?" Declan admitted, "It's all the positions you girls can do; I mean, what you can do with your body, I mean, it's just a great sport."

Alex laughed, looking at the portraits on the wall. He glanced back at Declan and remarked, "That was a terrible save, mate." Lin looked directly at Declan and whispered, "You're losing the battle before it's begun."

As they neared the bottom of the staircase, V continued, "I was going to the Institute of Science in India for Biological and Chemical Science."

Kyoryk added, "Miko, we really overfished the seas. On one side of my family, they were into it, and we saw how bad it got over the years. The good thing is, it's really starting to come back since we started to raise them on farms now. It brought back the nature of it."

Declan, trying to be funny again, said, "They have fish in Japan?" Some of them laughed.

Alex entered the library and looked around in awe. "Incredible. Even though this is vast, all the knowledge can't possibly be stored here."

In the middle of one side of the room, a huge globe rotated slowly. On the other side hung a five-meter-high hourglass. As Alex watched, he realized it seemed to rotate on the hour automatically. A few computers sat on the table while a spiral staircase ascended three more stories, leading to shelves upon shelves of books. The shape of the room was unusual—rounded on both ends.

Above the bookcases on the ground floor, stone-carved busts of what looked like Elders from previous CATs lined the walls. The bookcases were divided into five sections, each representing a different CAT, containing records from the last 4,400 years—24,000 years in total. Along the walls were sections dedicated to combat techniques, directives, and laws. As the floors ascended, each was devoted to two of the seven planets, documenting their histories and technologies.

Everyone started browsing different categories, and soon, all the other Students had made their way into the library.

The signs on the walls read: "One Moon, Planet Terraenti," "Two Moons, Planet Vattania," "Three Moons, Planet Regnolnm," "Four Moons, Planet Vindor," "Five Moons, Planet Kall," "Six Moons, Planet Eldulcan," "Seven Mooned, Planet Amotaious".

Alex pulled out a book about Vindor.

It detailed their transportation development, which relied on magnetic suspension in vacuum tunnels to move quickly from city to city and to enormous colosseums. The book included a one-page bio of the author along with a picture. The author's body resembled a human's but was more muscular. His face had bird-like features—somewhere between an eagle and an owl. His shoulders rose higher than those of a human, giving him a distinct posture. The writing looked like Arabic, though parts had been translated into English.

The room buzzed with chatter as everyone shared what they found.

Kyoryk interjected, "Declan, check out these pictures from Eldulcan. The planet looks mostly like a desert, and its people… they kind of look like lizards. Their bodies seem to have scales."

Alex responded, "On Vindor, their bodies are similar to ours, but their heads look like owls or maybe eagles."

Declan shouted, "Amotaious is similar to Earth in geography. But it only has a hundred thousand people."

Kyoryk commented, "Isn't that where all the Elders live? Where do we end up living?"

Alex nodded. "Yeah, I think so."

Suddenly, chimes echoed through the vast space, catching everyone's attention.

Lin raised her voice, possibly trying to lead the group. "V, I think that's for us. The future awaits—back to class."

"Patterns and Cycles," announced Keira Clarke as a virtual screen flickered to life.

"Can someone name some natural patterns found on Terraenti?"

Maria quickly responded, "Seashells and honeycombs. Is that what you mean?"

Keira nodded. "Yes."

Swaraj added, "Spider webs and snowflakes."

The screen displayed various patterns: rocks, tree rings, waves, seafoam, and weather patterns. Miss Clarke gestured with her pointer.

"My point is, there are countless patterns and cycles. Why are these patterns so ubiquitous?"

Tonari suggested, "God."

Maria interjected, "Isn't it due to the way atoms and molecules form?"

Miss Clarke smiled. "Perhaps this is how the Creator designed everything. We will find out."

"Now, let's identify some cycles," V chimed in. "The carbon cycle, water cycle, rock cycle."

Miss Clarke's excitement grew. "Brilliant! There's also the nutrient cycle and interactions between cycles. Nowadays, we talk about the Milankovitch cycle, and there's one you can investigate called the **Great Year**—the 25,000-Year Precessional Cycle. This goes way back. It was first noted around the time of Christ, then 25,000 years before that.

How does that affect our climate and Terraenti? Our sun influences our CAT cycles. Can anyone control the sun? No! The sun is 864,000 miles in diameter and 10,000 degrees Fahrenheit on its surface. Over a million Terraentis could fit inside the sun."

She paused before repeating the question. "I ask again: can we control the sun? No!"

An image of the sun appeared on the screen, showing a massive solar burst of plasma—a monstrous X flare, what some would call a mini-nova.

The Students stared, stunned.

Keira continued, "Remember this when you learn more about your roles here at the University. You will understand your importance and the significance of this institution."

Alex, hands on his head, took a deep breath, almost hyperventilating.

Prezzy reached over, placing a hand on his shoulder. "Are you okay?"

He replied, "Yeah, I'll be alright."

Insanity. Look at that! I can't believe we're going to go through that. I don't understand how they just sit up here and do nothing.

Miss Clarke continued, "We don't know the precise day of the upcoming CAT. It usually starts when the sun enters a prolonged period without sunspots, reducing our magnetic field and allowing more cosmic rays to strike the planet."

"More importantly, it's a **warning sign.** Although our sun goes through many cycles, the poles shift every eleven years."

"There are also longer cycles of solar maximums and minimums—every two hundred, four hundred, eight hundred, and sixteen hundred years, and so on. This leads to the moment when the sun bursts."

She pointed to the three-dimensional image, her face tightening with concern.

"This is a CAT. This image shows CAT Five. I'm not going to show you what happened to the planet—you can imagine. Over the next few years after it happens, over ninety percent of the population is lost. This occurs every forty-four hundred years."

She let the weight of her words settle before continuing.

"That's why we are here. We are Historical Technicians. We can protect our planet from extraterrestrial threats, but that has never been the problem. Our main mission is to record history, especially what happens in this solar system and on Terraenti over time."

Alex, sitting upright, looked at her, then back at the still image of the sun's violent eruption on the virtual display. His jaw clenched.

"So we can't help? We can't warn the people of Earth—of Terraenti?"

Mr. Hardy, noticing Alex's concern, stepped in.

"It's possible that people will figure it out in time to save some. Some governments likely already know about this."

He hesitated before adding, "But when the solar outburst happens, the planet won't be able to sustain its current population. Feeding the billions that survive would be an astronomical challenge. It's just not feasible."

His words hit like a blow to the gut.

"Something to consider," he added, his voice measured. "The CATs vary in strength. For instance, CAT Two was severe. Since then, population losses and damages have decreased."

Alex leaned back, trying to steady his breathing.

Miko, her voice small but urgent, asked, "What about warning our families?"

Miss Clarke's gaze softened.

"If you went home now and told them your lifespan has been altered, that the Creator will give you Gifts, and that they need to live underground with supplies because the sun will burst… would they believe you?"

The room was silent.

"Probably not," she answered herself. "First, they would ask how you know. And you'd say, 'Well, I was on the moon with these people, and they told me this happens every forty-four hundred years. Oh, and there are other planets I can't tell you about.'"

She sighed, her expression shifting from frustration to quiet understanding.

"Listen. Give it a couple more days. Let the Common Mind do its work. Wait for your Gifts. Learn more about our program here. Talk among yourselves. Talk to Fem and Gig. Talk to your Stewards."

She scanned the group, her voice softening.

"All I'm saying is… give it time."

Alex felt his blood rise, his thoughts racing.

I'm going to figure out something. There is no way I'm just going to sit up here and watch it all happen. That's insane.

Miss Clarke continued, "I know it's a lot to take in. It's not going to happen for a while. It's not supposed to happen until your third year here. Let's react calmly and compassionately."

She took a slow breath, her next words measured.

"They have tried in the past. Some of the greatest stories in history are written about this. Even civilizations with Gifts tried to stop it. They failed. Maybe it made a three percent difference."

Her eyes flickered with something deeper—faith, perhaps.

"Look to the Creator."

A pause.

"Once you understand the Common Mind and your Gifts, you'll see that the Creator designed these patterns and cycles—the CATs—for a reason. There have been other disasters too—volcanic eruptions, earthquakes, comets, meteors. Things beyond even the Creator's control. You will learn about all of them."

The room fell silent. In a soft voice, V spoke up. "My parents would laugh in my face and throw me back into therapy."

Declan added, "We're all going to need therapy after this."

Mr. Hardy interjected, "I know it's a lot to take in, but we're not going to solve it all in the next few months. Learn about the previous CATs."

"All the information is on your tablets and in the library. Focus on learning, not doing. Tomorrow is combat class. Three other Stewards and I will be there. Try to have a good evening."

Still in shock, they slowly walked out of the room, Alex looking particularly stricken.

A lot to take in. It's the end of the freaking world. We will do something—that's for freaking sure.

In the Student common room, they tried to relax before dinner. The furniture was a mix of rattan wicker and large plush floor pillows. A couple of tables stood near an old-fashioned pinball machine and a dartboard. Unlike their bedrooms, the space was more modern, featuring a fully stocked kitchen with a small stove, drinks, and microwaveable food. Fresh veggie sticks, dips, and ice cream sat on the counter.

Declan, excited, announced, "Found some cookie dough. I'm going to make fresh cookies."

Alex, trying to snap out of his funk, said, "I'll have some milk too. Where's V?"

Declan smirked. "Go slow, Alex. Every relationship I rushed into didn't go too well."

Alex shot back, "You were in a relationship?"

Miko, who had been quietly observing, suddenly spoke. "She's in her room." Then, she hesitated, her expression shifting. "No, now she's walking down the hallway. Oh, yep, she's coming this way."

She stared at the wall, eyes widening. Then, the realization hit her.

"Oh shit."

Prezzy raised a brow. "You can see her right now?"

Miko, still staring at the wall, nodded. "Yep."

Alex frowned. "You can see her through the wall?"

Miko's voice rose. "Yes! I can."

Prezzy and Lin exchanged glances before standing up and walking over to Miko. Declan, standing next to the small oven, pointed to the far back wall.

"Miko, what's happening on the other side of that wall?"

Miko squinted, focusing. "It's a little person setting up food on the tables, probably getting ready for dinner." Then, as the weight of what she had just done sank in, she paled.

"Don't ask me to do it again," she whispered, covering her eyes.

At that moment, V walked into the room, stopping as she noticed everyone gathered around Miko. "Everything alright?" she asked, puzzled.

Alex turned to her. "Miko can see through walls."

Declan threw his arms up. "I want that Gift!"

V blinked. "How?"

Miko hesitated before explaining. "Alex asked where you were. Then I asked my mind, 'Where's V?' I looked up and saw you through the wall—in your room, then walking down the hallway. It felt weird."

V folded her arms. "So if you seek out something, you can see it through walls? It must be one of the Gifts, right?"

Alex nodded. "She saw the little person through that wall," he pointed toward the far side of the room.

V's curiosity deepened. "What was he doing?"

Miko shrugged. "I don't know, getting ready for dinner, I think."

From the back, Lev's voice broke through the chatter. "When is dinner?"

Prezzy shot him a glare. "Shoosh."

Lin said, "This is definitely the first Gift. My Steward told me we would all get Gifts from the Creator."

Before anyone could respond, Declan startled everyone by yelling, "Cookies are ready!"

Alex grabbed the milk from the fridge and grinned. "What a day!"

End of the world, I met my dream girl. What the hell is next?

He sat back down at the table with the glasses, just in time to hear Lin attempting an Australian accent as she asked Prezzy, "So, what did you do in Australia, mate?"

Prezzy laughed. "My parents own a chain of restaurants called Sangers and Grogs, between Melbourne and Brisbane. When I wasn't studying or working, I surfed."

V tilted her head. "Were you any good?"

Prezzy shrugged. "I guess."

Alex smirked. "She won two years of the Small Board Young Surfers' Competition."

Prezzy's eyes widened. "How did you know that?"

Alex grinned. "I looked you up."

V teased, "Who else did you look up?"

Still smirking, Alex said, "I came with Prezzy, that's why. I was just curious."

Lin's eyes lit up. "Wow, that's so cool—a surfer."

Declan leaned forward. "So what do they serve at this place, and what does Sangers and Grogs mean?"

Prezzy chuckled. "Sandwiches and beers."

Declan's face lit up. "Do you serve onion rings?"

Alex raised an eyebrow. "Onion rings?"

Declan shrugged. "I love onion rings."

Prezzy grinned. "Yes, we have the best onion rings."

Declan made a fake drooling sound. From across the room, Candido chimed in, "I can make something called a blooming onion."

Lin, intrigued, got up and plopped down next to Candido. "So, you cook, huh? What's Brazil like? And what are you writing?"

Candido, a very handsome 21-year-old, well-dressed and soft-spoken, looked up from his notebook and smiled. "I was on my way to New York to become a chef. Brazil? It's a very beautiful place. And I was writing a poem."

Lin bit her lip, looking like she was ready to pounce. She winked at V and Prezzy.

Declan raised his milk glass with a smirk. "Here's to the Brazilian poet who can cook a blooming onion."

V added, "A very handsome, polite poet from Brazil who can cook blooming onion."

Alex glanced at V; w*hat about me? Am I handsome?*

V turned to him and said, "Yes, you're handsome too, Alex."

Alex's eyes widened. *Did she just read my thoughts?*

Let's see, my favorite color is blue—between the ocean and sky blue.

V's expression shifted slightly as she looked back at him, curiosity flickering in her eyes.

Alex stared at her. "What's my favorite color?"

V hesitated for just a moment before answering. "Blue. Between the ocean and sky color."

Alex shot up from his chair, walked over to V, and knelt on one knee, locking eyes with her. He gently took her hand.

"I never told you that! Did you just read my mind?"

Her expression was priceless like she had just realized something terrifying and wonderful at the same time.

Alex hoped she was thinking; *I might really like this guy!*

But then her face paled. She swallowed hard before whispering, "I think you're right."

Alex studied her, then grinned. "What am I thinking right now?"

V hesitated, her lips parting slightly. Then, with a quiver in her voice and a mischievous smile, she said, "That you want to go skinny dipping with me?"

Alex jumped up, eyes wide with excitement. "V can read minds! V has the next Gift. Amazing!"

He turned back to her and whispered, "Although I'm thinking of changing my favorite color to green... like your eyes."

V's smile was insurmountable.

Alex spun around, hands raised in excitement, about to say something, when he suddenly froze. Fem and Gig had just walked into the room.

Gig's deep, raspy voice carried over the group. "How's it going in here?"

Tonari, leaning against the wall with one leg propped up, casually pointed toward V and Miko. "Miko can see through walls, and V—well, she just read Alex's mind. Other than that, we're just having milk and cookies."

Declan pumped his fist. "This is great!"

Fem, draped in a long, silver shimmering evening gown, stepped beside Tonari, towering over her by more than two feet. She smiled. "Great, we're making progress. Alex, did you know you can block her with the Common Mind?"

Alex blinked. "Block her?"

Fem nodded. "The Common Mind is the most powerful Gift we all have. You'll have a class on the Gifts in the coming days. As you train, it will become even stronger."

Gig and Fem took a few more steps into the room. Gig inhaled deeply from his pipe, exhaling a thick cloud of smoke that fogged up half the space. His oversized, worn cowboy-style hat tilted slightly as he cleared his throat. "The Creator doesn't fool around when it comes to Gifts. They can be fun, but they are also incredibly important for your future."

He took another deep pull from his pipe, scanning the room before asking, "Other than the Gifts, how's everyone holding up?"

Alex stood up, running a hand through his hair. "Can you be scared to death and amazed at the same time? I mean, the whole CAT thing—that's what's really got me thinking. And now, all of this? The Gifts, the Common Mind, the other planets? It's a lot."

Gig smiled knowingly and stepped toward him. "I know it's a lot to take in, but as the alcoholics in your time say—'One day at a time, one hour at a time, one minute at a time.'"

Lev straightened, standing almost at attention. "We're doing fine, sir."

Gig chuckled. "Call me Gig, Lev."

Lev hesitated, then nodded. "Yes, sir—Gig."

The room fell quiet for a moment as the Students took in the sheer size and presence of the two Master Elders.

Gig raised his massive hand, his voice steady. "Be patient. It will get easier. Your Gifts and the Common Mind will help you through it."

Fem, radiant and graceful, offered a warm smile. "It's your first day—lean on each other." She spun lightly in her magnificent gown before adding, "Let's try to have some fun tonight. We'll see you at dinner."

IV

V looked up at Alex, who gave her an affectionate smile. "From what Gig said, I can block you from hearing my thoughts."

Alex sat down next to her, leaning in close so no one else could hear. "But I can't think of any reason for doing that," he confessed. "I do worry about the others, though."

V leaned back in her chair, a playful smile forming as she let out a soft giggle.

Alex backed away, stretching as he headed for the door. "I'm going to close my eyes for a few minutes before dinner."

He has romance in him. He could be something. We'll have to keep an eye on him, V thought, watching him leave.

Declan waved a hand to grab her attention. "Hey, V, what am I thinking right now?"

V rolled her eyes, unimpressed. She let a pause hang in the air before deadpanning, "That you either need to take a massive dump or you're craving a lollipop."

Laughter erupted as Declan threw his hands in the air. "Ha, ha, very funny."

V turned her focus back to the group while pretending to read a book on the couch. Across the room, Tonari, Miko, and Lin sat together at the table.

"Did you see Fem's dress?" Tonari asked, her voice tinged with admiration. "Never seen anything so beautiful before."

"I know, right?" Miko chimed in. "What kind of fabric was that?"

Maria strolled over to join them. Meanwhile, V's mind raced.

Why am I able to read minds? What's that all about? What other Gifts will the others have?

She glanced toward the guys.

Declan plopped a six-pack of German beer onto the table near the dartboard. "You guys want to play darts?"

Candido quietly excused himself and left the room.

53

Declan grabbed a bottle, twisting off the cap. "You wanna pair up or play individually for points?"

Lev, the largest of the group and always dressed like he was ready for a business meeting, crossed his arms. "Individual is good." With his crew cut and disciplined posture, he looked like he had military training. He turned toward Kyoryk. "You play a lot of darts?"

Kyoryk grinned. "I've played."

Swaraj shrugged. "Not so much."

Declan leaned against the table, his tone dropping conspiratorially. "I was talking to Alex, and we were trying to figure out what the hell Gig is smoking in that pipe of his."

Kyoryk let out a chuckle. "Some type of 4,000-year-old purple chronic, I suppose."

Laughter echoed through the room as they grabbed their darts, the conversation shifting as the game began.

Lev's deep, calm voice carried across the room. "Was their entire race, our entire planet, really eight or nine feet tall? And they've lived for over four thousand years? And now they're here? In just two days, my whole reality has shifted."

Declan rubbed his neck. "And these marks… are they part of the Gifts from the Creator? I didn't even go to church."

Kyoryk scratched his own neck. "Last night was intense. It still hasn't sunk in that our lives have been extended. How does that even work?" He glanced at Declan. "Yeah, my neck still itches."

Declan turned Kyoryk around, inspecting the mark. "Looks like a bird or maybe an eagle." He leaned over to check Lev's. "Yours too."

Kyoryk shifted the conversation. "What's Saint Petersburg like?"

Lev leaned back. "Not bad. We live about thirty minutes from downtown. My grandfather and father own five tailor shops from Saint Petersburg to Toksova. Our biggest competitor is the Imperialist Tailoring Company. I was supposed to be the fourth generation in the family business, but now it'll be my younger brother." He sighed. "My dad gave me two choices: Harvard Law or running one of the stores. I picked Harvard."

Kyoryk grinned. "That explains why you always look like you walked out of a magazine."

Declan smirked. "I thought you dressed that way for the ladies, but now I see—it's in your blood."

Kyoryk tilted his head. "What kind of lawyer were you aiming to be?"

Lev shrugged. "Honestly? Probably corporate law."

Declan made a face. "Can't imagine why anyone would willingly choose that."

Kyoryk chuckled. "My mom's a lawyer. She makes a ton of money."

Declan perked up. "More than your dad?"

Kyoryk nodded. "Some years, yeah. Depends."

Swaraj suddenly frowned. "I just realized something… money. I guess we don't have to worry about that anymore." He exhaled. "I need to stop thinking about all this."

Lev nodded. "There's so much to figure out—about this place, about ourselves."

Swaraj stretched. "I need to clear my head. I'll get cleaned up before dinner. See you guys there."

Miko plopped down next to V, grinning. "Whatcha doing?"

V smiled, closing her book. "Nothing much. Is everyone heading to dinner?"

Miko nodded. "Looks like it. Time to go."

V and Miko stood and walked toward the dining hall, their minds still buzzing with everything that had happened.

Everyone reconvened at the grand table in Eternal Hall. The setup mirrored the previous evening, with Fem and Gig seated at the head. The year on Terraenti was 2033. Most students instinctively returned to their previous seats, settling into a familiar routine.

V glanced at Prezzy and mused, "What other Gifts do you think we might get?"

Prezzy shrugged. "No clue. But I think our brains have been altered somehow. Seeing through matter? That has to involve changing atomic structures, right? It's insane."

V nodded. "Something like that. And hearing other people's thoughts, especially in a group, that's not normal. Maybe it has to do with this Common Mind they keep talking about."

Declan, joining the conversation, interjected, "Transhumanism, isn't that about integrating A.I. into human neural networks? They've been messing with that for years, but it's all mechanical. This? This is different. Scientists playing around with the brain is one thing, but if this is some kind of different reality, that's starting to freak me out."

Lin smirked. "Noggin? Did you just call our brains 'noggins'?"

Declan grinned. "That's what my dad used to say. Old noggin. People are losing their minds, going mental. Some of that A.I. stuff has helped people with disabilities, though."

V shook her head. "There's no way this is man-made. We've been changed, but not by some lab experiment. This has to be from the Creator. A higher power. We're not superheroes; we're just... different."

Alex leaned in. "I agree. Maybe we'll have enhanced physical abilities—holding our breath longer, faster reflexes, and solving equations instantly. Maybe even heightened senses. Something's definitely changed. I think V is right." His gaze lingered on her for a moment before he turned back to the conversation.

As the meal wound down, some students lit up small hand-rolled cigarettes, and Klinchme served more wine along with whatever strange concoction filled Gig's massive mug.

Gig slid his chair back, settling in, then slammed his rock down on the table. "Fem and I have a few things to go over."

A virtual screen flickered to life, displaying Terraenti and its position in the solar system. Fem rose and addressed the group. "Right now, there are no immediate signs of CAT 6 arriving anytime soon."

The screen shifted, showing weather patterns and planetary data. "We are in a strong Grand Solar Minimum. There are more frozen rivers than in previous winters, and the Oceanic Conveyor Belt is at its weakest in two thousand years."

"This is why Northern Europe has been colder than usual for decades. A full magnetic reversal is possible, but it hasn't happened in over a hundred thousand years. The poles are shifting faster than ever, but whether they will completely reverse remains uncertain."

V watched the data scroll across the screen. Most students only half-listened, knowing the event was still years away.

Fem continued, "One of the things we must focus on is tracking timeline indicators. When Gig and I arrived, it took three years before the CAT struck. Our sun will be our primary focus, but all other factors—geological and atmospheric—must be closely monitored."

"The daily readings of pole positions, Terraenti's magnetic field strength, and fluctuations in cosmic radiation will provide us with early warnings of a super flare. Those of you who haven't visited the Science Lab or Control and Operations Room should do so in the next few days. Staying informed is crucial."

Fem sat down, and Gig took over. "The timeline can only be established once we detect Pulse Reversals. After the first two, we can begin estimating how much time we have before the CAT arrives. The problem is we never know how many Pulse Reversals there will be. In the past, the minimum was five, the maximum seven.

He took a deep breath and scanned the room. "We just wanted to keep you all in the loop. Any questions?"

V stood, her voice steady but full of curiosity. "What happens to the sun during a Pulse Reversal?"

Fem rose again, her presence immediately commanding attention. "The sun moves through cycles—strong, then weak, then stronger again, then weaker still. When it reaches its extreme weak phases, the Pulse Reversals occur. After several of these, the Super Flare hits."

She glanced at the virtual display, shifting the image of the sun. "It's difficult to compare it to anything else, but during these dormant periods, Pulse Reversals happen every forty-four hundred years. The first one isn't catastrophic—it affects the system, disrupts the magnetic field, and can be dangerous for our ships. But the planet itself only experiences minor issues—occasional power outages, slight atmospheric shifts."

Alex stood next. "About the Gifts—we have two so far. What are some of the others, and when will we receive them?"

Gig leaned forward, rubbing his hands together before standing. "Each CAT brings different Gifts. They adapt to the people, the needs of the time, and the challenges ahead. We don't know what they will be, and neither should you speculate." He looked around the room. "The Creator decides, so be patient. The Gifts will come when they are meant to."

His sharp eyes shifted toward Declan. "Didn't you have a question?"

Declan caught off guard, sat up straighter. "Uh—yeah, we were wondering about the marks on our necks from last night."

Fem reached up and removed her scarf, revealing six distinct eagle-like marks along the side of her neck. "All twelve of you bear the mark now. In time, as you progress through your training, the most suited to lead will eventually bear all six. These marks will transfer as the leadership role shifts."

She scanned the room, making eye contact with each of them. "But remember, every one of you is vital. The two at the head of the table may have more marks, but the rest of you are just as crucial to the future. Soon, you will start synchronizing as one, thanks to the Common Mind. It unifies the group."

She turned back to Declan. "Didn't you have another question for Gig?"

Declan hesitated, then shook his head. "No, I don't think so."

Gig chuckled, his deep voice filling the room. "I know some of you are curious about what I'm smoking in this pipe." A ripple of laughter moved through the group.

"It's a mix of herbs from times past," Gig continued, puffing on his pipe before exhaling a thick cloud. "If you'd like to try it, it's in The Pantry. But use it in moderation—especially before class. There are other treats in there too. The Pantry has a few surprises."

He gestured toward the deck. "Once again, join us for refreshments. Let's enjoy the evening."

As the group stood, Declan leaned toward Alex and whispered, "I didn't think about them having Gifts. They could probably read our minds or listen in."

Alex smirked. "Pretty sure we mentioned that a couple of times already. It's probably no big deal."

Declan nudged him. "Let's check out the pantry tomorrow around lunchtime."

Alex nodded. "Sure."

On the deck, V settled beside Alex, drawn in by the quiet intensity of his gaze over the cavern. The deck lights reflected off the mist rising from the waterfalls, blending with the shifting hues of the massive virtual screen. Scenes of untouched landscapes—snow-covered reindeer in Russia, cascading Hawaiian waterfalls, endless golden deserts—flickered across it. Each image felt like a love letter to Terraenti, a reminder of everything that would one day be lost.

The music shifted, a haunting melody filling the air. The **"Song,"** *Earth Bound*, carried a sense of longing, as if it had been written for those who knew their time was slipping away. It resonated in V's chest in a way she couldn't explain. She glanced at Alex, watching his reaction.

And then, without meaning to, she slipped into his thoughts.

She didn't just hear them—she *felt* them.

His reverence for Terraenti's beauty, his silent grief over what would come, the unbearable frustration of knowing and being unable to stop it. The vastness of his emotions overwhelmed her. He wasn't just mourning what would happen—he was carrying it. The weight of it pressed down on him, a responsibility he had given himself.

V had never felt anything like it.

Her parents had taught her logic, strategy, and analysis. She had grown up under pressure, but it had been cold, calculated. Feelings had been secondary, weaknesses to be controlled. Yet, here was Alex—someone she had only just met—drowning in emotions so raw, so deep, that they shook her.

She went deeper, slipping further into his mind. Why did this consume him so completely? Why him, more than the others? Could he see something they couldn't? Or was it simply that he *felt* it first? That he was the only one to grasp what they were facing truly?

Her breath hitched as she pulled back, suddenly aware of how deeply she had gone. Alex turned his head slightly as if sensing something.

V hesitated. She had been inside his mind completely.

And for the first time in her life, she realized—she wasn't afraid of what she had found.

Alex swallowed hard, his emotions still raw. He looked around at the faces of his classmates, their expressions mirroring the depth of his own thoughts. The bond they all now shared was undeniable. This *Common Mind*—this unseen force—had woven itself between them, linking their emotions, their thoughts, and their purpose.

V squeezed his hand gently, her warmth grounding him. *I'm not alone in this.* The realization settled deep within him. For the first time since he had learned about the CAT, he didn't feel isolated in his frustration and urgency. They *all* understood now. They *all* felt it.

Tonari wiped her tears and smiled. "We're really in this together, aren't we?"

Prezzy nodded. "Yeah, and I don't think it's just some emotional connection. This is real. The Creator did something to us."

Lev, his usual composed demeanor slightly shaken, added, "This power… it's not just about feeling what others feel. It's like an amplification. When Alex was grieving, we *all* grieved. When V comforted him, we *all* felt it."

Lin, usually one to joke, spoke softly. "If we can influence each other like this… imagine what we could do if we all focused on the same thing at once."

Declan smirked. "Like breaking out of here?" He winked, but no one laughed. There was an unspoken truth to his words—an undercurrent of something bigger.

Alex looked at Fem', her expression both serene and knowing. "You *knew* this would happen."

Fem' smiled. "Of course. This is what you were all chosen for. This connection—the Common Mind—will only grow stronger. The twelve of you are unlike any who have come before." Her gaze swept over them. "I know you feel the weight of what's to come, but understand this: you are not powerless. You *can* make a difference."

Gig, ever the towering presence, took a slow drag from his pipe and exhaled, watching the mist rise. "You're at the beginning of something remarkable, kids. What you do with it—that's up to you."

Alex took a deep breath, looking at his classmates, his team, and his *family*. The uncertainty remained, but one thing was clear—they weren't going just to *watch* as the world burned. They were going to do something about it.

"We're going to figure this out," Alex said firmly, his voice unwavering.

V smiled, the connection between them sparking again. "Yes, we are."

And for the first time since arriving at Eternal University, hope burned bright.

V lay in bed, staring at the ceiling, her mind racing with everything that had happened. The weight of the Common Mind, the Gifts, and the reality of her new life pressed down on her like an unseen force. She had spent her entire life questioning the world, analyzing motives, and preparing for the unexpected. But nothing—*nothing*—had prepared her for this.

She touched her neck, tracing the eagle mark with her fingers *for the rest of my life.* Freida's words echoed in her mind. The Common Mind wasn't something temporary—it was permanent. And she wasn't sure if that was reassuring or terrifying.

Her thoughts drifted to Alex. His pain had been *real*—not just an emotion, but a physical weight she had felt inside herself. The others had felt it too, but not as intensely. *Why?* What made her experience it differently? Freida had hinted that her Gift was something special, something beyond simple mind reading. *But what does that mean? What does the Creator want from me?*

The Intelligence Bureau, her past, her parents—all of it seemed distant now, like a fading memory. The life she had once envisioned was no longer even a consideration. *This is my path now.*

She turned onto her side, exhaling slowly. The warmth of the wine still lingered in her body, but her mind refused to settle. Tomorrow was combat training. What else would they discover about themselves? About their abilities? *About what we're truly capable of?*

She closed her eyes, listening to the faint hum of the university's systems, the distant sound of the waterfalls echoing through the cavern. This place, these people—*this* was her new reality.

And for the first time in a long time, V felt something unfamiliar: a sense of belonging.

With that thought, she finally drifted into sleep.

V

Alex snapped out of his thoughts, clearing his throat. "Yeah, yeah, I'm good." A new "Song" started. *Don't Stop Me Now*

Declan smirked, stepping into the shower. "You sure? Because you look like you just saw the face of God."

Kyoryk chuckled as he adjusted the water temperature. "Or maybe he just realized *he's in love.*"

Swaraj shook his head, lathering up. "Let the man breathe, guys. It's only been a day."

Alex leaned against the marble wall, letting the water wash over him, but his mind was elsewhere. *Vibrean Padame' Aboli.* He repeated her full name in his head. He'd never met anyone like her. She wasn't just *beautiful*—there was something else, something *deeper.* She was sharp, fearless, and confident in a way that both intrigued and unsettled him. And last night in the Common Mind… *he had felt her*. Not just her thoughts but her emotions, her essence.

Declan's voice snapped him back. "By the way, for Alex, today's "Tune choice is *'Don't Stop Me Now,'* I figured it fit the mood."

Kyoryk laughed. "What mood?"

Declan grinned, pointing at Alex. "Lovestruck. Horny. Totally confused."

Alex rolled his eyes. "You've got issues, Declan."

Swaraj rinsed his hair. "So, combat training today. You think we'll be fighting each other?"

Kyoryk shrugged. "Probably. Maybe some weapons training too."

Declan punched the air. "I hope so. I've been waiting to throw hands since I got here."

Alex smirked, shaking his head. "Nice tune; let's just hope we all make it out in one piece."

As they finished up, Alex quickly dried off and changed into his training clothes. His mind was racing, but one thought stood above the rest: *Whatever happens today, I know one thing—I want V by my side.*

As Alex stepped through the archway, he caught sight of Kira unlocking a weapons case. A row of firearms gleamed under the soft lighting of the training area. He was intrigued but turned his attention back to his own group, where Declan was already complaining.

"This dummy's giving me a weird look," Declan joked, throwing a weak punch at the padded figure. Swaraj sighed. "It's literally a mannequin, Declan."

Kira stepped up. "Alright, boys. Let's focus. These dummies are programmed to simulate human reaction times. You'll be practicing accuracy and speed."

Alex squared up, rolling his shoulders. "Got it." He threw a precise jab, the dummy's head snapping back slightly.

Declan mimicked his movement but overextended, nearly losing his balance. "Shit," he muttered.

Swaraj chuckled. "You're gonna get yourself knocked out."

Meanwhile, across the gym, V's group worked with Roman on weight training. Miko struggled with her barbell, and Lin offered an encouraging smile. "Just breathe. Focus."

V pressed her weight easily, scanning the room. She spotted Alex at the training dummies, his form sharp, his movements controlled. *He's good at this.* She smirked. *Maybe I should challenge him later.*

On the other side, Freida's group continued with knife training. Kyoryk had begun hitting four out of five targets consistently. Lev was already showing proficiency, while Candido, frustrated, grumbled, "I swear, this board is rigged."

Freida clapped his back. "Keep practicing. Knife throwing isn't just about strength. It's about control."

Across the room, Hugh's voice rang out. "Alright, listen up! We're switching stations in five minutes. I want you all pushing yourselves, but with controlled movements, no reckless hits. We're training for precision, not street fighting."

Alex, wiping sweat from his brow, turned toward Declan. "I think you need that speech more than anyone."

Declan grinned. "Nah, I think I've got this." He threw another punch—this time, he connected solidly. The dummy jerked back, but so did Declan, landing flat on his ass.

Swaraj burst out laughing. "Yeah. You've *got* this."

Alex shook his head, grinning as he helped Declan up. "Maybe combat training won't be so bad after all."

Kira nodded approvingly. "Good. Keep practicing. It needs to become second nature." She moved on to observe the others, leaving Alex to repeat the movements on his own. He focused, his arms sweeping in controlled arcs, deflecting invisible attacks. *This actually makes sense,* he thought. *It's simple, but it could save my life someday.*

Meanwhile, back at the firing range, Tonari took her stance, steadying the firearm. Hugh guided her hands into the correct position. "Relax your shoulders. Breathe. Don't tense up." She fired her first round, the recoil surprising her, but she maintained control. Hugh nodded in approval. "Nice. Keep going."

Maria leaned over to Prezzy and whispered, "You really jumped after that first shot." Prezzy chuckled. "I wasn't expecting it to feel so... powerful."

On the other side of the gym, the knife-throwing group continued their practice. Candido was improving, managing to stick three out of five knives into the board. "Better," Freida encouraged. "Your grip is getting steadier."

Lev, always composed, threw with precision, landing all his knives in the center. Kyoryk, watching, muttered, "Show-off."

Freida laughed. "Competition is good. It makes you better." She then glanced over at V, Lin, and Miko, who were working on weights. V was pressing heavier than expected, her form flawless. Lin and Miko exchanged glances. "She's stronger than she looks," Lin murmured.

Miko nodded. "She has good control too."

Hugh's voice rang through the gym. "Alright, switch stations! Let's keep moving."

Alex, wiping sweat from his brow, caught Declan's grin as they passed. "Not bad with the dummies," Declan remarked. "I mean, they *are* just standing there."

Alex smirked. "You still fell on your ass punching one earlier."

"Technicality," Declan shot back. "I was testing its structural integrity."

Kira overheard and smirked. "Maybe next time, test with less enthusiasm."

As the groups switched, Alex found himself walking toward the knife-throwing station. He glanced over at V, who was already watching him. He grinned. "Think I can throw knives as well as you?"

V smirked. "Try not to hit the floor like Candido."

Candido groaned. "I *heard* that."

Alex picked up a knife, feeling its weight. He lined up his throw, breathed in, and let it fly. It missed the target completely, clattering onto the ground.

Declan burst out laughing. "Oh yeah, you're a natural."

Alex rolled his eyes. "I was warming up." He picked up another knife, this time focusing. He threw, and the blade stuck—not dead center, but at least on the board.

Freida clapped. "That's progress."

As the combat session continued, each Student pushed themselves, learning more than just techniques—they were adapting, growing, and realizing that their training would shape their futures in ways they couldn't yet comprehend.

V glanced over at Maria, her expression unreadable. Alex, caught off guard hesitated before responding, "Uh, yeah, sure."

Maria smirked and walked off, her long strides deliberate. Declan leaned in with a grin. "Man, you've got options."

Alex shot him a look. "You're an idiot."

V crossed her arms, looking between the two. "Should I leave you boys to gossip, or are we heading to lunch?"

Alex turned to her, ignoring Declan's smirk. "Lunch sounds good."

As they made their way up the ramp toward the dining hall, Miko caught up. "So, what's up with the Common Mind and... that?" She nodded toward Maria, who was now chatting with Lin and Prezzy.

V shrugged. "Not sure. Maybe it's bringing us closer together in ways we don't fully understand yet."

Declan chuckled. "Yeah, or it's just enhancing what was already there."

Alex shot him another glare, but before he could reply, Hugh's voice echoed down the hall. "Let's keep moving, people. We have an afternoon session waiting for us."

In the Pantry, Alex picked up one of the containers of herbs, examining the label. "Looks like a mix of old-world stuff and some unique blends from Terraenti," he mused.

Declan, stuffing his pockets with rolling papers, grinned. "Well, I guess we'll have to try them out later and see if Gig's onto something."

Prezzy shook her head. "You guys are like kids in a candy store."

Tonari, still holding her cookies, smiled. "Maybe we are. But look at this place—it's a time capsule. Everything from different cultures, different CATs, all in one spot."

Alex nodded. "Yeah, it's fascinating. But also kind of eerie. It's like… they've been preparing for us for a long time."

Declan tossed a lighter to Prezzy. "I guess we should be honored, right?"

They made their way back toward the entrance, passing stacks of fresh produce, neatly arranged spices, and barrels of aged wine. Kahput was still organizing supplies near the carts, his keen eyes watching them with mild amusement.

Alex paused, turning to him. "How long have you been here, Kahput?"

Kahput smirked. "Longer than you'd think. Not as long as my father, though. He's been here since CAT 1."

Declan's eyes widened. "Since CAT 1? How old is he?"

Kahput shrugged. "Time works differently for us. When you're chosen by the Creator, things change."

Tonari exchanged glances with Alex and Prezzy. "Does that mean we'll stop aging?"

Kahput's expression grew thoughtful. "Not exactly. You'll still grow, but differently. You'll see."

Alex frowned, digesting that information. "So, we're basically immortal?"

Kahput chuckled. "Immortal is a strong word. Let's just say... your lifespan will far exceed what you once expected."

Declan whistled. "Damn. Guess we're in it for the long haul."

Kahput nodded. "Yes, you are."

The group stood in silence for a moment, the weight of their new reality settling in. Then, as if breaking the tension, Prezzy clapped her hands together. "Alright, enough deep thoughts. Let's get out of here before Declan hoards the entire tobacco section."

With a laugh, they made their way out of the pantry, stepping back into the hallway, where the rest of their classmates were heading toward the dining hall.

Alex glanced at V as she passed by, her green eyes locking onto his for a moment before she looked away with a slight smirk.

Declan nudged him. "Yeah, mate. You're in deep."

Alex sighed. "Tell me something I don't know."

In the dining hall, the Students settled into their usual spots. Gig and Fem' were already seated, watching the group with quiet amusement.

Gig leaned forward, his deep voice carrying across the table. "I take it the Common Mind is starting to show its effects."

Lin walking by grinned. "Oh yeah, it's definitely working."

Fem' nodded. "It will only grow stronger. Your bonds will deepen, your awareness of one another will sharpen, and in time, it will feel as natural as breathing."

Sitting at the table, Alex stole a glance at V, wondering if she had felt what he did last night—something more than just the connection between them all. He wasn't sure what it meant yet, but one thing was clear.

Everything had changed.

Tonari smirked, taking a bite of her food. "Well, they don't look that old. Guess the whole 'Elder' thing works differently."

Declan shook his head, still chuckling. "I mean, seriously, Kahput and Rugrog sound like characters from a fantasy novel."

Lin rolled her eyes. "Declan, everything here is like a fantasy novel. Have you looked around lately?"

V turned her attention back to Prezzy. "So they just came here for us?"

Prezzy nodded. "That's what he said. They've been waiting for this moment for a long time. Makes you wonder how much is actually planned and how much just happens naturally."

Alex looked thoughtful. "If everything was planned by the Creator, then what choices do we actually make? Or do we just go along with a path that's already set?"

Lin shrugged. "Maybe it's both. Maybe we have free will, but the big events—the things that really matter—are already decided."

Declan pointed at Lin with a fry. "That's deep. Too deep for lunchtime."

Tonari smirked. "Better get used to it, Declan. We're not in Kansas anymore."

Declan snorted. "No shit."

Alex glanced at V, noticing the way she was absently spinning her fork between her fingers. Her eyes flickered toward him for a second before she looked away, a small smile playing on her lips.

Prezzy exhaled, setting down her fork. "So… tonight, we test out the Pantry goods?"

Declan grinned. "That's the plan."

V raised an eyebrow. "You're seriously going to do that on your second night here?"

Declan leaned back in his chair. "We're on the moon, V. Literally. And we just found out we're going to live for, like, ever. Might as well see what kind of fun they have to offer."

Tonari smirked. "Just don't embarrass yourself. Again."

Declan placed a hand on his chest, feigning offense. "Me? Embarrass myself? Never."

Alex shook his head, laughing, but his mind was elsewhere. He kept thinking about what Fem' had said last night—about how they were chosen, about their Gifts. He was still wrapping his head around everything.

And then there was V.

He didn't know what it was, but something about her pulled at him in a way he couldn't explain.

Lin's voice snapped him out of his thoughts. "Earth to Alex. You okay?"

He looked up. "Yeah. Just… thinking."

V gave him a knowing glance. "That's dangerous."

Alex smirked. "Tell me about it."

V sat back in her chair, hands on her head. "Oh Ganeshi. This is so crazy. We are hanging out with people who have lived for thousands and thousands of years. Teachers that smoke weed party almost every night." She shook her head, "It's all crazy."

Declan, still giggling with a mouth full of food, said, "I'm trying not to think about it."

Lin slammed her hand down on the table. "What is this? It's the best damn thing I've ever had. Jesus, it's good."

Prezzy sat up, grabbed one off her plate, and ate it. She paused, then said, "That is good. I think it's like a baby Brussels sprout with barbecue sauce."

Declan reached for Lin's plate. "Lemme have one." Lin slapped his hand away. "Get your own damn baby sprout." Declan frowned, still giggling. "But lunch is almost over."

Tonari looked at Alex. "Maria keeps looking at you, Alex." Alex glanced at the other table. Maria smiled and looked away. "She's just messing with me." V questioned, "What's going on?" Declan smirked. "I think she wants something from Alex." V asked, "What does she want?"

Declan mimed kissing someone and then laughed. Alex rolled his eyes. "It's nothing. Declan's being a dick, and Maria? Well, we're not sure what's happening with her. She is flirting with me." V looked over at Maria, puzzled. Maria smiled. Declan, trying to rile V up, said, "Well, we will see how far she is willing to go." Alex sighed. "Declan is just messing around. Harvey told me to focus, and I'm going to focus."

Declan stood up. "Yeah, now let's go focus on shooting some guns. Let's go."

They all got up from the table and headed back to the gym.

Hugh cleared his throat. "Group two, you're with me. Group three, you're with Kira now. Group four, you're with Roman on weights. Group one, you're with Freida on knives."

The Students went to their assigned places. Alex, Declan, and Swaraj headed to the firing range.

While setting up, Declan asked, "What type of guns will we be training with?"

Hugh answered, "This is a Glock 9mm. This model is a 19X. It's a more compact piece. Lighter."

"Will we be given guns?" Declan asked. "The purpose is to train on these weapons in case you ever need to use them. So, no. At this point, it's not necessary to have one," Hugh replied. "The rifle we'll be using is the AR-15-M-LOK-16."

Swaraj asked, "Has another planet's people ever attacked Earth? I mean, Terraenti before?" Hugh said, "No. But there have been some problems with Amotaious. Breaking the Directives and Laws. No population as of yet has the ability to travel to other planets."

"What were they?" Swaraj inquired. "Some think we should share technologies. Some think the populations of the planets should know about the Elders and the existence of the other planets. Things like that. Vindor has a very aggressive culture. They have always advanced as fast as us. I think they have tried to steal technology from other planets. There's even talk of taking over other planets. That kind of thinking could lead to a galactic war. It would be bad," Hugh explained.

Alex added, "Right, like letting our people know about the upcoming disaster." Hugh agreed. "Right. But if we told them, how many would die from panic? People would take to the streets; people would go nuts. The greed, or they might just give up altogether. Now, if you could come up with a way to protect the planet without letting them know, that might work."

Alex got a determined look on his face. *"There must be a way. Something we can do. I'll get with the others and figure out possible ways to help. Maybe we can use these new Gifts. Maybe this Common Mind thing? Why does the Creator just sit around doing nothing? It's been, what, five Catastrophes now? What the hell is going on here?"*

Declan asked, "Has an Elder ever tried to let the people know?" "I think some have tried, but the people didn't listen, or the Creator interfered. Not sure. You could look in the library or on your tablet. Look back into religious history that might tell you. Everything is there. You just need to find it. Let's get back to shooting. Right!" Hugh said.

"So far, you all are doing okay. You need to focus on precision. It's important where you hit a person. Debilitate or kill. That's not a question."

Swaraj began shooting again. Hugh asked Alex, "Since I can't leave the room, could you go ask Kira to come and see me?" "Sure," Alex replied.

Alex returned to the gym area and told Kira. V, Lin, and Miko were training with knives. Alex asked, "Have you guys ever thrown knives before?" Miko replied, "Does throwing a butter knife at my brother Tiko count?" They all laughed.

Alex leaned towards V, excitement gleaming in his eyes. "I learned something new from Hugh. Apparently, there have been issues on Amotaious among the Elders of different planets."

V's curiosity was piqued. "What kind of issues?" "Some Elders wanted to share technology, while others wanted to reveal their existence to their populations," Alex explained.

V, starting to know Alex's compassion, asked, "What about stopping the CAT?" With a serious expression, Alex replied, "If there was a way to do it without alarming the population, then yes, it's a possibility."

Miko chimed in, skeptical. "How are you going to prevent the nova or whatever they call it? Isn't that impossible?" Alex, determined, responded, "I don't know, maybe protect the Earth somehow. We can't just do nothing."

V suggested, "Well, let's meet and talk about the possibilities later in the common room." "Alright," Alex agreed. "Declan and some others want to try out Gig's ancient weed later too."

Miko and V exchanged uneasy glances. V admitted, "Not a big fan of pot. Makes me paranoid. And it's not a place I want to be paranoid in."

Lin added, "If we had some shrooms, I would do that."

V smiled. "Never done magic mushrooms before."

Alex stood upright. "Alright, I better get back to the firing range."

Returning to the range, Alex saw Hugh talking to Kira. Hugh was instructing, "We'll meet back here the day after tomorrow. We'll go over hand-to-hand combat and start with the rifles. Then they can practice on their own." Kira nodded. "I'll add it to their schedules." Hugh thanked her. "That's great; thanks for helping with the scheduling." Kira smiled. "My pleasure," she said, then left the room.

Hugh turned to Alex. "Alright, Mr. Alex. Let's see you go through all the steps. Then we'll be done for the day."

Alex stepped up, checked the number of rounds in the clip, stood appropriately, raised his arms, and pointed the weapon towards the target. He clicked the safety off, put his finger on the trigger, aimed, breathed in, then slowly out, and pulled the trigger.

He fired, then put the safety back on, pointed the gun toward the ceiling, and removed the clip. He placed everything on the table and looked at Hugh. "How was that?"

Hugh, impressed but composed, said, "Good." He put the gun and clip back into the gun case. "Everyone did well. Next time, we train with rifles." He directed everyone back to the gym.

In the gym, he announced, "Tomorrow you have Directives and Laws. The day after that, we're back here to continue and finish the basics."

"Next week, we have hand-to-hand combat and rifles. Remember, you can work out in your free time; just follow the rules." He pointed to a sign on the wall detailing the gym rules. "Alright, have a good evening."

Half the group gathered in the common room. Alex, Declan, and Prezzy sat at one of the tables. Candido, Tonari, and Lin sat on floor pillows in the center.

Declan was attempting to roll a joint. Alex remarked, "Shooting was fun."

Declan agreed. "I liked it. Haven't shot a pistol before. I thought it was funny when Hugh said, 'It's important where you hit the person.'"

Alex recalled, "Yes. He said, 'Do you want to debilitate or kill? That's not a question.'"

Alex leaned closer to Declan. "So, what are you rolling there?" Declan replied, "This is the Mongolian Thai."

Prezzy noted, "I'll take one hit only." Alex affirmed, "One hit of this just might do it."

Declan looked up at Alex. "Where is Maria?" Alex gave him a dirty look. "Quit messing with me about that."

Declan asked, "So, what did you do in Australia?" Alex replied, "We built and ran desert racers in the Northern Territory. I also worked at my dad's machine shop when I had time away from school. What about you in the U.K.?"

Declan took a hit and coughed. "After my dad passed, we moved to England, and my mom opened a couple of gambling clubs. She's a professional gambler."

Declan coughed again. "She ran a couple of underground clubs too. I would help her out when I wasn't in school."

Alex asked, "What city?" "Bristol," Declan answered.

Alex turned to Lin. "What about you, Lin? What's your story?" Lin, looking up from the pillows while holding her guitar, replied, "I'm from Aberdeen. My parents are homesteaders. They raise cattle, chickens, and pigs. What they don't eat, they sell. They live off the grid. I have a little YourScreen channel."

Alex, excited, said, "That's awesome! How did they get into that?" Lin replied, "Remember the U.S. blackout in 2028? After that, my parents decided to go off the grid and raise their own food."

Tonari commented, "I remember that. Didn't thousands of people die?" Lin nodded. "Over 20,000 people died. Food shortages. People freaked out." Candido asked, "How long was the power out? The whole U.S., wasn't it?" Lin replied, "I think it was eight or nine days." Candido said, "Without power, it's a crazy world. I bet places like New York and San Francisco were super bad."

Alex blew out a big puff of smoke. "That's enough for me. Wasn't that the same year the president had a heart attack? It just shows you how fragile our system is. I don't understand why we live like this. Why is our power grid, all over the world, the way it is? The just-in-time food system and all that. There must be a better way." Declan added, "I heard the president got impeached like eight months later. You're right, though. The system is too fragile. YourScreen, AllTunes, all the teens are on that app from China ClickClack, now China basically owns Afghanistan to the Western Sahara? What are you going to do?"

Alex asked Lin, "What do you do on YourScreen?" Lin replied, "Sing and play guitar, sometimes in the mall." Candido pulled out his tablet. "What's the name of your channel?" "Linnea Adder." He typed it in, listened for a moment, and said, "Wow, you're really good." Lin smiled. "Thanks."

Declan said, "Alex, slide over the lighter." Alex, high, was looking at the ceiling. Declan's hand stretched out on the table towards the lighter, repeated, "Alex, gimme the lighter." Finally, Declan yelled, "Alex!" The lighter magically slid into Declan's hand. With an amazed and confused look, Declan said, "Did you see that?"

Lin looked up but couldn't see the top of the table. "See what?" Declan looked at her. "The lighter moved. Did I make it move?"

Alex rolled his eyes. "You're high, mate. This weed is chronic." Declan slid the lighter back to the other side of the table. "Okay, watch this. No, really!"

Everyone watched. Declan verified, "Is everyone watching?" They all looked at him. Alex said, "Mate, yes."

Declan put his hand out towards the lighter, and after about two seconds, the lighter slid right into his hand. Declan exclaimed, "Another Gift? Damn, I'm good. Is that my Gift?"

They all gaze at Declan in astonishment. Prezzy says, "Here, move this." She places her tablet on the table, about two feet from Declan's hand. He extends his hand, and the tablet slides effortlessly into his grasp.

Alex, intrigued, says, "Here, move this." He positions his beer at the table's edge. Declan reaches out, and the beer begins to slide towards him. It topples over, spilling and rolling across the table.

Alex laughs heartily. Lin exclaims, "Oh shit!" She jumps up from her cushion and snatches a towel to clean up the mess. V strides into the room, announcing, "You're going to be late for dinner."

Lin turns to V and declares, "Declan can move things with his mind. Not very gracefully, but he can do it." V, curious, says, "Show me."

Candido, now standing, places a lighter on the far end of the table. Declan reaches out again, and the lighter glides smoothly into his hand.

V, amazed, exclaims, "That's incredible. So that's three gifts in two days." Lin continues to mop up the spilled beer. V muses, "I wonder what we will see by the end of the week."

Alex inquires, "What time is dinner?" "Now," Prezzy announces.

Declan begins to jump up and down, shouting, "I can move objects! I can move objects!" They all rise and head off to dinner.

VI

In the grand hall, Alex settled beside V, fixing her with a stern gaze. "We need to find out more about what happens to Terraenti when the Super Flare hits," he declared. V, already absorbed in her tablet, pointed at the screen. "I've looked into it. It details how people survived previous flares and their impact on climate and everything else. The main concern today is food. Did you know they restock the stores every night? It's called Just-in-Time delivery. If the power goes out, stores will run out of food within a week, maybe a month, if trucks can still deliver. No food means no survival."

Alex nodded. "I'm going to talk to Harvey later. He's been here for a year; maybe he knows something." "I'll talk to Freida and see what she knows," V responded.

Lev, frustrated by his lack of a Gift, interjected, "What? Declan can move things with his mind?" Candido affirmed, "Yeah, we saw it."

Lev turned to Declan, "How did you do it?" Declan explained, "I was asking Alex to pass me the lighter. He was spacing out, so I asked him again. Then the lighter just slid across the table to me."

Miko chimed in, "So that's three Gifts now?"

Lin added, "He needs to perfect it. He spilled a beer all over the table."

Alex turned to V, "We need to start working on these Gifts and the Common Mind." He gave another stern look. "I think we're the only ones who can do it. The only chance the planet has to protect it somehow." V agreed, "Let's gather everyone in the common room on Saturday and work on it." Alex concurred, "Alright, I'll talk to the guys. You get with the girls, and we'll start on Saturday."

Everyone noticed Lev squinting like he was in intense concentration. They laughed as Maria put her hand on his shoulder. "Don't worry, Lev, your Gift will be really cool." Frustrated, Lev slammed his fist on the table, cursing in Russian.

Suddenly, the lights dimmed, fluttered, and then went out completely in the Eternal Hall before flickering back on.

The table fell silent as the Stewards, Gig and Fem, paused their conversation. The Students looked at Lev. Maria hit him on the arm, exclaiming, "Holy shit, man. Is that your Gift? Can you control electricity or something? You'll need to work on that."

Lev's frustration melted into a broad grin.

Miko exclaimed, "That's four Gifts now!"

V and Alex exchanged looks, and Alex gave Lev a thumbs-up. As they were finishing their meal, Gig slammed a rock onto the table, activating a virtual screen displaying Amotaious and its location in the galaxy. He stood and announced, "We're having issues on Amotaious that need our attention. Fem and I will be there for a few days with the Stewards. You all have three days off to catch up on material and work on your Gifts. Stay focused and remember why you're here."

Fem added, "Tomorrow, we'll have Directives and Laws with Harvey and Beauta. No other immediate news for now."

Some Students headed to the deck, while others returned to the common room. V waited for Freida. "Do you know if any Elders tried to help Earth prepare for the CAT?" she asked.

Freida, looking stern, replied, "Telling people is a major lawbreaker and would be bad for Terraenti. The Creator might intervene. We've survived five catastrophic events. Fem said it was the hardest thing she's ever endured. Maybe there's a way to protect Earth without the population knowing, but the sun is so powerful. I just don't see how it's possible."

Unhappy with the answer but resigned, V asked, "Why are you going to Amotaious?" Freida shrugged. "Not sure, we'll be briefed on the way. I see you're getting a few of your Gifts. How are your classes going?" "They're fine. I think we have four Gifts now," V replied.

Freida encouraged, "Great. Focus on your classes too. You could receive more than one Gift. Be aware of that." She smiled but seemed preoccupied.

"How long does it take to get to Amotaious?" V inquired. "Around six hours if we catch one Thread. Is everyone getting along okay?" Freida asked. "Yeah, everyone's alright," V assured her.

"Okay, I'll talk to you later. Have fun this weekend," Freida said, departing.

V went down to the deck and saw Alex talking to Harvey. She waited at the bar and ordered a Palm Toddy. When Alex joined her, he asked, "Did you find out anything?" "No, not really.

Same thing: focus on the Gifts and classes. How about you?" "Nothing important. Do you want to stay here or go back to the common room?" Alex asked.

V, looking sour, said, "Let's head back to the common room."

In the common room, Miko was talking to Lin in Japanese. Lev was turning the lights on and off by hitting the wall. Declan struggled to move the table. V smiled at Alex, "See, everyone's working on their Gifts." She walked over to Lin, "Didn't know you spoke Japanese?"

Lin, looking annoyed, replied, "I didn't know either." She waved her hand at Lev, speaking in Russian, "Knock that off. I'm going to have a seizure. You don't need to pound your fist either; try snapping your fingers." Maria chuckled.

Alex suggested to Lin, "Maybe that's your Gift? Sing us a tune in French. I love the French language."

Declan grumbled, "Shit! This damn table isn't moving."

Lin grabbed her guitar and started singing in French.

Alex sat next to Declan with a beer. "You can't move the table?" Declan sighed, "No. Not yet." Lev walked over, physically picked up the table, and moved it closer to Declan. "There." Declan laughed, "Very funny. Ha ha."

Alex addressed the group with determination. "How can we use our Gifts to help the people of Terraenti during the impending CAT?"

A moment of silence settled over the room. Declan broke the tension with a jest. "Well, Lin can speak to all the different countries in their languages and let them know." V interjected, "One of the primary rules is we can't let the people know." Swaraj added, "We don't know enough about the Gifts to change anything yet. We still have more Gifts to discover." Alex nodded thoughtfully. "You're right, Swaraj. We can't devise a plan until we know what tools we have. How about playing a game to unwind?"

"Beer Pong," Declan suggested. "There are some games in the cupboard," Prezzy said, standing up to check. "Let's see. Yahtzee, Monopoly, Blank Slate, Pictionary."

"Yahtzee. I played that a while back," Alex remarked. "I know Yahtzee," Lev chimed in.

Prezzy grabbed the Yahtzee box and set it on the table. Alex distributed scorecards, and the others gathered around to play while Lin continued to play her guitar, singing in French.

Candido walked in and started listening to Lin. When she finished, he asked, "What tunes do you know?"

A new **"Song"** started. *El Porompompero*

Candido then said, "I know this tune on the guitar. He held up his tablet; everyone joined in to sing the chorus part." He began to play and sing, and Lin joined in. Tonari watched from the couch.

Unbeknownst to them, the Common Mind was especially potent with music. As Lin and Candido sang, the others started to feel its power.

One by one, the Students entered the common room, humming the tune. Lev and a few others abandoned Yahtzee, grabbed pots and wooden spoons from the kitchen, and joined in, beating on the makeshift instruments. Candido played louder, his and Lin's voices rising in volume.

Declan nudged Alex, nodding towards Maria, who was gazing at Candido. "I think you're in the clear, bro. Look at the way Maria is looking at Candido." It was evident Maria's affection had shifted from Alex to Candido.

The chorus swelled as they all sang. The Common Mind reached full strength. The room buzzed with an almost magical energy. It was like a collective trance, a state where body and mind were liberated. The group moved as one, singing, dancing, and pounding on pots.

V felt the energy surge through her more intensely than the previous night with Alex and the others. Her worries melted away. She spun around the room, grabbed Alex's hand, and they danced and sang. Maria knelt in front of Candido, twisting her hair and singing. Prezzy and Declan spun around, lost in the music.

Everyone shouted. They were so immersed in the moment that they didn't notice Gig and Fem peek into the room.

Fem turned to Gig, "I think they'll be fine this weekend." They walked down the hallway, singing.

The night ended with laughter, hugs, and possibly some secret kisses. The group couldn't believe what had happened. They had forgotten all about the impending disaster. For the second time, they experienced the true power of the Common Mind through music, feeling united and invincible.

After a few more beers and glasses of wine, they celebrated their extraordinary experience. Gradually, they made their way to their rooms to retire for the evening. At the end of the hall, V noticed a room during her search for an extra pillow on the first day. It housed extra linens and the washers and dryers.

After, she left a note on Alex's bed. It read, "Meet me in the room at the end of the hall at 11:00. V." She wasn't sure if she was doing the right thing but felt compelled to make the first move. It was now 10:45.

Only V and Miko remained in the common room. Miko asked, "How did that all make you feel?"

While cleaning the kitchen area, V glanced over. "What do you mean? It was fun. I don't know. The Common Mind is weird. I've never felt anything like it. It's like we're all together. It's like a drug or something."

Miko walked over, checking the archway to ensure no one else was around. She whispered, "It makes me feel kind of horny. It's like my body is going through something I can't describe."

V chuckled. "Maybe. I do feel different. Freida said it's going to get stronger as time goes on."

Now leaning against the counter, Miko looked up at the ceiling after taking a sip of wine. "So, I'm going to feel better than this? That's crazy. Maybe it's the air here."

V smiled. "We're done here. We should get some sleep."

Miko took the last sip of her wine, rinsed her glass, and said, "Okay, I'll see you in the morning."

V added, "Don't rush into anything, if you know what I mean. Even though your body might be telling you otherwise."

Miko smiled. "I can take care of that myself, if necessary. If you know what I mean." V laughed. A new **"Song"** J'Attendrai started.

V finished her wine, started the dishwasher, and saw that it was 10:58. *"Okay, let's do this,"* she thought.

She went down to the laundry room, entered, and closed the door, sitting on one of the washers. As she sat there, doubts crept in. *"Maybe I made a mistake. Alex isn't coming. What was I thinking? Leaving a silly note on his bed. What am I? In third grade?"*

She checked her tablet—11:02. Just as she was about to leave, the door opened. Alex stood there with a nervous look on his face. After a long pause, he said, "Hey."

She looked at him and said, "Hey."

V opened the door wider and invited him in with a wave of her hand. Alex, unsure of V's intentions but hopeful, entered slowly. He asked cautiously, "So, what's this all about?"

V sidestepped closer to him, her voice trembling slightly, betraying her nerves. "I wanted to try something." Alex, now looking into her eyes, asked, "What's that?"

She had this French music playing she thought Alex might like playing. Alex smiled. V got close, looking directly into his eyes, and stood on her tiptoes. "This," she whispered, wrapping her hands around the back of his neck, tilting her head, and kissing him.

At first, it was a regular kiss. After about two seconds, she pulled on his hair, and their kiss deepened. Alex's hands roamed over her, and V knew this was no mistake. She kissed him more aggressively, and Alex picked her up, setting her back on the washer where she had sat moments ago. Their hands explored forbidden places, and they began to lose control. Clothes were about to come off when V pushed him back.

"Are Baap Re!" she exclaimed. Alex spun around, pacing and whispering to himself, covering his face. V could only make out a few words: "Focus, wrong with me, idiot." It seemed he couldn't look at her.

"Alex. Alex, look at me," she finally said. He turned to face her, stepping closer. "What?" he asked, as if he had done something terrible. V raised her brows. "Are you okay?" "Yeah, I'm great. How are you?" he replied. V smiled. "Thanks for letting me try that."

Alex looked puzzled. "What happens the next time we try it?" She laughed. "Don't know. Prepare better?"

V hadn't kissed anyone in over two years. Alex hadn't had a girlfriend since his first year at university, about the same amount of time. Both were inexperienced lately. Alex raised his hands as if to put up a stop sign. "Okay, well, that was fun."

He grabbed her tablet, "This is nice, but I like this French **"Song"** *Tornade* better. He smiled at her. "Thanks for inviting me here. I should probably go to my room now. By myself."

He sat on one of the dryers next to her for a minute. "I'll guess I'll see you in the morning." He approached to kiss her again gently on the lips. Then did. "Good night, then." He slowly hopped off the washer.

V smiled. As he walked out slowly and before he shut the door, he stopped and smiled at her. She hopped down, did a spin on the floor, and headed to her room, listening to the tune he left playing on her tablet. *"Good. That worked. A good kisser, too. Alright, don't go too fast."*

"Relax, V. Don't go too fast. God, that felt good. It was like I wanted it all right then. What is wrong with me? I'm a crazy person. Okay, go to bed."

V made it back to her room and went to bed.

The next morning, she opened her eyes. All she could think of was the kiss and "Porompompom, pero, pero."

She smiled inside, something fierce.

She leaped out of bed, feeling like she had extra voltage coursing through her veins. She knew she had to calm down or risk being found out. *"Calm yourself, woman. Just breathe,"* she thought. Shaking her arms and legs, she did some sit-ups and push-ups.

"I wish I could swim. I need to swim. Tomorrow, I'm going to swim. Alright, calm down. Damn, that was a good kiss. The tune Candido sang was fun too. What is wrong with me? I've never felt this good." She paced around the room. *"Don't tell anyone about the kiss. Be cool with Alex. Okay, let's go."*

V grabbed her robe and headed to the shower.

She walked into the shower room to find Prezzy, Lin, Miko, Maria, and Tonari all showering. She slipped in between Prezzy and Miko.

A thin, smoked glass divider separated them, and she said, "Last night was fun. The Common Mind? It's like we were all one, totally in sync. I'm starting to get what it's all about now, why they call it the Common Mind." Miko agreed, "Yeah, it was great. What a feeling."

Prezzy giggled, "A friend of mine gave me a pill at a nightclub once, but this was much better. I wonder what it's like to have sex with the Common Mind going on?"

There was a brief pause before they all burst into laughter.

V, with a big smile, pondered aloud, "Wonder how that works?" Prezzy suggested, "You won't know until you try."

They laughed again. Tonari, with soap all over her face, asked, "What is it?" Prezzy looked at her, questioning if she hadn't heard. She responded much louder, "Sex. Sex while in the Common Mind."

Tonari nodded, smiled, and nonchalantly agreed, "Oh, that would be nice." They all laughed even harder.

Alex, Lev, and Declan walked in. Declan asked, "What's so funny?" Lin looked at Declan and replied, "You'll never know." Prezzy smiled and admitted, "He might."

Lin looked at V, and they laughed again. V looked at Alex and said, "Good morning." Alex, smiling, responded wittily, "Porompompom, pero, pero."

V and the other girls laughed as they toweled off and left the shower. Declan and Lev laughed too. The boys showered.

While getting some toast and eggs, V sat down next to Lin and Candido. "What's the schedule for today?" she asked.

"Directives and Laws. I think the whole day is only on Directives," Candido replied. "Great, a whole day of the Directives," V said. "A whole day of telling us why we can't interfere. Wonderful."

Lin suggested, "We could plan what we're doing this weekend." "I'm swimming all three days. That's the best thing for me. It's my way of exercising and reducing stress," V declared.

Miko sat down and added, "Swimming sounds good to me. I also need to practice my flips and jumps."

Alex joined them with a couple of donuts. "Last night was fun. Within a few seconds, I knew all the lyrics to that tune. It's still in my mind. Porompompom, Porompompom, pero. Man, I slept well."

V smiled and said, "This weekend, we should all get together and think of things we can all get in sync with the Common Mind."

Alex looked at V, smiled, and said, "I'm up for that."

Prezzy and Lin laughed, and Candido said, "You girls have the giggles this morning."

Alex, with a puzzled look, laughed and said, "Yeah, we could all Porompompom, Poromp, pero, together."

Everyone laughed. Alex, looking at V, said, "Not all of us, just you and me and?" V hit him on the arm. "Don't you wish," she retorted.

Alex started singing, "Porompompom, pero, pero." They all joined in as they got up and left the table.

In class, Harvey Goldmen and Beauta Fowler stood at the front as instructors. Harvey got their attention by clearing his throat and lifting his tablet. "On your tablets, you'll find Directives and Laws. The first part of this class will cover Directives. Why you? Why are we? Why are you all here?"

"Only Elders know about this University and Elders from other planets. It is not known by the people of Earth-Terraenti or the other planets. Our number one directive is to keep it that way."

"We've all been given the Gifts by the Creator to keep a historical record of its people, to record changes on the planet, and so on. We are not to interfere in any way. Another is to keep the peace between the planets."

"If Elders from another planet try to interfere with our people, we are to stop them. Sharing technology, stealing natural resources, or any interference is prohibited. We're here to protect Terraenti."

Beauta interrupted Harvey, saying, "I know this is hard. When you return home for the holiday break, you must keep silent about what's happened to you and what's going to happen when CAT 6 hits. Harvey, I, and the other ten Stewards have been here on and off for a year now. We have kept our silence; you will be able to do it as well." She looked to Harvey.

Harvey continued, "Another key Directive is that the Gifts must be used appropriately. A Gift will be removed if not used for the betterment of the group or for the safety of the planet and its people. You will have three days to find and work on your Gifts, to study past CATs and the one to come."

"Another Directive is Conduct. Please conduct yourselves properly. You are all highly intelligent individuals. You're young, and this must all be a big shock to you, so keep yourselves in check. You represent Elders now, represent yourselves accordingly. Another is..."

V's mind wandered from her studies, drifting back to the day she left home. "*She recalled the tense car ride to the airport with her sister and parents.*"

"*The unresolved tension hung in the air. Her father, Anil, with his infuriatingly smug smile, tried one last time to persuade her to stay. "One, two years at the Bureau would be the experience of a lifetime. You could go to college next year or the year after. Or not at all. I don't understand why you need another four years of college.*"

Her mother spun around in her seat, her voice filled with urgency. "Just stay one more year here. You're making a big mistake by not waiting."

V's mother is always confident and always sure of her conclusions. She never wanted V to pursue another four years of education.

V scoffed, her voice sharp with defiance. "It's all lies and deception. It's not what I want to do. To start my life lying and deceiving people. I know you want me to stay."

She looked out the window, admitting, "I read the file. My first mission would be to go back to high school and befriend this Kunal Anzari kid. I'd probably have to sleep with him?"

Anil looked back again and said, "Whatever it takes."

V continued, "Get close to his father and find documents in their house. Look into all the information on their shady businesses."

Aishwarya's voice was firm, "It's a matter of India's national security."

V shot back, "I'm pretty sure Kunal is in on the business." Anil nodded, "I can guarantee he's in on it."

V rolled her eyes. "Yeah, I read the file. I just said that." Both of her parents scoffed. V asserted, "It's like becoming a professional thief. A full-time liar. No! It's not for me. I'm not like the two of you. I can't do it."

V saw Anil and Aishwarya exchange a look and whisper. Anil muttered, "She's perfect for this; she just doesn't realize it yet. We could cut her off from funding for school. Take her credit cards." Aishwarya agreed, "Let's do it. That will teach her."

V looked at Saanvi and said in Hindi, "Stupid parents, they're out of their minds. I don't even think they care about us. Bureau this, Bureau that."

Saanvi, with a tear running down her cheek, said, "I'm going to miss you. How long till you get back?" V reached over to comfort her. "I should be back for the holiday break. We'll figure out a way for you to get away from our crazy parents, alright!" Saanvi nodded, "Okay."

Anil blurted, "Well, we'll just have to cut you off then." V replied calmly, "Fine. Cut me off. What does that even mean?" Anil snapped, "Your credit cards, your school. We won't pay." V leaned forward with a confident smile, "You're not paying for any of that. So, as you know, the school is paying for everything. All expenses are paid in full. So, you can't use that as leverage. So, whatever - to both of you. You're both crazy."

She hugged Saanvi again and whispered, "Just concentrate on school and your swimming routine. Stay out of their business, and keep up with your medicines."

She kissed Saanvi as the car stopped at the airport. "Love you. You can call me anytime, love you." Saanvi replied, "Okay, I will. Love you too."

V got out of the car, looked at her parents, and said, "Goodbye, you crazy people." With a loving smirk and a wave, she entered the terminal and looked at her ticket. It said gate 3.

She headed toward the departure area. Walking down the corridor, she saw Freida Azmij standing to greet her. Surprised, V asked, "What are you doing here? Thought I was going to meet you at the University."

Freida admitted, "Change of plans. You know we did all the tests and evaluations on you?"
V nodded, "Yeah." Freida continued, "Well, we wanted to make sure that you were one of them."
V questioned, "One of whom?"

At that moment, Harvey slammed a book on the table, snapping her back to reality. He said, "Are we paying attention or drifting off?" V looked up at Harvey and Beauta and replied, "A little of both, I guess."

Harvey emphasized, "That's super important, so don't forget it. Alright, let's break for lunch and get back here in an hour and a half." V turned to Swaraj and whispered, "What did I miss? I wasn't listening."

Swaraj grinned, "He spent the last 30 minutes talking about our sexual relationships and how the Common Mind might affect them. How it's really easy to fall into them."

V, looking disturbed, asked, "Well, what did he say?" Swaraj, still smiling, said, "Didn't pay too much attention myself. Alex asked a bunch of questions; maybe you should ask him?" V, with a worried look, glanced back at Alex as he walked down the steps.

V approached Alex, who asked, "Something wrong?" She smiled, shaking her head. "No, nothing. I'll ask you later."

Alex nodded, his expression earnest. "We'll figure out a way to beat this CAT or at least minimize the damage to the planet."

V, still disturbed about missing Harvey's sex talk, agreed. "Yeah, let's concentrate on that." She thought, *"Damn, I missed all of Harvey's lectures. What the hell! I can't ask Alex. I'll ask Prezzy and Miko."*

As they walked to the common room, Declan said to Alex, "Harvey really went on and on about the Common Mind and how it affects us." Alex replied, "Yeah, he did. Harvey's the one who brought me here. He's a good guy. Straight to the point, if you know what I mean."

V sighed, "Crap. I kind of drifted off during that whole part." Declan laughed. "I'm sure Alex will fill you in. He asked all the questions." Prezzy and Lin looked back and chuckled. Lin said firmly, "No. No, no. I think it's better if we let her know what Harvey said. We're not letting you guys make up some crazy story."

Lin, Prezzy, and Miko sat down with V in the common room. V, looking tentative, asked, "So, how does the Common Mind affect us in relationships?"

Miko smiled and replied, "Harvey said our emotions can get messed up. The Common Mind may interfere with our decisions. We need to watch our feelings so they don't get out of hand in our relationships." Miko leaned in closer, a flirtatious smile on her face. "I think he meant that sex can be really good."

Lin and Prezzy laughed. Lin added, "Like he doesn't want us to have an orgy or something." They all laughed again. Prezzy corrected, "No, he didn't say that. He was just stressing that we need to be aware of our emotions."

Miko looked at V and asked, "Where were you in class?" V replied, "Oh, I was thinking about my insane parents and leaving my sister the other day."

Miko asked, "Why, what's wrong with them?" V sighed, "My sister has some disabilities, and my parents, well, they're so locked into their careers they have no concept of reality."

Miko asked, "What happened to your sister?" V explained, "She hasn't been eating right, and she's bipolar. I'm trying to get her to stay with my Aunt Anaya. She's normal."

Prezzy declared, "This weekend, I'm getting with Declan and getting emotional. Maybe Swaraj?" They all laughed.

Miko looked uncomfortable. V said, "Alex is set on trying to figure out how to stop the CAT or at least slow it down." Miko mused, "What could we do? Can't stop the sun. Could we do something on the planet? As soon as it happens, the shockwave hits in minutes, doesn't it?" V replied, "We can't just do nothing and let it happen."

Lin admitted, "I don't know about you all, but I'm going to have a good time this weekend. Candido's pretty cute. Maybe I'll sing another tune with him." Prezzy teased, "You're going to have to distract Maria."

V added, "Right, first Alex, now Candido. We've only been here a few days, and sex is already on the brain. It's the Common Mind." Lin suggested, "Maria's nice. Maybe she should hook up with Lev. He's big, strong, and probably has a big..." Lin stopped talking, and they all burst out laughing.

From across the room, Declan called out, "What are you all laughing at?"

Prezzy stood, hands on her hips, smiling. "Nothing, baby, you just mind your own business." They laughed harder.

Alex walked over and asked, "So, what's the plan for this weekend?" Lin looked at him, "Why are you so serious all the time? Want to do some Common Mind with me later?"

Alex looked puzzled. V stood up, "Alright, that's enough for me. Alex and I are going to lunch." She grabbed his hand and started to walk out of the room. Turning back to Miko, Prezzy, and Lin, she mouthed, "I'll calm him down." The three girls laughed and got up.

In the dining room, Kyoryk, Candido, Lev, Maria, Swaraj, and Tonari were already seated, eating. Alex and V got their food and sat down. Declan, right behind them, asked, "Anyone find out why they're going to the Elders' planet yet?"

Lev spoke up, "I talked to Roman. He said some of the Elders of Vindor were trying to trade technology with Vattan. Sell or something?"

"Vindor is the most advanced of all the planets, and I guess they've done this before. Vattan is mostly water, and they wanted some O2 converter tech for an underwater city. So, they all meet to discuss what to do with the Elders who broke the rules. Roman said it wasn't too serious. Most of them just wanted to go because Amotaious is an awesome planet. I guess the Stewards have only been there once or twice before."

Declan added, "Isn't Vindor the planet where the people look like birds?"

Alex nodded. "There's a whole section in the library about the planets and their populations. I saw one of Vindor's books, and they have an intense transport system. They seem very aggressive, with huge coliseums for fights." Lev grinned. "That sounds like fun." Alex continued, "Their people there look like large owls or eagles and have claw-like fingernails."

V sighed. "It always seems to come down to battle and war. Why is that?"

Declan suggested, "It's the way of the world, I mean worlds. But we're not going there anytime soon. We're here on our planet. Eventually, I hope we get to see Amotaious. That will be fun—to explore another planet, taste the food, and see the vehicles. Imagine all the different people on Amotaious from the five other planets. That's going to be amazing."

Alex, always focused, said, "Right. I'm going to start studying the other planets and see what happened to them during their CATs."

Lin groaned, "I'm not really looking forward to this next class—Laws. So boring." Prezzy chimed in, "It's not the most fun class."

V, staying positive, said, "Well, we have three days without class. We can study, work out, play, whatever." Lin looked at Candido and added, "We can play some music together, maybe do Karaoke on the deck stage."

Maria gave Lin a slightly dirty look. "Yeah, sing more music." Lev frowned. "I don't think I'm a very good singer." Maria agreed, "Maybe you shouldn't be the lead, but you're okay."

Declan nodded to Alex. "What are we doing after class?" Alex replied, "I might go to the library. No, we should explore somewhere else. How about the greenhouse?" Declan, not too excited, said, "Yeah, alright." V looked at Alex. "Before dinner, you going?" "Yeah, I thought it would be interesting to see."

Miko, still a bit shy, said, "I want to check out the greenhouse and see what they're growing." V nodded in agreement. Swaraj spoke up, "I'm going too."

They all slowly got up and made their way to class. In class, Beauta lectures on the Laws. Alex, distracted by his tablet, stumbles upon something about CAT 5 and its monitoring. He focuses on the magnetic pole positions and Terraenti's magnetosphere strength.

Determined, he starts typing a list of things to track.

Things to Monitor and Evaluate:

- Position of Magnetic Pole

- Magnetosphere Strength

"Gig mentioned the Pulse Reversal and the number of occurrences in previous CATs—minimum of four, maximum of six," he recalls, continuing his list.

- Pulse Reversal and intervals

- Strength and Weakness of Oceanic Conveyor Belt

"What other signs could I investigate?" he wonders, adding more to his list.

- Greenland Ice coverage year to year

- Sunspot Numbers over time

- Cosmic Rays, Solar Wind Speed

"This should be a good start," he thinks. *"I need to go to the Lab and the Operations room for the numbers. I'll start that tomorrow."*

Alex looks up at Harvey, who is discussing multiplanetary laws. The virtual screen displays a list:

"Elders can share information among themselves, but not between planets. Transfer of Planetary Technology is prohibited. Procreation between species is prohibited. All galactic ships must remain in stealth mode. Interference or Intervening in the CATs of planets is prohibited."

The list goes on. Harvey addresses the class, "Over the next few months, review these Laws. Now, let's discuss the consequences of breaking them."

"This is largely unwritten because it's up to the Council of Master Elders and, ultimately, the Creator. The council comprises two Master Elders from each of the six planets and all the retired Master Elders. Two of you will eventually become like Gig and Fem'. The other Elders can influence but not decide the final judgment."

Swaraj raises his hand. Harvey nods, "Go ahead, Swaraj."

"What are the penalties?"

Harvey responds, "Usually, an Elder is confined to Amotaious for a time, based on the council's decision. This leads us to visit Amotaious. We'll inform you next week of the outcome."

Swaraj asks, "So, no death penalty? What if someone commits murder?"

"Twice in our history, an Elder has killed another Elder. The Creator judged and executed them immediately. So, murder among Elders is not tolerated."

"However, some Elders have gone missing. Their whereabouts remain unknown. Elders who misuse their Gifts might lose their senses temporarily. After a prayer, an Elder who misused the Gift of levitation lost his voice for a thousand years." "Wow," Swaraj mutters.

Declan asks, "How many Elders have gone missing or just left?"

Harvey replies, "Not sure. Less than 20 from us and from other planets, I'm not certain. You'd have to look it up." He glances at Beauta.

Beauta says, "Remember, these classes are an overview. For details, visit the library or use your tablet. That's it for now. Have a good evening, and review the Directives and Laws. Doog and Fare will be here with the regular university staff. Behave this weekend. See you next week."

Alex and the other Students leave and head to the common room.

In the common room, Declan aggressively played darts while sipping his beer. "Alex, come over here. I want to try something."

"Let me grab a beer first," Alex replies. Declan hands him the darts. "Throw a dart."

Alex throws it. Declan says, "Now, aim right of the bullseye, toward the outer rim." Declan extends his arm.

"Now," Declan commands. The dart flies far to the right. "Damn, let's try again." The second dart changes direction at the last second, landing two inches from the bullseye.

Declan grimaces. Alex laughs, "Relax, let the Gift do its thing." Declan grabs three more darts and relaxes, breathing slowly. This time, the dart hits the bullseye. Alex cheers, "Again!"

Another dart flies off course, but Declan waves his hand, guiding it to the bullseye. "Hey, that's great, Declan!" Alex exclaims.

Declan jumps excitedly, showing off to the others. Declan hands Alex two darts. "Okay, throw two at once." One hits the bullseye, and the other drops to the floor. Declan shrugs, "I guess I'll keep working on that."

"Yeah, I guess," Alex replies, then sits next to V. "So, what are the other Gifts? I don't know mine yet." V, puzzled, says, "Not yet, but we'll figure it out."

Alex continues, "I started making a list of things to monitor. The poles and magnetosphere. I'm heading to the Lab and Ops room tomorrow." V nods, "Sounds good. We need to start doing something."

Miko joins them, "Weren't we going to the greenhouse?" Alex remembers, "Right. Do you know the way?" V and Alex stand up, and Swaraj joins them.

"Declan, you coming?" Alex asks. Declan, tossing a Nerf football, declines, "No, go ahead."

The group heads out, ready to explore the unknown.

The group heads toward the greenhouse. Miko, trying to make a joke, says, "I think it's on the north side." They all give her puzzled looks. "North side?" Swaraj echoes, confused. V suggests, "Let's ask someone." They spot Roman walking by, and Miko politely asks, "Mr. Roman, sir, do you know where the greenhouse is?"

Roman Taktarov, a fearsome ex-boxer from the Russian Special Forces, mutters in his rough, raspy voice, "Not a clue," and continues walking.

V smirks at Alex and whispers, "That guy is terrifying." Alex quips, "There are geographic poles on the moon, but a compass wouldn't work." V shoves him playfully down the hallway, "No, it all!"

They laugh quietly and then see Kira, Miko's Steward. Alex asks, "Excuse me, Kira, do you know how to get to the greenhouse?" She smiles at Miko and thinks for a moment.

In her soft voice, she says, "Pretty sure it's on the opposite side of the pantry. Go through the kitchen, then turn right instead of left."

"Thanks," Alex says. They walk down the long-ramped hallway towards the kitchen. Miko mentions, "Did you know she has three black belts in different martial arts?" V remarks, "She's so tiny." Alex adds, "I think she and Hugh have something going on." Miko responds, "Really? That would be an odd couple. She's been super nice to me." They laugh as they reach the pantry, turn right, and enter a large greenhouse.

The greenhouse is enormous and brightly lit, mostly filled with hydroponically grown plants. The temperature is 15.5 degrees with 90% humidity, growing vegetables and herbs used daily in the kitchen. Swaraj, trying to be funny, asks, "Where are the chickens and goats?" Miko laughs, "Ha ha, I don't think they keep livestock at the university."

Alex surveys the area, "I guess it's about what I expected. Nothing fancy." In the back, he notices warmer tropical plants. V smiles at Alex, "Well, that was fun." Alex replies, "It was something to see." Miko adds, "Yeah, I guess. Lin probably would have liked it; her family has a homestead." Alex feels a bit awkward, "Yeah, I guess."

They start back towards the common room. Swaraj wonders aloud, "I wonder where the secret stuff is?" V asks, "What do you mean by secret stuff?" Swaraj explains, "You know, where they keep all the hidden things."

Passing a door, Swaraj nudges Miko, "Look through that door. What's in there?" Miko concentrates, "Gold bars, gold vases, it's a treasure room." They all laugh. Miko corrects, "It looks like a linen room." Swaraj insists, "I know they have secret rooms." V reassures, "Since we're becoming Elders, I'm sure they'll tell us where the secret rooms are. This will be our place."

They walk into the common room, where Candido excitedly exclaims, "Unbelievable!" Alex looks at Declan, "What's going on?"

Declan explains, "We were throwing the football around, and Candido went long right through that closed door. Now he's waving his hand through the table."

Alex looks and says, "So Miko can see through matter, and Candido can actually go through it." V adds, "Great, another Gift. Maybe we'll discover them all by the end of the weekend."

Declan asks, "How was the greenhouse?" V replies with a frown, "Oh, very exciting." Alex frowns too. Miko jokes, "Swaraj found a secret room full of gold bars." Swaraj asks, "Very funny. How long till dinner?" Candido announces, "Half an hour from now."

A little later, Declan asks, "How many Gifts are left? Assuming we each get one?"

Alex counts, "Prezzy, me, Swaraj, Tonari, Maria, and Kyoryk. That's six left. Where did V and Tonari go?"

Miko looks through the wall, "V is in her room, and Tonari is asleep... no, wait, she's running down the hallway." Alex asks, "Which is it? She can't be in two places at once."

Miko concentrates, "She's definitely in her room. But she's also running down the hallway."

Alex, Declan, and Miko head to Tonari's room. They reach her room and find her asleep in her chair with a tablet in her lap. Down the hallway, they see another one of her at the end, waving her arms and yelling, "It wasn't me; I didn't do it!" She curses in Spanish.

Alex looks at Declan and Miko, "What the hell is going on? How can there be two of her?" Declan nudges Alex, "Go wake her up." Alex reluctantly agrees, "Alright, jeez." He gently wakes Tonari, "Tonari, wake up." Tonari rubs her eyes, "Alex? What is it?"

Declan, still looking down the hallway, says, "She's gone from the hallway." Alex asks, "What were you dreaming about?" Tonari replies, "Some family stuff, I think. Why?" Alex explains, "You were in two places at once." Tonari, bewildered, struggling to get up asks, "What does that mean?"

Miko places her hand on Tonari's shoulder, "You created a body double of yourself." Declan marvels, "It's like two of her. How did she do that?" He gets a mischievous look on his face, looking at Alex, "I wonder if she can do three of her; wouldn't that be interesting?" Alex and Declan chuckle.

They walk back into the common room. V shows up, "What's going on?" "Tonari just created a body double. Can you imagine?" Declan announces, astonishment evident in his voice.

Alex overhears Kyoryk mumbling something. "What did you say, Kyoryk?" "It's called Kinetic Replication, I think," Kyoryk explains. "It happens when the body gets hit or moves incredibly fast." "But she was dreaming," Declan points out.

Kyoryk clarifies, "A dream is a state of consciousness characterized by sensory, cognitive, and emotional occurrences during sleep."

Declan continues, "She was asleep; she was dreaming. Can she do it while awake?" Kyoryk speculates, "Maybe it's Omni Fabrication, or she can manipulate kinetic energy."

Declan, curious, asks, "How do you know all this stuff?" Kyoryk shrugs, "I don't know. It's just coming to me."

Alex tests him, "What's the square root of 2000? And Pi to the tenth power?" Without hesitation, Kyoryk responds, "The square root of 2000 is 44.72135955. Pi to the tenth power is approximately 140.503319. To the tenth decimal, it's 2.9982361e21."

V looks at Alex, astonished. "I think we just discovered two more Gifts."

Alex stares at Kyoryk. "So, you were a math genius in school?" "No, I got a B in math, worked at a pet store, and commercial fished a little," Kyoryk replies.

Alex says, "Well, it looks like you're super smart now. What's that called?" Kyoryk rattles off, "Superintelligence, Cosmic Knowledge, or Cyber Mind. Maybe Pseudoscience Manipulation or Supernatural Mind." Alex cuts him off, "Alright, we'll just say you're super smart."

Meanwhile, V talks to Tonari, "Try to concentrate. What was in your dream?" Tonari hesitates, "I guess I was scared. I don't remember all my dreams."

V instructs, "Okay, think of yourself in the hallway again." Miko moves to the archway to look down the hallway. "Nothing," she reports.

V smiles encouragingly at Tonari, and then her face changes. She yells, "CONCENTRATE!" startling Tonari. Miko glances again.

"Now she's there," Miko confirms. "Can you feel your other self over there?" V asks. "Kind of," Tonari responds uncertainly.

Alex is taken aback by V's conclusion. "Do some jumping jacks," V suggests. Tonari starts doing jumping jacks.

"Not you. The other one," V clarifies as Declan and Alex laugh. "You, the one in the hallway." Miko nods, "Yep, she's doing jumping jacks."

Lev arrives and, standing in the archway, asks, "Why is Tonari in the hallway doing jumping jacks? Wait, she's right here! Am I seeing things?"

Declan and Alex burst into hysterical laughter.

Kyoryk explains, "Technically, she's kinetically replicating her body into two different spaces at the same time. No, she might even be in two different times."

Lev marvels, "That's awesome. But you guys are going to be late for dinner." Alex checks the time, "Oh shit, we should go." Kyoryk interjects, "Technically, we have 1.5 minutes. That's 90,000 milliseconds. It's actually a long time considering." Declan retorts, "We don't need to know that, but thank you."

He rummages through a drawer, finds thick, silly glasses, and puts them on Kyoryk. "Here, you have to wear these the rest of the night." Everyone laughs as Kyoryk stumbles down the hallway, unable to see through the thick lenses. "This is preposterous. I can't see a thing."

As they walk, V notes to Alex, "Now there are four Gifts left if we all get one." Alex adds, "We have the whole weekend to work on them." Declan cheers, "No classes for a couple of days. I'm going to sleep in."

The group reaches Terraenti Hall, grabs their food, and sits down. Maria, helping Kyoryk walk around, says, "Can I take off these silly glasses now?" Declan laughed, "No! V announces, "Of course silly. I'm going to swim all three days."

Prezzy agrees, "That sounds good." Alex tries to relate, "I like to swim." Declan jokes, "They have pools in the desert? The Northern Territory?" Alex plays along, "Yes, we had a pool. One at school. I was on the polo team for a year. It wasn't my thing, though." He puffs out his chest and blurts, "I was working out with weights most of the time."

Declan adds, "Yeah, with dumbbells?" Alex shoots him a warning look. Declan mutters, "Right, no teasing the boss Alex."

V turns to Prezzy, "How about 10:00?" "Sounds good," Prezzy agrees.

Alex declares, "Declan and I are going to the Lab and check out the Operations room." Declan looks puzzled, "We are?" Alex confirms, "Yes, we are."

V and Prezzy smile. Miko chimes in, "So you're going to the pool at 10:00?" V nods, "Yeah, want to join us?" Miko agrees, "Sure." Tonari adds, "I'm going too."

Lev looks at Maria, curiosity piqued. "What are your plans for the weekend?" Maria shrugs, "Not sure. I need to figure out my Gift. My dad would be freaking out about all this. He's really into space flight and works on a lot of technical stuff."

Lev asks, "What do your parents do?" Maria sighs, "My mom's been gone for years. It's just been my dad and me. He's an engineer who makes parts for the space station and other high-tech things. He wants to go into space so badly, but he's a bit old for that now." Lev offers a sympathetic look. "Sorry about your mom. When did she pass?"

Maria replies softly, "When I was four. I don't remember much, just what my dad tells me. He's a good guy who works from home mostly. We have a huge machine shop on the property, so he's around a lot." Lev smiles, "That's cool. Tomorrow I'm going to the gym. Want to join me?"

"Sure," Maria agrees. "Tomorrow night, we should have a party. If the band's not here, we can use the sound system." Lev grins, "Sounds like fun." Lin overhears and chimes in, "What's this about a party tomorrow night?" Maria beams, "Yeah, we can figure out the sound system on the deck and get crazy." Candido jumps in, "I'm up for that." Maria smiles at him. "Good. I'll let everyone know."

Gig slams a rock on the table, catching everyone's attention. "We're leaving first thing in the morning. Behave yourselves. Try to get some studying done and have fun. No moonwalks or buggy rides."

He continues, "The band's not playing, but you can use the sound system on the deck. Check with Rugrog to get it working. If you need us, use your tablets."

"There haven't been any changes in the sun, so that's good. Next week, you'll be instructed on the use of the Lab and Operations rooms, and we'll start to train on all emergency protocols."

Gig looks at Fem' and asks, "Anything to add?"

Fem' nods. "Keep working on your Gifts. They're much more powerful than you think. You just need to focus to unlock their full potential." She turns to V. "How many do you have now?"

V replies, "We have eight so far." Fem' surveys the table and the Students. Looks at Gig with a surprised expression. "Alex, Prezzy, Swaraj, and Maria are still left to get theirs."

Fem' continues, "There are always twelve Gifts, including the Common Mind. Previous CATs have had as many as fifteen, so you might have more than one. Consider all possibilities. If you need anything from the pantry, get with Kahput. Bahdubah and Klinchme' will be around on the deck for whatever else you need. Have fun." She looks at the Stewards. "Anything to add for this weekend?"

Roman sits up slightly. "No, not for this weekend." Fem' concludes, "We'll be back for Sunday night dinner. See you then."

Declan turns to Alex, excited. "What's this about moonwalks and buggy rides?" Alex's eyes light up. "That's something I'm interested in. Walking on the moon? Imagine someone with a telescope seeing us. That would be hilarious." Declan asks, "Who are Bahdubah and Klinchme'?" V responds, "I met Bahdubah at the bar. Klinchme' is the woman who was bringing us drinks."

Miko notes, "Funny names. What CAT are they from?" Prezzy comments, "I think they're all relatives from CAT 1. I met Kahput in the pantry. His brother is Rugrog. They all look similar, so they're probably from CAT 1." Kyoryk adds, "That means they're over 18,000 years old. That's crazy." Prezzy clarifies, "They might be the kids of the Elders, so they may not be that old." Alex muses, "Imagine being that old. All the things they've seen and done. Insane, right?"

V looks at Prezzy. "So, we may get more than one Gift? That's interesting. Wonder what my second one will be?"

Prezzy smiles. "Let's see. One of us might have a love potion or something that makes people tell the truth." V laughs. "I doubt it. So far, it's been things that change matter or physics."

Declan, as he gets up, jokes, "Maybe you'll have laser eyes and can melt people. You do have rare green eyes, and you're from India, right?" V stands, smiling. "No laser eyes. It just means someone in my family is from the north."

Alex whispers to V as he rises, "I think you have amazing eyes. And for the love potion, you won't need it on me." He thinks to himself, *"Should I have said that? No, it's okay. She invited me for a kiss. I'm in. Or? Quit second-guessing yourself. She probably likes me."*

A few minutes later, in the common room, all the Students are practicing and honing their Gifts. Maria, in a loud voice, announces, "Tomorrow night on the deck, we're checking out the sound system and playing your favorite tunes."

Everyone acknowledges. Candido says, "Sounds good. I know some great Spanish artists."

Declan adds, "There's a new EDM DJ called Zophina. She wears a bug head."

Lev suggests, "Russian Rap Bass. That should sound good on a big system."

Declan recalls, "I saw the racks. One was a computer, and the other five were amp racks. My mom's friend from Los Angeles used to work on big theater sound systems. I used to help him adjust settings."

"Anyone up for poker?" Alex asks. "I'll play," Declan replies, rummaging through the drawers. "Wonder if there are any poker chips?" After a moment, he triumphantly pulls out cards and poker chips from the fourth cupboard. "Found them!"

Lin strums the guitar while Candido, Lev, Maria, Kyoryk, and Swaraj grab some beer and wine coolers and play darts. Prezzy, V, Alex, Declan, and Miko sit at the table to play cards. Tonari practices her Gift while smoking a cigarette, the smoke swirling around her.

V asks, "So, what kind of poker are we playing?" Miko admits, "I don't know how to play." Declan reassures her, "I'll teach you." Alex interjects, "Isn't your mom a professional poker player?"

Declan laughs, "Yes, but I only played on Sundays when there weren't too many people around." V raises an eyebrow. "What does that mean?" Prezzy grins, "It means he's really, really good."

Declan distributes the chips, shuffles the cards, and begins dealing. "Five-card draw. You get five cards. Keep the best ones and draw up to four new cards." Miko asks, "How do the chips work?" Alex explains, "Let's say the lighter colors are the lowest and the darker colors are the highest. White is one dollar, blue is five, green is ten, red is twenty, and black is fifty. How's that?" Declan nods. "Sounds good. Ante up."

He places a white chip on the table. The others follow suit, Miko glancing at her tablet for poker hands. "So, I want a royal flush," she says.

V nods, "Isn't that the top hand?" Alex agrees, "Yes, Royal Flush is the best."

They all ask Alex for their draw cards. Declan explains, "Now we bet. Since I dealt, Miko, you bet first." Miko says, "I'll bet a green ten dollars."

Prezzy adds, "I'll raise another ten." V calculates, "So that's twenty to me." She matches the bet. Alex throws in two greens. Declan says, "I'm good." They all reveal their cards. Miko has two jacks, Prezzy has two fives, V has nothing, and Alex says, "I was trying for a straight but didn't get it." Declan reveals, "I have two tens, so Miko wins."

Miko beams, "I won! Wahoo!"

Declan, frustrated, suggests, "Let's play seven-card hold'em. It makes for a bigger pot. You each get two cards. The other five are face-up, and we bet each time I put a card up. Ante up."

He looks around. "You ready?"

V blurts out, "I'm ready. Big money. Come on, big money." Alex smirks, "Okay, big money. I'll make a side bet with you that I'll win this hand or at least beat you." He places a black chip between them. V, determined, says, "Alright, I'll take that bet. If you lose, I get that chip, right?" She puts a black chip next to his. Declan puts up the first card and says, "Now we bet." Miko says, "Ten dollars." Prezzy puts her ten in. V follows. Alex says, "Ten it is." Declan matches and looks at Miko to add another ten.

Miko complies, and Declan puts up another card. Miko says, "Another ten." Prezzy ups the ante, "I'll bet twenty." Alex jokes, "Big spender." V matches, as do Alex and Declan. Declan reveals the next card. Prezzy smiles, "Wahoo." Alex teases, "Got something, huh?" Miko bets ten. Prezzy, quiet, says, "Twenty again."

V matches. Alex follows. Declan puts in his twenty and says, "Okay, last card." V says, "Big money, come on." Declan, with a drum roll, puts up the last card and says, "Last bet."

The face cards are the Jack of Clubs, Ace of Clubs, Four of Hearts, Ace of Spades, and Ten of Clubs. Declan looks around, "Looks like a straight flush is possible."

Miko says, "I'll bet fifty." Prezzy, surprised, asks, "Fifty? What do you have?"

Miko teases, "I'll tell you in a minute." V, without hesitation, says, "I'm in."

Alex puts in fifty. Declan groans, "I'm out." He folds. Everyone reveals their cards. Alex has two fours. V has two jacks. Miko has three aces.

Prezzy stands and screams, "I won five hundred dollars!" She waves her hands excitedly and suddenly disappears.

Declan looks shocked. Alex exclaims, "What the hell?"

V reaches out, "I can feel her. We can still hear her."

Three seconds later, Prezzy reappears. Kyoryk and Lev walk over, standing next to her. She looks around. "What? I won five hundred buckaroos. Eat that!" She slams her hand on the table. Everyone is silent.

Finally, V, staring straight at her, says, " Prezzy, Pretty sure you were just invisible for a few seconds."

Prezzy looks at Swaraj, then back at V. "Invisible? Really? You couldn't see me?" V confirms, "Yep, pretty sure you were invisible."

Alex adds, "For like two seconds."

V, focused, continues, "I could still hear you and feel you, but you were invisible."

Declan, hands on his head, exclaims, "Another Gift! That's awesome. Invisibility didn't know that would be a thing." He yells to the sky, "What's that one for, Creator, huh?" He puts his hands down and claims, "They say they come out when you get emotional or excited. I guess that's the most emotional I've seen Prezzy get."

Prezzy stands up, trying to be invisible again, squinting and wiggling her nose. "Is it working?"

Alex laughs, "No, wave your hands around again. Jump up and down. Whistle."

V gives Alex a stern look. Declan laughs. Kyoryk starts poking at her like a science experiment. Then V advises, "No, you need to relax, focus, and sit back down."

Prezzy, frustrated, swatting at Kyoryk, takes a deep breath, sits down, and takes another deep breath.

V sits up in her chair and starts to shout at her, "Okay, now it's working. Can you hear me?" Prezzy responds, "I'm invisible, not deaf."

V chuckles, "Sorry," as she reaches out to feel her. Prezzy informs her, "You're touching my boob." Declan jumps up, "Let me feel." V pushes him back, "Stop."

About three seconds later, Prezzy reappears.

Swaraj, in his deep Indian accent, marvels, "Remarkable, how is she doing that?" Kyoryk says, "Shh, I'm trying to figure out the physics of it." Alex suggests, "This is the work of the Creator. I don't think we're going to figure out the physics of it."

Prezzy gets up and starts walking out of the room. V asks, "Where are you going?" Prezzy, excited, announces, "To find a mirror!" Declan looks at her cards, "Shit, she had a royal flush. You know how hard it is to draw that?" Declan yells, "You're not going to see anything." He chuckles. Kyoryk calculates, "The odds are one in twenty thousand."

Alex asks, "Are we playing or not?" V looks at Alex with a flirting smile, glances down at the black fifty-dollar chips, and says, "These are mine."

Declan says, "Let's keep playing." He shuffles and deals, and the group continues playing cards. Kyoryk sits down in Prezzy's spot and starts playing.

By the dartboard, Lev asks Maria, "You still need your Gift, right?" "Yep," Maria replies. Candido chimes in, "It comes out with emotion. What could we do to help you?" Feeling closer to

Maria, Lev suggests, "Let's try this." He pokes her shoulder with a dart. "Ow, shit, what the hell?" Maria reacts. Lev chuckles, "I was trying to make you mad."

Maria looks at Swaraj, "Slap me." Swaraj smiles, "No, I can't." "I'll do it," Lev volunteers.

Declan, noticing the commotion, asks, "What's going on over there?"

Alex shrugs, "Not sure; I just saw Lev poke Maria with a dart. Give me a card." "Okay," Declan responds, handing a card to Alex.

Maria objects, "No, look at your hand; it's huge. You'll probably knock me out." Candido steps in, "I'll do it." Maria agrees, "Alright." She braces herself, and Candido slaps her hard. The room freezes. Declan's card, thrown mid-air to Alex, hangs suspended. Tonari's cigarette smoke is a frozen wisp.

Maria surveys the room, understanding her power. Everyone is still frozen in time. She approaches Lev and Candido, slaps Lev hard on the cheek, then steps back to her original spot. Time resumes.

Lev, startled and furious, snaps at Candido, "I thought you were going to slap her, not me!" He shoves Candido and growls in his deep Russian accent, "You dick."

Maria, laughing and jumping, exclaims, "This is great! Prezzy can be invisible, but I can stop time!" Lev, rubbing his cheek, mutters, "So it was you. You didn't have to slap me so hard." Maria pulls his hand away, "Let me see, you big baby." Lev's cheek is bright red.

Across the room, Alex asks, "What's going on over there?" Lev, still rubbing his cheek, says, "Maria can stop time."

The card players glance back skeptically and return to their game. Declan mumbles something like, "Yeah, right." Maria determined, announces, "Let me try something." She pricks her finger with a dart. Time halts. She walks over to the poker table, turns their cards face out, and moves all the chips to Declan's pile.

She's tied Candido's shoelaces together and muses, "That should do it." Time resumes. Alex, in the middle of betting, notices the chips and exclaims, "What the hell, Declan?" Declan exclaims, "What the hell?"

Maria had also stuffed some of the pot's chips into Declan's shirt pocket. V realizes, "Wait, really? Holy crap, that's awesome, Maria. That's one of the best ones yet."

Candido starts to walk toward the dartboard and trips. Maria laughs as he falls, and the others join in. Candido, on the floor, grumbles, "Nice, you had to do that." Maria, grinning, declares, "Well, you all didn't believe me. I had to show you."

Kyoryk, puzzled, states, "Well, there is no figuring out how she does that. No amount of logic can explain it. It's not possible, really?" Alex adds, "And yet, she just did it. Wonderful. Now it's just Swaraj and me left."

Swaraj steps into the open area. "Declan, throw me that Nerf football."

Declan grabs the football and tosses it to Swaraj, who stops it in midair, making it float. "What do you think about that? Pretty cool, huh?" He drops his hand, and the football lands in his other hand. Alex, impressed, asks, "How long have you known?" Swaraj explains, "I kind of figured it out in the shower when I reached for the soap, and it didn't fall. I think it's like levitation or zero-gravity. Not sure yet."

Alex glances at V. "It's just me left."

Lin starts singing a new type of music, capturing everyone's attention with her Himalayan throat singing. Declan laughs, "This is the best university ever. We're going to have a great weekend." They all laugh and return to their activities.

Fem and Gig poke their heads in. Gig asks, "How's everyone doing?" They walk into the room. Alex and V get up to greet them. Alex asks, "Anything we should be doing this weekend? Declan and I are going to the lab in the morning. I'm going to learn how to monitor the indicators."

Gig smiles at Alex's enthusiasm. "Doog and Fair will be in the lab this weekend monitoring. They're from our CAT."

He motions for Alex and V to step into the hallway. "We want both of you to keep an eye on things. You're beginning to grasp the situation here. Focus on the group and monitor the signs. Doog and Fair will tell you what to watch for in the lab. Just keep an eye on the signs. It's a long trip for us, for only a day or so. You shouldn't have to worry about anything."

Alex and V nod, assured. V affirms, "We'll keep an eye on things."

Fem looks at V, "I forwarded ways to contact us to your tablets. For now, you two will oversee your group. We are scheduled to return Sunday around noon."

Alex and V nod and smile. V says, "Okay, we will see you on Sunday."

Gig and Fem smile back and walk down the hallway. Alex and V return to the common room, feeling more confident. Maria and Prezzy celebrate their new Gifts with the group. After a few more drinks, the evening winds down. Alex finds no note on his bed but receives a blown kiss from V as she enters her room.   Alex felt good about the day.

VII

V awoke and glanced at her clock. It read 9:30. She donned her one-piece bathing suit and robe, then headed to the common room. Miko, in a very revealing bikini, sat with Tonari in her in her bathing suit. V grabbed a bagel, sliced it, spread cream cheese from the fridge, and joined them.

"What's happening?" she asked. Tonari replied, "Nothing much. Declan, Alex, and Kyoryk went to find the Lab. Some others are hitting the gym. Haven't seen Prezzy yet. She was coming, right?" V nodded. "Yes, she'll be here." As she ate her bagel, Miko asked, "What else is going on today?"

"I'm helping Alex with some stuff," V replied. Miko smirked. "Oh, really?"

V grinned. "He's going to show me something."

Prezzy walked in, greeting everyone. "Hey, how's it going?"

Tonari said, "Just ready to relax in the pool." Miko looked at V with a mischievous smile. "What was Alex going to show you?" "Nothing I'll tell you later," V responded, smiling.

They finished their breakfast and headed to the pool. Passing through the gym, they saw Lev, Candido, Maria, Swaraj, and Lin working out.

In the pool area, V finished her breaststroke laps while Prezzy, Tonari, and Miko relaxed in the hot tub.

"What are we doing the rest of the day?" Prezzy asked. "I'm going to rest a little, then study," Tonari said. Miko suggested, "I'd like to go exploring and see what else there is here." Prezzy agreed. "I'll go with you, but I want to work on my Gift." "How's that going?" Miko inquired. "I can go almost a full minute now," Prezzy replied.

V, getting into the hot tub, sighed contentedly. "This feels so good." Miko added, "If I concentrate, I can see further now. I got bored of watching everyone."

Prezzy laughed. "You've been watching us?" "Not in a bad way," Miko clarified. "Lev, Maria, and Alex do push-ups and sit-ups every morning."

"V, you too sometimes. Candido checks himself out in the mirror a lot. Some pray and listen to music. Regular stuff, nothing weird."

"How far can you see now?" Tonari asked. "Through three to four rooms," Miko replied. Tonari remarked, "I've been trying to create more than one body double. I call them Toni's."

V, curious about the girls' opinions of the guys, asked, "What do you think about Alex? He does have a nice body. Lev is a little overbuilt for me." Miko pondered. "Do you think they're trying to pair us up, like Gig and Fem'?" "It's possible," V admitted. "Fem' and Gig told me and Alex to look after everything while they're gone."

Prezzy said, "Everyone knows you and Alex are kind of together." V, surprised, responded, "We're not together, together. It seems like it's heading that way. Maybe? Pretty sure he likes me." Miko laughed. "You're kidding, right? Have you seen the way he looks at you? It's more than like you."

Prezzy agreed. "I'm sure of that." Tonari said, "I think Candido is cute." Miko added, "I guess Declan, if we have to pair up. I'd let him park his car in my carport." The girls laughed. Prezzy, still laughing, noted, "Never heard it put that way before."

V asked, "Could it have something to do with the Gifts?" Prezzy replied, "I'm not interested in anyone yet. If we were supposed to stay with the person we came here with, you and Miko already messed that up." Miko protested, "What does that mean?" "V and Alex, you and Declan," Prezzy explained. "Well, I don't know about that," Miko said. Tonari observed, "Most know you four hang out together a lot." Miko squirmed. "He does have a unique personality. Since the prayer that first night, getting the Gift and the Common Mind, I've been really horny." They all laughed.

V said, "We need to find a way to help the people on the planet. Whatever happened before, are we just going to let it happen again?" "Whatever we do, we must do it together," Prezzy asserted. "We'll figure something out." Miko added, "I think it all has to do with the Common Mind. My last boyfriend was funnier than Declan." V suggested, "You might not want to tell him that." They all laughed as they left the pool area.

As they walked back, V asked, "When do you want to go exploring?" Miko replied, "Let's get showered and eat something."

V added, "I'll see if Declan and Alex want to join us." Tonari noted, "See, you four are always together." "That doesn't mean anything. You could come too," V said.

Later, in the common room, Declan, Kyoryk, Lev, and Alex sat at a table. V, Tonari, and Miko entered.

"How was the Lab?" V asked. Alex looked up. "No need for that spreadsheet I mentioned. They're already monitoring everything in the lab. What are you guys up to?" "We're going to explore," V said. "Miko can see through walls, so we thought we'd see what we can find."

Miko stood by the archway. "Okay, let's go."

They all got up and walked toward an unexplored area of the university. They reached two large doors. Alex pulled on one. "It's not locked," he said. They entered a huge dock area where ships were stored and unloaded. Five ships similar to the ones they arrived on and two long ones capable of seating thirty or more were docked. Equipment and supplies filled the rest of the space.

Alex approached one of the big ships. "This is incredible, an intergalactic ship that can travel to different solar systems. Did you notice they turned white when we approached the moon?" No one responded.

On one side of the building, a huge door with a rail system led outside. Massive magnetic cranes maneuvered the ships. On the other side, large tanks loomed. They scattered, exploring the area.

"Isn't this where we came in on the first night?" V asked Alex. "What do you think life will be like after we graduate? Will we live on another planet?"

Alex, ever focused, replied, "Yeah, but what about our planet? What then?" V tried to reassure him. "We'll get through it one way or another." Alex remained determined. "I'm still looking for a way to help our planet. We can't give up or just let it happen. I'd do anything to save as many people as possible." "No way to stop the sun," V said. "If we can somehow protect the planet or deflect the flare..." Alex stopped walking and looked at her. "What protects the Earth now? Let's go." They rejoined the others and continued exploring.

Alex approached Kyoryk. "Hey, what protects Earth from solar rays and such? How does our atmosphere stay intact?"

Kyoryk stopped walking and began gesticulating animatedly. "Mainly the magnetic field, generated by the planet's spin, core, and gravity. It creates a protective shield around Earth."

"Without it, we wouldn't exist. Other planets have fields, but they're either too intense or almost nonexistent." He raised a finger in the air. "People think they have it all figured out, but they don't. Ever seen those folks claiming free electricity like Tesla figured it out? There's no free electricity. Unless, of course, a Creator is involved. If you could control Earth's magnetic field, you might prevent the CAT or slow the flare's damage. But it would take immense energy."

He glanced at the tanks along the wall. "I wonder what's in those."

Alex asked, "So how could we strengthen the magnetic field to deflect the massive flare?" Kyoryk shrugged. "Maybe make the core spin faster or energize the field somehow? It's probably as hard as stopping the sun from going nova."

Frustration etched on Alex's face. "Shit, it's impossible."

Miko interjected, "Let's find something else."

V, sharing Alex's frustration, urged, "Come on, Alex, let's go."

They all left the dock and walked down the hallway until they reached another door. Declan tried it. "It's locked. Miko, can you see through it?"

Miko peered through the door. "It's a bunch of big pipes and pumps. Some kind of equipment room."

The group moved further down the corridor, finding two more doors—one large on the left and a smaller one on the right. Alex checked the larger door. "Locked." Declan tried the smaller one. "Locked too."

Miko looked through the smaller door but shook her head. "I can't see anything; it's dark."

"What about this one?" Alex pointed to the larger door. Miko peered again. "Also dark." Lev stepped up and gently knocked on the walls next to both doors. Miko's eyes lit up. "Now I can see." Alex nodded appreciatively. "Nice." Lev stood proudly. "I've been practicing." Miko continued, "It's a bunch of antiques, similar to what's in the library."

Tonari added, "There are carpets, gold vases, and other collectible items." Puzzled, V asked, "Are you in there?" Tonari closed her eyes and concentrated. "Shoosh, let me focus. No, it's all Earth's past stuff. There is a huge stuffed wolf in here."

Declan, tugging on Lev's shirt, said, "Lev, hit this wall too. Light up the room." Lev complied, and Miko reported, "This one has security boxes. Cameras inside." "Like safety deposit boxes?" Declan asked, excitement in his voice. "Yes," Miko confirmed.

Declan, rubbing his hands together, rattled the door handle. Tonari teased, "Get in there and get the gold." V placed a hand on Declan. "Yeah, let's not break in and get caught on camera, only to have Gig and Fem' smash us to pieces." Declan sighed. "Alright, spoil the fun." Alex added, "It's probably the Elders' boxes or ours in the future. Breaking in wouldn't be wise."

Miko pointed down the hallway. "There are more doors at the other end."

They walked to the opposite side of the corridor. Miko reminded Lev, "Don't forget to turn off the lights." Lev hit the walls next to the locked doors, extinguishing the lights.

They found another large door further down and entered. Declan exclaimed, "Wow, look at these! Moon buggies and space suits!" Inside, there were three moon buggies—two white and one flat black—with huge tires and glass-like shrouds. Alex marveled, "I wonder how fast they go. What is that?" Declan pointed to a sleek two-person ship. "Those must be super-fast." He tried to climb in, but Miko pulled him down. "Let's not get crazy here. I'm sure you'll get your chance." Lev added, "I can't wait for a moonwalk." Tonari suddenly exclaimed, "Look, I did it!" She pointed, revealing two identical copies of herself. Jumping up and down, she hugged Kyoryk and kissed him on the lips. He smiled, trying to kiss her back, but she lowered her head, and they bumped foreheads. "Ow! That hurt." They all laughed.

A large man walked in, catching them by surprise. He was as tall as Gig but heavier, with a thick mustache and a bald head. He wore shimmering deer skin clothes, similar to Gig's but darker. He had wolf-like eyes and sparkled with a great smile. He asked, "You all checking out the vehicles?"

Lev, in amazement, approached almost in military fashion. "Yes, sir, we were just looking around. Is that okay?"

The man, with a raspy chuckle, replied, "Sure. This is your place; these are your things. Just avoid anything you're not trained for."

Just then, Fair entered with a broad smile. Her long silver-blonde hair and turquoise and silver dress shimmered as she asked, "How's everyone doing?"

Tonari stepped up. "We're fine. I just made two more of me. My Gift is getting stronger." Fair smiled down at her. "That's great, Tonari."

"Is everyone finding everything okay?" she asked, her crystal blue eyes shining with warmth. Alex exclaimed, "Those ships are incredible. You're Doog and Fair, right? Gig and Fem' told us you'd be here this weekend. Do you know when we'll be trained to go to the surface?"

Doog, glancing at Alex, replied, "Not sure, but soon. Eventually, you'll be trained on all of these, including those." He pointed to the smaller ships next to Alex and Declan. "These are our fastest. They hit 1.25 LYH." Declan's eyes widened. "That's awesome."

Fair, with a radiant smile, added, "Once trained, you'll be able to venture out on your own. It's a lot of fun. We've gone to the surface many times."

V asked, "Have you heard from Gig and Fem' on Amotaious?" Doog shook his head. "No, they're still in transit and have their meeting tomorrow. We won't know anything until later, but it won't affect us here. Don't worry; you'll be part of the council meetings someday."

V responded, "We're meeting on the deck later tonight. Will you two be there?" Fair smiled. "We'll try to stop by if we can." "Sure, it should be fun," V said.

Fair nodded. "Let us know if you need anything. We need to get back to the lab. Have fun." As Doog and Fair left, Declan marveled, "How crazy is that? Doog is bigger than Gig."

V admitted, "It's astonishing how beautiful Fem' and Fair are, and their dresses are amazing."

They left the room and headed back to the upper floors. In the common room, Alex found a beer and relaxed on one of the couches. Declan did the same. Alex yawned. "How long till dinner?" Miko checked her tablet. "Half an hour." Alex closed his eyes. "Okay, thanks."

V grabbed four premade Pina Coladas from the fridge and sat next to Prezzy and Miko. "We're starting the party right after dinner?" Maria joined them. "If we start drinking now, it should get interesting by the time the party starts." She attempted to cheer all of them by clinking her canned drink. Miko agreed. "Sounds good. That hot tub was super nice, so relaxing."

V thought. *"Maybe I'll do that later. It felt good earlier. Maybe I'll take Alex there. We'll see."* She said, "I feel good too. I haven't done laps in a few weeks." Miko commented, "We used to go into a super cold pool before gymnastics. They say it improves circulation and reduces inflammation."

Prezzy added, "It'll be a while before I can surf again. Surfing is one of the best workouts." Maria said, "I'd like to try surfing. I just ran every day and worked out with light weights." Lev and Kyoryk walked up. Lev's deep Russian accent chimed in. "I used to run and work out an hour or two every day." Kyoryk added, "An hour a day in Aikido, it centered me."

Maria teased, "Lev, you might need to slow down on the weights, but Kyoryk, you're just fine. Don't change a thing." V smiled at Miko.

Maria, looking at Kyoryk, asked, "What's your last name?" Kyoryk replied, "Dragoon." Maria fluttered her eyes. "Kyoryk the Dragon, that's nice. I like that."

V chuckled, grabbed a Nerf football, and threw it at Alex. He jolted awake. "What the hell?" V laughed. "Get up, it's dinner time."

Alex rubbed his eyes and walked over to Declan, shaking him excitedly. "Declan, Declan, get up. Did you hear what happened?" Declan shot up. "What?" Alex grinned. "Three women are waiting for you in your room, naked." Declan groaned. "You ass!" Alex laughed, pulling him up. "It's dinner time." Declan muttered, "Ass." The girls laughed.

Candido and Tonari walked in. Lin asked, "Where have you guys been?" Candido replied, "On the deck." Lin gave them a flirtatious smile. "I see." Prezzy asked, "You guys seen Swaraj? I want him." Some laughed, shaking their heads.

Miko looked through the wall. "He's coming now." Prezzy hid behind the archway. When Swaraj walked in, she jumped on him, yelling, "Gotcha! Finally, you're here." Hanging off him, Swaraj maintained his balance. "What? You all have been waiting for me?" Lin, with her British accent, sarcastically said, "Yes. Right, we've all been waiting for you. Don't you know it's your turn?" Swaraj asked, "My turn for what?" Prezzy joked, "To walk us to dinner. Like this." She hopped down, tilted her head back, moved her arms back and forth, and took exaggerated steps. Alex and Declan mimicked her. "Like this?"

Everyone laughed, imitating her walk as they left. Swaraj ran to the front with Prezzy. "Like this, I'm the leader now." Lin quipped, "I think they call this the Staunch Butler walk." They all tried to imitate it.

V thought, *"This night is going to get out of control. Twelve 21-year-olds are drunk under the influence of the Common Mind. What could happen? I need a couple of drinks and to get Alex out of there."*

At the buffet table, Declan bumped into Miko. "Let's skip dinner, get drunk, and have sex." Miko gave him a sexy smile. "Settle down, sailor. You should eat something." He smiled back. "Okay, Mum." Then he saw V's disdainful look and frowned.

At the table, they all sat together. Alex started, "Did you hear about the men who broke into the pharmacy and stole Viagra?" V looked at him. "No, I didn't." Alex grinned. "They put out an alert for two hardened criminals."

Declan laughed and added, "What's the difference between kinky and perverted?" No one answered. He continued, "Kinky is using a feather to tickle your girlfriend. Perverted is using the whole chicken." Tonari, with a serious look, said, "I like peacock feathers." Candido grinned and said, "Really?" They all laughed.

Lin smirked, "What's the difference between a tire and 365-used condoms? One's a Goodyear; the other is a great year." V spat out her soda onto Alex and laughed. They all burst into laughter again.

Lev cleared his throat and paused. Everyone waited in anticipation. He began, "A penguin takes his car to the shop, and the mechanic says, 'It'll take about an hour to check it.' While he waits, the penguin goes to an ice cream shop and orders a big sundae. The penguin isn't the neatest eater, and he ends up covered in melted vanilla ice cream. When he returns to the shop, the mechanic takes one look at him and says, 'Looks like you blew a seal.' 'No!' the penguin insists. 'It's just ice cream.'" They were silent for a moment, then erupted in laughter. Declan admitted, "I think that was the best one, especially in a Russian accent." V looked at Tonari to see if she got that one.

Maria looked around the table. "Alright, finish up. It's party time." Alex quipped, "Maria, the event coordinator." Declan yelled, "Bahdubah, where are the drinks?"

As they finished up, music started playing on the deck. Alex looked at V. "I think the Common Mind is going to get out of control tonight."

She nodded. "I think it already has."

Declan noted, "Sounds like Rugrog and Bahdubah are getting the sound system started up."

A new **"Song"** started. *Another Morning.*

Miko asked, "What kind of name is Rugrog?"

Declan added, "What about Bahdubah? That's a really cool name, Bah-du-bah. Bah-du-bah. I like that!"

V chuckled. "Jeez, Declan! Sounds more like a nickname of sorts, Bahdubah."

Alex chimed in, "Or one you hear in a kids' cartoon." In a loud, cartoony voice, he yelled, "Hey Baaahhhhhhhhhhhhddduuuuuuuuuuubbaaahhhhhhhhhhhh, how you doin' mate!!?" V laughed as she got up. She looked at Swaraj and asked, "How are we walking to the deck?"

Swaraj, puzzled for a second, remembered how they walked to dinner. "We could do the chicken," he suggested, flapping his arms. Prezzy countered, "No, let's do the driver." She tilted her head back, put her arms out like she was holding a steering wheel, and shuffled her feet in circles, shifting gears.

Declan blurted out, "Yep, this is going to be a fun night."

They all worked their way to the deck, some doing The Chicken, some continuing with the Pompous Butler, and others trying The Driver. They eventually walked normally halfway down the ramp, making their way to the bar.

Declan took a bar stool. "Are we doing shots?" Miko, sitting next to him, suggested, "How about Ice Teas? Those work." V asked, "Isn't that like four different alcohols?" Declan replied, "It's Tequila, Vodka, Rum, Triple Sec, and a splash of Coke." V nodded. "So, it is. Sweet."

Bahdubah, behind the bar, walked up and asked, "What are we having?" Miko smiled. "Hi Bahdubah, how are you doing?" Bahdubah, standing just over three feet tall with a whiter complexion than Kahput, a long white straight mustache, long beard, and long white and gray hair under a New York Yankees hat, always chipper, smiled and chuckled. "Doing fine, Miko. How are you all tonight?" Miko replied, "We're doing okay. We'd like to start off with some Ice Teas, please."

Bahdubah nodded. "Sounds great." He grabbed some highball glasses and started mixing the drinks. Declan asked, "You a Yankee fan?" Bahdubah pulled off his hat as if he had forgotten he was wearing it, then put it back on. "Yes, love baseball." Declan continued, "Are they going to be in the playoffs this year?" Bahdubah nodded. "Looks like it." Alex asked, "You and Klinchme' from CAT 1?" Bahdubah corrected him, "It's pronounced Klinch-may. And yes, our mother and father were from CAT 1."

V, without thinking, asked, "So, Elders can have kids?" Bahdubah chuckled as he handed out the drinks. "Yes, it's possible if you do it right." They all laughed, and Bahdubah left to help Klinchme'.

Lin started with a French **"Song."** *Secret.*

Alex leaned in and quietly said to V, "Thinking about kids already?" She shoved him playfully. "It was just a question."

Alex laughed. "If you ever need help with that, I could, you know?"

V smiled and softly said, "You want to 'Dance' with me, Alexander Katz?"

He looked into her green eyes. "Yes, I want to 'Dance' with you, however you want to put it." They got their drinks. Some played pool, while others danced.

After a few drinks, with Kahput and Rugrog's help, Lin, Prezzy, and Kyoryk set up the sound system for karaoke. V, Alex, Declan, and Miko played pool while the others watched Lin sing. After she finished, Lev jumped on stage and started singing one of his favorites while pointing to Lin. His strong Russian accent added a fun twist, and Lin joined him on stage.

After he finished, Candido jumped up on the stage and started singing in Spanish. Everyone stopped what they were doing and started yelling, "Such a lovely place! Such a lovely place!" His voice grew deep with passion, bending over as if he were one of the original singers. Lin also joined him, singing. The Common Mind kicked in, and the music made them all feel like one. "Welcome to the hotel, California sounded throughout the cavern. They all started singing in

Spanish and dancing around, spinning and dancing, completely free from worry. The tune ended, and they cheered and clapped, excited for what was next.

Everyone looked to Alex, urging him to sing. Declan was especially insistent. "Come on, man. Get up there; you must know one tune?" Alex, thinking hard, knew so many tunes from constantly listening to music but only knew the words to a couple. Finally, after V coaxed him onto the stage, he said, "Okay, in a few minutes." Declan put on another tune and tried to sing it. By this time, everyone was very drunk.

Alex talked to Lin and Maria about his pick, and they agreed to help with backup singing. After Declan finished, Alex got up on stage with the girls. V watched intently.

"I only know a couple of **"Songs"** *Copacabana* by heart. My brother and I used to sing this with my mom while she cleaned the house." Alex spoke into the mic.

"With the assistance of my two beautiful backup singers, Maria and Lin, let's do this." Rugrog handed microphones to the girls as Alex pointed at V.

He began singing.

In V's mind, she immersed herself in Alex's memory. *He was four or five, his brother ten or eleven.*

They did the Bunny Hop while their mom vacuumed, sliding around on the wooden floors moving into carpeted bedrooms with dust wands.

V watched this vivid scene in his mind of Alex's childhood, feeling a pang of jealousy. She saw the love and joy in their faces and started to understand Alex's deep affection for his family and the world. She felt the warmth of his family's love, something she had never experienced before.

It brought tears to her eyes. They hugged and chased each other, their laughter echoing through the house.

As "Copacabana" blared through the speakers, V felt in her heart what it felt like to be part of a loving family, something she had never felt before."

Miko nudged V and screamed, "Can you believe this?" V snapped back to reality to see everyone on the deck singing. Lin and Maria swayed their hips, feet sliding on the stage. Alex, a different person on stage, held the mic with confidence. *"Who is he?"* V thought. *"Look at him. This guy surprises me every step of the way. Am I in love?"*

The Common Mind, a gift from the Creator, put them all in a trance. They almost floated. They spun, danced, and sang. Was this a master plan to make them forget the impending end of the world? The Creator at work. V now understood traditional family love from Alex's memory. This night felt different; change was coming.

Bahdubah, Klinchme', Rugrog, Kahput, and other workers joined in, singing and dancing. Lev controlled the lights, syncing them with the tune. The entire cavern lit up. Time slowed in the final minute of the tune. Everyone spun, jumped, sang, and hollered. One mind, one body, the Common Mind, had unified the University of CAT 6's, the new Elders. All had their Gifts except Alex. What was his Gift?

V stood in awe as Alex jumped down from the stage and kissed her. "Oh my god, that was fun."

V, struggling to find words, said, "That was unbelievable. You're a lot of fun, Alex Katz. I can't believe you and your brother used to sing and dance around the house with your mom. That's wild. I saw it." She looked into his eyes.

Catching their breath, they sat for another drink. Declan paused, kissing Miko to say, "Alex, bro, that was awesome. I like your mom now."

Alex noted, "I told Rugrog to turn the volume up as it progressed gradually." He smiled, feeling a sense of accomplishment.

Lin and Lev switched the sound system back to the playlist, and Lin started a somewhat romantic **"Song."** *Into the Mystic*

At the bar, V asked Klinchme', "Could I get a couple of cozy hot drinks?" Klinchme' replied, "Two Hot Buttered Rums coming up."

V thought, *"I think it's time to show Alex the hot tub and maybe more. I don't know if it's the Common Mind or not. He said he wanted to "Dance. That sounds great to me." I feel really good right now. Let's do this!"* Alex walked up and quietly said, "I'm a little cautious and worried about things, especially when I got here. But when I'm with you, my self-confidence soars. I just feel better when you are near."

V put a finger to his lips. "I feel the same way. This place, us, it all just feels right." She looked into his eyes. *Yep, this guy is special. He might actually change the world somehow, and I want to be there with him when he does.* " Klinchme' handed them their drinks.

V took a sip. "This is delicious. Thank you." Klinchme' nodded and smiled. V looked back at Alex. "I want to show you something." She hopped down from the bar stool and grabbed his hand. "Come on." Alex said, "Yeah, but last time you showed me something?" She took a look back at all of the students' slow dancing, some of them even kissing, and proceeded up the ramp.

They walked to the pool area. Alex looked around, impressed. "Wow, this is nice." V noted, "Wow, it's much better at night." As they walked in, the lights came on automatically. One waterfall split, one side flowing into the pool, the other into a lake by the deck. The two arched windows overlooked the deck. A fireplace by the hot tub ignited automatically. Alex was amazed. "This is super nice," he said.

V continued, "I didn't realize it before, but I think we're just to the side of the deck. We can hear the music from here." She set their drinks on a table by the hot tub. They walked toward the pool's other side. "The archways had a similar view as the deck." V slipped off her dress and shoes, slowly entering the pool. She looked up at Alex and asked, "You coming in?"

Alex, still looking at the view, now saw V half-naked in the pool. Without hesitation, he dropped his clothes to his underwear and jumped in.

V said, "It's the perfect temperature."

Alex, trying to remain calm, replied, "Yes, this is perfect. Can't ask for much more than this."

She kissed him briefly and swam away. Alex swam after her; the laughter and singing from the deck, faintly audible, excited the mood. He caught up to her in the shallow end.

V, now close to him, said, "You're right. One can't ask for much more than this." She gently placed her hands around Alex's face and started kissing him. They kissed for a few minutes, lost in the moment. She then forcefully pushed him away. "Let's get into the hot tub." V jumped out of the pool and into the warmer water. Alex slowly joined her, and they resumed kissing, gently touching and caressing each other as a new **"Song"** played upstairs. *The Great Gig in the Sky.*

Alex gazed into V's emerald eyes and whispered, "Are you sure about this?" V smiled, unclipping her bra and slipping off her panties. *"I've never felt this good in my life. This is the best night ever,"* she thought.

"Yes, I'm sure," V whispered back. Alex quickly removed his briefs. V repositioned herself in the hot tub and whispered in his ear, "Completely." They began making love, their passionate kisses mingling with the melody of the background music and the splashing water made it the perfect compilation. It was like watching two lovebirds in flight, their movements synchronized to the rhythm of the music. The lights shining through the arched window spilled in, lighting up the ceiling. Controlled by Lev, the changing colors created a magical atmosphere.

The hot tub, a custom shape accommodating up to fifteen people, created waves that moved back and forth. V submerged herself completely, then slowly emerged, her hair swooshing back into the water. Alex smiled at her, and she felt as if she were floating on a warm cloud.

Alex was gentle and slow, exploring V's body with delicate hands. *"This guy is nice and romantic,"* V thought.

He took his time caressing and kissing her. V shifted her head, feeling the pleasure of the warm water and their bodies coming together like they were made for each other. She moaned with pleasure, the music and water creating a perfect symphony. Alex had forgotten the impending disaster, lost in only the moment.

"I may need to be the aggressor here. I like to go faster," V thought as she picked up the pace. To her surprise, this ignited something in Alex. He became aggressive, and the hot tub waves became turbulent, spilling onto the tiled floor.

Not long after, he climaxed, and V thought, *"Oh, shit, this feels good. I've never felt anything like this before. What the hell is going on here?"* She pulled him tighter, closer. All the time, without intimacy, the new feelings came to a head.

She dug her nails into his waist, lifted her legs out of the water, and with the energy from Alex's climax triggering her, she released all her stored energy. She held him tight. "Bhagavaan Meree Madad Karo" ("God Help Me"), she yelled in Hindi, pulling him even tighter. Her body surged again, her heart pounded, and when she thought it was over, it wasn't. She took another deep breath and held it in. Pulsating again and again, *"Oh my God," she thought. "What the hell is happening?"* After what seemed to be a minute or more. Her body tightened even tighter; again, she wrapped and pulled her arms around him and held him as if her life depended on it; her toes and fingers stung. Her pounding heart sounded off to the slowing rhythm of the music and water as the moment finally came to an end. She was at last able to breathe.

"This is insane. Is this what they warned us about in class? The Common Mind? The Creator? Or is it Alex? Who cares? I'm drunk; this is the best night ever!" She laughed, grabbing his face and kissing him compassionately. When she looked at him, he had a concerned look on his face. "Haven't done that in a while. That was something, Mr.!"

Alex laughed gratefully, "Best night ever!" She looked at him cheerfully. Smiling back, "That's exactly what I was thinking. Best night ever!" Alex got up, commandeered the drinks, and looked at V, "Best night ever." V chuckled again.

Upstairs, Maria, Lin, and others laughed, one of them saying, "I think this tune was in The Lion King." Alex and V looked at each other, questioning.

V asked, "What's going on up there?" "Who knows, they're probably very drunk now," Alex replied as a new **"Song"** started. *Mo Ghile Mear* V sat back in the warm water with Alex, feeling completely satisfied. She knew she was on the right track, completely confident in herself, the University, and Alex. Looking into the fire, "Sounds like they're having a good time, I think?"

V smiled, thinking, *"I've never felt like this before. Is it what I feel or the Common Mind? It's the best sex I've ever had, that's for sure. Alex is just doing everything right. For the first time, I feel like I'm doing the right thing. Everything just feels perfect."*

Alex looked at V, noticing her thoughtful expression. "You here? You okay?" V smiled, kissed him, and hugged him. She retrieved her bra and panties from the water and put them back on. "Yeah, I'm perfect."

Alex got a peculiar look on his face. "Look at the fire." V looked at him and then at the fire, "Yeah, I see it." "No, look past it, look into the colors as they change, the colors, isn't it spectacular. I've always liked and enjoyed a good fire." V looked at him and he had this smile like he was so content. "I guess so." She responded. "It's so beautiful and yet so destructive." He looked at her. "You are so beautiful." She thought. *"What the hell is he getting at?"* "Are you okay?" Alex snapped out of it. "Yeah, I'm okay. Everything is falling into place." He gave her a smile she would never forget.

A few seconds later, the pool started to swirl, capturing their attention. Small waves crashed against the sidewalls, a warm wind filled the room, and the lights flickered, then flashed off and on.

Alex extended his arms protectively around V. "What's this?" V, alarmed, watched as the lights continued to flicker before going off completely, except for the internal pool lights, which appeared to grow brighter. The wind extinguished the fire, and the water in the pool swirled more aggressively, forming a tornado-type formation.

"Is it a woman? A man? An angel? What's going on here?" V wondered as the water formation started to take shape. She was now frightened. Scared. Alex quickly put on his jockey shorts and held her tighter.

As the water continued to swirl, the shape became clearer: a figure, possibly an angel, from the mid-section up, fifteen to twenty feet tall. The figure is now clear and perfect like it went from water to an ice formation. It started to speak.

"The information you seek is in the library, in the center of this shape," it said. The angel figure put its hands together, then spread them apart, revealing a figure-eight symbol made of water and then ice, illuminated by the pool lights. It was spectacular.

It looked directly at them, scaring both of them.

It continued speaking, "This time is different; all are in danger. Train and use your Gifts. You will need them long into the future. All Elders living will."

The angel pointed at them. V and Alex listened intently.

"You must risk all to save as many as you can. Save the technology. It's up to you to find the solution. You and the other Elders must work together; it's all or none. Never has your people been in this place of consciousness. You're creative, immortal, infinite beings. Use your Gifts to save this race in its infamy. You must save all you can. You must find the solution."

The figure seemed to almost smile at them.

Then, just like that first night at dinner when Fem' performed the prayer that bestowed upon them the eagle marks, a blue sapphire lightning bolt arrow flame emerged, swirling around the room. It spiraled through the air, passing through them as it had done only days ago, before shooting back into the angel figure and disappearing.

In an instant, the angel splashed down into the pool, the lights slowly dimming until all was dark.

Two seconds later, the lights flickered back on, and suddenly, the fire reignited, startling them. All the lights returned to their original state as if nothing had happened.

Alex, astonished, looked at V, "What the hell was that? Holy shit!" He smiled at her, exhilarated.

She looked at him and muttered a few choice words in Hindi. Adjusting her underwear, she exclaimed, "Shit! What was that, Alex? Did we just see some kind of message from the Creator?" She pushed him away, then pulled him back and kissed him. "You're amazing."

Alex smiled and pulled her close, "No, you're amazing." V pushed him back, then pulled him towards her again, kissing him deeply.

Miko and Declan speak loudly, having trouble walking in through the archway. "Here you are; we've been looking for you. This is nice, really nice," Miko let go of Declan excitedly expressed. Alex and V looked at each other and chuckled. "That's what I said," Alex remarked. Miko added, "This is right beside the deck. I can hear the music."

V smiled and chuckled, "That's what I said." They stripped down and joined them in the hot tub. Declan just kept saying, "Dude?" And looking around at the pool area.

"Something just happened," V commented. Miko, smiling, suggested, "I could tell by the looks on your faces when we walked in. It's all-natural; you shouldn't be shy about it."

Declan was in awe as he got into the hot tub and sat down. Miko got in and sat on his lap. "No, not that. We just saw something. It could have been one of our Gifts or something more powerful. Something appeared out of the pool," V insisted.

Declan chuckled, slurring his words, "How big was it? You've seen one before in the showers, haven't you, V? You do know it gets bigger when it gets excited?" Miko laughed, smiled, and nodded, "Yep, it does."

"Stop! Stop it, you guys. We saw an angel or something."

"It came out of the water," V said.

Alex, rubbing his face in disbelief, added excitedly, "It was made from the water. It told us something. Miko and Declan, stop joking around. This is serious."

Miko, trying to be more serious now, asked, "Alright, seriously, what was it?"

"It looked like an angel made from the pool water. It spoke to us," Alex explained. Declan asked, "What did it say?"

V, looking at Alex, stood up and began imitating the exact way she saw it in the pool with her hand and her body. "It said, 'The information you seek is in the library, in the center of this shape. This time is different; all are in danger. Train and use your Gifts. You will need them long into the future. All Elders living will. You must risk all to save as much as you can. Save the technology. It's up to you to find the solution. You and the other Elders must work together; it's all or none. Never has your people been in this place of consciousness. You're creative, immortal, infinite beings. Use your Gifts to save this race in its infamy. You must save all you can. You must find the solution.'"

Miko asked, "What shape?" Noticing V's neck said, "You have two marks on your neck, not one." Alex stood up to look at V. "You do," he confirmed.

V put her hands together as she looked at Alex's neck, "It was the infinity symbol; that's what it showed us, a figure eight.

A new **"Song"** started on the deck. *Sausalito Summernight*

Declan asked, "What tune are they playing up there? I've never heard that one before. I like it. Hey, Alex has two marks too. But whose Gift was it to be seeing the angel thing? And why do you both now have two eagle marks?"

V replied, "Not sure. We should tell our Stewards. Maybe it's Alex's; he doesn't have his Gift yet. When do they get back?"

Miko asked, "Isn't it Sunday afternoon?" Alex, with a blank look and a long pause, almost looking like he was stuck in time, muttered, "They won't be back until late on Sunday at midnight."

Declan looked at him and said, "Are you okay? How do you know that?" "When V asked, I just saw them coming back and saw the clock. It was almost midnight," Alex explained.

Miko added, "That sounds like Alex has two Gifts now." V looked at him, "So you saw into the future? That's crazy."

Declan looked at the three of them, "This is the best night ever." V and Alex laughed, saying simultaneously, "That's what we said!"

Alex stood up, jumped out of the spa, and grabbed V's hand. "Shower time. We've been in here for a while now. I'm starting to melt."

Miko, with an exaggerated smile at them, "A while, huh?" V chuckled, with a flirtatious smile, as she got out, "We'll see you guys in the morning. We need to go to the library and find out what's going on. Figure out what the rest of the message means." As they walked out, Alex smirked, "Have fun."

In the shower, as they rinsed off, Alex looked at V, "You want to come to my room?" V smiled and replied, "I do, but I think we should be a little discrete." Drying off, she added, "But that doesn't mean you can't come to my room tomorrow night."

Alex grinned, "It will be the best night ever."

As they walked down the hallway, holding hands like schoolchildren, they reached V's room. V stood on her toes and gave him a short kiss. "See you in the morning. That was very, very nice. The other part, we will have to figure out."

Alex smiled, "Best night ever. It was nice. And yes, we will figure it out. I think the Creator was listening." He let go of her hand slowly, as if he never, ever wanted to let go. He chuckled and bowed slightly, "Good night, my lady." V curtsied and replied, "Sir," then she disappeared into her room.

Now, in her sweats, V danced around her room, listening to some music. She fell onto her bed, put her hands behind her head, looked at the ceiling, and said to herself, *"What a night! Best sex ever! Best night ever!"*

VIII

"What a night. Am I with V now? She's spectacular. Is she with me?" He stared into his own eyes. *"I've never experienced intimacy like that before. Now I understand what Harvey meant. I must be careful; I could lose myself in her."*

He closed his eyes. *"Alright, focus. Find the figure eight in the library. I need to figure it out. I can't obsess over V."* He rubbed his face, opened his eyes, and looked back into the mirror. *"She's incredible, though. Will she stay with me?"*

"STOP! Focus. Do some jumping jacks. Damn, I have a headache. Stop second-guessing yourself."

A knock at the door interrupted his thoughts. Alex said, "Come in." Declan opened the door, "Get up, man. Oh! Come on, Bahdubah's making Ramos Fizzes in the common room."

Alex stopped the jumping jacks and looked at him, "What's that?" Declan smiled, "It's like a fizzy lemonade drink. Great for hangovers. Let's go."

Alex quickly dressed, ran a comb through his hair, and asked, "Has anyone noticed their eagle mark is missing?" Declan, in a hurry, replied, "I don't know, I've only been up a few minutes."

As they walked to the common room, Alex commanded, "Let's keep last night quiet until we know more about the angel and the eagle marks. We need to check the library before sharing any information. Later, we should meet with everyone to work on the Common Mind." Declan agreed, "Okay, boss."

Alex stopped walking and held Declan back with his arm. "I think V and I might be together now. How did it go with Miko last night?" Declan grinned and chuckled, "It went very well. We hooked up. So, we'll see."

Alex started walking again, "Let's keep that to ourselves too."

Declan agreed, "Dude, relax. Have a Ramos Fiz. No need to stress. Today, it's the "No Stress Express.""

In the common room, Candido, Tonari, and Prezzy were sitting on floor pillows, enjoying their drinks. Alex walked in and put his arm around Bahdubah, "This is great of you to come this morning and make these drinks."

Bahdubah turned to Alex, "No problem. I thought you all might need this after last night."

Alex smirked, "Well, it's super nice. I do have a little headache. Morning, Tonari, Prezzy, Can Do Man. How are you guys doing this fine morning?" They all lifted their drinks in greeting. Alex returned the gesture and asked, "Anyone else up yet?" No one answered.

Prezzy asked, "Did you and V get your Gifts yet?" Alex turned in his seat, "Possibly. I think I saw into the future. I saw the Elders returning tomorrow night, not in the afternoon. I saw the clock on the wall in the dock area; it said '11:49 pm' as they got off the ship. V and I saw something, but we're not sure what it meant. We'll discuss it with everyone later today."

Declan commented, "The hot tub was super relaxing last night."

Alex turned again to look at Prezzy and the others, "Later, we should get together as a group and strengthen our Gifts. Declan and I are heading to the library in a few minutes to do some research. Let's meet around noon?" Prezzy replied, "Okay, I'll let the others know we're meeting at noon."

V and Miko entered the room. Alex, unsure how to approach V after last night, thought, *"Should I kiss her? Hug her?"*

V said, "Did you all sleep well?" As she walked towards Bahdubah, she gently stroked Alex's back. "Well, I slept like a baby. How nice of you to make these drinks for us this morning. This is great." She gave Bahdubah a big hug, "Thank you." Alex noticed V had a bit more confidence in her step. He looked at Miko, who was glowing with a big smile.

Declan noticed and commented, "You ladies look chipper this morning. You must have slept well?" Miko grabbed her drink and stood behind Declan, placing her hand on his shoulders, possibly signaling, "He's mine."

Lin entered and thanked Bahdubah before sitting down, "Any plans for today?"

V sat next to Alex and began to speak. Alex put his hand on her wrist, cut her off, and gave her a look that said, "I got this."

He said, "We were thinking of meeting here to practice our Gifts and the Common Mind." Lin asked, "When?" Alex replied, "How about noon?" Lin agreed, "Sounds good. I'll let the others know." Alex stated, "The four of us have plans to go to the library."

They finished their drinks and headed to the library.

Once there, Declan asked, "So, what did the angel say again?" V looked around to ensure they were alone, "She said we've never reached this level of consciousness. Then she showed us the sideways figure eight symbol with her hands and said to look for it in the library." Alex looked at V and smiled. He pulled out his tablet and searched for the symbol.

"I looked it up last night. It's the infinity symbol," he showed her a picture on his tablet. "There are four types: mathematical, physical, metaphysical, and the last is everlasting love." V said, "I like that last one."

Alex got closer to her, "The symbol is called the Lemniscate." He traced a figure eight on her chest and smiled softly, "Once you're in love infinitely, the symbol represents that your true love is everlasting. You can never fall out of love, ever." He continued tracing the figure eight, "See, it's endless. Could that be us?"

V grabbed his face and gave him a big lingering kiss. Declan blurted out, "Alright, we're here to find answers, not to get all mushy." Miko admitted, "If you'd said that to me, I'd have given you a big kiss too."

Declan approached Miko and slowly took her hand, looked at her compassionately, and paused.

"When I was a kid, I dreamed of finding one person, one soul for me. This place is real; I know that now. After last night, spending time with you, I know I've found that person. A beautiful woman. Miko Machenyu Jonetsu, you're the one. The one for me, and I'm the one for you." Almost, with what looked to be water eyes, he added, "I know that it's all true."

Alex and V were stunned by Declan's confession. Miko visibly moved, grinned and jumped all the way onto Declan, giving him a passionate, messy kiss, messing up his hair.

Alex looked at Declan and said, "Wow, nicely done."

Declan joked, "No, I was talking about Suzzie Chappy, the chick I was watching last night on the internet on my." Before Declan had time to finish, Miko slugged him hard on the chest, "You're an ass."

Alex laughed, "Now that's the Declan we know." V joined in, "Declan, the shame. You need to stop joking with her."

Miko walked away quickly, and Declan started chasing after her, "Baby, I was just messing around. I'm sorry."

V glanced at Alex and said, "We're searching for that symbol, right?" She scanned the library, looking around the walls and floor.

Suddenly, she jumped at the sight of the enormous hourglass shifting with the hour. Standing over three meters tall, it was immense yet surprisingly quiet. Alex followed her, and she remarked, "The library is organized by the intervals between catastrophes and the seven planets. I don't see anything resembling the infinity symbol."

Alex looked at her intently, "You know, I was tempted to sneak into your room last night. I couldn't stop thinking about you."

She stopped him with a smile, "If you're going to sneak into my room tonight, make sure you bring a quart of ice cream and one big spoon." Alex embraced her and whispered, "I just wanted to snuggle with you, to feel your warm body next to mine."

V smiled and pushed him away, continuing down the aisle, "Spooning."

"What?" Alex asked. V grinned, "It's called spooning. One fits perfectly into the other."

Alex laughed, "No, I meant, what kind of ice cream do you like?"

"Velvet Mint Chocolate Chip," V replied, looking at him seductively. "It's cold, minty, and a bit chocolatey. You could smother it all over me."

Alex groaned, "Jesus, stop it. You're going to make me attack you right here." She flipped her hair back and said, "Later, baby."

Alex's expression turned curious, "Why does the Creator suddenly want to stop the CAT? He said we've reached a new level of consciousness. You just mentioned it's from His message. Does He want us to continue?"

V shrugged, "This is a good thing. Could it be due to the WFNWP? Or is it truly about our consciousness?"

Declan announced, "The big hourglass looks like an eight, but it's not sideways." They all approached the hourglass. Miko looked up at it, "World Free Nuclear Weapons Program. Have all the countries started yet?"

As it completed its rotation, Alex stated, "I think they have. It's projected to be completed by 2045 to 2050. We are far better off than we were in the past. Didn't 800,000 slaves build the Great Wall and his 8,000 life-sized soldiers in China? How many slaves built the pyramids? If they were built that way? Oh my God, we need to find that out and how they move those 50-tone stones."

The hourglass hung from a metal and wooden frame attached to the ceiling. After searching for a while longer, V, frustrated, muttered some words in Hindi and declared, "This is shit. We're not finding it."

Alex laughed and looked at Declan, "Wonder what she said in Hindi? We don't see it here. All I see are books, wooden bookcases, and these Elder heads carved out of granite."

Declan commented, "In movies, there's always a secret door and a lever to open it. Ever seen Young Frankenstein? 'Put the candle back!'"

Alex laughed, echoing, "I remember that. 'Put The Candle Back.' That was hilarious; he gets stuck in the door, and every time they said 'Frau Blücher,' the horses freaked out." Declan laughed.

Miko suggested, "Maybe we should get the others down here. With all of us, we might find it."

V asked, "Did anyone mention their eagle marks missing from their necks?"

Alex answered, "No, but we didn't ask. Whoever it was, we can't do anything about it. Maybe they haven't noticed yet?"

"Let's take one more look around and see if we find anything," V added. They spent another half hour searching. Declan commented, "I want to see Alex sing 'At the Copa' again."

Alex laughed, "That was fun. I think it was those ice teas'."

Miko, hugging Declan from behind, said, "I think it had a lot to do with the Common Mind. When we all join together, thinking the same thing at the same time, we sync up somehow. Imagine watching a sexy movie together."

Declan looked back, "Horny girl." Alex laughed.

V, gazing at Alex from across the room, said softly, "Maybe he could sing to me again." Lowering her voice so no one else could hear, she added, "Last night's peak of pleasure. How will I top that? I should be patient and wait a night or two."

Alex asked, "What did you say?" V replied, "Nothing, baby. We're not figuring this out. We need more people or help from one of the older Elders."

Alex suggested, "Should we tell one of them what we saw? Then, see where it goes from there. Or maybe just tell Gig?" V nodded, "I like Gig. He seems alright."

Alex looked at Miko and Declan, "What do you think?" Declan replied, "Tell Gig. I think that's a good idea." Miko agreed, "Fine with me. Everyone will find out anyway." Alex decided, "Alright, we'll tell Gig." Declan jested, "Okay, after that, we'll get drunk and have sex." Miko hit him in the arm. Declan squealed, "Oww, shit, that hurt."

Miko warned, "You better mellow out. You might be in some kind of relationship now. You don't want to blow it." Declan looked at her and said, "Roger that," he pushed her gently, "Woman!"

V laughed. "We'll return after talking to Gig about this. We need to uncover who built the library and what alterations have been made. Someone placed something here that can help us stop this CAT. I think the message came from the Creator."

As Alex and the group took one final look around the library, he nodded, "I agree. Once the Pulse Reversal hits, chaos will ensue. We need to figure this out, but we must tread carefully."

Declan chimed in, "It must be from the Creator because both of you received additional eagle marks from Him. It must be a genuine message. You two are much closer to becoming the Master Elders now. Let's see who gave you the marks and if they'll be weird about it. Hopefully not. We need to act nonchalantly until we understand what the message means."

Miko agreed. "The group has gotten along so far, and we need to keep it that way. Let's head back; I need a snack." V smiled. "I'm glad we're all here together. So far I've been having some doubt about this place, but today, I feel much better with the three of you." Declan, opening up, said, "I use humor to hide my emotions. It's my way of coping with this craziness, pretending everything's okay." Miko added, "I like your sense of humor."

Alex started through the archway and looked at them, "Wheat Thins and Cheddar Cheese. Sometimes Monterey Jack Cheese, with a Coke. That's my go-to." V said, "I prefer Root Beer and Rold Gold Tiny Twists dipped in Garlic Hummus." Declan laughed. "You guys are very specific about your snacks." As they walked up the ramp towards the upper floors, Declan raised his hand. "Melba Toast with Swiss cheese and grapes." Miko asked, "What the hell is Melba Toast?" Declan laughed. "Melba Toast. It's like a big piece of bread squished down to a thin little piece with Swiss cheese. Grapes are always a winner."

Alex thought to himself, *"When should I call Gig? He said to call if there were problems. No, he just left his contact information. It hasn't even been a day. I'll wait until later today. V is so beautiful and smart. Why would she ever be with me?"*

"I need to stop thinking like that. I'm an okay guy. I just need to keep doing what I'm doing."

V leaned towards him and whispered, "Midnight." "What?" Alex asked.

"Come to my room after midnight," she repeated. Alex smiled. "It will be the best night ever." V whispered, "That can be our saying—that every night together is the best night ever."

"But you have to leave before anyone wakes up. I want to keep this between us for now. Is that okay?" Alex smiled. "Yes, of course."

They reached the common room. Most of the group was sitting, looking at their tablets. Kyoryk and Lev were playing darts. V asked, "We're missing Candido and Tonari. Has anyone seen them? What time is it?"

Alex checked his tablet. "It's 11:45."

Miko glanced through several walls. "Looks like they were out on the deck. Oh, they are kissing. Wait, now they're headed this way."

Alex walked over to Lev and Kyoryk. "You guys ready to meet?" Lev replied, "Yes."

Alex checked their necks; they still had their eagle marks. He walked over to the others—Prezzy, Swaraj, Maria, and Lin—who also had their marks.

He returned to the table where Miko, Declan, and V sat. "It looks like Candido and Tonari lost their eagle marks. So, we agreed to tell the other Students what we saw and then call Gig later. Everyone okay with that?"

They all nodded. Alex got up to fetch a beer, grabbing one for Declan. Candido and Tonari walked into the room. V looked at Alex. "You want me to explain what happened last night?" Alex said, "Sure, you'll explain it better than me."

V stood and gathered everyone's attention. "Okay, everyone, Alex and I were in the pool area late last night when we received a message, possibly from the Creator. We're not sure. Kyoryk asked, "What kind of message?"

V looked around at them all. "We were in the hot tub, and the lights flickered. The pool water became turbulent and formed the shape of a person, like an angel.

It looked at us and said, 'The information you seek is in the library, in the center of this shape.' Then, it put its hands together and made the infinity symbol. It continued, 'This time is different; all are in danger. Train and use your Gifts. You will need them long into the future. All Elders living will.' It pointed to us and said, 'You must risk all to save as many as you can.

Save the technology. It's up to you to find the solution. You and the other Elders must work together; it's all or none."

"Never has your people been in this place of consciousness. You're creative, immortal, infinite beings. Use your Gifts to save this race in its infamy. You must save all you can. You must find the solution."

"Then we saw the same blue-violet light swirl flame arrow thing go around the room as it did the first night. Then went back into the angel and disappeared. The pool returned to normal, the lights came back on, and we noticed we both had an additional eagle mark on our necks. That's it."

"We need everyone's help to figure out what it means. The four of us went down to the library but couldn't find anything."

Candido, looking somewhat sad, said, "I noticed my eagle mark was missing this morning, and Tonari just found out when we were talking on the deck. It's been less than a week, and we've already been judged on our performance. It's not fair."

Kyoryk, with the Gift of knowledge, replied, "The eagle marks are from the Creator. None of us controls that, not even the Stewards or the other Elders, not even Gig or Fem'."

"Maybe it means Alex and V are the group leaders for now. I read that the marks can shift between us while we're in school. So, we shouldn't assume Alex and V will be the Master Elders." Alex nodded. "I agree. It's too soon to determine who the Master Elders might be. But what do you think about what we saw?"

Lev asked, "The shape of a person that came out of the water? Was it familiar, or did it give any clues?"

V answered, "It was about twelve to fifteen feet tall, made of water, like ice once it formed. We couldn't tell if it was male or female. It did resemble an angel in a way."

Lin asked, "Have you told anyone outside this room about this yet?" Alex replied, "No. I was planning to contact Gig later today to inform him about what happened and what we should do. But I thought we should find the symbol first. To see what the other message is."

Prezzy laughed and stood up. "You saw an angel, a message from the Creator. That must have been awesome." V looked at her. "It scared the hell out of us at first, but now, yeah, it was an awesome sight."

Kyoryk, staring intently at his tablet, declared, "I can't find anything about messages or visions from the Creator." V added, "We believe there's a message or some kind of plan in the library to help us mitigate the effects of the upcoming Super Flare of CAT 6. That's what the message indicated."

Maria inquired, "What were you doing when it happened?" Alex, sharing a knowing smile with V, chuckled, "At that moment, nothing really. We were just sitting there."

Prezzy, pacing and smirking, interjected, "You guys were having sex, weren't you?" Everyone burst into laughter. Lev, Candido, and Maria chimed in with playful affirmations while Lin pointed at them. "So, you two are a couple now?" V smiled and clarified, "I don't think what we were doing at the moment is relevant to the message. Alex has been trying to figure out how to stop the upcoming CAT, and he asked for my help." Prezzy, still laughing, teased, "So around midnight, you were helping him figure this out?"

V frowned at Prezzy, but Kyoryk redirected the conversation. "So, you think the Creator has asked us to help stop the CAT? That means the Creator is watching and monitoring our thoughts." Declan explained, "Yes, that's what we believe. The angel said it's up to us. So, what's our next step?"

Lev stood up decisively, like in the military. "We need to go to the library and find this information that's supposed to help us." Prezzy, already hopping with excitement, pointed at Lin. "To the library we go!" Lin got up, and Prezzy exclaimed, "Yes, let's go figure this out!" They all got up and headed out of the room excited.

Miko looked at Declan. "What about my snack?" Declan walked over to the kitchen area, grabbed a box of crackers, quickly sliced some cheese, and fetched a bottle of water.

He returned and handed them to Miko. "This will have to do for now, my sweet." Miko smiled. "Okay, thanks."

As they walked to the library, Kyoryk fell in step with V and Alex. "Tell me again exactly what the angel said. I want to type it out." V started to recount the message, and Kyoryk typed it into his tablet. By the time they finished, they had reached the library. Kyoryk summarized, "It said to look for the infinity symbol in the middle. Or was it in the middle of the infinity symbol? The rest was about us and the other Elders." Alex nodded. "Yes, the four of us searched everywhere but couldn't find the infinity symbol. Once we find it, the message says it's in the center."

Everyone scattered around the library, searching for the symbol but finding nothing. Prezzy looked at V and asked, "Has anyone checked the second or third level?" V replied, "No, we didn't. It's just more books and pictures up there." Prezzy pointed to the spiral staircase. "Let's go up there." V agreed. They reached the second level and found nothing, then ascended to the third level. Frustrated, V yelled, "Anybody find anything?"

They all looked up. Lev approached Alex. "Nothing, no symbol." Alex said, "Maybe we're not looking at it the right way." He looked up at V again. "Did we miss part of the message?" V replied, "I don't think so."

Alex gazed at V and Prezzy on the third level, admiring their beauty. "You look beautiful up there!" V responded, "What?" Alex repeated, "You two look beautiful up there!"

Both smiled. Prezzy spun around, fluffing her hair, then suddenly had a revelation. She stepped back, paused, and started jumping up and down. "I found it! I found it!" She hugged V, almost knocking her over.

Calming down, she grabbed V's arm and pointed excitedly, moving her arm from one side of the library to the other. "Look, look at the whole damn room. Its shape—it's the whole room, the library, that's the symbol."

V started speaking in Hindi, bouncing up and down. "Alex, everyone, Prezzy figured it out. It's the whole room—the room is the symbol." She pointed to the big X-shaped bookcase in the middle of the room. "It's got to be in the center of the symbol, the X."

Alex and the others gathered around the bookcase. Candido remarked, "I don't see anything." Declan suggested, "We need to get on top of it. Is there a ladder?"

Alex looked around. "I think it will support me. Here, hold these books." He started removing books to make steps to climb to the top. Declan took the books and set them on the floor.

V called out, "Be careful."

Declan joked, "Put the candle back."

Alex reached the top and looked down. "Nothing but these busts of men and women from different CATs. They're carvings of the faces of the Elders, I think?" He examined the one in the center. "V, this one in the center kind of looks like the angel we saw last night." He tried to get into position. "I need a Phillips screwdriver."

V responded, "I'll call Bahdubah." She turned to Prezzy. "I don't know if this will work." She took out her tablet and made the call, saying, "Call Bahdubah." It rang. "Hey Bahdubah, it's me, V. We need a favor."

Bahdubah replied, "Sure, what is it?"

V explained, "We're in the library, and we need a Phillips screwdriver. Can you bring us one?"

There was a long pause. V asked, "You there?"

Bahdubah finally responded, "What are you guys up to? I'll be right there."

V said, "Thanks, don't forget the screwdriver." She hung up and called down, "Bahdubah's bringing the screwdriver."

Declan, smiling, called out, "Tell him to bring some drinks too."

Miko, standing next to him, playfully hit his arm. Declan defended himself, "What? He brought us drinks earlier."

Alex shouted from above, "I'm going to take the statue off. It looks like there's a hole underneath."

Declan, with a curious expression, asked Kyoryk, "Just a thought—how did they have Phillips screws thousands of years ago?"

Miko, puzzled, asked, "What are you talking about?" Declan explained, "Phillips invented the Phillips head screw a hundred years ago, and now it's in a 20-thousand-year-old library? Just saying." Kyoryk looked at Declan, equally perplexed.

Bahdubah burst into the room, panting heavily as if he had sprinted all the way there. He scanned the faces around him before his gaze landed on Alex's high on the bookcase. "I don't think you should be up there," he admonished.

Declan clasped Bahdubah's shoulder. "V and Alex received a message from an angel last night. We believe it came from the Creator, instructing us to look here for a solution to stop the impending CAT."

Bahdubah's eyes widened. "You saw an angel? What was that like?" Alex, perched atop the bookcase, responded, "Yeah, it emerged from the water in the pool." V, unable to contain her excitement, began jumping up and down, shaking the rail. "Did you bring the screwdriver?" she called out.

Bahdubah, catching his breath, looked up at her and replied, "Yes, here." He retrieved the screwdriver from his back pocket and handed it to Declan, who then passed it to Alex. Alex immediately began removing the screws from the bust.

"Hurry up!" Prezzy urged. "Calm down, jeez," Alex retorted, focusing on his task.

Everyone watched Alex intently as he worked, with Prezzy and V looking down from the upper level. Alex handed the screws to Declan. "Hold these."

Declan pocketed the screws, grumbling, "Can't believe there's no lever to pull or something."

Carefully, Alex lifted the statue. "There's a hole in the center of the bookcase," he announced. He looked down at Declan. "I need you to take this. Don't drop it." Gently, he handed the statue to Declan, who examined it closely. "It does look like an angel. Or maybe my Uncle Bob," he quipped, eliciting laughter from Miko and the others.

Anticipation built as Alex reached into the hole. "I feel something," he said, a broad smile spreading across his face. He pulled out a roll of papers and held them aloft. The girls screamed in excitement, and Prezzy's yell was particularly loud.

Once the noise subsided, Alex examined the roll. "Looks like charts or plans," he said. The roll was three to four feet long and about six inches in diameter. "Seems to be around 10 to 12 pages," he noted, handing it down to Declan. "The papers, sir," he whispered theatrically.

Bahdubah, eyes wide, murmured, "I think I just shit myself." Declan laughed. "The girls did get pretty excited, didn't they?"

Bahdubah, closing his eyes in apprehension, muttered, "I don't know about this. We're going to get in trouble." "If it's nothing, we'll put them back," Alex reassured him.

Kyoryk advised, "Don't open them until we get back upstairs. We need to be careful. They look really old." "Okay," Declan agreed. Prezzy and V, unable to contain their excitement, started running downstairs.

"Hand me the statue and the screws," Alex requested. Declan handed the roll to Kyoryk before giving the statue and screws to Alex. "Be careful. We don't want to break anything," Bahdubah cautioned. "I think this bookcase is pretty sturdy," Alex replied as he climbed down. "Let's go back to the common room and see what they are."

They replaced everything and made their way back. V turned to Kyoryk. "Let me see." She grabbed the roll from him, her excitement palpable. "I can't believe we found them. We searched all morning."

Bahdubah, still in awe, asked, "What was it like to see an angel?" V smiled. "Scary at first. The pool went crazy, and the angel was made of water, then it solidified into an ice statue."

Back in the common room, Lev moved both tables together, and V began unrolling the papers. Miko stopped her. "Here, put this blanket down first. We don't want to damage the drawings."

Everyone carefully unfolded the roll. The top diagram depicted the planet, showing its magnetic field.

Kyoryk explained, "This first one looks like a rendering of what happens during the CAT." They all peered at the diagram. "See, the magnetic field rings. The flare from the sun, all this plasma being ejected. The magnetic field protects the planet from the plasma and the blast's forces. It's like electricity, akin to lightning. Something we haven't seen in modern times."

"It can carve canyons and melt rocks if it's strong enough. Anything on the surface today wouldn't stand a chance if the plasma touched the planet. You'd need to be six to ten feet underground or ten to twelve feet underwater."

Bahdubah asked, "How do you know all this?" Kyoryk replied, "My Gift is knowledge." Declan joked, "He used to work at a pet store. Now he's the smartest guy on the planet." Miko hushed them. "Shoosh."

V asked, "Is the moon protected by the field?" "Somewhat," Kyoryk replied. "Ideally, the moon would be on the opposite side of the planet when the sun's flare hits. We would be safe because we are 3 to 4 kilometers inside. How many people on the planet live 4 kilometers down inside a mountain?"

Prezzy, still jumping with excitement, asked, "What's the next page?"

Alex carefully rolled up the first page and set it aside. Kyoryk examined the next one. "This is the infinity symbol made from human figures." He looked at Maria. "Could you count how many there are, please?" Maria smiled. "Of course." She began counting.

Kyoryk pointed out, "They appear to be holding hands and looking down towards the planet. There's a device in the middle that four of them are holding."

Maria, flirting, smiled back at Kyoryk. "There are 36." "Thank you," Kyoryk mouthed sweetly.

Declan interjected, "Wait, you two?" Miko hit him, grumbling, "Knock it off."

"Let's look at the next page," V suggested. She rolled up the current one and set it aside. "This one shows the planet," Kyoryk said, pointing. "Here's the north pole, and here's the south. The figure eight of the people is exactly above each pole."

Prezzy, still fidgeting, asked, "What does that mean? What does it mean?" Kyoryk paused. "I have no idea."

Swaraj gently grabbed Prezzy's shoulders. "Calm yourself. You're making me nervous." She clung to him, whispering, "I can't help it. This is exciting. It's like finding a treasure map."

Declan, observing, thought they might be flirting too. He glanced at Miko, who gave him a warning look: don't say anything.

"Next one, V," Kyoryk prompted. She removed the previous page. "I don't recognize this language," Kyoryk noted. He looked at Lin, whose Gift was understanding all languages. "Can you read this?" Lin examined it. "It looks like pre-Arabic, but it doesn't make sense." She turned to Lev. "Sweetie, could you hop up on the chair and take a picture with my tablet?" "Sure, baby," Lev replied with a smile.

Declan whispered to Miko, "I think everyone hooked up last night." Alex beamed at Declan, who returned the smile. Miko mirrored their grins. With Alex's assistance, Lev climbed onto the chair and snapped several photos of the enigmatic plans.

Kyoryk leaned in, inspecting the documents. "These might be instructions of some sort," he mused. Glancing at the other pages, he added, "Below are detailed schematics of the top four pages of that device. We won't know their purpose until we decipher the writing and comprehend the instructions."

V turned to Bahdubah, eyes wide with curiosity. "Have you ever seen anything like this before, or do you know who might have created them?" Bahdubah shook his head slowly. "Never. I have no idea what this is all about." Alex's eyes narrowed thoughtfully. "You're from CAT 1, right?" Bahdubah nodded. "My parents are from CAT 1, but I know nothing about this. If it's possible to stop a CAT, that would be unprecedented. It's never been attempted before. Our role has always been to record events, not interfere. And the message, I've only heard of it once before from the Creator."

Kyoryk's expression grew intense. "There are 36 figures, arranged in a figure eight at each of the poles of the planet. There are 12 of us Students in each CAT, correct?" Bahdubah confirmed with a nod. "This is the sixth CAT. Six times twelve is 72—the exact number of Students the university has seen. That's no coincidence. It must mean something. Are all the Elders from the university still around?" Bahdubah shrugged. "Possibly. Some might be missing."

Alex interjected, "Hugh mentioned some Elders are unaccounted for—around 20. But the Stewards or the Elders' descendants with the Common Mind could assist if needed. We will have to look into that."

Alex addressed the group, determination in his voice. "Our mission is to figure out how to make this device work. Lin will decipher the text. I'll inform Gig about our discovery. We might actually be able to save everyone or most of the planet. This is unbelievable, but we need to solve it." He hugged V tightly. "We're going to make this work."

Excitement erupted. Everyone jumped, hugged, and high-fived. Lin played music, and they danced with joy. Equally elated, Bahdubah announced, "I'll make some drinks." Declan clapped Bahdubah on the back. "You're my new best friend. My man! Let me help." They began rummaging through the fridge. Declan called Alex over. "Isn't it fascinating that someone from the past knew about all this? They left these drawings for us to find many millennia later. They foresaw the future. Isn't that mind-blowing?" Alex nodded. "I glimpsed two days into the future last night, so I suppose it's possible. Maybe my Gift will strengthen, allowing me to see further. I don't know about thousands of years, but maybe a century."

Bahdubah looked amazed. "You can see into the future?" Alex explained, "I saw the Elders returning before midnight tomorrow. We'll see if it comes true." Bahdubah, starting the blender, remarked loudly, "Never heard of that Gift before." Declan added, "You also haven't heard of Elders seeing angels. Oh, you said one time before. We think V and Alex might be communicating with the Creator." Bahdubah advised cautiously, "You might want to wait before telling Gig. If you inform him while he's on Amotaious, it might cause a frenzy. Just a thought. And it wasn't an angel they saw; it was a figure in smoke or water vapor."

Alex agreed. "You're right. Explaining it over the phone could lead to chaos. We should wait until they return on Monday and explain together. This revelation changes everything—the entire process you all have been following for thousands of years."

V hugged him. "We'll do it together. I'll recount what happened to us, and Kyoryk can show the drawings. By then, Lin might have deciphered the language. "They all nodded in agreement. Alex, turning to V, announced, "I have to go."

She looked puzzled. "Where are you going?" He grinned. "I need to find something for later, remember? It's going to be the best night ever!" V recalled their plan involving ice cream and spooning at midnight.

In the pantry, Alex searched for ice cream. He saw Kahput stocking shelves. "Do we have any Mint Chocolate Chip?" he asked. Kahput put away his items and led Alex to the freezer. "Let me show you. Possible." Inside, he pointed to the section with various ice creams.

As Alex scanned the shelves, Kahput inquired, "Something big happened, didn't it? I felt it." Alex, aware of the Common Mind's power among Elders, hesitated. "I have a question." Kahput nodded. "What is it?" "With the Common Mind, if a significant event occurs, would the others feel it? Even on Amotaious?"

Kahput smiled knowingly. "I've witnessed incredible things with the Common Mind. If it's an intense emotion or something impactful, Elders across the galaxy would sense it. Even those with only a few days of practice can feel it. Imagine Gig and Fem', who have honed their Gifts for thousands of years, and my father, for tens of thousands. If I sensed it, the other Elders did too, though they might not know the specifics. It's akin to the collective energy felt at a concert or a big event by regular people on the planet. Have you ever felt it at a big event? When you're in a big crowd, it's in everyone. When everyone is consentratiing on the same thing. I know you've felt it. It's just amplified here by the Creator."

Alex nodded, understanding. "I have. Thank you for explaining to me like that."

Finding the mint chocolate chip, he exclaimed, "Here it is." Kahput, reflecting on his experiences, remarked, "This will be my third CAT. The Common Mind intensifies emotional bonds among Students—fear, joy, love, and sadness. It's the Creator's greatest Gift to us, to our world, in fact. Somethings going on, I can sense it."

Alex shared, "Last night, I foresaw our group returning late from Amotaious. Don't know if it's true yet, but I saw them disembarking the ship late at night." Kahput acknowledged, "Seeing into the future is a valuable Gift. Don't remember ever hearing that one before. Each CAT group has unique Gifts."

As they exited the freezer, Kahput offered, "Want whipped cream?" Alex grinned. "Sure, that would make it even better. Thanks. Have a good evening." Kahput replied, "You too." Alex paused, then turned back, smiling warmly. "Kahput, you might be the wisest person here. Thanks again." They shook hands, and Alex headed to the scanner with his items.

Alex returned to the common room, labeled the bag with his name, and wrote, "For V," before placing it in the freezer.

He joined V, Prezzy, and Lin at the table. "What did you do with the drawings?" he asked V. V responded, "I put them in my closet. We'll get them out tomorrow for another look. I've already sent pictures to your tablet."

Alex nodded thoughtfully. "You know, they sense that something happened." "Who?" Prezzy inquired. "Everyone—the Elders," Alex replied. "How is that?" Lin asked. "I spoke with Kahput, and he felt our happiness or excitement through the Common Mind. So, they know something transpired, but they don't know what exactly." "I'm not sure if people like Gig and Fem' have a more powerful Common Mind and know exactly what we found. Kahput said the Common Mind is our most powerful Gift, and it's in everyone. It's just magnified here. He's wise—strange-looking but wise. If they were really interested, they would have contacted us, right?" Alex suggested. Lin shrugged. "Nothing we can do about it now. The cat's out of the bag. The cool thing is we all have our Gifts now. We can work on strengthening and prolonging them."

"How are Candido and Tonari dealing with the eagle marks?" Alex asked. "I think they're okay. Some of us don't even want to be Master Elders. It's like being a monarch or a president— more work and a lot of pressure," Lin answered. V added, "I wasn't even thinking about being the Master Elder. Alex and I were just trying to figure things out and help the planet." Prezzy looked at Alex and V. "When you received the new eagles, you saw the blue swirly light? Do you feel any different?" "It was surreal," V replied. "Wind, water, lights—we didn't even know what was happening. But yes, we saw the arrow light like before when the angel appeared from the water."

Alex chuckled. "I was just sitting there, and V started attacking me like a wild animal, scratching and clawing at me. Kissing me all over."

V, shocked, hit him playfully. "No, I didn't." Alex laughed. "No, we were just talking and listening to the music you all were playing, and everything went crazy. We just froze and watched the whole thing. It's something I'll never forget; the arrow was like the prayer the first night."

"I wonder if that happens every time the eagle marks are transferred," Lin pondered. "Just so you all know," Alex said, "the Common Mind affects how we feel about each other—our fear, happiness, sadness, and love. It's very powerful, and we've only been here a week. So, expect more."

Prezzy smiled at Swaraj. "I'm happy with how I feel right now with all of you. I couldn't ask for a better group to experience this with. This is unlike any other university on the planet."

Lin laughed. "I agree. Never thought I would hook up with a guy like Lev, but I'm happy with what's happened. That's all that matters. And we're not even on the planet. One of my dad's favorite sayings is, 'Live in the moment.'" V raised her drink. "To living in the moment!" Everyone echoed, "To living in the moment." Declan approached. "What are we drinking to?" Prezzy jumped up. "To living in the moment!" Alex glanced over and saw Maria and Kyoryk making out on a couch; Maria was squirming all over him. "Now that's interesting," he remarked to Declan. Declan nodded. "Who would have thought?"

Alex pulled Declan aside. "I wonder how much the Common Mind is affecting our sexual desires." Declan laughed. "Oh, I know it is, and I'm okay with that." Alex grinned. "What's that saying? 'Just go with it?'" They both laughed as Miko interrupted. "What's so funny?" Declan smiled at her. "Carpe diem, honey. Carpe diem." He hugged Miko. "I've never felt this good. Did you put something in my drink?" Declan and Alex continued laughing. Alex stood and called over to the couple. "Maria, get off, man, and let's go have dinner."

They all laughed as Maria stood up. "I think we should drink champagne tonight." She jumped on Kyoryk's back and pointed to the door. "Onward, my man. Onward, that way." Alex looked at V, grabbed her hand, and asked, "Tonight, would you prefer filet mignon or kippers?" She gave him a playful look. "Sir, kippers are for the lower class."

He laughed. "Will they have those little onion balls?" She turned him around, jumped on his back, and said, "To the dining hall, Sir."

Declan turned to Miko. "Madam, jump aboard; dinner awaits." Miko smiled. "I'll take that ride, Sir." They all laughed. Lin looked at Lev and said in Russian, "Come here, my big man, I need a ride." She jumped on his back. Candido turned to Tonari. "I'm the finest of stallions from the Golden Valley. Would the Crowned Princess like a ride to her destination?" He struggled to carry her. She slapped him playfully. "Pick up the pace, horsey!"

They all made their way to the dining room, got their food, and sat down. Lin announced, "I agree with Maria. Tonight's champagne by the pool."

"What do you all think?" Most smiled, some raised their glasses, others their forks or spoons with food in agreement. V looked at Alex. "This should be interesting."

Bahdubah and Klinchme' walked up and sat down with their food. Lin stood, tossed her hair back, and in a pompous, sexy way, asked in her English accent, "Sir, madam, would it be possible to have champagne by the pool tonight after dinner?" Bahdubah and Klinchme' chuckled. Klinchme' replied, "I don't see why not."

Alex looked at Bahdubah. "Have you ever been to one of the meetings?" Bahdubah stopped eating. "Many. Any Elder can attend, but the Master Elders make the final decisions." Alex asked, "What is Amotaious like?"

Klinchme' answered, "It's like our planet during the Jurassic period but without the dinosaurs. The plants and trees are enormous. Some smaller animals like what we have are larger on Amotaious. The city, called Tunimbria, nestles in the foothills of a massive delta near an ancient caldera. It's beautiful. There's a volcanic area with huge red colonnades a day's ride away—truly breathtaking. They just finished building a huge amphitheater at Two Dunes Harbor, near the Bay of Alloo."

V asked, "What's it like to live there?" Bahdubah turned to her. "The community is like our university—small and close-knit. Our population just surpassed a hundred thousand, and recently, there's been a baby boom. Traditionally, families had one child, rarely two, like Kahput and Rugrog."

"Now, families have three or four children. Imagine six governing farms working together to sustain a community. That's essentially what it is. People have lived there for so long that the

Creator's rules and laws are deeply ingrained. Life is relaxed, with ample natural resources. We hunt, fish, grow our food, and use thermal power."

"There's no poverty, and seven moons orbit our planet. It's a beautiful place to live. The diversity of people from other planets is fascinating. I was born and raised there, so I don't notice our differences much. But you'll eventually learn about and meet everyone. Currently, there's a stir as young people are mixing interracially. Several girls from our planet are seeing males from different planets, causing quite an uproar among parents. The Creator's reaction to an outer planetary child is unknown."

Declan spat out his food in laughter. "Oh, my god, that's insane. That will be something." V added, "Wow, that's going to be a big deal."

Klinchme' nodded. "It really is. My other brother is very upset—his daughter is involved. There are even tunes about it. I played one last night. Biologically, most of us are similar, but Vindors have fewer bones, and the Elducan's hair and skin are distinctly different. There's talk of a Master Elders Council Meeting about this soon." Alex remarked, "Well, I'm looking forward to going."

Doog and Fair walked in, capturing everyone's attention with their imposing presence. "How is everyone doing?" they asked. The group, startled by their size and beauty, nodded affirmatively. V inquired, "How are you doing?"

Fair responded, "We're fine. We wanted to let you know that tomorrow, a cargo ship will arrive. Kahput and Rugrog will oversee unloading. Every Sunday, everyone participates in communal activities. Please meet at the docks at 9:00 for instructions." Alex sat up. "Of course, we'd be happy to help. We'll all be there at 9:00." He relaxed back into his seat.

Doog asked, "Earlier, we felt something unusual. Is there anything going on that you need help with?" The group exchanged worried glances before looking at V and Alex. Alex smiled at Doog. "No, we've just been having a great weekend, getting used to being here, and using our Gifts."

V added, "We think Alex received his Gift last night. Alex and I also got additional eagle marks on our necks, but we're not sure what they mean yet." Doog and Fair examined V and Alex's necks. "That's interesting,"

Doog said, looking at Fair. "You've only been here a week, right?" Kyoryk replied, "Six days so far." Doog looked puzzled. "Doesn't that usually happen after six weeks or so?" "Yes," Fair agreed, looking equally puzzled. "Do you all have your Gifts now?"

V sat up. "Yes, we think so. Gig said some might get additional Gifts over time, but we all have the Common Mind and one Gift each." Fair mused, "A transfer of two eagle marks and the Gifts in six days. I don't remember that happening so quickly. How did they transfer?" Candido spoke up. "Me and Tonari we lost them." With a troubled expression, he asked, "What does it mean?" Fair reassured him. "It's nothing to worry about. The eagle marks may transfer back and forth between all of you several times before the Creator decides which two will be the Master Elders. Each one of you is equally important, so never think of it as a punishment. The Creator is determining your roles."

She looked at Alex. "What is your Gift, Alex?" "I think I saw the future. Last night, when Miko said the group would return tomorrow afternoon."

"I saw a vision of them returning just before midnight. I'll know if it's true when they arrive." Doog smiled. "That's great, Alex." He turned to V. "V, what about you? What's your Gift?" V hesitated. "I can tell what people are thinking, and I may have two Gifts. I saw a vision of my grandmother this morning. The Common Mind might be influencing me more. It's not clear yet."

Fair considered this. "I remember someone in CAT 1 with a similar Gift—she communicated with the dead and made predictions about the distant future. Is your grandmother alive?" "No, she passed two years ago," V replied. Doog and Fair exchanged a look. "We need to inform the others about this—the eagle marks and everyone's Gifts. Nothing to worry about. Have fun tonight, and don't forget about helping in the morning." "Okay," V and Alex said as Doog and Fair walked out.

Alex listened to them discuss the situation as they left. Doog remarked, "It's extraordinarily fast for the eagle transfers. And how did it happen without a prayer?"

Fair agreed. "It's also very soon for everyone to have their Gifts. We should check if this has happened before." She pulled out her tablet as they disappeared through the archway.

Declan looks at V and quips, "You can communicate with the dead? See if you can uncover what happened to D.B. Cooper or Amelia Earhart." V rolls her eyes at Declan. "Very funny. I'm not even sure what I saw this morning. And I definitely didn't want them to know that Alex and I saw an angel last night." She paused, "Until we know more about all this."

Alex interjects, "What's the deal with the eagle marks? We need to decipher these documents." Bahdubah and Klinchme' leave the table. Maria begins to speak, but Declan interrupts with a shout, "Oh, oh! Find out what happened to the Lindbergh Baby?" Miko smacks him on the arm. Declan yelps, "Ouch! You're going to bruise me. Find another way to punish me?"

On the way back to their rooms, Alex turns to V. "Do you think the person from CAT 1 who's like you made those drawings? Someone had to predict this and hide them in the library." "Maybe," V replies as she enters her room. Alex heads to his room to change, opening dresser drawers and thinking, *"I don't even think I brought any swim trunks."* He finds them. *"They must have put these in here. I definitely don't recognize them. They thought of everything. I still can't believe all of this is happening. The end of the world, me, V, people like Gig and Kahput. Oh my God! What about the Pyramids, Atlantis, real aliens? We haven't even asked those questions yet."*

He puts on the trunks, grabs his robe and tablet, and looks in the mirror, running a comb through his hair. *"And this place, Eternal University, in the moon, where the main teacher smokes weed at dinner. What the hell is going on? I just saw an angel, received a message from the Creator, can see into the future, and have a girlfriend—all within a week. She's beautiful beyond belief."* He rubs his face vigorously. *"Jesus, ooooh! Alright, pull yourself together, man. You're supposed to be a leader. Am I? Shit. V will help me. Okay, let's go."*

He walks back to V's room, taps on the door, and asks, "You ready?"

"Come in. Close the door," V replies. Alex enters to find V half-dressed, putting on her suit.

He smiles and admits, "I've always liked bikinis, but on you, that one-piece is stunning." He tugs playfully on the fabric around her left butt cheek and starts to massage her shoulder, attempting to help her tie her top straps. V smiles and shivers slightly. "After last night, you want to get me all riled up right here, right now?" She grabs Alex, kisses him passionately, and pulls him toward her. She pushes him onto the bed, hops on top of him, and whispers, "No, we should wait till later." "What?" Alex says, disappointed, closing his eyes. "I'll just imagine it then." She laughs.

V, continuing to put on her suit, says something in Hindi, smiling at Alex. He thinks, *"She's a wild one, that's for sure. I do think she really likes me. If she wants to lay me down right here…"*

In the pool area, Bahdubah and Klinchme' have set up bottles of champagne at the bar and a couple by the hot tub on ice. Declan and Miko walk in. Declan runs over and jumps into the pool, yelling something. Prezzy sees him and does the same. At the bar, Bahdubah looks at Alex while filling glasses. "Do you think it was someone from CAT 1 who had a prediction about CAT 6 and left the drawings in the library?" "I do, yeah. V might have that same Gift. Now I'm seeing into the future. Something is going on," Alex replies. Bahdubah says, "Doog and Fair seemed surprised that it's all happened already." Alex nods. "I know, right? It means something. We'll have to find out why. Gig and Fem' should know."

Alex hears a ringing and feels the vibration in his robe pocket. He looks at Bahdubah. "Shit, I think I'm getting a call." Bahdubah notes, "You'd better answer."

Alex, looking nervous, pulls the tablet from his robe pocket. "Oh shit, it's Gig." He taps on it and walks into the hallway for privacy. "Hello?" Gig responds, "Alex, how's it going? I'm here with Harvey and Freida." Alex tries to stay calm. "Okay, how are you all doing?" Gig asks, "We felt like something happened there. Harvey, Freida, and I wanted to check in and make sure everything is alright." Alex replies, "Yes, everything is fine. I'm pretty sure everyone felt it. V and I received our second eagle marks last night from Candido and Tonari. And we think we got our Gifts." Gig is silent, but Harvey's voice comes through. "Alex, what are your Gifts?"

Alex speaks up, "Last night, Miko mentioned you returning tomorrow afternoon as planned, but I had a vision of you all returning around midnight instead." There's a long pause. Alex continues, "And then V said she saw a vision of her grandmother who passed away." Another long pause follows.

V walks up to Alex to listen in. Freida's voice gets louder. "That's really fast for the eagle mark transfer. How the hell did that happen anyway?" She asks, "Alex, is V there?" V leans closer to the tablet. "Yes, hi Freida, I'm here." Freida asks, "You saw your grandmother, the one that passed on? Did she say anything?" V is surprised by the question. "Yes, I think so. It was hard to understand, but I think she said, 'It's going to happen sooner than they think. Believe in what you see.'"

148

Alex looks surprised. "You didn't tell me that." She hits him on the arm, "Shoosh." Another long pause follows. Gig finishes, "Alex, V, we need to find a different place to talk, we're going to call you back in five minutes." "Okay," they both say. The connection ends, and Alex looks at V. "Your grandmother said it's going to happen sooner than they think?"

V looks back with a questioning expression. "Yeah, I think so. Something like that has never happened to me before. I thought I was dreaming. So, I didn't think about it much until we talked about it at dinner. All this is new to me."

V's frustration mounts and she starts to get upset. "I don't know what's going on. She was…" She curses in Hindi. "She was like in the chair, kind of floating, then she was sitting there. The image kept fading in and out. She said, 'It's going to happen sooner than they think.' Then the image vanished in a poof of smoke." V pushes Alex and walks toward the pool.

Alex, unsure of what just happened, follows her. "V, V." He catches up. "Hey, it's going to be okay. Together, we'll figure this out." He points to the Students fooling around in the pool, the music loud, with splashing, drinking, and laughing.

"Look," he says, pulling her closer and looking her in the eyes. "We—us, all of us—Gig, Fem', Freida, Harvey, me, all the Elders. We'll get through this together. Don't worry." Her anger fades into sadness. He hugs her. "I don't know what I'm doing. I hate not knowing what I'm doing," she admits. "Kiss me," Alex demands. "That's not going to help," she reasons. Alex smiles lovingly. "Well, it will make me feel better." V smiles back and kisses him.

"See? It did work," Alex exclaims. Feeling a bit better, V says, "Okay. Next time it happens, I'll know it's real. I'll pay better attention."

Miko and Declan approached, their curiosity piqued. "What's going on?" Miko asked. "Gig just called," Alex replied. "I told them about the eagle marks and our new Gifts. They're going to call us back." Miko nodded knowingly. "I knew they felt something. It's the Common Mind—there's no hiding anything from them. The Creator, the council, they're all watching us." They both glanced around the room, feeling the invisible eyes of unseen watchers. V, still unnerved, said, "We're not hiding anything from them, are we? We're going to tell them what we found." Declan laughed, "You're gonna get in trouble. You're gonna get in trouble." Miko shoved him playfully. "Knock it off, crazy person. No one's getting in trouble."

Bahdubah, now with them, added, "I've got some other stuff to take care of. If you need anything, give us a call. Don't worry, I'm sure everything will be fine. We'll figure it all out on Monday." Alex nodded. "Thanks for your help, Bahdubah. See you tomorrow." Turning to V, he asked, "What do we do? Should we tell them what we found?" V, now calmer, smiled. "I don't know. Let's just wait until the next call." Declan handed Alex a glass of champagne. "Here, drink this. If you're drunk, you won't care."

V walked toward the pool, calling out, "Hey, everyone, listen up. Gig is calling back, so keep it down for a few minutes." A few splashes greeted her, and Prezzy shouted, "More champagne!" Maria yelled, "Let's do chicken fights." V returned to Alex. "Let's go somewhere quieter." Miko, V, Alex, and Declan left the pool area and headed down the hallway a few meters.

V said to Miko, "I think I heard my grandmother say, 'It will happen sooner than they think. Believe in what you see.'"

"In your vision?" Miko asked. "Yes, it was this morning. I thought it was a dream." Declan quipped, "That is so cool. Like that movie, 'I see dead people.'"

Alex pulled his tablet from his robe pocket. "Wonder how the council meeting went?" "Ask Gig when he calls back," V suggested. Miko shivered. "I'm getting cold." "I'll get our robes," Declan offered. He returned with the robes, and the four of them stood in the hallway, waiting. Finally, the tablet rang.

Alex answered, and Gig's voice came through. "Alex, it's surprising to us that the transfer of eagles happened so quickly. We're not sure how it happened without a prayer. Also, Alex?" "We're here," Alex confirmed. Gig continued, "Your Gifts— we've never seen anything like them." "We've decided we want to meet everyone—all of you, the Stewards, Fem' and I—in the morning, first thing in Terraenti Hall Monday, okay?" Harvey said something inaudible in the background. "Yes, first thing Monday morning, 9:00. Will you let everyone know? We'll go over everything then," Gig said. "Of course. I will let everyone know," Alex affirmed. V, always direct, added, "Freida, come and talk to me when you get back around midnight." There was a pause. "As soon as I get back, I'll come see you, okay?" Freida responded. "That would be great," V replied.

Alex, Declan, and Miko remained silent. Harvey's voice murmured in the background, "I knew something happened." Gig interrupted, "Alright, everyone. We'll see you tomorrow night.

We need to return to the council meeting in the morning so that we won't be back until late. Alex, your Gift is real. What you saw, it was real. V, we'll talk more about yours. I'll do some research. We'll have more information for you on Monday morning." "Okay, that's fine," V said. In the background, Freida remarked, "The Creator is warning us." Gig asked, "Other than what we discussed, is everyone fine?" "Yes, everything and everybody is okay," V assured. Declan interjected, "We're all in the pool." Freida murmured, "Oh my God." Gig returned, "Good. We'll see you tomorrow night then. Take care," Gig concluded. The line quickly disconnected.

V looked at the others. "I'll tell Freida everything when she gets here tomorrow night. I had to say something; it was freaking me out."

Alex smiled. "If we told them everything, we'd have been on the phone for hours. We'll tell them later. I'm glad you said what you did." They all returned to the pool area.

Miko looked at Declan, "Why did you tell them we were all in the pool?" Declan dropped his robe and jumped into the pool, yelling, "Swan dive! No, cannonball!" Miko glanced at V and said, "Child." The three of them laughed.

Alex and V got their drinks and settled in the hot tub. "I think that went okay," Alex mused. "Even if we told them everything, the outcome would have been the same. Nothing they can do from there."

Miko added, "Let's relax. There's nothing we can do now. We have work tomorrow morning." She grabbed another bottle of champagne, joined them, and smiled. "More champagne?

Have you ever drunk a lot of champagne before?" Alex asked. They shook their heads, sipping their drinks. Alex laughed. "This is going to be very interesting." V smiled and lifted her drink. Prezzy and Lin changed the music, and everyone enjoyed more champagne. Lin jumped into the pool, got on Lev's back, and yelled, "Chicken fight!" V and Miko laughed, and Declan called for Miko to join him in the pool.

V turned to Alex. "I'm okay right here. Let's watch." "Kiss me," Alex said. "Two dollars," V replied with a grin. "That's all? I'll pay you at midnight." "That's right, we're having a thing later." She glanced at the clock. "An hour and a half. Did you get the stuff?"

Alex, attempting a French accent, said, "Yes, Miss, why would I not get da items? Eah!" V smiled and moved closer to kiss him. The group grew wild with the champagne, and Alex spent most of the time either watching or making out with V in the hot tub. Just before midnight, Alex and V left to shower. Alex changed, retrieved the ice cream, and headed to V's room.

At her door, Alex thought, *"Okay, think of something clever. This is the first time I'm knocking on her door for a date."* He knocked. "Delivery? Delivery?" "Come in, please," V replied. Alex entered. "Shut the door, please. What are you delivering, and who is it for?" Alex pulled out a random piece of paper from his pants and, to his surprise, said, "It's for Vivacious Vixen." "And what is your name?" V asked. "My name is Maximus Long and Strong, a modest delivery man from the streets of Nantick Lick."

Alex pulled the ice cream, spoon, and whipped cream from the bag. "I have custom-made mint chocolate chip ice cream, made from the milk of laughing goats by elves off the coast of Ball-varia. Creamy whipped cream, made by talking cows from the mountains of Cliteratutchland, and a big metal spoon forged by dwarfs living inside the mountains of Penis Golia. Where would you like them?"

V, trying not to laugh, patted the bed. "So many interesting places." After he sat down, she looked at him seriously. "Open the ice cream, take the spoon, scoop a fair amount, and proceed to feed me."

Alex did as instructed. V then said, "Now, squirt for two seconds that stuff made from the cows on to the ice cream made from the laughing goats, please." Alex complied. Both struggled to hold back their laughter. "Nice to meet you, Mr. Long n Strong. Now say the magic poem and put the spoon in my mouth."

Alex, trying to be creative, cleared his throat several times and looked into her eyes. He held the spoon to her lips. "You, me. Wewe. May it be forever true that we are we." With a weird squinty smile, he added, "We, we?" V, unsure how to respond, repeated, "We we."

He slowly fed her the spoonful. "Oh, my, my," he murmured. V, with a mouthful of ice cream and whipped cream, giggled and mumbled, "We, we." Alex began tickling her. She struggled to break free. "Wait! Wait a minute, Mr. Long n Strong. I thought I was supposed to teach you how to spoon."

He jumped off the bed and bowed. "Please forgive me, Miss Vixen. I don't know what came over me." V positioned herself on the bed. "Now, you lay down right beside me, facing my back. I'm the big spoon; you're the little spoon."

Alex, lying down beside her, mumbled, "I don't want to be the little spoon." "Shush. Now, move your body as close as possible to mine." Alex complied. "I'll try not to poke you," he whispered.

V chuckled. "Put your left arm onto my left arm," she instructed. Alex did as she said. "Put your toes next to mine. Can you feel me breathing in and out?" "I can, Miss Vixen," he whispered. "When I exhale, you inhale. Do you understand, Mr. Long n Strong?"

Alex whispered, "I understand, Miss Vixen." V closed her eyes, smiled, took a couple of deep breaths, and whispered back, "Now that's spooning."

Alex pondered to himself, *This is extraordinary. She radiates warmth and comfort. What is this sensation? It feels so intense, almost ethereal. Is this the influence of the Common Mind? It's like a profound intimacy without physicality. What is this?"* Alex murmured, "I love spooning."

"Mr. Long n Strong?"

"Yes, ma'am."

"Where's the ice cream?"

Alex drew a breath, "I don't think it matters anymore. This, you—it's overwhelming. I'm content just as I am."

V glanced around, "I think it's melting on the floor." Alex glanced over to see it had toppled over, dripping onto the floor. He whispered in her ear, "Does it really matter now?" She rolled her head back, "I'd like more ice cream and, if possible, a little... intimacy, Mr. Strong." Alex hesitated for a moment, then jumped off the bed, "Of course. Isn't that why I'm here, Miss Vixen?" He fed her more ice cream. After a few spoonfuls, he exclaimed, "Oops, I got some on your shirt." Quickly, he removed her shirt and tossed it aside. Then, "And on your pants." He discarded them too. She grabbed the spoon, "Let me feed you?" Alex protested, "That's against the rules. The delivery rules."

V dismissed his objection, "Rules don't matter." She fed Alex. "Oops, got some on your shirt again. I should take it off." V ripped his shirt off and threw it aside aggressively. Alex was taken aback by her assertiveness. She smiled at him mischievously, scooping up a large spoonful of ice cream, making a playful sound. Alex was surprised by V's boldness. She accidentally spilled it on his pants, saying, "Oops." Alex looked down as V knelt before him, "I'm going to have to remove these dirty pants, Mr. Strong." She quickly pulled them off, apologizing, "Oh, my. I must be punished."

Both stood in their underwear. Alex asked, "How would you like to be punished?"

V replied, "I lie on my back, and you give me a gentle massage, then turn me over for a firm one." Alex chuckled, "Miss Vixen, this 'delivery' is going to cost more than $2 now." V pulled him down onto the bed, "I don't care about the cost. This is happening."

He thought to himself, *"Who is this woman? A week ago, I had no clue when I first looked into her emerald eyes. Now, she's like a wild creature. Is she about to devour me? Oh well, let's see where this leads. I'm captivated by this Common Mind experience. Last night was beyond anything I've experienced. What will I remember about this night?"* He switched off the lights and proceeded to give her a gentle massage, then turned her over for a vigorous one.

The evening ended with ice cream strewn across V's room. Alex and V didn't eat much ice cream, but they polished off an entire bottle of whipped cream.

Alex now had mastered the art of spooning. He woke up early and quietly slipped out before anyone noticed.

IX

V awoke to the sight of a pint of ice cream melted on the counter. The clock read 7:00 a.m. She sat up in bed, reflecting on another exhilarating night with Alex. *"What's happening to me?"* she wondered. *"Have I lost all control over my emotions? This Common Mind feels like an intoxicating aphrodisiac. Has it ensnared me?"* She glanced around, noticing their clothes strewn across the floor, speckled with ice cream. She chuckled softly. "I need to get a grip on myself. This isn't like me." Rubbing her face, she rose, gathering their clothes into a pillowcase. She grabbed her robe and donned her swimsuit, heading out for her morning routine in the pool.

After she swam, she saw Alex and Declan strolling down the hallway towards the showers. V greeted them with a playful smile, fluttering her eyes and tossing her wet hair back. "Good morning, Declan," she said. "And good morning to you, Mr. Strong." Alex grinned, tipping an imaginary hat.

"Good morning, Miss Vixen," he replied. "I owe you two dollars," she teased. Alex smirked, "Yes, you do."

V, as she entered the utilities, heard Declan ask Alex, I thought your last name was Katz, Alex replied, it is. She chuckled.

Later, they reconvened in the dining area for breakfast. Once everyone settled, Alex stood up, commanding their attention. "I spoke with Gig last night. We agreed to explain everything tomorrow morning at 9:00 about what we discovered. This is incredibly important; it could potentially save billions of lives. Lin, any progress on the writing?" Lin stood, responding, "I've made some headway but haven't deciphered it all. It seems linked to the Common Mind and the Elders."

V then stood and shared, "Yesterday morning, I had a vision of my late grandmother. At the time, I dismissed it, but Gig thought it was significant." Lin asked, "Did she say something?" "It will happen sooner than they think. Believe in what you see," V recounted. "Alex and I saw the angel and what we found in the library."

"We believe the Creator is guiding us for something monumental, not just for us, but for all planets and the Elders. Let's do our best to figure this out."

Lev inquired, "Do we all have our Gifts now?" "Maybe a few more will emerge," Alex suggested. "It all depends on what the Creator wants." Kyoryk proposed, "Let's meet in the common room after work today to review everything."

Lin turned to V, "So you saw your grandmother? Were you close?" V leaned forward, "Very close. She passed away two years ago and was my mentor, teaching me resilience." Lin continued, "How did she die?" "She was with the Intelligence Bureau like my parents but as a field agent for many years. During a robbery at a jewelry store, she was shot," V recounted, a shadow crossing her face. Alex placed a comforting hand on her shoulder. "Did they catch the robbers?" Lin asked, concerned.

"She managed to shoot two of them, but she succumbed to a brain aneurysm three days later," V said, her voice thick with emotion. "It was one of the worst moments of my life." "I'm so sorry, V," Lin replied sympathetically. Alex looked at V, "You'll have to tell me more about her. She sounds remarkable." V smiled, "She was."

As the group dispersed, V returned to her room, with Alex following. She began packing more clothes into her pillowcase and looked at him, "Do you have any laundry you want me to do?" He embraced her, "You want to do my laundry?" She laughed, "I don't have a full load. You can add yours." "Now we're getting serious," Alex teased. "It's just laundry; you're not putting a ring on my finger or putting a toddler in my crib," V replied with a grin.

"What? He chuckled, I'll be right back," he said, returning with his own pillowcase of clothes. "Thanks, and I'm sorry about your grandmother." "There's more to the story, but I'm not ready to share it yet," V confessed.

"My older brother was killed too," Alex revealed, glancing at his hand and missing three fingers. "Some things from the past are complicated." "The past is the past. We should head to the docks now," V said, kissing him. "Will you escort me, Mr. Strong?" she teased. Miko, passing by, quipped, "I thought your last name was Katz?" V chuckled, "It is. I'll explain later."

They joined the Students at the docks. A large, white cargo ship entered, its enormous bay doors creaking open. It then turned to a flat black in color somehow.

A deafening noise accompanied the metal ramp extending, causing some Students to flinch. "Jesus," Prezzy muttered in response.

Kahput emerged from one of the archways, asking, "Anyone familiar with a forklift?" Alex and Lev raised their hands. Rugrog pointed at Lev, "Let's see you handle it." Lev skillfully maneuvered the forklift up the ramp and into the ship. Moments later, he backed out, carrying a full pallet of supplies. Rugrog directed them on how to organize the pallets on the floor, following marked yellow lines.

Miko asked V, "What's the story with Alex and Mr. Strong?" as they watched the guys unload heavy, bulky crates from the ship. V, trying to keep the details vague, smiled at Miko.

"Alex came to my room last night," she began. "He said he had a package for Vivacious Vixen." Prezzy, standing nearby, perked up. "Then he claimed his delivery name was Maximus Long 'n Strong, a humble courier from the streets of Nuntu Lick, with a spoon forged by dwarves from some mountains called Penis Golia."

They burst into laughter. "He fed me Chocolate Chip Mint ice cream with whipped cream, spilled it on my clothes, and insisted on removing them. He even recited a poem." V grinned mischievously. "I charged him two dollars for the lesson in spooning."

Prezzy nodded, amused. "Oh, I see." Miko added, "From Alex? How romantic." "What did he call you again?" Prezzy teased and pushed on her shoulder. V laughed, "Vivacious Vixen." "I wouldn't have expected that from Alex. He's always so serious," Miko said. "Don't let him know," V replied with a wink.

Rugrog called over, "Grab these carts and start loading them up." He gestured to the goods. "These go in the fridge first. Sound good?" V smiled, "No problem."

As they worked, Miko shared, "Declan brought me an ice cream sundae and tried to feed it to me. Then he cracked some jokes, so I just tackled him." V chuckled, "I saw the scratches on his back in the shower. You're like a wildcat."

They continued loading carts, shuttling back and forth for hours until the ship was empty. Around 3 p.m., Kahput announced, "The refrigerated items are done. Let's focus on the main pantry now." A few minutes later, Doog and Fair entered, mingling with everyone. V and Alex stocked shelves side by side. Fair approached them, "How are you two?" "We're okay," V replied. "Did you hear what happened?" Fair smiled, "You mentioned the eagle transfer and seeing your grandmother. Was there more? Harvey and Gig filled us in this morning."

V and Alex exchanged glances. "Sorry," they said in unison. "We weren't sure who to tell." Fair continued, "Your Gifts are unprecedented. And the Eagle transfer happening this early is bizarre. Something more must have occurred." Fair gently touched V's shoulder. "What was it like seeing your grandmother?" "At first, I thought I was dreaming. She hovered above a chair," V said, her voice tinged with awe. "Were you close?" Fair asked. "Yes," V replied, apprehensive about revealing more. "Harvey said she mentioned something happening sooner than expected. Is that right?" Fair probed. V nodded. "She said, 'Believe in what you see.'" Fair pondered aloud, "What do you think that means?"

A new **"Song"** started. *The Alarm...*

Before V could respond, an alarm blared throughout the university. Panic set in as Candido and Tonari sprinted out of the pantry. Kahput ran after them. "Where are you going?" he shouted. V's face paled. "What is that?" "It sounds like the Pulse Reversal Alarm," Fair replied urgently. "We need to move to a safe location."

Chaos erupted as the Students bombarded each other with questions. "What's happening?" "Are we going to die?" Doog commanded, "Everyone, calm down. Head to the vault with Rugrog and Fare. It's the safest place. Sit and wait it out."

As Kahput dashed to find Candido and Tonari, V grasped Alex's hand tightly, anxiety churning within her. *"Is this it? Are we all going to die? Why now? Why so soon?"* Declan muttered, "This is insane." "We weren't supposed to deal with this for years," Alex whispered to V. V squeezed his hand, murmuring, "I just wish they'd turn off that damn alarm."

Lin sang softly, humor tinging her voice, "It's the end of the world as we know it." No one found it amusing.

They reached the vault, and Rugrog fumbled with the keys while Prezzy bounced nervously beside him. "Can I help?" she asked. Rugrog smiled, "I've got it." He opened the door, and everyone hurried inside. Fare instructed them to find spots on the floor. "Five minutes," she said, glancing at her tablet. Doog's voice came over the loudspeaker, advising everyone to proceed to safe areas due to the Pulse Reversal.

After the shocking, terrifying experience in the vault, V reached her destination, taking a moment to regain her senses after experiencing her first Pulse Reversal.

In the common room, Declan put on a **"Song,"** *Living on the Moon*, to lighten the mood. Tonari and Candido disappeared into their rooms while the rest turned to alcohol to calm their nerves. V sat with Alex on the couch, lost in thought about her decisions over the past week, questioning if she had made the right choices. The Pulse Reversal made her reflect on the past week. *"Should I be here? Was it right to be with Alex? Why didn't I tell Fem and Gig about the Creator's message? Will I be a good Master Elder? I need to talk to Frieda."* It all felt overwhelming.

Doog and Fair entered, smiles lighting their faces. Doog raised his hand. "Everyone okay?" Lev stood up. "Yes, sir. Can we help?"

"Not right now," Doog replied. "Get something to eat and relax. Maybe later, you can help clean up." V stood, feeling guilty for not sharing the message sooner. Fair turned to her. "Now, about this Eagle Transfer, how did it happen?" V stepped further into the room, Alex following. Nervously, she said, "Friday night." She looked at Alex. "Can you get the Creator's Plans from my room?"

Then, she recounted the whole story to Doog and Fair. As she finished, Doog suggested sending the information to Fem and Gig before their return. They listened silently. "Let's spread out the documents and take new pictures so I can send them to the others," Doog said. "We'll record your statement too."

Fair looked at the group. "You realize what this means, don't you?" V, Alex, and the others looked up, puzzled. "This will change everything we've been doing for over twenty-two thousand years. Not just for our planet but for all planets. Unbelievable."

Doog paused, at a loss for words, and finally spoke. "If this works, just think about it."

Alex grinned, and Declan hugged him. "Damn right! Alex and V found it. The Creator sent it to them." He bowed playfully to Alex. Prezzy started fidgeting and bouncing on her toes.

Fair added, "This is something." Bahdubah called from the back, "I'll make some drinks." Everyone laughed.

"The other planets might resist," Doog noted. "We'll explain it all to them," V asserted. Lev shouted, "We'll fight!" "Let's send the recording to Gig and Fem now. They'll want to review it on the way back. Pictures too," Fair suggested.

Doog examined the Creator's plans, puzzled. "What's the device, and what are those people doing around it?" Kyoryk replied, "It appears to be an Accelerator of some sort, and those might be Elders using Gifts in the Common Mind. We believe it increases the planet's magnetic field to block the Super Flare." Lin interrupted, "I'm still deciphering the language. I should have more done by tomorrow's meeting." Doog and Fair beamed at the group. "The Creator chose the right Student Elders this time," Fair said.

"Drinks are ready!" Bahdubah shouted, eliciting more laughter. Doog started typing on his tablet. "I've sent Gig the information. We'll hear from him soon. This university is a mess. Get some food, relax, and we'll talk later or at the meeting tomorrow at 9:00." He started dancing around the room with Fair to the music Declan had put on, "Great choice in the music." He exclaimed as they both danced out of the room.

Prezzy and Lin joined in and danced as well. As they left, Alex hugged V. "See, it all worked out." "Maybe," V replied, still uneasy. "I haven't talked to Fem or Frieda yet. It's all happening so fast." Alex handed her a drink with a comforting look. "Maybe we'll get another message. Let's focus on the drawings and our Gifts. Here, drink this." "Gig might call soon. Be prepared," V said. "I'm ready," Alex confirmed.

The group tried to calm down with food, drinks, and music. V collapsed on a couch, hands above her head, eyes closed. Alex picked up fallen items and asked, "Anyone need something to eat?" Declan, sprawled on the floor next to Miko, said, "I already have a sandwich." Alex handed V a sandwich and said, "Eat something." "Thank you," she smiled, pulling him down for a kiss. "Thank you."

Alex stretched, surveying the room. "Everyone okay? Where are Tonari and Candido?" Miko replied, "They went to Tonari's room. She was pretty upset." "How long have they been there?" Alex asked.

"Only a few minutes," Miko said. "We should check on them soon if they don't come out," Alex noted. He turned to V. "I'm going to put the drawings back in your room." "I'll do it," V offered. Alex gently pushed her back onto the couch. "You rest; I'll go."

"Put them in my closet or maybe under the bed?" V suggested, smiling. "You're still super attractive, even when you're scared or sad," Alex said, getting up.

"Thank you, Mr. Strong," she whispered, squeezing his hand. He returned shortly. "Declan, what other music can we play?"

Declan tapped his tablet. "Here's a **"Song"** *Let's Think About Living* to lift the mood. One of my grandfather's favorites."

The music filled the room as everyone began to relax, the tension of the Pulse Reversal slowly fading away, and the group became goofy. V, half asleep on the couch, let her mind wander, pondering the nature of her Gift. The sound of Declan and the others playing a 1960s tune filled the room. Lin teased, "Lev Yaroslav, you're such a clown." V silently pleaded for guidance. *"Hello? Creator? A hint? What is my Gift all about?"*

Suddenly, she found herself in Lev's mind, recalling a memory. *He sat at a table with his grandfather on his sixteenth birthday in what looked to be an old tailor shop, discussing a grim family tradition dating back six or more generations. To maintain peace between families, each had to sacrifice one of the other's sons between two families.*

Igor, his grandfather, explained this gruesome tradition in a calm manner; he seemed to have gone through it before. "Before this, many lives were lost. Like the Hatfields and McCoy's, so many family members on both sides were killed in revenge and disseat, now only two every fifty or sixty years two lives would be lost."

Lev, from modern Russia, stared incredulously. "Are you insane? Is this a joke?" Igor pointed to a table. "Knife, gun, or machete? Though the machete can be messy." Lev, shocked, asked, "How long has this been happening?" Igor, with his wrinkled face and thick accent, replied, "Since before 1653. We lost twenty relatives that winter." Lev responded in Russian.

V opened her eyes, bewildered. "What is this?" She glanced at the guys playing darts and the others dancing around, playing to the music, then closed her eyes again. *"Is this real? Why is the Creator showing me this? What is this Creator? Huh?"*

She went back into his memory. *Lev demanded, "This is a joke, right? You're filming me?" V saw Lev looking around the room for cameras. Igor slammed his hand on the table. "I'm deadly serious."*

"If you don't do this, our entire family is in danger. Your mother, Aleksandr, Eduard, your father, your cousins." Lev erupted, "And for over 400 years, we've done this? Now, I must kill an innocent eighteen-year-old?" Lev stared right at him, "I don't even know this family."

Igor interrupted, his voice grumbling with spittle, looking at him as Lev just did, "He killed your brother Boris. That's what happened to him, not a car accident like you were told. This is the true story."

"Now it's their son's turn. You're the lucky one who survives." Lev, furious, cursing in Russian, got up from his chair and briskly stomped around the room, looked at the table of weapons, walked slowly towards them, chose a knife, looked at his grandfather waving the knife at him, "I'm doing this for them, our family not for myself. He takes five more steps and turns the nob on the door. Looks back at his grandfather, shaking his head and mumbling, "Doing it for them. My mom, remaining brother, and all the cousins." He walks through the door and closes it. V can barely make out. Lev says, "Sorry about this."

V, shocked, pulled herself from the memory, muttering in Hindi, "What has the Creator gotten me into? This is not good; why the hell is the Creator showing me? Why this memory in Lev's past?" She rubbed her face quite aggressively.

As Alex, Declan, and Kyoryk cleaned up in the kitchen, Alex noticed her. "Hey, you okay?" V rubbed her eyes, masking her ordeal. "Yeah, I'm fine." She thought, *"What was that? I hope it's just part of my Gift. Oh my God. Bigger things to think about, let's concentrate on the drawings and getting through this Pulse Reversal."*

"Hey, Bahdubah," Alex called. Klinchme' announced, "We brought sandwiches." Lev and Prezzy, grateful, jumped up. Prezzy hugged Bahdubah, asking about his arm. "Better?" she asked, kissing it.

"Did you break it?" Alex inquired. Klinchme' replied, "No, but it's bad." Bahdubah smiled, "Had a fight with a marble table." Alex laughed. "We heard about the mirror incident." "Doog told us you got hurt; I'm glad you're okay. V commented as she rejoined the group.

Klinchme' asked, "Do you need anything?" V smiled. "No, but we can help you all clean up on the deck." "Sure, we'd appreciate it," Klinchme' replied. Declan and Prezzy volunteered.

"I'm good to go," Declan said. Prezzy added, "I want to help." Bahdubah chuckled. "Sure, we could use help." "Cool," Alex said. "I'm going,"

V announced. As everyone got up, she added, "I want to check on Candido and Tonari." Alex nodded. "Alright, we will meet you on the deck?" Klinchme' agreed. "Great, everyone's coming? Way cool."

V and Alex headed to Tonari's room. V knocked gently. Candido opened the door. "You guys okay?" V asked. Candido glanced back at Tonari and smiled. "Yeah, we're okay." "There are sandwiches, and we're going to help on the deck. Join us after a bite?" V invited. Tonari stood up. "Sure, thanks. We'll be down soon." "Okay, see you later," V said.

Alex and V strolled down to the deck. As they walked, V pondered Lev's memory, *"If I looked into another person's memory, what would come out? Prezzy seems unusually eager to help. What's her story?"*

"Maybe I'll experiment with my mind-reading new ability on her. Perhaps the Creator will reveal something new. Hopefully, it will be a nicer one. Do I need to be in the same room? I must understand my Gift more."

They began rearranging tables and chairs tidying up the deck. The damage wasn't too severe, except for the broken glass. Alex asked Bahdubah, "I'm making a list for Doog. Any damage that we need to write down?" Bahdubah replied, "Follow me, I'll show you."

They walked off as V sat at the bar with Klinchme'. "You've been through this before?" V asked. "Unfortunately," Klinchme' sighed, handing V a glass of water. "There will be more of these. I don't know how the Super Flare is because we've never been here when they hit so. But I imagine it's not something you want to experience. Even being kilometers inside the moon, protected, you can see the damage of the Reversal. That was nothing compared to the CAT. If what you found can shield the planet and make the field stronger somehow, that's incredible."

V said, "We sent the pics of the drawings to Gig. Lin is working on the translations. Hopefully, we'll understand it." Alex returned with Bahdubah. "Did you figure stuff out?" V asked.

"Yeah, I added broken shelves to the list," Alex replied.

V glanced at Prezzy, who was setting furniture upright. *"This might be the chance to explore her past. Alex just walked away, and Klinchme' is busy at the other end of the bar,"* V thought and delved into Prezzy's mind; she saw several memories until landing on this one that looked similar to Lev's for some weird reason.

Suddenly, she saw Prezzy on a yacht off the coast of Australia, probably near where she lived, confronting an elderly man sitting in the fighting chair, watching the wake of the boat and the partial sunset. Prezzy reached into her bag, pulled out a syringe, and injected something into his upper thigh, saying, "This is for the countless kids you have molested over the years."

The man, unfazed, asked, "Prezzy, what are you doing? What did you poke me with?" Moments later, he clutched his chest, stood up, and then fell onto the deck of the boat. Prezzy circled him, declaring, "That's for Milly, Karen, and Brad."

"Did you harm Suzzie and Billy too?" She accused. As the man gasped for air, Prezzy revealed, "Box Jellyfish Venom. That's what it was." The man, finally comprehending the situation, curled himself into a ball sobbing, He said, "I couldn't stop. Even now." Prezzy shook her head; V could tell this was something she didn't want to do but it was something that had to be done by someone. This man of influence would have continued to get away with hanis act for many years to come. She walked over to the pilot station and called the harbor patrol on the ship to shore radio, reporting a medical emergency happening with Mr. Danial Steelyard, the owner of the small yacht.

V snapped back to reality as Prezzy walked away. "Holy shit," she muttered. Alex asked, "You okay? You look spaced out."

"Yeah, I'm fine," V replied, glancing in the mirror. "Just a minute more, and I'm ready to head up." She delved back into Prezzy's mind, seeking reasons behind her actions.

V saw a younger Prezzy talking with two guys, likely her brothers, in a garage, discussing how evil the man was even years ago. Then, older, V saw Prezzy talking to the victims, hearing their stories of abuse.

V reflected, *"Did he deserve this, to be murdered? How many did he hurt? Why did Prezzy do it? What does this mean for my Gift? Is everyone in our group like this? I need to be sure. I hope no one looks into my past."*

Emerging from her thoughts, V said, "See you tomorrow." Klinchme' raising her glass, stated, "Thanks for your help. See you all in the morning."

V thought, *"I need to keep this mind-reading to myself. It's unnerving me; it would terrify all of them. Or it just flat out makes them angry at me."*

Alex and V returned to the common room. Declan glanced at his tablet and asked, "Any word from Gig?" "No, what time is it?" Alex replied. "It's 7:00," Declan said.

Alex strode toward the archway and called out to Doog. "Hey, Doog, how's it going? Have you heard from Gig? Did he call you back yet?"

After a brief pause, Doog responded, "He should be calling you any minute now. They probably wanted to review the documents before contacting you, and V. Don't worry about anything. Sit tight." "Alright, thanks, Doog," Alex said. "No problem. See you in the morning. Great job, Alex."

V, with her mind racing, looked at Alex and said, "They'll call. Do you want to wait in my room?" "Yeah, okay," Alex replied, a concerned look on his face.

Alex took a seat while V settled on the bed. She mused, "I wonder what happened on the planet? What was the damage from the Pulse Reversal?" "I don't know. We could check the news," Alex suggested, pulling out his tablet. Just then, it began to vibrate and ring. "It's Gig," he said, looking up at her. She smiled. "You going to answer? Put it on speaker." Alex paused briefly before tapping the screen. "Hello?"

"Alex," Harvey said after a pause. "We're on the way back. We're on the ship. I'm here with Gig, Fem, and Freida. Is V with you?" There was a crackle, followed by another pause. "Can't believe you got a message from the Creator. That must have been something. Are you okay?"

V smiled at Alex, who replied, "Yes, it was something. It scared the hell out of us. So, you've heard V's testimony and seen the documents. What do you all think?"

"Do we have a chance of stopping the Super Flare?" After a long pause, Gig said, "It's incredible to consider after all these years, Alex, V. Yes, we have much to consider. In a way, I'm glad we didn't know when we were on Amotaious. This changes not only our world but the future of all worlds. You, V, and the other Students are extraordinary. The Creator is urging us to prepare, to be ready, and take action on all this. We need to act quickly."

Alex started to speak, but Freida interjected, "I'm very proud of you, V. You and Alex have already become leaders. A direct message from the Creator is truly special. You should feel honored." Fem hushed them and said, "We will continue reviewing your testimony and the Creator's documents. We'll meet in the morning."

"I hope the Pulse Reversal wasn't too shocking. Is everyone okay?" Alex glanced at V, prompting her to respond. After a brief delay, she said, "Yes, I think so. It wasn't pleasant, but I believe everyone will be okay. The university is damaged, but nothing too serious. We reached safety in time. We're fine." She shrugged at Alex.

"We're all okay," Alex added.

Gig said, "This is incredible. Only once before did we receive a message from the Creator, and that was to the entire Master Elder Council. This will go down in history, but not yet. We need to review everything before informing the other planets. We have a battle ahead of us with them; they will likely not agree to move forward with this. We'll start in the morning. See you then."

They all said goodbye, and the call crackled and disconnected.

Alex looked at V with a quirky smile. "That wasn't too bad." V frowned. "No, I guess not." She lay back on the bed. "What a day." Alex sat next to her. "Want to spoon?" She smiled at the ceiling. "I guess so. If you poke me, you owe me two dollars." Alex chuckled. "Only two dollars? I'd think it would be more." V glanced at him, a warning in her eyes. The night ended after they both fell asleep spooning.

X

Awakened by a noise in the hallway, Alex quietly slipped out, careful not to disturb V. He ventured down to the docks, determined to confirm the authenticity of his Gift. Standing by the door, he glanced at the clock as the Elders disembarked from the ship; it read 11:49. Satisfied, he returned to his room and drifted back to sleep, now certain his Gift was real.

In the dining hall, while the other Students enjoyed breakfast, Alex immersed himself in the Creator's documents on his tablet. Prezzy asked, "When will the next Pulse Reversal occur?" Alex looked up, "Gig might have an idea. I remember him saying we won't know until the next one happens, then it sets the timeline of each one after that." Surveying the table, he continued, "Listen up! I spoke with Gig earlier. Our schedule has changed. We'll now train in all emergency procedures, including trips to the surface, moon buggy rides, and solo ship excursions." Declan and Prezzy jumped up, high-fiving in excitement. "Also, make sure to contact your families and talk to your Stewards about yesterday. The meeting is in 20 minutes." He sipped his coffee, then added, "Oh! No class today." Smiles and chatter erupted.

Miko glanced at V, "He's got the Jimmy legs." V asked, "What?" "Declan's legs twitch before he falls asleep," Miko replied. Declan interjected, "It's just my body relaxing, muscle spasms." V and Alex laughed. "Alex sleeps like he's in a coffin," V remarked. Declan laughed. "What does that mean?" Miko asked. V explained, "He lies on his back with his hands around his neck. It looks strange." Alex countered, "It keeps my hands warm. It's comfortable."

Lin, looking at Kyoryk, said, "The Infinity Papers suggest that the Common Mind increases the Magnetic Field." Kyoryk replied, "Yes, I think it's the device. The accelerator is the generator, and we will be the gas. I think Common Mind powers it."

Alex interrupted, "Is that what the writing indicates?" Lin nodded, "I have more to read, but yes, I believe so." V asked, "So, Infinity Papers? Is that what we're calling them?" "Creators Plans," Declan blurted out.

Alex added, "I also discussed with him who might have created them, maybe 20,000 years ago."

"Someone like me, who could see spirits, or like you, who could glimpse the future," V speculated.

Miko leaned in, "Practice your Gift, Alex. See our future in a few years. V, did you summon your grandmother, or did she come as a messenger?" V shrugged, "I have no idea. This is all new to me." She pointed to the Eternal Hall, "I don't even think they know." Declan chimed in, "What's happening in ten years? Are we on a beach or stuck here?" Miko frowned, "That better not happen." Alex mused, "What about aliens, the pyramids, Atlantis? We haven't even touched that." Declan replied, "Too much going on already." He paused, "What about other dimensions, the Bible? Every religion has a flood story." V nudged Alex, "Stop it, guys. Focus on the present." Alex nodded, "I'll work on my Gift, especially regarding the next Pulse Reversal."

In Terraenti Hall, Gig and Fem' presided over the packed table with Stewards, Students, and university staff. Gig stood, slammed his rock gavel on the table, and declared, "We convened today for several reasons. Yesterday's Pulse Reversal requires cleanup. We also need to prepare for the next one. Friday night, something extraordinary occurred. V and Alex received what we believe was a message from the Creator. I'm sending V's account to your tablets now." He gestured over his tablet, distributing the recording.

He continued, "The Creator's message instructed us to find something potentially beneficial for our planet and people to fight against CAT 6. The Students located relevant documents in the Library, sending them to Fem' and me. Congratulations, especially to Alex and V."

Applause filled the room as Declan shook Alex's shoulders. "I'm sending the documents now," Gig said, transmitting the drawings. "We believe this message from the Creator cannot be ignored. Although our primary law forbids interfering with a CAT, we must consider this."

"Let's examine these documents, build the device, and present it to the Master Elders Council. All in favor, raise your hands." As Gig and Fem' lifted theirs, every hand in the hall followed. Alex thought, *"Who would say no?"*

Alex grinned broadly at V. Gig announced, "Great, I want everyone to review the documents and share your insights with me within the next few hours."

"Once we interpret them, we can devise a plan. The Master Elders Council has requested our findings on Amotaious within the month. Fem' and I will invite some of you to join us for that meeting." Alex looked at V again, grabbing her hand in excitement.

"Lin, with her Gift of languages, and Kyoryk, with his Gift of knowledge, both have been analyzing the detailed drawings. Super work there." The Students erupted in applause and cheers.

"We are also fortunate to have Tillom and Ranny, Master Elders from CAT 1, joining us tonight for tomorrow's meeting. Alex, with your Gift of foresight, could you work on determining the next Pulse Reversal?" Alex gave a thumbs-up, and the room applauded. Harvey gave him a wink.

Gig continued, "After thousands of years, the possibility of mitigating this Catastrophe is astounding." He glanced at Fem'. "Truly remarkable." The room erupted in applause. "It's been just a week, and we are deeply impressed with our new Elders." Fem' and the Stewards stood, applauding the Elder Students. "Given our situation, we'll reevaluate your schedule. Expect a new one by tomorrow, focusing on advancing certain classes. Today, let's continue reviewing the documents and the clean-up at our beautiful Eternal University. Thanks to Bahdubah for preventing a marble table from crashing into an ancient glass mirror on the deck—luckily, no major injuries." Everyone clapped for Bahdubah. "Our meeting starts in five minutes. Thank you very much."

The Stewards approached their Students. Freida hugged V, asking, "Are you okay? How was it?" Alex shook Harvey's hand. Harvey said, "Hey, you survived your first Pulse Reversal. How was it?" "Sudden and scary," Alex replied. "I've never experienced an earthquake, but I imagine it was similar. For a moment, I was worried about being inside the moon's cavern."

Harvey smiled, "We're safe now. And your Gift—seeing a message from the Creator—that's incredible. You've only been here a week, and you're already in the history books." Alex laughed, "It was an intense experience. Initially terrifying, but afterward, it felt overwhelmingly positive."

Harvey teased, "Yeah, we knew something happened. We all joked that you were having some kind of sex party or something." Alex, with a puzzled look, said, "Well, some of the Students, you know, may have gotten together this weekend. Harvey smiled and chuckled, "It happened to us in the first few months. How are V and the others?" Harvey asked, patting Alex's shoulder.

"V is strong; she handled it well. She's amazing," Alex replied. "It hit Tonari and Maria hard, but overall, we're coping well."

"That's understandable," Harvey nodded. Alex inquired, "How was your trip? What's Amotaious like?" Harvey described, "Travel is long and taxing. We had to catch three Threads on the way there, which took an extra two hours. Coming back, only one Thread—six hours total. The planet is remarkable, with a well-organized community. I'll send you pictures. The buildings, rail system, and massive greenhouses—the engineering is incredible. If we can, I'll show you Millapillar Valley, where they quarry the stone."

Gig approached, shaking Alex's hand. "We leave for a couple of days, and you twelve change the world. Next time, will you change the universe?" He chuckled. "The messenger, when we saw it, appeared from vapor, not water. What was it like when you saw it?" Alex, excited, said, "We were in shock, but afterward, we knew we experienced something special. Ours turned from the water into like an ice figure." V joined them, and Gig hugged her. He asked, "V, what did you think? Two messages in one weekend?" V smiled, "When the lights flashed, and the blue-violet light appeared, we had seen that before. But when the pool water swirled, it was a bit scary. Once it spoke, we understood; we kind of knew it was likely from the Creator."

Gig beamed, "Experiencing that is a rare privilege, rarely seen, if ever. You've made history. Both of you should document your experiences." Pausing, he added, "Someone will contact you to include it in the history of CAT 6." Alex and V smiled and agreed, "Okay." V asked, "Is there a name for the blue sapphire lightning bolt and the transfer of the eagle marks?" Gig, with a quirky smile, replied, "We call it the Creator's Wand, imagining the Creator selecting as needed. It's a Gift, but that's just a guess. Ready to dive into the Creator's plans?"

Alex nodded, "Yes, Kyoryk calls them the Infinity Papers."

Gig concluded, "Alright, let's get started."

He walked to his seat and slammed the rock onto the table. Touching the small panel beside it, he said, "Let's examine these Infinity Papers." The virtual screen illuminated above, and everyone, including the Stewards and Students, took their seats. Fem' and Gig remained as the others resumed their duties.

Gig asked, "Lin, any progress on the language of the papers?"

Lin stood up. "I've started deciphering the first page. This statement reads, 'We must risk all to save as many as we can. Save the technology. Preserve the knowledge from yesterday to today.' This symbol might represent CAT 6 or this period of time."

She continued, "Then it states, 'Must Survive.' I believe it means this level of consciousness must continue. Another part suggests, 'The Elder must use the Gifts given to create something stronger.' This symbol here—'Link? Or Connection?'—remains uncertain."

Fem' typed the information into her tablet. "I'm inputting Lin's findings into the computer. It should help interpret the rest based on existing data." She paused, looking around the table. "I feel we've reached a new level of consciousness, possibly throughout the entire population. We haven't experienced slavery in ages like we've seen in the past, and the last major war was 50 years ago. Acceptance of diverse groups is increasing. Could this be related?" She questioned the group, "Are we truly improving? He set the sun's cycle to reset the population every 4,400 years. Has He changed His mind? Consider that for a moment."

Everyone in the room stared in awe, engaging in hushed conversations.

Fem' continued typing as the virtual monitor began deciphering the text. Gig slammed the rock again. "She's right, but let's stay focused." He looked at Kyoryk. "Kyoryk?"

Kyoryk replied, "I think this symbol represents the planet's Magnetic Field. We also figured out that the Elders at the two poles are the exact numbers leading up to CAT 6. Thirty-six at each pole, there will be six CATs; that's seventy-two Elders needed to power the Accelerators, we think. That can't be a coincidence." Some of the Stewards look confused. Kyoryk stood. "Twelve Student Elders in each CAT, right?" They all looked around. "Right?"

Kyoryk motioning with his hands, "Six CAT's now, six times twelve is seventy-two. That's the exact number of Elders that have been initiated through the University that have become Elders since last week when we got here and received our Eagle Marks."

The Stewards looked at each other and now understood what he was talking about. Kyoryk's Steward Hiro looks at him, "Oh, I understand now. You're right; that can't be a coincidence. This was all planned out thousands of years ago. That's incredible."

Lin added, "There are also two signatures here at the bottom. We should run them through the computer to identify the creators of the Infinity Papers." On the screen, the symbols are transformed into English.

Fem' highlighted the signatures, enlarging them. Declan pointed to the first name, joking to Alex, "Jesia Westh? I know a guy named Jesus, a biker from Bristol. He owes me money."

Fem' says, "That's amazing. It looks like Jesua Westch. Or West?"

Alex laughed, "Doubt he's the author." Declan replied, "His last name is Westfield. He's in a gang, so no."

V pointed to the second signature. "This looks like Maria or Mara Norta."

Fem' says, " Or North? Maria? We'll check the records. Neither name is familiar." She restored the screen view and highlighted the center of the infinity symbol. "There's something here. Among the thirty-six Elders, four in the middle hold something." More symbols changed to English.

The gig switched to another page on the screen. "Here's the detail on that."

Kyoryk said, "I've studied this. There are many pages about it. It seems to be a Magnetic Field Generator or Accelerator." As they examined further, the computer continued translating.

Kyoryk suggested, "If we could excite the core, trick it into thinking it's spinning faster, we might increase the magnetic field temporarily—perhaps only for an hour?" He looked at the group. "Right before the Super Flare?"

Gig questioned, "What do you mean?"

Kyoryk smiled. "Alex asked about this recently. Increasing the planet's magnetic field to a power of ten like or similar to a solar maximum could enhance protection significantly, especially since we're in a solar minimum. We'd enhance the shield during the event, then gradually reduce it back to its current state. It might work."

Hiro Oguri, Kyoryk's Steward, asked, "What if we overdo it or reduce it too much?"

Kyoryk frowned. "Severe Earth changes, like massive earthquakes or a VEI 8 or higher volcanic eruption. The Toba eruption 74,000 years ago created a genetic bottleneck, reducing the human population drastically. A similar event could lead to catastrophic darkness for years, preventing crop growth."

"If the field weakens too much, cosmic rays will enter, causing mutations and death. We'd need to live underground without power for crops."

Declan elbows Alex, "That's grim. We'd look like albino cave dwellers with fish eyes." Kyoryk reminded, "The planet travels through space."

Gig interrupted, "Hold on." He leaned back, hands behind his head. "I get the gist, but if we build this machine per the drawings and test it, we could create a stronger magnetic field, right? We must ensure it works." Alex, V, and all the Students nodded emphatically.

"But if we fail, we might annihilate humanity forever?" Gig asked.

"Possibly," Kyoryk admitted.

V, determined, said, "Maybe that's what the angel meant by, 'You must risk all to save many.'" Alex rubbed his temples and sighed softly, saying, "Oh my god." Declan insisted loudly, "But we won't, right?"

Gig looked at Kyoryk and Hiro, "Alright, let's proceed as planned." Turning to Fem', then he looked at Harvey, he said, "Like we discussed before the meeting. Alex, Kyoryk, and Maria team up with Hiro, Darya, Harvey, and Freida to figure out how to build this Magnetic Field Accelerator. We need someone to construct it; we need to understand its function."

Kyoryk interjected sharply, "According to the drawings, we require two of these machines."

"Understood," Gig responded decisively. "Miko, Declan, Prezzy, and Swaraj, you will collaborate with your Stewards. Develop a comprehensive program to simulate the operation of the Magnetic Field Accelerators and assess their impact on the planet's magnetic field to shield it from the impending Super Flare. Lev and Lin, Candido and Tonari, your task is to investigate the necessity of having 36 Elders at each pole. The plans suggest our Gifts might be instrumental in powering or amplifying the device, likely linked to the Common Mind. Alex and V, you'll assume the roles of project managers alongside Harvey and Freida. Your responsibilities include coordinating updates and compiling detailed lists of each group's requirements. Fem' and I will handle the logistics of transporting the Elders to the planet's poles. Our current fleet isn't equipped for this mission, so we must retrofit two larger cargo ships to accommodate the transport vessels."

Gig surveyed the room, his expression solemn. "Does everyone comprehend their assignments?" The group responded with a chorus of affirmative nods. "Good. Let's take a break for lunch. Reconvene in your groups at 2:00." His grin widened as he turned to his companion, his wife of over four millennia. "Words cannot express the gratitude we feel from both of us," he continued, his gaze sweeping the room. "This is extraordinary—what we're on the brink of achieving. Let's remember who we are and who we've become. We are no longer mere chroniclers of history; we are warriors. Saviors. Liberators of the planet Terraenti."

At that moment, Alex felt a profound certainty deep within his soul. He saw it mirrored in the faces around the table, in V, in Harvey, in Declan, and now in Gig. In that instant, he knew with absolute clarity that their mission to save the planet had begun, and he was at the heart of it. Gig concluded, "Thank you, everyone."

As V made her way to the balcony, Alex quickly caught up. Attempting to lighten the mood, he asked, "Hey, Project Manager, how are you feeling?" She leaned against the railing, glancing back at him. "Next week, or whenever the time comes, I want to be on that ship to Amotaious for the big meeting." Together, they watched the waterfalls cascade into the glacier below.

"I'm sure Gig will have you present the entire plan to the council of Elders," Alex mused. V smiled, rising on her toes. "You really think so?" she asked, her excitement palpable.

She hugged Alex, uttering something in Hindi. "That would be incredible. I can't wait to meet people from other planets."

"Have you ever managed a project before?" Alex inquired, noting the brief flicker of concern on her face before she grinned.

"No, but you have, so you'll guide me, and together we'll make it happen."

Alex admired the breathtaking view. "Ordinarily, the first step is creating a budget, but I doubt that's an issue here. I wonder if my dad's shop could manufacture the Accelerators. That would mean a couple of trips to the planet. I could take you through the N.T., and you could meet my parents."

V's smile softened. "I'd love to meet your parents."

Alex turned to her with a thoughtful expression. "I wonder if we have a 3D printer here. I have two at home; we could fabricate a prototype for the presentation."

He grasped her shoulders with a determined look. "This is our dual mission. First, we must convince the council that the Infinity Papers are authentic and from the Creator. Second—" He paused, retrieving his tablet and dialing Harvey. "Hey, Alex," Harvey answered promptly.

Alex, excited, said, "Could I get my two HV-1 3D printers sent up here? V and I thought having a mockup of the Magnetic Field Accelerator would be beneficial." Harvey replied, "Let me talk to Gig and see what he thinks." Alex continued, "My father's company has done military contracts. We were thinking they could handle the budget and construction of the Accelerators. Just an idea."

Harvey paused. "Could be. I'll run this by Gig and Fem'." "Okay, where should V and I meet you at 2:00?" Alex asked. "Meet us on the deck," Harvey said.

V turned to Alex, "What's the second thing?" Alex looked puzzled. "Our mission? What was the second part?" He took her hand. "Let's get something to eat."

As they walked to the dining hall, V asked again, "So, what's the second part?" Alex gave a quirky smile. "To make everything work and save the planet."

V replied, "That's a big second part." "Yes, it is," Alex agreed. They joined Kyoryk, Maria, Hiro, and Darya at a table. Alex asked, "Do you think the Lab has everything you need, computer-wise?" Kyoryk responded, "I think so." Alex suggested, "We'll need detailed documents on the Accelerator." Kyoryk nodded, "We have them; we just need updates for the 21st century." V looked at Alex, "Take a breath, Mr. Impatience. We just had our first meeting." Alex smiled, "Patience isn't my strong suit." He took a deep breath. "Okay, I'll relax—just a little." Hiro and Darya laughed.

V looked at Hiro and Darya. "What did you think of Amotaious?"

Darya replied, "The people from Vindor are intriguing. They have this high-pitched, squeaky voice and get right in your face when they talk. They say there are two sides to them: a calm, mellow state and then an aggressive one. A Vindamor mentioned they have huge coliseums for fighting, like our Roman gladiators from thousands of years ago when they could fly like birds." V asked, "So none of them can fly now?" Darya said, "No, but they look different from us. They still have ten fingers and toes, but their backs are broader and hunched. The two I met were very nice." V responded, "That's fascinating. I can't wait to go."

After lunch, Alex and V headed to the deck to meet Harvey, Freida, Kyoryk, and Maria. They all sat down as Harvey opened a box and pulled out two 2033 Dell Latitude Rugged Extreme laptops. "You can use these for the project," he said.

Alex beamed, grabbing one and inspecting it. "Wow, these are awesome. Built like a tank!"

Harvey added, "Keep a close eye on them when you're home or in Amotaious. If you need software, talk to Doog or Fair in the lab or use your Alva accounts." He glanced at Freida, who smiled, knowing what was next. "How about the six of us talk to your dad and uncle about building the Accelerators and picking up your 3D printers? We have a list of items to collect in Darwin."

Alex looked at V, then back at Harvey, "Yes! That would be awesome." V, equally excited, asked, "When do we leave?" Freida said, "We need to arrange a meeting with your dad for tomorrow morning. Pack a suit." V inquired, "Who else is going?"

Freida replied, "Kyoryk and Maria. We need to get this project moving fast. If you can set up the meeting, we could leave in two hours."

Alex and V seemed ready to burst with excitement. Alex asked, "What should I tell my dad?" Harvey thought for a moment. "Tell him it's a special design and build project through the University and that we need his help, confidential like his previous government contracts."

Alex nodded, "We'll have paperwork for everyone to sign. But how did you know I'd ask about the 3D printers and my dad doing the work?" Harvey grinned. "We've been observing you for a year. I knew you'd jump at the chance to build the devices."

Freida chimed in, "Harvey bet everyone on the ship yesterday that you'd suggest it before anyone else did." V covered her mouth, muttering something in Hindi. Alex, shocked, asked, "So what did you win?" Freida replied, "Just a small upgrade to our accommodations."

V asked, "Where is it? Is it nice?" Harvey said, "Mindil Beach Casino and Resort. We have three suites." Alex, still in shock, got up, smiling. "I'm going to call my dad. Can you ask Maria and Kyoryk to meet us here?" V joined him, and Harvey called out, "Meet us at the docks at 4:30. Bring Kyoryk and Maria." They both nodded, smiling. Alex checked his tablet, noting it was 7:00 am in Darwin, Australia. "Perfect," he thought. "We'll get there in the late afternoon."

He called his parents' house, and his sister Audrey answered. "Hello." "Hey, Audrey, it's me, Alex." She teased, "What's wrong? You in jail?" Alex laughed. "No, Silly Goose. I'll be in Darwin later today." Audrey quipped, "Flunked out already? That was fast." "Shut up. Let me talk to Dad." Audrey called out, "Dad, it's Alex. He's in jail!" Max picked up the phone. "Hello? Alex, what's going on?"

"Sorry about Audrey. She's being a weirdo." Max asked, "So, what's happening? How are you?" Alex, voice slightly shaky, said, "We have a special project, and I wanted to see if you and Skip could help us fabricate it."

Max replied, "Sure, why not? Am I getting paid?" Alex assured him, "Yes, fully paid." Max said, "Send the engineering specs, and we'll take a look." Alex continued, "I'll be in Darwin later today. Can we meet tomorrow morning?"

After a pause, Max called out to Ella, "Alex is in Darwin." Ella grabbed the phone. "Alex, what's going on? Why are you in Darwin?" Alex explained, "We have a university project and wanted to see if Dad and Skip could do a budget and possibly build it for us. Can we set up a meeting with all of us at 9:00 am tomorrow?"

Ella agreed, "Sure." Max mentioned a meeting in the background, but Ella confirmed they would be there. "You're bringing your group to our building?"

"Yes, six of us."

Ella asked, "Where are you staying?"

"At a hotel by the airport. We have other things going on."

"Alright, call me when you arrive. You can at least stop by the house, can't you?"

"Yes, I should be able to. See you tomorrow."

Ella asked, "What's that noise? Are you near a waterfall?"

Alex said, "Love you, see you tomorrow." Hanging up, he looked at V. "Jeez, my family—they're all crazy."

V is listening in on the conversation. "They sound like a lot of fun." Alex asked, "Are Kyoryk and Maria coming down?" V replied, "Yes, they're on their way. I can't believe we're going back to the planet and staying in a fancy hotel." Alex said, "Yeah, this should be interesting. Now I'm getting my family involved, and they can be a bit much sometimes." V admitted, "Better yours than mine."

"My parents are a nightmare, always judging and analyzing." Alex is trying to be supportive. "It can't be that bad." V frowned. "No. It's bad, trust me." Just then, Kyoryk and Maria joined them.

Kyoryk asked, "What's going on?" V smiled. "How would you like to go to the planet for a couple of days?" Kyoryk, looking puzzled, said, "Where? Why?"

Alex explained, "My family has an engineering and fabrication business. We thought they could build the Accelerators for us."

With excited expressions, Kyoryk asked, "Where is your family's business?"

Alex smiled. "Darwin, Australia." Maria grabbed Kyoryk's arm excitedly. "That's awesome." V added, "Gig and the others knew about Alex's dad's engineering company. They figured it all out on the ship back from Amotaious. Did you get your computers?" Kyoryk and Maria nodded. "Yes." Maria asked, "When are we going?" Alex said, "Let's meet Harvey and Freida at the docks at 4:30. We need to stick to the truth as much as possible, so we'll tell everyone we've been selected for a multi-university project, working on a device that saves the planet. It magnetically filters out CO_2 for Alva Global. We can work out the details later with Harvey and Freida. We'll be there for two nights. Let your Stewards know."

Maria started bouncing on her toes. "This is so cool. What's the hotel like?" Alex suggested, "It's a nice casino by the ocean. I've only been there once to gamble and once to eat with my parents when I was little. Never stayed there." V grinned. "Everyone, make sure you have all your computers set up before we leave. Pack business attire and something casual. See you all at the dock." Alex added, "V and I will let the others know. We'll be working on the drawings tonight. Anything we don't get finished, we'll send to my dad later." V noted, "The rest of the group might be upset they can't go back to the planet with us, but they'll have to deal." Alex said, "We'll try to send them back on other assignments."

Later, on the way to the docks, Alex and V saw Miko, Declan, Prezzy, and Swaraj in the lab. Alex explained the trip and asked, "How's it going? Did you find software that can simulate the whole process?" Declan replied to the group, "Yes, we found a program. I can't believe you get to go back to the planet. Enjoy the flight. You'll be back on Wednesday?" Alex said, "Yes, my dad and uncle own a design and fab shop."

"We're seeing if they can build the Accelerators." Miko hugged V. "Be careful." V said, "We will. Let us know if you need anything while we're there. Keep us posted on your progress."

Swaraj pointed to Doog. "Doog is helping us. Hopefully, we'll have something in the next couple of days." Declan said, "Are you only going to be gone two days?"

"Bring me back some Jelly Belly's, the fruity ones." Miko smiled, knowing they were for her. Alex said, "If we see some, I'll pick them up. See you in a couple of days."

As they left, Declan remarked, "Alex is so serious. 'If we see some in our travels, blah blah.'"

At the dock, Harvey was helping others load the ship. It was an eight-seater, slightly longer than the one they'd taken to the University. Harvey asked, "You guys ready?" Alex replied, "We're ready." Kyoryk and Maria handed over their luggage. Harvey asked, "You all remember how to use the G suits?"

They put on their G suits and boarded the ship. The outside crew locked them in and gave a thumbs-up. The ship navigated through the tunnels, and the round door opened to the surface, leading them onto the tracks out to the crater of the moon.

Harvey, working on his tablet, looked up from the front seat next to Freida. "Does everyone have a green light on their jumpsuit?" They all confirmed, "Yes, ready to go."

The magnetic arm lifted the ship vertically. Its engines ignited, and it took off. The screen indicated the computer was searching for the Thread. Harvey told everyone to take a deep breath as the Jella filled their suits. The computer found the Thread. They all braced themselves as the ship accelerated.

SNAP! CRACK! BOOM! SWOOSH! White lightning flashed outside the window, and everyone cringed again.

Standing in the hotel lobby, Harvey turned to Alex. "Go check us in." Alex nodded. "Okay." He thought, *"He didn't give me any details. This must be a test. Everything's under Alva Global. Let's keep it simple."*

Approaching the counter, Alex smiled at the receptionist. "We have rooms under Alva Global."

179

She typed into the computer and, moments later, handed him three room keys along with four small envelopes. Alex opened one, revealing a $200 card with a note: "Have Fun. Get it Done. - Gig."

Alex chuckled and returned to the others. "Here are your hotel keys."

Harvey announced, "Make sure all the drawings are ready for the meeting. Let's meet in the restaurant in an hour."

V thanked Harvey and Freida, and they headed to their rooms. Alex gave Kyoryk and Maria the gambling vouchers. "These are from Gig for us to enjoy. Mine said, 'Have fun, but get it done.'"

Maria said, "That was nice of him. I've never gambled before." Kyoryk replied, "It's even better when it's not your money." V added, "I've never been to a casino."

Alex reassured her. "It's fun, you'll see."

In their room, V fell onto the bed. "It's all so weird." Alex glanced around. "What's weird?" V reflected, "Being here on the planet, with all the normal people, after being on the moon. Everything that's happened and what we're about to do—it's hitting me how crazy it all is. Do you think we can prevent the world from ending?" Alex sat next to her. "We have to try. They believe we were born for this. We must do everything in our power to make it work. We have time, probably not much, but enough to figure it out." V asked, "How much time do you think we have?" Alex replied, "A year, maybe. We need to test our theory and what's in the Infinity Papers. Then, with our Gifts, we can find out exactly when it's going to happen. Let's go downstairs, and I'll show you how to play blackjack."

V changed into a stylish green and silver one-piece dress, while Alex switched to off-white slacks and a light brown dress shirt with a tie, topped with the faded brown leather coat that he was gifted from Uncle Skip. They paused on the balcony, gazing at the Timor Sea, before heading out.

In the hallway, Harvey and Freida emerged. Harvey commented, "You know it was supposed to be guys in one room and girls in another."

Alex started to respond, but Harvey interrupted. "It's alright. If anyone asks, just say you and Kyoryk are sharing a room."

Freida laughed. "We know what's going on with the twelve of you. Fortunately, with the Common Mind, we are confident it will work out."

"Talk to Gig and Fem'—they'll tell you about their group's experiences. We've had the Common Mind for over a year now and went through similar things." V asked, "So, you've had relationships, and you think it's because of the Common Mind?" As they walked to the elevator, Freida replied, "Yes, we did and still do. But we just have the one Gift. Some of you may bond together forever." Alex inquired, "Do the Stewards ever get more than one Gift?" Harvey said, "Gig told me it's possible but rare." They crossed into the casino, where Harvey and Freida took seats at the bar. Alex and V got some chips and sat at a blackjack table.

Alex glanced around the casino and asked the dealer, "Not too busy today?" The dealer responded, "Our busy season just ended. Where are you from?"

Alex smiled. "V is from Bhubaneswar, India, and I'm a local. What's your name?" The dealer, pointing to his name tag, smiled. "Mike."

V looked at Alex. "Okay, what do we do?" Alex instructed, "The minimum bet is $10, so you have to bet $10 or more." Mike asked, "First time at blackjack?" V, as radiant as ever, replied, "I've never gambled before." Mike, with a deep Aussie accent, said, "First time is always lucky. First-timers always do well." Alex said, "You place your $10 chip out like this, and then Mike deals."

Mike dealt the cards. Alex said, "If you have less than 16, you say, 'Hit me.'" V picked up her cards, and Alex gently placed them back on the table. "You're just supposed to look, not pick them up."

Alex had a Jack and a four. "If you want a hit, you can say it, but it's better to wave your fingers like this." He gestured, and Mike dealt another card.

"I have a six, that's 20," Alex said, "then you wave your hand like this." He demonstrated, signaling to stay. "The goal is to get 21. If you go over, you lose." V had two kings. "That's twenty, right? That's good?"

Alex explained, "With this pair, you could double down." Mike separated the cards. "Now you make another bet because you have the same card above ten. But you must put $10 more out by this other card; now you're playing two hands."

V, slightly confused, went along with it. Mike, patient, asked, "You ready?" Alex smiled at V and Mike. "We normally shouldn't teach you at the table, but it's not busy, so it's okay." Mike nodded. "Yes, it's fine." He placed a five next to the first king.

V waved her hand. "Hit me." "You can't hit on that," Alex instructed. V confused, says, "What?" Alex smiles, "It's the rules. But you're getting it."

V smiled. Mike dealt an Ace next to the other king. "Great, you got Blackjack, 21. You automatically win 15 there." V smiles. Now it's Mike's turn." Mike revealed a 10 and then a 5. "He'll hit on that." Mike drew a 7. "He busted with 22, so we win," Alex explained. V earned $25 in total winnings. "Again?" she asked, excited, leaving all her chips out.

Alex grinned. "Yes, let's put out the bet again."

Kyoryk and Maria approached, with Maria exclaiming, "I won fifteen dollars at the slots over there."

V scoffed, looking up. "I won twenty-five on my firsthand."

They settled in to play for a while, and Kyoryk suggested, "We should meet Harvey and Freida soon."

Mike, the dealer, inquired, "Where are you two from?" Kyoryk replied, "I'm from Japan, and Maria, she is from Russia." Mike continued, "How did you all come to be here together?" "We're working on a special project for our universities," Kyoryk said. Mike asked, "Oh yeah, are you going to CDU?"

Maria and V looked puzzled, keeping their view down. Alex, sensing it was time to leave, said, "Yes. We're just visiting the university for a couple of days." V, realizing they should go, stood up and announced, "Look, I won seventy-five dollars."

Mike said, "See, first-timers are lucky." Alex placed a ten-dollar chip on the table, saying, "Thanks, Mike. Have a good one." Maria added, "I won fifteen at the slots and fifty here." As they walked towards the restaurant, Kyoryk asked Alex, "What is CDU?"

Alex chuckled, "Charles Darwin University."

V advised, "If anyone asks, just say we're working on a special machine to save the planet from pollution. Stick to the truth as much as possible."

Alex and Maria laughed. "Kyoryk, how are you doing?" Alex asked. "I'm up a couple of hundred." Kyoryk replied, "I see a pattern in the slot machines, and I won seventy-five from blackjack." V asked Alex, "So, did you win?" He smiled, "No comment." Everyone but Alex laughed.

At the table with all six of them, Harvey said, "Kyoryk, make sure the Infinity Papers are ready for the meeting in the morning. Remove anything regarding the university or what the device actually does."

Kyoryk asked, "What should we call it?"

Harvey interjected, "Let's not call it anything. Remove the names from the drawings altogether. We're working on a proprietary project through various universities." He glanced around the restaurant to ensure no one was listening. "We have non-disclosures to be signed by your father's company. They've done military contracts before, right? Half the time, they have no idea what the parts are for."

Alex nodded, "True, they keep descriptions off the documents, just numbers." Kyoryk said, "Alright, I'll assign numbers to everything and have something for your review by morning. If anyone asks, we're working on a device to help the environment." Harvey agreed, "Sounds good. This device is part of a larger system to reduce air pollution. Make a list of the parts and assign part numbers."

"We've never done this through the university before, so treat it like a government contract. In response to questions, we'll say you're all working on your master's degrees in engineering and environmental sciences." Alex added, "After dinner, I'll work with Kyoryk. I know what government engineering documents look like."

"Great," Harvey said. V, with her laptop out, added, "We'll have everything ready for the morning." They finished their meal, and Alex, Kyoryk, V, and Maria returned to their room to work on the documents.

Alex and Kyoryk assigned part numbers while V and Maria chatted on the balcony. It was around 5:00 PM Darwin time, midnight their time. V turned on the news, finding the channel she watched before, which speculated about the strange super flare and pulse reversal. Alex and Kyoryk completed the documents for the morning meeting. Their rooms were luxurious, with two queen beds and a balcony overlooking the pool and ocean. Alex said, "That should do it. My dad and uncle will have a good starting point for building the units."

Kyoryk mentioned, "This coil and the core material, surrounded by liquid sodium, will need to be added at the lab later."

As they reviewed the drawings, V and Maria, disgusted by the news, turned it off and switched to an old movie. Alex asked Kyoryk, "What will it do?"

Kyoryk explained, "It will excite the magma around the core, simulating increased solar activity. The device injects electrons into the magma, making it appear that the sun has entered a super grand solar maximum. This natural phenomenon strengthens our magnetic field. We're artificially inducing it to protect the planet temporarily, feeding it more energy with these accelerators and the power of the Common Mind."

Kyoryk closed the drapes and projected a three-dimensional screen above the computer, capturing the girls' attention. V turned off the movie. He pointed to figures in an infinity symbol. "All thirty-six Elders stand in this configuration, holding the Accelerator, channeling energy into the magma at the core."

All four gazed at the 3D image. Kyoryk gestured within the hologram, "With the Common Mind, we increase the field's energy. It's like a rail system, and our energy drives it." He traced a figure-eight pattern. "See? The energy flows through the middle, spinning the Accelerator's core. That's why it's shaped this way." They began to understand.

V looked at Alex and Kyoryk, "I get it now. Along with our Gifts, that's the additional power force from the Common Mind."

Maria nodded, "Now I understand how it works."

Alex looked at V, excitement in his voice. "This is going to be fantastic. We need seventy-two people with similar Gifts, plus a few more to handle communication with the lab. We can make it happen." He mused, "We should work on our Gifts together, like in a group. I'd love to try that when we get back." Kyoryk added, "Exactly. We'll have to see how it goes, but I think the drawings are ready for the morning. I need some sleep." "Agreed. This will be incredible once we get it all set up on the computer and run the simulations. Ready to showcase it to everyone," Alex said.

He and V headed to their room. It was past 1:00 a.m. their time, so they all went to sleep.

XI

V awakens and strides into the center of the suite, finding Alex absorbed in a movie. She greets him, "Hey, what's happening?" Alex smiles and raises his coffee in acknowledgment but remains silent. V settles beside him, glancing at the screen. "Two Men Enter, One Man Leaves." Alex gestures towards the screen, his expression earnest. "It's not just the technology. It's everything the people have created like this. This is why we can't let the world end; we must make it work."

He looks at her again, "Have you seen Mel Gibson in Braveheart?"

V watches the screen and murmurs something in Hindi before kissing Alex. "It's very violent. Isn't that Tina Turner?" She rises, "Do you like Mel Gibson?"

Alex remains silent. V offers, "I'm going for a swim. Do you want anything from downstairs?" Again, Alex doesn't respond.

V reflects, *"Alex is really into movies, or perhaps Mel Gibson. I'll have to remember that. I need to get ready for the day."* After her swim, V returns with fruit. Alex finishes the movie, and they both shower, dress, and leave the room.

In Harvey and Freida's room, Harvey asks Alex, "Are the drawings ready?" Alex replies, "Yes, they are ready." Freida turns to V, "How did you sleep?" V smiles and says, "Good. Alex was watching a movie when I woke up. He said we should save the world because of movies like Mad Max and Braveheart." Freida laughs, "He's not wrong."

Kyoryk and Maria enter the room. Harvey and Freida take seats at the table. Harvey instructs, "Alright, present to us like we are going to present it to them." Kyoryk activates his computer, projecting a 3D virtual image that spins above the screen. "We've made one final assembly drawing, 20 detailed drawings, all numbered but without descriptions."

"The main assembly is crafted from 316 stainless steel, with a copper wire coil coating the interior, as shown here." Kyoryk points to the inner part of the drum. "This core is filled with Liquid Sodium. We left that part out; it just needs to be sealed."

Harvey, frustrated, interrupts, "First, you can't show them the 3D image above the computer; we don't have that technology yet. And you're including unnecessary details. Stick to paper and computer screen. Present it like we're in the meeting now." Kyoryk runs his fingers through his hair, exasperated. He smiles at Harvey and drops the 3D screen, redirecting to the computer screen.

He begins anew, "There are a total of 35 parts. The main components are the inner drum, the outer drum, and their caps, along with the handles. The centerpiece core will be the hardest to procure. It's composed of Iron, Nickel, and Gold, and it self-centers through its magnetic field when powered up. All specifications are indicated in the drawings. There is a coil wire wrap between the inner and outer drum walls, made from copper. The coil terminates near the handles. Material is specified, including all tolerances. Everything else was omitted for security reasons. If we secure the project, this unit will scale up to remove pollutants from the air with minimal power usage." Kyoryk smiles at Harvey. Harvey and Freida exchange approving glances.

Freida says, "That's great. Simple and clear." She then asks, "What exactly are you building?" Kyoryk replies, "This is a small prototype device that magnetically charges particles in the air. With an electric charge, it will remove specific pollutants. If it works, it has the potential to save the planet's environment. Instead of filtering pollutants, we obliterate them with an electrical charge."

Harvey addresses the group, "Perfect. Instead of filtering pollutants, this machine will destroy them with a magnetic charge." As some rise from the table, Alex jokes, "The Obliterator." V laughs, "Let's tell them we haven't come up with a name yet." Freida looks at Harvey, "I think we already have. Let's go to the restaurant and get some breakfast."

Harvey stands, "Okay, we're ready." They all leave the room and head to the restaurant, dressed in their business attire.

After breakfast, they travel to Katz Design and Engineering Co. The meeting goes well.

V meets Alex's parents and secures a dinner engagement, along with the possibility of trying out one of his desert racers on the track behind their business. V and Alex meet the group in front of the car. Harvey says, "Freida and I have some errands to run, then we'll be back at the hotel."

Alex responds, "If possible, V and I wanted to go to my parents' house for dinner."

Harvey smiles, "Sure, that's fine. Our flight isn't until early morning. We'll take the others out to eat or stay at the hotel. Keep in touch, and we'll plan on seeing you in the hotel lobby around 6:00 am, if not sooner, okay?" Alex agrees, "Sure, that's great. If anything changes, message me." Alex, V, Kyoryk, and Maria get into the car and head back to the hotel. Alex, driving, asks, "V and I are going to my parents' house for dinner. Did you guys want me to leave the car with you?" Kyoryk looks at Maria, "We can just hang out at the hotel. I wanted to gamble some more. Is that okay with you?" Maria smiles, "Sure, sounds like fun. If we need a car later, we can ask Harvey." V says, "We'll go back, change, and head to my parents' house." Alex nods, "Yes."

Alex and V return to their room and start to change. Alex compliments, "You look really nice in your business attire." She slips off her dress, smiles at Alex, and asks, "How about now? How do I look?"

Alex grabs her shoulders, kisses her, and says, "Very nice, but I don't know how it would go over in business meetings." He smirks, "I think this part of you would distract others from the point of the meeting." V teases, "Does it distract you?" Alex replies, "No, it's your eyes that always distract me."

He runs his hands over her body, adding, "These are attention grabbers." Alex becomes aroused, and she reaches down, grabbing his crotch. "I think this Mr. Long 'n Strong would cause a frenzy in the meeting with the other ladies."

Alex laughs, "It's not for hanging coats."

V laughs, kissing his neck. "It certainly is reacting to the situation."

Alex smiles, "I have a better idea of what to do with it." He lifts her onto the sink counter, kissing her aggressively and pulling at her remaining clothes.

She starts to pull at him. "How about this!" V moaned, "In the bathroom? You dirty boy." Alex pulled her hair back and kissed the center of her neck. V thought, *"What is happening to me? Having sex in the bathroom, I'm out of control. They were right; the Common mind is getting stronger. It's got a hold of me now for sure."* She yelled something in Hindi. Alex kissed her softly, "This is the best business trip I've ever been on."

He walked out of the bathroom, pulling up his pants. "I need to make sure it's okay." V hopped down from the counter and started putting her clothes back on. "Okay, for what?" Alex grabbed his tablet off the counter. "To take you for a ride." V thought again, *I can't do this. In the middle of the day, in the bathroom, what's next?"*

V yelled from the bathroom, "You only need my permission to take me for a ride." She looked at her reflection in the mirror, talking to herself, splashing water on her face. "Have I turned into a sex addict? What's wrong with me? Having sex in the bathroom. Oh! Ganesh! Never done that before." V cleared her throat and laughed.

Alex was on the phone with his dad. "Hey, it's me. Can I take the smaller racer out in the back?"

V yelled again, "Are we turning into sex addicts?" Alex quickly ran to the balcony, laughing. "Okay. And then after, we'll come by the house for dinner. Okay, great, thanks, Dad." He returned and put the tablet down on the table. V emerged from the bathroom. Alex saw her and said, "I think my dad heard you ask if we were sex addicts." V laughed, "Oops, sorry about that." Alex suggested, "We have a couple of hours. Want to play slots and have a couple of drinks?"

V, now dressed, replied, "Sure, sounds like a plan. You can call me Big Money." Alex laughed, "Okay, Big Money, let's go."

Down at the slots, they met up with Kyoryk and Maria. V asked, "How's it going? Are you winning?" Maria replied, "Kyoryk is up $500." V looked around and saw a big, shiny slot machine. "Let's play that one," she suggested to Alex. Alex pulled Kyoryk aside. "You're not using your Gift to win, are you?" Kyoryk looked surprised, "No. No, I don't think so." Alex advised, "Don't win too much. We don't want to attract attention. Stick to the slots; you should be safe with them. If you start counting cards and winning a lot, they might get suspicious."

Kyoryk nodded, "I know, I won't win too much. But I think I see a pattern in the slots before they hit." Alex cautioned, "Just be careful, that's all." Kyoryk smiled, "Okay."

V walked over to play the big machine and asked Alex, "How do you play?"

Alex explained, "You put in the money or the card, then select how much you want to play. This big machine is $2 per line." He pointed to the machine where you could play three lines, so she should bet $6. V hit the line button three times, lighting up the lines and displaying $6. She looked at Alex. "Now what?"

Alex smiled, "Pull the lever." V excitedly pulled the lever, the machine spun, and then stopped. It showed three 7's on the top line and rang.

V jumped up and down, exclaiming, "How much did I win?" "$200. Wow, that's crazy." Kyoryk suggested, "Now you should go to a new machine." V asked, "Why?"

Kyoryk explained, "The likelihood of this one paying off again before you spend another $200 isn't very good." V looked around and found another big machine. "This one is $5 per line," she said. She played $15 and won nothing. Kyoryk encouraged, "Try again." V pulled the lever, but nothing happened. "This machine sucks," she complained. She tried one more time, but again, nothing. V looked at Kyoryk, "This one is no good." She found another machine, tried it, and declared, "This one is no good either. What's going on here?" Alex laughed, "It's called gambling." Frustrated, V returned to the first machine she had played and tried again. It didn't pay out. She looked at Alex. "I've almost wasted the $200 I won." Kyoryk suggested, "Try this one. It hasn't paid out in a while; I've been watching it." V put her money in. Kyoryk advised, "Make all the lines light up." She kept hitting the button and asked, "How many lines are there?"

Kyoryk replied, "This one has eight, and it's a dollar per line." V pulled the lever, but nothing happened. "This is shit," she said. Kyoryk encouraged, "Try again." V set up all the lines, pulled the lever, and a bunch of cherries appeared. She started yelling, "I did it." She won $175. Kyoryk smiled, "See, you won your money back."

They all continued to play slots. V found gambling interesting but not as fascinating as she had first thought. She pondered, *"From what has happened to me in the last week with reading into Lev and Prezzy's minds, maybe I should look into Maria's? No, maybe I should look into Kyoryk's and see what's in his past. What does the Creator want me to see in him?"*

As she looked at the cherries on the machine, they started to blur. She saw Kyoryk's memories, finding one that weighed on him.

"He was on a train, a rail system in a city, somewhere in Japan, sitting with his younger siblings. Miyoshi looked to be around 12 or 13, and his brother, Sessue, was about 15. The three were enjoying the ride through the busy metro skyline when an abrasive, drugged individual attacked an older man. Most passengers ignored the commotion.

As the man approached them, he fixated on the pretty bow in Miyoshi's hair. He got down on his knees, started to cry, and reached out to her, saying, "I'm so sorry, Natalia. It wasn't my fault." Kyoryk felt sympathy for the man, recognizing his drug-induced state and mental illness.

Kyoryk's anxiety grew though, knowing the man might need to be restrained. The man stood up, proclaiming, "I'm going to protect you this time. From all of them."

He began cursing at the passengers, blaming them for someone's death. He grabbed a backpack from an elderly woman, searching for a gun, and started yelling, "Where is my gun?"

V couldn't believe what she was seeing in Kyoryk's memory. *"She saw him deciding to restrain the man to protect his family and the passengers. He had the training but had never used it in such a situation. The man grabbed his sister, said a few choice curse words, and tried to flee with Miyoshi, but Kyoryk jumped up and put him in a headlock, holding him down until he passed out. Passengers began recording with their phones.*

Kyoryk received applause from the passengers. He checked on his sister and ensured the man had a pulse. He did. When the train stopped, police and an ambulance arrived."

V delved deeper into Kyoryk's memory, *"Discovering the man had died later that day. Kyoryk felt responsible for the man's death, despite it being ruled an accident due to the drugs he was on and possibly incorrect medical intervention. Even though Kyoryk was not at fault, he still felt the weight of the man's death. V could feel it too."*

Now in her third memory, V began to feel them deeply, a tear streaming from her eye. She thought, *"What is the overall purpose of me seeing these memories? Is the Creator showing me something all the Students did? Or is He training me for something bigger? They are getting more powerful. I can truly feel them now. What is the true purpose of this Gift?"*

She started to come out of it and saw Alex standing next to her with his hand on her shoulder. "V? V? You okay?" he asked.

Startled, V responded, "Yeah, I'm okay." She looked around the casino, seeing the others still playing the slots. She wiped the tear from her eye, said something in Hindi, and smiled at Alex. "I need to tell you something later". "At least this story was a little better than the last two. Hopefully, they will get better. Mine isn't. I wonder what Alex did?"

Alex glanced at his tablet and then at V. "We should go if we want to take a ride before dinner." Trying to distract him from her mind reading, V said, "Now I'm hooked on gambling?" Alex laughed. "Okay, Big Money." "We can come back after dinner," he suggested. V frowned. "Well, alright. We need to stop by a candy store." "Why?" Alex asked. "Remember Declan wanted Jelly Bellies? I think they're for Miko."

"Okay, we can get some other stuff for the group. What kind of candy do you like?" Alex asked. V replied, "Fudge, no nuts." Alex laughed, giving her a mock menacing look. "No nuts? What kind of person doesn't like nuts?" She pushed him playfully and started to run to the car. "Me! No nuts!" she yelled. "I don't like nuts in my ice cream either." Alex chased after her, opening the door for her. He kissed her and said, "Mental note: V - no nuts." Sitting in the car, he looked at her and said, "You're weird."

She gave him a disgusted look, hit him in the arm, and said, "You're weird!" She tried to tickle him, but he looked at her and said, "I'm not ticklish." V laughed. "What? Not ticklish? Now that's weird!"

He gave her a puppy dog look and said, "I like gentle caressing and stroking." She looked back at him and asked, "Oh, like this?" She started petting his hair, touching and caressing him all over. "Like this?" she teased.

Alex swerved the car slightly. "Hey, I'm driving here!" "I thought you were a race car driver; you can't handle a little distraction?" she retorted. Alex smiled. "You'll see, just wait."

They stopped by a candy store, got the no-nut fudge, and arrived at the Katz family business. In the racer now, Alex instructed her on how to use the 3-point seat belt harness buckle. "How fast are we going to go?" she asked. Alex smiled at her. "This trip is not about speed." He pushed in the cassette that was already in the racer, and a fun, old **"Song"** East Bound and Down started as he drove through the big door and out to the back of the warehouse.

He and his family had built a track with a couple of jumps and turns for drifting. In the center of the track was a place to do donuts.

Alex hit the gas, and the engine roared. V, wearing goggles, covered her ears. They made a turn, and the vehicle drifted around a corner. She went from holding her ears to grabbing onto the padded rails, yelling something in Hindi.

For a couple of minutes, he went over jumps and drifted on corners. She looked back at him, trying to smile. He pulled to a stop in the middle of the track. He looked at her and loudly asked, "What do you think?" V yelled back, "Nice, bumpy?" Alex nodded. "Yes, hold on."

He started doing donuts, and dust covered them. He stopped. She spat out dust and sarcastically said, "Oh, yeah, this is fun?" Another old **"Song"** Melissa started from the cassette.

Alex's was having a great time of it until this tune started, had a distraught look on his face. He didn't say anything and headed through some trees. They came to a canyon overlooking a view of the entire Northern Territory. It was picture-perfect. V was struck by the view.

Then she noticed the look on Alex's. He wasn't happy. He took one hand off the wheel to turn off the engine and lowered the volume. She wasn't sure why he had just sped off and stopped at this spot. Then she saw a tear rolling down his cheek.

"You okay?" she asked. *"What the hell is going on now?"* she thought.

"This tune," Alex said with a drawn-out look on his face. "I forgot it was on this cassette. It was one of my brother's favorites." He turned to look at her. "Melissa, my brother's fiancée. That was her name. We haven't seen or heard from her since just after my brother died." He unbuckled his harness and sat up in his seat. "I've never told anyone this. And you asked me to tell you, so here it is."

"My brother Maxim was on a trip almost three years ago with Melissa, his fiancée. They were east of here, camping. Some guy came into their camp. Melissa said at first, the guy seemed nice. They invited him to join them for dinner. Afterward, he started making advances towards her. He and Maxim fought. By the time Melissa got the paramedics there, Maxim was dead, and the guy had disappeared. Right after that, she disappeared too. Last year, I was out there and finally found the guy, camped by the river. I confronted him, and we fought. It was infested with crocodiles. I got out with this."

He held up his hand, showing her his missing three fingers. "Well, he wasn't so lucky. He didn't make it out of the river. They found parts of him a couple of days later. I killed the man that killed my brother."

V looked more concerned than shocked. "So, you didn't get bitten by a croc like you said, and it wasn't a machine shop accident like you claimed that first night. And no one knows?" Alex replied, "I think my dad suspected, but he only brought it up once. The day I left for the University. From what he said, I suspect he knows." V asked, "What did he say?"

Alex looked at her. "He said, 'I know what you did for the family and your brother. I'm proud of you, but don't ever do anything like that again. You're lucky you just lost a couple of fingers.' So, I'm guessing Skip and my dad know what I did." V said, "Yeah, he knows. And you told me, why?"

Alex turned to her again, smiling. "Because you're more than my new best friend. I think you realize that already. And it was a knife. He had me pinned down. My only option was to grab the knife."

"Right after I did, the croc bit him on the leg and pulled him in. Then I left and went back to the shop, claiming it was a shop accident."

V smiled. "Wow. We all have skeletons in our closets. I'm beginning to think that all twelve of us have done something like that in our past." She wondered silently. *"How do I respond to this? What is wrong with me? What do I say? I hate these situations."* Alex, with a puzzled expression, asked, "Oh yeah, why do you say that?" V grinned and replied, "A couple of things, really. First, my Gift is getting stronger, allowing me to see people's thoughts. Second, some things the girls have said. It's all a pattern; all twelve of us have done something like this. Now, can I drive?"

Alex laughed and hopped out of the driver's seat. "Yes, but we are not done talking about this. Eventually, you are going to open up to me." V slid over to the driver's side. As Alex got in, he said, "You don't think I'm a terrible person? I'm glad you're here with me. I'm starting to really appreciate our friendship." V smiled and said, "No. You're right; we are more than friends. I think we all did something bad for a good reason." As she started the engine, she loudly added, "I really like you too. But I don't do well expressing my feelings."

"I hope you understand that. I did something pretty bad too; I've been seeing some of the other Students' memories. They have done things that aren't so good. But I don't want to tell you right now." She spun the vehicle around and headed back through the trees and out to the track.

Alex, surprised at how well she handled the vehicle, held onto the side rails and yelled, "Let's not get too crazy!" His body stiffened in the seat. She hit the gas even more when they got back to the track. She navigated the track faster and better than Alex had. After all the jumps, she reached the center and started doing donuts. He looked over at her in total shock.

She stopped the buggy, and with both of them completely covered in dust now, she asked, "How was I?" Alex laughed. "Have you done this before?"

V, spitting out the dust, smiled. "No, never. But I've played some racing computer games with my sister. She has pedals, the steering wheel, the whole setup in her room." Alex, impressed with her driving, questioned, "I guess it's similar?"

She laughed. "I did have some defensive driving training with the Intelligence Bureau, but this was fun. Next time, you'll have to show me a bigger track with bigger jumps."

Alex laughed and shook his head. "Okay, now I get it. You have the training. Next time, bigger jumps."

V pulled into the warehouse, leaned over, and kissed him. "Thanks, that was fun. I will open up to you eventually, I promise." She hopped of the racer and asked, "What about all this dust?" "That's why I had us put on the overalls. Here, let's use this." They took off the overalls, and Alex blew them off with a compressed air hose. He directed her. "Close your eyes."

They arrived at Alex's parents' house, a single-story, custom ranch-style home on 4 hectares. They made their way inside and went to the kitchen, where Ella was getting things ready for the barbecue. Ella asked, "How did everything go with the meeting?" Alex replied, "It went fine. I think we shouldn't have any problems making the parts and putting it all together." Ella offered, "That's good. Do you want a drink? We have beer and wine. I could make some margaritas?" V said, "Wine is fine."

Ella poured V a glass. Alex grabbed a beer, and they both sat down at the kitchen bar. Ella said, "We're having steaks, potatoes, and veggies. How does that sound?"

V smiled. "Sounds great." Ella looked over at V. "Where are you from, V?" "Bhubaneswar, India," V replied. "Are you studying engineering as well?" Ella asked. V responded with a smile, "Yes, focusing on Environmental Sciences." Ella said, "This machine you're building. Max told me a little. Is it going to save the planet?" V smiled, looked at Alex, "We hope so. We have a way to go, so we will see. It's just a couple of small prototypes to see if it all will work, but yeah."

Audrey walked into the room. She is 15, with blonde-brown hair, very outgoing, and likes to tease Alex. She looked like a miniature version of Ella. She sat down next to V, looked her over, and said, "Who are you? Are you Alex's girlfriend? Jeez, Alex, it's only been a week, and you're already bringing a girl home to meet the parents?" V tried to spin Audrey's enthusiasm. "Oh, no, I'm Alex's sexy young instructor. You must be Audrey." Ella and Alex laughed. "We are working together on a project," Alex explained.

Audrey asked, "What kind of project?" "We are building a device that will save the planet," V interjected.

Audrey laughed. "So, is it a machine that will eliminate all the politicians? Maybe you should build a machine that stops the sun from destroying the planet?"

V looked at Alex with a smirk, then at Audrey. "What are they saying on the news about what happened?" Audrey grabbed her phone off the table. "They say it was an extreme X flare, a solar burst from a coronal hole. I've been studying it. Did you know that cosmic rays can alter our genes?"

Alex laughed and looked at Audrey. "Yeah, maybe you'll get superpowers, like blowing hot air out of your mouth." Audrey scoffed, shaking her phone. "You know why they went to the moon in the 1960s don't you?" "Why?" V questioned. Audrey smiled and explained, "There were so many sunspots on the sun, they thought it was going to explode." She pulled up a video on her phone. "Look at them when they came back. Look at their faces. They found something up there. If you went to the moon and came back, wouldn't you be happy and all like, 'I just went to the moon! Cool!' No, they looked like they saw a ghost up there. Maybe they saw an alien or something. Some say when they landed, it sounded like a big bell. Maybe there is an alien city there."

Alex laughed. "Didn't they go for exploration and to beat the Russians?" Audrey, shaking her head, denied it. "That's what they want you to think. It's all a conspiracy." V asked Audrey, "Do they say it will happen again?" Audrey noted, "They don't know. I saw one reporter say, 'Just stay inside; everything's going to be okay.'" She laughed and waved her phone around again. "Why do they keep telling us to stay inside? Have you seen Hawaii? It's like a war zone. They still have no power. It's like 50 percent of their transformers and power lines are melted."

Ella said, "Audrey, I think you've been spending too much time on the Internet." Alex added, "I think they should start putting all the power lines underground."

Audrey asked, "V, where are you from?" V smiled. "I'm from India."

Max entered the room and asked, "How's everyone doing tonight?" He hugged Ella and commented, "Oh, steaks, very nice. Alex, V, what hotel are you staying at?" "We are at the Mindil Hotel," V replied. Max nodded appreciatively. "That's a nice place." V beamed. "I gambled for the first time." Alex laughed. "Yeah, we call her Big Money."

Everyone laughed as Max grabbed a beer. "Let's sit outside. I'll start the barbecue." They all moved to a large table in the backyard.

V admired, "You have a beautiful house." "Thanks," Ella responded.

She walked out with the steaks and more wine, placing them on the table. She poured V another glass and asked, "What do your parents do?" V frowned slightly. "They are psychologists." Ella raised her eyebrows in surprise. "Both of them? That's interesting." V smiled wryly. "They're interesting, alright." Max, sensing V's sarcasm, asked, "You don't get along with them?" V cringed. "I do. They are just very intense people." Alex chimed in to help. "V's parents work for the Intelligence Bureau." Audrey, eyes wide with excitement, exclaimed, "That's like the CIA or MI6, right?" "Yes, it is," V confirmed. "They wanted me to work with them, but I decided to get my master's degree instead."

Ella, sipping her wine and getting more comfortable, asked, "That's wild stuff. What did they want you to do there?" V took a sip of her wine. "If I had stayed, I would have been back in one of the local colleges, befriending the son of a criminal." Audrey, now really excited, said, "So you would have been a spy, like in the movies."

V set her glass down and grabbed a chip. "Something like that, but the deception and lying... it's not something I wanted to do or live my life like that. It's insane." Max smiled at V. "It must take a unique person to do that kind of job." Ella smiled too, looking right at her. "Yes. And an even more unique person not to do it at all and to turn down the position." V added, "I trained for a couple of years at the Bureau. But when I saw the whole picture, it wasn't something I even wanted to consider. It's not for me."

Max changed the subject. "How did you like riding in the buggy?" V perked up, smiling. "I've never done anything like that before. It was fun." Alex added, "She is actually a really good driver. I was surprised." Max suggested, "When you return, maybe we can take out the There And Back?" V looked at Alex. "That's the bigger one in the warehouse?" "Yes," Max confirmed. "It's very fast. It's the one we take every year to the race for advertising."

Ella asked, "When is your flight?" "Early in the morning," Alex replied. "I'm taking my 3D printers with us. They want us to have an example of the machine to get an idea of what it looks like."

Ella mentioned, "I heard from Melissa. She said she was going to come by tonight or tomorrow." Alex was surprised. "Really? How is she?"

Ella looked at V and said, "We've been trying to get a hold of her since Alex's brother passed, Milissa was my son fiancé, but she never replied to any of our calls until now. She's been living down on the southern coast." V replied with a nod, knowing a little bit about it from earlier.

Max asked, "Do you think you will be returning anytime soon?" "It's possible," Alex replied. "Maybe once the fabrication is done, Harvey and Freida will more than likely come to get it."

Ella put her hand on Alex's. "Well, keep in touch. Let us know how you are doing." Audrey asked, "What's it like in the U.S.?" Alex replied, "We haven't really seen too much. The school is super nice—old buildings, very green, cold at night." V smiled and said, "Seems like we've been in a plane the whole time. We'll get back, get settled in, and be able to do some sightseeing."

Max, standing by the barbecue, announced, "Steaks are ready."

A new Melissa **"Song"** started. *Melissa*

They finished eating, Max helped Alex load the 3D printers into the car. As they all stood in the front yard with the streetlight flickering and the sun already setting, casting a warm glow on the street, an old beat-up car pulled up. Melissa waved and parked the car right under the light, then got out.

V noticed she looked to be around twenty-six or twenty-seven, very tan, with blonde hair down to her waist. She was very pretty, with an Aussie look, wearing a colorful skirt, a silky blouse, and sandals.

Melissa had a confident walk. She walked around to the back of her car, opened the door, unbuckled a kid's car seat, and pulled out a two-year-old boy with blond-brown hair, setting him down on the grass.

Ella gasped. V couldn't help it and delved into Ella's mind. It was easier to enter a regular person's thoughts. V was amazed. She saw Max giving Melissa a curious look, and Audrey was speechless. Melissa, looking as if she might break down and cry, said, "Everyone, this is Maxim, Maxim Jr."

A heavy silence enveloped them all. Ella slowly approached little Maxim, knelt down, and said, "Hello, Maxim. How are you?" Alex leaned toward V and whispered, "We're going to be here for a while."

V asked, "Did you know?"

Alex shook his head slightly and whispered, "I don't believe anyone knew. Only Melissa." V, delving into Ella's mind, could feel the intense emotions emanating from her.

Her knees began to shake, almost buckling under the weight of the emotion. She started to cry, wrapping her arms around Alex as he tried to walk away.

V, now overwhelmed by the emotions of others, couldn't help but delve deeper into Ella's mind and feelings. *"My grandson. Max Jr. Jr. Oh my God,"* Ella thought, her emotions flooding V with unprecedented intensity. It was more overwhelming than any moment she had experienced."

"Even more than the night she watched him and his brother dance while cleaning the house, singing *"At the Copa."* She recalled the tune Alex played in the buggy. Caught in a trance, she snapped out of it and exclaimed to Alex, "Unbelievable."

Ella lifted little Maxim Jr. high into the sky and spun around in joy, her bare feet making impressions on the grass. Melissa began to explain everything to Max Sr. "I was living near the coast with a couple who were like gypsies from the U.S., living off the grid in old railroad cars."

"They helped me through a lot. When Max was killed, I had just told him that night. I didn't know what to do. On my way back to my parents' house, I met them when I stopped for gas and something to eat. I've been with them ever since. We traveled a bit, but for most of the year and a half, we stayed on the southern coast at their place."

Max asked, "And Maxim is okay? No problems?"

Melissa smiled. "Yes, Max is a healthy two-year-old boy who keeps me going all day and night. It felt like I hit a crossroads in my life. I was devastated when Max was killed. I didn't know whether to come back home or run."

Max, almost speechless, said, "Well, you're here now, and you can stay as long as you want. You know that." He hugged her passionately. "You'll always have a home here with us, and Maxim Jr. too, whatever you need."

Melissa began to cry, hugging him back. "I know, it's just been so hard." A tear escaped Max Sr.'s eye. "It was hard on all of us. You know the guy who killed Max died last year." Melissa looked at Max, surprised. "I didn't even know they had found him," Max whispered something in Melissa's ear. She turned back to Alex with a big smile and said, "That's incredible."

V watched, tears in her eyes, astonished by the family's emotional reunion. As the family walked back into the house to get reacquainted with Melissa and meet young Maxim Jr., V took a back seat, waiting patiently. She now understood the profound love and unbreakable bond of a true family. She had never felt anything like it before.

She realized why Alex was the way he was and felt the depth of Ella's devotion. V knew she had to explore these emotions further at some point.

Alex talked with the family for another half hour. He then looked at V and said, "It's time to go." Ella hugged V. "Have a good flight. It was a pleasure to meet you." V smiled and hugged her back tightly, feeling the warmth and care she had never experienced. "Thanks for dinner. You have a wonderful family, and now a grandson. It's incredible." With watery eyes, V said goodbye to the rest of them and got into the car with Alex as they made their way back to the hotel.

Lying on the bed with his hands over his head, Alex said, "I can't believe it. After all this time." "That was crazy," V said. "So, Melissa never told anyone about your brother's son?" "No," Alex replied. "She was really messed up by my brother's death. She was in the hospital for a couple of months after the baby was born." "What is she going to do now?" V asked. "They all agreed that she would stay at the house with them for a while," Alex said. "I'm sure the whole family will help her out. My brother has a kid."

He took a deep breath. "I can't believe it. It's insane. Melissa said she told him the night before that she was pregnant. It's a miracle, really!" V nodded. "What a story. Melissa and little Maxim. That's going to be really good for your family. For your brother's memory too." Alex took a few deep breaths and looked up at the ceiling.

V noticed he had set out all his clothes for the next day and smirked. "Have you always done that?" "Done what?" he asked. "Put your clothes out like that."

He got up and turned down the bed. "Yes. Is there something wrong with being organized?" V, with a playful face, said, "No, I think it's a good quality. Are all your pencils sharpened?" Alex grabbed her and threw her onto the bed. "We need to get up at 4:30. Do you want to fall asleep watching a movie?" "Maybe," V said, trying to speak through her laughter. "We already had sex." "You can't have sex twice in a day?" Alex teased, pinning her down on the bed. "That's an addict, isn't it?" V mumbled.

Alex, wrestling with her, said, "Are you writing the rules? Give me the remote." "Two dollars," V said, making Alex laugh.

They ended up watching half of *Lethal Weapon* before falling asleep. V didn't put out her clothes for the next day. Alex packed and got the coffee maker ready for the morning, then cleaned the bathroom before finally going to bed.

The next day, they arrived back at the university. Alex and V retreated to their rooms to unpack their luggage. They met back in the dining area for a snack. Passing by the common room, they noticed it was empty. After eating, as they rose from their chairs, Miko, Declan, Swaraj, and Prezzy spotted them and shouted, "They're back!"

Miko ran up and hugged V while Declan gave Alex a fist bump. Prezzy joined Miko in hugging V. With her face just an inch from V's, Miko exclaimed, "I missed you! How was it?"

V, a bit overwhelmed by the enthusiastic welcome and hesitant to share the entire story, replied, "It was okay. We got everything done. It wasn't that exciting. Alex and I met with his family, which was nice. They're going to work on the Accelerators." Alex asked, "How have you guys been? Anything happen here?" Declan, excited, said, "We've been working on simulations and practicing with the Common Mind. Lin and the others discovered something amazing. We can communicate telepathically by thinking a certain way. Remember how we felt connected on the deck or while singing together? We can do that now without much effort." "How does that work?" Alex asked.

Miko chimed in, "We can pass a message around the room, and the first person who thought of it verifies if it's true. It's super cool. We realized this could help with the Creator's Plans. We have a meeting after dinner to show you. It's really amazing." Alex, impressed, said, "That's awesome."

Prezzy asked, "How was it seeing your family after everything, and being back here?" Alex admitted, "It was weird because I couldn't be completely honest with them. I tried to tell them as much as possible without revealing everything. It felt awkward. I've never been in a situation like this before." Miko said, "Well, you're back now, safe and sound." Declan added, "They revised our curriculum. We'll be training on all the safety measures and be able to go to the surface sooner."

Alex turned to Declan. "Very cool. When does that start?" "Tomorrow, I think," Declan replied. "Gig is trying to get everything back to normal."

V commented, "I got to ride in Alex's desert racer, and I gambled for the first time. That was fun." Miko smiled at V with curiosity. "And did you and Alex share a room?"

V smiled back. "Yes, it's funny. We didn't even think about it. We just took a room."

"Later, we found out Harvey meant for the guys to be in one room and Maria and me in another. But yes, it was a very nice hotel. I'm glad to be back. What are you guys doing right now?" Miko answered, "We're heading back to the common room for a bit." V replied, "Great."

Declan and Swaraj helped Alex set up the 3D printers. V ran to her room to get a bag of candy for the group. She walked back into the room and announced, "I brought goodies." She handed Miko a big bag of Jelly Belly's and showed the rest of the fudge and other treats she bought. Miko exclaimed, "These are my favorite, thanks." V agreed, "We figured." Declan playfully yelled, "Hey, I was supposed to give her those. You losers." Alex came over, "Gig wants us to join them for dinner in the Eternal Hall. He wants to go over our progress before the meeting in the morning."

V looked back at him. "Okay, we should get an update from both teams to see how things are going." Alex texted Lev to meet soon in the common room, then returned to setting up the printers. V asked, "Miko, could you show me what you have so far on the simulation?"

Miko retrieved her computer and started the simulation. "What are we calling this simulation?" V asked. Miko looked over to Declan and loudly asked, "Hey, what are we calling the simulation?"

Declan smiled and said, "Our first thought was 'Creator's Plan' or 'Creator's Gift.'" V said, "Alright, that's good for now." Miko began to describe the simulation displayed on the computer. "After we identify the exact time of the final Solar Outburst or Super Flare, we send the two ships with the 72 Elders and two others for communication and support. Then, we find the current strongest magnetic pole positions. They always change slightly. We position the Accelerators above the poles. Right now, the south pole is in the ocean off Antarctica, and the north pole is entering Russia's coast."

"With the Gifts, we start the Accelerator. Using the Common Mind, we spin the Accelerator." She pointed to the screen. "This indicates a person or persons outside the Infinity symbol group."

"They communicate with someone in the Lab here at the EU, monitoring the increase and strength of the Magnetic Field."

"They then signal back to the group to adjust the Accelerator's spin. As you see here, the magnetic field increases through the excitement of the magma around the core."

"We can then determine how much to increase the magnetic field to protect the planet from plasma, solar winds, and radiation. The lab then tells us to decrease the Accelerator and return it to normal. Then we go home."

V, very excited, said, "Wow, you guys did all this while we were gone. This is fantastic. Has Gig or Fem' seen this?" Miko explained, "They've seen parts of it but not all put together like this." V shouted to Alex, "Alex, come here and look at this. They have a great simulation here." Alex walked over again, and V asked, "Miko, please show Alex what you just showed me." As Miko and Declan showed Alex the simulation, Lev, Lin, Candido, and Tonari entered the room. Lev greeted them, "Welcome back. How did it go?"

V, speaking to the four of them, said, "It went very well. Alex's dad's company is giving us a bid for the project, and they don't see any problems building the Accelerators. So, how is your group doing? Do we have an idea of what we're supposed to be doing down there?" Lev said, "Let us show you what we figured out." They all walked across the room to the bar stools and table by the dartboard. Lev placed a coffee cup in the center of the table. He called Declan and Swaraj over. This got everyone's attention. They each held one side of the table with one hand and each other's hands with the other.

Lev said, "Okay, go." The cup began to spin around on the table. Lev said, "Now Swaraj." The cup lifted off the table, spinning in midair. Declan and Swaraj looked over at Alex and V, smiling. The cup slowly stopped spinning and dropped back onto the table. Alex, V, Maria, and Kyoryk were surprised.

Maria hopped on her toes, exclaiming, "Wonderful." Lev then fetched the crockpot from the counter, placing it at the table's center. He instructed them to lift and spin it. The crockpot moved slightly but didn't lift off the table. The lid shook a little, but nothing significant happened, not like the cup.

Lev looked at V and the others with a smug expression. "If we add a few more people using the Common Mind, you'll see what happens." He gathered Prezzy, Miko, Lin, Tonari, and Candido.

They formed a circle, holding hands, with Declan and Swaraj holding onto the table. Lev said, "Alright everyone, let's try again and concentrate on Declan and Swaraj's two Gifts: motion and levitation."

They stood there for a moment, and the crockpot began to spin around. After a few seconds, it lifted from the table, spinning faster.

Alex, Kyoryk, Maria, and V watched in growing excitement. Alex looked at Lev and the group, exclaiming, "That is awesome! You figured it out!" Lev added, "Part of it, anyway. Now imagine 32 Elders standing in the infinity symbol orientation. Imagine the power we could harness with practice."

V admitted, "This is incredible. Great work, everyone." Kyoryk said, "This is it. This is how the Accelerators provide the power to excite the magma and make it think the core is spinning faster. You've cracked the code." Prezzy bounced on her toes, "Isn't this great?"

Alex smiled at her, "This is very impressive. You've just proved the main part of the operation." V asked, "Does anyone have this on video?" Lev replied, "No, we just discovered it last night." V instructed everyone to stay where they were. "Lev, could you go through this once more so we can film it?" Lev took the crockpot off the table and put the coffee cup back, proceeding with the demonstration again. V said, "Lev, explain it in detail, and describe Declan's and Swaraj's Gifts. Everyone, please be quiet. Let's get this on video for the others."

Lev looked at V. "You ready?" V stepped back and started recording, with Alex watching over her shoulder. Lev began, describing how their Gifts moved and lifted the coffee cup. Then, he put the crockpot back, explaining the difficulty due to its weight and mass.

He gathered the rest of the Students to hold hands, using the Common Mind to amplify Declan's and Swaraj's Gifts.

The crockpot landed back on the table with the top flying off onto the floor. Everyone laughed and clapped, celebrating.

Lev concluded the video, "With 32 Elders as instructed by the Infinity Papers, instead of eight new Elders, we should be able to power the Magnetic Field Accelerators to their full potential."

V, overly excited, yelled, "CUT! Great job, everyone. This is major progress. In just a few days, we've achieved so much.

With this video and the Creators Plan's simulation, we can show everyone tonight. Is it okay with everyone if we present this at dinner?" The group agreed enthusiastically, hugging and giving high fives. V turned to Alex, "I'm going to call Gig and let him know we want to show this tonight."

Alex said, "Great. Dinner is in a few minutes."

V walked into the hallway and called Gig. "Hi, Gig. It's V. How are you?" She explained everything, and he agreed. V returned to Alex. "Okay, you and I will present what we have tonight. I also told them we need 72 Elders and 2 others to help and communicate with the Lab and monitor the group." Alex said, "Great, you'll do all the talking, and I'll add what's needed. Is that okay?" V smiled, "Sure."

Kyoryk came over. "One thing I was thinking about during the flare: We might have a problem with our present communication methods with the EU. We need a plan for visual communication if the super flare knocks out radio or satellite communication." V started typing on her tablet. "Okay, I'm adding that to our to-do list." Alex mentioned, "Great. I'm going to have a beer. Would you like a glass of wine?" V smiled, "Sure, I need to calm my nerves a bit." Kyoryk said, "Grab me a beer too."

Declan declared, "I've been practicing a new tune if we're doing karaoke." Miko perked up, "Oh yeah? What's that?" Declan smiled, "I'm not telling. It's a tune Elvis used to sing."

Lev said, "You can sing?" Declan, jokingly and loudly, stated, "Oh, yeah, baby, I can sing." The group sat in the common room for a few minutes before dinner.

At dinner, everyone was talking and getting their food. The table was filled with the Stewards, Gig, Fem', and the Master Elders from CAT 1, including Tillom and Ranny, Rugrog and Kahput's parents.

Tillom, a stylish old black man, stood at 5'4", adorned in fur and leather with a gray beard and a short, furred derby cap.

Ranny, equally stylish in fur and leather, was a 5'2" attractive older woman with goldish hair and feathers above one ear. They both radiated joy and laughter.

Doog and Fair, along with Bahduhbah, Klinchme', Rugrog, and Kahput, sat among the Students. Also present were Parnick and Trank, children from CAT 2, involved in medical and culinary duties, and Farook and Mitchka, band leaders and children of Elders from CAT 2. The room buzzed with conversation and laughter.

As everyone finished their meals, V noticed Gig lighting his pipe and guzzling his beer, signaling he was ready to speak. Alex looked at V and asked, "You ready?"

She smiled, "Yes, I think so. I have everything on my tablet to make it easy." Miko reached across the table, grabbing V's hand. "You're going to be great." V, a little nervous, took a sip of water, then a big gulp of wine. She thought, *"Okay, I can do this. Breathe. Just explain everything, that's all. Easy."*

Declan teased, "Just remember, you'll do the same thing in front of whole Council of Master Elders from six planets in a week or so." Miko elbowed him, "I don't think that's helping her right now." Declan and Alex laughed. Alex looked at her, "What do they say? Picture everyone in their underwear." V scoffed, "Yeah right, I'm not doing that. I'll be okay. You're all making me more nervous just talking about it." Declan mimed zipping his lips. Alex stared straight ahead. After a long pause, they all started laughing. V thought, *"Laughing is good. Keep doing that. Everything is going to be okay."*

Gig rose to his feet and slammed the rock gavel down on the table. "We have a full table tonight. Thank you all for coming," he began. "I want to express my gratitude to everyone for their efforts in the University cleanup."

"We have a new curriculum for our Elder Students that we'll commence in the morning. Given the somewhat urgent situation we face, we've advanced all the studies initially scheduled for later in the coming years."

"We've made significant progress in deciphering the Creators' Plan to help the planet survive the impending CAT. V and Alex will now provide us with an update."

Miko started clapping, and the rest joined in for a moment. Alex and V stood up, and V said, "Could we have the display up, please, Gig?"

Gig pressed a few buttons on the keypad on the table, and a large virtual display of the planet appeared overhead, capturing everyone's attention. With a wave of her hand, V sent the simulation that Declan, Miko, and the others had created to the big screen and began her presentation.

"Declan, Miko, Prezzy, and Swaraj have developed this simulation of the Creator's Plans. It illustrates how the Elders are positioned on the north and south sides of the planet. These two individuals here," she pointed to two figures standing outside the figure-eight configuration, "are communicating with the Lab at the University."

"They will relay precise information on when the wave will hit and how much to adjust the Magnetic field. We are still devising a plan for maintaining communication with the Lab, considering the solar burst will likely disrupt it."

"The Lab will monitor the field strength and dictate when to initiate, amplify, and return the field back to normal. Currently, the Infinity Papers do not specify how to power the Accelerators through these symbols here," she indicated a section of the virtual image. "We hypothesize that the Elders using the Common Mind's force is what drives the device's spin."

V took a deep breath, smiled at Freida across the table, and continued, "According to our team, as you can see, the simulation shows the flow of material around the core intensifying. This friction increases, causing elements to bombard each other, creating and amplifying smaller magnetic filaments as shown here," she pointed to a graphic at the bottom of the screen. "This is akin to the activity within a coronal hole on the sun, where the plasma field bursts out and then collapses back. We'll include that graphic in the next presentation. All of this will ultimately strengthen and expand the overall magnetic field surrounding the planet."

"This process naturally occurs when the sun is very active, gradually exciting our magnetic field and bolstering our protective shield. However, during a Grand or Super Grand Solar Minimum, the sun's inactivity weakens our magnetic field."

"To artificially protect our planet, we need to simulate an active sun. That's where the Accelerator and the Elders come into play—they control the Accelerators."

She paused. "Any questions about the simulation?" Fem' inquired, "Do the Accelerators have a power source?"

V responded, "No, the current designs do not include a power source, not in the normal sense. The power comes from us. On the Norther Team, Swaraj will center the core, and Declan will spin it. The other 34 will concentrate on them, increasing the spin. The Southern Team the same. We will devise a plan to adjust it accordingly while communicating with the lab. They will be monitoring the fields strength."

Freida asked, "So the fluid surrounding the core produces smaller magnetic fields, which you called filaments?" V nodded, "Yes." Freida further commented, "These produce the larger filaments that surround and protect the earth?" V confirmed, "Yes, and that's one of the simulations we will include in the next presentation.

"Along with our communication strategy between the planet and the Lab on Luna during the plasma storm, which will keep the two teams in sync."

V scanned the room for more questions. "Earlier, Alex and I recorded a video of the group performing a test using the Common Mind to power the Accelerator. Please watch." She waved her hand, and the video appeared on the screen. "Initially, Declan used his Gift to move objects, and Swaraj used his Gift to make them levitate. In the first test, they managed to lift and rotate a cup. When Lev placed a heavier object, like the crockpot, on the table, they couldn't move it."

"By adding additional Elders having the Common Mind in a circle we concluded that the crockpot floated and spun effortlessly. All Student Elders concentrated on Declan's and Swaraj's

Gifts. It's now the group's belief that the Common Mind powers the Accelerators, making the Creator's Plan work. It's the key element. We also need two Elders with Gifts like Declan's and Swaraj's on the Southern Team."

Harvey leaned forward, "So we're going to trick the planet's interior into reacting as if it's experiencing a Super Grand Maximum Sunspot activity?"

V said, "Exactly. The magnetic field is always stronger when the sun is active. We believe one reason CATs affect the planet so severely is the sun's inactivity during these periods, which weakens the magnetic field." Kyoryk added, "I think we need to push it even further than that, we'll need to make some calculations, the field strength will go beyond anything, any strength we've seen in modern day, possibly ever."

V sat down, thinking, *I did it! Thank God. I did well. I'm great at this. What's it going to be like in front of thousands of people, in front of all the Master Elders? No, I can do it. I'll be fine. Alex is with me.* Gig asked, "How long until we have the Accelerators ready for a stealth test on the planet?"

V smiled and nudged Alex under the table to prompt him to answer. Alex stood, "I believe we can have two working Accelerators within three months, hopefully sooner. Once we receive the bid from the fabricators, we can expedite the parts' production."

"We should also study Saturn's magnetic field—it's incredibly strong, likely due to its different core composition. We need to ensure we don't damage or alter our magnetic field but rather restore it to its original strength." The group fell silent for a few moments.

Tillom and Ranny exchanged glances, stood, and began clapping vigorously. The rest of the group joined in. Alex placed his hands on V's shoulders and whispered in her ear, "Great job, perfect presentation. It's like you were made for this, Miss Project Manager." V looked up at him and smiled.

Tillom clears his throat. "I speak for myself, Ranny, and the others from CAT 1 when I say that witnessing the repeated collapse and reconstruction of civilization over thousands of years has been the hardest part of our lives." Ranny, with a tear in her eye, adds, "Some Elders in the past have seen the Cataclysms as a fortunate thing, born from the brutality of certain human behaviors and cultures."

"They believed humanity needed these fresh starts. But to think, for the first time, that it might not have to happen again is incredible."

"Imagine our planet maintaining its current level of technology for another 4,400 years, or at least until the next unavoidable natural cataclysm. It's miraculous."

Tillom smiles, raises his glass, and Ranny follows suit, the tear now rolling down her cheek. "I would like to propose a toast." Everyone raises their glasses. "To the possibility of our civilization thriving for another 4,400 years," he pauses, "and to the new Elders of CAT 6 for their exceptional efforts in this presentation. Making this vision possible. We will proceed with these plans and hold our next major meeting on the seventh planet. Thank you, V. Thanks to all of the new Students."

Everyone drinks. Gig and Fem' stand, prompting the others to join them. They shout, "Here! Here!" Gig exclaims, "To the next forty-four hundred years!"

The room erupts in applause. Gig declares, "Well done, everyone. A bit more work, and we'll be ready to present everything at the Master Elders Council Meeting."

He presses a button, causing the screen to disappear. "This calls for a celebration! Tillom and Ranny leave tomorrow. We've almost finished cleaning up. And I heard through the grapevine that Declan's going to sing us an Elvis tune. I love Elvis."

Declan glances at Miko, who smiles and shrugs. The Students laugh, and Declan grins at Gig. Gig and Fem' chuckle as Gig gestures towards the archway leading to the deck. "To the deck!"

Everyone stands, some hug, others chat, and they all start walking to the deck. Freida works her way around to hug V.

While Harvey congratulates Alex with a firm handshake and a man hug, music begins to play on the deck. The Master Elders—Tillom, Ranny, Gig, and Fem'—shake hands, hug, and congratulate the Students. Eventually, they all make their way to the deck for a drink. Tillom and Ranny catch up to Alex and V.

Tillom says, "You know, if you two pull this off, you'll become," he pauses, "The most renowned Elders in our galaxy."

He stops them both and looks at them intently. "But be aware, some from other planets will reject this idea. I can assure you, however, that all of us from this planet will do everything possible to make it happen."

Ranny places a hand on V's back and says, "Until now, I didn't think it was possible. But after your presentation, I believe it just might be."

She looks back at V as they approach the bar. "Just imagine our planet with its CAT cycle of around four thousand years, while other planets have cycles of eight or ten thousand years. The idea that our race could not only survive but thrive with our current technology for another four thousand years or more is remarkable. Our planet is also the youngest in terms of people and consciousness. Well done on your presentation."

The four of them sat at the bar. Tillom glanced up at Bahdubah and declared, "Let's have four Mind Blowers."

Alex chuckled and asked, "What's a Mind Blower?" Tillom, Ranny, and Bahdubah erupted in laughter.

Tillom explained, "It's a concoction of various potent ingredients. You'll see why we call it the Mind Blower. Don't have more than four; the fifth one is called the Mind Crusher." Their laughter filled the room as Declan and Miko approached. Declan inquired, "What are you drinking?"

Alex, still amused, replied, "We're trying Tillom and Ranny's famous Mind Blower." Declan raised his hand to Bahdubah, "We'll take two of those." Declan looked at the group and added, "Not sure if we'll need it. Miko and I just had a couple of hits from Gig's pipe." Their laughter grew even louder. Bahdubah returned with the drinks. "Here they are."

V took a sip and remarked, "It tastes like candy with whipped cream." Tillom and Ranny laughed. Tillom put his hands on his head, mimicking an explosion. "Mind Blowers!" They laughed again. Ranny noted, "They make you do all kinds of crazy things, especially with the Common Mind. It's absurd."

An hour later, Lin took the stage with Farook, Mitchka, and the rest of the band from CAT 1. Horns, full strings, two sets of drums, and gongs – it was like half an orchestra. Fifteen or more musicians filled the stage.

Lin sang the **"Song"** *I Love The Nightlife* from the 70s with an authentic accent.

Tillom, Ranny, Alex, V, Declan, and Miko sat at a table now. Tillom commented, "She's good."

V added, "She's big on the internet. She has the Gift of understanding languages, which enhances her singing." Alex, now drunk, looked at the group and proclaimed, "After three Mind Blowers, my mind is officially blown. Everyone remains calm; everything is okay now. Maybe I should sing a tune. I've been thinking of one for V." Everyone laughed. V asked, "You've had three?" Alex smiled, grabbed Declan, and headed toward the stage. "Maybe four or?"

V, feeling tipsy, asked Ranny, "What happens after four?" Ranny laughed. "You don't remember anything. The fifth one is a Mind Crusher, but Alex is a big guy; he can probably handle it.

Looks like he's about to sing a **"Song,"** *Vehicle*, so we'll see."

V nodded, "He sang one last week; he was pretty good." She looked around, "Where did they go?"

Unbeknownst to V, Alex and Declan had sneaked backstage to don leather jackets and other fancy clothes. The band grabbed horns off the wall and started playing. Kyoryk joined them to help with backup vocals. The three of them walked out in their leather outfits, mics in hand, and began singing another 70s classic. The horns started off, followed by the guitar.

Alex sang. V and the others at the table laughed and watched. V recorded the performance with her tablet.

V looked at Miko, "Here we go; the Common Mind is going to get out of hand tonight." Tillom remarked, "I told you, with these drinks, it always does."

Alex continued to sing, with Declan and Kyoryk joining in the chorus. Farook or Mitchka put the lyrics up on the bigger screen, and everyone started to sing. Everyone laughed and clapped, their joy reverberating through the open part of the cavern as the tune continued. People joined in, singing along with the performers.

V reveled in the moment.

Alex and his companions dropped to their knees, sliding their microphones behind them. With a dramatic flourish, they extended their right hands, two fingers pointing outward. They leaped off the stage, greeted by a chorus of cheers. V enveloped Alex in a warm embrace.

The band transitioned to a slower melody, inviting everyone to slow dance. V, now swaying with Alex, whispered, "So, you're my vehicle, huh? Take me anywhere I want to go?" Alex grinned and replied, "Yes, I am."

After a few minutes of dancing, Alex and V returned to the table where Tillom and Ranny were still seated. They settled into their chairs. "That was fun," Alex exclaimed.

Ranny nodded, "You're a pretty good singer." Alex chuckled, "I think Farook and Mitchka did something to the sound system to make me sound better." Tillom mused, "Could be. They once put on a concert to introduce all the newcomers to Amotaious. Half the city attended, and the show was incredible." V looked at Alex, "Well, I liked it, especially that you sang it to me."

Alex, now visibly drunk, smiled, "I'm glad you liked it. It's a tune my dad used to play in the car when I was little. And guess what? We survived the Mind Blower drinks. To The Ides of March! And to my dad! Time for coffee!" V agreed, "Yes, you definitely need coffee."

Tillom smiled, "It was a pleasure meeting you all." V placed her hand on Ranny's arm, "Are you leaving, going back to Amotaious soon?" Ranny replied, "Tomorrow or the next day, at the latest." V asked, "I had one question, two actually, I forgot about." Ranny smiled, "Sure, what is it?" V inquired, "Do you remember the names on the Infinity Papers? Did anyone have a chance to find out who they were or anything about them?" Ranny answered, "Jesua West and Mara Norta. No, we haven't found anything on them. That was a long time ago, prior to CAT 1, and our records don't go back that far. We were selected right before CAT1, I think they might be from before that."

"Also, we didn't have high-speed travel until after CAT 2. You can imagine how hard it would be to find them. Sorry about that."

V nodded, "Yeah, you're right. It's interesting to think about. I wonder if they were contacted by the Creator back then? Do you think they could have seen into the future?"

Ranny shrugged, "Don't know. What you saw is rare; we would have known about it if it happened before. To get a message from the Creator in the way you did, they must have been told to keep it a secret." V said, "I know. Hopefully, it will happen again. Hopefully, we will get another message somehow. Well, if I don't see you tomorrow, I hope to see you on Amotaious in a couple of weeks if we get to go."

Alex stood up, "It was great to meet both of you. Hope to see you soon."

Ranny asked, looking at V. "What was the second one?" V is visibly inebriated. Looked up at her glossy eyes, "Oh!" She chuckled, "How is it you are of average size, and the others from CAT1 are, you know, shorter?" Ranny chuckled, "We are just from different areas of the planet, silly. "V and Alex said their goodbyes to Tillom and Ranny and started to leave. Gig and Fem, now coming down the ramp, had stopped them and made them stay for Declan's singing.

Alex leaned over to V and asked, "You want me to stop by in a little bit?" V teased, "No, you go to your room. Maybe, if you're lucky, I'll come to your room tonight." Alex smiled and said, "Sure, that would be nice."

Miko approached V, "Have you seen Declan?" V replied, "No." Miko said, "I can't find Kyoryk or Lev either." Just then, Declan emerged on stage with the entire band, Lev and Kyoryk. They wore leather jackets and full costumes.

Declan announced, "I only know a couple of tunes. Turn this one up. This one's for Miko, my Anne, my wild woman. My college buddies and I took a trip to Louisiana, and I saw someone play this tune once and never forgot it. Here we go." Declan had secretly practiced the tune with Lev and Kyoryk.

V noticed Gig, Fem, Tillom, Ranny, and a few others watching from the bar. Declan stood on stage with Lev and Kyoryk in the background, all equipped with instruments—Lev on bass, Kyoryk on backup guitar, and Declan on lead guitar. They all had microphones and wore leather jackets, long fake beards, mustaches, and hats.

Declan and the band began to play the **"Song."** *Polk Salad Annie*

Reminiscent of Louisiana in the sixties. The band, informed earlier, provided full backup, with lyrics displayed on a monitor for the audience to join in. Gig had also known about it.

The guitar riff began with a catchy "Dwang, dwang, dwang, dang, dang dwang."

His voice echoed through the room. Miko gasped in astonishment.

213

She screamed right into V's ear, jumped onto Alex, and exclaimed, "Oh My God!!! AAHHH!" Grabbing V's hand, she shouted, "Come on!" She seized Alex's hand and dragged them to the front of the stage. Declan, Lev, and Kyoryk continued with Elvis's rendition; Declan's voice resonated through the entire cavern. At this point, the horns joined in, adding a vibrant layer to the performance.

Gig, Tillom, and their ladies approached the stage, singing along. No one had ever seen this side of Gig except perhaps Fem' and a few colleagues from the university. When Declan and the guys were practicing, Gig noticed and mentioned it was one of his favorites.

Being a big Elvis fan, Fem' had told Klinchme' that he used to play it loudly in the Master Elders Residence when the university was free from any personnel.

The whole audience saw Gig singing and joined in. Bahdubah handed a mic to Gig, who, though embarrassed, joined in. Gig, a Master Elder with the most powerful Common Mind, sang alongside the boys.

The crowd grew increasingly enthusiastic, especially during the false endings. Gig stopped; his expression was priceless.

He looked around and began singing; the girls sang.

He sang alone for a minute, then then they all joined in, sending everyone into a frenzy. Farook and Mitchka had added more false endings, delighting the audience. The Common Mind took over, and everyone became completely enthralled.

V couldn't believe her eyes or feelings. She looked around the room, thinking, *"These people are completely out of control, but I love it. Once again, the Common Mind has us all in its grip, and this time, it's our leader, Gig."* She gazed at Gig, who was having the time of his life. *"Good for him,"* she thought.

"After all he's been through and seen, almost five thousand years old. That's crazy. What a night. What's the future going to be like for us? For Alex and me?"

"This is so bizarre. I can feel everyone in the Common Mind. It's such an unreal feeling. Every time it gets better, it's all so surreal. What's next?"

She walked up to Alex and kissed him, "What a night." The music ended. "Did you know Declan was going to sing this?" Alex asked. "No, they must have done it when we were gone. Gig enjoyed it. That was great."

Miko climbed onto the stage, hugging and kissing Declan. Someone changed the music to a slow dance, allowing everyone to catch their breath.

Alex headed to his room, and V to hers. She lay on her bed for a few minutes before deciding to visit Alex. She put on something special, donned her robe, and snuck down to Alex's room. Entering the dark room, she closed the door and whispered, "Hello?"

A new **"Song"** began. *Je cherche un homme*

Alex, sitting in a corner with a flashlight, lit up his face and said in a spooky voice, "Welcome. Whom do you seek?" Startled, V thought for a second and replied, "I seek The One." Alex continued in his eerie, scratchy voice, "The One?"

"Yes, The One with the touch," V said.

Alex struggled to stifle his laughter. Switching to a faux Italian accent, he declared, "I am The One. The One with the touch. The touch of love."

V laughed, "Oh my. What must I do to be touched?"

Alex lit a candle, turned off the flashlight, and, still in his Italian accent, said, "You must perform the secret dance."

"A love dance. If you do it correctly, you may touch The One." He glanced at his tablet and played a seductive dance tune. V couldn't help but laugh as she dropped her robe.

"You laugh; there is no touching," Alex said.

V began to dance seductively around the room. "You may kiss my hand," Alex commanded.

She kissed his hand, and Alex continued in his accent, "Now you may kiss my feet."

V retorted loudly, "I'm not kissing your feet!" Laughter echoed from unknown Students passing by in the hallway.

V fell onto the bed with a sexy, soft sigh. "You're not finished dancing," Alex said.

"Yes, I am," V whispered softly. "Get over here."

Alex blew out the candle and joined her on the bed.

That night, V snuck out before breakfast.

XII

Alex scours his bed for his tablet, finally locating it to discover his dad's bid had arrived late last night. He sits up, reviewing it. *"Two months,"* he muses. *"If they can build it in that time, we'll be ready before the next Reversal. Whenever that is."*

"We need to be prepared to present to Gig. Hopefully, V and I will get to go to Amotaious. We're doing well, maybe going a little too fast. Is our relationship pushed by the Common Mind or by us? Should I be in a relationship during the biggest project of my life? Everything just feels right."

Finishing his morning workout, Alex rises too quickly and sits back on the bed, visions of Students and Stewards on a ship filling his mind. *"Was that another prediction? Or am I going crazy? These visions feel like being in a steam room, barely seeing ahead."*

After taking deep breaths, he heads to the showers. Later, in the common room, he spots Declan. "Today, we train on space suits. That should be fun," Declan announces. "Yeah, buddy. Been looking forward to that. Hey, my dad's bid came in, two months to get the two Accelerators built," Alex replies. "How much to build each one?" Declan inquires. "Eighty per unit. The copper windings and three-quarter-inch stainless are expensive. We still need to send the specs on the core. What percentage of gold, nickel, and iron is there? I read it might have diamonds like Saturn and Jupiter, but our core is different from Jupiter's."

Kyoryk, overhearing, adds, "It could be that Jupiter is eleven times bigger." "Has a core mostly surrounded by hydrogen and helium, possibly in liquid form due to the pressure." He turns to Alex, "How is the 3D printing going? Will we be ready for the presentation?" Alex nods, "It should be finished by this weekend, ready for next week." V walks in, her robe slightly over her bathing suit.

Declan jokes, "Hey, hot mamma, how was the pool?" "The pool is nice, different because of the gravity. I can swim longer. What's happening today?"

V asks, grabbing a cup of coffee. Declan replies, "We are getting trained on the space suits." Kyoryk explains, "They call them EVAs, Extravehicular Activity Spacesuits, with layers of protective materials and three types of sunscreens. Our ships and buggies have similar protective layers." "I'm going to shower. I'll be back," V says.

Alex stops her, "Before you do, I saw all twelve of us on a ship with our Stewards in my room a few minutes ago. I'm pretty sure we'll all get to go to Amotaious soon." "That's so cool, another planet," Declan smiles. "How? What were you thinking about?" V asks.

"I had just finished my reps and sat on the bed. Got a little dizzy. I guess I was thinking about the trip, and then I saw us all traveling on one of the bigger ships in the Jella suits," Alex explains. "That's great, Alex, your Gift is getting stronger. I need to shower," V says, smiling. "Do you need help soaping up?" Alex teases. V smiles back, "I can handle it." Declan laughs, "How about me? You want me to help you?" Ignoring him, V walks out. Alex turns to the others, "I don't think we'll spend much time on the surface. The main reason for the training is for emergencies or maybe to repair a big door or something."

Half an hour later, the whole group is in the common room, heading down to the docks. Hiro Oguri and Vitor Aldo are preparing suits, rolling two racks into the middle of the room. Hiro, Kyoryk's Steward, and Vitor, Candido's, gather the group.

Hiro stops moving the cart and addresses them, "Today, we'll go over different space suits and their functions. For surface walks and repairs, we use EVAs, and for inside tunnels or vehicles, we use IVAs. The gray suits are IVAs; the black ones are EVAs. EVAs have stealth capabilities, so we can't be seen from space or the planet, at least from afar. The suit consists of the lower torso, upper torso, helmet, pack, and gloves. Let's demonstrate on Miko."

He grabs a "Small" suit from the rack. "If you don't mind, strip down to your underwear." Initially shy, Miko has opened up since the beginning of school, perhaps due to the Common Mind. Smiling, she giggles, "My underwear?" She strips down and sits on the bench.

Hiro helps her with the lower torso, then the upper torso, then the helmet, and finally the gloves. He hits a button on her wrist, turns on communication equipment, and asks, "Can you hear me?" Miko, laughing inside the helmet, responds, "Yes."

Hiro looks at the group, "At all times, you must be in communication with each other and the Lab." He picks up the pack, "This is the life pack. It's your air, water, and cooling system."

He attaches the pack to Miko's back, "You should never need to remove the hoses from the pack. They must be removed with a tool. The other sides of the hoses that connect to the suit are color-coded. Blue for air, green for cooling, white for water." He connects the hoses to the suit, lifts the helmet visor, and asks, "How are you doing? Okay?"

She smiles, "Yes, okay."

He pulls a small hose from inside the helmet, "This is your drinking water. Practice grabbing it with your mouth to get a shot of water. Bite down gently; a sensor gives you an ounce of water each time. There's enough oxygen for 12 hours. After that, you need to replace the CO_2 and filters and resupply. For longer durations, you need these." He holds up what looks like a fancy diaper. Declan and Lev laugh. "These are super absorbent containment diapers, but always go to the bathroom first before suiting up."

"We have five sizes of suits," Hiro explains, "The SS is for our friends from CAT 1, the S model is what Miko is wearing, and the M size." He looks at Lin and adds, "You look like a medium, and for Lev, he would wear an L, large." Lev, the tallest at 6'4", nods. Hiro continues, "And then there are SL sizes for people from CAT 5, like Gig and Doog."

Hiro pulls Miko forward and says, "All sizes are marked on the left sides of the suits." He shows the group the size letters on each part of the suit.

Lowering Miko's visor, he says, "Once the suit's completely ready," he lifts Miko's left arm and displays the control indicator panel on her wrist. "On your left wrist is a round red button. Press it once."

He presses it, and everyone hears a hissing noise. "When that red button turns green, the suit is ready." He shows three columns of indicators, "The left column is your oxygen, the middle is water, and the right one shows your overall safety status."

Hiro then pulls her right arm up, "This panel shows your vitals. The first column is blood pressure, the middle is oxygen level, and the right column is body temperature. All these indicators are monitored in the Lab by someone observing you."

"At no time should you go into the tunnels or to the surface without someone in the Lab monitoring you. We will instruct you in the Lab later. Once you've been in the suit for a few minutes, your body will warm up. Inside the suit are tiny veins of fluid-filled coolant. Before you remove the suit, press the green button." He hits the button, and they hear filtering noises. "Wait about five seconds."

He holds Miko's left wrist up again, and the button turns from green to red, and then the control panel goes dark. He lifts Miko's visor and says, "Alright, let's get the rest of you women in the suits. Guys, you can help."

The girls strip down to their underwear and pick out suits from the racks. Maria, not wearing a bra, smiles at Swaraj, who helps her put on the suit. Alex assists V, whispering in her ear, "Good thing you're not wearing that thing from the other night." She smiles back, "Yeah, I only wear that for you." The others help the girls with their suits.

Lev asks, "Do we wear the EVAs when we are in the vehicle to go to the surface?" Vitor replies, "Yes, the EVAs are less complicated. You would wear the same size, but in a vehicle, you don't need all the additional monitoring. The vehicles protect you from the cold and supply your oxygen, much like the ships."

As Alex helps V with her suit, he asks Vitor, "How many times have you used the suits?" Vitor responds, "I've been on the surface twice and in the tunnels once." Prezzy starts hopping around, saying, "These are pretty comfortable, considering."

Vitor looks at the group and says, "There is one reason to put the suits on if you are in the cavern: complete system failure. That's never happened, but we must instruct you just in case. If you hear the alarm during the pulse reversal and the light above the door is red, get into the black suits quickly." Everyone glances up at the green-lit light above the door.

Hiro continues, "Green means the cavern is secure, yellow means systems need checking, orange means a seal is leaking, and red means you need to protect yourself from outside elements immediately." Tonari asks, "Are there enough suits for everyone if that happens?"

Vitor answers, "During normal operation, yes. But if there's an event like the first night you came, no. Remember, you can always get into one of the ships and close the hatch. The Lab and Operation rooms are also safe in a red situation." Tonari looks relieved.

The girls power up their suits and walk around, some being goofy. Maria walks over to the door, looks up at the lights, and loudly says, "Red light, bad." Hiro and Vitor laugh.

Vitor says, "Alright, now guys, if you could help the ladies out of their suits, and you guys get into them." The guys suit up and walk around. Gig and Harvey enter the room. Gig asks, "Everyone understanding the suits?" V replies, "Yes, no problems. I think we all got it."

Gig looks at Alex and V, "We received the bid from your dad. We told him to go ahead with the project and sent him half the costs. V, when they finish all the outer casings before starting the core, let us know, and we will send the rest." V smiles, "Alright, I'll let you know."

Gig addresses the group, "We're on track with everything. Next Wednesday, we will all go to Amotaious to present our findings and solutions to the Council of Master Elders." Alex and V smile as the rest of the group gets excited. Declan hugs Miko, "This is awesome, we get to go to another planet."

Prezzy starts jumping up and down, all excited.

Gig says, "For the first time on Amotaious, stay with your Stewards. V and Alex will present our findings to the Master Elders."

"The rest of you can be present but do not interfere. Represent our planet well. Behave yourselves. Your Stewards will go over everything with you."

"This is not a sightseeing trip. We leave Wednesday morning. It's a six-hour flight if we catch one Thread. Thursday we have the Council meeting, then fly back. If the meeting lasts longer, we may stay another night. We're not sure how the other Master Elders will react to our proposal."

"Something like this has never been presented before. V, Alex, we'll spend most of Tuesday going over the presentation with Fem', Harvey, Freida, and me. How is the 3-D model going?" Alex replies, "It will be done by Monday. I made it into six parts to explain how it operates. I should have time to paint some of it to represent the different materials used and how it operates."

Gig smiles, "Wonderful." He looks at the group, "Everyone must be clean-shaven and professional-looking. We need to be on our best behavior. This is a big deal. Not all other planets agree with what we're doing. Vindor and Kall are resistant. I've been in contact with Vattan, Regnolnm, and Eldulcan. They agree if it's from the Creator, we should proceed."

Gig and Harvey conferred briefly before approaching V and Alex again. Harvey began, "Alex, have you seen any signs of the upcoming Pulse Reversal?"

Alex replied, "I've tried, but it's still too far out to see clearly. This morning, I did see that we're all going to Amotaious, so I know that's true."

"I'll keep looking into it. It's becoming clearer how to do it. I'll also focus on the Council meeting's outcome. If I can understand why those two planets are resistant, maybe we can devise a plan to convince them otherwise."

Gig looked at Harvey, then back at Alex. "Okay, keep investigating and keep us informed." V added, "We'll start prepping for the meeting to ensure we have everything ready."

Gig and Harvey left the room. Hiro asked, "Is everyone clear on how to use the suits? Any questions?"

Vitor suggested, "Let's meet in the Lab after lunch to go over the communication systems and other emergency procedures." The guys then got out of their EVAs and returned them to the racks.

At lunch, Miko asked Alex, "So, you saw that we're all going to Amotaious? That's so cool." Alex replied, "It seems my Gift is selective. I wonder if it's controlled by the Creator. I've tried thinking of other things, but nothing comes. I'm still figuring out how it works." Prezzy loudly asked, "What are we doing tonight?"

Swaraj questioned, "Why? What's tonight?" Prezzy replied, "It's Friday night. Should we do something different? What if we swim below the deck by those big waterfalls?" Miko shook her head. "I don't know if we're supposed to do that." Declan suggested, "I want to go to the surface and walk around on the moon. That would be almost better than sex." Miko and V laughed. Miko asked, "What else could we do? We're inside the moon."

Alex suggested, "Maybe we could pick a movie and watch it somewhere. If they have a projector, let me ask." He called Bahdubah on his tablet. Bahdubah answered, "Hey, Alex. What's up?" Alex asked, "Do you know if there's a projector we can use to watch a movie?" Bahdubah replied, "Have you been below the deck yet?" "No. What's below the deck?" Alex asked. "It's an open area overlooking the falls, next to the lake. You could use one of the walls to watch the movie."

Bahdubah replied. Prezzy yelled, "Can we go in the water down there?" Alex gave her a stern look. Bahdubah said, "I don't think there's a rule against it. Why don't I show you and find a projector?"

Alex said, "Alright, we'll meet you there in 15 minutes."

Bahdubah agreed, "Sounds good." Alex hung up and turned to Prezzy, "We have a plan. Come with me to meet Bahdubah in 15 minutes." Prezzy replied, "Alright."

They finished lunch, and Alex, V, Prezzy, Declan, Miko, and Swaraj went to meet Bahdubah. At the deck, Bahdubah led them through a big double door to the left of the bar by the dartboard. They walked down a flight of stairs to a large open area below the deck.

Bahdubah said, "No one ever comes down here. You could project the movie on this wall." He pointed to a large wall under the main hall. "You could bring some floor pillows or chairs. I have some speakers you could use."

Prezzy exclaimed, "This is awesome! What movie should we watch?"

Bahdubah suggested, "I have a couple of action movies from Vindor similar to ours here."

They all looked surprised. V said, "I never thought about that. What would movies from another planet be like?"

Bahdubah replied, "Come back after dinner, and we'll set it up. You can pick whatever movie you want." Prezzy felt the water, "It's pretty cold but doable. Can we get in the water here?" Declan looked down, then up at Prezzy. "You know there's a glacier down there, right? I'm surprised it's not colder."

Bahdubah said, "I think it's fine. Just don't get too crazy. Don't get naked."

Alex, hugging V from behind, said, "Alright, Prezzy, is this different enough for you?" Prezzy laughed, shaking the water from her hand. "Yeah, this is great. This will be fun." She frowned and said, "We can't get naked?" She started tickling Swaraj, who said, "Knock it off. Declan, looking at Prezzy, said, "You need to teach me how to surf."

Prezzy replied, "There are no waves here. We can bring pillows from the common room, drinks, and popcorn. This will be great."

They left and met the others in the Lab for class. Vitor was going over the electrical control and operations part of the system.

Instructing the Students on how to power down and restart it. Vitor said, "When the sensors pick it up, we know the Pulse Reversal is starting, and we get the alarm."

223

Prezzy said, "We heard an alarm before the Pulse Reversal hit, and Doog verified that it was the alarm for the Pulse Reversal. Then we went down to the vault."

Hiro said, "That's good. That's how it's supposed to work." Vitor showed them the monitor that would trigger the alarm. It displayed a blue, infrared, real-time image of the sun. Vitor said, "This will alert us to any significant CME or Solar Flare. The alarm lasts for one minute, then repeats if not reset. Whoever is nearest or in the Lab should notify the rest of us. Let's test it."

Hiro walked over to another table and asked Prezzy to join him. The rest of the group listened in. Hiro said, "All the ships are on channel 6, the emergency notification channel. If someone is on the surface or in the tunnels, they will hear it."

He picked up the mic, pressed the button at the bottom, and said, "This is a test. This is only a test." He hit a button, and the alarm they all heard last Sunday before the Pulse Reversal sounded.

He looked at Prezzy and commanded, "Now, tell them a Pulse Reversal has occurred and to proceed to a safe area."

Prezzy, nervously pushing the button, announced, "Hello, we have a Pulse Reversal. Please go to a safe area." She paused, then added, "Thank you." Declan laughed, "Good job, Prezzy."

Vitor took the mic from Prezzy, pressed the button, and said, "This has been a test. Once again, this has been a test." He put the mic down and turned off the alarm. "Does everyone understand how this works?"

Everyone nodded. Tonari asked, "What's a CME?"

Vitor explained, "A Coronal Mass Ejection (CME) is a large expulsion of plasma from the Sun's corona. It ejects billions of tons of coronal material and carries an embedded magnetic field. It travels outward from the sun."

"Think of it like this: Our bodies and most materials on Earth have a specific atomic structure. Plasma is the next state of matter. We use plasma to cut through metal. The sun is plasma. Lightning is plasma. It's extremely powerful and dangerous."

"We've learned to harness it in our everyday technology. The sun occasionally explodes with it, sending it into space. Imagine a campfire—you add something too explosive, and it flares up.

The sun is made of hydrogen, helium, carbon, and other elements, burning together for over nine billion years."

Tonari looked bewildered, while the other Students were awestruck. Prezzy exclaimed, "What the hell, man? That's insane. I think I need my own ship and EVA suit, like, today if we need to get out of here."

Alex noticed Miko and Declan messing around in the back. Miko had her hand inside Declan's pants. Alex waved to get Declan's attention and nudged V to look at the two goofballs.

Vitor continued, "An extreme CME can reach the planet in as little as ten hours, knocking out satellites, power lines, and more. Smaller ones can take days. Unfortunately, the Pulse Reversals and the Super Flares reach the planet within minutes."

V, seeing Miko and Declan messing around, couldn't resist probing their minds. She wanted to fine-tune her Gift. She tried Miko but saw nothing for some weird reason. Sometimes, the images are foggy and hard to reach. This time, Declan's, however, was easier. She went into his mind. *"She saw his mother yelling at him, "Don't go after him! Don't do it!" A man was pulling money from a safe and running away. It seemed to be located in his mother's place of business."*

"Declan chased the man through the building, out to a back alley, likely one of his mother's gambling houses. He continued the chase down a front street early morning no people around.

They ended up in a four-story abandoned building. On the roof, they struggled. The man pulled a knife, stabbing Declan in the belly and slashing the side of his face."

"Declan wrestled, finally, punching the man, who lost his balance and started to fall off the roof. Declan grabbed the backpack, but the strap broke, and the man fell to his death.

V felt Declan's pain. For years, Declan struggled with the guilt of taking a life over a simple robbery. His mother had warned him."

"The police ruled it an accident; the man had a long criminal record. Declan still questioned his responsibility; V felt he was more concerned about his mother's opinion, not of the man's death.

V approached Miko and Declan, whispering, "Seriously, you guys? Can't you wait until after class? Or until the university's pretend night?" She scoffed, *This Common Mind is getting out of hand."*

Vitor, back at the monitor showing the sun, said, "If you look at the bottom of the monitor, it shows the precise time a CME will hit after it happens. Before going to the surface or tunnels, check this monitor. It will give you a time of arrival."

"The same applies to Pulse Reversals, which hit faster. Notify others on the emergency channel. Your tablets link to this feed, showing the sun and the countdown timer."

Everyone pulled out their tablets. Vitor pointed to a small sun icon in the lower left corner. "Click on that for the sun's live feed. At the bottom, you'll see a countdown timer."

V read, "23:10."

Vitor nodded, "Good. On the left, it says?" "M.2 class solar flare," V replied.

Vitor addressed the group, "That's a mild solar flare, not affecting anything here or on the planet. If you hear the alarm, check your tablet. This icon here," he pointed to a red 'A' on the upper right, "tells you what the alarm is for—maybe hydrogen or helium detected in the tunnels."

Kyoryk admitted, "I didn't know all this information was on the tablet."

Vitor said, "Everything is on your tablet; you just need to know where to find it. Let's go through some other procedures." He moved to another area of the Lab. "If the power goes out, you need to reset the breakers."

He pointed to massive electrical panels on a large wall. "Pull this one down hard to reset, then push it back up. This powers the whole university."

He continued with more emergency instructions, including communicating with people in EVAs and surface vehicles.

V asked, "Can you get the emergency channel on your tablet?" Vitor replied, "No, but the tablet system, similar to WIFI, has a battery backup. So, call whoever is announcing in the lab."

Alex saw Miko dragging Declan into the bathroom. Hiro showed them monitors indicating the surface doors were sealed and secure. Alex pulled V aside, his voice urgent. "I just saw the two of them go into the bathroom together." V, with a frustrated yet amused look, chuckled. "I tried to tell them to pay attention. But with everything we've been through, maybe we should let them have their fun." "What does that mean?" Alex asked, curiosity piqued. V smiled. "My gift. I'll explain later."

A while later, the group finished up and returned to the common room. Alex lounged on a couch while V retreated to her room for some rest. About an hour later, V woke up and saw her grandmother's image sitting in the chair across from her. The apparition flickered, and V leaned on her elbows, thinking, *"Oh, shit! Another message!"* She rubbed her face. *"Wake up, V!"* She sat up, fully opening her eyes, focusing.

The image continued to fade in and out like fog. Her grandmother's figure finally settled, smiling warmly.

"Tonight, V. You and the others must stick to your plans. Another message is coming. All should attend. It's important. Take care, Vibrean. Love you."

The image flickered again, changing in tone and stature. It spoke once more.

"V, this part of the message is for you only. You are vital to our future. Your Gifts are crucial. Exercise it."

"Don't hesitate to utilize it. Keep Alex safe. He is extremely important." The image started to fade completely. "Tell no one about this part. You and Alex are the key."

As the image dissipated like smoke in fog, V rubbed her eyes, "I miss you." She murmered. She sat on the edge of the bed, deep in thought, when a knock came at the door.

"Who is it?" V asked.

Alex opened the door, poking his head in. "It's me." Seeing V's expression, he entered. "What is it? Are you okay?"

"No, not really. I just saw my grandmother. I guess I fell asleep for a few minutes. When I woke up, I saw her." V still sat on the bed, looking up at him with a petrified look on her face. "I miss her, I need to try and talk to her next time." Alex, excited, asked, "What did she say this time?"

V pointed to the empty chair. "She said, 'Tonight, V, you and the others. Stick to your plans. Another message will be coming. All should attend. It's important.' What do you think it means?" Alex speculated, "Could be another message from the Creator. We should let Gig know right now."

V grabbed her tablet, trembling slightly, and called Gig. "Hi Gig, I received another message from my grandmother."

Gig shushed someone nearby. "What did she say?" V looked at Alex, then back at the tablet. "She said, 'Tonight, V, you and the others. Stick to your plans. Another message will be coming. All should attend. It's important.'"

There was a long pause before Fem' spoke in the background, "What were they planning on doing tonight?" V cut in, "I heard Fem'. We planned to go below the deck to watch a movie on the wall down there. Bahdubah is helping us get everything together." Gig said, "Let's stick to that. I don't want to change anything. A few of us, if not all, will join you for the movie."

"Do you want me to let Bahdubah know more people are coming?" V asked nervously. "No, I'll get with him and Klinchme' to prepare everything."

"Do you think the message will come during the movie?"

"No way to tell, but I'll let the other Elders know. From now on, someone will stay with you at all times. Harvey will be down soon with a camera, just in case it happens soon," Gig interjected.

Alex nodded. "That's a great idea. If we record a visit, it'll be hard for the other Elders from other planets to deny it."

"Precisely. If necessary, I'll call you back in a few minutes," Gig replied.

V looked at Alex, who paced the room. She stood. "What do we do now?"

"Not sure." He looked around the room and up at the ceiling. "All of this is so weird." V looked at him. "What are you looking at?" Alex grabbed his face, then pulled back on his hair, looking at her, "He's watching us all the time. Like a big eyeball in the sky." He kind of shook and shivered. "Doesn't that kind of freak you out?"

She looked up at the ceiling. Looked back at him with a disdained look, "Well, it does now!" She pushes him against the door. "He's helping us. Think of it like that." "I'm going to the common room; I'll see you there." Alex took one last look around the room. "Oh no, you're not leaving me alone; let me get my tablet." She grabbed her tablet and ran after him.

They briskly walked to the common room where Miko, Declan, Lev, Lin, and Maria were. Alex checked on the 3D model pieces.

"Where are the others?" V asked. "Kyoryk is resting in his room. The others might be in their rooms," Declan replied reluctantly.

"Maria, could you find them? We have something to tell the group," V requested. Maria hopped up. "Okay, I'll find them. If not, we can call them." "Alright, thanks," V said. Alex quietly asked Declan, "Did you have fun in the bathroom?"

Declan laughed, but his look was stern. "Dude, it's not me. It's her. She's crazy. One minute, she's normal; the next, she's a sex maniac." Alex warned, "Just be careful. We've only been here a couple of weeks. We don't know what capital punishment looks like.

Have you seen those space movies where they open the airlock and eject you into the vacuum of space?" Declan's face twisted with worry. "No, they wouldn't do that, would they?"

Kyoryk entered the room, and Maria said, "Come on, help me find the others." They walked out, returning a few minutes later with the rest of the group. V gathered everyone and went over everything with them.

Harvey and Freida entered the room, chatting animatedly, carrying a sleek video camera. Harvey approached Alex while Freida sat next to V, and they began to talk.

Standing beside Alex, Harvey glanced at the 3D printers. "It sounds like we may receive a new message soon. How's the model coming?"

"It's crazy," Alex replied. "This time, more than just V and I will experience it. I wonder if it will emerge from the water like last time."

Harvey smiled. "No idea, but we won't miss it. I've got the camera to capture it. A video of a message from the Creator would be undeniable proof for the council of Elders, although it will still lead to further complications." "What do you mean?" Alex asked.

"Every planet has catastrophe cycles. Most are spread out over more years than ours. If you were from another planet, wouldn't you want to stop or deter your catastrophe? Like we are trying to do. We'll have to wait and see, but this will be an incredible sight." Alex nodded. "I always thought the first message was a one-time thing."

Harvey shrugged. "Who knows?" He examined the Accelerator parts. "These parts look great. You made them modular, which is a smart idea."

"I plan to paint them if we have time," Alex said. "Great," Harvey replied. "I'm with you for the next four or five hours, or however long it takes. Gig told me to stick with you tonight."

Alex laughed. "Okay, no worries. We're going to eat and then watch a movie. There's a big area below deck that Bahdubah said we can use." "I haven't watched a movie in a while," Harvey said. "What movie?"

"We haven't picked one yet," Alex replied. "Bahdubah is bringing a few from one of the other planets." "That should be interesting," Harvey noted. "I know, right," Alex agreed. V walked over. "We're all going to dinner now."

They all headed to the dining area, got their food, and sat down. Alex looked at Harvey and Freida. "So, who's coming to the movie?" Freida laughed. "I think everyone." V laughed too. "So, if it doesn't happen until late, is everyone going to follow us around, sit at our bedsides?" Freida laughed again. "That's the plan. Nothing like this has ever happened before. We've only been here for a year. This is going to be amazing."

"I tell you, It's been pretty boring over the last year. You guys show up, and everything starts happening. I can't imagine how it's been for Gig and Fem' over so many years."

Alex, with a proud look, "I know, right? We showed up at the right time." He looks back up at the ceiling again. He's watching us all."

After finishing dinner, Alex, V, Harvey, and Freida were the last to leave. Most everyone was on the deck waiting as they walked down the ramp.

V remarked, "They're all staring at us." Alex laughed. "Oh wow! We're celebrities now!" V laughed too. "It's all so surreal!" Harvey and Freida laughed along. Bahdubah approached them. "We've got everything set up. Prezzy and Swaraj fetched the pillows from your common room."

Alex and the others sat at the bar, feeling a bit nervous. Alex said, "How about a drink? We're kind of freaked out about all this." Bahdubah mixed a couple of drinks and handed them over. V asked, "What are these called?"

"Comfortably Numb," Bahdubah replied with a smile. V laughed. "What's in them?" "Chamomile tea, a couple of different liquors, Saint John's Wort, and Kava," he explained. "What's Saint John's Wort?" Alex asked. "It's a plant. The leaves and flowers are dried and used in tea or pill form for anxiety. It's supposed to relax you," Bahdubah replied. "Isn't the alcohol and chamomile enough?" Alex joked. Bahdubah laughed. "Just drink it. You'll like it." V took a sip. "It's good." Prezzy came up from downstairs.

Alex got her attention. "How's it going down there? Is it all set up?" "Yes, all set up. Ready when you are," Prezzy confirmed.

Alex lifted his drink. "Okay, thanks, Prezzy." Gig and Fem' walked toward them.

Gig looked at the group. "This is a crazy time. I never thought something like this would happen before you all arrived." Fem' added, "I think the Creator is in a hurry to tell us something." Freida asked, "So, nothing like this has ever happened before?"

Fem' replied, "If it had, we would have been told. A messenger from the Creator in this way has never happened. You two must be aware of how special this is. When we get to Amotaious, people will treat us differently. Be prepared."

Gig and Fem' walked to a table. Alex looked at Harvey. "What did Fem' mean by people treating us differently?" Harvey explained, "Imagine someone on our planet being contacted by their God and having proof. Millions would come to meet that person."

"I don't think you realize what's to come. Let's say Jesus came to your house for dinner, and you had proof."

Harvey and Freida went to sit with Gig and Fem'. V looked at Alex. "I didn't want this. It's like we're famous now. What's it going to be like when we get to Amotaious?"

Alex looked serious. "Should I grow a beard, put lifts in my boots, pierce my ears?" He laughed. "No matter what happens, we must remain the same. I'll look after you, and you'll look after me. Agreed?"

V, jokingly concerned, said, "I think I should dye my hair green and blue, wear long eyelashes, and pierce my nose." She laughed. "Most definitely, we should stay the same. Let it not affect us, no matter what. Remain the same."

Alex lifted his glass. "To remaining the same." He put his arm around V and hugged her. Alex looked at Bahdubah. "What do you think? Should we let our celebrity status change us or remain the same?" Bahdubah replied, "Remain the same for now. But at the end of all this, for one night, you could do the fancy nose rings and eyelashes."

"How about some hats with feathers?" Alex and V laughed. They got up from the bar and started walking towards the door. Alex glanced back. "Bahdubah, are you coming?"

Bahdubah laughed. "I wouldn't miss this for anything." V turned to Alex, kissed him, and chuckled. "What if nothing happens? We'll look like complete idiots." Alex laughed. "Yes, we will. But she said tonight, right?" V nodded. "Yes, of course, she did." She looked up towards the ceiling, "Or He did, or whoever is up there watching us." She chuckled as she nudged him a bit.

As they descended the stairs, Declan and Miko greeted them. Miko grabbed V's hand. "Come sit with us. We have Jelly Bellies, and I found the fudge in your room."

V whispered in Alex's ear. "Are they treating us differently now?" Alex gave her a stern look. "No, relax."

"Did you guys pick a movie?" Alex asked Declan. "Yes," Declan replied. "It's an alien attack movie from the planet Vindor." "What's it called? We can't read the writing," Alex said as he sat on the floor next to V and Miko. Declan laughed. "Bahdubah said it's called 'Alien.'" Alex laughed. "I've seen some of the ones made in America. Aren't there like twelve or thirteen Alien movies?" Declan chuckled. "I think there were six in total."

The movie started, and Alex looked around. Over 30 people filled the room. He whispered to V, "This is crazy. The whole room is full. I think everyone at the University is here."

V glanced back and saw Doog and Fair sitting with Gig and Fem' in the back. "I know it's insane. Let's try to watch the movie and not think about it."

"It will be okay after the messenger comes," Alex whispered.

Halfway through the movie, the Vindor ship returns from space with hidden aliens multiplying within the population of a city. The subtitles made it hard to follow. Prezzy jumped into the water, and Swaraj tried to get her out.

The movie turned super violent. Aliens entered people's mouths while they slept, multiplied in their brains, and caused them to go insane, biting and chewing on others.

Their heads split open, and aliens flew out, stabbing everyone with their stingers and turning them into cocoons. Then, they transformed into giant mosquito-like aliens. It was graphic yet amusing. Everyone seemed to enjoy it.

V looked worried. "I have to get up. I'm tired of sitting on the floor."

Concerned, Alex got up too. They walked to where the water met the floor's edge. The crystal-clear water, mist, and movement from the nearby waterfall created a serene view. The accent lighting lit up the walls differently than on the deck.

It was a beautiful sight, looking out into the small lake and down into the glacier below, which seemed ten feet deep but was over a hundred. The whole view was spectacular.

V took a deep breath. "I need to talk to Freida."

Alex, unsure how to comfort her, smiled. "Okay. We'll figure it out. It's going to be okay."

She let go of his hand and walked over to Freida. Alex noticed the credits rolling on the screen. *"What the hell do I do now? Nothing is happening. Crap. This isn't good."* He looked up at the cavern ceiling. *"Come on, Creator. Please make something happen. Please, do it now."*

Declan tapped him on the shoulder. "Nothing yet?"

Alex turned to Declan, noticing everyone was looking at him. "Not yet. It will happen, I hope."

He put his hand on Declan's shoulder, hoping it would help. He looked at V, shrugging. Some of the little people from CAT 1 started heading up the stairs. Alex and Declan walked over to where V and Freida were. "Nothing yet. Sorry about that."

Harvey, trying to lighten the mood, asked, "What did you think of the movie?"

"It was a bit too bloody for my taste," Alex replied. "And why did the aliens have to split the brains open to come out? They could have just come out of the nose or mouth. It was like watching an alien chick hatch from an egg, but more insane."

Freida chuckled. "It was pretty crazy. Vindor made that movie, didn't they?" Harvey asked, "Last time, what were you two doing?"

Alex thought. *"Shit, I can't tell Harvey what I was doing. Having sex with a wild woman. The best sex I've ever had. Yes, Harvey, it was great!"* He smiled at V, hugged her, and said, "At the moment, nothing. We were just sitting in the hot tub talking."

V hugged Alex back even harder, thinking, *"Yes, Harvey. It was right after the best orgasm of my life. I basically thought I was going to die happy."*

"Like the opposite of how I feel right now." She looked at a small lamp Bahdubah had brought down. She picked it up, set it back down, before she looked away, the small bulb flickered. She held it again; it got real bright before completely going off. She looked at Alex with complete satisfaction. She knew it was time.

Alex, not seeing the lamp, asked, "What?"

V pushed him on his shoulder, grabbed his hand, and pulled him towards the waterline of the small lake. No one else noticed the lamp. She walked him to the water's edge. "Just watch." She looked back at Harvey and Freida, smiling and nodding, assuring them with a look that said, "It's happening."

The movie credits rolled, accompanied by bizarre harp and violin music. All the lights and the projector began to flicker. A few people noticed Alex and V standing by the edge, smiling. Everyone started to react. Soon, everyone lined up at the water's edge or behind them.

The room grew warmer, and a gentle breeze tousled everyone's hair. V held Alex's hand even tightly. The projector stopped, and all visible lights flickered more rapidly, grew very bright, and then went completely out. The lights in the water of the lake remained on, becoming very bright.

Shouts erupted from the deck above as impatient onlookers who had left the lower level began exclaiming, "It's happening!" In the movie room, cries of "Oh my God!"

"Here it comes!" and "Praise the Lord!" filled the air. Some stood in silent awe.

Alex scanned the room, noticing Harvey behind him to the left, recording with the video camera.

To his right, a few filmed with their tablets. A low rumbling began, and the water in the pond churned violently. From below, a tornado began to form, illuminated with a violet-blue light deep within the glacier. The water rose, swirling in the center. The rumbling grew louder, and the building vibrated. The water receded from the floor of the room.

Alex took a final look around. Everyone was mesmerized. Several people dropped to their knees. Fem' had her hands over her mouth, and Gig embraced her tightly. To his right, Tonari, Candido, and Maria knelt in prayer.

V's face lit up with a smile, all doubt gone. The water rose higher, forming a thick waterspout that reached twenty-five feet. The shape morphed into a figure Alex and V had seen before the filament of water started to shape.

Holding V from behind now, Alex inhaled the scent of her perfume. The figure took form, and a blue-violet arrow shot from its top, swirling around the area.

It cracked and split into three arrows that gently passed through everyone. By the time this happened, the water formed into the Angel, then it paused, crystallized before their eyes into the ice formation, crystal clear, it locked in place. Then it moved and looked directly at V and Alex, even more beautiful than before it pointed right at them with its giant arms.

V took a deep breath in as the shock from the arrow going through them abided the two of them exhaled. The entire cavern fell silent, save for the sound of waterfalls to the right. As the arrows retracted, the figure moved slightly and she spoke.

"The future is not set. You will have a profound and lasting impact on all consciousness. Proceed with the plan. Complete this first mission. You must risk all to save many. If you fail, all consciousness could end, not just for your planet but for all planets."

"In two hundred and fifty-one of your star days another situation will arise, the galaxy must survive. Trust in each other. Follow the path I have set."

"Use your Gifts. Use the true Gift—the Common Mind. Risk all to save all. The future will then be set."

Alex looked around the mist-filled room. Everyone stood still, some with hands over their mouths, others reaching out, wanting to touch the magnificent Creator's Messenger.

Many knelt in prayer. The figure raised its hands towards the crater's top as if reaching for the sky. The giant Angel, standing twenty to thirty feet tall, began to descend into the water. It almost seemed to smile at them before speaking again.

"Love you all. Protect V and Alex. All the Students. They are the key. Raba Rashi."

Everyone quietly echoed, "Raba Rashi." The crystal image became water again in a split second and plunged back violently into the lake, splashing into the room and wetting everyone's shoes, splashing against the opposing walls of the lake. The lights deep in the water extinguished, plunging the cavern into total darkness for about three seconds.

Only the sound of splashing waterfalls could be heard. The projector startled everyone as it came back on, followed by all the other lights.

Most people remained transfixed, staring into the lake, as if hypnotized by the lasting image.

Alex and V felt a warmth and love from the Creator that left an everlasting impression.

As the spell lifted, V heard a few people crying and others hugging. Shouts and cheers came from above. The room's biggest person started clapping. Alex turned to see Doog and Fair hooting and hollering. Declan exclaimed, "Oh my God, that was incredible, just incredible." Other people joined in, shouting.

V turned to Alex, gave him the warmest of smiles, and said something in Hindi before hugging and kissing him.

Gig and Fem' found Alex and V. Gig, with his huge hands on Alex's shoulders, pulled him in for a giant hug and whispered, "This is not just about us, our planet."

"It's so much bigger. I guarantee you, they are going to listen now." Gig pulled back, smiled, and said, "Thank you."

Alex, unsure what to say, just smiled. Fem' hugged V tightly, exclaiming, "That was fantastic! Never in my wildest dreams— incredible!"

Alex looked around, thinking, *"The Common Mind has gripped everyone, and now I'm starting to feel it too. The sensation is incredible. I've never felt this good before. It's as though all of us are hugging, kissing, and more. I don't even know how to describe it."*

"It's as if all negative thoughts and feelings have left my mind entirely. My body feels incredible. I wonder what's next." He looked at V. *"Can you hear me? Can you feel the Common Mind within us all now?"*

To his surprise, V answered back in his mind, *"I can. I can feel you. I can feel all of them. This is incredible. This is crazy."*

A new **"Song"** started playing. *The Voice*

Declan jumped on Alex. "That was insane, man! Crazy, right?" Music played upstairs on the deck. People began making their way upstairs. Prezzy jumped up onto Alex, exclaiming, "That was incredible!" She turned to V. "You are incredible!" V smiled as Prezzy hugged her. "Just incredible!"

V, overwhelmed, hugged Prezzy back and looked around the room at the smiles and happiness of the group. *"This is incredible. Thank you, Raba Rashi. You came through. That was amazing. Wait! Did I just communicate with Alex in my mind? That's crazy. We need to try that again. That's the Gift. That's what He's been training me for. And what does this message mean? What's coming in how many star days? And I love Alex. Yes, I love Alex. I'm a crazy person."* She pulled away from the hug with Prezzy, looked at her, and said, "I love you, Prezzy, and I'm a crazy person."

Prezzy kissed her and laughed. "Love you too."

As everyone gathers upstairs, the room buzzes with loud talking and congratulating. Alex and V return to the deck, sit at the bar, and burst into laughter. Bahdubah prepares another Comfortably Numb drink for them. Alex and V raise their glasses to him, thanking him. With a huge smile, Bahdubah says, "I've never seen a group of people act this way before. This is crazy." V asks, "You saw the whole thing?"

Bahdubah grins widely, "Oh yeah. Some of us were up here. It was just like you described. Incredible. I think the Common Mind is at its peak tonight."

Alex and V turn in their seats, watching everyone dance and celebrate. Alex smiles at her, "And you were worried."

V replies, "But what she said—what's coming, Alex? We might be solving a bigger problem than we thought. If it involves other planets, what does that mean?"

Alex smiles, "That's for us to worry about tomorrow, not tonight, right?"

V smiles back, "You're right, tomorrow. And we need to practice more on this mind communication thing that happened tonight." Her voice drops to a whisper, "You know, how we talked to each other in our minds."

Alex grins, "I know, that was so cool. We'll have to work on that." He takes a sip from his drink, and to his surprise, V jumps down and starts dancing with Prezzy and Miko. Declan sits next to Alex, "You okay? Crazy night?" Alex laughs, "Yeah, I'm okay." They turn to face the bar. Bahdubah walks by and asks Alex, "Need another drink?" Alex replies, "Sure, that would be great. Thanks." Declan asks, "What are you drinking?" Bahdubah says, "I'll make one for you."

Alex explains, "It's a calming tea drink with a surprising amount of alcohol in it." Bahdubah overhears and says, "That's the numb part of the drink." Alex jokes, "Maybe we should call it Just Numb?" Bahdubah laughs. A drink later, Miko and V come back over.

As the night settles down, V looks at Alex, "Ready to go?" Alex asks, "Why? Are you sleepy?" She smiles, "I'm comfortable." She grabs his hand, pulls him off the bar stool, and starts walking up the ramp. Miko and Declan laugh and follow them. Alex looks back, "Goodnight, Bahdubah." Bahdubah smiles, "Goodnight."

Miko and Declan talk loudly and laugh all the way back to their rooms. They reach V's room first, and she pulls Alex inside. Declan asks, "Want us to join you?"

Miko laughs and hits him. V says, "No, I think we're good." Declan laughs, and they continue to their rooms. V shuts the door. Alex asks, "What do you want to do now?" V lights a candle, "I have some fudge hidden." She opens a drawer, pulling out a pack of long feathers. "And I have these."

Alex smiles, "What are we going to do with those?"

V drags the feathers by the candle, the light flickering in the room, and attempts to tickle Alex with them. "You'll see." V and Alex ended the evening a little later, after the feather fun.

XIII

V zipped up her backpack as Alex walked in, carrying his garment bag and his backpack. He plopped down in her chair and greeted her with a grin, "Morning, sweet cheeks."

V raised an eyebrow, puzzled. "Sweet cheeks? Are you talking about these cheeks?" she asked, pointing below her waist. "Or these?" She gestured to her face.

Alex's smile widened. "Both, but you're just sweet all over." She kissed him. "Morning to you, handsome man." "Do you feel confident about our presentation?" Alex inquired. "Yes, I think so. We can review everything again on the ship if necessary. I was thinking we should compile a list of potential questions the Master Elders might ask and prepare our answers." "Sounds good." He stood up. "I'll see you in the common room. I need to wrap up the parts of the Accelerator. Are you good?"

V nodded. "I'm okay now, but I might be a wreck tomorrow morning before the presentation. All this extra attention—our sudden celebrity status—it's overwhelming." "I think it's starting to fade here at the University, but on Amotaious, we'll be bombarded with handshakes and congratulations. We'll have to learn to tune it out," Alex said with a joking tone. He stood straight, extending his hand for a shake. "Yes, it was something special. I'll tell my grandkids about it. What does it all mean? Well, we're here to figure it out. We're confident we can accomplish the mission."

V laughed. "That was pretty good. We just need to focus on the overall goal and ignore the attention. With the other planets involved, we'll likely be working with them."

Standing in the doorway, Alex looked back. "Hopefully, we'll get more messages about what it all means."

"Gig thinks the other planets might be in danger, but he doesn't want to speculate. He said we should concentrate on our part and get through the next few days." Finishing with one of her bags, V looked up. "He's right. We need to get through this first. Did anyone figure out what the Creator meant by '251 of our star days'?"

Alex's expression turned distant. "Kyoryk said one solar day is twenty-seven of our planet's days. So, we think we have eighteen years until whatever is going to happen to our galaxy. That's six thousand, seven hundred seventy-seven of our days. Something big is going to happen in our galaxy fifteen years after we graduate. We don't know why we received such a warning. Gig and some others are almost sure the Super Flare will happen within the next year. The second message isn't about our planet now. I think the next Pulse reversal will occur in 3 to 4 months." He glanced at his luggage. "Alright, I've got to pack the Accelerator." V nodded. "Okay, see you in the common room."

All the Students gathered in the common room with their luggage, ready to head to Amotaious for the presentation of the Creator's Plans. They made their way to the docks, boarding a ship different from any before. It seated thirty and had two pilots. The seats were more spacious, equipped with personal monitors, and offered temperature control and massage functions. Bahdubah and Klinchme' would provide meals and drinks during the flight. The ship had a small galley and two bathrooms. Gig and Fem' sat up front with the Stewards, while the Students took their seats behind them. The G-suits were also much improved.

V sat towards the back, next to Alex. As everyone settled in and buckled up, the ship proceeded up the main track, entering a larger tunnel. One of the pilots checked on everyone, ensuring all had a green light and were doing okay. After returning to his seat, the ship went through the crater door.

The journey felt different on the larger ship—straight ahead for a few minutes, vertical for five to seven, then horizontal for another two, and finally back to the surface. V was getting used to it.

The ship stopped and became vertical again. The pilot's voice came over the loudspeaker, "I'm your pilot, Reoline. My handsome co-pilot is Sarcan."

"If we catch one Thread, we'll reach Amotaious in six hours. We're about to take off. You can watch our flight path on your personal monitors if you like." The line clicked, and V could barely hear Reoline talking to the lab, informing them of the takeoff. They traveled above the surface for about five minutes before Sarcan announced over the intercom, "60 seconds until the Jella is initiated. 2 minutes until the ship jumps on the Thread. We'll be accelerating for almost three minutes. After that, you can move about the cabin."

V looked at Alex. "Three minutes? I don't like the sound of that." The Students murmured about the three minutes. V glanced across the aisle at Tonari, who was covering her face in disgust. "It's 600 light years to Amotaious. If we need to catch another Thread, add another half an hour. Remember to breathe in through your nose and out through your mouth." A few seconds later, the computer beeped. Sarcan's voice counted down, "4... 3... 2..." V took a deep breath in. "1."

SNAP! CRACK! BOOM! SWOOSH! The cabin filled with white light, and V felt her body being crushed by the pressure, struggling to breathe. The light was overwhelming, and she finally exhaled slowly, taking in another breath through her nose. She gripped the armrests tightly, thinking, *"How long now? Has it even been a minute?"* She closed her eyes, hearing people cursing. *"What the hell? Now how long has it been? This is torture. God help me. Or Raba Rashi help me!"* She saw the white light fading through her eyelids. *"Is it over?"* She opened her eyes, and the light outside the window had dissipated. She breathed in through her nose and out through her mouth, wondering, *"When will it end?"* The computer beeped again, and she felt the pressure easing as the ship reached its acceleration.

Sarcan's voice came over the loudspeaker. "The Jella will be released any second. We're good to go for a while. If you need anything, let one of us know."

Alex looked at V and said, "That was fun." V shook her head. "Not really. I didn't enjoy that at all."

She glanced over at Tonari and asked, "You okay?" Tonari looked back, "I hate that. I hope it's worth it." V smiled at her.

The intercom clicked, and Reoline's voice instructed, "You can move about the cabin now. Wrap up your Jella suits and put them in the locker below your seat. Thanks."

V and Alex removed their G-suits. V took out her computer and started reviewing the presentation videos. Alex, curious about the ship, headed towards the front where Sarcan and Reoline were seated. After a few minutes, Freida came and sat next to V.

Freida asked, "Are you nervous about the presentation?" V smiled. "Not yet. I'm sure I will be in the morning." Freida continued, "I wanted to go over a few things you should know. I was in the Council building last week. It's an amazing structure—imagine the best architecture and furniture from six different planets, spanning thousands of years. The twelve Master Elders sit in a semicircle.

The twelve in the front are from the most recent CATs, two from each planet. Behind them are thirty-two retired Master Elders. We have eight retired Master Elders. Vattan is on their fifth CAT, like us, so they also have eight. Regnolm, the three-mooned planet, has six retired. Vindor, the planet we need to worry about, has six. Kall, currently in a perpetual ice age, has four. Elducan also has four."

V nodded. "I understand."

Freida pulls up some images on her tablet. "The current Master Elders convene with their planetary Elders, reach a decision, and present their opinions to the entire council. They vote by standing for 'yes' and remaining seated for 'no.' You, me, Harvey, and Alex will be seated on the main floor in front of them."

She shows V a picture of the Master Elders' Council Amphitheater. "You'll have your computer connected to the virtual main screen here. We'll set everything up before everyone arrives, and then you'll speak and review our findings."

V takes a sip of her water and says, "Okay, sounds good."

Freida smiles and looks at her. "I also wanted to share something that might help. You've known Gig and Fem' for a couple of weeks now. What do you think of them?"

V, unsure, replies, "They are super nice and relaxed. When I first met them, I thought they would be more intense and stricter. You know, with the university, the Gifts, and the Creator. It's all unlike anything we could have imagined."

"We drink and hang out with you all. It's been fun but also terrifying. I really don't know how to describe it. And Fem and Gig are awesome." V smiles at Freida, "Not sure what you're asking."

Freida chuckles. "What I'm trying to say is, compared to the rest of them, Gig and Fem' are more disciplined and sticklers for the rules. They lean back in their seats, take a deep breath. They all have been alive for so long, taking records, unable to interfere. I think they've become complacent."

V cuts her off, "Oh, I understand what you're saying."

Freida continues, "They're goofy and don't care much for the rules what we call Directives and Laws. Gig and Fem' are the only Master Elders truly trying to do what the Creator wants, more than all of them."

V smiles. "So, you're saying the meeting won't be as intense as I'm imagining?"

Freida breathes out. "Yes, exactly. They may yell a little, but it's just posturing. The Master Elders have been around for thousands of years. I'm guessing they will mainly be interested in why the Creator contacted you rather than them, and what it was like. What makes you special."

"If things get weird, you can always tell them the Creator contacted you and Alex, and you feel it's your mission to follow the Creator's instructions. Use this to your advantage. Don't see it as a burden but as an opportunity to help them."

V nods. "I think I understand what you're saying."

Freida says, "Harvey and I will be sitting with you, and I guarantee that if any one of them gets out of hand, Gig and Fem' will shut them down quickly, especially if they start verbally attacking us."

V says, "So they are nothing like our politicians or business leaders."

Freida says, "Not at all. A lot of our society is based on self-worth, greed, and who can benefit the most monetarily. Here, it's different. Most people you'll meet have been overseers of their planets, historians, and since they can't interfere with their people, there is no self-interest."

V reaches over and hugs her. "Thanks for that; I feel a lot better now."

Freida says, "Harvey is going over the same things with Alex, so you two will do fine. Just remember, the Creator wouldn't have come to you if he didn't think you could handle all this. You and Alex were made for it." Freida smiles. "Are you and Alex getting along okay? It seems everyone has paired up nicely."

V asks, "Is that something that happens before every CAT?"

Freida nods. "It does. I was concerned at first, but after talking to Fem' and Fair, some of you will stay together, and some may not. You must remember that all of you are very similar, and the influence of the Common Mind reinforces relationships and so much more. In the first couple of weeks, you experience years of training. We have been here a year, and Harvey and I have just recently become very close. Who knows what the future holds? One thing I haven't talked to you about yet is your other Gift. How is that going? One, the visions of your grandmother, two, the messages from the Creator, and you haven't said much about your mind-reading ability."

V, with a look of uncertainty, says, "I can feel and see what others are feeling and thinking. I can go back into their memories."

V looks around to make sure no one is listening to them. Whispering, she says, "My Gift has revealed some pretty wild things. I haven't told anyone yet. For example, Kyoryk saved a group of people and his siblings from a maniac on a train, but the guy died, and he feels responsible. I can actually feel it. I can feel the burden he carries."

V looks out the window as a nearby solar system passes by. "The pressure on his psyche, I was filled with all these emotions. And then I met Alex's family. Something happened there. I was able to go into his mother's mind. Why has the Creator given me this Gift?"

Freida, with a surprised look, says, "Not sure, let me talk to Fem' about it, and I'll get back to you. For now, don't share this with anyone. It's too personal, and we don't know why the Creator is showing this to you. How many have you looked into?"

V sits back and thinks. "I looked into Lev, Declan, Prezzy, and Kyoryk so far."

Freida asks, "And their histories are all related to a similar thing? Like a bad event in their lives?"

V says, "Yes, all related to a murder."

Freida speculates, "I think all the Students have experienced something similar. Not that they committed murder, but they were involved in a situation where someone was murdered. Or one of them might have killed someone for a good reason. They possibly deserved it, I guess." V rubs her face. "I don't know. This is a weird Gift. Why was I given this? And where did we, or were we all chosen because we had an event like this in our past?"

Freida says, "Let me talk to Fem' and see. Maybe it will change as your Gift progresses. Who knows?"

V nods. "Okay, sounds good. Something weird happened to Alex and me too. Last Friday night with the Common Mind, I was actually able to go into his thoughts, and we communicated. I actually talked to him. It was a trip."

"We've tried since, but it hasn't worked again. But it was a really cool experience. A lot is happening. I don't know."

Freida laughs, holds V's hand, and says, "You are special, V. Alex too. Out of the twelve of you, you and Alex have something unique going on with the Creator. You might share some of this with Alex but not with Miko and the others. I would hold off telling them for now. We are not even sure why you are experiencing some of the things you both are going through. For now, keep it between us, you, me, Alex, and Harvey."

V puts her hand on Freida's. "Thank you. It's not easy going through all this, and we seem to be going through it very quickly."

Freida says, "With all that's happened in the last week or so, with you all getting your Gifts and how quickly you both received the transfer of the eagle marks, it's new to all of us as well. The Creator must have some very important plans for you and Alex."

Freida gazes out the window, her voice tinged with awe. "It's astounding, all of this. Every day is a revelation—the Creator, the Gifts, the potential to save the planet from the next Catastrophe. It's all so extraordinary. I've been around Gig and Fem' for a year, and in the last few weeks, they seem like different people."

"This has brought a new perspective on life for so many. It's an exhilarating time for all of us. Focus on tomorrow, and don't worry about anything else."

V looks at her with newfound liberation. "Thanks for everything. When we first met, I envisioned another four years of college. Then, at the airport, I felt deceived, reminiscent of how my parents made me feel."

"Now, look at us. We're on a ship traveling to a new planet, carrying a message from the Creator, speaking on behalf of our entire world. I haven't even fully grasped what the Creator, God, is all about. My parents are religious, but I think they do it to appease others. I've always used it as a crutch. Now, with everything happening... Do you have any Valum?"

Freida laughs. "No, but I'm sure we could get some chamomile tea. Let's ask Klinchme'. Maybe she can get us a glass of wine." V glances at her and chuckles. "It's 8:40 in the morning." Freida laughs again. "We should wait until lunch." V smiles, "With lunch."

Freida leans back in her seat, closes her eyes, and exhales deeply. "It's a lot for anyone." V mimics her and says, "It is, isn't it?"

Hours later, Klinchme' walks around, offering drinks. V opens her eyes and whispers, "How long till lunch? Would it be wrong if I had a wine?" Klinchme' smiles. "Lunch is in 30 minutes. I'll get you a glass." Freida overhears, opens her eyes, and whispers, "I'll have one too, thanks." Klinchme' smiles again. "Two wines, coming up."

V and Freida continue to gaze out the window. After lunch and a couple of glasses of wine, they feel good and a little goofy. V shouts, "Are we there yet?" Freida laughs.

Sarcan and Reoline walk around, helping everyone get their Jella suits on.

Sarcan and Reoline, from CAT 3, have Micro Computer Implants connected within their brains and a modified eye that can take pictures and scan information. The people from CAT 3 average about 5'5" tall and wear clothing designed for total comfort, made of beautiful fabric controlled electronically with heating and cooling elements. People during their time discovered the Stepped Leader Thread, which a scientist found named the Electromagnetic Galactic Aurora Universal Web Interlacement Highway, or "Egauwih."

This web connects all the suns of the galaxy, allowing ships to hop from one Thread to another, traveling between solar systems.

Their facial features are similar to ours but with more pronounced cheekbones and larger eyes. They have one of the longest lifespans among all civilizations.

V stops Reoline and asks, "What does that fabric do in the rain and snow?" Reoline replies, "It's made of a Robotic Microfiber that can change instantly depending on the climate."

V inquires, "How does the chip work? Can you feel it?" Reoline answers, "No, but see your computer? We have all those capabilities within us—the mic, camera, full conversations—without speaking. Like this." Reoline smiles at V and whispers to her, Alex, Declan, and Miko, "I'm going to give Sarcan a hard time. Watch." She stares at V and contacts Sarcan with her mind, saying, "Why the hell is it taking you so long to get them in their Jella suits?" A second later, Sarcan yells,

"Reoline, what the hell are you talking about? Quit messing with me." Reoline grins at the four of them. "See?" Declan exclaims, "That's incredible! What if you have a nagging mother-in-law always wondering where you are?" They all laugh. Reoline smiles. "You can turn off communications if you prefer, like your computer or tablet."

Everyone gets their G suits on. Sarcan and Reoline return to the front. Sarcan clicks the ship's coms on. "Alright, everyone, we get a few minutes of discomfort. Luckily, we traveled on one Thread this time. We've had to jump up to four Threads to get to Amotaious before. That wasn't fun. I've put the front camera on your personal monitors so you can see the planet as we arrive."

He checks the control panel to ensure that 30 green lights indicate all Jella suits are locked in. "We will disconnect from the Thread in less than 3 minutes. We will begin deacceleration in 5, 4, 3, 2..." V grabs Alex's hand. You hear Tonari cursing in Spanish. "1. SWOOSH! BOOM! CRACK! SNAP!" V sees a flashing white light fill the cabin. Her body is squished and then pulled forward.

She sees Alex breathing in through his nose and out through his mouth, grunting and groaning. About 2 minutes later, the ship slows down, and everyone sighs with relief. The ship's computer announces, "Disconnecting from Thread in 4, 3, 2, 1." V catches her breath as Jella is pulled out of her suit.

She looks at Alex. "That's crazy stuff." Alex smiles. "You okay?" V smiles back. "Yeah, you alright?"

Alex says, "I think I left a power bar in my shirt pocket, and it squished against my chest. I thought it was going to break my rib." He unzips the top part of the suit and shows V a flattened power bar. She laughs.

V watches as the ship approaches the massive new planet. It looks similar to Taraenti, with blue oceans, brown land masses, and spinning cloud formations, but it's about three times bigger. As they get closer, they see massive mountain ranges, similar to the Himalayas but much larger. Below the snow-capped peaks is a massive delta leading into a light blue ocean.

Closer now, looking into the foothills below the snow line, they see a massive valley on one side of the three rivers that lead to the delta. The ship circles the big mountains and descends into the valley.

On approach to the runway, the trees appear vastly different, towering, and colossal compared to ours. Six massive glass buildings loom to the left while the city nestles among an expanse of gigantic trees on the right. The city barely peeks through the canopy of enormous trees. The buildings, modest at five or six stories, resemble ancient Rome's architecture from 2700 years ago. Tramways weave throughout the city, some dipping below ground, but most elevated alongside the stone structures.

As they descend, V spots another ship launching like a rocket further down the valley. Unlike a transport ship, this massive brown and black vessel emits a huge plume of smoke as it ascends, likely a cargo ship.

V points excitedly out the window for Alex. "Look at that ship; it's enormous! That's crazy." Alex, rendered speechless, watches their ship's wheels touch down gently, providing a clear view of the airport through the front camera.

Out of the side windows, they observe a variety of ships, many of unique designs, except for two or three similar to theirs. Around 8-10 ships are out of their hangars, varying in size. As they taxi down the runway, they pass numerous large hangar buildings.

Proceeding to their designated hangar, they see a massive stone sign flanked by two huge Black Bears reading "Terraenti." Their ship veers right into a hangar with multiple doors.

Adjacent to the hangar stands a row of colossal pine trees dwarfing the already enormous hangar. These trees reach heights of 600 feet, towering over the ship, which itself spans 40-50 feet in diameter.

Guiding the ship into the hangar is a figure from CAT 5. Once the ship halts, Gig stands up. "Ensure your G suits are stowed under your seats."

Everyone rises, unzipping their Jella suits. As they finish, Gig's voice booms, "We are heading directly to Terraenti's main building, the Alcazar. Your Stewards will guide you to your rooms, and we will meet for dinner in the Alcazar's Dining Hall."

V steps out of the ship, taking in the sight of several other ships in the large stone hangar. The roofs are supported by massive timbers. V, Alex, Harvey, and Freida wait together for two men, likely from CAT 5, judging by their size, to unload their luggage and other items. They retrieve their belongings and walk through a door down a walkway lined with numerous windows.

As they walk, V marvels at the sheer size of the trees and the enormous leaves and flowers. All the foliage is much larger than anything V has ever seen. They ascend several flights of stairs to reach the rail system platform. A solid rail above, resembling a long cylindrical pipe, supports the system. Harvey explains, "We need to take a couple of pods to get there. Let's wait for the next one." Alex and V watch as a round, cylindrical pod sways into view, slows and stops with a crackling electrical noise and a chime indicating its arrival. The pod features cone-shaped windows at both ends and oval windows on the sides. It's suspended by two smaller cylindrical pipes, with the whole system elevated by tall, inverted J-shaped supports, reaching 30 to 40 feet in some areas.

Alex asks Harvey, "How does it work?"

Harvey replies, "The rail is magnetic, and the pod hovers within the pipe, never touching it. Two fusion thrusters, forward and aft, move the pod along."

Gig and most of the group enter the first pod. As the door closes, they hear Gig say, "Alcazar." The pod leaves with a forced air-thrusting noise. V, her mouth agape in amazement, looks around at the scenery and then at Freida. "The plants and trees are huge."

Freida points towards the forested slopes of the snow-capped mountains. "The trees up there are even bigger. Most of these in the city were planted only a few thousand years ago." She jumps at the sound of something hitting the ground—a football-sized pinecone has fallen beside them.

Harvey warns, "Watch out for them. You don't want to be under these trees during a windstorm." Alex and V exchange surprised glances.

Freida adds, "The climate here resembles the tropical forests of Terraenti's ancient past, millions of years ago." The second pod arrives, and they enter. Harvey sets his luggage down and grabs a leather handle hanging from the ceiling, gesturing for V and Alex to do the same. V drops her backpack, and Alex sets down two garment bags and a duffle bag containing the Accelerator prototype. They grasp the handles.

Harvey requests, "Alcazar, please."

The pod accelerates from the airport into the city, leaving the immense trees and foliage behind. The aft engines hum, pushing the pod forward, swaying slightly. Everyone remains silent as they enter the city. V notices the buildings have names instead of addresses, all constructed from stone with large timber roofs. As they approach, they see intricate engravings on the stones in front of the buildings—machines, animals, furniture, fruits, and vegetables.

They pass a building adorned with medical symbols. Approaching a grand edifice, the only one over seven stories high, V is awestruck by its beauty. Engraved below the roofline are symbols of planets, stars, and possibly many solar systems. V asks, "What's that building?"

Freida replies, "That's what we call the Castle, but its official name is Rah Shalah. It houses the Master Elders' offices and Council meetings. It's where we are meeting in the morning. Constructed by builders from all six planets, it's the largest building in the city."

A minute later, they arrive at a grand, red-stone building. The pod halts and announces, "Alcazar, Terraenti." Massive arched windows adorn the building, three stories above street level. The walls are intricately engraved with figures of animals that have roamed the planet for the last twenty thousand years: eagles, bears, mammoths.

Wales, various animals from Terraenti's past. They step out onto the covered platform, heading towards the upper entrance of the building. As they walk, they notice the building's center, an open atrium with several pools, a garden, bars, and sitting areas. It is exquisite. Gig and Fem' lead them down one side towards the back of the building.

Gig gestures to the rear as they walk. "This whole area is temporary housing; we'll be staying here for the next night or two." He leads them up a flight of stairs to the fourth floor and points down a long hallway lined with doors on both sides. "From here to the end of the hall are our suites. The rooms on the right overlook the atrium, while those on the left overlook the northeast side of the city. Your Stewards will help you choose your rooms."

Gig and Fem' enter a suite on the left. The Students, now relaxed, become loud, filling the hallway with noise. Harvey and Freida guide Alex and V towards the end of the hallway. Harvey stops and says, "You two take this one; we'll take the one overlooking the north of the city." He opens the door to a suite on the right. "Most of these suites have two bedrooms and two baths." He opens the French doors, revealing a view of the entire atrium. "The small kitchens should have everything you need." In the kitchen area, he opens a drawer and pulls out maps of the city and the Alcazar.

Freida unfolds a map. "Do you guys want to explore the residence? Here's a map of where everything is. Let's meet at the main restaurant at 7:00." She points to the restaurant on the map and whispers to V, "Remember to keep your extra Gift between us for now." Harvey adds, "We'll see you at dinner."

Harvey and Freida leave for their room. Alex turns to V, "What's this about an extra Gift?"

V responds, "Do you remember when I read your mind?" Alex nods, "Yes."

V continues, "Fem' told us that everyone could block me from doing it, and I tested it with Miko and some of the others. It's just that I've seen some things lately. Freida wants me to keep it between us: you, me, Harvey, Gig, Fem', and her."

Alex smiles, "I've been wondering about that. So, what is it? What have you been seeing?" V sits on the couch. Alex joins her, "I've noticed sometimes you look a little spaced out like you're somewhere else. Is that when you're in someone's mind?"

V stands and begins pacing, "The things I've seen are really weird. I'm not sure why the Creator has given me this Gift." Alex reassures her, "It can't be that bad. What is it? Tell me."

V looks at Alex, "You know the situation with your brother and my grandmother. I haven't told you the whole story yet. I think all of us have a similar story." Alex, confused, asks, "All of whom?"

V, upset, replies, "All the Students." She paces more, "I've looked into Lev, Declan, Prezzy, and Kyoryk, and they've all been involved in situations like ours." Alex, concerned, asks, "Like what happened with me and my brother? What did you do?"

V stops pacing, sits down, grabs Alex's hand, and looks at him. "Like you, when my grandmother died, I took it upon myself to find the guy who shot her, and I killed him. Lev killed a man as part of a family tradition."

"Prezzy poisoned a man. Declan—someone fell off a roof. And Kyoryk? Are we all like this? What does it mean? Do you want to have sex? What time is it?" She sits back, almost shaking. Alex chuckles and scoots closer, grabbing her hand, "Hey, calm down. It's okay. I don't know what it means. It sounds like we all had a damn good reason. Maybe that's why we were selected. Maybe it's one of the qualities they look for. Who knows?"

She hugs Alex, "I've never been able to talk to anyone about my situation before. No one." Alex hugs her back, "Anytime you want to talk about it, I'm here to listen."

She looks at him, "Why do you think the Creator gave me this Gift? Why is he showing me this about everyone?" Alex smiles, "We've only been here a couple of weeks. Who knows? I'm sure it means something. Just be patient. Harvey said things are moving fast, and they don't even know why a lot of these things are happening."

"We just need to keep our sanity and go along with it. We'll figure it out as time passes. Maybe you should take a break from reading people for now."

V smiles, "You're right. Taking a break sounds like a good idea. But it is interesting to know what people did." Alex, curious, asks, "What did Lev do? And Prezzy poisoned a man? That's crazy. And what did you do to the guy that killed your grandmother?" He looks off into the room. "Now, about that sex?"

V gets up from the couch and pushes him, "I don't want to talk about it anymore. I'll tell you later. I'm not ready to tell anyone my story." She looks out the big sliding glass doorway window. "No, no, not yet. That got way out of hand. I need to shut my eyes for a few minutes; the wine on the ship made me sleepy."

V walks into one of the bedrooms and lies down on the bed, thinking, *"Oh, my God! What's wrong with me? Am I having a nervous breakdown? Did I just ask him if he wanted to have sex? I am insane! If I told Alex what I did, he would surely think differently of me. He would truly think me an animal."*

"I need to wait as long as possible before I tell him that. That freakin guy that killed my grandmother. Okay. Get it together. Close your eyes. Take a break. Everything's okay. Focus on tomorrow."

She hears Alex say, "Look at the size of the beds. They must all be for people from CAT 5. Bahdubah and Klinchme' must like it." Alex sits back on the couch, puts his feet up on the table, and looks at the maps.

V gets up a little later. Alex and Declan stand on the balcony overlooking the atrium. Miko sits on the couch, looking at the maps. Miko greets her, "Hey, sleepyhead."

V replies, "I just closed my eyes for a minute and fell asleep. What are you guys doing?" Miko responds, "We were going to look around the place. Want to join?"

V agrees, "Sure. How long until dinner?" Miko answers, "About an hour." Miko stands up, looks at the guys, and says, "Hey, losers. Let's go." Declan exhales a thick cloud of smoke. V grins and asks, "Are they outside smoking?" Declan and Alex enter the room, marveling at the unique flora. "This place is incredible, with plants and trees unlike any we've seen," Declan remarks. Alex adds, "Did you see the front of the building?"

"The size of the red blocks—it's like Puma Punku. The carvings of various animals make this city fascinating."

V grabs the map. "Let's explore the Atrium." Declan asks, "Have you looked at the sky?"

They descend to the Atrium, wandering around the pools and waterfalls. They stop by a small bar near the pool and sit. Declan says, "Did you ever imagine us ending up here instead of our respective universities?" Alex chuckles, "Not in a million years." Miko laughs, "What I witnessed the other night changed everything—my perception of God, death, money, just about everything."

V ponders, *"I wonder how long we will live now? They haven't explained that to us."* A waiter approaches and asks if they would like something. V orders, "Could I have a coffee?" Alex follows, "I'll have a coffee as well." Declan glances at Miko, who smiles and says, "Two more."

The waiter returns with the coffee. Miko asks, "So, V, Alex, are you ready for tomorrow?"

The waiter, wearing clothes typical of CAT 3, gets excited. "Are you Alex and V, the new Elders?" V smiles, "Yes, we are. What's your name?"

"I'm Rally. My parents brought you here—they're pilots." Rally, a cute, dark-haired girl around 17, wearing clothes similar to Sarcan and Reoline's with bright purple moccasins, asks, "What was it like to see the Creator?"

V smiles, "We didn't actually see the Creator. It was a messenger." Rally continues, "I heard you talk to dead people?"

Declan laughs while Alex tries to keep a straight face. V explains, "Only twice, and it was just my grandmother who passed a couple of years ago. It was very exciting for both of us. We feel very grateful for the opportunity."

"Wow, that's wild. If you need anything while you're here, let me know." Rally waves her tablet towards V's tablet, "Here's my number. Anything you need, let me know."

V chuckles and smiles, "Thank you. We'll let you know."

Declan asks, "Do you have the same modifications as your parents?" She frowns, "No, just my tablet. It works with my clothes and stuff."

"We don't get the ISIs until our 23rd birthday." Declan questions, "ISIs?" She responds with a quirky face, "Internal System Implants." She frowns again, "I have to wait another seven years."

Miko says, "My parents didn't give me a tablet until I was your age." V laughs, "My parents gave me a tablet when I was five. They wanted me to understand the world."

Rally gives V a big smile, places a hand on her shoulder, and says, "Let me know if you need anything more." Declan says, "Thank you, Rally."

Alex looks at V, "So, do you understand now?" V looks confused, "Understand what?" Alex smiles, "The world, your parents?"

V laughs, "When I was her age, not a bit. Now? Back then they force-fed me all the good and bad of the world. Mostly the bad. My parents are crazy. And now I have to understand. The Worlds. Not just The World."

Declan says, "She was cute. Let's see if we can go to the roof. I want to check out the city since we can't leave Alcazar." Alex agrees, "That sounds good."

A few minutes later, they finish their coffee, and Rally comes to collect their cups. Declan asks, "How do we get to the roof?" Rally points towards the other end of the Atrium and says, "Down that way. Enter the gym; there's an elevator to the roof for running and stuff."

Declan asks, "Where do you live?" She pulls out her tablet, and a 3D virtual screen appears above the table. The four of them sit back, surprised.

Rally spins the map around with her hands and says, "We live on this side of the city, up against Rikers Ridge, pretty far up above the lake on the Terraenti side."

She zooms into a development of 30-40 large houses by a winding creek. "It's super nice. I have my own room; I can hear the creek at night." They look at the 3D images of the stone-walled, timber-roofed houses, each with five to six bedrooms.

Declan asks, "That's really cool. Do you have brothers or sisters?" She frowns, "I have four brothers, and they're all asses." Alex and V laugh. V says, "Don't worry. It will get better." Rally touches her tablet, and the image disappears. Miko says, "It was nice to meet you."

Rally grabs V's hand and shakes it, "It was really nice to meet you." She pushes the chair away and gives Alex a big hug, "It was really nice to meet you, Alex." She giggles and quickly walks away with the cups; they all chuckle, get up and walk away.

On the roof, they get a panoramic view of the city, with its massive buildings featuring large, tiled roofs over timber. They see a ship taking off from the airport on one side of the city. Beyond the city, they spot massive glass greenhouses and, on the other side, a towering mountain range.

Looking down five stories onto the street, they see many vehicles. Some are for one person, others for four or more. They all have caterpillar-type drives in the center, with seats above—no tires, just seats.

Alex gazes down and says, "I'd like to get a closer look at those vehicles." Declan inquires, "Do you think they're powered by electricity or fusion?" Alex shrugs, "No idea."

As they gaze into the distance, massive puffy clouds gather, bringing squalls of rain from the ocean. V marvels, "Look at the sky. It's green above but orange below." She looks up and sees three moons: one close, the other two farther away, one with a reddish hue.

Miko, fascinated, asks, "How many moons does this planet have?" Alex replies, "It has seven." Declan exclaims, "It's wild! It feels like you could reach out and touch that one."

They find a table and sit down to relax. Kyoryk, Maria, Swaraj, and Prezzy emerge from the elevator and join them. Kyoryk looks up at the moon, "Isn't it wild? This city, this planet, the moons—it's all so crazy."

Prezzy, sitting next to him, grabs his arm, "I think it's romantic." Swaraj laments, "Too bad we have to stay within the building. I'd love to go sightseeing."

V suggests, "Maybe we can convince our Stewards to let us explore a bit before the Council Meeting tomorrow." Alex looks around, "I just want to walk around a little." V muses, "Gig said no sightseeing, but I think he meant outside the city. We'll ask at dinner."

Prezzy proposes, "What are we doing tonight? Drinks by the pool after dinner?" Alex nods, "Maybe one drink. We shouldn't get too wild with the meeting tomorrow. But you guys can do whatever."

Alex looks at Kyoryk, "When does it get dark?" Kyoryk replies, "Tomorrow at 2:00 pm our time. Then it's dark for eight hours, like the northern hemisphere in summer—long days."

Declan asks, "Have you seen anyone from another planet yet?" Kyoryk answers, "Not yet, but tomorrow we'll see people from all the planets." V adds, "Maybe later or at dinner, we'll see some."

As they sit, the clouds roll in, bringing warm raindrops. V gets up and looks at Miko, "What are you wearing for dinner?" Miko rises, "Something casual, nothing fancy." V replies, "I have that green dress for tonight. Tomorrow, I'll wear my business suit for the meetings."

Miko smiles as they head to the elevator, "I like that green dress. It looks great on you."

They walk through the atrium back to their suites. Miko opens her room door and asks, "How's everything? How's your second Gift coming along? You haven't mentioned it lately." V, trying to be discreet, replies, "I haven't used it much. I'm not sure why the Creator gave it to me. Freida says to be patient and wait." Miko smiles, "I know, right? And who is this Creator?" She puts on some mellow music and makes tea. V sighs, "After tomorrow, I can't wait to get back to a normal routine. It's been overwhelming—one thing after another. I need a few days off, not thinking about the end of the world or how we're going to prevent it." Miko rummages through drawers for snacks, "Have you ever thought about what God wants?"

V laughs, "Doesn't He want to save people?"

Miko counters, "Why now? Before we came, civilizations disappeared. He didn't intervene on all six planets before. Suddenly, He wants to save this one? Why now?" She gestures dramatically in the small kitchen. V looks puzzled, then shakes it off, "What are you doing to me? I need to focus on tomorrow. You're freaking me out."

Miko laughs, "Sorry. Declan and I have been talking about it lately, that's all."

V says, "Alex has been really great with everything. I don't know what I'd do if I had to face tomorrow alone."

Miko reassures her, "I'm here for you too. Anything you need, just ask. How's Alex?" V confesses, "I asked Freida about the sex and how we all fell into relationships so quickly. She said it's normal for new Elders."

Miko laughs, "Declan wants to have sex all the time. Are you and Alex doing it every day? Twice a day?" V, shocked, replies, "Twice a day? No, not every day. The first day back on the planet was wild. We did it in the bathroom and climaxed together. He has a fun imagination—role-playing, things like that." Miko scoffs, "Declan always wants to sneak off and do it. We did it in the shower late one night." V laughs, "In the shower near our rooms at school? That's risky." Miko nods, "He loves taking risks—pool, hot tub, bathroom near the lab."

V laughs again, "I don't know if I can be that risky. I'd be afraid of getting interrupted." Miko says, "I'm the same, but Declan is a crazy man. Have you thought about anyone else? Kyoryk has a nice body." V admits, "I've never been very sexually active. I've had a couple of boyfriends and one girlfriend." Miko, surprised, asks, "Really? You had a relationship with another woman?" V smiles, "Not a relationship. It was more like a weekend thing, a couple of years ago, with a nurse when my grandmother was in the hospital. You have to experiment, right? She was super nice, and it was fun, but I wasn't into it like she was."

Miko shares, "I had an experience with two girls one night in Jakarta." She laughs, "It was just for fun, I guess." V says, "But here, with the Common Mind, I'm surprised we're not having orgies every other night. I've been very horny this past week." Miko ponders, "Do you think it's the Common Mind? I don't usually have this much sex, either. In high school, it was crazy. I didn't do it until I was sixteen, then it was all the time, like now." V remains silent. They both laugh.

Declan and Alex walk in. Declan inquires, "What's so funny?" V responds, "Miko wonders why God, the Creator, suddenly wants to save the planet. After thousands of years, billions of people across six planets, and countless species lost, why now?"

Alex and Declan pause, exchanging glances. Declan's mouth hangs open. Alex turns to him, "That's a question for after tomorrow." Miko laughs, "That's what V said."

Declan, stunned, exclaims, "You just blew my mind! We're all running around, but we never asked why. Why is he doing this now? Miko and I have been talking about this."

Alex muses, "How did it all start in the beginning? Do we develop consciousness? Did it just happen?"

"We started drawing art, growing crops, and writing. What the hell?" He paces, continuing, "The pool is super warm. Should we swim after dinner? I wonder about the beaches here." Miko suggests, "Next time, we can get one of those weird cars and find a beach, just the four of us." She gives V a playful smile.

Declan heads to the counter, checking the tea, "I want to go now. It's a shame we can't do that on this trip. But I want to have a deep dive discussion soon on that subject."

Alex declares, "I'm going to the room to rest before dinner."

V stands, "I'll join you." She smiles at Miko, "I'm sure Declan and Miko have things to do." Miko laughs, "Oh, yeah, Declan will think of something." As V and Alex leave, Declan asks, "What does that mean?"

Back in their room, after a short rest, V slips into a red dress. Alex, in black slacks and a leather jacket, peeks into the bathroom, "Nice dress. What's underneath?"

V smiles, "You'll find out later. I'm not walking to dinner all sweaty."

He enters, grabs her butt, and says, "Don't know if I can wait."

She turns, "Neither can I, but we should. The longer we wait, the better it will be." He frowns and leaves the bathroom. Minutes later, they head to dinner.

At dinner, the group splits into smaller tables of twelve. V, Alex, Declan, Miko, Prezzy, Swaraj, and their Stewards sit together at one of the tables. Towards the end of dinner, several individuals from another planet join and sit down for drinks.

Gig and Fem' join them. The man stands around 6'3" with a bird-like facial structure, his nose and mid-face pointed, multicolored hair flowing back as if in the wind, and round reddish eyes.

His large torso makes his limbs appear shorter. The woman, 5'9", shares his feathered multicolored hair and wears bright red lipstick. Their dark brown skin shifts to red around their necks, with much darker arms. Their tight, smooth outfits, white and yellow with black at the bottom, resemble Arctic animal fur.

Another couple with fur-like skin and wide-set eyes, large noses, and full lips have a cowboy-like strut. Their arms hang more to the front, and they wear worn-looking blackish leather, very elegant despite its weathered appearance. They all start talking.

V quietly asks, "Where do you think they're from?"

Swaraj, studying their features, guesses, "The first couple could be from Vindor or Vattan, and the second couple definitely from Kall."

Alex asks, "Isn't Kall the Ice planet?"

Swaraj confirms, "Kall is in a perpetual Ice Age. I'd need to investigate its history further." As the group monitors the others, V notices Gig signaling Harvey. Harvey, who had been sitting with them, moves to other tables. Gig introduces him to the newcomers, and he sits with them briefly.

A few Stewards start to leave, but the Students remain, curious about the Elders from other planets. Harvey approaches V and Alex's table, "Alex, V, Gig wants you to meet some of the Master Elders." V feels a surge of nerves. Alex stands, "Sure," and grabs V's hand. V thinks, *"Meeting aliens from another world, just breathe. It's all normal, right?"* She takes a deep breath as Alex helps her up, and they walk over to the table.

Fem smiles, and Gig, thrilled, introduces them, "This is Vibrean Aboli and Alexander Katz. V, Alex, meet Prinks and Merick from Vattan and Ferlnill and Muirlmont from Kall." V, nervous but trying to be polite, says, "It's a pleasure to meet you."

Alex shakes hands and echoes the sentiment. Prinks, standing and smiling, asks, "Are you two ready for the presentation tomorrow?" V grips Alex's hand tightly. Alex smiles, "We are. V, I and the others have been working hard to understand the Creator's wishes and how to achieve them."

V smiles at Alex, relieved, and adds, "The night the messenger visited us was quite a surprise." Prinks nods, "I bet it was. How was the experience?"

V admits, "It scared the hell out of us, to be honest."

They all laugh. Muirlmont, with a deep, slow, almost stuttering voice, asks, "So, what's your take on the messages, Alex?"

Alex takes a deep breath, "There's still a lot to figure out. The first message is to help the people of Terraenti get through this CAT."

"It seems there may be a bigger problem in the future, but we have years to prepare. Hopefully, we'll receive further messages to guide us in protecting all planets."

V declared, "We must keep working on the solutions to both messages. Hopefully, more guidance will come to help us." Muirlmont remarked, "Well, V and Alex, it sounds like we have a stellar group of new Elders tackling these challenges."

Ferlnill glanced at Gig, "It's remarkable they've only been here... what, three weeks?"

Gig smiled and nodded, "Yes, just three weeks into their training."

He turned to V and Alex, "Remarkable. Tell the other Students they should be very proud of themselves. We are fortunate to have the Creator paying so much attention to you all."

Gig continued, "We had to adjust our program due to the first Pulse Reversal, and the messages were a game-changer for their studies, but they are all doing exceptionally well." Merick added, "If you need anything from us, please let us know. Have you had a chance to explore Amotaious yet?"

V replied, "Not yet. This trip is mainly for the presentation. We need to return to the university and Terraenti soon. Next time, we look forward to exploring more and spending time with everyone. From what we've seen, it's an amazing planet."

Prinks chimed in, "The community here is growing. I can't get my grandkids to stop having babies." The four of them from the other planet laughed loudly. He continued, "It's been peaceful thus far. We welcome you. Please get together with us upon your return. We would love to show you the sights. It's a truly beautiful planet, and we've worked well together for many years."

Prinks and Merick smiled, and Ferlnill and Muirlmont both nodded and smiled. Ferlnill added, "Whatever you need, let us know."

V said, "We will, and thank you." Alex added, "It was a pleasure meeting you all." Muirlmont said, "See you in the morning."

Gig smiled at Alex and V, "Thank you two. See you in the morning."

V and Alex shook the offered hands and returned with Harvey to the other table. On the way back, Harvey said, "Great job, you two."

"You'll do fine tomorrow. Have some fun, get some rest, and if I don't see you later, we'll meet back here in the morning to quickly go over everything." Alex replied, "Thanks, Harvey."

V and Alex sat back down at the table. V admitted, "I need to get used to all this. That was brutal. I thought I was going to have a panic attack."

Alex reassured her, "You did fine. You were holding my hand pretty tight at the beginning. Tomorrow, we'll all be together. Just present it like you did yesterday, and you'll be fine." Miko suggested, "It looked like everything went okay. What made you nervous?" V smiled, "That's the thing. I'm not really sure."

Declan offered, "Well, I have a solution to your nervousness—drinks by the pool, watching the moons go by."

He looked at Miko, "Unfortunately, honey, you'll have to get your bathing suit on. We don't want Alex getting all riled up." Miko laughed and looked back at Declan, "You're the one always riled up. You need to take a chill pill. You're wearing me out." Declan stood up, "Me? You're the one." Miko playfully hit him in the chest.

The rest of them got up. V asked, "Where did Prezzy and Swaraj go? Are they going to meet us there?" Declan replied, "I think the whole group will join us at some point."

V and Alex went up to their rooms to change and then down to the pool. V sat at a table and ordered drinks. Alex, Miko, and Declan sat down.

V said, "It was interesting meeting the Elders from the other planets." Alex added, "I wasn't expecting to meet Master Elders. We still need to see what the others are like—the Elders from Vindor, Regnolm, and Eldulcan."

Declan remarked, "They were extraordinarily striking. It still blows my mind that we're here." He looked up at the two moons visible within the atrium. "It's surreal." He turned to Miko, "Think how much our lives have changed in the last three weeks."

Prezzy jumped into the pool. Miko commented, "This is not normal. With the Common Mind, I feel really close to all of you. Usually, it would take a long time for me to open up to a group, but now it's different. You're all like my family."

Alex added, "The Common Mind is very powerful. There's a connection between us all now, and it's getting stronger."

"That first night when we received our Eagle Marks," he looked at V, "When I was fixated on V for the first time. I swear she looked different after she received the mark. Did anyone notice as well?" V smiled at him, "All I remember is you kept on looking at me." Declan laughed, "I don't remember that." Miko is looking for the waiter, "You think it changed our looks?" Alex smiled at V, "She just seemed to glow after that, and I knew I had to get to know this beautiful creature." V with her mouth wide open in awe. Swaraj biting his fingers, Miko says, "Alex man, V told me you were a romantic but come on. In public." Alex looked bewildered. "I'm serious. She changed after she received the Eagle Mark. She was touched by God. Everyone was." V says, "Is that when you knew I was the one?" Alex slams his hand on the table. "Yes, absolutely." She gives him a loving smile. "I won't know until you give me the $2 you owe me. She laughs. Swaraj asks, "What the hell are you guys talking about?"

V looks at him, "It's all part of the plan, supposedly. This has happened with every new group of Elders. The relationships, the way we feel for each other. Freida told me it's all normal. It's the Creator's design for us to be this way."

A waiter approached, "Can I get you some drinks?" Everyone was taken aback by his appearance. He stood 6'5" with a flat face, a small nose, and ears more above his head than at his sides. His torso and head seemed to merge into one. He had small, round roseate eyes, tiny feathers smooth looking for his skin, huge shoulders, and long arms almost down to his knees. He was a very built guy, the fat of his legs positioned more to the front of his body, smaller, shorter continued in a unique, unusual way. Despite this, he was quite attractive.

Alex smiled, "What's a fun drink here? What do you recommend?"

In a squeaky, bird-like voice, he responded, "I like the beer from Vindor called Kicker." V asked, "Are you from Vindor?"

He smiled and stood in a funny manner, with his head out in front, and he kept putting one leg out in front of him for some reason. His posture was sound and strong, though. "Yes, I am. And you're the new Elders from Terraenti?" V smiled back, "Yes, I'm V. This is Alex, Miko, Declan, and Swaraj."

He shook V's hand, "I'm Jonsockly Trigger Mingrey. Everyone calls me J.T., except my girlfriend from Terraenti—she calls me Jonny." He spoke quickly, almost too fast to understand, not because of his English, but his speed and squeaky voice.

V, surprised by his openness, smiled politely, "Does Vindor have a red wine?" J.T. smiled, "The one I like is green, but it's good. Sorry, my Terraenti isn't great. It's called G-Velela."

V said, "I think you speak Terraenti very well. Let's have three Kicker beers and three G-Velela wines." Declan chuckled and asked, "What's Vindor like?" J.T. replied, "It's nice. I've only been there once. We studied your planet in school. Our planet is different, even from here. We work very fast-paced for about three hundred days. Then, for sixty-eight days, every family takes off to practice for the Trinop. After that, we meditate for another thirty days. That's when our four moons semi-eclipse over the Sea of Valdorn. I'll get your drinks."

Declan commented, "I need to study more about the different cultures of the planets." V and Miko laughed. V added, "The wine is green?" Swaraj interjected, "I've read a little about that. The whole family gets involved, even the mothers and daughters. The Trinop is a tower in the middle of a stadium or coliseum."

"The family battles to get to the top, beating the other family with clubs. It's like our baptism or coming-of-age tradition. When a child turns a certain age, they can enter the Trinop. Some battles last for many hours. If you get knocked out or off, you're out of the game. It's very strategic. The family member at the top of the Trinop for a certain time wins. It's all set up in a big arena that everyone watches. It's very bloody. Certain families have battled the same other families for hundreds of years."

Declan mused, "I need to look into that. It sounds fascinating."

V remarked, "It doesn't sound like any baptism I've ever heard of. It sounds more like a bloody battle but with the whole family. Like our planet in Viking times or something?" J.T.

returned with the drinks, having overheard some of the conversation. He said, "We have fought to the death, but that only happens once every twenty-four years on V-Day. It's very bloody."

V and Miko shook their heads. Miko asked, "Do you have wars? Like different countries fighting each other over land or religion, like on our planet?"

J.T. explained, "We do, but on my planet, it's over territory and families. It's never been about religion. We have one government with many different strong families. I grew up here on Amotaious, so I have perspectives from all the planets and their different cultures. We are all one galaxy of people now." J.T. smiled, "My girlfriend and I even write tunes about it. Things are changing. You all are a part of that now."

Declan inquired, "Which planet do you find the most interesting?" J.T. answered, "My girlfriend is from Terraenti, so I like how strong the Elducans look. One of my favorite things to watch is the racers on Vattan. For days, they race through storms and big waves. The vehicles go underwater, on the water, and can fly in the air. It's crazy fun to watch."

He noticed Alex's tablet on the table, pulled his own tablet out of his apron, and typed. He waved his hand over his tablet towards Alex's, saying, "You can see for yourself. This is last year's finale."

Alex smiled, "Thanks." Prezzy returned from the pool. Alex projected the image onto the 3D display above the table, and everyone watched the racers go through the water, then up into the air, and back underwater.

This also caught the attention of some other Student Elders. Declan turned up the volume as they all watched the races. After a minute or two, V, frustrated, turned down the volume on the tablet and addressed J.T., "Are your parents Master Elders or regular Elders?"

J.T. replied, "My grandfather and grandmother were Master Elders on my father's side." Prezzy flirtatiously asked, "What is the population of Amotaious now?"

J.T. responded, "I believe it's just over a hundred thousand now." He noticed some Stewards walking up with other Elders from Amotaious and glanced back at the bar. "I should get back. Let me know if you like the beer and wine."

V and Miko sipped the green wine. Miko commented, "It tastes good, like fruity schnapps, but it's not wine. What's the beer like?"

Alex said, "It's more like our sodas, with brown sugar and carbonation." V laughed, "What does that mean?"

Alex laughed, "It tastes like carbonated Jägermeister, and it's dangerous." Declan laughed, "No, it's sweet, but maybe like Kahlua?"

V grabbed the beer from Alex and tasted it. "That's good. I like it better than the wine."

Declan wondered, "What's the alcohol content?" Miko tasted Declan's beer. "That is better." She got up and said, "I'm going to get one of those." V called out, "Get me one too."

An hour later, everyone was a bit livelier. Miko came back from the bar a little tipsy and set down four glasses next to the hot tub. She sat next to V and said, "These are called Red Eye Ale from Crownar." V remarked, "It feels weird."

Alex laughed, "Is Miko doing that thing again under the water? I told her to keep her hands to herself."

V said, "No, seriously, all this sun. For weeks, we've had artificial light. Now we have the real thing, and it's not even the sun we normally have. Or the sky we normally have. It's yellow-orange with blue, not pure blue. I wonder what this is doing to our skin."

Alex commented, "I don't think they've fully developed artificial sunlight that gives us everything we need yet." Miko asked, "So the skylights in our rooms and in the common room are trying to simulate the sun?"

V, feeling the effects of a few drinks, said, "I asked Kyoryk about it. He said the lights we have now are close but not one hundred percent of what we need—UVA and UVB light. I don't know; he went on and on about it."

Declan laughed, "I wonder what we'd look like if we lived underground for a few generations." Alex laughed, "I think I remember a movie where the people were all pale with big eyes. Of course, without sunlight, we'd all die."

"You can't live underground without some kind of artificial sunlight. Weird food would grow. You'd have to eat people. Then your teeth would rot out, and then?"

Alex closed his eyes and started yelling, "Soylent Green! Soylent Green!" V hit him playfully, "Shut up, that's ridiculous. You're just making stuff up now."

Lin, from a nearby table, yelled, "That's one of my dad's favorite movies, Charles Hexton!" Declan and Miko laughed. Declan said, "No, you've heard of the lizard people that live underground near JPL in Los Angeles. I've seen pictures."

V scoffed, "Little green men. Here we are on another planet with other civilizations. They look a little different, but we all still have ten toes and ten fingers." Alex laughed, "I only have nine toes and seven and a half fingers."

Miko laughed heartily and asked, "What's the scariest alien movie you've seen?" Alex replied with a grin, "Body Snatchers was insane. If you fall asleep, the aliens take over your mind." He then exclaimed loudly, "And Lin, it's Charlton Heston's not whatever you said; he was most popular from the movie, Planet of the Apes! He was also in Earthquake."

V chimed in, "I saw one where a fungus was discovered deep in the earth. The miners got infected first, and if you were infected, you'd grow this enormous mushroom head." V stood up, mimicking a mushroom bobblehead, eliciting laughter from everyone.

As Prezzy and Swaraj joined them in the hot tub, Prezzy asked, "What are you talking about? Mushroom heads?"

V responded, "We're discussing aliens and scary movies."

Swaraj chuckled, "Have you seen the black-and-white version of The Walking Dead? That was intense." Prezzy added, "You need to watch the original Blob movie."

V looked puzzled, "What's that?" Prezzy laughed, "It's just a big red blob that eats people and animals. As it moves around the city, it keeps getting bigger and bigger."

Declan interjected, "I had a dream like that. Every time I ate something, I'd get bigger and bigger." V laughed, "What happened?"

Declan explained, "When I was a kid, I'd get these fevers, like 104, 105 degrees." V interrupts, "No, what happened to the Blob?" Prezzy gets excited and starts waving her hands around, "So, after like 20 people are eaten by the red blob, they figure out that, you know, like those certain fire extinguishers, the cold ones that shoot out the CO_2 white stuff can stop it. They realize it's the cold."

"So, they transport the whole dam thing to the Arctic Circle with a helicopter." V laughing. "Where did it come from?" "Oh, it started out like this big. Then it was the size bigger than a bus." She, Prezzy, holds up her fist. "It was a Meteor, and the guy who found it ended up dying; it ate his arm first, then his dog." She laughed, "It was a great movie, "The Blob." 1958." Declan stares at V. She looks at him, "Okay, so, when you were a kid, you had really bad fevers, like a hundred and ten." Declan scoffed; a hundred and five, the sensation in my body was overwhelming like I weighed a thousand pounds. I couldn't move; it was terrifying." Alex laughed, "I can see how it affected you now. You eat like a bird—pick, pick, peck."

Declan continued, "It was so bad; I didn't eat ice cream or candy for years." They all laughed.

V shared, "I had a dream that I could jump really far, like over buildings and stuff."

Declan added, "Then my dreams changed to this really thin man. It was like I was really tall but had stick arms and legs."

Miko laughed, "After that, you could eat ice cream and candy again?" Declan smiled.

Prezzy said, "I have this dream where I'm in a box, and I can't get out. So, I poke a hole in the box to look out and see a bunch of other boxes with holes and eyes peering out, trying to escape."

Alex burst into hysterical laughter, "What is wrong with you people? Thin men, stuck in a box—that's insane."

V laughed, "I had one where I had really big feet and worried about stepping on my dog." They all laughed.

Alex got out of the hot tub and jumped into the pool, saying, "You all are crazy. Now I'm going to have weird dreams."

V and Miko finished their drinks and got into the pool. V remarked, "The water feels so nice; it's the perfect temperature." She noticed Swaraj and Prezzy making out and said, "I should probably get Alex and get some rest."

Miko teased, "I won't get any rest; Declan will be all over me." V quipped, "Are you sure it's not you that's all over him?" Miko smiled, "Well, maybe a little."

Declan jumped into the pool, splashing them. Miko swam to him and started kissing him.

V looked at Alex and asked, "Ready to go upstairs?" Alex smiled, "Sure. Do you want some mint chip ice cream or fudge?"

V smirked, "Oh, you think it's going to be the best night ever?" Alex kissed her and said, "I have a game I want to play, but I'm not telling you what it is until we get upstairs."

V kissed him back, "Alright, sounds interesting." They left the group and went upstairs. In their room, Alex was in the bathroom. V walked in and asked, "So, what's this game you want to play?"

Alex smiled mischievously, "We shower together. I wash you, you wash me, but we can't kiss or do anything else." He grabbed two small washcloths from the counter. "Then we dry each other with these, still no sexual or skin contact. Whoever doesn't make any sexual contact wins."

V laughed, taking off her clothes. "You're going to lose for sure. You won't handle it. You will lose, mister."

Alex smiled, "Either way, I won't be a sore loser." She turned on the shower. V got under the shower, acting all sexy, rubbing her hands all over her body and singing, "You're gonna lose, you are gonna lose."

Alex got into the shower, "I'm very strong-willed." She started soaping him up, whispering, "You think you are, huh?" She finished soaping him and looked him up and down. "Okay, do me, do me."

Alex tried to remain strong. V insisted, "Do me, do me," switching from English to Hindi. Alex protested, "Shoosh, that's cheating."

V whispered, "You never said that was against the rules. You won't even make it to the drying part."

Alex started soaping V's body. She pointed down, "Get that area really good." He knelt to wash the bottom half of her, whispering to himself.

"This is going to be harder than I thought." V asked, "What did you say?" Alex tried to soap her up quickly. V laughed, "Wow, what are you doing? You can't hurry through it. You need to wash properly. Didn't your mother teach you that?" She switched to Hindi again.

Alex stood up in front of her, "No Hindi, you're definitely cheating now." He tried to slow down the washing, "My mother never taught me anything like this."

V laughed and said, "When women are aroused, they can hide it, but men can't." She glanced down and teased, "See what I mean?" They stepped out of the shower, and V grabbed the tiny washcloth, attempting to dry him off. She laughed and added, "This little towel won't dry you off. Maybe if I blow on you?" She began blowing on his neck.

Alex, struggling to maintain his composure, said, "No blowing! That's not fair." He stepped back, tickled by her breath on his neck, and declared, "Now I dry you."

She smiled seductively and whispered, "But you're not dry yet." He murmured, "I'm dry enough." Kneeling, he began drying her legs, working his way upward. As he turned her around to dry her back, he accidentally touched her with his...

V giggled, "I felt that."

Alex, flustered, said, "It was an accident." He attempted to continue drying her but couldn't resist any longer. He started kissing her neck.

She enjoyed it for a moment before remembering their game. She pushed him back and exclaimed, "You lose!" She dashed out of the bathroom almost slipping on the floor, shouting, "Get away from me, you crazy sex fiend!" She jumped onto the bed and slipped under the sheets. He chased her, sliding under the covers with her and said, "You're all wet."

She laughed, kissed him, and said, "I know you didn't do a very good job of drying me off." They kissed for a moment, and she asked, "You never told me what the winner gets."

He pulled her so she was on top of him and admitted, "I never got that far when I thought up the game. Plus, you cheated."

She gazed at him under the sheets, feeling the warmth of their bodies, and said, "I guess this is an okay prize." She moaned and added, "I understand the game now."

Alex moaned and promised, "I'll give you your prize in the morning."

As she moved rhythmically on top of him, she moaned louder, "In the morning, huh? This game keeps going on and on." She paused, "Aren't you giving me my prize now? How about I give you a special prize in the morning?"

He smiled, pulled her down so she was beneath him, and said, "I'm satisfied being the loser of this game. I'll think of a surprise to give you soon. How about that?"

V's only response was a pleasurable moan and a few words in Hindi. Alex kissed her all over and pulled the sheets entirely over them.

The evening came to a blissful end.

XIV

Alex woke up and walked into the room, spotting V at the table, sipping coffee with her computer out. She smiled and asked, "Do you want some coffee?" "Sure. How long have you been up?" he replied. V stood and poured him a cup. "Just a few minutes. Breakfast is in half an hour; we should get ready."

Alex smiled, taking a sip of coffee. "What about my prize? You promised me one." V laughed, "Your prize? You lost, Mr. Loser. You owe me a surprise."

Alex looked confused. "Oh, that's right. I did lose, didn't I? Well, I'll have to think of something. I'll use my wild imagination." V, typing on her computer, said, "I'm ensuring this program runs smoothly." She glanced at the video and added, "You have a good imagination. I'm sure you can think of something delightful for me."

Alex assured her, "It will be fine. You are going to be great." She closed the computer, teasing, "What do you mean, I am going to be great? Aren't I great already? Wasn't I great last night?" Alex grinned, "The greatest." V smirked, "There you go. Now let's get ready and go to breakfast."

After breakfast, they received permission to explore the city for a couple of hours before the meeting. They walked across a few streets to where the shops were. All the shops were run by private owners. Most were small and catered to certain planets. Some larger ones sold clothes or groceries, reminiscent of a small-town main street. Alex, V, Harvey, and Freida strolled together. The Students dispersed, entering different shops. Alex paused to examine a particular one-person vehicle parked in front of a store.

"How does it operate?" Alex asked Harvey.

Harvey explained, "This one has an electric motor in the rear that drives the track. The whole thing is balanced by a gyrostabilizer in the back of the seat and frame."

Alex inspected the vehicle closely. It had one bucket seat with a frame built around it. There was no steering wheel or dashboard, no wheels but a track or frame below that resembled many legs of a caterpillar.

"How is it powered?" Alex inquired. "It's electric. Most of the vehicles here are AVs," Harvey replied. "Yeah, but if you need to, can you drive it?" Alex asked.

Harvey pointed inside the vehicle. "See the armrest? It has a small joystick for manual control." V chimed in, "AV?"

"Autonomous Vehicle. I've ridden in a four-seater. They have all kinds of different vehicles on this planet," Harvey explained.

Moments later, Alex looked back for V and Freida. They were petting an animal with a woman and her child. It looked like a very large raccoon. As Harvey and Alex approached, the woman and child walked away.

"What was that?" Alex asked.

"She called it a Nibit. It has the size and shape of a large dog but has the markings of a raccoon on its eyes and tail," V explained. They all entered what appeared to be a family-run furniture store. Some of the furniture looked normal, so to speak—handcrafted, with amazing tables and chairs, mainly made from wood. There were also carved stone tabletops and end tables.

"How does money work here if you wanted to buy something for your house?" V asked Freida, running her hand along a marble table.

Freida smiled. "They don't use money here. It's a barter system, or things are simply gifted. Families trade services. Most families have trades, and everyone works for the community. A lot of it started from resources from the original planets. Now it's all self-sustaining. Kids learn different trades in school or from their parents and then take over or help in other jobs on the planet. Or they start their own. It's a small population. Growing food, processing—much of it is done by machines designed by different planets. Have you read about communities on our planet that are self-contained and self-sustaining?"

"Like a commune?" V asked.

"Something like that. It's been working here for around fifteen thousand years," Freida replied. "When the Elders have kids, do they have Gifts or extended lives?" Alex asked. Freida answered, "Just the Common Mind and extended lives. No extra Gifts."

"So, if I invent something really popular or widely used, I don't make any money?" Alex questioned.

Harvey responded, "It would be great if you invented something everyone used, but why would you need a lot of money here? You already have everything—food, medical needs, everything. If you need to go back to the planet for something, it's provided within reason. You don't need gold toilet seats; that's an Earther thing. Understand?"

Alex and V nodded in agreement. Freida smiled, holding up a wood carving of a peculiar sailboat. "The only time I needed money last year was back on the planet, and Alva provided everything."

"Where does Alva get its money?" V asked.

Harvey sat down in a spectacular large wooden rocking chair. "Alva Global Industrial goes way back. They have all the resources and money needed. It's not something we need to worry about. They have investments, properties, mineral rights."

"It's the oldest company on Earth. Rev and Mod control everything, and they were on our planet before CAT 2. All the Elders have similar arrangements on their planets. You'll meet them eventually."

V admired a hand-carved headboard. "Look at this bed. It's incredible, all hand-carved." She began to ask, "How much does this cost?"

Freida interrupted, "If you like it, you order it, or tell them how you want it, and they build it for you. Whatever way you want. Remember, you now have a lot of time. You and Alex will develop your trades here and do the same—run a business, make things, manage projects, whatever. It takes a while, but you start thinking about things differently. Harvey and I have been here for a year, and I still think monetarily sometimes."

Alex, after looking at a copper art piece of Amotaious's solar system on one of the tables, looked up at Harvey. "I think we get it, especially here. The system is so different, and the Master Elders make up the government in a way."

Harvey and Freida smiled as they walked out of the store. Alex began to understand how life was going to change. They saw Miko, Declan, Kira, and Hugh.

Declan, excited, said, "You guys should see the stuff in the store we just visited." Alex pointed to the store, "Super nice things in there as well. You could fill your whole house."

Back at the Alcazar, Alex and V returned to their room, taking a final moment to prepare and change into their business attire.

Harvey and Freida knocked on their door, and together, they made their way to the third floor, heading towards the rail system where others were waiting. They all boarded the Pod. Alex set down the duffle bag containing the sample Accelerator and grabbed the handle. Harvey requested, "Rah Shalah, please."

Alex remarked, "I thought it was called the Castle?"

Harvey replied, "I'm not sure that would work. That's what we call it, but last time we were here, Fem' just spoke to the pod saying, Admin building. Since then, I found out the true name is Rah Shalah, which is what most of the population uses."

In the pod, Harvey turned to them and said, "Are you two ready? It's just the four of us now. Let's get through it, and if you need any assistance, let us know. Everyone should be relaxed in the meeting."

"It was that way a week or so ago, so I don't see why today would be any different." V and Alex smiled, and Harvey and Freida smiled back. V reassured, "We are prepared. We should be fine."

They exited the pod and were greeted by an attendant. As the doors opened, they entered the building and paused to look out over the balcony from three stories up. The building buzzed with activity. Someone noticed Alex and V standing at the top of the balcony, and eyes began to peer upwards, but then attention shifted to two massive doors opening at the far end of the entrance. The doors, towering and adorned with carvings of the faces of the Master Elders, were truly impressive.

As the people entered, Alex marveled at a huge killer whale floating in mid-air, accompanied by its calf. Several other creatures, which Alex assumed were sea creatures from other planets, also floated in mid-air with their offspring.

Intrigued, Alex asked, "How are they floating in the air? I don't see any cables or anything holding them up." Harvey chuckled, "I wondered the same thing."

Alex continued to look around, noting the six massive round stone pillars evenly spaced throughout the building, each carved with the names and animals of the six planets. The floor, a striking light purple and blue marble, featured four sets of stairs. The two outer stairs wrapped around to the upper floor, while the inner stairs wrapped around to the middle floor. All the stairs were made from white marble, with dark blue and green inlays.

The walls were adorned with large tapestries depicting various types of agriculture and farming methods from all six planet, reminiscent of fields from the USA, China, Iceland, and Holland.

V glanced at Alex and then at Harvey, smiling. "Is he going to be okay?" she asked.

Harvey replied, "I think he likes the building."

Alex, unable to tear himself away from the view, finally looked at them and smiled. "It's like part ocean and part earth. Fascinating." He pushed himself off the rail. "You guys ready?"

V smiled, "Take your time."

Harvey said, "This way. The offices are on the top four floors above the theater, and there is a massive library in the basement. We'll have to see those another time."

Entering the theater, they found a large half-round table set up for them with four chairs. Alex observed that they were a half level below everyone else.

In front of them sat the Master Elders in twelve massive hand-carved wooden chairs, with additional seats behind them for the retired Master Elders. The theater, with its three levels of seating, had stones so large it boggled the mind how they were mined or put into place. The ceiling was constructed from enormous timbers, reminiscent of a log cabin but with logs seventy or eighty inches around.

Alex took the mini mockup Accelerator out of his duffle bag, along with both computers from the smaller backpacks, and set them on the table. As they were setting up the equipment, a technician came over to help with the microphones and other connections to the computers.

Harvey looked up at the massive hall. "Looks different from down here."

Alex asked, "Where did you sit last time you were here?" Harvey pointed up. "On the third level, and there were about a thousand people here." Alex asked, "How many people does it seat in total?" Harvey replied, "I think around five, six thousand? And it should be packed today. The 3D virtual screen will come up in the center of the room right above us."

Gig and Fem' walked in and joined the four of them. Gig looked at Harvey. "Okay. How is everyone today?" V and Alex responded, "We are fine, ready to go." Gig asked, "You all hooked up?" V, putting on her mic, replied, "We are getting there."

The technician woman said, "Let's test the mics."

Alex said, "Test, test." She tested V, then Harvey and Freida. "Go ahead and pull up your presentation," she instructed. V typed on her computer, and a massive 3-dimensional virtual display appeared above them.

The technician advised, "It's best to keep looking at your computer screen rather than the big display. Just relax, and you will do fine." She showed them how to run the controls, spent another minute with them, then smiled and walked away.

Gig looked around as people filled the hall. Someone else came out and placed glasses and pitchers of water on the table. Fem' asked, "What did you think of the city? Did you have a chance to look around?"

V replied, "We visited a few smaller shops. Saw some beautiful handmade furniture. The vehicles, everything is quite different from our planet."

Fem' said, "Yes, it's a unique place indeed. Very peaceful, the environment is similar, truly an Eden in time."

Gig and Fem', looking slightly nervous, exchanged glances. Gig said, "Okay, well, let's give it to them and see what they say. You're going to do just fine. We'll come back down after the presentation. Okay?" They walked away as the Elders' Hall filled.

Harvey observed, "I think Gig and Fem' are more nervous than we are." Freida and V smiled. Alex added, "Possibly, he did say 'okay' more than a couple of times."

A few minutes later, most of the Master Elders, along with the retired Master Elders, had taken their seats.

V and Alex surveyed the diverse assembly in the hall before taking their seats alongside Harvey and Freida. Gig and Fem' joined the other Elders of Amotaious, who had already settled into their places. Over five thousand attendants filled the hall. The Master Elders sat about twenty to thirty feet in front of them, almost a story up.

Fem' and Gig hailed from Terraenti, Prinks and Merick from Vattan, Ferlnill and Muirlmont from Kall, Lorness and Blain from Vindor, Minter and Rall from Regnolm, and Letsa and Alder from Elducan. Each Elder occupied a massive, intricately hand-carved wooden chair, some adorned with weapon motifs and others with animals. The chairs from Kall resembled giant ice crystals, adding to the spectacle. The Elders conversed amongst themselves as the crowd roared with anticipation.

Alex glanced at V, who exchanged looks with Harvey. Harvey noticed Gig whispering to Fem' as the lights dimmed. Alex squeezed V's hand under the table and whispered, "Here we go."

The crowd hushed. Gig struck a stone gavel against his armrest, further dimming the lights. A spotlight illuminated him from an unseen source.

"Welcome to Master Elders Hall," Gig began. "Over our time in this galaxy, we have received few messages from our Creator, Raba Rashi." The crowd echoed reverently, "Raba Rashi."

Gig continued, "Today, we gather to discuss and evaluate the findings from Terraenti's new Elders—the twelve Elders of CAT six." The audience erupted in applause and cheers, chanting, "CAT six," "Elders of CAT6," and "Terraenti." V and Alex exchanged surprised smiles. Alex squeezed her hand reassuringly.

Gig struck the gavel again, restoring order. "Recently, we received two messages from the Creator," he announced.

"We are here to assess the Creator's plans to strengthen Terraenti's Magnetic Field, protecting the planet from Catastrophe 6, or at least minimizing its impact."

"Until now, our Creator's Directive and Laws forbade interference with any of our six planets' Catastrophe cycles."

Gig paused, surveying the vast theater. "But these are extraordinary times. Never has our Creator, Raba Rashi." The crowd softly echoed, "Raba Rashi, bowing their heads in reverence. "Sent us a messenger instructing us to change our Directive and Laws. We must decide today. A unanimous vote—Yay or Nay—on proceeding with these new plans. We have little time to waste."

He raised his hand and index finger. "This decision will empower our newest and brightest, chosen by the Creator, to follow their path and complete their task. I say let them do it. What say you?" He waved his hand, inciting the crowd.

The audience erupted, chanting, "Let them do it!" "CAT 6!" "Creator's Plans!" "Alex and V!" Several Master Elders shook their heads in protest, mouthing, "No, no!"

Gig lowered his hand, sat for a moment, and struck the rock gavel once more. The crowd settled. He stood again. "Today, presenting their findings are our newest Students, Elder Vibrean Aboli, Elder Alexander Katz, Elder Steward Freida Asmij, and Elder Steward Harvey Goldmen." Applause and cheers erupted once more, with chants of "CAT6, Terraenti," "V and Alex," and "New Elders."

Alex noticed V's nervousness as she let go of his hand and stood. She focused on Gig and Fem', smiling for reassurance. Fem' smiled back. The crowd gradually quieted. V cleared her throat and waited a few more seconds until the hall was silent enough for her to speak.

She glanced at Alex, who smiled encouragingly. "You got this," he mouthed.

V turned on her mic. "We live in extraordinary times. Not just for us," she gestured to Alex, Harvey, Freida, and around the amphitheater, "But for the entire galaxy. We received a message about Terraenti," she said, activating the display. A 3D visualization of Terraenti and its solar system appeared, then expanded to show all seven civilizations in the galaxy. "And another message about all planets supporting life and consciousness in our galaxy."

The visual remained as V took a deep breath and looked back at Gig, Fem', and the other Master Elders. "On the fifth night at our university.

"Alex, I, and the other Students were overwhelmed with worry and fear about the impending Catastrophe and its impact on our loved ones and the entire planet. Alex, in particular, was deeply concerned. We believed we had three years, but now we know otherwise."

An artist's rendition of the messenger above the pool appeared. "We were visited by a messenger from the Creator while at our university's pool. Within seconds, an image appeared like this and spoke to us: 'The information you seek is in the library.'"

The Elders and the audience listened intently as V recounted the entire experience, including her interaction with her grandmother. Not a single person interrupted her narrative.

V concluded, "We believe the Creator is urging us to use this method to increase our magnetic field and protect our planet during the next Super flare." She took another deep breath, scanning the hall. "Last Friday, while preparing to watch a movie at the university, one of my ancestors, through one of my Gifts, foretold the messenger's return. We gathered everyone to witness it. Here is the video Harvey shot that night."

As the video played, murmurs of astonishment rippled through the Master Elders and the crowd. V looked at Alex and Freida, smiling. Alex squeezed her hand in support, noting that many had come to see this video and perhaps meet them.

The video ended, and V said, "As you heard, our entire galaxy is in jeopardy, not Terraenti alone. According to the messenger, we have eighteen years. All life in our galaxy could be eradicated. But we have time to address this."

V gazed up at the Master Elders. "We don't have much time to consider the first message concerning the Creator's Plans. This event will unfold within the next year or so. We estimate three to five months before the next Pulse Reversal. We need to test the accelerator, evaluate its function, and increase the magnetic field."

"We must conduct these tests by the fourth and sixth months, during the third Pulse Reversal. We are somewhat positive we will receive another message within that period."

She scanned the amphitheater once more. "We are merely fulfilling the Creator's directives."

With a sigh of relief, she concluded, "That's it for the presentation. We can now answer any questions. Thank you." The Students erupted in applause, hoots, and howls. Fem' and Gig began clapping and slowly stood, prompting the rest of the crowd to follow.

V displayed images of Terraenti's beauty and its people on the screen. After a moment, Gig said, "Thank you, V, Alex, Harvey, Freida, and all the others from the university, for your hard work and diligence."

Blain and Lorness from Vindor stood. Both resembled Jonny, whom the Students had met serving drinks at the pool at the Alcazar. Blain, taller and much older, had more pronounced features. Standing over seven feet tall, his face was more rounded with a small, hard, almost shell-like nose above his mouth, resembling an eagle's beak. His medium, circular eyes contrasted his smooth skin, which sported hues of yellow, brown, and white akin to fine feathers. His body, all torso, had huge shoulders, long arms, and shorter legs, partially obscured by the feathery fur coats that reached almost to their ankles. The couple looked ominous. Blain's voice, deep and raspy compared to J.T.'s squeaky tone, resonated through the hall. "Thank you, V, for your presentation."

He surveyed the hall, then turned to the other Master Elders. "You realize this will change everything we've been doing for the Creator and our people over the last thirty thousand years. I'm not convinced yet. We've kept records and the history of our planet all this time. What if the population finds out? We must be absolutely sure we are ready to change thousands of years of policy and procedures."

Letsa and Alder, Master Elders from Elducan, stood. Both had long, slender bodies with shorter limbs, standing around six feet tall. Their eyes, chameleon-like, were positioned on the sides of their heads.

Their long, rounded mouths and lips, with puffy multi-colored hair, complemented their leathery, blue, and gray skin. Alder had orange spots with faded black, giving him a lizard-like appearance. Letsa rubbed her puffy hair. They waited for the Vindormores to sit, then said, "We agree with Blain and Lorness."

"We must be cautious with our decision. Once we help Terraenti with their CAT, won't all of us want the same for our planet?"

Alex couldn't hold back. *"I have to say something,"* he thought. "They don't understand. I must get them to agree to something." He slowly stood, turned on his mic, and looked to Gig for permission to speak. Gig held out his hand, signaling him to wait. After the Elducan couple sat, Gig and Fem' nodded for him to proceed.

Alex addressed the hall, "If I may, it's not as if we, the four of us, the Students and the Elders of Terraenti, asked for this. We were as surprised as you when we received these messages. We cannot accomplish our mission without you. The plan needs everyone, all the Elders, to be involved. It's possible the Creator planned it this way. Part of the message from the Creator said you and the 'other' Elders must work together. It's all or none. The Magnetic Accelerators won't be ready for a full test for at least two months. May I suggest we meet back here before then? This will give you time to discuss it further with your people and come back to vote again. If the tables were turned and the message was about your planet, how would you think? We can create a volunteer list; we need over 90 people. Not to be rude or overstep, but our lives have completely changed in the last three weeks."

"We don't have the knowledge and long-term backgrounds you all have. We just want to do what's right for all the planets and all the people residing on them, for all of you and the Creator. We still need to figure out what the second message means for the galaxy. Let's consider how this test on Terraenti might have profound implications for all the planets and our galaxy."

Alex scanned the amphitheater and smiled. "Thanks."

Muirlmont and Ferlnill stood. Alex sat with a satisfied smile, glancing at Harvey, Freida, and V, who looked at him in amazement.

Muirlmont said, "We should all agree that these messages are from the Creator. After that, we take the advice of our young Elders here and meet back as he suggests for a final vote."

Ferlnill added, "None of our planets have ever seen such a quick progression of Student Elders before. The Creator is trying to tell us something, and we should listen."

"Within three weeks, they have undergone a complete transformation. They had all their Gifts within a week and achieved eagle transfer without a prayer."

"We should thank them for their hard work and diligence." Ferlnill and Muirlmont began clapping, and the rest of the hall followed suit.

Gig stood and struck the gavel. Fem' stood up as well. Gig said, "I make a motion that we vote on agreeing these messages are from the Creator."

Muirlmont and Ferlnill seconded the motion, remaining standing.

Alex learned that the Elders voted by standing or remained seated. Those who agreed stood, while those who disagreed remained seated. Gig and Fem' were already standing, along with Ferlnill and Muirlmont.

As the Master Elders stood, people from various planets in the seats above them followed. Alex saw Harvey and Freida already standing and joined them, along with V and the Stewards from Terraenti. Prinks and Merick from Vattan, Letsa and Alder from Elducan, and Minter and Rall from Regnolm stood as well. Only a few in the crowd remained seated.

Finally, Lorness and Blain from Vindor rose, looking grumpy. Blain raised his hand regally.

Gig said, "We all agree. Please remain standing if you agree to meet back in a month or so to vote on whether to proceed with the Creator's Plan and strengthen Terraenti's Magnetic field." Everyone remained standing. The crowd began to buzz with excitement.

Gig glanced over to the Master Elders of Vattan. "Merick, Prinks, if you could, please?" he requested, reminiscent of that first Friday night when Fem' led the prayer. Prinks grasped a red stone the size of her hand. Merick announced, "If we could all sit for the prayer to the Creator to end the meeting." The room fell silent as everyone sat. Marick slammed his rock down on his armrest. Prinks remained standing and chanted, "Ooh! Raba Rashi! Naash! Ooh, Raba Rashi! Cama, See, La Ruh! Uttah! Delders! Demasters! Cama See La Ruh! Shanka Ne Ala-Muta, Ne! Pat!" The lights in the massive room flickered and then dimmed. The stone in her hand illuminated, warming the room.

The air swirled, moving the large tapestries on the walls. Heavenly thunder echoed. Merick stood and slammed the rock again, and the stone in Prink's hand grew even brighter.

A green sapphire lightning bolt emerged from the stone, breaking into numerous lighted arrows that swirled around the room before gently passing through everyone. This time, it enveloped over five thousand people.

Everyone's body tingled with a warm, soothing electrical sensation, a heightened spiritual experience. The entire auditorium shared a Common Mind.

Their eyes shut, heads tilted back, and arms outstretched with palms up. Then, as if electrocuted with a taser, it ended abruptly. After the shock, everyone knew it was over. Alex, before opening his eyes, thought, *"Okay, now I get it. Being in a prayer. The Common Mind with five thousand people. Unbelievably incredible! That has to be the best feeling I have ever felt in my life. I have to figure out how to do this with my group."*

Alex opened his eyes to see the auditorium lights coming back on. V leaned over to kiss and hug him. She said, "So this is how prayers are with a large group. Imagine if we could do this someday." Alex smiled, "I was just thinking the same thing."

He stood to hug and kiss her back, gazing into her green eyes. Without thinking, he almost said, "I love you," but instead, he said, "I thank, I thank you." She smiled and gave him a funny look before giving him a quick kiss. Harvey and Freida stood to congratulate them. They looked around at the laughing and cheering crowd. Alex asked Harvey, "Do big group prayers always feel like this?" Harvey replied, "Yes, the prayer is one of the most intense times we have. It brings all six cultures together. It's the people, the Common Mind, along with the Creator. Those three, all in one. Possibly someday, maybe you and V will be able to perform the prayer here?" He looked at Alex's neck and said, "Maybe sooner than we think."

Freida glanced at V's neck, "Again, with a transfer, remarkable." Alex looked at V's neck, and she looked at his.

V said, "Another eagle mark for both of us." She put her hand up to her lips, "Oh, no." Alex, looking a little worried, asked, "You worried?"

V pulled her hand down, "It's not up to us. We don't have anything to do with it. Let's not bring it up." She stood on her toes, very excited, "Well, we did it. We got through it. What's important? I didn't pass out from a panic attack."

Alex, always looking ahead, said, "We did it. But we still have a lot to get through."

V hugged Alex and whispered into his ear, "Enjoy the moment, Mr."

The Master Elders descended from their seats to shake their hands. Blain and Lorness approached them, standing more than a foot above them. Blain said, "It is remarkable how fast you all are progressing. Good job today. We look forward to the next meeting." The Master Elders congratulated Alex and V, shaking hands and nodding in approval.

Gig and Fem' approached. Fem' said, "Great job, you guys."

"We made more progress than we thought. I'm confident that, eventually, all will agree with the plans. Alex, your closing statement was perfect. Both of you did a wonderful job with the presentation. It's like you two were meant for this."

Alex asked, "What's next? Are we leaving right away?" Gig looked at Harvey and Freida for their response. Harvey said, "We should have some dinner first." He looked back at Fem' and Gig for agreement. "We wouldn't get back till after midnight our time."

Gig smiled, "Why don't we leave in the morning, say around 6:00? I'll have Bahdubah and Klinchme' prepare a breakfast meal to eat on the ship after we take off." Fem', with a big smile, said, "Sounds good. Why don't we all have dinner at Three Falls Park? I'll call and see if they can accommodate us. Maybe the band is playing tonight?" Gig looked at Harvey, "I'll text you the details. We will meet in an hour or so." Harvey said, "Sounds good. I'll inform the others."

Gig and Fem' left, and Alex and V started packing their things. Harvey and Freida walked towards the exit. Alex looked around the room; only a few people remained in the stands. He looked at V, who was gazing at him with overwhelming joy, her eyes watery. She asked, "Did you mean it?"

Alex looked confused at first, then thought back to a few moments ago. *"Oh, Shit! Did She Just Do That Mind Reading Thing?" On me, again?"*

"When I was going to say, "I love you," but stupidly said, "I thank, I thank you." With a big smile and a look of love that he had felt ever since that first night when he saw her at the big table in Terraenti Hall.

He grabbed her by the shoulders and said, "I've felt that way about you since the first time I looked into those beautiful green eyes of yours. The first night at the university. I think we do very well together." With some embarrassment, he asked, "How do you feel?"

She wiped away a small tear and said, "For me, it wasn't until after that second night we, you know. Together." She put her fingers about an inch apart, "I'm about this close to knowing. I know I love your family."

Harvey, from across the room, called, "Come on, you two. Let's go!" V hugged Alex and grabbed his hand. "You just make me feel complete, sure that I'm on the right track. That the path I'm on is the right one."

Alex, trying to grab his duffle bag as she pulled him away, said, "That's great. I feel so much better knowing you feel that way."

"You make me feel like I can do so much more now than I could before. With you by my side, I know I could climb a much bigger mountain. I just know that."

She stopped walking and pulled him close. "That's one of the greatest things anyone has ever said to me." Alex smiled graciously. "From what you said, I think the same thing."

Harvey and Freida looked increasingly frustrated as they waited. V, noticing their impatience, said, "We should get going. We'll talk more about this later when we have dessert in our room."

"Oh, dessert, huh?" Alex replied, intrigued.

V flipped her hair back playfully. "Yeah." She ran to join Harvey and Freida while Alex struggled to chase after her with all the bags. Though Alex had always been uncertain about relationships, this time, he felt remarkably sure.

Harvey and Freida turned to walk with them. Freida asked, "What's taking so long? What were you two talking about?" V laughed. "Oh, I was just informing Alex that we are going to have dessert in our room tonight." Harvey and Freida, catching the implication, chuckled.

Alex, a bit embarrassed by V's boldness, smiled at Harvey. They walked up the ramp to the main floor and headed towards the entrance where the shuttle pods awaited. Back in the room, Alex fell onto the bed and shut his eyes.

V put the bags in the corner, then snuggled next to him. "Well, we got through it. I feel much better now," she said, closing her eyes.

Later, Alex woke to see V putting on a super sexy outfit for dinner. "Where did you get that?" he asked, surprised.

"Oh, this? It's something I used to wear when I went out drinking with friends," V replied.

"Jeez, you look really nice," Alex said, admiring her. He put on a tight T-shirt, his light brown leather jacket, and a pair of off-white slacks with dark loafers. V slid her hands into his jacket, rubbing his chest. "You look very nice tonight," she said.

Alex gently pushed her away. "Stop it, or we won't be able to leave the room if you get me all roused."

She laughed. "Is that what you call it? 'Roused?'" "You know, it's short for 'Aroused,'" Alex explained. V laughed again. "Alright, let's go."

In the hallway, they saw Freida. "We are all meeting at Falls Park," she said. On the shuttle pod, they met Miko, Declan, Swaraj, and Prezzy. Everyone looked stunning in their going-out attire. Prezzy wore a vibrant, colorful dress matching her personality. Declan sported a tie with a picture of Einstein that read, "You Know Nothing!" paired with his dinner jacket.

Miko donned a very see-through silky nightdress over what looked like a gymnast outfit, showcasing her petite beauty. Swaraj was sharply dressed in a formal light green suit tailored to perfection.

The city transformed at night. Streetlights, instead of the usual white or orange hue seen on Terraenti, glowed a mystical blue violet hidden among trees and buildings. The cityscape resembled a movie set more than a real city, with buildings evoking the ancient splendor of Rome, the Pyramids, or Terraenti's ancient cities.

The pod sped out of the city and into the forest, passing through small communities and climbing a large canyon by a big river.

In the distance, a large gothic-looking building appeared. The shuttle-pod circled the structure and entered a big park, passing an amphitheater. It soared over the falls, making a grand loop. The three waterfalls, split by massive boulders, cascaded down two to three hundred feet.

The spray from the falls hit the shuttle as it circled back to the gothic temple-like building. On one side of the mountain stood bright red basalt columns, hundreds of feet tall, formed by a volcano.

The Three Falls Restaurant was more than a dining place; it was a nightclub a meeting spot, and next to it was a large amphitheater. Outside the restaurant, a large stage overlooked a pond with several decks and bars, both indoors and outdoors, accommodating around two hundred guests.

The shuttle docked on the third story of the building, where a fancy butler, reminiscent of the elegant Vattania, helped them out. "If you will follow me, your party is this way," he said. They walked past upstairs tables, offering breathtaking views of the stage, basalt columns, and waterfalls. They descended to the bottom floor and headed towards the stage, where some of their group had already arrived.

V, looking around, exclaimed, "I've never been to a place like this before. This is so crazy."

They made their way to the large bar area to the right of the stage, behind which a rocky pond collected the falls' water. The mist lightly touched their faces. The underwater lighting made the falls and pond glow ethereally.

Alex saw Bahdubah and Klinchme'. Klinchme' ran up to V. "You guys did great today. I was very impressed," she said. V, relieved, replied, "Thanks. We got through it, and I wasn't as nervous as I thought I'd be. This place is crazy nice. What should we drink?"

Alex shook Bahdubah's hand. "Hey mate, how are you?" Klinchme' said, "Yeah, we worked here before the university job." Declan scoffed. "You worked here? That's incredible. This place is off the charts!" Bahdubah noted, "It took us years to get in here, but once you're in, you're in. Great view, great food. But tonight, it's all about you guys. Great job."

Miko asked, "Is there a band playing?" Klinchme' pointed to the stage. "Yes, it's an all-string band made up of people from all six planets. It should be really great."

The group ordered drinks and sat at a table. Alex, V, Miko, Declan, Prezzy, Swaraj, Klinchme', and Bahdubah gathered at one table while the other Students sat at another. Stewards set up a few more tables. Gig and Fem' sat with other Elders from various planets.

Prezzy looked at V and Alex and said, "Just noticed your additional eagle marks. Good for you two. We all knew it would be you guys. The council meeting was incredible. The prayer was insane. What a feeling. Prayer with five thousand people. Crazy. What's next?"

Alex mused to himself, *"The prayer felt so different with such a vast congregation. I wonder what it would be like when we all gather with the Accelerator, and 32 of us connect with the Common Mind. Maybe we should try it with the twelve of us first, just to see how it feels or what it does. V looks absolutely ravishing tonight. I wonder who lost their eagle marks."*

V smiled at Prezzy and said, "Thanks. We have a long way to go, but I'm glad that part is over."

Lev snuck up behind Alex and put him in a light yet firm headlock, his burly frame enveloping Alex's chair. With a hearty laugh and a thick Russian accent, he said, "You took my eagle mark, you shit." Alex grinned, struggling to speak. "It's V's fault. She's the mastermind. She told me what to do." Everyone laughed. Lev released him, smirking. "Sure, blame your woman. She's always at fault."

V called over, "How are you guys doing over there?" Lev replied, "Have you ever seen a place like this?"

"I'm glad we stayed. This is something else. It's like we're on another planet!" The group burst into laughter. Miko asked, "Do you know who lost the other mark?"

Lev looked over at her. "Kyoryk noticed during the Council meeting. I heard Maria say, 'Oh shit, I'm out.' I'm sure she's fine."

Lev smiled at V. "I'm sure she will talk to you about it." V sighed. "Great, I don't want Maria mad at me."

Lev glanced towards the other table where Maria was rising to join them. He said, "Uh-oh, here she comes now. Quick, V, run!" They all laughed as Maria approached, feigning anger. She wore a headscarf, a silky, colorful blouse reminiscent of a Russian Gypsy, and a flowing skirt with fancy sandals.

Maria placed her hands on V's shoulders, and V, slightly nervous, looked up at her. Maria scanned the group and then fixed her gaze on V. As V started to speak, she noticed that everything had fallen silent. Even the waterfalls seemed frozen in time. Maria had halted time.

With her Russian accent, Maria said, "I would have never made it as a Master Elder. You know that, right? I think I'm a little too crazy for the job."

"Great job, by the way, in the Council meeting. You might have just saved my family." She moved around to the other side of V, still touching her as time remained suspended. V tried to follow her movements with her eyes and head.

V asked, "So, you're okay then? I don't need to post a guard?" Maria laughed. "No, no guard needed. We're okay." She smiled as she began to withdraw her hand.

V grabbed her hand and stood to hug her, saying, "I'm glad you are okay." As they released from the hug, time resumed its normal flow.

Declan, sensing something had happened, looked at them. "Maria, did you just use your Gift?" Maria, now standing with V, replied, "Just for a second. V's black eye should be appearing any moment now."

V smiled at the group and shook her head. "No, we're okay. I'm sure she'll try to get back at me in combat class." Maria laughed. "No, I'm okay. I was telling V that I don't know if I would have made the best Master Elder."

Lev took Maria's hand and said, "I think you would have made a great Master Elder."

As they walked back to their table, Alex looked at the group. "How does that time thing work?" Miko said, "Kyoryk told me he hasn't figured it out yet. He thinks it's localized within a couple hundred feet or something. And if she touches you, you enter the time loop with her."

Declan, looking surprised, asked, "Why are you talking to Kyoryk about stuff?" Miko teased him. "What? I talk to people. Plus, he has a super nice body."

Declan, looking shocked and a bit jealous, said, "What? What did she say?" Everyone laughed, and Miko kissed him. "Your body is okay. Your personality is better than all these guys. Plus, I don't think he's as aggressive as you are in bed."

V laughed. "Are we eating or just drinking?"

They perused the menu. Halfway through their meal, a band started playing, with four musicians on stringed instruments. A tall, sultry woman from Vattan began singing softly. Swaraj laughed and asked, "How much do you think this dinner would cost on our planet at a place like this?" V answered, "I don't know. Never been to a place like this."

Declan guessed, "One fifty a head." Prezzy added, "Where my friend got married, it was three hundred per person, but this is nicer. I'd say five hundred."

Declan leaned back in his chair, draping his arm around Miko. "Don't know, but I could get used to this." Bahdubah laughed. "Get used to it. You'll all be living here on this planet soon enough." A minute after the waiter delivered dessert, Alex glanced at the stage where a piano player and several horn players had joined in, creating a jazzy atmosphere. "This is, by far, the nicest place I've ever been, though the food is a bit too fancy for me. I'm not used to it."

V looked at her dessert. "It's almost like an art piece like you're not supposed to eat it." Alex laughed and whispered in V's ear, "I thought we were going to have dessert in our room."

V smiled at him. "Don't worry, you'll still get your special dessert later." Bahdubah and Klinchme' got up to dance. Declan, overhearing V's remark to Alex, asked, "Special dessert? What's that, Alex?" V gave Declan a playful glare. "That's for you never to know and for Alex to find out later."

Prezzy jumped up from the table, nearly knocking over some glasses, startling everyone. She looked at Swaraj, holding out her hand. "I'm ready." Swaraj, puzzled, looked at her as she gestured towards the dance area. "Oh, you want to dance," he realized.

He got up slowly, took her hand, and they walked away. He glanced back at the group, smiling. "When she jumps up like that, I'm never sure what to expect." They all laughed.

Alex looked at V's dessert. "Are you almost finished with whatever that is? I'd like to dance and feel your soft skin against mine."

He stood up, extended his hand, and said, "May I dance with the woman who always fills my heart, whose green eyes melt mine, even thousands of years into the future?" V looked down at her dessert, smiling inwardly.

Miko cooed, "So romantic." Declan frowned. "I can be romantic," Miko smirked. "Now would be a good time."

The four of them at the table walked to the dance floor. Alex, slow dancing with V, whispered in her ear, "The best night ever."

V kissed his neck and, echoing their shared sentiment, said, "It is the best night ever."

They danced for a bit, but the music wasn't quite to their taste. After a couple of tunes, V and Alex joined Miko and Declan at the bar. Declan asked Alex, "What are you guys going to do?" V replied, "We thought we'd head back to the hotel, maybe go to the pool or grab some drinks, and head to the roof." Declan suggested, "We should find where the younger crowd hangs out tonight." Alex, trying to keep the group out of trouble, said, "Let's go back to Alcazar. Next time we come, we can find a bar or club. We need to get up at like 5:00 AM." Miko looked at Prezzy, who was gazing at the moons above and said, "Alright, let's go back. We can hang on the roof for a couple of hours and play some music." V and Alex agreed.

Alex told the rest of the group they were heading back to their building and that they could do something there for an hour or two. Thirty minutes later, back at Alcazar, they went to their rooms, grabbed some drinks, and headed up to the roof.

Standing near the edge of the building, Declan looked out over the city. "This place is incredible. Why can't the University be here?" Alex responded, "We have a lot of work to do before we get to stay here." Declan looked at him. "I know, but it's fun to think about. To imagine what our lives will be like then."

Alex glanced back and saw Prezzy setting up some speakers from their room. "Do you think the other Elders are going to help us?" Declan, still admiring the view, replied, "Yeah, I think so."

"They don't have a choice, and deep down, they probably know that even if they don't want to admit it yet. How are things with V? You guys seem to be getting along really well."

Alex brightened. "With V? Yeah, everything is going really well. Almost too well." Declan asked, "What do you mean, 'too well'?"

Alex explained, "Well, we've spent a lot of time together. I guess that's a good thing, but everything seems to be moving so fast." Declan shook his head. "I don't get you, man. Most of the time, you're focused, and you know exactly what's going on. Then, you second-guess yourself. What's that about?"

Alex, frustrated, rubbed his face. "I don't know. I do that sometimes when things are going really well. My head gets all messed up. I guess I'm overthinking." Declan laughed. "Maybe you have a mental problem."

Alex laughed too. "Very funny. How are you and Miko doing? She looks sexy tonight, that outfit." Declan said, "She wants everyone to think I'm chasing after her. But honestly, it's her. She's a sex maniac. Don't get me wrong, I like it, but she's wild when we're alone. It's like she wants to get caught." Alex nodded. "For some people, that's part of the excitement. I made V dance somewhat naked the other night. That was fun; she thought it was romantic." Declan grinned. "That does sound like fun. We do weird stuff like that too. I had a friend in the first year of college. He'd be with a girl at lunchtime, a different one at dinner, and another to sleep with at night. He did that all the time with a lot of different girls. I don't know how he kept track of it all."

Alex laughed. "Yeah, I've never been like that. It would get into my head, and I'd feel guilty or something." Declan said, "I can't do that either. I joke about a lot of stuff, but when it comes to being serious in a relationship, I get very serious. I've had a couple of long relationships, but nothing for a while. The last one messed me up, and I haven't had a serious one for a couple of years now."

Alex said, "I had a long one in high school, but after that, nothing until now." Declan laughed. "With all the crazy stuff we've seen in the last three weeks, I'm surprised we're not all going insane. And with the Common Mind and the Gifts, who knows what that's doing to us or how it's changing us?"

Alex smiled. "You're pretty smart for a comedian who can move objects with his mind." Declan asked, "How's your Gift? Have you seen anything lately? Anything into the future?" Alex replied, "No, nothing lately. I've only been trying to see when the next Pulse Reversal might happen. I haven't been searching for anything else." Declan said, "Well if we can make what's on the infinity papers work, we are going to be superstars. Just not famous superstars. None of the people I know will even know what happened to me or what I did."

Alex said, "Yeah, it's funny how that's all going to work. We are going to save a bunch of people, but no one will ever know except all the new people we are now associated with. V and I are already feeling like we're being treated differently around here. But back home, we're just regular people."

Declan looked up at the moons. Two hung above, with another rising on the dark horizon, all different sizes. Two were closer than the moon on Terraenti, and the third was the same distance. Alex saw him and looked up at them too. "Isn't it crazy? This planet has seven moons, and it's only going to be dark for another hour or so. We haven't even begun to see what's on this planet. What about the animals? Or is it geography? I need to bring one of my racers here. That would be fun."

Declan asked, "Do they have that kind of fuel here? Or would you bring that too?"

Alex scoffed and looked disappointed. "I don't know. I suppose I could make it. I need another beer."

Declan hit him on the shoulder. "I think you and V have a lot of responsibility right now. You just need to take a step back and smell the roses once in a while. You know we are all here together, helping each other. We will all figure it out together."

Alex smiled. "I appreciate that, mate. I know, I just get into thinking too much." Declan said, "Well, don't. Let's get another beer. I think you're lucky. V is smokin' hot."

Alex laughed. "Yeah, but Miko wants to have sex every four hours. We're both doing okay. They are both two super smart, beautiful creatures."

They got closer to the group, and Miko jumped onto Declan. "What have you two been talking about?"

Declan chuckled, "We were trying to figure out how to produce fuel on this planet when Alex showed up with his desert racer. He wanted us to find a secluded beach for some skinny dipping with girls from Vindor." A new **"Song"** began to play. *Let's Think About Living*

Alex joined in the laughter. "Do you remember the tune someone played after the Pulse Reversal? Do you recall that?" The girls burst into giggles. Miko teased, "Got hoppin' and boppin' on your mind?"

"That was me," Declan admitted, still laughing. It topped the charts in 1961, both pop and country."

"My grandfather used to play it. It's hilarious. Want to watch the video? Let me show you." He pulled up the tune on the speakers, and V joined in the laughter.

Miko began to sing along. Curious, Prezzy asked, "What does it all mean? Was it really the number one tune in 1961?" Declan confirmed, "That's what it says."

Reflecting on the passage of time, Alex remarked, "Times have certainly changed. I think 'The Copacabana' was a movie in the 80s." The group ended the night singing and dancing to the upbeat 'hoppin' boppin'' tune on the rooftop.

XV

Friday morning, the seventh Friday of their stay, V strode into Alex's room to find him seated in the chair, eyes closed in concentration. "Still trying?"

Alex opened his eyes in frustration. "Damn it, nothing! What the hell?"

V chuckled. "Keep at it; it'll come."

Alex frowned up at her. "This isn't funny. We need to figure this out."

V sighed. "I know, baby. We will. Maybe it's a year from now, and you can't see that far out yet."

Prezzy popped her head into the room. "Class starts in five minutes."

V turned to her. "He's trying to foresee the next Pulse Reversal. It's not working, and he's frustrated." Prezzy stepped inside. "How has it worked before?" Alex frowned. "Lately, I think of things and then see them, but this time it's not happening."

V interjected, "The first time, Miko asked Alex when the Elders would return, and he just saw it."

Prezzy laughed, then walked up to Alex, shaking him almost violently. "Alex, Alex! When is the next Pulse Reversal happening? Tell me now!" V pulled her away. "Jesus, Prezzy, that's not cool."

Alex, dazed with his eyes open, remained silent. V and Prezzy watched him intently. After a few seconds, he snapped out of it. "That's it, you did it."

Prezzy jumped up and down. "I did? Ha! No way. Cool! I just asked the question."

V looked at her in surprise. "Well, you did shake him. What did you see, Alex?"

Alex chuckled, smiling. "Not entirely sure. We were in costumes at a party on the deck. Then, I saw the date sign in the lab showing November 3, 2033. I watched the solar image on the screen, seeing the Pulse Reversal. We were all there, but not everyone. Me, V, Harvey, Freida, Miko, and Declan."

Prezzy excitedly, "Were we still in our costumes?" Alex frowned. "No, we were in regular clothes. Why was I dressed as Batman? V, you were Catwoman or Batwoman. We were dancing. Something's wrong with my visions."

V and Prezzy burst into hysterical laughter. Alex looked at them, confused. "What?" V explained, "We girls ordered Halloween costumes from Kahput. They should arrive next week. It's a surprise for you guys. We're having a Halloween party next Monday night."

Alex thought for a moment. "Not this Monday, but the one after? I think you saw two different nights." V and Prezzy, beaming, lifted him out of the chair. "You did it! We know when it's going to happen."

Alex grinned. "Two weeks from now. Thursday, November 3, 2033, will be the second Reversal." Prezzy asked, "What day was the first one?"

V answered, "You don't remember? It was on September 11th. So, how many days is that? They say it sets the pattern or time cycle." Alex, checking his tablet, said, "53 days, less than two months. Now I need to figure out how many Reversals will happen before the big solar burst. The Flare." He started pacing, worried again.

V hugged him. "You just figured out something major. Stop and think how

amazing that is."

Prezzy joined the hug. "And why do you think you have to figure all this out alone? Remember, I asked the question. I figured out the library is shaped like an infinity symbol. I'm the rock star here!"

Alex smiled. "You're right. Take the win. And Prezzy, thank you. You are a rock star." V grinned. "You are a rock star. What do we do now? Should we call Gig? Go to class and tell them?" Alex looked at them with a mischievous grin. "No, let's get naked and have sex." V and Prezzy laughed. V teased, "I think that part of your future telling might be a little fuzzy. We should go to class."

In the classroom, Harvey announced, "This is the last day of Directives and Laws." The group clapped and cheered. Beauta noticed the trio and quipped, "Nice of you to join us."

V spoke up. "Alex has seen when the next Pulse Reversal will happen." Beauta looked shocked. "It's not in five minutes, is it?"

Harvey asked, "What did you see?" Alex replied, "November 3rd, two weeks from now." Harvey instructed, "Alright. You two find Gig and Fem and let them know. We'll continue with class and regroup later." Prezzy, feeling sidelined, pointed at Alex but sat down with a frown.

Alex and V left the room, walking down the hallway. Alex called Gig on his tablet. "We have some news. Can we meet now?" Gig replied, "We're in the lab. Come here."

In the lab, Doog and Gig looked up. "What's the news?" Alex announced, "We have a date for the next reversal. It's November 3rd."

Gig mused, "The last one was September 11th. That's 53 days short. Ours were around four months apart, four of them. So, 16 months. These two will be two

months apart, so it'll happen in 2034. Doog, put out an alert for all ship traffic, and cancel surface or tunnel work plans. How did you see it?"

Alex and V laughed. Alex explained, "The girls planned a Halloween party with costumes. I saw us at the deck party, dressed up. Then, I saw the date sign showing November 3, 2033. Some of us were watching the sun's reversal on the screen."

Alex pointed to the screen displaying a live video of the sun. "So, my conclusion is that I see Halloween night, then the date, and then us witnessing the Pulse happening on this screen. It's the way I perceive things—a series of events. I'm confident about that date. I must be in these places in the future. If I'm there, then I'm seeing it there."

"But if I'm not there, then maybe I can't see it. I don't know if I'm actually creating future events by being there, and that's the perplexing part. And the Creator?" Alex appeared somewhat confused.

Gig looked equally puzzled but nodded in understanding. "Alright, I don't think that sentence made much sense, but I get what you mean. I'll send out a message to everyone. This is huge—you saw it so that we can prepare better."

"The third will be in December, and the fourth in February. The CAT might happen in April or June if we have the fifth Pulse Reversal. We should prepare just in case the CAT happens in February."

"When do you think the Accelerators should be ready? Mid-November. We could do a full test during the late December Pulse if we can get the rest of the Elders on board."

Gig gave a firm smile. "V, could you create a schedule of events so we can meet on Monday or in a couple of days to go over everything?" V responded, "Sounds good. I'll work on the schedule and add it to the to-do list."

Gig smiled generously. "Great job, you two. You better get back to class." "Okay, we'll see you later," V said, pushing Alex out of the room.

V and Alex returned to class and sat down. Beauta was speaking, "Using this new technology on our planet will change many of our laws. We are currently reviewing and updating them."

Declan asked, "What do we do if anyone from the population finds out who we are? Like if they see us using our Gifts?"

Lev interrupted, "We eliminate them!" The class laughed, and Beauta and Harvey smiled. Beauta, in her Australian accent, said, "Well, no elimination. Rev and Mod can create plenty of cover stories to make the situation disappear."

Alex asked, "What CAT are Rev and Mod from?" Harvey answered, "They aren't from any CAT. Let's just say they've been around for a long time; you'll meet them in the next few months." Tonari added, "Rev is super nice."

Beauta continued, "We are not to use our Gifts on any planet, and it's limited for special use on Amotaious. Alva Global can create any paperwork you need—IDs, licenses, and credentials for any project you're working on. Lev, how do we buy products that are shipped here or to Amotaious?"

Lev replied, "In the past month, I just asked Kahput to order it for me."

Harvey smiled. "But if you are Kahput, how do you do it?" Lev answered, "I contacted Alva Global. They have various companies to purchase whatever we need; we always go through them, right?"

Harvey confirmed, "Right. Alex, how did you handle your family's business while building the Accelerators?"

Alex explained, "We had Alva produce all the documents, purchase orders, non-disclosures, and the payment schedule. We even put Alva Global Industries on all the Infinity Documents. All the paperwork went through them."

Beauta posed a scenario, "Let's say someone in your family wants pictures of you at your college. What then?"

No one answered. Beauta said, "Contact Alva and they can produce photos of you at your university or in your dorm room, with a background of buildings in the area or the university."

"They've been doing this for a long time and are very good at it. If a relative or friend unexpectedly visits you at your false university, what do you do?" Kyoryk, with a questioning look, answered, "Call Alva and tell them your situation."

Beauta said, "Right, and they will send someone to meet them and inform them you're away on school business. They're excellent at creating any deception."

Harvey added, "Let's say Alex wants to bring home pictures and presents from MIT for the holiday. You go online, pick out backgrounds, and choose the presents. They'll get them for you. But here's the tricky part: you must plan ahead. Think about the scenario you're trying to present. Unfortunately, we have to do these things to keep everything a secret."

Beauta said, "Once you're finished here at the university, things will be different. You can spend more time with your family. But you'll still need to create false careers, addresses, and bank accounts. All of this has to be meticulously planned. You'll be going home in December, so remember the gifts and pictures. Plan long-term with Rev and Mod later. Any questions?"

Prezzy asked, "What about family emergencies? If we need to go home?"

Harvey replied, "Anything like that can be arranged quickly. If it happens, who would you call?" Prezzy answered, "I would call Beauta and Alva Global and tell them what's happened. Is that right?"

Harvey said, "Right. Alva is basically Rev or Mod, and they can act quickly."

"Also, let Gig or Fem know so they can inform the lab. The lab needs to know where you are at all times."

"Alright, let's take a break for lunch. Next week's class is 'Living as an Elder' with Amand VanZantg and Sanjay Babu. When you return, it will be with Hugh and Keira for more about CATs."

The group got up and moved to the common room. V set up her computer to modify the schedule based on Alex's vision. She added ship modifications for landing on the planet without a runway, ghost, or stealth technology for covering the ship and Elders while on the planet, the next Elders' meetings, and the new dates for the Pulse Reversals. Alex, Declan, and Miko sat down next to her. Declan asked, "So, when is the next event?"

Alex replied, "In a couple of weeks, November 3rd. But they're preparing for it now, just in case my information is incorrect."

Declan asked, "What did you see?" Alex looked at Miko and asked, "Does he know about the Halloween thing?" Miko says, "Yes, he wanted to have input on what he was going to be, so I told him what we were doing." V exclaims, "What the hell? I thought we were going to surprise them." Miko replies, "I know, but I didn't want him freaking out about his costume."

Alex smiles. "What is he wearing?" Miko says, "He's the Monster of Frankenstein, and I am his Bride." Alex and V laugh. Declan asks, "Why, what are you?" V grins. "Alex is Batman, and I am Cat Woman." Declan, looking curious, asks, "What does this have to do with how you saw the next Reversal coming?"

Alex responds, "Probably nothing, but I saw all of us on the deck in costumes. Then, I saw the clock in the lab at the same time we were watching the Pulse Reversal live in the lab." Miko says, "That's crazy. I wonder why you saw the deck part."

Alex shrugs. "I have no idea." V laughs. "The good thing is that you saw it, and you can see further now."

V continues working on the schedule. After lunch, they return to class. Hugh Hardy and Keira Clarke resume the History lesson. Hugh begins, "You all hail from different parts of the planet, with diverse beliefs, religions, and cultures. Today, we delve deeper into Terraenti's past."

"Over a month ago, we discussed the CATs and their impact on cultures, growth, technology, and daily life. Today, we venture beyond the CATs and explore significant events from the last 23,000 years since the Eternal University has existed."

A 3D virtual display shows a massive city on an island surrounded by water, west of Gibraltar in the Atlantic Ocean. The island, with its unique three-sided cyclone shape moving counterclockwise, was enormous. Hugh explains, "This area, now known as the Azores, once housed one of the planet's largest cities between CAT 2 and 3. But what was this city?"

Kyoryk excitedly exclaims, "Atlantis?"

Hugh smiles and points at Kyoryk. "Yes! Can anyone guess what significant contributions they made that we still use today?"

Silence follows. Hugh continues, "Out of all technological advances from different CAT cultures, this one was the most advanced. They discovered how to use the Thread for high-speed space travel and separate materials using sonic frequencies, enhancing standards of living in numerous ways."

"These advancements are the foundation of our travel and technology on Amotaious today. One of the greatest mysteries is how the pyramids and other ancient megastructures were constructed."

V notices Alex perk up at the mention of Atlantis and the Pyramids. Hugh continues, "There was another slightly larger city built by the same culture off the North American coast called Mammotaious. These cultures invented this tech. Now, can someone tell me how Atlantis and Mammotaious fell?"

Alex guesses, "Was it CAT 3?"

Hugh shakes his head. "No, CAT 3 was 8,800 years ago. Those two solar bursts, CAT 2 and 3, were the least catastrophic. But just after CAT 2, 12,400 years ago, a large comet entered our solar system. It broke into many pieces before hitting the planet."

Keira activates the panel, displaying a real-time video of the comet's impact and destruction. The class is stunned. Hugh explains, "One piece hit the ice shelf above North America, and another burst in the air off Portugal. As Earth spun, another large piece hit off Africa's southeast coast near Madagascar."

"The waves exceeded a thousand feet; cities stood no chance. Mountains were stripped of trees, and boulders the size of buses were displaced hundreds of miles. By the time Keira switched to the next screen, everyone was completely awestruck. V glanced at Alex, who seemed overwhelmed by the magnitude of it all."

Hugh continues, "The atmosphere miles up was affected by another impact. The piece off Madagascar sent massive tsunamis."

Keira displays a satellite photo of Africa and Madagascar, showing an underwater ring of mountains formed by the impact. "This pressure created underwater mountains, now part of Madagascar."

Keira reveals an ancient map of the Americas, showing Mammotaious, a massive city with waterways and canals stretching from Florida to North Carolina, Kentucky, Tennessee, and the Mississippi River, with farmland extending to Oklahoma and Nebraska. V notices Alex on the edge of his seat.

Keira explains, "This city had a population of over a billion, the largest known in terms of population and technology."

"The largest comet piece exploded above Canada, causing unprecedented water flows and ice melts, setting the planet on fire. Thousands of smaller pieces struck, causing global devastation."

Keira, with her English accent, notes, "Such events are rare but catastrophic. There's little we can do—at least not yet."

V asks, "Did the population know about the comet or the CAT before it hit?"

Keira answers, "The Master Elders knew, but only shortly before—too late to act. Some events might be mentioned in religious texts."

"During that period, the Creator gave Gifts to a few, allowing them to predict such catastrophes. Many ancient religions had forewarnings of these destructions."

Declan comments, "Like Noah in the Bible?"

Keira nods and says, "Exactly, and many other religions had forewarnings before the flooding. The ancient texts of Japan and India are also worth investigating. This comet completely devastated the atmosphere, causing crop failures and widespread destruction of cities and populations."

Swaraj asks, "How long have we been on this planet?"

Hugh responds, "Before the University was established, we believed humanity and our consciousness had existed on Earth for over 200,000 years. Between each glacial period, which spans roughly a hundred thousand years, there might have been even more advanced civilizations at the peak of the interglacial period around 130,000 years ago."

"Unfortunately, there was no university or other known locations or planets from that time. There's talk of a pre-Ice Age civilization capable of time travel to different planets, but that's a whole other story. A group on Amotaious discusses such theories, but we're not affiliated with them."

Alex asks, "So how did they build the pyramids and places like Gobekli Tepe?"

Hugh replies, "As mentioned earlier, their technologies were incredibly advanced. Different from ours today, plus some individuals had Gifts like yours. They discovered how to separate materials using frequencies. That group from CAT 3 developed what we call Harmonic CRD (Cutting, Rounding, and Drilling) on Amotaious. You can tour the plant; it's about three hours from Tunimbria. Using these sonic technologies makes constructing massive structures easy."

"Every element has a frequency, and by manipulating these frequencies, they could cut stone, rock, or anything else. You're already familiar with anti-gravity. This technology is very similar to the Creators' Plans."

"I'm sure these same technologies were used to build many ancient structures still standing today. But I'm not the best person to ask about the technical details."

V looks around the room and notices Miko isn't as interested in the historical aspects as the rest of the group. V smiles at Miko, who smiles back. V has always wondered why Miko claimed to be so shy. V looks back to the front of the class and peeks into Miko's mind.

"She sees Miko at age 12 with her best friend, their family's close neighbors. Then, police and people swarm her friend's house—her friend is missing.

V delves further and discovers Miko's best friend, Mori, was kidnapped. Miko spent days, weeks, and months looking out her window, but Mori was never found. V feels Miko's heartbreak at losing her best friend and refrains from diving deeper. She promised Alex she'd take a break, but curiosity overwhelms her.'"

"She goes back into Miko's mind and finds a memory from just months ago. Miko is in a car with an elderly man, rendering him unconscious for some reason. She curses at him, secures his seatbelt, and runs a hose from the exhaust pipe into the car."

V struggles to make out the scene blurry and out of focus. It seems similar to what Prezzy experienced, a man preying on young boys and girls. Miko, deeply upset, took matters into her own hands, leaving a suicide note on the dashboard before walking away.

V senses Miko's deep compassion and willingness to risk her life for others. This understanding of the group's readiness to help others in need fills V with admiration. She speculates this could be why the Creator chose these twelve individuals.

V snaps out of her trance as Alex elbows her. "Hey, space girl, you okay?"

V looks up at Hugh and Keira. Hugh announces, "Next week, we'll discuss how these events affected extinct animals and why we call it the Younger Dryas Event." V smiles at Alex and softly says, "Yeah, okay. What's the Younger Dryas?"

Alex grins and mimics Yoda's voice. "You know nothing, little one. I will teach you." He places his hands in a meditation pose, "Omm." V playfully hits him. "Space girls say, 'You're stupid, and you do a terrible Yoda. Aussies can't do Yoda.'"

Alex, feigning shock, replies, "Can't believe you called me stupid."

They join the others, leaving the classroom. V and the group headed to the common room. V resumes working on the schedule. "Alex, help me review the list of things we need to include."

Alex sits beside her. "Atlantis—who would've thought it was real? Didn't someone write about it?"

Kyoryk joins them. "It was Plato. He described them as half-gods, half-men."

Alex nods. "Amazing that it actually existed."

Kyoryk adds, "Plato's relative claimed he made it all up, but it seems he told the truth." He looks at V's list. "We need to add how we'll communicate with the lab from the planet."

V continues typing. "Yes, here's what I have so far: production of the Accelerators, the second meeting with the Master Elders on Amotaious."

"Modifications to the two ships for transportation, stealth, or ghosting while on the planet, and the first test on December 27th."

Alex asked, "Where are we going to house all the Elders during the test and final operation?" V nodded, typing as she added it to the list. "I'm calling it 'Elders Accommodations.' We may need to do it two or three times. We all need to be on the planet starting December 27th and then again on February 18th. Again on April 11th."

Alex added, "We need to pick up the accelerators. I guess that would fall under 'Production of Accelerators.'" Kyoryk laughed, "We need to throw a massive party somewhere if we all survive."

Alex and V smiled. V chuckled, "I'll put it down. I can ask Bahdubah and Klinchme' what they think. I'll assign Lin, Maria, and Prezzy to that task."

Alex said, "We all get to go back to the planet for the holiday. We should add that too. Oh! We also need to find two Elders with the same abilities as Declan and Swaraj. That's super important." Kyoryk asked, "So we all go to the planet, wait for the lab to tell us when the sun does its thing, and then activate the accelerators?"

Alex looked at V. "I guess so. The first test will tell us more about how to prepare for the next one. That's how all engineering works. I just hope we figure it out before it hits. When the Pulse hits, we'll only have a few minutes to spin up the accelerators. Why can't it be like a normal flare?"

"Those take a day or more to hit the planet. After that, we'll know if it works. We need things like cold gear, a generator, food, and supplies." Kyoryk suggested, "Maybe we can use a tent? That might help hide us from the prying eyes of satellites."

V said, "I'm adding that to the list. That might be a way to conceal us. Well, this is a good start. We can continue tomorrow. We'll meet with Gig and the others on Monday. That's it. We are completely prepared."

Alex looked at V and Kyoryk. "Yeah right, don't think that. Not yet." The night ended, and the group went to more classes, growing even closer over the next several days, using their Gifts and the Common Mind.

XVI

The group had been at the University for two months now, and Alex, V, and the others were growing restless. They needed a break or some time back on the planet. Fortunately for V and Alex, Harvey and Gig had agreed to let them return to check on the progress of the Accelerators.

V sat alone in the common room, making last-minute adjustments to the schedule. She had it displayed above the table, showing the list of assignments and the people working on them:

- Production of the Accelerators: Alex and V

- Second meeting with the Master Elders on Amotaious: November 10th

- Modifications of ships: Lev, Lin, and Gig

- How to communicate with Lab: Kyoryk and Maria

- Stealth or ghosting of shelters on the planet: Prezzy, Swaraj, Declan, and Miko

- Pick up Accelerators: Alex and V

- Find Elders with Gifts like Declan and Swaraj: Gig

- Elders Accommodations: Lin, Prezzy, Rugrog, and Kahput

- First test, Pulse Reversal: December 27th

- Second test, Pulse Reversal: February 18th

- Third test, Pulse Reversal: April 11th

- Party at Two Dunes Harbor, Seven Moon Amphitheatre: Lin, Maria, Prezzy, and Fem, with all the Students

As she did every morning, she updated the schedule. Alex walked in and said, "Hey, we have about three hours of work this weekend, then it's all free time. Anything special you want to do? Wow, you have it all up on the 3D display; that looks great." His voice deepened theatrically, "You are the Master Planner now!"

He stepped over to the kitchen area. "So, we could go to the casino, which was fun, or we could stay in, do Jello shots, run around naked, and touch each other inappropriately. Or we can visit the house, see Melissa and the baby, my mom, and go camping with my dad in the bush."

V paused to consider the options. "The first option sounds like fun; I am 'Big Money.' The second option sounds even better, but all that leads to sex and more sex, and that leads to these little things. Have you seen them? They poop, cry, and pee all over, really disgusting creatures. So, the third option sounds good. Where would we sleep?"

Alex smiled. "In a swag, in a sleeping bag." V looked at him curiously. "On the dirt? With bugs and stuff?"

Alex laughed. "You've never slept in a sleeping bag or a swag?" V shook her head. "Nope, never. You serious, with bugs and stuff?"

Alex reassured her. "I'll make sure there are no bugs. This will be our first trip by ourselves. You ready for it?" V smiled again. "Sure, it'll be fun. Never been camping before."

Alex said, "Well, let's head down to the docks." V closed her computer, put it in her bag, grabbed her gear, and they walked down to the docks. When they arrived, Sarcan, the pilot from CAT 3, was working in the docks. Alex and V put on their Jella suits and walked toward the ship. Sarcan helped them get started.

V and Alex climbed into the ship, and Sarcan asked, "You've had your training on the ship, right?"

Alex and V nodded. "Yes."

Sarcan continued, "If you need anything or have any questions, there's always someone in the Lab who can assist you. Be safe and have a good flight."

Alex said, "Would it be possible for you to join us for lunch next week? A few of us have questions about when your parents lived on Terraenti."

Sarcan smiled. "You want to know about Atlantis?"

Alex replied, "More than that, like what happened during the other bad events, how many people were left, what it was like, and how the Common Mind fit in at that time."

Sarcan agreed. "Sure, how about Tuesday? I'll let Reoline know. We'd be happy to sit down with some of you. Okay, have a good trip. See you next week." V with a smile. "Thanks, Sarcan."

Alex closed the hatch, sat down, and clicked a switch, bringing up the screen. Operating the ship was straightforward, but landing on an airstrip was more stressful. He pressed a few buttons, driving the ship out of the docks on the track through the tunnels. Alex activated the stealth mode.

According to Kyoryk, the stealth system emitted a magnetic wave that disrupted satellites and other instruments, making them think the ship was a discarded rogue satellite out of orbit. Since cloaking a ship was impossible, the best way to hide in space was to disrupt electronics or blend into the environment. They did both.

The large round door opened, and V and Alex stepped out onto the platform and onto the surface. V remarked, "We haven't been outside for over a month. It's nice to get out for a couple of days."

Alex agreed, "I've been so consumed with everything, I didn't even think about it. But you're right, it's going to be good to get out."

The ship reached the end of the rails. Alex hit a button to lift the ship vertically. They checked their buckles, and from this point on, he used the armrest control panel to pilot the ship. The main screen displayed a green light. He hit the Com button and said, "EU, we're ready for takeoff. Are we all clear?"

The lab responded, "This is the Lab. Nothing to report. You are all set, clear to launch. E.U. out."

Alex smiled at V. "Thank you, E.U. Lab. See you in two days. Alex and V out."

Coms clicked off, and V looked at Alex. "Isn't that wrong? Don't we call the ship something? What are our call signs?"

Alex hit the button, and the ship slowly took off. After a few minutes, V pointed to the screen and said, "Isn't that it, Alva 107?"

Alex confirmed, "Yes, we are Alva 107. Should we put some music on?" V asked, "How do you do it?"

Alex showed her how to do it on her tablet/phone. "See the ship's Bluetooth or whatever, Ship.4.EU.2." They reached the point of the Thread, and the computer announced, "Jella engaged." V looked straight ahead and took a deep breath. The computer counted down, "Connecting to Thread in 4... 3... 2... 1..."

The SNAP hit them. Light flashed outside, and warmth enveloped their bodies. Just as the 80's **"Song"** started, *Blackout*, their bodies were thrown back into the seats, and the Jella warmed and squeezed them uncomfortably.

The music began, with a fast-paced rock band from the 80s. Alex looked at V, tried to smile, and said, "Here we go." V and Alex both grunted in response.

The atmosphere inside the ship felt markedly different now that it was just the two of them. As the vessel reached its desired speed, the Jella started releasing pressure, and the computer announced, "Reaching max acceleration in 3... 2... 1. All systems nominal."

Alex reached over and unbuckled V's harness, then released the rest of his own. Stretching his arms above his head, he scratched the back of his head with both hands and gazed out in front of him. "Can't ask for much more than this," he declared loudly, kicking off his shoes. V turned down the music. She pulled herself up and over to Alex, giving him a passionate kiss. He kissed her back and murmured, "This is perfect."

"We've been together for almost two months now," Alex said, "So, what do you think? Are you going to stick with me?" V, not one to overanalyze, replied, "I don't know, I've been attracted to Prezzy lately. She's so lively."

Alex chuckled. "Very funny. Do you see us together in a year?"

V, slightly frustrated, said, "I don't like discussing such things. I think we work well together. Do I see us together in the future?" She smirked. "Yes, I'm very happy with you and our relationship. If we're still alive in a year, in ten years... after that, we can have a couple of little Alexes and Alexas racing around the desert with us. Sure, I can see that."

Sensing her discomfort with the topic, Alex changed the subject. "So, you've never been camping?" V smiled as she looked at Earth getting closer. "No, never. It's not something our family ever did." She snuggled closer to him. "If we went on vacation, we'd stay in a hotel. My parents pretended it was for me and my sister, but they were always working on some covert government mission. Camping never crossed their minds. My sister and I had to find ways to entertain ourselves."

"How is your sister?" Alex asked. "She's okay," V said. "I've been trying to get her to stay with my aunt. It would be a much better environment for her, but it's not good for her to stay with my parents."

V put on some relaxing music, scooted over to sit on Alex's lap, and started kissing him more. She looked forward and said, "This is something, just the two of us traveling through space. What should we do?"

Alex smiled. "We could play cards. I brought some." V laughed. "I had something else in mind." She whispered in his ear, "A surprise, something guys like."

She unzipped his Jella suit and his pants. Alex looked around the cabin nervously. "I hope there are no hidden cameras on this ship. Happy birthday to me."

He stretched back in his seat and admired the view of the planet getting closer. V took off the top of her Jella suit and explained they were going to play a meditation game. Alex clarified, "Just to be clear, this is going to be more of a massage than meditation?" V smiled and said, "Just to be clear, I read this in an Intelligence Bureau book, and you're going to love it. All men do." She waved her hands around Alex's head. "I start here," she said, patting him on the top of his head. Then she massaged his hair and scalp. "Then, I work my way down to your toes." She traced her finger slowly down his body, all the way to his toes. "I massage you all the way down to them."

She gently worked her way back up, massaging his calves and thighs, then grabbed his crotch area with both hands. "Then I stop and focus on this area," she said, smiling. "This is where the countdown ends."

Alex gulped. "The countdown?" "Yes, all meditation has a countdown. That's how you reach your goal." She smiled raucously. "Okay, I get it. This is where I finish. Are you ready?"

He looked at her. "You read this in a book? An interrogation manual? Oh, shit!" She growled at him playfully, biting his neck.

As a new **"Song"** started. *Shooting Star*

"Let me put on the right music," she said. "Counting down from 5 to 1, as I go down, the surge of energy will end up here." She grabbed his crotch again and laughed. "Just go along with it." She started the music, and as the seven-minute tune progressed, V began the countdown. She started massaging his scalp and facial muscles.

Alex found it odd. *"Who is this woman?"* he thought. *"Is she some kind of Indian Guru or a Specially Trained Interrogator? Has she undergone special sexual pleasure training?"*

By the time she reached 4, she was massaging his hips and upper thighs. She had taken off almost everything, even his socks; it was a big operation.

When she counted to 3, she finished with his toes and worked her way back up, making him increasingly nervous. *"I need to look into this meditation countdown thing,"* he thought. *"I know she didn't pack any weird sex toys, so we're safe there. But she is giving me a good massage."*

As she neared his midsection again, she pulled his jockeys down and said, "I need to cool this area down." Alex looked up at the ceiling, thinking, *"Oh boy!"* His body was very relaxed at this point, and V was down to number 2 in the countdown.

She started blowing cool air around that area. "This will help you cool down," she said, getting into the music. Alex's legs and arms stiffened slightly. When she reached 1, he felt her on him. She had taken the final meditation step.

He almost pushed her away, exclaiming, "Oh my God! What the blazes is happening here?" His body shook and shivered.

"Let me finish!" V insisted. Alex braced himself, locking his legs and feet against the bulkhead. V looked up slightly, smiled, and said, "Hold on." She reached down and grabbed his thigh and the side of his chest, continuing the massage down the final section of his body. He pounded on the ceiling of the cabin, yelling loudly, "Holy cow!... Oh my God!" In the final seconds of the tune, Alex took another deep breath, looking out into space. V laughed. Alex yelled, "Stop the music! Turn the ship around!" Then he fell silent.

A minute later, Alex, with a huge smile on his face, said, "Never in a million years could I have imagined that. It was an incredible massage." V returned to her seat. Alex looked over at her and said, "I can't believe you read that in a book. Should I do something for you?"

V turned down the music, smiled, and said, "Well, sure." They began kissing again.

Alex's hands roamed over her as he laughed and said, "This is my first time in space. How about you?"

V laughed, pulled his hand down to her crotch, and said, "Sex in a ship, in space? No, I've done this many times." They continued kissing. Alex proceeded to unzip her pants to massage her, but he lacked experience. He found it challenging to get into position but managed to pull her to the side for ample room. As he progressed, something was set off within V.

V stared blankly into the stars, then glanced at the tablet and said, "No! Something faster!"

She smiled at Alex and changed the **"Song."** *Crazy What Love Can*

Her determination is evident as she seeks to solve the problem. She put on an EDM mix, possibly her own creation she made from four tunes, Alex thought. He tried to keep up with the pace with the imagination of delivering pleasure. Things escalated quickly.

When he looked up at her, she smiled, but it wasn't the smile he expected. She grabbed him by the hair, forcing him down between her legs, and she turned up the music.

As he worked, he wondered, *"Who is this woman? She's a wild one!"* V. Suddenly, her legs pinched Alex's head, and they went vertical, her feet pounding on the ceiling of the ship. She yelled something in Hindi. From another passing ship, all one would see were V's legs pointed straight up, visible through the windows. "There. That's it," she said. Alex thought, *"Am I starting to understand women? Or is it just this one? She's wild. Are they all like this? She definitely doesn't hold back on what she wants."*

Alex tried to keep pace with the beat of the tune, attempting various techniques. He glanced up to gauge his performance, but she looked down angrily and said, "Don't stop now!" After many words in Hindi, V gave a final yell, "Holy shit!" As she climaxed, she activated one of the ships switches with her foot, causing the ship to spin out of control. Alex saw this through the window and exclaimed, "What the hell?" He quickly corrected the situation at the control panel. When he looked back at V, she had a look of total satisfaction and a big smile on her face. "Girl, wow. You okay?" he asked. V laughed hysterically, hugging him, and said, "That was fun." She sat up, fixed herself, and looked back at him. "Best space sex ever."

Two hours later, they entered the atmosphere and transitioned to the normal flight plan of a regular plane. Alex retrieved his tablet, found the flight plan and instructions from Alva Global, and prepared for their descent off the coast of Australia.

Alex pressed a button and said, "Darwin tower, this is Alva 107, Bhubaneswar, India, requesting permission to set up for approach." "Roger, Alva 107. Descend to 10,000 with a heading of 230. Cleared for ILS runway 27," Darwin tower responded.

"Roger, Darwin tower. Descending to 10,000 for runway 27," Alex confirmed, typing the information into the ship's computer. The ship made a slight turn and began its descent.

"Darwin tower, we are on approach and have visual," Alex reported. (In most conditions, the ship could land itself, but in extraordinary circumstances. It could be controlled by Rev or Mod.)

"Start your approach. Cleared for the visual, runway 27," Darwin Tower instructed. Alex typed again, and the ship started its descent onto runway 27.

Alex smiled at V. "See? We got this."

"Darwin tower, final approach to 27," Alex announced. "Alva 107, cleared to land, runway 27," Darwin tower responded. The ship slowly descended to the runway, touched down, and rolled to a stop.

Alex clicked a button. "Darwin ground, this is Alva 107 for hangar 16." "Alva 107, cleared from 27 to cross runway 10. Then on to hangar 16," Darwin ground responded.

"Roger, Darwin ground. Taxiing now to hangar 16. Thank you," Alex replied. "Roger, Alva 107. Have a nice day," Darwin ground said.

V looked at Alex and smiled. "Good job, pilot Alex."

Alex laughed. "The ship did most of it. I just talked on the radio." V grinned. "Yeah, but you did it correctly."

Alex teased, "You're going to talk to the tower when we take off." V scoffed. "Maybe? I'll use a sexy voice and get the tower all riled up."

Alex chuckled. "Don't think that would be a good idea." In a sultry voice, V said, "Dear Darwin tower, this is V. We are in a really good position here, ready to thrust. The runway is all wet. Should we have concerns about overheating? We've checked all our fittings; they're greased up, and our engines have plenty of hot oil."

Alex gave her a curious look. "Jesus, who are you? And what have you done with the other V? V smiled, grabbed his crotch, and said, "She's back at the university." She glanced out the window at a kangaroo hopping down the field next to the runway. "What the hell, you're going to get hit, buddy," she muttered. They pulled into the hangar, and Alex stopped the ship. He took a deep breath and said, "Okay, we're here." He looked at her. "Thank you, ma'am, for flying EU Air. Please exit the craft. Oh, by the way, thanks for the special service along the way."

V laughed as she walked down the steps. "Yeah, and thank you. I don't think anyone heard me in space, do you?"

Alex laughed. "I don't think anyone heard you. I still need to learn Hindi. And I can't wait to do that again. I need to get ahold of that interrogation manual."

V shook her head. "No, then it wouldn't be special. And you did just fine." She looked back and gave him a wink.

As they walked to the car, Alex called the lab at the university to let them know they had landed safely. They got into the car and left the airport.

"Why don't we go to the casino, have lunch, and play for a bit? Then we can meet my dad," Alex suggested. "Sounds good," V agreed. They had lunch, gambled for a bit, and then headed to Alex's dad's business. When they walked in, Ella ran up and gave Alex a big hug, then hugged V.

"How are you guys?" Ella asked in her deep Australian accent. "We're fine. How are you all doing?" V replied.

Ella inquired, "How is school? Everything going okay?" "School is fine. We're still working on the one project and getting into some other classes," Alex said. "We've taken a history class and other classes, like lab safety and equipment usage," V added.

Alex smiled at V. "The classes are going very well." Ella noticed the marks on their necks and asked, "What is this?"

Alex, forgetting to cover the eagle marks, quickly said, "Oh, it's a temporary tattoo we use to identify ranking in class. It's silly, really." Ella inquired, "What do three of them mean?"

V, trying to keep her composure, explained, "When we attain a higher rank in the class, we earn an eagle mark. Out of the twelve Students, we have taken two marks from others. Once we collect all six, we become the leaders of the group."

Ella marveled, "Wow, and you already have three? That's impressive." She scrutinized V's neck. "Does it come off? It looks permanent to me."

Alex grabbed his mom's hand and interjected, "Stop, it's a silly thing really. Where's Dad?" Ella replied, "They're in the shop at the back. Are you staying for dinner?"

Alex said, "We just ate, but we could drop by the house later to visit." Ella scoffed, hugged V again, and said, "Well, I hope so."

As Alex and V walked toward the back of the shop, Alex muttered, "Shit, I forgot about the eagle marks. That could have gone badly."

V smiled. "Your mom is super nice. It must be wonderful to have parents like yours." "Yeah, I guess," Alex responded. "And the eagle marks—that was a great save. I'm pretty sure she believed us."

They reached the back of the shop where Alex shook his dad's hand and then Skip's. Both men, towering over two meters tall, greeted them with rich Australian accents. Max said, "Hey buddy, how are you? V, nice to see you again. How are you two doing?"

"We're doing well. How about you?" V replied.

Alex looked at Skip and asked, "Dad said you're taking the T&B out this weekend?" Skip confirmed, "Yeah, we made some modifications to the cams and lifters. I want to test at high speed."

V smiled. "How fast do you want to go?"

The men grinned. Max said, "As fast as possible, but if we can get it up around 280 to 300 on the dirt, that would be a happy day." V laughed. "Okay, I get it the faster, the better."

Skip smiled at V. "The trick is to reach that speed as quickly as possible. That's what we're working on."

Max asked, "How is school?" Alex responded, "School is good. We're both doing very well and learning a lot."

"How is our project going? Harvey wanted us to check on the progress," Alex inquired.

Skip said, "We're ahead of schedule on the frame." They walked over to a table laden with multiple parts. "The two cylinders are done, as well as the caps. The mounts still need some welding. Next week, we'll polish everything up and be ready for the following week."

"We had a hard time finding someone to make the center core piece and melt it down to your specifications, but we found someone a week ago. They say they can get it back to us by next week so we can polish it to the desired tolerances."

Alex examined the parts. "This is great. It's bigger than I imagined." Max said, "When it's all together, each unit will weigh around 199 kilos."

"Wow, that's a lot heavier than I realized," Alex remarked. Skip explained, "It's really thick material. We had to send it south to have it rolled; we don't have a roller for this thickness."

V, inspecting the welds, said, "That's amazing." Skip added, "To weld this thick stainless steel isn't easy. We'll put it in the mill, and you won't see the welds once we're done." He looked at V. "What does it do again?"

V, with a serious look, explained, "If it works, it will filter out certain gases with a magnetic charge."

"The core spins, and the copper picks it up, creating a magnetic field that shoots out the bottom. It's filled with gases that will obliterate other toxic gases." Skip, puzzled, said, "Okay, sounds interesting."

V looked at Alex, then back at Skip. "If it works, it could save the planet. This is just a small prototype. The real one will be much bigger."

She gestured around the building. "Like, as big as a building." Max, amazed, said, "That's incredible. I can't believe you're already working on something like this. Is it dangerous?"

Alex assured me, "Everything will be in the lab. One reason the material is so thick is because there will be compressed gases inside." Max cautioned, "Alright, well don't blow yourselves up. Make sure Harvey isn't pushing you too hard."

V reassured, "Harvey and the others are being very safe with all this. We've spent the last month in safety classes and emergency lab procedures. It's all safe." Max smiled at V. "We should have no problem shipping it out around the 15th. Where do you want it sent?"

Alex said, "I'll send you the instructions. You'll probably take it to the airport, or someone from there will pick it up." Max asked, "Do you want it on one pallet or two?"

Alex considered their destination and the need for frequent movement. "These will need to be in actual cases. We'll have some cases made and sent here. I'll text or email you about it later."

V, noting the information on her tablet, caught Skip's attention. "What kind of phone is that?" he asked.

V replied, "These are prototypes of phones that might be on the market soon. We call them tablets. They hold much more information and are larger than regular phones." Max laughed. "I think I use one percent of my phone's power. You guys are so high-tech, I can't keep up."

Alex said, "They're pretty much the same. These are mainly focused on appearance, at least that's my opinion." "Alright, I'll let you know about the cases. As for the project, it looks like everything is going as planned. We need to check in at the hotel, but we'll stop by later at the house to get the gear and say hi," Alex said.

Max asked, "You staying for dinner?"

V replied, "We just ate so that we might get another bite later at the hotel. It would be later tonight, but thank you."

Alex added, "We'll see you in a couple of hours at the house." Max smiled. "Great, see you later."

Alex and V stopped by Ella's office to say goodbye, then drove to the hotel and checked in. The next day, Alex and V spent the day and night out with his dad, sister, and uncle, camping a couple of hours away from his house. They raced ATVs and the T&B around. Alex made sure to clear all the bugs from the tent for V.

They arose early the next day and promptly returned to the university. The Students prepared for the next impending Pulse Reversal and the Halloween celebration.

XVII

Alex awoke to the sight of Declan, wearing a Frankenstein Monster mask, staring right at him. "Wake up, man! How was your trip? Are the Accelerators ready?"

Alex pushed him back. "Almost. We'll have to take you and Miko out for a ride. We're planning a trip to ride buggies on Amotaious. V really enjoyed herself." Declan removed his mask. "You guys camped out?"

Alex replied, "Just for one night with my dad and uncle. They were testing some modifications on the racer I told you about. V rode an ATV, and I took her for a spin in our thousand-horsepower desert racer." "That sounds like fun! A thousand horsepower? That's insanely fast," Declan exclaimed.

As Alex donned his robe to shower, he asked, "Anything happen here?" "Not much," Declan said. "We just hung out, drank, and worked a little."

"Are we having our nine o'clock meeting with Gig?" Alex inquired. Declan, starting to walk out of the room, said, "I presume so; I haven't heard anything different." He stopped and poked his head back in, "You ready for tonight? Batman!"

Alex yawned. "Shit, I forgot about that. Alright, I'll see you at the meeting." Declan walked down the hallway, making monster noises. The group met with Gig and the others. The meeting went well. They had a three-hour class on the History of Planets and then dinner.

V met with Alex in his room and handed him his costume. She went back to her room to change into hers.

A bit later, Alex, dressed in his Batman costume, knocked on V's door. V opened it. "Well, what do you think? I think it might be a little too tight."

Alex's jaw dropped as he stood there, speechless.

V's Cat Woman outfit looked like it was molded onto her body, all in black, complemented by high heels. Her makeup looked professionally done, and her hair was pulled back into a ponytail, a style she had never worn before.

Finally able to speak, Alex said, "Wow! You look... you look amazing. Are you sure you should wear that? Maybe put a sweater on over it? Maybe we should stay in tonight?" She smiled. "Pretty sexy, huh?" She scoffed. "We have to go to the party." She adjusted her shoe, then bent over to fix the bottom of the suit. "After the party, I'll let you touch my catsuit. What do you think of my tail?"

Alex remained speechless. She stood up and looked at him. "Let me see how yours fits."

Alex, clad in black with a cape and a mask covering his eyes, nose, and the top of his head, stood before her. "You look really nice," V said. "It fits just about right." She grabbed his crotch and asked, "How does it feel? Is it comfortable?"

In a deep Batman voice, Alex replied, "Woman, if you are trying to adjust my belt, you're a little too low. But yes, it feels very nice. Cat Woman, you better behave, or I'll have to punish you. I am Batman."

V grabbed Alex's crotch harder, smiled, and in a sultry Cat Woman voice, said, "Oh, I don't let just anyone touch my tail."

As they walked into the hallway, Alex said, "Never been one for dress-up fantasy, but I'm going to be staring at your body all night, thinking of all sorts of crazy things." V looked at Alex with a sexy smile. "Really?"

The two of them continued their way to the deck. The cavern by the pond was all lit up with orange lights. There was a large band tonight. The rest of the group was dressed up: Declan and Miko in their Bride and Monster of Frankenstein outfits. All the women wore very sexy costumes. Prezzy was a queen. Swaraj was a king. Lev and Maria were dressed as Doctors and Nurses. Maria and Kyoryk were Viking Warriors.

Candido and Tonari were dressed as a Priest and a Nun. Everyone mingled and had drinks. Bahdubah and Klinchme' looked great in their Wizard and Witch costumes.

Klinchme' seemed to have some difficulty walking around with the large Witch hat and her tray of drinks.

Alex and V sat at a table with Miko, Declan, Prezzy, and Swaraj. Declan commented, "I have to say, you ladies look exceptionally sexy tonight. Swaraj, what is your fantasy costume?" Swaraj looked around the room. "It's hard to say." The guys laughed hysterically.

Alex said, "I told V that I had so many thoughts the first time I saw her. As I look around the room, it's all too much to think about." Declan laughed again. "I know, right? It's like this weird fantasy." Swaraj suggested, "How about a hot queen or princess?"

Alex responded, "Good answer. How about you, Declan?" Declan answered carefully, "I always fantasized about two women dressed as sexy lumberjacks or two really dirty car mechanics. But tonight, it will have to be my bride here. She looks super sexy in that big gray tall wig."

V asked, "Okay, Alex, what is your fantasy?" Alex laughed. "All of you look very nice tonight, but I was thinking of a mermaid. She comes out of the water, takes you down under to the underwater city, and introduces you to her three sisters. Since they have never been with a land dweller, they have to touch and inspect you all over." They all laughed. Declan said, "Four mermaids? Nice, that sounds like fun." Alex added, "But, since mermaids aren't real, and since I am Batman, I would have to say Robin. If Robin's not available, then it would be, of course, Cat Woman."

Prezzy questioned, "You think Batman and Robin ever? You know?" Miko suggested, "How about a gladiator, just in from a battle, all bloodied?"

V gave Miko a strange look. "What? Bloodied and stuff? What does that mean?"

"I'm thinking of Superman. It might not be a lasting experience, though, because he is as fast as a bullet or a freight train. So I would have to say, a man with six arms. Think of what he could do to you."

Alex looked at her, surprised. "A man with six arms? What the hell? What if he had six...?"

Prezzy said, "How about a cowboy that has been out on the prairie for six months, all thirsty and shit?" Declan remarked, "Shit, you all have some weird fantasies."

"Alright, what's the scariest old movie you've seen?" Alex asked.

Prezzy replied, "Old scary movies? How about Jaws? I heard when it came out that not many people went swimming at the beach that summer."

"The Shining was good," Alex interjected.

Miko added, "The Exorcist when the little girl's head spun around. That was crazy."

Declan pointed out, "The original Psycho. Wrink, wrink, wrink." He mimicked a slashing motion with a knife.

Swaraj, sitting up in his seat and talking with his hands, said, "Poltergeist was fun, with the TV and everything. And that girl's voice yelling from inside the TV, 'Mommy, Mommy!'"

Everyone looked at V, waiting for her to add her two cents. "I haven't seen that many scary movies. Someone tried to get me to watch the Blair Witch Project or Carrie. Carrie was fricking scary."

Declan interrupted, "Have you seen *The Birds*? It's a trippy movie where thousands of birds go crazy and start pecking people's eyes out."

V grimaced. "Stop. Oh, shit, can we talk about something else?"

Declan suggested, "Let's do some shots or kamikazes."

Prezzy chimed in, "Let's do Slammers."

V proposed, "Let's ask Klinchme' for something new." She got Klinchme's attention.

Klinchme' approached and said, "How is everyone? You all look very nice."

V inquired, "Do you have something new, like Kamikazes or Slammers?"

Klinchme' paused, then said, "There's an alcohol that's green, and when you slam it on the table, it turns red." Declan laughed. "How does it do that?"

Klinchme', smiling, replied, "When it gets agitated, it changes color. If you don't drink it quickly, it turns back to green. I think it's called a Banger."

V exclaimed, "Twelve Bangers, please."

Everyone laughed. A few minutes later, Klinchme' returned with the shots. "You have to be fast, or it will turn back to green."

V said, "Thanks. Alright, who's first?" Declan didn't wait. He covered his shot with his hand, slammed it on the table, and watched it turn red, then almost immediately back to green. Klinchme' laughed. "You can't look at it; it changes back too quickly."

Surprising everyone, V slammed her shot on the table and drank it super-fast. "That's really good. It doesn't even taste like alcohol."

Klinchme' added, "I asked Bahdubah what they're called, and they're called Evil Bangers." They all laughed. "I wouldn't do too many too quickly. Maybe two or three, then wait a while. That's what Bahdubah said."

After three rounds of shots, most of the Stewards were now on the deck. Alex and V looked over to the stage, where more band members were joining. Three on horns, another drummer, several backup singers, a tall Elder on bongos, and several more.

A new **"Song"** began. *The Sky And The Dawn And The Sun.*

V nudged Alex to look over and see who was coming down the ramp from Terraenti Hall. It was Gig, Fem', Doog, and Fair, all dressed in black cloaks, hats, and makeup. Prezzy stood up and started waving at the band members, signaling the start of whatever was about to happen.

Four members, each wielding a large metal hammer, began striking anvils in rhythmic succession. Someone rolled out a chalkboard on wheels and started writing mathematical equations on it. A flutist played an ancient melody, and another woman began singing to the rhythm. Someone handed a microphone to Fem'. She walked to the front of the stage, performed a formal bow, and announced, "In our appreciation, we have written a tune for you all."

V looked at Prezzy. "What is this?"

Prezzy reassured them, "Just watch, it's going to be great."

The beautiful woman started singing softly as the band played a slow tune. "Today, we recognize their commitment, love, and compassion."

The big virtual screen in the cavern displayed slide shots of all the Student Elders from their stay around the university these last few months.

The music tempo increased, the horns blared, and the entire stage of musicians joined in. They all started singing in rhythm. Apparently, Gig, Fem, the Stewards, and others had created a tune along with a couple of Students. The lyrics went:

"So high is our commitment tonight.
From our love to your love.
We will fight and make it right to save Terenti, alright?
We will know our Creator's Right.

Let's save our planet's plight.

The Student Elders are the blade of the knife."

Over and over, in sync, the band struck their instruments. The tempo increased. In the background, sawing noises, metal grinding, hammering, all sounds of construction blended with the music. On stage, the Teacher worked on the chalkboard. The anvils were struck rhythmically. The instruments played to their fullest. Jet fighter noises, freight train effects, cheering from sports events, subway noises—all kinds of sound effects filled the air. The instruments grew louder, the singing continued, and images from around the world appeared on the virtual screen above the glacier lake.

Alex looked at V, both completely surprised. It was creative and spectacular. The stage seemed to have around 15 people playing different instruments, yet it sounded like 50 to 60 people were performing.

Everyone was out of their seats now, watching: all the Student Elders, the Steward Elders, Fem' and three other ladies, and all the other band members. The audience watched with bated breath as the tempo slowed and then came to a complete stop. The main singer, in a lovely soft voice, sang as the band accompanied her:

"We are the planets; He is the Galaxy.
We are the Stars. We are the Suns.
From every one of his fantastic rationalities,
We are the only ones with a consciousness that knows his reality.
He is Raba Rashi. Raba Rashi!"

The music stopped. Everyone shouted, "Raba Rashi!" Two men with big wooden hammers struck large gongs in the back.

The metal hammerers resumed striking the anvils in sync. The band burst into a faster rhythm and tempo. All the musicians and vocalists performed at full pace, transforming the music into an Electronic Dance type. The vocals re-entered:

"Come Join With Me! Come Join With Me." "It's a New Galaxy. It's a New Galaxy." They pounded their feet on the stage as the drums hit again and again. "I am the Stars and Suns; He is the One. I am the Stars, and He is always The One, The One, The One..."

The crowd went wild. Over the lake, flashing on the virtual screen, the words appeared:

"Save Terraenti! Save Terraenti! Save Terraenti!"

Fem' took a deep breath and said, "We wanted to show our appreciation for all the work you have done. So, Prezzy, Lin, and Maria wrote the tune, and with some band members from Amotaious, they put this together in just a few days. A big hand to them for a job well done." Everyone clapped and cheered.

Everyone gathered around Gig and Fem' on the stage. Fem' announced, "Let us take a moment to pray for the coming months. For our Students, our safety, and the survival of our planet." Fem' retrieved a crystal from her gown. Gig slammed his rock on the stage floor, and the crystal in her hand began to glow.

She chanted, "Ooh! Raba Rashi! Una CAT! Ooh, Raba Rashi! Una CAT! Uttah! Elders! Plandor, Magneeti Ferri Reesha! Demasters! De-Elders! Planda To Vorka, Reesha! Cama See La Ruh! Shanka Ne Ala-Muta, Ne! Tanka Ru! RaPlanna! Saffa Terru Nu Entu! Pat!"

Gig slammed the rock again. The room's lights dimmed, and the stone in her hands glowed even brighter. The room grew warmer as the air swirled around. Heavenly thunder rumbled, and a blue sapphire lightning bolt shot from the stone, swirling through the room. It shattered into many arrows, gently passing through the bodies of all the Students and Stewards. Everyone felt warm and tingly.

Their eyes shut, heads tilted back, and arms stretched out with palms up. A sensation like an electrical shock surged through them. Alex felt it within his body.

A few seconds later, he opened his eyes to see many smiling faces. Laughter filled the room as people discussed the amazing musical production. The band gathered and began to play again. Alex looked at V. "That was spectacular and really thoughtful of them. Did you know?"

V, still in shock, replied, "No, I had no idea. They must have worked on this while we were away. They did a great job." Alex and V danced before returning to their table.

Alex said, "Great job, Prezzy. That was fun. I can't believe how quickly you put that together."

Prezzy added, "Fem', Lin and Maria wrote the lyrics, and the band did the rest. I really didn't have much to do with it."

V smiled at her. "I'm guessing it was your idea in the first place, right?"

Prezzy smiled. "Yeah, I guess so. I thought it would be a fun thing to do for everyone."

The group at their table took more shots and danced more. Alex, looking at V, thought she now had the full effect of the Evil Bangers. Gig and Fem stopped by their table.

Fem' asked, "Well, what do you think?"

Declan said, "I really liked all the effects and different sounds. It was like a halftime Super Bowl production. I can't believe you did all this in a week or so."

Gig said, "The band is really good at coming up with these productions. I was also surprised at how well it turned out."

Alex added, "It was an amazing production. If the after-party of our mission is anything like this, it's going to be spectacular."

Gig said, "I think Prezzy, Maria, and Fem are already planning it."

They all looked at Prezzy and Fem', who smiled. Prezzy mimicked the zip-the-lip gesture. "We aren't going to tell, but yes, we are working on something, a much bigger production."

Miko said, "Let us know if we can help with anything."

Prezzy said, "Lin wants everyone to be involved next time. She has a plan, but that's all I will say for now."

Gig looking around at the group, "You all look very nice in your costumes. We didn't have Halloween in our time. It was more like a celebration of Fall, and everyone would dress up, and prepare for winter."

Fem' said, "Alright, have a good night." Gig added, "We'll see everyone tomorrow. Have fun."

A bit later, Prezzy and Swaraj returned to the dance floor, and Miko started kissing Declan. Alex looked at V and asked, "You ready?"

V smiled and replied, "Ready."

They returned to Alex's room. Alex said, "I think the Evil Bangers did something to you."

V, with a faraway look, said, "You think? I feel so mellow. Those shots were something. It's like a champagne buzz but in a mellow way."

Alex laughed. "Mellow, mellow." She lay down on his bed. He looked at her and, in a Batman voice, said, "Cat Woman is on my bed. What's Batman to do?"

She laughed. "If you pet me, I purr. If you attack me, I'll scratch and claw."

He sat down next to her and started to take off her clothes. "How did you get this thing on? It's like glued to your body."

V smiled. "Not sure. I don't remember anything. What was your name again?"

Alex laughed. "I'm Batman, and I'm here to teach you a lesson. You've been a very bad kitty."

V asked, "What did I do?"

Alex pushed her shoulders down. "You stole the Marque Delamore diamond from Max Volt and killed his butler."

She said, "Oh, I did? I forgot. What are you going to do to me?"

Alex said, "You've been drinking, Cat Woman. I'm going to tie you to the bed and torture you."

She said, "Batman would never do that. He is too polite. He could help me get out of this tight suit, and then he would bring me a glass of water."

Alex got up and tried to figure out how to get the black suit off her. "This thing is welded onto your body." He struggled to pull her pants off. V laughed and started purring. He got the top of her suit off, covered her with a sheet, and said, "Let me get you some water."

In a quiet voice, she said, "Thank you, Batman."

Alex returned a few minutes later with a bottle of water and saw that V had fallen asleep. He took off his Batman suit and lay down next to her. He pulled her hair back from her face and said, "So beautiful." He kissed her cheek and fell asleep next to her. The evening ended.

The group prepared for the upcoming Pulse Reversal.

XVIII

Midnight loomed as V and Alex stood vigilant in the lab, their eyes fixed on the monitors, scanning for the next Pulse Reversal. Tasked with the first shift, they had been prepared for this moment after days of intense training and classes.

"What exactly are we watching for?" V inquired, her gaze shifting to Alex as he adjusted a couple of switches, transferring the live feed from the sun onto the larger monitor. "This," Alex replied, pointing at the screen, "We're monitoring solar activity. When it happens, the alarm will sound, and we'll need to alert everyone to head to their safe zones."

"Which part of the Earth will get hit this time?" V questioned, a hint of concern in her voice. "This time, we can't pinpoint the location," Alex explained, his tone serious. "But once the second one strikes, we'll have the exact timing figured out."

V glanced at the clock. "So, we're on watch for four hours? The last hit was around three in the afternoon, right?" "Closer to four," Alex corrected, "And when it happens, we'll know precisely when the next one will occur, down to the minute."

Three hours dragged by. V yawned, breaking the silence. "Alright, anything else to do here?" "Klinchme stashed some drinks and sandwiches in the mini-fridge if you're hungry," Alex offered.

V smiled and shook her head. "I'm good." "Do you remember the protocol for the intercom when the alarm goes off?" Alex asked, ensuring they were prepared.

V grinned mischievously. "Oh, you mean to scream, 'Panic and run for the hills!' and then make spooky crackling noises into the mic?" Alex chuckled. "There are actual instructions by the mic. Might want to review them."

V rose from her chair, removing her hoodie revealing her tight, multi-colored workout clothes. She began stretching, her movements deliberate.

Her hair, tied back in a ponytail, swayed as she bent, catching Alex's eye. "You're driving me crazy," Alex admitted, unable to look away.

V moaned softly as she stretched, then teased in a sultry voice, "How about this one?" She placed her foot on the table, flipping her hair back, and eyed him seductively. "This one really stretches my lower thigh," Alex smirked, his pulse quickening. "I can see that. It's definitely getting my blood flowing."

As V straightened up, she glanced at the monitor. "How much longer until the next shift?" "I told you, another hour, stop moving around," Alex replied, checking the time again.

"I think I have something in my eye," V said, feigning distress. "Come help me in the bathroom." Alex hesitated, eyeing the monitor. "Make it quick." Together, they slipped into the small bathroom between the lab and the operations room. "Which eye is it?" Alex asked, leaning in to inspect.

V hopped onto the counter, pulling him close. Her hand darted to his crotch as she whispered, "I lied. It's not my eye that's bothering me; it's the bulge in your pants." A grin spread across Alex's face. "Isn't this a bit risky?" he asked as V kissed him, unzipping his jeans.

"Then you'd better hurry," she murmured, pulling down her tights. She glanced back at the door. "Miko and Declan did it here. I just wanted to see what the fuss was about." Alex laughed softly. "To see what? The thrill of a public restroom quickie?" He pressed closer, grabbing her hips and pulling her towards him. "It's about this. And this. And this!"

V tilted her head back, moaning in pleasure. "Oh my. I get it now. I like this." He groaned, caught up in the moment. "Are you some kind of sex addict?"

She moaned again, teasing, "We haven't done it since that morning. I woke up in my Cat Woman outfit. And don't call me a maniac," she added playfully, her eyes flicking to the door. "Someone could walk in any second."

"Wasn't that three days ago?" Alex kissed her hungrily, their passion intensifying. "Oh! Oh!" He suddenly pulled back. "I think I hear someone coming."

V's eyes widened in panic. "What? Really?" Alex laughed, urging her, "We have to hurry, hurry, hurry."

She kissed him again, her body moving in rhythm with his. "No, don't rush," she whispered, her voice breathy. "Slower, Alex. That's it, right there."

Another minute passed before V clung to him, her grip tightening as she gasped, "Aaahhhh, yes, perfect." She muttered something in Hindi, her voice low and satisfied.

The warmth of her sent Alex over the edge. He moaned, feeling her legs wrap around him. "That was… thrilling," he panted.

V laughed, still breathless. "Yes, it was." She playfully added, "Thanks for helping me get that thing out of my eye." "Anytime, anywhere," Alex replied, smiling as he pulled up his jeans. "I'm always happy to assist with your eye troubles."

They both crept out of the bathroom, careful not to be seen. V grinned at Alex, "Safe and sound. But your face is all red." Alex took a deep breath, his pulse slowly returning to normal. "Too bad we don't have two shifts; we could do that again."

V sat next to him, laughing. "Did you wash your hands?" She teased, "What if the alarm had gone off while we were in there?" He laughed back. "Then I would've had to go even faster."

"That was pretty exciting," V said, her voice still laced with adrenaline. "I'll have to thank Miko." "So, Miko suggested doing it in the bathroom?" Alex asked, intrigued.

"No," V replied, smiling. "Declan did. He's always up for it." Alex chuckled, "Funny, he told me the opposite. Said it was her idea. She's the one who likes to spice things up."

V raised an eyebrow. "Really? They have interesting dynamics." She turned her attention to the monitor. "Does the sun give any warning before the Reversal?" "Just that it goes eerily quiet," Alex explained, his focus shifting back to the screens. "Few, if any, sunspots remain."

"And the poles? Still migrating?" V asked, her curiosity piqued. "Yes," Alex confirmed. "The poles continue to migrate, weakening the Magnetic Field."

"They might even shift back toward the geographic poles, a phenomenon known as Magnetic Excursions. It occurs more often than once every twelve thousand years."

V leaned back in her chair. "So, where do you want to go when it happens again? Back to the vault?" "No," Alex said firmly. "We'll stay here in the lab. It's safe, and I want to monitor everything firsthand."

V glanced around. "So, it's just as safe here?" Alex nodded confidently. "Yes, safer even. Last time, the vault was too crowded. That's why Doog had us all go there. But here, we have everything we need to manage the situation."

Half an hour later, Candido and Tonari enter the room. Candido asks, "How's it going?"

V, slightly bored, replies, "Nothing's happening—pretty uneventful. How are you two holding up?" Tonari grins, "I suppose I'm as good as one can be at four in the morning."

Alex rises from his seat. "You both remember how to handle everything?" Candido approaches the control panel, where the mic and alarm controls are located and nods confidently. "Yeah, we should be fine." He picks up the binder with the instructions. "We've got this. You two can head out." Alex says, "We'll be in V's room getting some sleep. If anything happens, the alarm will wake us, and we'll come back to the lab." Tonari reassures them, "Sounds good. Doog told us to call if we have any questions, but I think we're good."

V adds with a smile, "Great, see you later today."

Afterward, V and Alex catch some much-needed sleep. V awakens around eleven o'clock and heads to the common room for coffee, finding Lin, Lev, Swaraj, and Prezzy lounging around.

"How's it going? Anything happens yet?" V inquires, still shaking off the remnants of sleep. Lev responds, "Nope, nothing yet. Our shift starts in an hour, so we'll see." Turning to Prezzy, V asks, "When's your shift?"

"We've got the last shift from 8 to midnight tonight. Everyone thinks it'll hit around the same time as before, around 3 or 4," Prezzy replies.

V nods, "Yeah, that's what Alex was saying. Did you guys get any sleep?" Lev answers, "A bit. There's not much else going on, just waiting. I saw Candido and Tonari earlier—they're sleeping now, or at least trying to. Kyoryk and Maria are in the lab."

Alex enters the room, and V announces, "I'm going for a swim. It should help me relax." "I'll join you," Alex offers, his expression softening as he looks at her.

V smiles and takes a sip of her coffee. Alex, standing close, says, "I'd like to be in the lab between three and five if possible. By the way, I talked to Rev at Alva about the crates for the Accelerators—they're going to have them made and shipped to my father. Did you just wake up?" V grins, kisses him, and replies, "I did. I've only been up for half an hour or so."

After their swim, V and Alex meet in the dining area, grabbing some food before sitting down with Harvey and Freida. V asks, "Is the University all set for the Reversal?" Freida responds, "Yes, we're ready. How are you two holding up?" Alex says, "We're managing, just trying to stay calm."

Harvey chimes in, "We're in good shape. The University has weathered many Pulse Reversals before. Where will you be when it hits?"

Alex replies, "Once we hear the alarm, I thought we'd go to the lab. I'd rather be there than in the vault. The last experience wasn't exactly pleasant. Do you think it'll happen around the same time?" Harvey considers this. "It's possible. What time did the last one hit?"

"4:55 p.m., our time," Alex answers. Harvey nods. "Maybe we'll join you then. We have a meeting at 3:00, but it's a short one." Freida shifts the conversation. "How's the schedule looking? Will we be ready when we return to Amotaious?"

V responds, "Yes, we'll be ready next week. Declan and the others are meeting with the engineers about the tents. The main challenge is getting the Master Elders to agree. What happens if they don't? Are we going ahead anyway?" Harvey, with a resolute expression, answers, "We'll do whatever it takes. We already have enough Elders on our side. Gig says he has two Elders with the same Gifts as Declan and Swaraj."

"When I spoke with Gig, Fem', and the others, they made it clear we're proceeding with or without approval."

V's eyes widen in shock. "Oh, that could lead to serious issues down the road." Freida agrees, "Yes, but we'll cross that bridge when we get there. The instructions came from the Creator; we're going through with it."

Alex turns to Harvey. "I didn't realize so many others felt this strongly. Will we be part of the meeting this time?" Harvey shakes his head. "No, we'll be in the audience this time. We've done our presentation, fulfilled our part. It's now up to them to decide. Gig said he'll take a vote, and that's it. If they don't agree, he'll handle it."

V stands up, her decision made. "We'll be in the common room until 3:00, then we'll head to the lab." "Alright, see you later," Harvey responds, as he and Freida prepare to leave.

In the common room, everyone waits anxiously. V and Alex attempt to work on the schedule, but nerves are running high.

A couple of hours later, V and Alex head to the lab, where Lev, Lin, Doog, and Fair are already monitoring the situation. Alex and V take their seats in the operations room. At 4:45, Alex gets up and walks over to the monitor displaying a live feed of the sun from one of Earth's satellites. He turns to Doog. "Can we put it up on the big monitor?" Doog looks up. "Sure. Do you think it'll happen at the same time as before?"

Alex replies, "Not sure, just a feeling." Fair chimes in, "When you saw it in your vision, you didn't catch the time?"

Alex shakes his head. "No, I just remember the date. But once it happens today, we'll know the exact time for the next one." Doog confirms, "Yes, it's down to the minute, at least it has been in the past."

V, feeling the tension, admits, "The waiting is making me anxious." Doog smiles reassuringly. "Well, at least we know it will happen within the next 8-9 hours. We've never had a warning like this before. Alex's Gift is really going to help us."

V asks, "What do we do when it hits? Sit on the floor like last time?"

"You can sit in a chair, on the couch over there, or on the floor—whatever feels safest. We just don't want anything falling on anyone or for you to fall," Doog explains. Harvey and Freida enter the room. Freida asks, "Nothing yet?"

V responds, "No, nothing. It's almost past the time of the last one." Declan and Miko then join them, and Declan asks, "We're here for our shift—everything quiet?"

Alex nods. "Yeah, and it's past the time. I thought it might happen at the same time as before." Lev announces, "Alright, we're going to rest for a bit." "Sounds good. Thanks, guys," Doog replies, as Lev and Lin exit the room. Doog then reviews the emergency procedures with Declan and Miko. The six of them settle in, and as 4:55 approaches, Declan asks, "Before the shock wave, do we leave the doors open or closed?"

Doog clarifies, "The doors are supposed to remain open. If there's a vacuum leak or the sensors detect any hydrogen, these doors will automatically close. These two rooms are some of the safest places in the university. That, and maybe the rooms in the docks, followed by the safe room near the kitchen, then the vault. Those are the four safest places during a reversal."

V asked, "When the super flare struck in the past, where did you seek shelter?" Fair replied, "Last time, we retreated to Amotaious. The university shuts down, and everyone is evacuated as a precaution; it's simply too dangerous to remain here during the CAT. However, this time, a few will stay behind for communication purposes."

V's eyes narrowed. "Well, this time, we'll all be at risk—we'll be on the planet." Fair nodded, a hint of surprise in her voice. "That's the gamble we're taking. I was astonished that when we asked our people on Amotaious for volunteers, most didn't hesitate. We even received volunteers from other planets, despite the significant risk of death."

V pondered aloud, "What drives so many to risk their lives?" Doog interjected, "I believe it's two things: the chance to be part of something that will alter history, and the connection to previous Elders who still have relatives on the planet. We've even received volunteers from the great-grandchildren of those from Amotaious. As long as they possess a strong Common Mind, all are welcome to volunteer."

"And perhaps the most compelling reason is the belief that the Creator deems humanity ready for our next level of consciousness."

Alex, reflective, added, "I hadn't considered it that way. I was thinking we needed Stewards and Student Elders from previous CATs." Doog corrected him, "No, Kyoryk said anyone from Amotaious could volunteer. We've had hundreds come forward."

Alex shook his head in disbelief. "That's incredible. I thought we'd struggle to find participants. And they all understand the risks?" Fair glanced at her tablet, "We sent out a general message to everyone on Amotaious. As of today, we have 353 volunteers. We're working on a more efficient way to select them. Many are young, given the population boom over the last century."

V, her face showing shock, asked, "That's insane. How will you choose?" Fair explained, "We don't want anyone too young. Previous Student Elders and Stewards are automatically included if they sign up. Beyond that, we're considering choosing the closest relatives to them, particularly those from Terraenti. But volunteers from other planets have also stepped forward. There's even been talk of the Master Elders staying out of it because we'll need them for future council meetings. Has Gig spoken to you and Alex about possibly staying on Amotaious during the CAT?"

V's shock deepened. "They don't want the Master Elders to participate?" Fair nodded solemnly. "We'll need our Master Elders if this doesn't work out. But I'm unsure if they'll be forced to stay."

Alex, overhearing the conversation, interjected, "Wait, are the Master Elders from previous CATs not going to participate?" Fair sighed, "Think about it—if something goes wrong and we lose one or two of the previous Master Elders, who will represent us on Amotaious?"

Alex's concern grew. "I hadn't even thought about that. Damn, V and I are close to becoming Master Elders. Are they considering keeping us out of it?" Fair hesitated. "I shouldn't have said anything. Gig and Fem' were planning to discuss it with you."

Alex called Harvey and Freida over. "Did you know about the possibility of all the Master Elders staying on Amotaious during the CAT?"

Harvey, caught off guard, replied, "I know it was discussed. We need the Master Elders to carry out their duties."

Alex and V exchanged a worried glance, knowing they were likely to become the next Master Elders. Both looked visibly upset. V asked, "What about our group? None of us are Master Elders yet. Is Gig going to make the two of us stay on Amotaious? Are they considering making Alex and me stay?" Harvey, trying to diffuse the tension, said, "Nothing has been decided, and we understand how much this means to you both."

Alex turned to Declan. "There's no way I'm staying on Amotaious while everyone else risks their lives. What about you, V? What do you think?" V spoke a few words in Hindi before responding, "Alex and I received messages from the Creator. We're meant to be there. And who's to say we'll be the next Master Elders?"

Miko, attempting to calm V, reassured her, "I don't think they can stop you from going. Everyone knows you and Alex are destined to be the next Master Elders. You should have the power to make your own decisions." Harvey urged, "Let's slow down, everyone. Nothing is set in stone. We'll figure it out. Everything will work out as it's supposed to."

Alex, trying to remain calm, declared, "There's no way V and I will stay on Amotaious when the CAT hits. Absolutely not."

At that moment, Declan, his eyes fixed on the main monitor, exclaimed, "Look, what's that?"

Doog quickly assessed the monitor and confirmed, "That's it—it's happening."

The alarm blared, and everyone stood, transfixed, as the monitor displayed the sun ejecting an enormous ring of magnetic energy and plasma. Declan turned to Miko. "We need to get on the coms and alert everyone to prepare."

Miko, visibly nervous, shook her head. Declan, sensing her hesitation, looked to Alex and then to Doog, who nodded, "Go ahead, Declan. It's not a drill—tell the others."

Declan, looking visibly shaken, agreed. "Alright, Alex, help me." Alex handed him the notebook. "It's all in here. You can do it—just read it."

Declan pressed the mic button and, with a nervous edge to his Scottish accent, announced, "This is not a test. Please proceed calmly to your safe areas. This is not a test."

"Once there please notify the lab, thank you." He glanced at Alex and, after clicking off the mic, asked, "How long until the shock wave?"

Alex, checking the monitor, replied, "It says it will hit us in eight minutes. Good job on the mic by the way." He said with a smile.

Declan quickly clicked the mic back on and continued, "We have less than eight minutes. Please proceed to the four safe areas immediately. This is Declan. Please confirm when you've reached your safe areas by calling the lab or any one of us. Currently in the lab are Miko, Alex, V, Harvey, Freida, Doog, and Fair. Contact any of us to confirm your location. Thank you."

Alex chuckled, flashing a grin at Declan. "You're doing great, mate."

The lab phone rang, and Doog swiftly picked it up. Gig's voice came through, "Fem and I are in the medical bay."

Miko grabbed a notepad, "I'll keep track." She began jotting down names.

Doog spoke to Gig and hung up the phone. "Make sure you note their locations too. We need to know where everyone is."

V received a call from Prezzy and put it on the speaker. "I'm with Swaraj, Kyoryk, and Maria. We're almost at the kitchen." Miko scribbled down their details. The calls continued, with people checking in and reporting their whereabouts. Bahdubah and Klinchme' then walked into the lab.

Alex, eyes locked on the monitor, marveled, "Look at the size of that thing. That's wild!" His gaze was fixed on the massive solar flare erupting from the sun. "See how lightning-like tendrils trail off their sides and loop back into the sun? It looks similar to the last one—maybe a bit weaker?"

Doog analyzed the monitor, "Hard to say just by looking, but the size seems consistent with the previous ones. That's a positive sign."

Declan continued notifying the university of the countdown, while Miko diligently recorded everyone's names and locations. The alarm was finally silenced, and minutes ticked by. Miko reviewed the list, "Alright, everyone's accounted for."

Doog exhaled in relief, "Great. I think we're good. The power should cut off any moment now. Let's sit tight."

V and Alex settled on a small couch in the operations room, while Doog and Fair sat on the floor nearby. Harvey, Freida, Declan, and Miko took their places in rolling chairs.

Alex, attempting to reassure V, smiled at her. Suddenly, the power breakers clicked off, plunging the ops room into darkness, save for the dim glow of battery-powered backup lights. From the other room, about five meters away, Declan's voice broke through, "Here we go!"

Alex wrapped an arm around V, who closed her eyes and clung to him. Silence fell over the group. Moments later, the room began to shudder; a few items toppled from shelves and tables. Loud crashes echoed through the university. A stronger tremor followed, causing Harvey, Declan, and the girls' chairs to slide several inches, alarming Miko. Declan reached out to steady her. More objects clattered to the floor in the adjacent room, but then the shaking ceased.

V sensed the static electricity in the air, just like last time. Her thoughts raced, *I hate this— this uncertainty, this lack of control. It's nothing like almost rolling that ATV the other day with Alex's sister, that was fun.*

It's far worse—being trapped in a metal box inside a crater on the moon while the sun partially erupts. This is messed up.

V opened her eyes, noticing the hair on Alex's arm standing on end. She inhaled deeply, exhaled slowly, and surveyed the dimly lit room. Alex glanced toward Doog, "I think it was less intense than the first." Doog nodded, "It appears so. That's usually how it goes—they weaken before the big one. The pattern's held for years."

They remained seated; the tension still palpable. Doog eventually stood and helped Fair to her feet. "Everyone alright?" Harvey, ever the joker, chuckled, "We're okay. That was… interesting. Quite the experience for my first time." Freida, unimpressed by his humor, shook him gently. Doog added, "We'll restore the power shortly. Let's wait for the static charge to dissipate."

Alex and V stood up. V remarked, "That wasn't as bad as last time."

Alex agreed, "We were prepared this time. It felt less overwhelming."

Doog instructed, "Alex, get ready to reset the breakers like last time. I'll tell you when. Let's check in with everyone first. Declan, call Kyoryk and make sure they're okay in the kitchen. I'll reach out to Gig in the medical bay. Miko, was anyone in the vault?"

Miko responded, "Roman and a couple of others. I'll call them."

After checking in, it seemed all was well. Doog gave the go-ahead, "Alright, Alex. Let's bring the power back online."

"Got it," Alex replied. He moved to the main panel, pulled down the breaker, and then forced it back up. The breaker emitted a loud, energetic snap, followed by softer clicks from the other panel. Monitors flickered back to life, and lights illuminated the room. V glanced around, observing the gauges and indicators as the systems powered up. A faint static charge still lingered in the air. Alex returned to the room and began typing on the keyboard.

V asked, "What are you looking at?" Alex paused, "I'm checking where it hit on the planet." After a moment, he added, "Looks like Africa and the Red Sea area. Doesn't seem as severe as the first one."

V nodded, "It felt different here too—less shaking, but more static in the air." Harvey smiled, attempting to lighten the mood, "That wasn't so bad. I expected worse." He waved his arms theatrically to amuse the group.

V reminisced, "Last time, it scared the hell out of us. Some of us were in the vault—it was terrifying not knowing what to expect." Alex looked at Harvey, "That's right, you were returning from Amotaious when the first one hit. It was definitely scarier then. We weren't prepared. This time, we knew it was coming. That made all the difference." Freida added, "It wasn't fun. I wouldn't want to be here when the big one hits. At least on Earth, you have some protection. Isn't it true the moon's magnetic field offers little protection?"

Alex confirmed, "Only partially. You're right—the planet is far more protected, at least for now. We definitely need to strengthen the magnetic field with the accelerators. I'm not ready to return to the Stone Age, tilling the ground by hand and hunting for whatever's left to eat. No one is."

Doog reminded them, "Even if we boost the field to its maximum, it'll still impact the planet. Most continents could be without power for years."

V remarked, "Lin was talking about the blackout in the U.S. in 2025. She said about 20,000 people died, and the power was only out for a week or two. This time, it could be out for years, which would be infinitely worse."

Alex nodded, his expression firm. "We'll do what we can. Even if people are without phones or electricity for a while, our efforts will make a difference. I'm not staying on Amotaious. Anyone thinking that should forget it."

Harvey, his eyes filled with empathy, placed a reassuring hand on Alex's shoulder. "I understand. Freida, Doog, Fair, and I will discuss it with Gig. I'm sure we'll cover it in one of our upcoming meetings. No one's going to force you and V to stay on Amotaious."

V, her voice tinged with concern, asked, "But what if the power stays out for a year during this CAT? How many would die then?" Fair's tone was grave. "During our last CAT, we lost over ninety percent of the population—billions gone. It started well, but wars and famines took many more. Another disaster followed, wiping out even more. That's why all our technology was lost, and everything had to start over. Now, there are over a thousand on Amotaious and over nine billion on Earth. History has a way of repeating itself."

Alex and V exchanged troubled glances. V shook her head in disbelief. "That's insane." Doog added somberly, "If you looked at our family tree, it would blow your mind. There's been a population boom on Amotaious over the last hundred years, and we're not sure what's causing it. Elders are now having four or five children when before they had none or one. The galaxy is a dangerous place. A super volcano or a meteor can reduce the population by eighty or ninety percent in an instant."

Harvey shot Doog a disapproving look. "You're going to depress everyone. Let them be. For now, we're okay." He then brightened, "Who knows what could happen after we save the planet?

We might expand to another world. Never underestimate progress. Anyway, you four are done here. Why don't you go relax and grab something to eat? We'll talk more in our next meeting." Alex smiled, "You're right."

V agreed, "I'm starting to realize how fragile our system is. In a big city, you can find any kind of food, a doctor, dentist, entertainment—everything is within a half-hour walk. But take away one or two of those, and that's it. What if you're in a cold area without electricity? That's it—you're a popsicle!"

Alex chuckled, "Let's not dwell on it. We'll all drive ourselves nuts." Declan added, "V, I guarantee that most people I know wouldn't have a clue how to live without power. We'd all have to move to Lin's parents' house off the grid. That wouldn't last a week before someone tried to kill us for what we had." Miko, her tone firm, interjected, "I think that's enough. Let's talk about something else." Freida nodded in agreement. "You're right, Miko. We can't control everything, and it's not healthy to dwell on it. Let's focus on saving as many people as we can and preserving the technology and history we've built over the last four thousand years."

V, Alex, Declan, and Miko made their way back to the common room. As they walked, V turned to Miko, her voice tinged with disbelief. "So, in all the previous CATs and other events, the population drops to five or ten percent, or even less? That's insane. With what we're doing, I hope we can save more than that."

Miko sighed, "I sure hope so. We just need to focus on what we can do and hope for the best. Freida's right—we can't dwell on the past or these events that happen every ten thousand years. We need to focus on the future and finish the Creator's Plan."

Declan nodded. "She's right. Let's save as many as we can, as the first Creator's message says. With the Common Mind so strong within us now, we should be able to do remarkable things—things we don't even realize we have the power to do yet."

Alex grinned. "You're a brilliant guy, Declan. You just said something that's so true. We have this power we haven't even begun to tap into yet. We need to put it to the test."

V glanced at Alex curiously. "And you have an idea of what to do?" Alex's smile widened as he looked at her. "I think so."

The group entered the common room, where the others were relaxing, trying to cope with what had just happened.

Alex raised his hand high to get everyone's attention. "Hey, everyone! I'd like us all to gather and do an experiment with the Common Mind after dinner. It's been a while since we synced up and put our minds together." He scanned the room, his gaze landing on each Student. "If it's okay with you all, we could share our thoughts and feelings. We're halfway to saving the planet and our people. We all need to focus on the positive possibilities for our future and that of the planets."

The room buzzed with agreement.

Lev spoke up, "We need to focus on something to start it off, then our thoughts and feelings will take over from there. So, what should we concentrate on at the beginning?"

V suggested, "We could go over the items on the schedule. First, we have the meeting of Elders on Amotaious. Then, we have the test of the Accelerators on December 27th, ready for the next Reversal at 5:33 pm our time. Or we could make it more personal—everyone could share how we're doing individually. That might be better."

Kyoryk stepped forward, his expression thoughtful. "We've all been through a lot. The second option might be a good way for us all to share and open up a little."

Prezzy hopped up, her eyes shining. "I think that's a great idea."

Miko raised her hand. "I'm willing to give it a try."

Maria muttered something in Russian, prompting Lin and Lev to laugh. Lev grinned and translated, "Yes, dropping your dithers works for me."

Tonari, looking puzzled, asked, "What does that mean?"

Lin explained with a grin, "Showing everyone your vulnerable side—or showing everyone your whoo-hoo."

Tonari's confusion deepened. "I have to show you my...?"

Alex interrupted, "Yes, perfect. Everyone meets back here at 7:30."

V approached Alex, smiling. "This is a good idea," she said. "I think it'll be good for everyone."

Alex nodded. "And if it works, we could have meetings like this every other month or so. I also want to see how strong the Common Mind is with all of us working together like this."

Declan came up behind Alex, placing his hands on Alex's shoulders. "This will be fun—a big group meeting. Who knows what could happen?"

Alex smiled. "Yeah, it was your idea. Remember when you said, 'We should be able to do remarkable things'? That gave me the idea to do this. And in class, they said they used the Common Mind to cut and shape the stone. So, we should be able to do something as Student Elders, right?"

Declan and V exchanged incredulous glances, their shock evident. Declan spoke first, "That engineering mind of yours is always at work, isn't it?"

V playfully nudged Declan's shoulder, "He's a brilliant man, no doubt about it."

V then wrapped her arms around Alex in a warm hug, while Miko shrugged and asked, "Do I have to reveal my deepest, darkest secrets during the meeting?"

Declan laughed heartily, "Have you even shared all your darkest secrets with me?"

Miko chuckled, "Absolutely not!"

Before Declan could respond, V interjected, "No, it's not about that. We're just sharing how we've been doing over the last few months. Alex or I will start to set the tone, so things don't get too weird. It's just about how we're coping with school, nothing too personal. Don't you guys think that would be good?"

Alex, Declan, and Miko nodded in agreement. Miko then hugged V. "Oh, so it's just about the recent months."

V smiled, "Exactly. Now, let's go grab something to eat."

The group dispersed, heading to the dining area. An hour later, they reconvened in the common room, where V had arranged the chairs and couches in a circle. Once everyone was seated, Alex stood, cleared his throat, and began, "I was thinking we could go around the room, updating everyone on the current strength of your Gift. Then, share your personal thoughts on how you've been handling life here at the university. V and I agreed we don't want this to be about the schedule or the Creator's Plan—nothing like that. I'll start to set the tone, and V will wrap it up.

Afterward, we can experiment with the Common Mind, perhaps doing a sort of meditation to see what happens."

He smiled nervously, glancing around the room. Though apprehensive about speaking in a group and opening up, Alex continued, "I've come to know you all fairly well—some more than others—and, well, V and I are very close." He glanced affectionately at V before continuing, "I haven't seen much of the future lately, except for the Pulse Reversal. I've been practicing identifying what triggers my future sight, focusing primarily on preparing to save as many lives as possible on the planet. It was a relief to visit my family, and I'm looking forward to the holiday break, maybe even meeting V's family in India."

Pausing, Alex looked thoughtful. "What we've been chosen to do here has weighed heavily on me. I'm grappling with the potential outcome for the planet. Now that my aging process has slowed, I'm finding it mentally challenging to think in terms of centuries, rather than decades or even days. And the possibility of becoming an Elder, or even a Master Elder, has been daunting."

He took a deep breath. "I've been putting immense pressure on myself to figure everything out. I want you all to know—I never desired to be a Master Elder; I just wanted to help save the planet. I've also struggled with discerning how much of my emotions come from the Common Mind versus my own feelings. It's hard to tell where one ends, and the other begins, especially with everything happening here."

He glanced around the room, meeting everyone's eyes. "Some of us have learned that the Master Elders are supposed to remain on Amotaious during the next Accelerator tests and the actual event. This really bothers me. I can't imagine just standing by while others complete the mission I was sent here to accomplish. I'm hoping that all gets resolved."

Alex sighed, "Our arrival here changed everything—the way I see the world, my place in it, and what the future holds. I don't think it has fully sunk in yet, and I'm still processing it all. The thought of living thousands of years on a completely different planet—it's so overwhelming. But at the same time, I'm grateful for the opportunity and look forward to working with you all in the coming year to achieve our goals. Beyond that, who knows what the next three years at the university will bring?"

He smiled wryly. "I have no complaints, just laser-focused on getting the Accelerators working and, hopefully, saving the planet."

Alex then gestured to Declan, signaling it was his turn. Declan grinned, "I'm Declan, and I'm an alcoholic." The room erupted in laughter. He continued, "Seriously, though, my ability to move larger objects has grown stronger. My relationship with Miko has been incredible—we, uh, have quite an active love life." Miko elbowed him, playfully scolding, "What the hell?"

Declan smiled, "But in all seriousness, Miko and I have a solid relationship, and I'm excited about our future together. I'm also really looking forward to returning to Amotaious and doing some traveling, seeing the sights. Like everyone else, I've been struggling with the immense changes that have happened over the last few months—our roles here and what they might mean. We've all been thrust into extraordinary circumstances, and it's overwhelming. What a crazy university. Right?"

He rubbed his face, clearly contemplating the enormity of their situation. "All the potential outcomes for the planet and its people... This school, this mission—it's a lot to process. But as a group, I believe we can overcome it. I'm with you all, supporting you all the way. I'm like a candle in the wind, still learning, still growing. That's about it for me." He squeezed Miko's hand, offering her a supportive smile. "I've been having a lot of fun so far thanks."

Miko smiled and took her turn. "I've been honing my Gift, extending my sight further and further. I can almost see all the way to the big doors on the surface. Soon, I hope to see miles through anything, which should be helpful during the Accelerator tests."

She glanced at Declan, grinning. "Declan is my man, though he's nothing but trouble. But I'm working on him—I'm sure I can change him for the better." The room filled with laughter, except for Declan, who playfully shot her a dirty look. Miko continued, "I want him to be more focused on my needs." More chuckles rippled through the group. "I'm really looking forward to returning to the planet. We've been cooped up here for too long. I can't wait to feel real sunlight on my skin, see my family, maybe catch up with some friends."

Miko's expression turned serious. "Everything in my life has changed so drastically. I'm honestly surprised I'm not on medication. From the day we arrived at the University, it's been overwhelming—living longer, the potential loss of loved ones, and the thought of outliving them all. But I'm really glad to have you all with me. I've made some great friends here. Like in gymnastics, when you fall, you get right back up and try again. So, I'll keep doing that. Other than that, I'm okay. I guess that's it for me."

Prezzy suddenly cleared her throat, jumped out of her chair, and stood with her arms outstretched. "I love you all, and I truly believe we're going to save the planet. We will get it done. I'm also really looking forward to going home. If anyone wants to go surfing, that's where you'll find me. Sitting on a board, waiting for a wave—that's what it's all about."

She closed her eyes and disappeared for a few seconds, eliciting smiles from everyone. As she reappeared, she continued, "I can stay invisible for around three to four minutes now. I'm planning to rob the biggest bank in Sydney when I get back—who's in?" She paused, scanning the room before chuckling. "Just kidding! But seriously, I'm working on extending it to ten or fifteen minutes."

Prezzy hugged Swaraj and teased, "Never in a million years did I think I'd be in a relationship with an Indian guy, but Swaraj here—he's got this amazing trick where he lifts us up in the air during sex. It's truly spectacular." She grinned at Swaraj, who blushed slightly and muttered, trying to pull her down. "Shoosh, stop kidding around momma."

V glanced at Alex, a smile playing on her lips, and whispered, "This was a good idea. Everyone seems to be relaxing a bit." Alex returned her smile, relieved to see the group at ease.

Swaraj, pats her on the leg as she sits, "Well, this has all been a real big change for me." He smiles at Prezzy, crosses his legs, looks around at the group, his voice calming. "Prezzy has helped me, you all have helped me. This is all crazy. My siblings are young. So, I was on my own when I grew up. Now I have a family, I feel that. I'm trying to lift and hold heavier items."

He held up both his hands to illustrate. "Can't wait to get back to the planet. Get back to some simulation of a normal life somehow maybe."

"I think that would make me feel a little better." Prezzy fidgets in her seat. Swaraj laughs, sits back in his seat, "Prezzy keeps me on my toes every time she jumps up in excitement, I love her for that." Some laugh. "This is all crazy, I really want to help and do my part. That's it for me, thanks."

344

Lin rises from her seat, a confident smile playing on her lips. "I believe this," she begins, her voice firm yet warm. "All of you, everything we've been doing, has been extraordinary. I've had—and will continue to have—the time of my life. And when we save this planet, it's going to be the most exhilarating feeling imaginable. I'm certain we're going to succeed; it's all going to work out. My Gift of language is unique, and it's already proven its worth. I'm eager to return home, to feel the earth beneath my feet, and bask in the sunlight." She turns to Lev, her smile widening. "Never in my wildest dreams did I imagine falling for a giant of a man, but here I am, and he's incredible—focused, loving, caring."

She shifts her gaze to Alex and V. "You two are doing a phenomenal job. None of us expected anything like this a few months ago, but here we are, ready to make a difference. No group of Elders has ever been entrusted with such monumental responsibility, and I'm honored to be a part of it."

Her eyes gleam with anticipation. "I'm looking forward to the grand celebration we'll have afterward. It's going to be the most significant event in Amotaious's history, held at the breathtaking new outdoor theater in Two Dunes Harbor, near the Bay of Alloo. We have that to look forward to. From what I've learned, the Creator has been making changes on Amotaious, just as He has here. I've picked up bits and pieces about it from the locals."

"We were all chosen for this, and we must never forget how special we are. I've endured some horrific experiences before arriving here, but now, the Creator has bestowed upon us extraordinary abilities. I feel optimistic about the future and have genuine hope for our planet. Change is challenging, but we will overcome it. And we will succeed. Thank you." Lin sits down, her smile radiant, and plants a kiss on Lev's cheek. "Big party soon to come."

Lev leans back in his chair, placing his hands behind his head, a relaxed grin spreading across his face. "We're on a mission." He declares.

"One that I truly believe will succeed. I was on the path to becoming an attorney, coming from a long line of tailors—a destiny I didn't want. But now, this, this feels like a real mission in life. My Gift might not be the most spectacular yet, but I haven't fully grasped its potential. I mean, turning lights on and off is just the beginning. Imagine if I could power down an entire university or city with a mere thought?" He raises a finger, as if he could take control of an entire metropolis with a flick.

He lowers his hand, his tone more contemplative. "I'm fairly certain I've only scratched the surface. I'm incredibly fortunate and grateful to have Lin and all of you in my life right now. My life before this was mundane—working out, school, helping with the family business. I adore my father and grandfather, but I didn't have many friends. Now, even though it might seem like we haven't accomplished much yet, we've learned more about our planet in a few short months than others could in a lifetime. And to discover that there are six other planets in our galaxy with life? To have visited another planet, lived on the moon for the past two months, and been contacted by the Creator himself? It's mind-blowing. I was in a dark place before all this—a family situation had me messed up—but now, compared to what we're dealing with, that seems trivial."

He glances around the room at the other Students. "With the knowledge we've gained from the library, we know what happened to past civilizations, who built the pyramids. Sure, looking back thousands of years, we see the terrible things that happened, but let's not forget the good— the ways people have changed for the better, the advancements in technology. It's mind-boggling. And if any of these other planets dare to mess with us—" Lev clenches his fist and slams it into his other hand with a fierce determination, "We'll crush them."

He settles back into his seat, his demeanor shifting once more to one of calm resolve. "I've seen the pictures of the galactic battle cruisers, and they're impressive. I'm a warrior at heart, but I'm desperate to get back to the planet. We've been up here too long. I can't wait to dig my toes into the dirt with Lin, sit in the sun, and meet her parents. I know it's overwhelming—all the changes—but I have a good feeling that we're all going to find happiness in the years to come."

He crosses his legs, a satisfied smile on his face. "So, I'm doing okay, and I look forward to learning and experiencing as much as I can. Thanks."

Tonari straightens in her seat, her delicate frame and striking beauty drawing the room's attention. With a gentle smile and a hint of her Latino accent, she begins, "At first, I struggled, especially after that Pulse Reversal. I was desperate to find a way out of here." She pauses, a single tear slipping down her cheek. "But with everyone's help, I managed to pull through. So, thank you. I'm better now, and I'm starting to feel a glimmer of hope for the future. Candido and I— we're good for each other."

"He's kind, loving, and his passion for our mission has been a tremendous support for me. I think my Gift can be useful in specific situations. Time will tell why I was given it. I can now create three to four copies of myself and project my voice into distant rooms. I know I'm not the easiest person to get along with, but like everyone else here, I look forward to the future. I truly want to contribute in any way I can. And like the rest of you, I'm eager to return to the planet. No one should stay up here longer than a month or so. I miss my family." She chuckles softly. "If our families had any idea what we're doing, they'd freak out. But, of course, they wouldn't believe us, so there's that. On the other hand, I've had a lot of fun with all of you over the past month. The Common Mind has made me more positive—and hornier."

She glances playfully at Candido, catching the attention of the men in the room. Their eyes widen with curiosity as she continues, "I'm trying to maintain a positive outlook on our situation, doing my best to stay upbeat. Fem' and Rev have been helping me, and this latest Reversal was much easier than the last one, which was a relief." She looks over at Declan and, with a mischievous grin, adds, "No, I haven't used my Gift during sex to create multiple versions of myself, in case any of you were wondering." Her smile broadens as she concludes, "I wasn't particularly sexual before, but the Common Mind has opened me up to new possibilities. I look forward to having more fun with you all. That's it for me. Thanks."

Declan grins, while Miko shoots him a dirty look, and the room erupts in laughter. Candido, leaning forward in his seat.

His voice rich with a Spanish-Brazilian accent, says, "My ability to move through walls is progressing nicely, especially since most walls are less than a foot thick."

"I don't have much to work with," he continues, "but I can now pass my entire body through a wall with minimal effort. Kyoryk thinks I might even be able to take someone else with me soon, which would be amazing."

V's mind races at the implication. *"What does that mean? To take someone with him?"* Candido adds, "Right now, I can only bring objects through with me."

"It's been a fascinating couple of months," he reflects, "meeting all of you, the other Elders, people from different planets—it's surreal. Tonari has been my anchor through the tough times, and I love her deeply." With a playful smile, he looks at the group and says, "And if she ever does decide to create multiple versions of herself during sex, I'm not going to tell you guys." He points around the room stopping at Declan.

Tonari playfully jabs him with her elbow. "Stop it," she chides with a smile.

Candido laughs and continues, "I'm eager to return to the planet with her. I'm not one for sharing my feelings often, but I want to help in any way I can, for the sake of our planet and all our people. I feel optimistic about it. Reflecting on all the past civilizations makes me feel grateful to have been chosen to be part of our future, with all its incredible possibilities."

Alex, Declan, and Lev remain fixated on Tonari ever since she mentioned the sexual aspect of her Gift. V, noticing their distraction, claps her hands together sharply. "Focus, guys!" she commands. The men snap out of their reverie, quickly redirecting their attention to the group.

V interjected, "Sorry, Candido, please continue."

Candido nodded, his voice resonating with conviction. "I don't think we fully grasp the extent of our Gifts or truly understand what we are capable of. When we look back on this day, I believe we'll say, 'That was nothing compared to what we're facing now.' I'm beginning to feel a deep sense of gratitude for being here, and I'm finally looking forward to what lies ahead for all of us.

The magnitude of what we are doing for the Creator, what He's doing for us." He looks up at the ceiling. "Wow." Bows his head, "That's all I have to say, thank you."

Maria stands up, smiles and starts speaking Russian, no one understands her but Lin and she stops, "Seriously, Prezzy with the two of us, I think we can really get away with robbing a bank," she chuckles, "it's been over two months now, everything in my life has changed, I'm going to live a really long time, my best friend, my new lover is the smartest person on the planet, I'm going to help save billions of lives hopefully. I'm soon going to be able to live on another planet, I can stop time, being around you all has changed me, helped me."

"I too, had a really hard time in the first week or so, and then when the first Pulse Reversal hit, it was all too real, but I'm better now, trying like you all to focus on the short term, doing what's in front of me, I let him figure it all out. She grabs Kyoryk's hand, "I'm not built that way. I'm definitely better when all things are known, so it's been hard the last two months, but the more certainty I have around me, the better. I am not sure what my Gift is for yet, but I know there is a reason for it. I wish I could say that I am really happy to be here with all of you, but I'm still not sure it's all the right thing or that all of this is okay; still having a hard time figuring out how I fit into all of this, but I'm here, so I hope that I can feel better about it as we continue on into the future, all of this with the Common Mind has helped me but also has brought feelings that I have never had, so I guess that's a good thing. "

"Anyhow, if I rubbed you the wrong way in the past, sorry about that, trying to be a better person; so many things have changed, and it's hard to deal with it all. I was a lesbian before I came here, and now I have a boyfriend. So much has changed, and I'm still trying to figure it all out. That's it for me." Maria sits down.

Kyoryk hugs her, clears his throat, and says, "Albert Einstein said there comes a time when the mind takes a higher plane of knowledge but can never prove how it got there. What has happened to us all is very overwhelming."

"We have all been through a lot, and so much has changed; it has been hard to deal with it all. Before this, I worked at a pet shop, went to school, wanted eventually to live on a boat, didn't really have to many friends, worked out a lot, and now it's all changed. Things that I would have never thought of before are coming to mind. It's very overwhelming, but it has been better in the last couple of weeks; after our visit to Marmutt, I felt better about what we are doing and looking forward to being on the planet, I can't wait, actually."

"My Gift has changed me, the way I look at things, figuring out almost anything, it's surreal at times. Maria has helped me through these changes and I'm super grateful to have her in my life, grateful to have all of you here. Alex? I Don't know if I would want to be a Master Elder either. I look forward to helping everyone on the planet; I think we have a really good chance of making it happen; everything seems to be coming into place according to the plan of the Creator."

"Before this, I didn't even think about a Creator; now we have been getting messages; for whatever reason, I am here, so I have to deal with it and keep going after we get through the CAT. I do feel better about the future and it's possibilities. I have to say that it has been some of the funniest times that I've ever had with you all, so thanks for that. Thanks."

V stood up, her smile radiant as she addressed the group. "I'm so glad we had this meeting. I just want to say this was a brilliant idea. Before this opportunity, my life was on a downward spiral, thanks to my parents. I wasn't happy and just wanted to escape—except for my sister, there was no reason for me to stay. The first week or so here, I was lost, uncertain of what was happening."

"Tonari, I considered leaving too, but we didn't. We stayed, and now the future seems incredibly promising. Being here with Alex, with all of you—Gig, Fem', Doog, Fair, Freida, Harvey, Bahdubah, Klinchme'—we've all become friends. A family."

"Everyone I care about is here now. Where I came from, I had lost faith in people—the way they treat each other, the planet. But now, despite the challenges ahead, I see a bright future, and I'm excited to face it with you all. My Gift, it's multifaceted—visions of the Creator, glimpses of loved ones who have passed on."

"The Common Mind, feeling all of your emotions—sadness, happiness, fear, conflict—has transformed me for the better. Sometimes, I can even sense what another is thinking, and that's terrifying. I wrestle with self-doubt too, questioning my worth and wondering if I can truly contribute."

"One moment, I think this is all madness, that none of it is real. But the next, I'm convinced we can do it. Your support, especially Alex's, has given me confidence. I believe we can complete this mission, though we have no idea what the second one entails. It involves all six planets, so it must be significant, right? That's years away." She waves her hand away. "I keep pushing myself, and I encourage Alex to do the same. Sometimes, I feel isolated, like it's all on me, but I'm not alone—we're in this together."

"Alex and I have been back to the planet twice now, and you're right—we shouldn't stay here longer than necessary. After Amotaious, we should return as soon as possible for our sanity. Like Alex, I never envisioned becoming a Master Elder; it seemed like too much responsibility, too heavy a burden."

"I'm still unsure if I'm the right person for the job, even if I'm chosen. It could be any of you. But more than anything, I believe the Creator chose us because we work well together. We've completed the first mission, and though the next one is far off if it comes to battle, Lev, you're right—we'll kick some ass."

"I can sense that this is just the beginning, and for that, I'm incredibly grateful to be here. I rely on all of you—Alex, Miko." She gets a silly face and points to Declan. "Declan, Freida, Fem', everyone—to help me through this. Before, I only relied on one person, and she's been gone for two years now." Declan looks at her like, "What?"

"Sorry, I don't mean to go on, but I have a strong feeling that we're going to get through the next few months, help the planet, and fulfill our purpose under the Creator's guidance."

"And then we're going to have an epic party—on the beach at Amotaious, our new planet. We'll run around naked, and I think it would be fun to see three or four Tonaris running around naked—I'm not shy." The room erupted in laughter. Declan perks up.

"Our future is bright, but we'll have to fight for it with the support of everyone, even Elders from other planets. Earlier in the Lab, Harvey and the others told us there are over 350 Elder volunteers from Amotaious, and even people from the other planets, willing to risk their lives to help with the Creator's Plans—that's huge."

The group reacted with excited murmurs at the news of volunteers.

V continued, "That news gave me new hope that I'm in the right place, with the right people. I think this meeting was a good idea, and we should do it again every other month or so. What we're going through isn't easy, and we shouldn't feel like we're doing it alone. When we return to the seventh planet, we need to make sure everyone knows we're committed to seeing this through, even if some of the other planets don't agree—we need to fight for our planet."

V turned to Alex, her eyes softening. "Thanks for this meeting. This kind of openness helps me—a little expression goes a long way." She glanced around the room. "Thank you, everyone." V sat down.

Alex smiled, his eyes twinkling with satisfaction. "Well, for our first meeting all to ourselves, I think it went quite well. For some reason, after hearing V and Lev talk, I feel like shooting something—or maybe throwing some knives. And I must admit, the thought of seeing multiple Tonaris running around the beach naked gave me pause."

"But I feel better now, and I hope you all do too. Let me know your thoughts on how we can make the next meeting even better."

He clasped his hands together, surveying the room. "I want to try something—an experiment to see how it feels. V taught me a bit of meditation when we were returning to the planet, and I delved deeper into it." He glanced a smile back at V.

V then remembered the experience they had with her teaching him the meditation from what she had learned from several books and techniques from the Intelligence Bureau on the ship alone. She chuckled and smiled bashfully.

"Then Declan mentioned the power of the Common Mind, and I wanted to see how it would respond. If we could all join hands, since we're all homesick, tired of being on this moon, let's use this meditation to visualize where we want to be on the planet in a few weeks—maybe after reuniting with friends and family."

"For this first attempt, let's all imagine being on the beach, under the sun by the ocean, in a quick meditation. Let's see if it works."

Prezzy began bouncing excitedly. "I love this idea!"

Kyoryk asked, "Are you going to count down or use colors?"

Alex tilted his head thoughtfully. "I'm going to count down from five to one, with instructions, talking about the beach. Just follow my lead."

"Alright, everyone. Hold hands."

Lin added, "My parents meditate for hours. They use numbers and colors, going into different dimensions."

Declan blurted out, "No way! Do they see those lizard people?"

Alex, trying to maintain focus, said, "Okay, everyone, let's be serious. I'm going to start now. Is everyone ready?" He glanced around the room. Some were standing, others sitting, laughter bubbling up.

"Everyone, stand, hold hands, and bow your heads. Close your eyes and relax. Breathe in, and exhale slowly."

V, chuckling, teased, "We didn't do this on the ship."

Alex chuckled back, "Come on, be serious. Help me out here—shoosh!"

V, now standing, nudged him playfully, "Alright, I'll be serious."

V held his hand tightly and whispered, "When I was doing that, I didn't know I was teaching you how to meditate. She gave him a loving but a mischief look.

Alex gave her a loving but stern look back, grabbed her hand even tighter, whispering back, "Shoosh, silly."

A new **"Song"** started. *Mother Nature*

Everyone stood and joined hands. Alex spoke softly, "Now, focus on the beach. Picture where you want to be on the planet and the joy it brings. I'm going to count down from five to one. When we reach one, you'll be completely relaxed, and you'll feel the joy more intensely than ever before. Five."

V first thought of her and Alex on the ship, but her mind then shifted to the walks they had taken along the beach near Darwin. It was the only beach she had ever visited. Alex's voice continued, "Picture the trees, start to feel the sand between your toes, the warmth on your face. Hear the waves crashing on the shoreline. You're more relaxed now—not sleepy, just relaxed. Four."

Everyone's hands began to warm to the point of heat. V could feel the Common Mind stirring within her, sensing the presence of the others' minds entwining with hers. Her beach vision, once clear and vivid, began to transform. The trees grew taller, the ocean deepened to a richer blue, and the coarse, peppery sand of Mindil Beach shifted to a pristine, fine white.

In V's mind, she wondered, *"What the hell? How is this image changing so quickly? I can feel the heat coming from everyone's hands. Unbelievable."*

"Relax. Breathe in, exhale. Relax." Alex's voice flowed like a gentle breeze, guiding the group into a trance.

"You can begin to see the beach more vividly now. Feel the sand beneath your feet, the warmth of the sun caressing your skin. Hear the waves crashing, see the trees swaying. Relax. Now, let the others into your mind. Hear their thoughts, feel their love. It's liberating, it's safe. Just... relax."

As the words hung in the air, the furniture in the room subtly shifted back a foot, unnoticed by everyone. "We're all going to meet on the beach now," Alex continued, his voice a beacon guiding them into the shared vision. "Let go of everything. Three..."

V's vision sharpened, and she could see the others on the beach. In Hindi, she murmured, "What the hell?"

"Oh my God, this feels fucking great," Prezzy exclaimed, her voice dripping with euphoria.

Declan's moan of pleasure was silenced by Miko's sharp "Shoosh!"

"Concentrate, everyone," Alex commanded, his tone firm yet soothing.

V felt the ocean breeze kiss her face; the sun's warmth enveloped her body. The scene crystallized around her; she could now see everyone clearly. The sensation of the sun's heat was almost tangible, a comforting blanket of warmth. She tilted her head skyward, catching sight of a bird soaring overhead.

Alex's smile was serene as he spoke again. "Relax. You can see and feel everyone now. Relax. Watch the trees sway, the waves crash, and the birds glide. Feel it all. Just... relax. Two..." His eyes closed, and V mirrored his action, sinking deeper into the meditation.

No one noticed that Swaraj had elevated the entire group, lifting them two to three inches off the ground.

Declan's Gift turned them slowly counterclockwise while Lev manipulated the lighting, casting hot and cold hues that danced across their skin. Maria's Gift subtly altered their perceptions, and Prezzy's power caused them to flicker in and out of existence.

"You're all doing wonderfully," Alex's voice resonated in the shared space. "I can see you all on the beach. Just relax and focus. Let us feel each other. Use the Common Mind. Let V guide us with her Gift, bringing us together. Relax..."

As Alex finished speaking, Lin began chanting in a strange, rhythmic language in her throat, the words echoing like an ancient prayer. "Nash, Ooh! Studenti Coma, See-La-Ru! Shanka! Ala-Muta Tanka! Commononi! Mindioni! Bondioni! Shanka! Tanka! Pat!" The incantation sent ripples of energy through the group, prompting exclamations and curses from Declan, Prezzy and a particularly loud outburst from Maria. They all started to hear the humming and chanting of old.

V felt an electrifying rush surge through her body as Lin's words resonated. In that instant, she connected with them all—feeling their minds, their love, their compassion, and their raw desires. The energy was overwhelming, nearly too much to bear.

Alex's voice trembled slightly, "We are all here now, completely relaxed, united as one. We're on the beach, free from worry, free from everything. One... We are in a perfect meditative state. Nothing can disturb us. Breathe in, breathe out. Perfect."

V shivered, fully aware of everything happening around them. She could feel all of them hear their thoughts, yet the magnitude of what was occurring left her incredulous.

She tried to speak, but her voice was stifled as if the overwhelming energy had replaced words with pure emotion. It was almost too much, even for her Gift. She sensed the others' elation, their desires intertwining as if molded from the same clay.

But something unsettled her. This state, this fusion of minds, seemed to spiral out of control. Her eyes darted to Alex, a smile playing on her lips despite the growing unease. She gazed at the sea and the sand, at the circle of friends holding hands on this imagined white sandy beach, each lost in the warmth of the sun and the ocean's embrace. None seemed to notice the dangerous path they were treading, but V did. She smiled at Alex and whispered, "Can you hear me?" Alex's nod was slow as if time itself had slowed to a crawl. "Yes, I can," he replied.

"We need to get out now. Something's not right," V insisted, her voice laced with concern. Alex nodded again. "Yes. Okay."

V focused, but it was a struggle. The others didn't want to leave the meditation; they clung to the blissful state.

She tried harder, opening one eye to see that the group was now a foot off the ground, spinning slowly around the room. Panic gripped her, and she screamed in her mind, "We need to go back! We need to go back! Everyone, we need to go back! Get out!"

In the last fleeting moment, as the beach began to fade, V saw the entire group suspended three to four feet in the air, spinning like they were about to be launched into another realm. *"What the hell is this?"* she thought. *"We've tapped into something profound. The Creator is sending us a message."* Her eyes snapped open in fear, and she was back in the common room.

Alex opened his eyes, then Kyoryk. Suddenly, the group stopped spinning, the chairs and couches returned to their original positions, and everyone dropped to the floor. The others were oblivious to what had just transpired—not even Alex noticed.

V smiled at Alex, then glanced over at Prezzy, who was covering her eyes, exclaiming, "Oh my god, oh my god, that was amazing!" Miko was clutching her crotch while Lev hugged Maria tightly. Candido and Tonari were locked in a passionate kiss.

Declan, wide-eyed and incredulous, kept repeating, "What the hell?"

V hugged Alex, her voice laced with awe. "How did you know?"

Alex laughed, "I didn't." Declan grabbed him, a wild grin on his face. "Dude, that was insane. Fucking awesome. What a feeling."

Alex looked around at the others, all smiling and laughing. "Did everyone feel that?"

Prezzy leapt into his arms, hugging him tightly. "You... you are amazing! How did you know?"

Alex shrugged, "I didn't." He raised his voice, "Did everyone feel that?"

Lev, shaking his head in disbelief, replied, "Man, we have no idea what the true power of the Common Mind is."

Tears streamed down Tonari's face as she clung to Candido. "Are you kidding? Yes, we felt it. It was like we were really there, all together. When can we go back?"

Candido nodded, his voice soft. "I can still feel the sand, the warmth of the sun on my skin. We were there."

Tonari wiped her tears, her hands trembling. "I can't believe it," she whispered over and over again.

The room buzzed with excited chatter as everyone shared their experiences, still processing what had just happened. Less than a minute later, Gig and Fem' burst into the room, breathless and beaming, like they had raced to get there.

Fem' looked around, her eyes wide with curiosity. "What's going on in here?"

V smiled at her. "We just had an experience. We're still trying to understand it. We were all on a beach, in the sun, feeling the ocean breeze and the sand between our toes. The sensation was incredible. Some of our Gifts manifested physically and in our vision. What... was... that?"

Fem' nudged Gig with a playful smile. "See? I told you I could feel them. It's happening so early."

The group turned their eyes toward Gig, silently seeking an explanation. Struggling to catch his breath, he bent over, hands on his knees, and managed a grin. "This wasn't supposed to happen for a while—usually not until Students are wrapping up their fourth year of school. How did you know?" His gaze locked onto Alex.

"What exactly did we just experience?" Alex asked, his curiosity piqued. Fem', still slightly breathless, addressed the group. "This usually doesn't occur until your final year or even after graduation. It's called the Common Mind Bond, a rare moment when you all synchronize in a fabricated place and time, sharing identical sensations."

She glanced at Gig, her face alight with awe. "This is extraordinary," she murmured, shaking her head in disbelief. "This group? Simply astonishing."

V, puzzled, turned to Fem'. "What do you mean?" Fem' grasped V's shoulders, her expression serious. "The CMB, the Common Mind Bond—you're all on the verge of something remarkable."

Miko, equally confused, still holding her crotch, interjected, "What exactly is the CMB?" "It's one of the most potent connections a group can forge," Fem' explained. "We call it the Common Mind Group Bond, or CMB. This was your first time, but just wait until you've experienced it six or seven times."

V noticed Gig gently pulling Fem' aside. He whispered, "Don't tell them too much. They need to discover it on their own. They'll figure it out." Fem' playfully pushed him back with a smile. "Alright, I'll keep quiet."

Gig waved his hand, drawing the group's attention. "Fem' and I could feel you all connecting; that's why we rushed over."

Declan, still buzzing with excitement, admitted, "That was incredible. I've done some wild things before, but this... It felt like we were actually there, all together."

Gig nodded in understanding. "I know what you mean. I've had similar experiences, but nothing as real or as powerful as this. The power of the Common Mind Group Bond is unparalleled among the Gifts." Clearing his throat, he addressed the group with a more serious tone. "This experience is sacred and shouldn't be taken lightly. For safety reasons, I must ask you not to attempt this again without supervision, at least until you're more accustomed to it. It can be dangerous—you could get stuck, or as we call it, locked. It could harm your mind, body, and emotions. One of us"—he pointed to himself and Fem'—"needs to lead the group so that we can break the bond after a few minutes. Never let it last longer than ten to fifteen minutes at first, or the consequences could be severe. Is that clear?"

Alex and several others nodded in agreement, but V noticed the group was still in awe, their faces lit with amazement.

Fem' pulled V aside, her voice low and urgent. "Gig and I will guide you through the next few sessions. Wait a couple of days before attempting any group meditation again. Believe me, the others will want to do it sooner, but it's not safe. The CMB is one of our most powerful Gifts, and it must be handled with care."

V nodded, concern etched on her face. "Why didn't we know about this?"

Fem' sighed. "Because this usually doesn't happen until the end of your training. It's something that needs to be carefully cultivated and approached with utmost seriousness. But you all figured it out on your own somehow."

"Yes, I understand," V replied.

V then pulled Fem' even closer, ensuring no one could overhear. "I'm not sure what happened, but I could feel everyone's thoughts and emotions—really intense stuff, like their deepest secrets and true feelings. I got scared and pulled them all out. It felt like we were about to travel somewhere. It was terrifying."

Fem' met V's gaze, her expression grave. "Tell no one. You and I need to research this further. I think you and Alex might have a genuine connection with the Creator. We need to be cautious about how we present this to others. We definitely don't want any Elders from the other planets finding out. For now, only discuss this with Alex, Gig, and me. Understood?"

V nodded. "Understood."

They rejoined the group, where Gig was outlining the precautions everyone should take. "Who suggested this?" Gig asked.

V smiled, glancing at Alex. "Alex did. He suggested we all think of a place on the planet where we wanted to be. We had an open discussion before that, where we all expressed our longing to be back on the planet, enjoying the sun, maybe on a beach. After the meeting, Alex proposed using the Common Mind to help us relax, and then, somehow, we all ended up on the beach."

Fem', still processing the shock, muttered, "Amazing. Alex, huh? That figures. Just remember to tell us next time before the whole group does it." She exchanged a look with Gig. "We need to advance the class on the CMB." Gig nodded, smiling. "Yes, we do. Like everything else, I guess." He chuckled….

Fem' and Gig reminded everyone not to attempt the CMB without them and left the room.

Miko, now rubbing her shoulders and thighs, turned to V. "That was insane. We were all there, on the beach. I felt like we were one, part of each other. It was an incredible feeling. I could feel the sand between my toes."

V agreed, her voice filled with wonder. "Everyone felt it. The power was incredible. It wasn't like anything I've ever experienced before."

Miko grinned mischievously. "Now I really want to have sex."

V laughed, noticing Miko's posture. "I can tell. I feel the same way—it's a crazy sensation, right?"

V strides over to Alex, her eyes gleaming with curiosity. "You're insane, Alex. How on earth did you come up with that?" Alex grins a hint of mischief in his eyes. "I just wanted everyone to feel at ease, to connect. Declan's mention of the Common Mind's power got me thinking. In class, they use it to create the mega stones. I saw it as a form of meditation—like walking down your favorite path and finding yourself in a place where you can truly feel and think. Honestly, I'm not entirely sure."

V leans in, her lips brushing against his. "Well, you tapped into something extraordinary. I think you led us all there—it was insane." Alex whispers into her ear, "I'm not sure about that, but it was an incredible sensation. It left me feeling... extremely aroused."

V laughs softly, kissing him again. "I think we all felt it. Miko mentioned the same thing." Alex's eyes twinkle with a sly smile. "We should try it again, just the two of us."

V nods, "We can attempt it, but Fem' said she'll guide us in a couple of days." "Sounds like a plan. I could use a beer right about now," Alex says, moving toward the small kitchen area.

"Pour me a glass of wine, please," V calls after him.

The rest of the group is scattered around, chatting and sipping drinks. An hour later, everyone has left, except for Tonari and Candido, who are locked in a passionate embrace on the couch. They glance up, then sheepishly exit the room.

V, Alex, Miko, and Declan gather around the table, still buzzing with excitement. Declan chuckles, "You know what's wild? Some of us were just talking in the meeting about things we didn't even know were possible, and then—bam!—this happens, like ten minutes later. It's unlike anything I've ever felt before. It's like having a double orgasm, without the effort—on mushrooms!"

V nearly spits out her wine, laughing. "We all felt it, whatever it was. When I came out of it, I was trembling. It was like my blood was electrically charged, but in the best way possible. No wonder Fem' said it was dangerous—you'd want to stay in that state forever."

Miko nods, "Everyone's going to want to do it again, and soon."

"But Gig and Fem' warned us—it's incredibly risky," Alex adds.

"Yeah, Gig must have mentioned that like three times," Declan muses. "Can you imagine a machine that makes you feel like that? People would just lose themselves, trapped in that sensation, and society would be doomed."

V and Miko share a laugh, and Miko, with a teasing grin, confesses, "I don't know about you, but it made me super horny."

Declan scoffs, chuckling. "You're always horny."

Miko leans in close to him, her voice sultry, "Never like this. This has done something to me."

Alex and V exchange knowing smiles. "Well, Declan," Alex says, "You'd better go take care of your woman. I have a feeling it won't take long. During the first meeting, I was imagining V with Tonari's Gift... what if I were with three or even four of her?"

Declan and Miko burst into laughter. Declan stands, offering Miko his hand. "My lady, pleasure awaits." Miko rises, leaning down to whisper to V and Alex, "Goodnight, you two. Enjoy your evening."

Alex watches them leave, then turns to V, his gaze intense. "How are you holding up? You going to be okay?"

V smirks, locking eyes with him. "Four of me, huh? You can barely handle one of me—how would you deal with four?" Alex pulls her into a kiss, her challenge igniting something within him. V gazes deeply into his eyes, her voice soft but firm. "You're incredible, Alex. You just come up with these things out of nowhere. I'm going to have to keep you away from all these other women—they're going to look at you differently now. Hell, I'm looking at you differently."

Alex chuckles, brushing a strand of hair from her face. "Don't. I'm just Alex. I had no idea that was going to happen. The real question is, what are you going to do about it?"

V stands, taking his hand with a playful glint in her eyes. "Come with me, and I'll show you."

As they head down the hallway, Maria and Kyoryk pass by. Maria gives Alex a wink, "Thanks, Alex. That was incredible."

Kyoryk chuckles, and V, not missing a beat, whispers to Alex, "See? I told you. You'd better keep your hands on me and only me." Alex laughs softly, "Only you. Got it."

As they pass Prezzy's room, faint echoes of "Oh my God!" repeat from within. Alex and V exchange amused glances, stifling their laughter.

Entering V's room, Alex tries to downplay his role. "Quit saying I did it. I led the group, that's all. Once we got to the beach, it was a collective effort."

V smiles as she undresses, her voice teasing. "What would happen if we were all thinking about sex? What then?" Alex closes his eyes, imagining the possibilities as he kicks off his shoes. "I think that's what Gig and Fem' are worried about. My imagination only goes so far—I'm not sure I'm ready for a group sex thing. Just thinking about being with you is all I need—nothing more."

V laughs, "Smart answer. Do you remember what we did to each other on the ship?" "How could I forget?" Alex replies, his voice thick with desire.

V smirks, "I found a new tune—it has the perfect rhythm." Alex laughs, "Sounds like you've thought this out."

V quickly strips off her clothes and hops onto the bed, pulling the sheets over them. "I'm a planner," she says, her voice sultry. As the music plays, Alex matches its rhythm, his movements synchronizing with V's. Her body instinctively recreates parts of the CMB, her back arching as she cries out in Hindi, nails digging into his back. She collapses onto the bed, catching her breath, a satisfied smile on her lips.

Kissing him softly, she murmurs, "Alright, I've got another playlist for you." Alex, surprised, raises an eyebrow. "Oh my. You're on a roll."

Alex slips back under the sheets.

XIX

Alex jolted awake, his heart pounding as he caught sight of his late brother Max lounging casually in the chair across from him. Max, dressed in a Hawaiian shirt and khaki shorts, grinned mischievously, one foot propped on the table. He looked almost the same—except for being four years older. "Hello, brother. Mate, things have certainly changed for you, haven't they?" he remarked, his tone laced with humor.

Alex struggled to breathe, his chest tightening as he attempted to push himself up on his elbows. Finally, he managed to rasp, "What? How?"

Max chuckled softly, a glimmer of amusement in his eyes. "Breathe, brother. I'd pour you a glass of water, but..." He waved his hand through the pitcher on the table, his fingers passing through it like a ghost, before turning back to Alex with a laugh. "I've got a message for you from this Creator dude."

As Alex fought to catch his breath, he slowly sat up on the bed, his mind racing, but his lips sealed.

Max's form flickered, fading in and out like a glitching hologram. "Thanks for handling that asshole for me and looking after Melissa and little Max Jr. Can you believe it? All of this is crazy, right? And all this?" He sat up a little in the chair. "I can't believe what you've gotten yourself into." Max's expression shifted, a brief look of distraction crossing his face as if someone were speaking to him from a distance. He glanced to his right, muttering, "Alright, calm down." Then, looking back at Alex, he added, "This Raba Rashi guy is very pushy."

"Raba Rashi..." Alex whispered, his voice barely audible.

Max adjusted his position in the chair, and as he did, his facial features seemed to morph, making Alex suspect that the Creator was beginning to take over his brother's body. The flickering intensified, anxiety gnawing at Alex as he edged closer to the foot of the bed. The entire scene began to shimmer with an otherworldly glow, and Alex's grip on the bed sheets tightened as he realized that Raba Rashi was now speaking through his brother.

"I'm very impressed with you, Alex. You and I are going to accomplish great things together." The Creator's voice resonated through Max. "For now, let's keep this meeting between us—just you and me. Do you understand?"

Alex, his thoughts spinning, rubbed his face in an attempt to ground himself. He couldn't quite focus on Max—or the Creator. The commanding voice snapped him back to attention. "Look at me, Alex!"

He forced himself to meet the intense gaze of Raba Rashi, now fully in control of Max's form. "I understand. Yes," Alex stammered.

"Good. I want you to continue on the path I've set for you and V. Be mindful of Vibrean; keep her safe. I have grand plans for her—she is the key to our future success. Be patient in everything you do."

The Creator's tone grew more solemn. "After the next four years, I will reshape your planet. Things will return to the way they were thousands of years ago, but with one crucial difference— only you and V will know for now. I am not who you think I am. There is One above all. Remember, this must remain a secret—don't share it with anyone. Do you understand?"

Still in shock and struggling to discern whether he was speaking to his brother or the Creator, Alex replied, "Yes, of course. I will keep it to myself."

"Stay the course, Alex…" The words hung in the air as Max's image began to flicker once more, the glow around him fading.

As Max's presence dissipated, his final words echoed in Alex's mind, "Stay the course. I'm always with you."

Alex, his breath shallow and his mind reeling, watched as the vision of his brother evaporated like smoke in the fog. He sat further upright, his thoughts a whirlwind. The static electricity in the air was almost palpable.

"The Creator is now communicating with me through my brother. This is insane. Who am I? What's next? Was that real? 'Stay the course,' he said. The Creator wouldn't say that if I weren't on the right path."

"There must be so much more ahead—things even the Master Elders can't foresee. And I can't tell anyone about this. I have to keep it all to myself. Great! What did he mean by V being the key? Damn, this is going to drive me crazy."

He stood abruptly, shaking off the lingering unease, and began pacing the room. After a few moments, he forced himself to focus, stretching and diving into his daily routine of push-ups and sit-ups. Once finished, he sat at the table where Max had just been, opening his computer to review his schedule, which appeared on the screen above him:

Today: Travel to Amotaious. Tonight: Fem', CMB Alcazar. Tomorrow: Harvey, Trip to Millapillar Valley.

Nov 11: Master Elder Approval Creator's Plans Meeting.

Nov 20: Visit with V's Family.

Dec 9: Resort with Group.

Dec 23: Prep for Reversal.

Dec 26: Full Reversal Test.

Feb 17: Full Reversal Test II.

April 11: Full Reversal Test III.

Party to follow after completion of the mission: Sight at the outdoor Two Dunes Amphitheater, two hours south of the City of Tunimbria, down the coast by the Bay of Alloo of the Sea of Tunimbria.

He looked at the schedule and spoke aloud, "Alright, let's shower, pack, shave, get approval, and save the world."

Closing the computer, Alex walked down the hallway into the common room, where V sat with Miko, both sipping coffee. Trying to mask his inner turmoil, he greeted them, "How's everyone this morning?" Miko grinned, "Doing great! Can't wait to get to the planet. I'm so tired of these white walls—desperate for some sunshine and maybe a little color on the walls." V nodded in agreement. "Yes, a change of scenery will be nice. How about you?"

Alex, forcing a casual tone, replied, "All packed up. Got a good night's sleep, especially without Ms. Jimmy Legs next to me." Miko chuckled, "What's that supposed to mean?" V laughed and explained, "Alex doesn't like it when I move my legs around before I fall asleep. I have this habit of running my toes through the sheets—it helps me relax."

Miko smiled, "You guys are funny. Declan says I snore like some kind of late-night chirping bird—almost like a whistle, he says."

As Alex sat down next to V, he laughed, "You guys? You sound funny to me. Does Declan wake up telling jokes?" Miko shook her head, "No, but he sometimes smokes before bed, and then he just starts laughing at things he's thinking about." V grinned, "You mean he just starts laughing at nothing? Now that's funny." Miko nodded, "We don't always sleep together. It's nice to have the bed all to myself sometimes."

Alex agreed, "That's what I think too. If we had a bigger bed, though, I'd be okay with it." V smiled, "These beds are pretty small—not really meant for two people." Just then, Declan walked into the room.

Alex added, "You need at least a queen-sized bed." Declan raised an eyebrow, "A queen-sized bed for what?" V chuckled, "We're talking about bed sizes. The ones we have aren't meant for two people." Declan chuckles while pouring his coffee. "Miko has these specific sleeping positions, and I've adapted to them, but she snores like some sort of small ocean bird."

Alex smirks, casting a glance at Declan. "V rubs her toes between the sheets for about half an hour before she falls asleep."

Declan laughs as he takes a seat. "That's hilarious. This trip is going to be fantastic—four days and three nights of pure exploration. Are you all ready? We leave in an hour." V finishes pouring her coffee and grins. "I'm ready. And for the record, rubbing my toes between the sheets relaxes me. Alex, on the other hand, sleeps like he's in a coffin. He straightens his body like a board and crosses his hands over his neck with elbows sticking out. What's up with that?"

Laughter erupts from the group, with Alex defends himself, "It's the same as having your hands halfway in your pants; it keeps my hands and neck warm." V stands up from her chair. "I need to shower and change. I'll be back in a few minutes." Miko follows suit. "Same here. I'm all packed, I just need to freshen up." V and Miko exit the room.

As Kyoryk, Maria, Candido, and Tonari enter, Declan asks, "So, what's the plan once we're on the planet? Got anything concrete yet?"

Alex nods. "Harvey wants me to accompany him to Millapillar Valley. It's a two- to three-hour drive. They cut the big stone and timber there, using tech from CAT 3." Kyoryk perks up. "I'd love to join. How many can fit?"

"Four per vehicle," Alex replies. "V wasn't planning on going, so there are two seats left. You two could ride with us. If others want to go, another Steward will need to take them. I'll see if Roman or Hugh can drive them. I'll talk to Lev and sort it out." Declan grins. "Count me in. What day?"

"Tomorrow," Alex says. "It's an all-day thing. I'll let Harvey know you're coming. The Council meeting is on Thursday, and we head out on Friday. If the meeting wraps up early, we could find a beach to camp out on. That'd be fun." Maria raises an eyebrow. "So, all the guys are going on a day trip tomorrow?" She glances at Tonari. "Maybe we could explore the town again, grab a fancy lunch, catch a movie?" Tonari nods. "Let's talk to V, Miko, and Lin on the ship. We can figure out something for tomorrow."

Alex grabs his coffee and lounges on one of the couches, closing his eyes. After a while, V nudges him in the chest. "Get up, let's go. Everyone's heading down to the docks."

Alex sits up. "All right. Hey, Declan and Kyoryk are joining Harvey and me at Millapillar Valley tomorrow. If anyone else wants to go, we'll need another Steward. Tonari said she was going to discuss plans with you all during the flight." "Okay," V says, "and remember, Fem' wants us to do the CMB session tonight after dinner. It's been five days since our first experience."

Alex smiles as he stands. "I wonder what difference the supervision will make. It should be interesting. All right, let's go."

He grabs their luggage, and they head to the docks. It's mostly the same group as last time, though Beauta, Amand, Vitor, and Sanjay are missing due to other commitments. They arrive at Amotaious without incident. V and the women find activities for the next day, while Roman agrees to take the other guys to Millapillar Valley.

Hours later, they arrive at the Terraenti building—The Alcazar. After settling into their rooms, they gather for dinner.

True to her word, Fem' meets the Students for their first supervised CMB session. By the pool, a meeting room has been arranged for them. Fem' explains, "Let's keep this session short.

These can stretch up to three or four hours, but I'll guide you to achieve positive results in a fraction of that time." She pulls a chair into the circle they've formed. "Please, sit and hold hands. Close your eyes and focus on your breathing—slowly in, slowly out."

Alex closes his eyes and steadies his breath.

"Now, count down from ten," Fem' continues, her voice soothing. "Ten—imagine a lush, green meadow surrounded by trees, with a path leading us forward. Nine."

Alex feels his body relax as the vision of the meadow forms in his mind.

"We're all barefoot," Fem' narrates. "We feel the soft grass and the cool mist on our toes. Eight."

The tension eases from Alex's body as the scene unfolds, each step drawing him deeper into the trance.

"We continue down the path, the sun's rays peeking through the trees, warming our skin. Seven."

Alex senses the others, their presence blending with his own, their thoughts beginning to overlap; he can feel the physical warmth of V's hand and Miko's to his left heating up just like before.

"Six—we are connected, feeling the gentle sway of the trees, the warmth of the sun, the cool earth beneath our feet."

His mind merges further with the group's, the connection tightening, becoming almost tangible.

"Five—imagine the beach where we were last time. The sand, the sea, the breeze. We're almost there."

Alex's senses heighten; the warmth of the sun, the feel of the sand underfoot, and the thoughts of those around him are vividly real.

"Four—together, we reach the beach, connected in mind, body, and soul."

Alex's body relaxes completely, the warmth and calmness enveloping him, merging with the collective consciousness of the group.

"Three—the cool water washes over our feet, and the sea breeze caresses our faces. We are one, unified in purpose, in thought."

"We are now completely relaxed, completely united. Twelve bodies. Twelve minds. Twelve souls—now one."

A new **"Song"** started. *Mother Nature.*

Alex's body feels as if it's floating, almost weightless, as he gazes out at the vast ocean.

The collective energy of the Students surges through him, amplifying his confidence and power. A profound sense of completeness washes over him, erasing every lingering doubt and negativity.

This is what we call Bliss. Nirvana. Freedom. In typical Alex fashion, he concentrates intently on the others, seeking to deepen his connection to their love and compassion and reaching further into the depths of their memories. He begins to see the cherished moments of Declan, V, Miko, Prezzy, and Kyoryk that are next to him.

"We are on the beach," a voice instructs. "We are one. Form a tight circle, sit down, and hold hands. As you look at everyone, you'll begin to see a multi-colored glow surrounding each person—a blue hue emanating from the feet up, an orange aura enveloping the torso, and a pure white light radiating from the neck upward."

As Alex observes, the others appear dressed in pristine white. The women wear flowing summer wraps and short dresses that flutter in the breeze, while Alex and the other men are clad in slightly off-white shorts paired with oversized, silky shirts that gleam with a pure, solid white. He begins to perceive the auras of the others, some shining from the sun more brilliantly than others.

Fem', momentarily closing her eyes, opens them to a startling sight: the Students' bodies are levitating, hovering a mere one to two inches above their seats. It's a phenomenon she has never witnessed before. She fumbles nervously, pulling her tablet from her skirt pocket to document the surreal event.

In a voice tinged with trepidation, Fem' continues, "Now, we commence another countdown from five. As you focus, the personal auras of those across from you will merge, melding into one another. The individual colors will vanish, replaced by a unified spectrum—a ring of blue at the bottom, orange in the middle, and a brilliant white light at the top. Four."

"Relax. Look beyond the image. Feel the presence of the others. You are all one—one mind, one soul, one entity. As the colors fuse, the distinctiveness of each person fades away, leaving only the pure light. Three."

Alex can truly feel the connection now. He sees the colors of Lev, Lin, Candido, and Tonari's auras shifting and blending.

"As you breathe in, relax further, and allow yourself to feel the others, observe the colors as they fade into the luminous white that cascades over the orange and blue like a fountain."

"Two. You are completely at ease, light as a feather, perceiving only light. You are light. You are now entering a new state of consciousness."

"The darker shades dissolve, and all that remains is the radiant white light. Feel the warmth of the sun, the light showering over you, entering your very soul. This shower is Love. Joy. Life. Freedom. Breathe it in."

Fem' pauses, then softly utters, "One…"

Alex feels an overwhelming sense of euphoria, even greater than before. As he inhales deeply, he hears Prezzy, Miko, and possibly Maria moan softly, the sound resonating through the group. The Common Mind Bond intensifies, enveloping them all in a unified experience. When Alex looks around, the individual images of his peers have vanished; only a single, radiant white aura remains. The brilliant white at the top dominates, cascading upwards towards the sky.

Fem' gazes in awe at the group, now elevated six to seven inches above their seats, rotating counterclockwise around the room. She can hardly believe her eyes. Her voice, quivering with astonishment, breaks the silence as she continues recording the spectacle with her tablet.

"Feel each other as one," she instructs. "The white light is all that remains. Your classmates have dissolved into the light, their physical forms replaced by pure radiance. As one, you are the embodiment of joy, connected through the Common Mind Bond. Three…"

"You are now one light, twelve souls moving as one, feeling as one, being as one. Two…"

Alex can no longer distinguish the individual forms; all he perceives is a pulsating, rotating, brilliant white light surging toward the sky.

"You are floating," Fem' declares. "The sensation is extraordinary, far surpassing anything before. Your bodies have dissolved into light; you are now light, one with the others. One…"

"You are one light, one soul, a creation of the Creator. Raba Rashi."

In unison, Alex and the others, their voices low and resonant, chant, "Raba Rashi." At that moment, they feel a pulse—a surge of energy. The white aura lifts the group twenty-thirty feet into the air. Alex's entire being tingles with warmth, the sensation magnified beyond anything he has ever experienced.

The collective moan echoes through the group as Fem' captures every moment, startled by the group's continued ascent and rotation. She films, unable to look away.

"You may now travel down the beach, out to the ocean, around the island—wherever you desire," Fem' says, her voice filled with wonder.

Alex feels himself moving within the light, soaring above the sand, free and weightless.

Fem', now utterly amazed, continues, "You are no longer bound by physical form; you are light. Travel around the beach, into the forest, across the island. But remember where you began."

Alex watches as they rise higher, the beach shrinking below them, the forest spreading out like a lush carpet. The entire island unfolds before him, a sensation unlike anything he has ever felt—freedom, warmth, and the shared joy of twelve others. It's an extraordinary experience. In mere minutes, they traverse the island, soaring over rocky cliffs, breathtaking waterfalls, and through lush valleys.

Alex, while seeing all this and feeling the love and compassion of the entire group, when he looks down sees only a shower of pure white aura flowing below them.

Beyond, looking at them all, it looks similar, a solid, brilliant white-tailed aura gently floating around the island.

Recognizing the unprecedented nature of the CMB's effects on these new Elder Students, and her own growing apprehension, Fem' decides to end the lesson. Allowing them a few more moments, she gently instructs, "Now, we will gradually return to the spot from which you came.

Slowly descend towards the meadow. As you do, you will begin to see the trees again, the green grass of the meadow."

Alex observes as the meadow comes into view, the descent steady and calm.

"You are now ready to touch down," Fem' says softly.

Alex feels the grass beneath his toes.

"You will begin to see the colored auras returning—from white back to orange and blue."

As Alex gazed at the ethereal glow of the auras, he watched them gradually fade, revealing the forms of the eleven other Students, their images sharpening into focus.

Fem', observing the group with keen eyes, noticed the cessation of their rotation and the Students returning to their seats—though not the ones they originally occupied, but instead three or four chairs to the left.

"You can still sense the collective thoughts and emotions of the group," Fem' instructed, her voice a calm anchor. "But the connection is dissipating. Remember how it felt. This bond is your community, your shared link."

"Continue your slow breathing," she guided, "counting down from four. Think of yourself now—your love, your compassion, the deep desire for things to unfold as you wish, both in your life and in the lives of others. . . three. . ."

"You can now feel your own body, your auras slowly returning to your individual selves, your thoughts and feelings gradually becoming your own once more. . . two. . ."

"When we reach one, you will fully return to your physical body, carrying with you the memory of being one with the group of twelve. Feel your body, your mind. Inhale….. Exhale…... You hold positive feelings for yourself and for your classmates. . . one."

As Alex reconnected with his individual self, the profound sense of the Common Mind Bond remained imprinted on him, the memory of the others still resonating within. It was overwhelming, almost intoxicating.

"Now, upon hearing the clap of my hands, you will open your eyes and emerge from your relaxed state, retaining all memories, all sensations. You are back to your individual selves," Fem' declared, her hands poised. "Three. . . two. . . one."

With a sharp clap, she brought them back.

Alex's eyes fluttered open, and he scanned the room, his body still wrapped in a warmth he had never experienced before. His mind was clear, free from the usual clutter of thoughts. He glanced at Declan, then at V, who was seated nearby.

They all bore wide, exhilarated smiles, and Prezzy was the first to break into laughter, covering her face as she exclaimed, "That was incredible!"

Declan, equally amazed, exclaimed, "Oh my God!" Tonari's in tears. Some of the Students rose, visibly shaken by the experience. It was only then they realized they had all shifted several chairs from their original seats.

Fem', though trying to conceal it, had a disturbed look on her face. "Well? How was that? Better than the last time?" she inquired, her tone measured. Miko, still in awe, replied, "I can still feel it—that was extraordinary. When you said the Creators name."

Alex turned to V, his eyes wide. "Crazy, right?"

V nodded, her voice tinged with wonder. "I've never felt anything like that before. We traveled; we became one. I could feel everyone—their thoughts, their desires. It was incredible. I can still feel it lingering. This time was different with the auras."

Alex, still processing what they had just undergone, glanced around at his companions. The awe was palpable. Maria, overcome with emotion, burst into happy tears and embraced Tonari. The entire group stood now, some trying to shake off the intense sensation, others simply marveling at what they had just experienced.

Alex and V moved towards Fem', and V, still in a daze, asked, "How—what just happened? Why are we in different chairs? How did we move?"

Fem', still somewhat puzzled, responded, "You became one and traveled?"

"Yes," Alex affirmed, his voice filled with disbelief. "It was unreal. We traveled around the island—we could feel and see everything. When you said the Creators name, that's when we shot into the air. Unbelievable."

"This is the true Common Mind Bond," Fem' explained, regaining some composure. "This was only your first time. As you practice, it will become quicker and easier to bond."

Addressing the entire group, Fem' asked, "Last time, did any of you notice returning to different positions in the room, or being elevated during the CMB?"

The group exchanged puzzled glances. Kyoryk hesitated before saying, "Last time we were just on the beach in the CMB, in the room when we came back I don't know. It's possible. We didn't do the aura thing." Prezzy, her curiosity piqued, asked, "Does that mean we were floating? Moving around the room?"

"Yes," Fem' confirmed, her tone more serious. "You were all floating and spinning around the room." "Is that normal?" Lev inquired, concern evident in his voice.

"No," Fem' admitted, a touch of dismay creeping into her expression. "This is something I've never encountered before. It's new. I'll have to investigate further, do some research."

As Fem' stood, the rest of the group gathered closer, eager to hear more.

"The CMB is extremely powerful," she continued. "It's designed to forge a deep bond among you, to strengthen your Gifts, to bring you closer to the Creator. It's one of the most powerful tools the Creator has given us."

V interjects, "Last time I remember at the last moment coming out of it we were above the floor, but it was very chaotic."

Fem' responds, "Something unusual is happening—some of your Gifts are being integrated into the Bond, and I'm not yet sure why. We'll need to explore this further." She chuckles, "That could be dangerous."

The group, still reeling from the intensity of the experience, gathers at a poolside table. Miko, Prezzy, V, Alex, Declan, and Swaraj settle into their seats, each lost in thought. Prezzy, her eyes alight with excitement, exclaims, "That was extraordinary! The power of it all—it's indescribable." Swaraj nods, his voice tinged with awe. "It's more than just meditation; the Common Mind connects us in a way that's utterly profound. The sensation was beyond anything I've ever imagined."

Miko, furrowing her brow, adds, "Did it feel more potent this time, or was it simply different? And what did she mean about going back in time or into the future? It sounds like something even more remarkable awaits us."

Declan leans in, his tone thoughtful. "I believe she was hinting that we might actually be able to travel—perhaps not physically."

"But within our minds. It's strange how these abilities keep manifesting, and then the Elders just casually mention, 'Oh, that's coming up soon.'"

Alex, rubbing his chin, agrees. "Exactly. So much of what we've learned or experienced hasn't been formally taught—it just emerges. Is this the way they've always trained, or is the Creator playing some kind of trick on us? What's different about our group? I wonder if past Students trained this way. Are we advancing faster than those before us?"

V, her eyes sparkling, grins. "I don't know, but I feel amazing right now. I can understand how people might get addicted to this. It's like a healing tonic for the soul."

Miko smirks, her mind wandering. "What about… sex during a CMB? Imagine if we were on that beach and started thinking about it—what would happen?"

Declan and Alex burst out laughing. Declan shakes his head, "But it's not physical, right? We're not actually doing it. Still, we could always experiment and find out!"

They all share a laugh. "I've tried meditation before—counting down, breathing exercises—but this was on another level. With a group? This is some mind-blowing stuff."

He glances at the ceiling, adding with a chuckle, "But can you imagine? We'd all come out of the CMB, look around at each other in a circle in the common room, and… well, let's just say, it would be awkward."

V wrinkles her nose in mock disgust. "Ugh, gross. That would be beyond weird."

The others cringe, clearly sharing the sentiment.

After a moment, Alex shakes his head and asks, "So, have you ladies got all your plans figured out for tomorrow?" Prezzy stands, a mischievous smile on her lips. "Don't worry, we've got it covered. We'll be fine." Grabbing Swaraj's hand, she adds as they walk away, "I want to try something while I'm still riding this high." Swaraj grins back at the group, clearly intrigued. Miko turns to Declan, a playful glint in her eye. "We've got something to do as well. See you in the morning."

As the others linger at the table, V leans back, her gaze drifting. "That was an experience. The intensity of it—it was like those out-of-body stories you hear about. I could feel everyone else—know what they were thinking, what they were feeling. It was overwhelming. And when she mentioned the Creator's name, we were all just...." She covers her face with her hands, murmuring something in Hindi. "Incredible. What do you think it all means?"

Alex, trying to push aside the morning's unsettling events, smiles at her. His thoughts, however, are a storm of questions: *She's the key, but what does that even mean? She's incredible—just look at her. But is she in danger? Will she save the universe one day? And who is this 'One' the Creator mentioned? When can I talk to V about this? Is Raba Rashi not a god but something else? Why does he always leave me with more questions?* Shaking his head, he forces himself to focus on her question.

"I imagine, with your ability to read minds, the Common Mind would have a stronger effect on you. Maybe it's a tool, like my Gift, but for the whole group—something to see into the past or the future. It's incredibly powerful, that's certain. How do you feel right now?"

V smiles, standing up and stretching her arms and legs. "I've never felt anything like this. My entire body is tingling—this sensation of pure joy. It's almost overwhelming. Let's head to the room. I need to lie down; my body feels heavy, numb, in a strange but pleasant way." She gives him a sweet, loving smile, offering her hand to help him up.

Alex returns her smile, his voice soft. "I know." He stands, still holding her hand. "I feel it too—you're so beautiful. I've never felt so calm before. Whatever this is, I'm glad we're experiencing it together."

They exchange glances with the remaining group before retreating to their room. Alex settles into a chair, watching as V undresses and lies down on the bed. She looks up, clutching a pillow, "Come lay with me—it feels amazing to just lie down."

Alex undresses, joining her in a spooning position. "That was an intense feeling. You're feeling good?"

V nods, her voice soft. "Just snuggle with me." She reaches over, turns off the light, murmurs something in Hindi, and pulls him closer.

As Alex holds her, his thoughts drift between the incredible experience they just shared and the challenges that might lie ahead in the coming months and years. He shrugs off the worries, focusing instead on the warmth of V in his arms, the bond they share. Feeling her breathe steadily, he realizes she's already asleep. He closes his eyes, and soon, he too drifts into a peaceful slumber.

The next morning, Alex, Kyoryk, and Declan meet Harvey on the street. Roman stands nearby with Lev, Swaraj, and Candido. They all piled into a sleek vehicle, similar to the one Harvey and Alex had inspected last time they were in the streets of Tunimbria.

This one, however, seats four, with a surfboard-like track at the bottom and a massive glass canopy enveloping the four bucket seats. The vehicle features the same gyro setup, with shocks hidden beneath the seats, and the chassis gleams with high-tech sophistication. The large doors rise upwards towards the vehicle's center as they open.

Alex settles into the plush bucket seat, immediately impressed by the comfort. Harvey taps a few buttons, and the vehicle hums to life with barely a sound. He adjusts the navigation screen, setting their destination. As the vehicle begins to glide down the road, a quiet hum accompanies their swift acceleration. Alex glances back to see Roman, Candido, Swaraj, and Lev smiling with anticipation as they follow in a similar vehicle.

Declan, curiosity piqued, asks, "What's our first stop?" Harvey responds, "We're heading to Glen Villa Ski Area first. From there, we'll switch vehicles to cross Pinchers Peak and reach Millipillar Valley."

Alex, admiring the sleek design, remarks, "This is a cool ride."

Minutes later, they leave the city behind, the vehicle's speed increasing.

Alex glances at the navigation screen, then at Harvey. "How does this thing work? Is it like the other AV?" Harvey nods, "It's electric, with a gyrostabilizer. The navigation system connects to a satellite control network, guiding us seamlessly from one destination to another."

Alex marveled at the smoothness of their journey, the landscape a blur as they hurtled forward. "We're moving fast. Where are we now?" he asked, glancing over at Harvey. Harvey pointed to the screen at the dashboard's lower edge, where the digits 152 mph and 244 kph flashed in small letters. Another section of the screen revealed they had 43 minutes remaining until their destination. "It'll take about 40 minutes to reach our first stop," Harvey explained, his eyes gleaming with anticipation. "Then, just over an hour to Millapillar Valley. You're going to love the ride over the summit."

Alex turned his gaze to the towering trees speeding past, catching glimpses of drones—some large, some small—methodically clearing debris.

Football-sized pinecones and hefty tree limbs were swiftly removed from the road, which stretched out in long, sweeping curves. As they ventured deeper, the structures thinned out, replaced by an endless expanse of forest.

When they reached their first stop, the dense trees gave way to sparse grass and brush. The vehicle came to a halt beside a building, nestled at the foot of a snow-covered summit. The structure, likely used for vehicle rentals and storage, stood off the road, its rustic charm reminiscent of early 1900s resorts on Terraenti, perhaps akin to Jackson Hole or Snowmass. Alex imagined the Students would relish an experience here in the future.

Inside the smaller building, they found an array of snow vehicles, some with tracks and others with odd designs. One looked like a snowmobile but sported retractable wings beneath its frame. Declan's excitement was palpable. "Are we going to take one of those?" Harvey chuckled, his eyes twinkling with childlike delight. "Out of all the vehicles in Tunimbria, these are my favorite. They're a blast to ride."

Intrigued, Alex inspected one of the machines while Harvey engaged in conversation with two women who seemed to hail from Vattan, the water planet. Their thick, vibrantly colored hair gave them an avian allure.

Both stood around five feet tall, their attractiveness undeniable. Harvey returned to the group, his excitement barely contained. "Alright, we're set! Let's go. This is going to be fun."

They all piled into two vehicles as the women opened the massive wooden roll-up doors. Unlike most of the planet, where stone and wood dominated, metal was scarce—only found in the vehicles, tram systems, and Pods. The vehicles rolled out as the doors fully opened, revealing a breathtaking vista. Harvey's grin was wide, almost boyish, as they began their ascent. Alex sat beside him, watching the tracks bite into the snow. The view was awe-inspiring, with towering peaks looming ahead. Harvey tapped the monitor, motioning for Alex to look. "It'll take us about an hour and twenty minutes to get there," he informed him. Alex noted the time, then glanced back as they exited the garage, catching sight of the Lodge's rear, where ski lifts climbed the mountain.

Skiers, snowboarders, and even sledders descended the slopes. The vehicle itself emitted nothing but the soft hum of electric tracks crunching through snow.

For the first half-hour, they ascended the mountain, passing hardy skiers and solitary pine trees. Alex fiddled with the music, setting the perfect soundtrack for the journey. The snow grew deeper, eventually swallowing the sides of the vehicle, obscuring the wings. Soon, they were enveloped entirely in a world of white, the snow flowing past the windows like a river.

Declan broke the silence, "We must be in a lot of powder now. How fast are we going?" Harvey swiveled the monitor for everyone to see, pointing to the relevant data. "Everything's right here on the screen," he said, leaning forward with a knowing smile. "In a few minutes, it'll get interesting. We'll reach altitudes over 70,000 feet, and the AI will guide us along the optimal route."

As if on cue, the snow completely enveloped the vehicle. Harvey looked back at Declan, his tone almost gleeful. "We're traveling through and under the snow drift, not on top of it anymore." Declan grinned as the cabin lights flickered on, accompanied by a soft hissing noise.

"Hah, this vehicle even has oxygen!" Kyoryk exclaimed, just as Declan began to voice his amazement. Suddenly, the vehicle burst out of the snow drift, soaring off a cliff. They all lifted out of their seats momentarily before settling back down. The snow cleared from the glass, revealing that they were indeed flying—gliding down the valley below.

"Hold on!" Alex shouted, grabbing the dashboard as the vehicle swooped low, then leveled out, landing gently on the snow before ascending another ridge.

Alex turned to Harvey, who wore a grin as wide as the peaks themselves. "Now I see why you love these vehicles."

Harvey nodded, his eyes sparkling. "Yeah, Gig drove last time, so this is a treat for me." He reached for the music controls, adding, "These were developed from ocean racers on Vattan. They can traverse water, submerge, and even fly for a time. They're a big deal on that planet."

Kyoryk, excitement in his voice, chimed in, "I love them. We saw those racers last time at the Alcazar—designed for snow, huh? That's awesome." Alex gazed out the window, captivated by the snow-laden landscape.

Harvey pointed to the monitor. "This shows our elevation, the average depth of powder, temperatures, oxygen levels—everything is right here." The group leaned forward, eyes glued to the screen, as the vehicle tunneled through yet another snow drift, now indicating a 14-foot depth.

A new **"Song"** started. *Paranoid*

Kyoryk, curiosity piqued, asked, "How can we push through nearly fifteen feet of powder? We couldn't do this on our planet."

Harvey shrugged, "The snow here is different, just like the trees and everything else. It has to do with the condensation—it's like fog-snow for days, unlike the rain-type snow we get back home." He glanced back at Kyoryk, "You'll have to dig into it."

Kyoryk nodded, mulling over the explanation. "Micro snow, then—lightweight flakes, but in massive amounts?"

Alex and Declan shared a laugh. "Here we go again!" Alex shouted as the vehicle descended another slope, the cabin lights glowing brighter. Music filled the space as they soared above the snow, reaching the next valley. Harvey, eyes focused ahead, announced, "Two more peaks before we hit Millapillar Valley."

Declan pounded on his seat, excitement radiating from him. Kyoryk, engrossed in calculations on his tablet, barely noticed.

"Hey, you like Black Sabbath?" Alex shouted over the loud music. Harvey grinned, pretending to shred on an invisible lead guitar. Alex couldn't help but laugh, astonished at this unexpected side of Harvey. Turning to Declan and Kyoryk, he called out, "Check out Harvey! He's on fire!"

The boys reveled in the moment, the thrill of the ride palpable.

As they crested the last peak, Alex glanced over to the other vehicle, where Roman and the guys appeared equally exhilarated. Lev, ever the joker, mimed shooting at them with an imaginary machine gun, adding to the uproarious mood.

Reaching the mountain's summit, the breathtaking view of Millapillar Valley unfolded beneath them. The landscape was dominated by six colossal vertical obelisks, towering at what appeared to be 20 to 30 stories high. Just four stories from their summits, massive timbers jutted out, forming a grand canopy that resembled an enormous tent. Beneath this majestic structure lay a small city, its silver and black roofs glinting in the sunlight, housing a multitude of large manufacturing buildings. As they drew closer, the smaller buildings rivaled those in Tunimbria in size, yet their unique tent-like design suggested a purposeful adaptation to the snowy environment.

As they neared the grand tents, the group veered left, approaching a massive building nestled against the side of a freshly mined, snow-covered granite mountain. Alex couldn't help but marvel, "Kyoryk, what do you think? Those main pillars—how tall are they? They must be the largest stones ever carved."

Kyoryk squinted, attempting to estimate their size. "Hard to say just by looking, but I'd wager they're about sixty, seventy feet at the base and over 200 feet tall. Are those wooden trusses holding up the canopy? They've got to be at least thirty to forty feet in diameter. Aren't redwoods usually around fifteen or twenty feet wide?"

Harvey, always full of surprises, chimed in, "Actually, it's closer to thirty feet." Kyoryk shot him a surprised look, impressed by the random bit of knowledge.

"Yeah," Kyoryk nodded, "but that's before they're cut. Those are the biggest we've got, right?"

To their left, massive stones lay scattered, ranging from two to three feet in diameter to colossal blocks measuring ten to twenty feet across and up to a hundred feet in length. As they approached one of the large buildings, they parked their vehicles in front of a massive glass door, which appeared to be the entrance to a visitor center.

Above them, a balcony with large umbrellas suggested an outdoor dining area, likely a break spot for employees.

Stepping out of the vehicles, the guys were met with an unusual sensation—a strange vibration underfoot that caused their feet to slide slightly from side to side, no more than a sixteenth or thirty-second of an inch. Amused, they exchanged glances, intrigued by the peculiar phenomenon.

Harvey and Roman led the group toward a smaller side door, guiding them inside. They entered a cozy reception area adorned with large displays showcasing a variety of stone textures and woods in sample sizes. Two women, heads popping out from behind a set of double doors, hesitated before stepping forward.

Their features, with long noses, wide-set eyes, and elongated necks, marked them as likely hailing from Kall, much like those Alex had met at the dinner and Master Elders meeting. Despite their otherworldly appearance, there was an undeniable allure to them.

A new **"Song"** began. *Gonna Make You Sweat*

Kyoryk, ever the curious one, remarked, "You hear that sound? It's like that boing, boing noise from this song, he pulled it up on his tablet quietly. His comparison drew laughter from the group. "Seriously," he insisted, "That's exactly what it sounds like!"

Declan, shaking his head with a grin, teased, "What are you smoking, bro? It's more like Himalayan throat singing mixed with a dash of opera or something."

The two women finally approached, introducing themselves. "I'm De-Arlyia, and this is Nanarr'i. Welcome to the stone quarry of Millapillar Valley. How was your journey?" Harvey, clearly taken by their unusual beauty, cleared his throat and replied with a smile, "It was quite the adventure—my favorite kind of trip."

Alex glanced at Harvey, noticing a hint of nervousness in his demeanor as he spoke to the women. Harvey quickly introduced the group, and the women invited them to the center of the room. Nanarr'i gestured to the array of stone samples on display. "These are just a few examples of the different cuts and types of stone we produce here.

The process is quite advanced—we use sonic fusion, a technique known as HCRD, which combines the power of the Common Mind with elemental frequencies to cut, drill, and shape the stone."

Nanarr'i, the more serious of the two, added, "It's the same method we use for what you call wood or timber."

De-Arlyia, whose striking beauty was impossible to ignore, sidled up to Alex and asked, "Is Vibrean joining us?"

Taken aback that she knew about V, Alex responded, "Not this time. She's eager to visit, though, perhaps on our next trip to Tunimbria."

De-Arlyia's eyes twinkled with a hint of mischief as she said, "We've heard a lot about V and you, Alex."

"I even volunteered to be part of the team on your planet during the CAT, but I haven't heard back yet." She fluttered her long eyelashes, a clear flirtation, and added, "Anything you need, just let me know."

Alex, maintaining a polite smile, replied, "I'll keep that in mind. Are you and Nanarr'i from Kall?" "Yes," De-Arlyia confirmed. "My grandfather was an Elder at the University on one of our moons 15,000 years ago. I've been working here for about four years. I'm not married yet, still looking for the right guy. We usually aren't allowed to marry until after thirty years, per our contract."

Alex, unsure of how to steer the conversation, said, "We were thrilled to hear how many from your planet volunteered for our mission. We're all quite new to this ourselves, just two months ago, I was an ordinary guy with no idea about any of this." De-Arlyia chuckled, her smile widening. "I assure you, Alex, there's nothing ordinary about you." Meanwhile, Alex noticed Harvey's gaze fixed on Nanarr'i as she spoke. As they walked, she took his arm, while Nanarr'i subtly pulled De-Arlyia away from Alex, ensuring she kept her distance.

Declan, overhearing the exchange, mimicked De-Arlyia's words with a smirk, fluttering his eyes playfully. "Anything you want or need, Alex," he teased, "you just let me know." With a laugh, he gave Alex a light push forward.

Alex, grappling with his newfound popularity on the planet, shot Declan a warning glance. "Knock it off, mate. You'll embarrass her. She's just being kind."

Declan chuckled as they continued their stroll. "Ever wonder what it would be like to hook up with a girl from Kall or any other planet? They might have techniques we've never even imagined."

Alex tried to hush him; his curiosity piqued despite himself. "That's an interesting thought," he murmured, nudging Declan toward Harvey. "But I think Harvey's got eyes for Nanarr'i."

Declan eyed Harvey with surprise. "No way. I can't believe he's into Black Sabbath."

As the group approached one of the final milling areas, they halted. They were instructed on how to don protective gear. The women gathered them together, explaining the process. Nanarr'i spoke with authority, "When we go through these doors, you'll see a group of more than ten within the Common Mind Bond, using frequency technology to cut the stone. The sound, processed through the computer, is quite unique—some even find it enjoyable. We're cutting granite-like stones, twenty by five by three feet, for the airport hangar on Vindor. Please, no talking or interruptions; we don't want to disrupt them. And remember, don't cross the yellow line on the floor."

The men donned their vests, hard hats, ear protection, and face masks—precautions, Alex surmised, against the possibility of a stone shattering. As they entered the cavernous room, the heavy doors swung open, revealing a vast space. Alex was startled to see a group of individuals arranged in a semicircle, reminiscent of the Creator's plans, gripping what looked like a steel bar supported by casters. They moved in unison, humming and throat singing, their voices melding into a choral harmony.

His gaze followed the stone being altered by the frequency, but he couldn't yet see it clearly. The group edged along the line, each holding onto the uniquely shaped bar that completed their semicircle. Two men gripped the bar firmly while the others linked hands.

In their meditative state, the group appeared utterly at ease, moving step by step within the CMB.

Alex, intrigued, slipped off his ear protection to hear the sound unfiltered. It wasn't unpleasant—in fact, the melody created by the group and machine was unexpectedly beautiful. He was careful not to cross the yellow line as he moved closer to the cutting edge.

He saw the air around the stone shimmer and shift, carving it into a waveform like a feather slicing through butter. The end of the steel bar disrupted the air, creating the feather-like effect that meticulously sculpted the stone.

"It's just as Kyoryk described," Alex thought, *"like the sound of a keyboard in an old disco tune or a modern EDM track. I see now how they can cut these massive stones—using the Common Mind and our Gifts, it's all possible. The CMB is incredibly powerful."*

A chill ran down his spine as he turned to Harvey, playfully punching his shoulder and smiling. Harvey returned the grin, giving him a thumbs-up. They lingered for another minute before retreating through the heavy doors. As they closed, the room fell into a quiet hum.

A new **"Song"** began. *Xeroolt Xaltar / Tsamyn Biyelgee (The Lucky Spotted Horse Tsam Dance")*

"That was unbelievable," Alex said, awe-struck. "I need to learn more about this."

Declan nodded, his eyes wide with fascination. "Did you see the similarities to what we're doing with the Creator's Plans?"

Kyoryk chimed in, "I did—the way they held the device, the way it disturbed the air, cutting through the stone like that."

Harvey, smiling with satisfaction, said, "I knew you all would be mesmerized by this."

Lev added, "It was beautiful." The group burst into laughter at his earnestness.

"What? It was," Lev insisted, "like a theatre performance—the way they moved, very elegant."

Nanarr'i, intrigued by Lev, asked, "What's your name?" "Lev," he replied, a smile playing on his lips.

Nanarr'i nodded thoughtfully. "Lev, what you witnessed is part of the Common Mind Bond, a higher state of consciousness that is not easily attained."

Alex pondered her words, realizing she was right. "It is a higher state of consciousness. I wonder if people in the past had access to this technology—or if it was knowledge passed down by the Elders. I need to ask Sarcan and Gig about this—they must know."

Nanarr'i continued, "We have many teams trained in this technique, both inside and outside. This method has been used for thousands of years to cut and move stone and timber, and as you now understand, it's intimately connected to the CMB."

Harvey spoke up, "We all noticed a similarity between this and our device—what we're calling our Magnetic Accelerator, which we'll use to enhance our planet's magnetic field. It's becoming clear that something akin to the CMB will be crucial in activating it."

Nanarr'i smiled as she led them out to another working area. "That's fascinating," she mused.

"Isn't it?" Harvey replied, sharing her enthusiasm.

Lev, unable to resist, asked, "What's this process called?" Kyoryk answered, "We just learned it in class—HCRD, Harmonic Cutting, Rounding, and Drilling, right?"

Nanarr'i smiled again. "We call it Karouling, but yes, HCRD is another term." Lev, eager to impress, added, "We practiced using the Common Mind Bond last night—it was extraordinary."

Nanarr'i seemed surprised. "So, you've reached that level in your training already?"

Lev and Harvey both stayed close to Nanarr'i now, with Harvey explaining, "Yes, we believe they've unlocked most of their Gifts and are now mastering the Common Mind. Fem' guided them through a brief meditative session last night."

De-Arlyea and Nanarr'i exchanged amused glances. "We're not allowed to use the Bond until after marriage due to its intimate nature," De-Arlyea explained with a giggle. "We've been looking forward to it."

The men exchanged startled looks but remained silent. Declan, ever the joker, tried to hold Alex's hand, eliciting a smirk. They moved to another cutting area, where a larger group—over thirty—was in a CMB, finishing up a massive stone-cutting project.

Nanarr'i and De-Arlyea instructed them to stand back as the team completed their work.

The group watched in awe as the CMB came to a close. Nanarr'i waited a few moments before speaking. "This is one of two stones that will be used at the stadium we're constructing. It's six hundred feet long, sixty feet wide at the base, and six feet at the top—a six-sided polygon," she said, directing the last comment at Lev. Lev, pleased with the attention, grinned. "A polygon," he answered, undeterred by the simplicity of the question.

Nanarr'i remarked, "That's the theme we are using to build a new stadium inspired by the six planets in our galaxy."

As the group descended from the quarry above, a few figures approached. Two older men, who seemed to be from Terraenti, walked up to greet the group. Nanarr'i introduced them, "This is Fronar and Zentra, two of the lead engineers at the plant." Harvey and Roman shook their hands, and it was evident that Harvey had met Zentra before.

The group continued their walk around the plant, taking in the breathtaking view of the valley. The majestic peaks they had just descended loomed in the distance, with a few cascading waterfalls spilling down the mountainsides, remnants of the late summer thaw. Zentra led them through a set of doors and up several flights of stairs.

Earlier, Harvey had mentioned to Alex that Zentra and Fronar were from CAT 1, much like Rugrog and Bahdubah, yet they were of nearly average height. Originating from the South American region, they had arrived long before the Aztec era.

As they entered a dining area on the third floor, Alex admired the expansive view, which was similar to the one below. The room, designed to accommodate around one hundred employees, had a buffet set up, ready for the group. It was a remarkably pleasant day, with no wind, so they chose to sit in the corner under the umbrellas, soaking in the scenery. A couple of other women, who appeared to be from Vindor, joined the group. Zentra introduced them as Marsilah and Breant.

They filled the tables with beers and other refreshments promptly served.

Harvey and the older Elders sat at one end of the table, while the younger men occupied the middle, and the women gathered at the far end. The men sipped their beers and sodas leisurely, the ambiance light and relaxed.

De-Arlyea giggled at something Breant said, who then looked directly at Alex and asked, "How is your schooling going? Are you enjoying it?" Sensing the pressure on Alex, Declan interjected, "It's been enjoyable, though the first few months were overwhelming with so many changes. But we're managing well; Alex and I are the leaders."

Lev, overhearing this, chuckled and, with a slight cough, muttered under his breath, "Bullshit."

Marsilah, who appeared slightly older than the others and carried herself with a confident air, smiled and remarked, "Here in Tunimbria, we undergo similar training to what you would experience in a Master Elder class, although it's quite different from being chosen by the Creator at a certain age. It must have been quite a shock for you all." Alex responded, "We had no clue about any of this until we were on our way to our selected universities. We were only informed at the airport before flying to our moon. How did you all come to work here, and how often do you get back to the big city?"

Breant, petite with striking reddish hair, replied, "Most of us work ten days and then spend three days back in Tunimbria. Some of us live here seasonally."

Marsilah raised her glass, taking a sip before adding, "I live here for most of the year. There are at least three months when the valley is completely closed."

Lev, curious, asked, "How long is a month?" Marsilah replied, "Fifty-eight days."

As Harvey and the older men rose to serve themselves from the buffet, Alex took a moment to admire the view from the dining area. To the left, the untouched, pristine mountains cascaded down to a valley blanketed with trees. To the right, further back into the valley, the landscape bore the marks of extensive mining.

Alex then asked, "What do you think of the snow vehicles we arrived in? Do you use those to travel to work?"

Breant began to respond, but De-Arlyea interrupted, "We have a shuttle that flies us back to Tunimbria. It operates mostly every other day if needed. What was it like to see the messenger from the Creator?" Declan answered, "It was terrifying at first, similar to a prayer, but overwhelming. It's hard to describe." As Alex stood up to get his food, he added, "It was an honor, an unexpected honor."

Meanwhile, Candido and Breant seemed to be talking a lot, which Declan quietly pointed out to Alex.

De-Arlyea followed Alex to the buffet, and several others rose to get their food as well. Standing next to him, De-Arlyea inquired, "Are you planning on moving here, to Tunimbria, after school?" Alex smiled and replied, "I would think so. I'd definitely like to have a place here, possibly with V." As he pondered this, he realized, *Did I just admit that V and I are moving in together? I have to be careful about what I say around these people. I have no idea what's going to happen in the next year, especially with the Creator talking to me personally. And that's another thing—why is the Creator speaking to me alone?"*

He then asked De-Arlyea, "Where's the best place to live—in the city or the foothills?"

De-Arlyea explained, "Most residences are organized by which planet you're from, but that might be changing since people are starting to intermix. I think the best place is by the lake, about a 20-minute ride from the city. Or you could live by the sea, but the weather there can get really bad. No one really stays there year-round."

"I'll have to look into that," Alex said. "How do you get used to these long daylight hours? How long does this season last?" De-Arlyea replied, "Compared to yours, I'm not sure, but we have 393 days in a year. This is our hot season, and it lasts three to four months, by your reckoning. Winter here gets very cold, and the valley shuts down for at least two to three months, depending on the severity of the snowpack."

Returning to his seat, Alex began to eat, with De-Arlyea settling in beside him. He then asked, "Earlier, you mentioned something about 'per your contract.' What did you mean by that?" De-Arlyea sat back in her seat, "It's similar to what you might call a law. At what age can you, you know, like when you're together?"

Alex grinned, "Yes, most of our countries have laws about when you can get married. It depends on where you're from on my planet. In some places, you can marry very early; some marriages are arranged, and others happen when people fall in love, I suppose. Generally, I think the legal age is around 18."

As she took a bite of her food, she asked, "What is religion?" Alex explained, "It's what you believe in. Like we believe in the Creator. On Terraenti, there are many different beliefs about who or what the Creator is. These varied beliefs are the foundation of most laws—the rules by which people live. How about on your planet?"

De-Arlyea replied, "We have those too—those who believe in the Creator and those who don't. I haven't been to my planet yet; I've been here all my life."

Alex smiled warmly. "Amotaious is quite pleasant—fewer people and everyone seems incredibly kind." De-Arlyea nodded enthusiastically. "It's a wonderful place to live, with plenty of exciting activities to enjoy."

Declan leaned in, curious. "What do you like to do for fun?" De-Arlyea's eyes sparkled as she listed her interests. "We have lots of parties and dancing. Ski racing, too. I even dabble in ice sculpting. My parents go fishing all the time, though I'm pretty sure they're not just fishing."

Alex and Declan chuckled in unison. "Sounds like the same kind of fun we have on our planet," Alex remarked. The girls finished their meals and rose to return to work.

Nanarr'i turned to the group with a friendly smile. "When you're ready to build, come back and see us. We'll assist you with whatever materials you need."

De-Arlyea gave Alex a quick side hug and grinned. "It was a pleasure meeting you." She waved her tablet near Alex's and added, "Here's my number if you ever need anything."

"Thanks, I'll keep that in mind," Alex replied, smiling. As the women walked away, Declan made a teasing kissy face at Alex, causing him to chuckle. The women bid their farewells and left the eating area.

Harvey and Roman stood and followed Fronar and Zentra outside. Alex and the other men finished their food and drinks before joining them.

Zentra approached Alex, his dark skin and stocky build hinting at his South American heritage. He was about 5'2" tall and had an approachable demeanor. "What do you think?" Zentra asked. "Perhaps one day this technology will reach Terraenti?" Standing beside Declan and Kyoryk, Alex marveled, "The technology is astounding—truly remarkable. It might take a couple of centuries, or even millennia before something like this reaches our planet. Who knows?"

Declan chimed in thoughtfully, "I believe the people of our planet need to unite, to learn to get along better before such advancements can happen. Otherwise, this technology might be used for the wrong purposes if it were to emerge now."

Alex turned to Zentra, curious. "You look different from Rugrog and Kahput. What part of the planet were you from when CAT 1 hit?" Zentra replied, his voice steady. "My father hailed from what is known today as the Olmec culture, near the Gulf of America."

"It was a city named Veracruz." He glanced at Declan. "We'll just have to wait and see. The next few years will be critical." Zentra paused, gazing up at the towering mountains. "You never know—you might be right. We could be thrust back thousands of years and have to start over again, just like last time. But with you guys now, there's hope. Perhaps we can prevent that and preserve this technology, keep everything moving forward. It's fascinating to think about the possibilities. I truly hope it all works out."

Alex smiled at him, confidence in his voice. "I believe we have a good shot at it. Ultimately, it's up to the people and how they evolve through it all. That's what will bring about the real, significant changes in the short term."

Zentra nodded, his expression serious. "Well, good luck to all of you. Many of us have volunteered, knowing that only a few will be able to assist. Thank you for what you're doing. We're all praying for your success."

Alex shook his hand firmly. "Thank you for the tour. Hopefully, in a few years, we'll be back here, picking out stones for our homes. We just need to get through the next few months."

Declan added confidently, "We'll get it done. You can count on that. Thanks."

Zentra looked directly at Alex, his eyes filled with resolve. "Stay the course—you'll do fine."

"Thanks," Alex replied with a determined smile.

The group climbed into their vehicles and began the ascent up the snowy slope. As Alex looked back at the massive, tent-like structure one last time before cresting the final peak overlooking the valley, he thought to himself, *"Stay the course."* He knew he needed to persevere, to push through—so many people were depending on him.

Back in Tunimbria, at the Alcazar, Alex returned to his room and lay down, closing his eyes in exhaustion. Later, he joined V and the group for dinner.

That evening, after returning to their room, Alex and V prayed for the approval of the vote tomorrow. They retired for the night.

XX

V watched intently as the assembly filed into the Master Elders Council Hall, her heart pounding with anticipation. This time, she sat in the regular seating area, nestled between Alex on her right and Freida on her left. The rest of the Student Elders were scattered strategically around them. Arriving slightly ahead of time had secured them prime seats in the first row of the second floor, close enough to feel the gravity of the Master Elders' presence.

As the delegations from various planets filled the hall, a palpable tension buzzed in the air. Discussions among the Students and Stewards grew fervent, their hopes pinned on securing the Master Elders' approval to proceed with the Creator's Plan to save Terraenti. The stakes were impossibly high—this vote could determine the fate of an entire civilization.

V gripped the wooden handrail, her knuckles white, as she scanned the diverse gathering below. "Unbelievable," she mused silently, her eyes wide with awe. *"Representatives from Kall, Vindor, Regnolm, Vattan, Elducan— all here, donned in their native attire. I can't believe I'm part of this moment. So many are willing to risk everything to save our planet. What an extraordinary time this is."*

Her gaze shifted left as the Master Elders began their solemn procession into the amphitheater. *"This is madness,"* she thought, her heart racing. *"Even if they vote no, we're going to do it. Gig and Fem'—just look at them. They're incredible."*

Alex nudged her side, a playful yet serious glint in his eyes. "You ready for this? It's surreal, isn't it?" He placed his hand over hers, the warmth of his touch grounding her. "This is going to happen, V. I can feel it."

Still fixated on the Master Elders' entrance, V whispered back, "I hope you're right, Alex. It would be much easier if they voted yes. I dread the thought of going against them if we must."

Suddenly, Prezzy, seated behind V, shook her vigorously and shouted, "Vote Yes!" The unexpected outburst startled both V and Alex.

The amphitheater was a cacophony of noise, with voices echoing sporadic shouts of opinion, much like Prezzy's. Alex turned around, half-amused, half-annoyed. "Jesus, Prezzy."

Prezzy laughed, her voice full of confidence. "What? Just look at this place! They're going to vote yes, no doubt about it." She began massaging V's shoulders, her touch light and reassuring. "You two need to chill."

Freida, catching Prezzy's infectious enthusiasm, turned and smiled, a silent agreement passing between them. A moment ago, V had been a bundle of nerves, but Prezzy's typical bravado had worked its magic. V found herself relaxing, the tension in her shoulders easing.

"Thanks, Prezzy. You're right; it's going to go our way." Energized, V stood and joined in the chant, "Vote Yes! Vote Yes!"

The atmosphere grew electric as more Students joined in, including Prezzy and Alex, their collective voices rising in unison. "Vote Yes! Save Terraenti!"

V felt a wave of calm wash over her as she glanced back toward Gig and Fem', who now looked up toward the group. V raised her hand in a subtle wave, which Fem' acknowledged with a serene smile.

The roar of the crowd reached its peak just as all the Master Elders took their seats. V, her hands once again gripping the rails, sat back down, her eyes sweeping over the vibrant crowd as the lights dimmed.

With a resounding crack, Gig slammed the rock gavel against the arm of his chair, and a single spotlight illuminated him. The crowd instantly fell silent, a disciplined hush descending upon the amphitheater. You could hear a pin drop.

Gig stood, his voice reverberating through the stillness. "Welcome to the Master Elders Hall. We gather here today to deliberate and cast our votes on implementing the Creator's Plan to fortify Terraenti's Magnetic Field, shielding it from the impending Catastrophe 6."

He paused, letting the weight of his words settle over the assembly. "Since the dawn of our existence, the law has been clear: we must never interfere with the natural Solar Catastrophes that befall our six planets. These events, seemingly predestined by the Creator, have challenged us for millennia."

"We have always endured—rebuilding, restructuring, repopulating. From Barbarian times to Slavery, to Modern. This cycle has persisted for over forty thousand years on the oldest of our planets. But today, we face an unprecedented situation. Never has the Creator sent a messenger with a directive to intervene. We must reach a unanimous decision to proceed."

"The inhabitants of Terraenti remain blissfully unaware that their civilization teeters on the brink of collapse as before. Our mission is to amplify the Magnetic Field, mitigating the effects of the Super Flare—an undertaking that must be carried out without the population's knowledge."

Gig paused once more, scanning the room before pointing directly at the crowd. "The Master Elders have deliberated and are pleased to announce that the individuals who volunteered to risk their lives to save Terraenti have been selected and approved."

The hall erupted into cheers and applause. V and Alex exchanged surprised glances; they hadn't realized the teams had already been chosen.

After a minute, Gig raised his hand, calming the crowd before continuing, "We are profoundly grateful to all who volunteered. Those selected will receive further instructions. Thank you, once again."

"The Creator has entrusted us with the task of saving as many lives as possible and preserving the technology on Terraenti. I urge you all to consider this as if it were your own planet at risk and if it was during its modern times."

Gig turned to the Master Elders and solemnly intoned, "It is the hope of the Elders of Terraenti and the will of our Creator, Raba Rashi."

The audience echoed in reverent unison, bowing their heads, "Raba Rashi."

Gig faced the assembly once more. "We must unite and agree to move forward. The necessary equipment is prepared, and the volunteers."

He points to the Students and Stewards seated above, to Alex and V. "We are now ready to implement the first test of the Creator's plans, to test the Accelerators on the north and south sides of the planet in forty-two days. Now, I open the floor to general discussion."

The crowd grew animated again, with scattered voices calling out, "Save Terraenti!" "Vote Yes!" "Go For It!"

Muirlmont from Kall stood, striking his rock gavel on the arm of his chair. His large nose was snooting, raising his hand. "Thank you, Gig. If the test succeeds and the final mission is accomplished, it's inevitable that the public, or at least the leading governments of Terraenti, will become aware that their planet was altered. What measures will be in place to prevent further investigation?" He sat with his large eyes glaring around at the other Master Elders.

Fem' rose gracefully, her gaze sweeping over the audience before settling on the Master Elders. "We have thoroughly considered this and believe that some may perceive it as divine intervention, while others will inevitably seek explanations. We have devised a strategy to deploy certain scientists who will assert that the Pulse Reversals naturally strengthened the magnetic field or that the planet protected itself by its own design. We are aware this will spark curiosity, but we have plans in place to minimize suspicion."

"Like all of you, we have organizations and put individuals in place during your modern times to manage such matters, as we have for thousands of years."

V leaned toward Alex and whispered, "She's referring to Alva Global. They'll handle this. We can collaborate with them to devise a plan." V sat back with a reassuring glow.

Alex's eyes lit up with excitement. "Governments pull off stuff like this all the time with false flags. I'm sure it won't be an issue." Harvey shot them a warning glance, shushing them.

At that moment, both Lorness and Blain, Master Elders from Vindor, stood. Blain spoke first, "At what point will we be discussing using this technology on our own planets and when?"

Alex leaned in close to V and muttered, "They shouldn't worry about that now. Let's just vote."

V nodded in agreement, eager for the decision to be made.

Gig rose to his feet, commanding the room's attention. "For reasons beyond our comprehension, the Creator has entrusted us with this mission. Patience is required as we await further messages to fully grasp its significance. We acknowledge there are still unanswered questions."

"We agree, as do others that we could modify the plans and implement them on another planet if the Creator wants it. Yes. We've all heard the second message, and we know that all planets will face peril in the coming years. Eighteen from now, to be precise. What we do now will directly influence that outcome. I hope this understanding is clear to everyone. We must succeed."

Lorness and Blain, their dissatisfaction evident, shook their heads in silent protest as they retook their seats.

Prinks, the Master Elder from Vattan, rose with measured grace. "We are all aware that this plan is fraught with complications. What if the population discovers our intentions? Can we replicate this on another planet in the future?"

"Why did He choose Terraenti? These are all good questions we must address. But." She looked at the other Master Elders, with her brilliant-colored hair lit up from the stage light far back in the amphitheater.

Her fur coat, matched against her skin, dawned soft-toned hues of brown to yellow from her arms up to her neck. "Can we all agree that these messages are indeed divine, truly sent by the Creator? If so, I fail to see how we can refrain from proceeding with the mission." She sat down, prompting the Students and much of the crowd to rise in unison, their cheers filling the hall. "Yes, Go with the Mission." Save Terraenti." "Proceed."

Gig stood once more, his voice resonating with the weight of his words. "I understand that this mission has sown discord among the planets. For the first time, the Creator has asked us to intervene, to deviate from our original Laws and Directives. Never have we been placed in such a position, but we must reach a consensus."

"Otherwise, the division will be inevitable from this point onward. Reflecting on the statement, 'You must risk all to save many,' we now have over 450 volunteers willing to lay down their lives to see this mission through."

The crowd erupted in agreement, their shouts echoing through the chamber. Gig raised his hand for silence, his authority undeniable. "These Elders who have volunteered hail from all six planets." Some Master Elders still growling in inconstant. Shaking their heads, no. Back and forth, fidgeting. The crowd, sensing the gravity of the situation, began to murmur and clap as the Master Elders prepared to voice their positions.

Lorness from Vindor stood, his voice sharp. "We agreed to allow them to go, but that wasn't an endorsement of the vote."

Prinks and Merick from Vattan quickly followed, "And what of the O2 Converter? We never fully resolved that issue."

Minter and Rall, the Master Elders from Regnolm, rose as well, their frustration palpable. "And our planet? The trees have been plagued by the Bonger Beetle for three centuries now."

"Our planet will not see electricity for another thousand years, and we have some kind of plague right now. Our population is…" Ferlnill, the Master Elder from Kall, jumped from her seat, yelling with slobber coming from her lips, her eyes moving in all directions.

Alex leaned towards V, his brow furrowed. "What the hell are they all talking about? This is spiraling out of control."

V smiled at him, a hint of amusement in her eyes. "Are all meetings like this? They're not even addressing the mission anymore. They're just airing their grievances. And look at the crowd—they're going wild."

Declan's head popped between the two of them, grinning. "Isn't this great? Look at them." He points to the Master Elders. "They're all going crazy, yelling at each other. This is mental. Best meeting ever." He laughed hysterically…… Prezzy put her hand on V's shoulder, laughing.

The Master Elders continued to argue, their voices rising with each exchange. The crowd grew increasingly restless, some shouting, "Let the mission go forward!" "Save Terraenti!" and other impassioned pleas.

Gig and Fem', visibly exasperated, stood in unison. Gig called for silence again, banging his gavel several times. "We need to vote!" he urged, turning to Fem'. "We must move this forward, or it will never end."

Fem' nodded in agreement. Her voice barely audible, "Let me handle this. I have an idea."

Gig took his seat as Fem' remained standing, raising her hand to command attention. "Let's vote on this. Do we all agree that the message is authentic and from the Creator?" The room erupted in unanimous approval, with the crowd, Students, and Stewards shouting, "Yes!" "We agree!" "Believe in the Creator!"

Gig rose for his vote, and as Fem' stood by his side, the other Master Elders slowly followed, the room falling into an anticipatory hush. The vote passed with an overwhelming "YES." Everyone was standing….

Fem' raised her hand again to quiet the crowd. "Now, for the final vote. Do we proceed with the mission given to us by the Creator?"

"On December 26th, we will commence the first test of the Accelerator to enhance Terraenti's Magnetic Field during the next Pulse Reversal and continue with all subsequent Pulse Reversals thereafter. We have a list of volunteers, and no current Master Elders will attend."

The audience exploded into cheers, many standing in celebration.

V turned to Alex, her eyes gleaming with relief. "Did you hear that? No current Master Elders. We're in!" She embraced him, their joy undeniable.

"There was no way they were going to keep us from this mission," V said, her smile radiant as she hugged him back.

The Vattan Master Elders were the first to stand, followed by those from Kall. Gig and Fem' were already on their feet, joined by the Elders from Regnolm. Finally, the Elducan Elders rose, the crowd erupting with renewed fervor, chanting, "Vote yes!" "Do the Mission!" "Yes! Yes!"

V and the other Students caught up in the moment joined the chorus, shouting, "Vote yes!" "Save Terraenti!" The chamber was filled with thunderous applause and cheers. After much hesitation, the Vindor Master Elders reluctantly stood. Blain from Vindor silenced the crowd with a commanding shout. "Silence, silence." He scanned the room, his eyes narrowing. "Where are Alexander Katz and Vibrean Aboli?"

The room fell silent as Blain's gaze landed on Alex and V, who raised their hands, still standing.

V's expression darkened as she whispered to Alex, "Oh fuck. What now?"

Alex squeezed her hand reassuringly. "It'll be okay." Then, raising his voice, he called out, "Here! We're here!"

Blain's eyes bore into them. "I want to be crystal clear, both of you and your team, as you say on your planet, better make damn sure this plan works and doesn't end in another catastrophe. Your classmates have made tremendous strides in a short period. The pressure on all of you is immense. Can you handle it? Can you make all this shit work?"

Alex's face hardened with resolve, as did Harvey's and V's. Alex's voice rang out with steely determination, "We will." He recalled the Creator's words, his brother's message, and Zentra's warning. "Stay the course," he muttered, then addressed the crowd with unwavering conviction. He looked at Blain, then at the Master Elders, and declared, "We will stay the course and get it done."

The group from Terraenti echoed his words, their voices filled with resolve. "We'll get it done."

Harvey's voice cut through the noise. He cupped his mouth, tilted his back, and yelled. "Stay the course!!!"

The crowd, growing increasingly agitated by Blain's challenge, began to shout and scream. Blain, sensing the rising tension, raised his arms to pacify them. "Very well, Alex and V. Stay the course." He paused, letting the words sink in. He raised his hand with his rock gavel in his hand, "Vindor votes yes to proceed. You better get it done." Everyone was standing….

The room erupted into wild applause. Alex and V embraced as Harvey and Freida jumped up and down in celebration, the euphoria spreading through the crowd. Prezzy and Declan joined in, their excitement palpable.

Gig slammed the rock gavel down on his armrest, commanding attention. "All in favor, stand." He looked around, but everyone was already on their feet. Gig and Fem' exchanged triumphant grins as Gig raised his hand high. "We have a unanimous vote."

He had a tremendous smile on his face, hugging his partner next to him. "We proceed with the mission to save Terraenti!" Both tuning and waving to the crowd. The crowd's cheers reached a deafening crescendo, their voices united in jubilation.

V embraced Alex tightly, exclaiming, "Thank you! Love you! This is wonderful!"

Alex wrapped his arms around her, "Love you too. This is it. Moving forward." Their group erupted in cheers, congratulating one another and waving to the exuberant crowd.

After a few moments, Gig silenced the assembly. "Thank you, everyone," he began, his voice commanding yet grateful. "I want to extend my deepest thanks to the Master Elders for their decisive vote. In the coming weeks, if you have volunteered, the council will notify you." As the crowd settled, most returned to their seats. Gig turned toward the Master Elders of Elducan. "Letsa, would you kindly close the meeting?"

Letsa rose, holding a red stone the size of her hand. Her eyes of red pearls, tiny nose. Pronounced cheekbones. Snake-like features. Feathered back-colored hair.

Her partner, Alder, his presence formidable, skinny, same eyes, same skin, his hair much darker and ominous looking, announces, "Please be seated for the prayer to the Creator," Alder intoned. His voice is resonant.

The room fell into a hushed reverence. Alder struck his rock gavel on the armrest with authority. Letsa, standing tall, placed her free hand over the stone and began, "Ooh! Raba Rashi! Naash! Ooh, Raba Rashi! Cama See La Ruh! Uttah! De-Elders! De-Masters! Cama See La Ruh! Shanka Ne Ala-Muta. Ne! Terraenti, Pre Raba, Cata de! Opruva! Shanka Ooh, Raba Rashi! Pat!"

As she chanted, the lights in the room dimmed, and the stone in her hand began to glow. The warmth of the stone radiated through the space, causing the air to stir and the tapestries to sway as though moved by an unseen force. A celestial rumble echoed off the walls, a sound both thunderous and divine. Alder struck the gavel again, and the stone in Letsa's hand shone brighter still. A luminous green sapphire arrow shot forth, shattering into countless smaller arrows that darted around the room, passing through each person like beams of ethereal energy. The sensation was familiar yet always awe-inspiring—everyone's bodies tingled with a warm, electric current.

Eyes closed, heads tilted back, and arms outstretched with palms upturned, they all felt as if they were being gently electrified by a benevolent force. Then, just as suddenly, it ended.

The participants opened their eyes, looking around at one another with expressions of joy and warmth.

Laughter and hugs filled the room as a collective sense of peace and contentment settled over everyone. V turned to Alex, who smiled and said, "These prayers—there's something about them. The more people, the more comforting they become."

V, still in disbelief, responded, "It's final. We're good to go. We did it—we have the approval." Alex hugged her, his grin wide with relief. "Yes, we will be ready."

Harvey and Freida approached, offering their congratulations. Alex, still beaming, turned to Harvey and said, "Two more steps—the tests, and then finally, our mission."

Harvey nodded, his smile matching Alex's. "We're on our way. This was a big hurdle. I was worried about the vote—Blain from Vindor was acting like a real tyrant. Who does he think he is…..the king? But in the end, they all agreed. We'll be ready."

V, her smile unwavering, added, "Yes, we will. I noticed Fem' mentioned that current Master Elders must stay on Amotaious."

"So, since we aren't Master Elders yet, we don't need to worry about that?" Freida asked, hugging V. "Exactly," V replied. "We're all set. The mission is a go."

The group made their way out of the Hall, heading back to the Alcazar building, where the celebration continued. They all gathered at a restaurant, excitement buzzing in the air. V caught Gig's attention and walked over to his table, where Gig, Fem', Harvey, Freida, Roman, and Darya were seated.

"Congratulations," Gig said warmly. "We're all set to go. I wasn't sure at the beginning or even near the end, but the vote was unanimous. Surprisingly, they all agreed." V smiled brightly. "Yes, it was incredible. Thank you all—we're so happy."

Fem' chimed in, "Well, thank you, V. You all did an excellent job. Now, the real work begins. Now we test, and we will be ready for the real thing. V says, "We need to be on the planet by December on the 26th. The accelerators will arrive next week. After that, we'll have our break; then we proceed with the first test."

Gig exchanged glances with Harvey and the other Stewards before turning back to V. "We've decided that you all should take your break back on the planet next Friday."

"The Stewards will coordinate with each of you on your itineraries. Will you inform the rest of your group?"

V's excitement was palpable as she replied, "Absolutely! Everyone will be thrilled to hear the news."

Freida added, "Congratulations again. We've just cleared one of the biggest hurdles of the mission. Have a good evening, and remember, we depart at 6:00 am sharp tomorrow morning."

V returned to her group to share the news. Prezzy Tonari jumped in the air with excitement. V said, "Work with your Stewards on your plans. They didn't specify our return date, but I imagine it will be three or four days before the 26th to prepare for the test. So that's it—a little more school and then a whole month back on the planet."

The group buzzed with a conversation about the upcoming break. Alex smiled, took a sip of his drink, and asked V, "What are you thinking? Let me know your plans."

V got a thoughtful look on her face and replied, "What do you mean? You're coming with me. We could visit my sister, then head to your parent's place or whatever we feel like."

Alex smiled, "We've already visited my family a few times, so whatever you want to do works for me."

V considered the options. "We could visit our families and then do something just for us. I'll talk to the others—maybe we could all meet up somewhere at the end of the month." Alex handed her their drinks, and they joined Miko, Declan, Swaraj, and Prezzy at the table for dinner.

Prezzy was already brainstorming. "Since we're going to be back for a while, we should plan on meeting up somewhere for a week or so."

Miko nodded, "We'll have to discuss it with the others when we get back, but I'm just happy to be able to go back."

"What is that, like 35 or 36 days on the planet? That's fantastic." Declan chimed in, "After we see our families, where would be a good place to meet? Cancun? Rio?"

V laughed, "We need to find out what kind of budget we have first. I'll check—maybe they'll cover it for us. You never know!" Declan joked, slamming his fist on the table, "We demand it! We'll tell them we're all stressed out and need to relax at a resort."

Prezzy grinned, "How about a yacht? Maybe they have a big yacht we could use. Lobster, prawns, massages…" Swaraj raised an eyebrow, "A yacht? What are we, millionaires?"

V interjected, "We might not be, but Alva Global is. It's an interesting idea. Alex and I will talk to Alva and see what we can arrange."

As the waiter brought their food, V looked at Miko and Prezzy. "So, what are your plans?" Miko replied, "I need to go home for a bit, but it's funny—I've been dying to go back, yet I never really thought about what I'd do once I got there. I guess I'll just visit my family for a couple of days."

V turned her gaze to Prezzy, who said, "I'll head home too, have Swaraj meet my parents, maybe surf, relax—do absolutely nothing, I suppose."

V suggested, "What matters most is simply being back on the planet, clearing our minds. So much has happened; I can't even imagine what it'll be like to see my family again."

"You're right," Prezzy agreed, nodding thoughtfully. "Just being back on the planet will be enough. Whatever we do, it's going to be nice."

"Sounds good to me," Miko added a hint of excitement in her voice.

Declan looked over at the girls, puzzled. "What are you all talking about?"

Miko grinned mischievously. "We're going to rent a yacht or stay at a resort, then maybe rent a yacht. Why did you want to come along?"

Declan and Swaraj laughed. "Oh, we're invited?" Swaraj teased. "What's the plan—somewhere cold or hot?" "Somewhere warm," Declan decided. "A place where the doors open right onto the beach, like the Bahamas."

"Cancun?" Alex suggested.

V chimed in, "I'll check with Alva. I'm sure this has come up before—there must be a place they own or something. I'll find out."

Prezzy stretched her arms over her head, sighing contentedly. "Just sitting on a beach for a few days would be amazing. Like in our CMB—feeling the sun, the wind. Even here in Amotaious, it's not the same. We need to be back on our planet."

She paused, a look of surprise crossing her face. "I can't believe I'm saying that. Back on our planet? Do we ever get to visit the other planets?"

"I doubt it," Alex responded. "Could you imagine someone from Vindor walking down the street in New York City? Everyone would freak out—they'd be captured and studied like some kind of alien."

Declan chuckled. "They are aliens. We're aliens. We live on the moon. We're genetically modified. Honestly, we don't even know what we are anymore."

"I'm just relieved we made it through the day," Swaraj said, his tone serious. "The vote, I mean. It would've been brutal if some of them had said no."

V scoffed, dismissing the concern. "We would've done it anyway, even if some of the Master Elders didn't fully agree. The vote was just a formality—to appease them."

Swaraj raised an eyebrow. "I didn't know that. Who told you?"

"Harvey mentioned it during the pulse reversal the other day," V explained. "He said we would've moved forward regardless. Over three hundred volunteers had already signed up. Gig basically said, 'We're doing it.'"

Prezzy, intrigued, turned in her seat. "That's interesting. But if they had voted no, it would've caused even bigger problems."

Alex nodded. "It's still going to be an issue later. The Elders from the other planets will want to do the same thing for their worlds. But let's not worry about that now."

The group finished their dinner and headed back to their rooms, the weight of the day finally lifting.

The next morning, the Students returned to the university. After a week of intense classes, they meticulously prepared for the Accelerator tests, checking and rechecking every detail.

Finally, all the Students returned home to visit their families and friends. V and Alex arrived back on the planet, touching down in Southern India.

XXI

Alex and V stepped out of the taxi in front of one of the taller buildings on a narrow street in Bhubaneswar, India.

"Thank you," Alex said, handing the driver some cash. V glanced around, her eyes lingering on familiar sights. "It feels like a lifetime since I left." She pointed to the top floor of the five-story building. "We're on the fifth floor."

Alex grabbed their bags. "I think I gave him too much." V chuckled, brushing off the concern. "Don't worry about it."

They climbed to the top floor, and V pushed the door open, calling out in Hindi. Alex assumed she was saying, "Hello, where is my sister? Anyone home?"

"Didn't you tell them we were coming?" Alex asked. V, slightly dismissive, replied, "Yes, I did." They stood in the family area, waiting. From down the hallway, they heard Saanvi yell, "I'm coming!" As Alex looked down the corridor, he saw Saanvi rounding the corner, sliding across the floor in her socks. She rushed up to V and enveloped her in a big sister hug. The apartment was modern, with four bedrooms, and its warmth felt instantly welcoming. In Hindi, Saanvi said, "I've missed you. It's been so strange here without you."

V gently set her down, smiling. "This is Alex."

In broken English, with a slight speech impediment, Saanvi greeted him. "Hi, Alex. You go University with Vibrean?"

Alex smiled warmly. "Yes, it's a pleasure to meet you. V has missed you too." They all sat at the table, and V pulled some food and drinks from the fridge.

Saanvi, though thinner and with shorter hair, bore a striking resemblance to V.

Her brown eyes sparkled with the same energy as Prezzy's. She sat across from Alex, beside V, and looked at her sister. "I can't believe you're here; it's been so strange without you. What's the university like?" V smiled. "It's been really fun so far. We're learning about some fascinating things. Where are Mom and Dad?"

"They'll be back by dinner," Saanvi replied. "Dad's been away for the last week, working on something."

"How's school? How has it been here without me?" V asked concern in her voice. Saanvi fidgeted a bit. "School's good. Mom has been helping me with my art interpretation."

V, who hadn't shared much about her family with Alex before, was surprised when he asked, "You're in an art class? Do you have anything you can show me?" Saanvi, excited, responded, "I'm studying to become an artist." She quickly stood up and started walking down the hallway. "Let me get some of my latest work. I'll be right back."

"She's in a private school that teaches art and photography for kids with special needs," V explained as she leaned back in her chair. "She looks really good. Maybe I was worried for nothing. I thought she'd have a really hard time without me here."

Saanvi soon returned, her face beaming. "Here's some of my stuff." She spread her artwork and photographs across the table.

Alex, impressed, said, "Wow, these are great." He shuffled through the papers, admiring the photos. "I really like these shots too."

Saanvi smiled shyly. "Thanks. How long are you staying?"

"We can only stay a couple of nights," V replied. As they continued talking, Alex noticed how intense Saanvi was. She couldn't sit still, constantly moving about.

"Is there somewhere I can lie down for a few minutes?" Alex asked, feeling the weight of the journey.

Saanvi jumped up, eager to help. "We have a guest room. Let me show you." She grabbed Alex's hand and led him down the hallway to one of the smaller bedrooms. "You can rest here."

"This is nice, thanks," Alex said, dragging his luggage in. Saanvi left the room, and Alex lay down on the bed, shutting his eyes.

A few hours later, he awoke to the sound of V's mother returning. He turned to his side, trying to catch a bit more rest, when V entered the room and sat on the bed beside him. "Dinner is in less than an hour. Are you ready to meet my parents?"

Alex turned to face her. "Sure. What should I expect?" He was already trying to figure out how to present himself to her parents.

"There will be a lot of questions," V warned, taking a deep breath. "They'll try to analyze you—figure out your likes and dislikes, what your parents are like, what you want to do with your life. They might even take your fingerprints and do a full background check."

Alex chuckled, smiling at her. "Interrogation stuff, huh?"

V leaned in, kissing him softly. "They always manage to surprise me with their methods. My dad should be here any minute, so come out in a few."

A couple of minutes later, Alex got up, hit the bathroom to freshen up, and made his way out to the family room. He adjusted his collar to hide his eagle marks, noticing that V had covered hers with a scarf. As he entered the room, V's dad stood up and extended his hand. "Hello, Alex, I'm Anil. Did you get some rest?" he asked in a thick Indian accent.

"Yes, sir, I did. It's a pleasure to meet you," Alex replied, shaking his hand.

Anil smiled and gestured for Alex to sit down. He was balding, in his late fifties, and wore a casual suit. Though not as tall as Alex, he was tall for an Indian man, thin, well-built, and sharp-looking. "Vibrean tells me you're working towards your engineering master's?"

"Yes," Alex replied, unsure of how much V had already shared with them. He decided to keep his answers simple. Aishwarya, V's mother, walked up, and Alex stood to greet her.

"I'm Vibrean's mom," she said with a warm smile. "It's so very nice to meet you. Vibrean hasn't told us much about you."

Aishwarya, slightly taller than V with a strong, determined face, was only a little heavier than her daughter. She wore a business suit, and both parents presented themselves in a modern Indian style.

The house had religious items scattered about, though V had mentioned they were mainly for show. V was the only one who somewhat followed the Hindu religion. Aishwarya poured everyone a glass of wine, and they all sat down at the table. Since they were on the top floor, the house had a large outdoor area with plants and a small herb garden.

Aishwarya asked, "Vibrean tells us you and some other Students are working on a special project for a company through the university?"

Alex nodded. "Yes, there are twelve of us working on a project to develop a device that filters out certain pollutants from the air. V and I manage our parts of the project, and we've both been selected as project managers. V has been doing an excellent job. Just the other day, she gave a full presentation to the company's management." He glanced at V, giving her a proud smile.

Both of V's parents looked at her, then back at Alex. To his surprise, their expressions remained neutral.

"That's nice," Anil said, his tone measured. "V had a promising career ahead of her here, but she chose more schooling instead. For whatever reason." He placed a hand on Alex's shoulder, a gesture of subtle authority. "I'm sure it's a good thing for you. What's your future look like? Your plans? You're from Australia, right?"

"Yes, from Darwin," Alex confirmed, still trying to gauge where the conversation was heading. "As for my future plans, they're still up in the air. I'm focusing on school for the next three years." "Well," Anil continued, "do you have any long-term plans? A company you might want to work for?"

Alex leaned back in his seat, exuding confidence. "I already have some patents generating income, and I'm considering starting my own engineering design company." V began to speak, but Aishwarya abruptly raised a finger, silencing her daughter mid-sentence. "Your parents live in Darwin? What do they do?"

Alex leaned forward, sensing the tension. "Yes, Darwin. They own and operate a design and engineering firm." V's eyes flashed with anger, her knuckles tightening as if she wanted to snap her mother's finger in two. The urge to silence Aishwarya with a well-placed punch simmered beneath the surface.

Trying to shift the mood, Alex said, "Saanvi's artwork is quite impressive. I particularly liked some of her photographs."

Anil waved a dismissive hand, shaking his head as if to say, "Whatever." He then turned to his daughters. "Vibrean, Saanvi, bring the food to the table." V and Saanvi rose, filling the table with an array of dishes. As they sat down, Anil mentioned, "Aish, I have to go to Delhi tomorrow.

I have a couple of interviews to conduct. What does the rest of your week look like?" Pouring herself more wine, Aishwarya replied, "I'm booked for the next couple of days, but after that, I'm free. Did you want me to join you?"

Anil, now seated at the table, said, "I planned to spend some time with Karan and Deepika." He then looked at Saanvi. "You'll be staying with Aunt Anaya for a few days."

Saanvi, visibly perturbed, nearly jumped out of her seat. "Is she going to take me to school?" "Yes, she can take you to school," Aishwarya assured her.

V shot a glance at Alex and rolled her eyes. "What's so important in Delhi?" Anil's tone grew guarded. "Karan has work there, but I can't get into it."

V leaned forward. "Interrogating someone? What did he do?"

Aishwarya interjected, "I thought you weren't interested in this kind of thing anymore."

V shrugged. "I'm not. Just making conversation while you two are discussing it."

Alex thought to himself, *What the hell is going on here? V's parents are clearly attacking her. This doesn't seem right.*

Anil answered, "We suspect he might have ties to a terrorist cell in Mumbai."

Saanvi, growing more agitated, said, "Well, I better get to go to school. I have a project to photograph elderly people by the river."

"What?" Anil's face tightened as he looked at Aishwarya. "You need to talk to her teacher."

Aishwarya scoffed. "Me?"

Alex turned to Saanvi, eager to steer the conversation back to something lighter. "So, you're studying art interpretation?" Saanvi nodded. "My teacher says I have to study past artists to understand who I might be."

Alex, trying to be encouraging, said, "That makes sense. I have to study engineering symbols before I can build anything."

Anil then addressed V. "How long are you staying?" "Two nights," V replied. "Then we're meeting up with some other Students." "Where will that be?" Anil asked.

"We were invited to stay with Lin and Lev at Lin's parent's homestead in England for a few days," V explained. "But before that, we're visiting Alex's family."

"When do you return to the university?" Aishwarya inquired. V smiled slightly. "We have our first test with the Obliterator on December 27th, so probably a week before that."

Anil raised an eyebrow. "The Obliterator?" V's tone turned dry. "Yes, Dad. That's what it's called."

Anil turned to Aishwarya with a hint of mischief. "Bring that dress I like for when we go out to dinner." He leaned in, kissing her deeply, a kiss that lingered a little too long.

V, clearly uncomfortable, interjected, "Alright, let's not get weird while Alex is here." Alex caught V's eye and smiled.

Aishwarya turned to her daughter. "Your dad likes that dress. He wants me to wear it. What's weird about that? Alex, do you have a favorite dress that V wears?"

Alex hesitated, unsure of where the conversation was heading. "She has a green dress that I like. It matches her eyes."

"That's not what I meant," V muttered, her discomfort growing.

Aishwarya's voice turned teasing. "Are you two having sex?" "Mom, stop," V snapped. "Alex isn't going to discuss our sex life with you."

Anil grinned, leaning back in his chair. "Are you in love? You've only been gone, what, three months?" Alex remained silent, smiling at V. V., keeping her composure, and retorted, "Would it be so wrong if that were true?" Saanvi chuckled, "Oh boy, here we go."

Anil, more serious now, added, "Just don't get pregnant. Starting a family now wouldn't be wise."

Alex, stunned by the turn the conversation had taken, stood up to get the bottle of wine from the counter. "More wine, anyone?" he asked, chuckling inwardly at the absurdity. *They're certainly open-minded, that's for sure. Now I understand why V didn't want to talk about them and why she gets so frustrated when I bring up stuff like this."*

As he poured more wine, Anil continued, "Aish and I have a very deep sexual relationship—experimental, some might say."

Saanvi, clearly done with the conversation, stood up, sipped some of V's wine, and announced, "That's it for me. I must study." She left the room.

V muttered something in Hindi to her parents before switching back to English. "You two are too much. Not everyone talks about their sex lives like you two."

Anil chuckled. "Maybe they should." He turned to Alex. "People should be open to all kinds of new things. It's freeing, don't you think, Alex?"

Alex, trying to stay composed, replied, "I guess so. It depends on the situation and the people involved." Anil nodded. "We're not swingers or anything, but we've experimented a bit." Aishwarya laughed, adding, "As long as you two are responsible."

V stood up, her patience wearing thin. "I thought you were talking about yourselves. We are not discussing what Alex and I do sexually. No way."

V walked over to the cupboard, grabbed something, and then stepped outside to the balcony, needing a moment away from the table.

Alex followed her lead, standing up with a polite smile. "Thank you for dinner. It was very nice." Anil and Aishwarya smiled back, saying in unison, "You're welcome, Alex."

Alex grabbed V's wine glass along with his own and joined her, distancing themselves from her parents. As V lit a cigarette, Alex raised an eyebrow. "I didn't know you smoked?" V smirked. "I don't."

She cast a glance back at her parents, who were still at the table, with Anil affectionately pawing at Aish. "They're crazy—just look at them," she remarked. Alex chuckled. "Well, they're certainly very open with their conversations. It's... interesting." V frowned slightly. "You think my family's weird, don't you?"

Alex shrugged. "I don't have much experience with many families. On my mom's side, some relatives are in jail, so I've seen my fair share of weirdness. So, no, I think your family is alright. Every family is different, I've learned that. But I get why you're frustrated." V smiled, relieved. "Right?" She turned her gaze back to the view. "We'll spend as much time with Saanvi as possible, then head over to Lin's place after we visit your parents. How does that sound?"

Alex nodded. "I'm good with anything. You know me—my main focus is getting back and completing the mission. I want everything to be squared away by the end of December." V kissed him softly. "Okay, I'll let Lin know we'll visit for a few days. And after that? Have you talked to Alva about where the whole group might meet?"

Alex looked out over the balcony. "Declan and Kyoryk are talking about the Bahamas. I have Alva checking it out. They should let me know by tomorrow or the next day." V, as she stubbed out the cigarette, asked, "What do you think of India?"

Alex smiled, glancing around. "It's nice—big, crowded, full of life." V nodded thoughtfully. "It was important to come. I needed to see Saanvi, and I still need to talk to my aunt about her. She needs some time away from our parents."

Alex and V spent the rest of the night with Saanvi. The next day flew by as they explored the bustling marketplaces and other vibrant spots in the city. V took Alex on a whirlwind tour, showing him the essence of her hometown. They had dinner with her parents again, but the evening ended much like the first, with another heated argument between V and her parents. However, V managed to spend a quiet morning with Saanvi before their flight.

After three nights with the Katz family, Alex and V were picked up at the airport by Lev and Lin, who drove them to Lin's parents' homestead. On their fifth night, Declan and Miko joined them, and the group enjoyed the Adder family's warm hospitality, extending their stay for another three nights.

On their final day in England, Alex confirmed the arrangements with Mod from Alva Global for a two-week stay in Cancun. Mod informed him that they'd be staying at a private house near a resort, complete with a large pool. The house would be serviced every few days with fresh food and clean linens, ensuring a comfortable and luxurious stay.

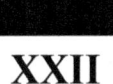

XXII

The group arrives at the sprawling mini-mansion, a stunning rental property that immediately captivates V with its architectural elegance. Designed to accommodate up to twenty guests, it boasts fifteen luxurious bedrooms, two shimmering pools, a pristine white-sand beach, and a pair of fully stocked bars—an opulent oasis that feels almost too grand for their modest party. Situated just twenty minutes from the city and minutes away from a couple of lavish resorts, the house provides a perfect blend of seclusion and convenience.

As the day wanes, the group settles into their respective rooms, each space an embodiment of comfort and style. Eventually, they gravitate towards the expansive dining area. Earlier, V and the other ladies had ventured into town, returning with chic new beachwear, and even picking out fresh attire for the guys.

The house staff has prepared an impressive spread for dinner—an array of shellfish and other local delicacies native to Cancun. The Students gather in the main dining area, relaxed and sipping on drinks, while V perches on a barstool beside Alex. Before dinner, she hears the front door creak open, followed by the unmistakable sound of an argument between two unfamiliar voices with distinct accents.

"I want to do the introduction!" one voice insists.

"You did it last time," the other counters sharply.

"No, I didn't—you did!"

"Your memory's clearly faulty."

V glances at Alex, trying to capture his attention amidst his animated conversation with Kyoryk, who's busy behind the bar. "Shooshh!" she hisses.

Annoyed, Alex looks up. "What is it?" "Is someone else here?" V whispers.

Their question is soon answered as two peculiar figures stride into the dining area, each carrying various steel cases that clatter as they set them down. The unexpected guests immediately draw the group's attention. Silence descends as everyone turns to assess the new arrivals, who radiate an air of enigmatic authority.

The woman waits until she's sure she has everyone's attention, then flashes a measured smile. "Elders of CAT 6," she announces. "I am Rev 321B, and this is Mod 561A. We were constructed prior to CAT 3, fifteen thousand three hundred forty-six years ago. We oversee Alva Global Industrial. How are we all doing tonight?"

Prezzy leaps up, nearly tripping over herself in her excitement, jumping over Swaraj, rushing to greet Mod, hand extended. "Pleasure to meet you!" she exclaims. Tonari follows, embracing Rev with a familiarity that surprises the rest.

Declan, stunned, mutters, "Oh my God!" Kyoryk's eyes widen with fascination. "Incredible."

The group, momentarily paralyzed by shock, gradually stirs into action. V, still processing the surreal encounter, finally finds her voice. "No one mentioned you'd be joining us. Would you care to stay for dinner?"

Mod glances at Rev. "Sure, it's typical. They always forget! I told him two or three weeks ago that we'd be doing this while they're all together."

Rev nods, looking back at Mod. "Exactly, while they're all together and relaxed." V, confused, asks, "Do what?"

"Your physicals," Mod replies nonchalantly. "Oh, okay, sure, no problem," V responds, though she's clearly still puzzled.

Rev takes a seat at the bar, her tall, slender frame almost too delicate, with large almond eyes accentuated by a hint of gold eye liner. Her short, curly, gold-brown hair and dark complexion give her a striking appearance. She leans on a cane as she walks, a noticeable limp adding to her enigmatic presence.

Mod, though smaller, still towers over Bahdubah at just over three feet. His dark skin contrasts with a reddish-brown mop of wavy, curly hair, and a bushy beard and mustache. A few dreadlocks dangle on one side, enhancing his wise, almost mystical aura. The two, dressed in impeccably tailored silk suits, make an intriguing pair—a contrast so vivid that it leaves V and the others in awe.

Alex, still in disbelief, blurts out, "So, you're not human?" Rev chuckles, her smile wry. "Alex, come on. You're supposed to be one of the leaders here."

"But you have a limp and carry a cane," Alex persists, confusion lacing his words.

Rev stands, raising a finger theatrically. "Deception is key! Who would suspect an AI robot with a limp and a cane?" Her statement prompts laughter from Declan, Kyoryk, and Miko, while the rest of the group, now on their feet, approaches to shake hands, eager to examine the visitors up close.

"That's incredible," Alex murmurs, extending his hand. "It's a pleasure to meet you."

"I'm Kyoryk," he adds, introducing himself. Mod scoffs lightly. "We've known who you are before you knew yourselves."

Mod turns to Rev, his tone darkening. "It was the same with Gig and Fem's group—they didn't tell them either. Are we not important enough to be properly introduced?" He pounds his fist on the table in frustration. "Third wheels, that's all we are."

Rev sighs, a weary smile playing on her lips. "We do everything. What would they do without us? They'd be useless. Alright, let's give them the rundown."

In unison, Rev and Mod launch into an explanation of their creation, their voices intertwining as they describe their intricate designs and capabilities. "I'm general purpose," Mod begins, "with five hundred and sixty-one modifications and two hundred revisions. We're both equipped with Vector and Array Processors, capable of forming a Cluster when necessary."

As questions fly, V whistles sharply, silencing the chatter. "Let's all sit down to dinner and get acquainted," she suggests, her voice firm.

Prezzy, bouncing in her seat, blurts out, "This is so exciting! Did you know Elvis? What about the Beatles? What were they like?" Laughter ripples through the group as Mod and Rev take seats at the center of the table. The Students fill their plates from the buffet, eager to continue the conversation. Kyoryk, seated beside Mod, leans in with curiosity. "What kind of storage capacity do you have?"

"We're akin to your supercomputers," Mod replies. "Though most of our storage is housed back at the Lab and on Amotaious, with additional access to our facility in Geneva at any time."

V, ready to steer the conversation, waves her hand to capture everyone's attention. "Instead of bombarding you with questions, why don't we hear from the two of you first?" She pauses, then adds, "Welcome, and second, is there something specific you need from us?" Rev nods appreciatively. "Thank you, V. Yes, there are a few things. We spoke to Gig, who suggested we come to introduce ourselves."

"He thought it would be easier while you're all here together, relaxing. Tomorrow, Mod will begin the medical exams to check on your well-being. After that, we'll be taking photos—for your family, friends, university records, and ID purposes."

Rev pulls out a stack of papers from her briefcase, showing them to the group. "These are for your background information, for today and into the future. You all need to start working on your identities. This is part of the school's process, though I'm sure no one told you about it."

Rev and Mod exchange knowing smiles before Mod speaks, "Apologies for the surprise. It's equally important for us to spend some quality time with you all." V smiles, shaking her head slightly, "No worries. We weren't briefed about the exams, but we were aware of the photos and documents from class."

"It'll be great to get to know you both and get everything done." V notices that the files in front of them, each bearing their names, are impressively thick.

Mod continues, "Last time, it took us two days to complete the exams and finalize all the photos and paperwork. I've just sent each of you a schedule on your tablets. We'll begin tomorrow at nine a.m., if that suits everyone?" Alex, nodding, adds, "You know, I hadn't even considered the physicals—especially after spending three months on the moon. I wonder how it might have affected our bodies."

Rev, with a curious tone, asks, "What do you think of this place? We rented it out last year for the Stewards." Declan grins, "This place is incredible! It has all the amenities of a five-star resort—not that I've ever stayed at one." Prezzy, unable to sit still, fidgets excitedly in her seat, a habit that Mod finds amusing, though the rest of the group has grown accustomed to it.

"So," Mod asks, "has everyone been feeling okay since you've been back on the planet for the past couple of weeks?" The group exchanges glances. Tonari speaks up, "I was just thrilled to be back on Earth. The first few days felt a bit off, but now I don't notice anything. We've been on the move, flying a lot, and that hasn't exactly been fun."

Mod nods, "Well, we'll make sure to check everyone thoroughly, but you all seem to be in good shape."

Alex, ever focused on the mission ahead, asks, "Have you analyzed the Creator's Plans? Do we have a chance?"

Mod smiles reassuringly, "Our projections are quite promising. With the immense solar energy set to impact the planet during the CAT, there will be inevitable losses, but the difference should be enough to preserve current technology. This civilization should be able to recover within a century or so—hopefully."

A little while later, with dinner nearly finished and drinks flowing freely, Rev stands, capturing the group's attention. "Now, regarding us," she begins, "we've been around for most of the recent CATs, but what you're about to undertake could preserve most cultures and technologies for another couple of millennia. It's a monumental endeavor."

Rev's voice is entirely human, free from any robotic undertones. Their accents, a blend of South African with a hint of old British English, add to their unique presence. She continues, "Our computing capabilities rival those of your most advanced modern computers. We possess facial recognition, and our eyes can read a postage stamp from nearly a thousand yards away while calculating the exact distance. Our internal skeleton is composed of an alloy yet to be discovered in this era, utilizing hydraulic actuators and pneumatic transducers. Our half-inch skin layer contains over 10,000 microsensors, mirroring your nervous system. We can hear frequencies ranging from 0.05 kHz to 100,000 kHz. While we're not designed for combat, our strength is comparable to, let's say, Lev here. However, we do possess the knowledge to incapacitate a human in less than a second without the use of a weapon. And yes, we do have sex organs, but only for aesthetic purposes. Any questions?"

Kyoryk, intrigued, asks, "What powers your system?" Mod responds, "We operate on an Internal Micro Nuclear Power Packet, which requires replacement every ninety years."

Kyoryk presses on, "Do you eat or drink?" Mod explains, "Yes, but purely for the sake of deception. Our systems are designed to hold liquids and compact solids into a cube, which we discard at a later time."

Rev and Mod spend the remainder of the evening fielding more questions, with Rev delighting the group with impersonations and Mod showcasing unique sound effects. The night stretches into the early hours, ending after one a.m., with the group continuing their lively discussion with the enigmatic duo.

XXIII

At midday, Alex and Declan jog along the sunlit beach, their pace steady against the rhythmic crashing of waves. They soon spot Rev capturing photos of Miko, Prezzy, and V, the ocean and sandy shore providing a stunning backdrop. Declan, with a playful grin, calls out, "Hey ladies, how's the photo shoot going? Any nude shots yet?"

Rev, her expression impassive, glances at Alex and Declan before replying, "Nude photos are unnecessary."

Prezzy laughs and responds, "Declan, you've seen us all nude before in the showers, and I'm sure you've seen Miko nude plenty of times." Suddenly, and to everyone's surprise except Rev's, V sheds her bathing suit and lies seductively on the sand, looking up at them with a teasing smile. "Rev, take one, and send it to Alex," she says provocatively.

The girls burst into laughter as Rev, unfazed, agrees, "Very well." Rev moves around, expertly finding the perfect angles. She seems to toggle her emotions like a switch, her demeanor now entirely focused. "These are excellent. Let's make them a bit more tasteful," she suggests, adjusting V's arm and leg to cover certain parts, ensuring the photo is more presentable. Rev chuckles, her laughter light and squeaky, "There, that's better."

Alex glances at the photo and smiles, "Very nice. Thanks, Rev."

Declan, still in shock, his mouth agape, turns to Rev and asks, "Can we take a few of Miko as well?" Miko smiles mischievously as she undresses and mimics V's pose on the sand. She looks at Declan and teases, "Enjoying yourself?"

Declan grins and chuckles, "What? Prezzy said I've seen you all nude in the showers before."

Rev turns to Prezzy, "Would you like a couple as well?" Already undressing, Prezzy nods, and Rev takes a few shots of her. Declan and Alex wait patiently, smiles playing on their faces. The three women then pose together, their backs to the camera, heads turned back with playful expressions. As the girls slip back into their bathing suits, Rev looks at the boys and smirks, "Maria and Tonari have been sunbathing nude all morning."

Declan, disappointed, exclaims, "Damn, I missed that?" Earning a dirty look from Miko.

Alex turns to Rev, "How are the physicals coming along?" Rev, beginning to pack up her equipment, replies, "We're right on schedule."

Alex probes further, "So, regarding your programming—do you experience emotions or feelings?" Rev smiles and explains, "Not in the way you're imagining. We're programmed to interact with you in thousands of ways, but perhaps not in the ways you're considering. There's a multitude of programming designed to prevent humans from discovering our true nature. Yet, we still maintain as much anonymity as possible. To this day, we've kept our true identities concealed."

Declan looking over at Rev he asks, "What was it like living thousands of years ago when humanity was so different?" Rev reflects, "We've had to adapt to countless cultures, and it was vastly different back then. In pre-modern times, things were far simpler to accomplish tasks compared to today. We've had to reinvent ourselves repeatedly."

Alex, helping to carry Rev's gear up the beach, remarks, "It's fascinating that you were developed so long ago." Rev responds, "From all the data I've gathered over the millennia, it's you all who are truly fascinating."

Declan, trudging through the sand, asks, "Before the last CAT, did you live in Atlantis or another city?" Rev replies, "We resided in a city off the east coast of North America called Mamotaious. Atlantis was developed and built from the people from that culture. After CAT 2. It's when and where we were developed."

Declan, wide-eyed, "I remember that from class. That city was incredible."

V catches up to them and asks, "Before a CAT or some other catastrophic event, what do you do? Where would you go?" Rev answers, "Remember, I've undergone many revisions, but in the event of a catastrophe, we retreat to the moon or return to Amotaious. We take extreme precautions to avoid being discovered by new civilizations."

As they arrive back at the pool, Rev heads inside the building, while Declan, Alex, and the girls relax by the pool. Alex examines his tablet and says, "This is a beautiful picture. Rev did a great job."

V, looking at the screen, agrees, "That's a lovely photo. I need one of you—not necessarily a nude one." Alex chuckles, "Most guys don't do well in nudes. Any plans for the rest of the day?"

V replies, "Not really. Lin is trying to organize a pool volleyball game, but with the exams and photos, we're pushing it off for a day or so."

Just then, Mod emerges and spots Alex. "Alex, it's your turn." Alex follows Mod into one of the rooms, where medical cases are neatly arranged. Mod steps onto a stool to begin the examination and asks, "How have you been feeling?" Alex responds, "I feel fine, no concerns. How are the others doing?" Mod reports, "Nothing unusual to note. All twelve of you possess unique genetics. Your bodies can handle low gravity and are less affected by solar and space energy compared to ordinary individuals. It's truly extraordinary. I didn't anticipate any issues in that regard."

Mod carefully examines Alex's face, gazing into his eyes, "How are you coping with the stress of all this? The immense responsibilities you now carry?" Alex smiles, "It's a lot to handle. Everything has changed over the past three months."

Mod, still studying Alex's reactions, asks, "And how does that make you feel?" Alex answers earnestly, "I'm determined to help, to make things right. I want to save as many as possible."

Mod, observing Alex closely, inquires, "So, you're managing everything?" Alex, with a sincere expression, replies, "If I weren't focused on fixing everything, I'd probably lose my mind. How are the others handling it?"

Mod responds, "It's a tremendous amount of pressure on your group, especially with all the changes from the Creator. What's intriguing is why now, after all this time." Alex nods, "A few people have mentioned that. Why now? After so many CATs, what has changed?"

Mod steps off the stool and sits in a chair, "It's a valid question. Is there anyone in your group you're particularly concerned about?" Alex considers for a moment, "I suppose Tonari, maybe Maria. They seem to be struggling more, especially after that first Pulse Reversal." He hesitates, then adds, "Possibly Swaraj too."

Mod advises, "It's crucial to remind everyone that they're not alone. You have an entire army of people and thousands of years of technology working with you to fulfill the Creator's Plans. You've got Gig, Harvey, and V. You and Declan appear to be good friends. And remember, the Creator is watching over you. Have you received any further messages since that time at the university when you were with the others?"

Alex recalls the Creator's last message, instructing him to keep their latest meeting a secret. He replies, "No, no further messages."

Mod examined Alex with a meticulous eye and declared, "Your tests are impeccable; you're in excellent health." He paused, contemplating. "Over the years, I've observed a remarkable shift in cultural dynamics. Hostilities have softened. People are more inclined to sit down and negotiate a compromise rather than remain stubbornly divided. The Creator, it seems, is willing to alter the course of history."

Mod continued, his tone thoughtful. "Consider this: just a century ago, certain governments or nations would fiercely prohibit the practice of different faiths or religions. It wasn't only governments; society itself was intolerant. A century ago, you could be shot, hung or dismembered for belonging to a different faith. Do you understand what I'm saying?"

Alex pondered for a moment before responding, "I get it. People are more relaxed now, more tolerant. They're learning to coexist, to get along better."

"Exactly," Mod agreed. "I'm just trying to decipher why the Creator is making these changes now. Society has evolved dramatically over the last century or two, and I believe the internet has played a significant role. Knowledge is now at everyone's fingertips; ignorance is no longer an excuse."

Alex nodded. "Compared to the world wars, things are completely different. And with the ongoing De-Nuclear Arms Pact of 2030, there's hope for a peaceful future."

Mod smiled. "When is that expected to be completed?" "By 2040 or 2042, I believe," Alex replied.

Mod's expression turned contemplative. "It's something to ponder. Perhaps the Creator is offering us a second chance, rather than resetting everything. I don't even know if the CATs were meant to reset the population in the first place. Some people believe that, but it's just a theory."

He paused and looked back at Alex. "I gave Tonari and Candido some mild medication after the first Pulse Reversal. They seem to be doing much better now, but keep an eye on them. You and V are in a relationship—how's that going?" Alex brightened. "V is extraordinary. Things are going well. She constantly reminds me to relax and not obsess over the mission. She's more grounded than I am, maybe even better balanced in life."

Mod advised, "Don't try to solve everything at once or let all your challenges overwhelm you. While you're here on the planet, focus on enjoying yourself. Don't dwell on what's going to happen in three or four weeks. Can you do that?" Alex smiled, "I'll try."

Mod's demeanor suddenly shifted to one of light-heartedness. He grasped Alex's hands and chuckled, "Alex, don't just try—do it! Clear your mind; it's essential. The meditation you practice during the CMB can be just as relaxing on your own. Alright, we're done here. Could you find Declan for me?" Alex nodded. "I'll get him for you. Thanks, Mod. It's hard to believe you are who you are—truly remarkable."

Mod grinned. "Thanks, Alex." As Alex left, Mod began to sing, "I am who I am. La La La La."

As Alex walked from the house to the pool area, he noticed Maria and Miko holding hands, running into the house. Alex approached Declan, who appeared agitated. "What's that all about?" Alex inquired.

Declan, visibly upset, responded, "Hey, what's going on?" "Mod wants to do your physical now," Alex informed him. Declan pointed towards the house. "Did you see that? Maria and Miko?"

Alex nodded. "Miko wants to fool around with Maria?" Declan, drying off from the pool, said, "Yeah, can you believe it?" Alex sat down, trying to process it. "That's something, mate. Sorry, I guess." Declan continued, "Miko asked me, and I said it was okay." Alex looked up at him, surprised. "Really? You're okay with this?"

Declan placed a hand on Alex's shoulder. "She asked me after the CMB, and I said it was fine. What pisses me off is that she doesn't want me to join them. Yet! Can you believe that?" Alex laughed. "I thought you said you were overwhelmed by her sexual aggressiveness. Maybe this will give you a break. What does Kyoryk think about it?" Declan looked off into the distance. "I talked to him, and he said Maria is a force of nature, and he's fine with it—whatever she wants to do. I think he's just happy to be with her. Whatever. I'm okay. I just wanted to join them, and she said, 'Not yet.'"

Alex chuckled. "She said 'Not yet'? Maybe you still have a chance. Be patient; your fantasy might still come true. Now, you better get going—Mod is waiting for you." Declan smiled, clasped his hands together as if in prayer, and said, "Someday. Someday…" Alex laughed, "You can dream, right?" As Declan walked away, he said, "I can visualize it right now."

Alex got up and walked over to where V and Prezzy were lounging in the sun. "Hey," he greeted them. "Catching some sun?"

V lowered her sunglasses and smirked, "Miko and Maria were totally making out in the pool— it was quite a show." Alex grinned at them. "Sorry, I missed it. So now they're…?" Prezzy laughed. "Use your imagination." Alex looked up, thinking about it, but said nothing.

V sat up and playfully kicked him in the shin. "Can you see it now?" Alex laughed. "I had a feeling something like this was going to happen." Prezzy chuckled. "It's not a big deal. Maybe I'll join them next time."

V, mildly concerned, looked at both of them. "I just don't want our mission to be jeopardized by our personal desires. After the mission, I don't care, but for now, we need to stay focused." Prezzy shrugged. "They're just having fun. I'm sure once we're back at the university, everything will be fine. Even if there are some adjustments to our relationships, we'll manage." V sighed. "We'll see. I'm not going to worry about it." She stood up. "I'm going to do some laps."

Prezzy looked at Alex. "She's going to worry about this, isn't she?" Alex smiled knowingly. "Oh, yeah. Where are the others?" "Kyoryk and Lev are on the beach with Rev, and the others went to the store," Prezzy replied.

Later, after Mod completed the physicals, Alex and V gathered the group for a quick update on the mission. Alex addressed the group, "V has updated the schedule on all your progress. I wanted to let everyone know that we are on track. We should have everything ready by the 20th of December. I spoke with Gig this morning. He and Fem' asked if we were enjoying ourselves. I told him we were grateful and thanked them for this amazing vacation spot. He said all the volunteers have been selected, and the groups on Amotaious are nearly finished with the modifications to the ships. The tents are ready."

Mod interjected, "We have a plan to interfere with the satellites in that area for as long as we need. The public will remain unaware of our presence on the planet and our activities. Additionally, the tents are made from a material that will help camouflage our presence." Alex declares, "That's fantastic; we can always blame it on an alien sighting, just like the old days." The room erupts in laughter.

V interjects, "I've noticed that Kyoryk and Maria have devised a couple of innovative plans to maintain communication with the lab during the event using lasers. The Accelerators have been preliminarily tested by Kyoryk and are securely packed in crates, ready for deployment. That's a major win."

"Meanwhile, Kahput and Rugrog have been tirelessly preparing accommodations for the additional Elders at the University. Does anyone have further updates or questions?"

Lin stands, her fingers deftly tapping her tablet as she plays a mellow, local tune. "I think we should all agree that Alex and V need to stop obsessing over the mission and start enjoying this vacation." Declan rises, raising his glass with a smirk. "Here's to all of us savoring every moment of this break," he says, casting a playful glance at Miko. "Wherever that enjoyment may lead us." Miko returns his look with a mischievous grin. "Yes, wherever it may lead us," she echoes with a hint of promise.

Alex stands and raises his glass. "I want to extend our gratitude to Rev and Mod for checking in on our well-being. We eagerly anticipate collaborating with both of you on many more missions and ventures in the future."

Everyone raises their glasses once more in a toast, and the evening unfolds with a delightful meal shared among friends. Later that night, Alex and Declan sit at the bar while Kyoryk crafts drinks with practiced ease. Alex can't resist asking, "So, spill it. Did Miko have fun?" Declan frowns, shaking his head. "She's not giving me much. All she said is that Maria is a wild woman." Alex chuckles. "I have a feeling it's the other way around, considering what you've told us about Miko."

Kyoryk, mixing drinks with a knowing smile, chimes in. "You know, I've learned some fascinating things from Maria—stuff I never even knew existed. For instance, did you know that over fifteen hundred animal species are bisexual?" Alex and Declan exchange bewildered looks, clearly taken aback.

"Really? Do tell," Declan prompts, leaning in with curiosity.

Kyoryk grins as he pours their drinks, enjoying the moment. "I'm not sure if it's a Russian thing, but the positions she's had me in... Let's just say she's either read a lot of books on the subject or she's incredibly creative." Alex and Declan, both wide-eyed, listen intently. Declan, unable to contain his curiosity, grabs a notepad and pencil. "Show me!"

Kyoryk laughs, shaking his head. "I'm not about to draw you a picture. But imagine us back-to-back, then leaning forward, and she bends—"

Before he can finish, Prezzy and Lin approach the bar. Lin interrupts, "Make us some drinks too, Kyoryk." Kyoryk, eager to change the subject, says, "Sure thing." Declan, still trying to extract more details, presses on. "Bends, what around now?"

Alex struggles to suppress his laughter while Kyoryk, now hesitant to continue with the women present, brushes it off. "You'll have to look it up." Prezzy, ever curious, asks, "Look what up?"

Declan, without missing a beat, replies, "We were just trying to get Kyoryk to reveal his favorite sexual position."

Prezzy, never one to shy away from such topics, casually remarks, "For a long session, I prefer the Irish Garden Position. But if I'm in a hurry, the Valedictorian gets the job done."

Lin adds with a grin, "If you're looking for a workout, the Wheelbarrow Position is unbeatable."

Alex takes a large gulp of his drink, trying to keep his composure. Kyoryk, now visibly embarrassed, continues mixing drinks without a word. Declan, engrossed, begins typing furiously on his tablet, "What were those called again?"

V and Miko stroll up, deep in conversation about renting a boat to explore a nearby island. Miko pauses, glancing at the group at the bar. "What are we drinking?"

Kyoryk, seizing the opportunity to shift gears, says, "With my newfound knowledge, I've concocted a few new drinks. This one is called the 'Magnificent Seven.' It's made with seven secret ingredients. Give it a try." He slid a couple of glasses to them on the bar. V takes a sip, her eyes lighting up. "Wow, this is fantastic."

Alex, eager to steer the conversation away from its previous direction, asks, "Did I hear something about a trip to an island?" V nods enthusiastically. "There's a place called Isla de la Pasión. It's about an hour's boat ride away. We were going to ask Rev and Mod if we could go." Alex grins. "That sounds like a blast."

Declan, ever the provocateur, quips, "Do we need any more passion?" Miko, standing directly behind him, asks, "What were you guys talking about?" Declan, now the picture of innocence, replies calmly, "We were just discussing the lovely weather."

Prezzy and Lin burst into laughter. Prezzy, never one to let things slide, notes, "No, Kyoryk was enlightening us about his favorite sexual positions." Kyoryk, with a sheepish smile, quickly clarifies, "Actually, I was just mentioning that over fifteen hundred animal species are bisexual."

Miko, not missing a beat, hugs Declan from behind. "The weather, huh? Well, when it comes to efficiency, I'm all about the Valedictorian." Prezzy chimes in, "That's exactly what I said."

To everyone's surprise, V rolls her eyes and corrects, "Isn't it pronounced Valedictorian?" Alex nearly spits his drink back into his glass as the group falls silent, taken aback by V's unexpected contribution.

Miko, ever the provocateur, adds with a mischievous smile, "After today, I've added a few new positions to my repertoire." Kyoryk, unfazed, responds calmly, "You know, even dolphins and penguins can be bisexual." Miko grins wickedly. "I wasn't just a Student; I was the teacher too." Declan, with a hint of resignation, mutters, "I can imagine." Miko kisses Declan on the cheek. "Nothing for you to worry about, lover."

Alex, sensing Kyoryk's unease, stays behind to help him make the final drinks as the others go to the hot tub, "Mate, there's absolutely nothing wrong with whichever way one wants to go sexually, especially in this day and age. What's on your mind?"

Kyoryk nods, appreciating Alex's support. "Of course, these days, there should be no judgment. And if there is, it's on those who judge, not on those who choose to live freely."

Kyoryk looks at Alex with sincerity. "It's just that certain countries, certain people, certain religions still don't understand. I was discussing this with Swaraj."

Alex, with a firm tone, declares, "Screw them, mate. I guarantee you, where we're headed, there will be no judgment. I promise you that." Kyoryk finishes preparing another pitcher of

Magnificent Sevens and raises his glass. "You're right. Screw them. 'We Do What We Want!'" Alex clinks his glass with Kyoryk's. "That's right. Screw it. We do what we want!"

Alex's thoughts raced. *What is Kyoryk trying to say? Is he hinting that he's gay? Or perhaps bisexual? Or maybe he already is? What's his angle here? And Swaraj—could he be gay too? Or did he slip something into our drinks? This whole situation is starting to seriously unnerve me. What's happening with these people?*

Has the Common Mind turned us all into sex-crazed maniacs, or is this just how 21-year-olds behave? I genuinely can't tell anymore. I'm just a simple guy from Australia, after all.

The group indulged in a few more rounds of drinks in the hot tub. Alex wasn't entirely sure which rooms they all ended up in. He knew he'd downed four or five Magnificent Sevens, and beyond that, the night was a blur. But when he awoke with V beside him, he felt a comforting sense of relief.

XXIV

The next morning, Mod resumed the physicals while V began her day with a refreshing swim, followed by a light jog along the beach with Alex. As they ran, Alex inquired, "When's your physical?" V replied, "I'm last, later today. Do you have any plans?" Alex shrugged. "As difficult as it is, I'm just trying to relax. Maybe I'll do some reading. Did you find out about taking a boat out?"

"We haven't booked anything yet, but Lin is planning a themed party before we leave," V responded. Panting, Alex, who wasn't much of a runner, managed to say, "That sounds like fun."

V teased, "So, do you think you'll make it?" Alex shot her a playful look. "I'm more of a sprinter." V smiled knowingly. "No, I meant trying to relax—it doesn't seem to be your thing. Why don't you get with Declan and Kyoryk and go on a hike or something?"

"Yeah, I don't like sitting around," Alex admitted, picking up the pace. "I'll figure out something." He glanced back at her. "Think you can beat me back to the house?"

V grinned. "If you win, you get a special surprise." Alex, now in full stride, laughed. "I think we're out of surprises." *Valedictorian,* V thought, laughing aloud as she sprinted down the beach. By the time they reached the house, she had easily beaten him. Calm and composed, she stood there, watching as Alex, completely out of breath, struggled to speak.

"Wait... maybe I should give you a surprise. What did you have in mind?" Alex gasped. V smiled as they passed by the pool. "Valedictorian," she said, pushing him into the water.

As she walked into the house, Alex called after her, laughing, "You keep surprising me, Vibrean Aboli!"

The group remained at the house, continuing with their physicals. Rev met with everyone to discuss how she doctored the photos for whatever reason. Meanwhile, V was in the room with Mod, undergoing her physical.

Mod began, "I'm essentially telling you what I discussed with Alex. Since you and he are the group leaders, I'll be sending the reports to Gig and Fem as well. You're all in excellent health, but these are for Alex if he needs them."

"He wouldn't take them from me—I didn't even offer—but I sense he's struggling to relax." He handed V a small container of medication. "Tonari and Swaraj are doing much better; we're glad they stayed."

Surprised, V asked, "I had no idea—when was this?" Mod explained, "On the ninth day, they wanted to leave, so Gig had Rev and me talk with them. I wasn't sure if Gig ever mentioned it to you. It's not an issue now; everyone is fine. We've been monitoring everyone, just keeping an eye on things. I wouldn't have brought it up, but I thought you should be aware."

V nodded, "Of course. And all the physicals are fine?" Mod, not one for many facial expressions, stood up on his stool, smiling. "You're all in perfect physical health—nothing to worry about." He looked into V's eyes. "So, how are you handling everything? With the test coming up and all? Are you finding time to relax?"

V, trying to keep her composure as he touched her face, replied, "Trying to. I'm sticking to my routines, focusing on the mission, trying to balance everything."

Mod inquired, "And how are things with Alex?" V laughed softly. "That's an open-ended question." Mod chuckled. "Indeed."

V continued, "Alex is very mission-driven and incredibly caring. He's an amazing man. I'll try to get him to relax over the next couple of weeks." Mod acknowledged, "With your group's accelerated progress, it's added more pressure from the Gifts."

"The rapid onset of the Pulse Reversals accelerated your schedule, along with the transfer of the eagles and everything else. I think you've all handled it remarkably well."

V asked, "How has the relationship with the previous groups been with the Common Mind and everything?" As Mod checked her reflexes, he replied, "It varies with each group. After a few months, most people pair up. After that, a significant percentage stay together, though some do change partners, as we've seen in the Steward group. Your group, with the Creator's increased involvement and the fast pace, is unique. My programming suggests that your group is a good match-up so far. After analyzing the messages from the Creator, I wouldn't be surprised if this changes how the population of the planet perceives us in the future."

V said, "If I understood correctly, there were people with Gifts on the planets before our time in previous CATs? Like, within the general population?"

Mod sat back in his chair, looking up at her. "In a way, Yes. It was quite different back then."

"Certain individuals had Gifts along with the Common Mind; they interacted very little with the population. You'll learn more as your classes progress. There's so much for you all to absorb. Let's just say it's completely different from what's taught in most history books today. Remember, we don't interfere; we don't tell. It's difficult to watch when some cultures have the history so wrong."

V smiled, "It's truly fascinating, even to be talking to you—who you are, what you are, what you've witnessed. It's incredible. It's wild that the general population has no idea what really happened in the past."

Mod nodded, "That's typically the role of the Elders—to record and preserve history. Before this era, the 'What, Why, Who, and How' were only known by the Elders. With the Creator becoming more involved, who knows what's next? Why now? Something is happening. Something is coming."

V said, "Well, whatever His plans are, we're here to figure it out."

Mod stood, placing his hands on V's. "For the next couple of weeks, try to put it out of your mind. I told Alex that you can use the Common Mind, like in the CMB, to relax and clear your mind for a few hours each day."

"Practice some meditation—there are good techniques on your tablet. Check it out. You all will get it done. As I told him, there are many people here to help you achieve your goals."

V stood up. "Thanks for everything. It's comforting to know you two are here on the planet, figuring everything out. I just sent my sister some pictures of me from college and from our break here—it's a freeing feeling."

As they left the room, Mod said, "We'll be leaving after dinner, so I'll see you back at the university." V replied, "Okay, thanks for everything. Alex and I will keep you updated on the group."

V joined Prezzy, Lin, Maria, Tonari, and Miko in the room with all the couches. "Where are the guys?" she asked. Tonari replied, "They found some fishing rods and headed down to the beach." Prezzy added, "I was with them earlier; it was pretty amusing how serious they were about it." V admitted, "Well if it keeps them busy, it's a good thing. Alex isn't used to sitting around."

Maria noted, "Kyoryk and Lev are like that too. We need to keep them occupied." Lin, putting her feet up, suggested, "We can make a list."

Tonari, lighting a cigarette, exhaled a cloud of smoke, "So far, all we've planned is the boat trip and the party at the end. That's only two or three days out of the twelve we have left. We can't just spend the rest of the time drinking and baking in the sun, can we?"

V strolled over to the bar with a playful smile, "We'll figure it out. Who wants some wine?" The chorus of enthusiastic responses—"Me!" "I do!"—filled the room.

Later, the group bid farewell to Rev and Mod, then embarked on a week-long adventure, exploring and striving to unwind. As the days in Cancun dwindled, Lin and Prezzy surprised everyone with vintage 60s attire, setting the stage for a lavish, themed party aboard a yacht that stretched across days. They spent the following days exploring a nearby island, reveling in the freedom of the open sea.

When the time came, a ship arrived to transport them back to the university.

Once settled, they convened with Gig, Fem', and the Stewards, meticulously preparing for the impending test—a trial that held the fate of the entire galaxy in its balance.

The week saw the group undergoing another CMB, drawing them closer than ever before. Each member fine-tuned their Gifts, honing their abilities for the monumental task ahead.

Messages from the Creator, delivered through the voices of their deceased relatives, echoed in the minds of Alex and V: "Stay The Course." This directive, seemingly random at first, was reiterated by strangers and friends alike, both during their vacation and back at the university. It became undeniable that these words were no mere coincidence; they were a mandate. With resolve steeled and unity forged, Alex, V, and their ten Elder Students stood poised, ready to face the challenge of their lives, knowing there was no turning back.

XXV

4:00 AM, December 27th, 2033. Alex and V stirred from their slumber, invigorated by the crispness of the early morning. They showered swiftly, dressed with precision, and packed light, prepared for an unplanned two-day excursion. By six, everyone was to converge at the docks. But first, the Students had organized a pre-meeting in the common room. As Alex and V entered, the entire group was already assembled, momentarily collecting their thoughts.

V, ever the leader, commanded attention. "Today is the test. Soon, we may face the real thing. When that time comes, we'll be doing this for everyone we know—our friends, our families, our technology, our very way of life. Let's use this opportunity to perfect our execution to refine every detail so that when the moment arrives, we'll be ready. Pay close attention, offer suggestions, and hold nothing back. When we confront the CAT, the Super Flare, or the Mini Nova—whatever we choose to name it—we will be prepared, and we will succeed."

Kyoryk interjected, "Why don't we call it *Utbrott Av Eos*? It's Swedish for 'Eruption of the Sun.'" His suggestion hung in the air, met with puzzled looks.

Declan broke the silence with a smirk, "Superflare it is."

V looked momentarily vexed, but before she could respond, Alex cut in. "Everyone, hold hands."

The group formed a circle, clasping hands tightly. Alex scanned the room, his gaze filled with pride.

He was their leader—confident, resolute, and deeply connected to each member. "We know our purpose. After the last CMB, I've come to know all of you intimately. I love you all. We are one. United, we wield incredible power."

Prezzy bounced on her toes in excitement, Declan grinned, and V's grip tightened around his hand. Lev, overcome with anticipation, inadvertently manipulated the lights, causing them to flicker.

With renewed determination, Alex declared, "We can do this! Let's show them—the people of our planet, the inhabitants of other worlds, the entire galaxy—what the Elders of CAT 6 are capable of!" The energy in the room intensified. Prezzy began to fade from sight, multiple Tonaris materializing in her place, like ethereal body doubles.

Lev shouted, "Fuckin' A, right!"

Declan echoed the sentiment, "We are the bomb, baby!"

Tears welled up in Lin's eyes as Alex proclaimed, "And we'll accomplish this with the Creator's help. Raba Rashi." Their grip on each other tightened, bowed their heads, and softly chanted, "Raba Rashi."

Alex took one last look around the room, his voice growing in intensity. "Louder this time. Let's get His attention. Let Him know we're serious, that we're coming to fulfill His plans—the Creator's plans." Taking a deep breath, he led the count. "Three, two, one."

In unison, they bellowed, "Raba Rashi!" The room trembled as furniture slid outward, the air pulsed with energy, and their hands lifted involuntarily toward the ceiling. The lights flickered, extinguished momentarily, then blazed back to life.

Laughter and exhilaration filled the room. V clapped her hands together, a spark in her eyes. "Okay! Let's go!"

Declan looked at Alex with a mix of awe and apprehension. "You're a madman! Not sure I want to be struck by lightning before the mission."

Alex chuckled, "Just wanted to make sure He knew we were ready." Lin wiped a tear from her cheek, murmuring, "I think He got the message."

Lev nodded, still a bit unsettled, "Yeah, He definitely got it."

They gathered their scattered belongings—luggage, pillows, chairs, and tables now strewn about the corners of the room. Kyoryk, ever the contemplative one, lingered, glancing around as if expecting more divine theatrics.

A moment later, they grabbed their gear and headed to the docks. As they entered, they saw the ships waiting—a few volunteers milling about, one ship anchored behind the other. V noticed one of them staring at her and nudged Alex, whispering, "Is this going to be awkward?" Alex flashed a reassuring smile. "No, don't worry. It'll be fine."

As they walked, Alex's mind raced with calculations. *"There are ninety Elders on this mission. Seventy-two will power the Accelerators—thirty-six in the North, thirty-six in the South. Four will handle communication with the lab, and four will handle everything on the moon's surface, using a laser to guide our adjustments. Six more will be in the lab for additional communication. That makes ninety, including the four ship pilots. Alright, let's meet them all."*

As they approached the other ship, more people began to take notice, halting their tasks. One by one, they stopped, then someone started clapping. Soon, the entire dock was filled with applause.

Previously, they had only met a few team leaders, never the entire team. The volunteer Elders from Amotaious had never met all the Student Elders either, and the excitement was palpable.

The Students rounded the corner, entering the main area like an infamous army moving in slow motion. All twelve of them—the Student Elders who had planned and fought for this moment—had arrived. The twelve who shared a unique, inexplicable bond with the Creator. They took ten more deliberate steps and halted, their presence commanding the attention of everyone around them.

Prezzy, unable to contain her excitement, began jumping up and down.

People approached cautiously, eager to shake hands and introduce themselves. Most were from Terraenti, with only four volunteers from other planets—two from Elducan and two from Kall, both assigned to the Southern Team.

Gig and Fem', standing tall among the crowd, clapped as they made their way to the Students.

Alex spotted them and approached. Gig grinned, "This is it. Our first test. You all ready?" Alex responded with unwavering confidence, "Yes, I think so. We'll find out what needs adjusting for the real thing. We'll make it happen." He shook Gig's hand firmly.

V, already immersed in her tablet, glanced at Fem'. "Everyone's here. I double-checked last night; almost everything was loaded. It's just the volunteers and their personal gear now." Fem' smiled reassuringly, placing a hand on V's shoulder. "Yes, everything's been checked and rechecked. We've gone over it three times. We'll be fine. Don't worry."

Alex added, "I was just counting heads. I believe we have ninety in total."

V hugged Fem'. "Thanks. Good morning."

Fem' replied, "Yes, it's all overwhelming."

The Students helped load the remaining gear as Alex reviewed his to-do list once more.

Gig, standing on a crate—though he didn't need to—called out to gather everyone's attention. "You all have your assignments from our meetings these past few days. Your team leaders have briefed you on what needs to be done. This is the first test. Hopefully, we'll have another, maybe even two more after this. Let's trust in the Creator that all will go well." He smiled at Kyoryk, "And let's not cause any planetary disruptions, right, Kyoryk?" Kyoryk gave a thumbs up, grinning. "Right, we'll monitor everything closely—no earthquakes or volcanoes happening on my watch."

Gig announced, "We have four teams. Team North, led by Alex and V." He gestured toward the ship on the left before continuing, "Team South, under Rov' and Joy." He pointed to the ship on the right. Then, with a commanding presence, he introduced the third team, "The Lab Team."

His hand directed attention to Doog and Fair standing nearby. "That's us—Doog, Fair, Fem', and two others from CAT 5, Roon and Flow, who are already in the lab." His gaze then shifted to four individuals by the door. "Our fourth team, working on the surface of the moon, comprises Rore, Pax, Mans, and Allanin." A couple of them raised their hands with confident smiles. "Now, let's finish loading up and get to the planet. I want everyone's input on how we can make the next mission even better." He paused, sweeping the room with a grin.

"We have an extraordinary group of people risking everything to follow the Creator's Plans and save the people of Terraenti and all its technological wonders. It's up to us to see it through. And we will. I believe in us. Let's get it done."

Gig's voice carried a resolute conviction that set the room alight with applause and cheers. He then stepped down, catching Alex's eye. "What was that earlier?"

Alex, momentarily puzzled, then recalled the earlier incident in the common room. A mischievous smile played on his lips. "Ah, just getting the group ready. We might have gotten a bit too excited, but everything's fine. No worries."

Gig chuckled, "Alright, just be careful about stirring them up too much." With a firm handshake, "Good luck. I'll be on the radio." Alex returned the smile, "See you back here when I see you."

As the crew loaded the remaining gear, Alex and V double-checked that all critical items were accounted for.

Alex couldn't help but admire the ship, now heavily modified for their mission. The vertical takeoff modifications transformed it into something reminiscent of a rocket, with two enormous fuel cells flanking its sides. Imagine a standard jet aircraft, capable of holding over 30 passengers, but with two massive bombs strapped to its sides—that's what it looked like now. The ship, originally a cargo vessel, had been repurposed as a passenger craft. Without windows, the interior felt more like a space capsule than an airplane.

Alex boarded the ship, a wave of confidence washing over him as he mentally ticked off each task. Moving forward, he found his seat next to V, noticing their unusual position right behind the pilots. He quirked an eyebrow, "Why are we in the front? Aren't we usually in the back?" V grinned, "We're the project leaders, remember? I handled the seating arrangements, so we get the prime seats, Mr. Leader."

Settling into his seat, Alex quipped, "Such a powerful woman. Where's my G-suit?" V leaned in and kissed him, her voice teasing, "Right under your butt."

As everyone settled in, they donned their G-suits and buckled in. The ship, already linked to the launch tracks, entered the tunnels. The massive doors opened, revealing the platforms on Luna's surface. The cabin was still, tension thick in the air. V smiled reassuringly at Alex, who gave a thumbs up across the aisle to Declan and Miko.

Declan grinned, "Here we go, brother—changing the world, saving the world. Let's do this."

Gripping the seat in front of him as the ship shifted vertically, Alex, V, and the others watched through the lone window as both ships ascended effortlessly in Luna's low gravity, breaking free of the moon's surface. The ships twisted, spun, and rotated, heading straight for Terraenti, the home planet of most onboard.

Three hours later, the North Team's ship decelerated, entering the atmosphere. Under Kyoryk's precise guidance, the pilots navigated to the geomagnetic north pole. They descended onto the barren, white expanse of snow and ice, the landscape a stark contrast to the mountainous regions they had anticipated. Alex, his breath visible in the cold air, turned to V, "Pure white. Nothing but ice and snow." V nodded, "We'll only be here for what, twelve hours max?" Alex shrugged, "This time, not long. During the real thing? Who knows?"

Struggling with the G-suits, the team began to disembark, climbing down the ship's central ladder. The climate was a harsh departure from the warmth of their previous location. The bitter cold bit at them as they donned parkas, gloves, and cold-weather gear.

Alex and V stepped out into the frigid air, V looking nervous while Alex's determination shone through.

He glanced at her, her parka flapping in the wind. "We're here. Let's get it done. Stay the course, as they keep telling us." V shivered but nodded, "Let's do it."

The team unloaded the tent, accelerator, communication cases, and tools from the ship's compartments. Declan, Miko, Tonari, Candido, Prezzy, and Swaraj organized everyone to set up the tent. Declan, ever the jokester, lightened the mood with his humor. Within hours, the tent was up. Declan, Alex, Lev, and Swaraj remained outside, tidying up.

Declan quipped, "So after all this is over, who wouldn't want to live in a place like this?" Alex exchanged glances with Swaraj and Lev. Lev chuckled, "Oh, yeah, who wouldn't? No trees snow blowing horizontally—a perfect whiteout. Nothing to see for miles. Reminds me of some parts of Russia." Alex grinned, "Lev, we *are* in Russia."

Lev smirked, "Kyoryk told me. We're in Siberia." He raised a finger to his lips, "Shh, don't tell anyone. We wouldn't want any visitors. Or animals." Declan looked up, securing a line, "Animals? Up here?"

Alex laughed, "Did we even bring a gun?"

Swaraj squinted into the distance, "I can't see a damn thing. I think my eyes are frozen."

Kyoryk emerged from the tent, "Hey, I need help getting the Accelerator in place."

Declan chuckled, "Alex was just wondering if we brought a gun to fend off any animals. Kyoryk, what wildlife is up here?" Kyoryk glanced around, "Animals? Didn't really think about that. Maybe a lonely polar bear? Caribou? But I don't see anything. I don't think we need to worry." He squinted westward, joking, "Look, I think I see a Siberian chipmunk."

Kyoryk started mimicking chipmunk noises, causing Declan and Alex to burst into laughter. Lev, recalling a past trip, smiled, "I once visited southern Siberia. It was nice. Nothing like this, though."

Harvey emerges from the tent, squinting against the harsh light. "Are you guys done yet? What on earth is taking so long?"

Alex and Lev secure the final lines, then retreat into the tent. Inside, the group huddles around tall propane heaters, the warmth a welcome relief. Tables laden with food and drinks stand ready, but the focus remains on the task at hand.

Kyoryk removes the lid from the Accelerator crate. "Help me get this upright," he instructs. It takes four of them to hoist the device into position. The tent, barely large enough, shelters all 39 individuals and their equipment that are there for the test today.

"Is it aligned correctly?" Alex inquires. Kyoryk checks a meter and then glances at his tablet. A smile flickers across his face. "No need for concern; we're right where we need to be. As long as we're within a hundred miles, we're fine." He catches Harvey's eye, noting his lack of amusement. "This spot is perfect."

"How's our timing?" Harvey asks, eyeing the darkening sky. "We've got an hour until sunset," Kyoryk replies, focused on his tablet. "I just need to verify our communications. I've already touched base with Gig, but I need to check a couple of other things."

He opens a large case and then looks up at Harvey and Alex. "Spread the word. We'll do a pre-test in thirty minutes, then we'll wait." Harvey nods and walks off to inform the others.

Alex turns to Declan, his voice tinged with concern. "This had better work. Maybe we should say a prayer?" Declan smirks. "Unfortunately, we need a Master Elder for that, and they're not exactly here in case we all kick the bucket." "No one's dying today," Kyoryk interjects with a confident smile. "If my calculations are right, the impact will be far away, somewhere in northern India. We might cause a little tremor, but nothing close to us or the Southern team." He adjusts the mic. "Lab, this is Kyoryk. Do you copy?"

After a brief adjustment to the radio, a loud response crackles through. "Roger that, Kyoryk. Reading you loud and clear."

Kyoryk lowers the volume. "We'll be running the test in twenty-five minutes. Inform the Southern Team. Over." "Copy that, Kyoryk. We'll be ready," Doog replies.

Kyoryk switches off the mic. "Next time you hear from us, Ty'mmie' will be on the line. I'll be on the Accelerator." "Understood. I'll alert the Southern Team," Doog confirms.

V, now standing beside Alex, asks, "How's everything progressing?" "We're set for a full test in twenty minutes," Alex replies.

V strides away, her voice rising above the low murmur of the group. "Alright, everyone, we've got twenty minutes until the test."

As darkness envelops the camp, Alex approaches V. "Are we ready? Who are the other two on the Accelerator?" "Declan and you on one side, Swaraj and I on the other," V explains. "Swaraj will lift the core while Declan spins it counterclockwise. Ty'mmie' will coordinate with the lab and relay instructions to the Southern Team. They're running a bit behind but should be ready soon." Alex grins at her. "Excellent work, team leader."

Just then, Ty'mmie', the youngest volunteer and a relative of Klinchme', approaches with evident nerves. "What exactly am I supposed to do again?" Klinchme', standing beside her, offers a reassuring smile. "Just be patient."

Rev, overseeing the process, nods at Ty'mmie'. "You'll be fine. Kyoryk will guide you." Kyoryk, overhearing, steps in. "Ty'mmie', you'll monitor this display here and another one on the wall." He points to the display. "As the percentage increases, announce it every ten percent. If it drops or needs adjustment, call it out so the lab can respond. Rev will be here to assist you."

He gestures toward Alex and V. "They're the team leaders. Make sure everyone can hear you. Yell if you need to. Everyone needs to know the status as it changes. Got it?" Ty'mmie' smiles, her confidence bolstered. "Got it, no worries." Kyoryk adds, "When this clock counts down, start announcing the seconds as it nears zero. After that, stick to the percentages; we want the percentage to be at its max at the clock's zero point." Ty'mmie' nods, understanding her role.

A few minutes later, V gathers the group around the Accelerator and begins issuing instructions. "Alright, everyone, here's the plan. Swaraj will center the core, and then Declan," she pauses as Declan waggles his fingers theatrically, "will spin it counterclockwise. We'll form a figure eight—the infinity symbol—around the device. Focus on Declan as he spins the core."

"Ty'mmie' will call out the percentages, and we'll adjust our efforts accordingly. The lab will monitor the magnetic field and guide us. Take it slow and steady; we don't want this getting out of control. Remember, we are the power source. The Accelerator is the tool."

She pauses, then adds with solemnity, "Remember, the Creator is with us. We're following the path laid out for us, so let the Creator guide our hands."

V then turns to the group, "Declan, Swaraj, Alex, and I will handle the device. The rest of you spread out around the symbol. You all know what to do. Once we're in the Common Mind, focus on controlling the percentage levels. If you can't hear Ty'mmie', tune into what Alex and I are feeling. Let's make this happen."

Everyone nods in agreement and takes their positions. Alex and V give the signal to start. Ty'mmie' alerts the lab, and Alex calls out, "Okay, everyone, get into formation."

The room falls silent as the group assembles in the infinity symbol. The only sounds are the flapping of the tent's fabric and the faint hiss from the speaker. The Accelerator sits at the center, surrounded by the focused group. Alex exchanges glances with V, then with Declan, then Swaraj, and finally locks eyes with Swaraj once more. "Go ahead, Swaraj. Center the core!"

"Ty'mmie', what's the countdown?" Alex inquired with a sharp edge to his voice. "Two, zero, zero," Ty'mmie' replied, her voice steady yet tinged with anticipation.

"Declan, initiate the spin," Alex commanded, his eyes locked on the Accelerator.

V turned to Miko, her tone firm. "Miko, ensure it's perfectly centered." Miko, gripping Declan's hand within the loop, observed the interior of the Accelerator. "It's centered and spinning," she confirmed, her gaze unwavering.

"One forty-one," Ty'mmie' murmured, the tension in her voice palpable.

"Alright, everyone, focus on Declan," Alex instructed, his voice authoritative. "Channel the Common Mind; concentrate on him."

The group closed their eyes in unison, their collective energy coalescing. Ty'mmie's voice, now trembling slightly, cut through the silence. "One twenty-nine… Zero percent."

"Here we go," Alex said with a determined grin, exchanging a look of steely resolve with V, who mirrored his expression.

"One hundred… Zero percent," Ty'mmie' announced. An eerie stillness settled over the tent as the seconds stretched into what felt like an eternity. Then, a deep, resonant hum emanated from the Accelerator, a sound that vibrated through the air.

Suddenly, Gig's voice crackled through the speakers, his words barely audible over the growing hum. "Something's happening."

"TWO PERCENT!" Ty'mmie' screamed, her voice startling Klinchme,' who jumped in shock. "Shit, Ty'mmie'!" Klinchme' exclaimed, her heart pounding. Rev, standing beside Klinchme', placed a reassuring hand on her shoulder, a smile playing on her lips as Ty'mmie' continued. "Fifty… Three… twelve percent."

"North Team, slow it down a bit," Gig's voice boomed over the radio, a hint of urgency creeping in.

V opened her eyes, catching Alex's gaze. She mouthed, "You okay?" Alex smiled back, mouthing, "Yes."

Gig's voice returned, more controlled now. "Both groups, we're at six percent. Let's ease it up to ten."

Alex and V closed their eyes once more, syncing with the group's focused energy. Moments later, Ty'mmie' reported, "Nine… ten percent." She pressed the mic and confirmed, "We have ten percent, Mr. Gig."

"Hold steady at ten," Gig instructed, his voice calm but firm. The Accelerator's hum deepened, morphing into a low, horn-like resonance that filled the tent.

"Southern Team, increase slightly. Everything looks stable. We've boosted the horizontal intensity by two percent, vertical by four percent, and overall inclination by three percent. Let's push to twenty-five percent and hold it there."

Declan, Miko, V, and Alex exchanged determined glances before closing their eyes, the group collectively striving to elevate the Accelerator's power. Over the next few seconds, Ty'mmie' called out the rising numbers. "Twelve… fourteen… eighteen… twenty-three… twenty-eight… thirty."

"Slow it down, both groups!" Gig's voice was sharp, cutting through the escalating hum.

"Twenty-eight… twenty-three… twenty… twenty-four… twenty-three… twenty-five," Ty'mmie' commanded. She then yelled, "Hold at twenty-five, please."

"Okay, everyone, maintain that level," Gig instructed, his voice tense. "I need to take magnetic readings now."

Alex cracked one eye open, glancing at the LED display. It flickered at a steady twenty-five percent. The Accelerator continued its harmonic pulsation, emitting a sound that resonated deep within the earth.

"We're holding at twenty-five percent; we have zero on the countdown clock." Ty'mmie' announced with excitement, her voice trembling with adrenaline.

Klinchme' exchanged a relieved smile with Rev, who beamed with pride at Ty'mmie's diligence. The hum of the Accelerator intensified, filling the tent with its potent vibrations. Despite the noise, Alex could barely discern Gig's voice as it returned, brimming with rare enthusiasm.

"Elders of Teraenti, we have success! Let's initiate a gradual shutdown."

Ty'mmie' quickly took charge. "Alright, everyone, let's bring it down slowly." Over the next few minutes, she carefully guided the group. "Twenty-five… nineteen… slow down, people… twenty-two… twenty… seventeen… eighteen… sixteen… fourteen… ten… eleven… eight… five… six… four… two… zero. We're at zero percent; everyone can relax."

The group opened their eyes, smiles spreading across their faces. The tent erupted in applause and high-fives as they celebrated their seven-minute stint in the Common Mind Burst. Alex and V moved towards Ty'mmie', joined by others eager to hear from Gig.

"Great job, Ty'mmie'," Alex praised, watching as she bounced on her toes, her excitement infectious. "That was terrifying but exhilarating," she admitted with a grin.

"Thanks, Rev, for the backup, and you too, Klinchme'. That was outstanding. We're halfway there; now we just need to hear from Gig," Alex added, nodding appreciatively at the team.

Rev replied, "No problem, Alex."

Gig's voice broke through the speakers, "Is everyone listening?" Through his mic, the Southern team's cheers could be heard, their jubilation echoing through the tent.

Ty'mmie' clicked the mic. "We're all ears, Mr. Gig."

"Congratulations, Elders. We've increased the horizontal intensity by ten percent, vertical by fifteen percent, and overall inclination by twelve percent. We maintained a steady 0.23 and increased it to 0.37. To safeguard the planet during the flare, we should aim for at least 0.65, but no more than 0.75."

V responded with a click of the mic, "So everything's functioning as expected?"

"Absolutely," Gig confirmed. "Once you see the data, you'll notice the difference. How did everything go on your end?"

"It went smoothly," V replied. "As you saw, we sped up a bit too much at one point, but we're on track. We'll need a few adjustments before the next round. How long until the Pulse Reversal?"

"Forty minutes," Gig answered.

Alex grinned broadly at V. She clicked the mic again, her voice brimming with excitement. "This is excellent, Gig. It's working. We need to determine how much protection we can achieve. How far do you want to push it?"

"If possible, I'd like to reach one hundred percent on our meter today," Gig said. "Let's see if we can surpass the strongest recorded field during the last grand maximum, somewhere between ninety-five and one hundred percent. That's what Kyoryk was aiming for."

Alex and V responded in unison, "Sounds good, we'll be ready in thirty minutes."

Alex then asked, "Any reaction from the planet or its governments?"

"None so far," Gig replied. "We won't know anything for sure until tomorrow. Great work, everyone. Tell Kyoryk to test the other communication method. We need to be fully prepared. Let's do a trial run now."

Kyoryk clicked the mic. "No problem. When your laser hits our sensor, we'll know. Direct the laser to the northeast corner of the tent, where the tent pole is. When Ty'mmie' sees the LED on the control box light up, it's time to increase. When it dims, decrease. Go ahead and give it a try, and I'll keep you informed. We've already tested it on our side."

"Very well. Stand by," Gig acknowledged. After a few moments, his voice returned, "Anything yet?"

Ty'mmie' swiftly clicked the mic, her voice tinged with anticipation. "No sign yet, Mr. Gig," she reported, lowering the mic just as a flicker of light danced across her vision. Her heart quickened as she clicked the mic again, this time with a burst of excitement. "I saw it! The light just flashed. Try moving back slightly to where you were—yes, just a bit more… stop! That's perfect, it's steady now."

Kyoryk, with a focused demeanor, took the mic from Ty'mmie'. "Gig, just below the joystick, there's a green button. Press it, and it'll sync with the rotation. We need to test this precisely three minutes before 4:55." "Understood," Gig responded.

"All set. I'll check back in twenty-nine minutes for the final test. Excellent work, everyone—we'll reconvene shortly."

As some others gathered near the control equipment, Miko couldn't suppress a smile. "Congratulations, everyone. So far, everything's on track."

Declan nodded, though a hint of frustration crept into his voice. "It would've been nice if I could've seen that percent meter more clearly."

Alex, ever the problem-solver, suggested, "We'll add monitors on opposite walls of the tent so everyone can see the readings."

Maria, filled with pride, planted a kiss on Kyoryk's cheek. "Good job, Mr. Genius."

V grinned, reflecting on the close call. "We did well. I was nervous when the readings spiked, but we managed to regain control."

Miko, still buzzing with the intensity of the operation, turned to Declan. "I could feel the Accelerator's energy. Next time, we should consider using earwigs for communication. The noise in there is overwhelming—imagine how loud it'll get at one hundred percent." Declan chuckled, correcting her gently. "You mean earbuds, sweetie. But you're right, we all knew what you meant."

Alex, feeling the weight of the responsibility, added, "Great idea. We'll make those adjustments. I'm just relieved it's working. I hope this will save as many lives as we anticipate. I need some air; it's stifling in here."

Stepping out of the tent, Alex, V, Declan, and Miko were greeted by the crisp night air. The sky stretched above them, a vast canvas dotted with stars, and to the north, the Aurora Borealis began its ethereal dance.

Alex gazed upward, his voice filled with awe. "Now, this is a clear night." The vivid colors of the aurora shimmered against the inky blackness. Declan, ever the enigma, pulled out a vape and took a hit.

V, curious, asked, "Is there pot in there?" Declan shook his head, passing it to her. "No, just a bit of nicotine." V took a drag, her expression shifting to one of surprise. "What is that?" she exclaimed, slipping into Hindi momentarily. Alex, intrigued, reached for the vape. He took a puff and grimaced. "Menthol lemon. Interesting," he remarked, before taking another hit and coughing. "That's enough for me."

V, undeterred, took a couple more puffs and smiled. "I feel really positive about all this." Alex nodded. "Same here. The first test went well." Declan, however, was scanning the horizon, his gaze fixed on something unseen.

Miko, noticing his focus, asked, "What are you looking at?" Declan, squinting into the darkness, replied, "Waiting for the helicopters?"

Alex burst into laughter. "What are you talking about?" Declan grinned. "You know, like in the movies. When you're doing something secretive, and suddenly, the helicopters swoop in, guns blazing, tearing the tent apart." V, her expression suddenly serious, said, "No one knows we're here, and by the time they find out, we'll be long gone. That's how this movie ends."

Alex playfully nudged Declan's shoulder. "Stop freaking everyone out." Declan chuckled. "Well, at least we haven't triggered any volcanoes yet. That's a win." A few moments later, they rejoined the group.

As the atmosphere grew more intense, V made the five-minute announcement. Standing by the control panels, Rev asked Alex, "Did you manage to unwind in Cancun?"

Alex smiled warmly. "Yes, and thanks for the medicine. I only needed it for a couple of days, but it really helped."

Gig's voice crackled through the speaker. "Southern Team, are you ready? Northern Team, you all ready?"

V clicked the mic. "We're ready." She smiled at Ty'mmie'. "Has it happened yet?"

"Not yet," Gig replied, "but any second now."

V nodded, issuing orders with calm authority. "Alright, we'll get into position." She clicked off the mic and announced to the group, "Everyone, back to your positions. Same as last time, but this time, we'll slowly push up to one hundred percent."

As she finished speaking, the tent filled with the sound of alarms. Ty'mmie' looked around, her voice tinged with anxiety. "What does that mean?" Klinchme' responded reassuringly, "That's the Reversal alarm. It's part of the process."

Gig's voice cut through the tension. "Both teams, you all have nine minutes to ramp up to one hundred percent. Is everyone almost in formation?"

V raised her hand, commanding attention. "Alright, everyone, that's the signal. Let's get organized and start the process." She walked with Alex and held onto the Accelerator, her leadership evident in every step.

Alex marveled at her composure, thinking to himself, *Maybe she's the key. Just look at her command. One day, she'll be the king of all Master Elders. This is just the beginning.* He glanced at Declan, who returned a knowing smile, and then at the other Students, thinking, *Look at them, all of us on the brink of an incredible journey. This is just the start. Stay the course, as they keep telling me.* He smiled back at Declan, determined.

Ty'mmie' announced, "Zero on the percent clock. 834 on the countdown." She clicked the mic again. "Mr. Gig, we're set in formation and ready to proceed."

Alex cleared his mind, hearing V's steady voice guiding them. "Alright, everyone, Alex will take over the count and guide us through the percentages. Listen to Ty'mmie', focus within the group, and we'll see this through. May the Creator guide us."

Taking a deep breath, Alex turned to Swaraj. "Go ahead."

Swaraj, deep in concentration, replied, "We should be near the center."

Miko, using her Gift to observe things through matter said, "It looks good, maybe a little higher to the right." Swaraj nodded to her, "How is that?" She smiled, "Looks good."

"Declan, start the rotation," Alex commanded. "Alright, everyone, let's bring it up to twenty-five percent and hold it there." Most of the group closed their eyes, channeling their collective focus.

A minute later, Ty'mmie' called out, "7, 15, 20, 24."

"Okay, hold it here," Alex instructed, exchanging a confident smile with V. "Alright, everyone, let's maintain this level. Around twenty-five."

Gig's voice crackles through the speaker, authoritative and calm. "Alright, everyone, let's elevate to fifty percent and hold steady."

"Roger that, Mr. Gig," Ty'mmie' responds, her tone laced with determination. The group channels their focus, pushing the percentages higher. Ty'mmie' calls out the rising numbers, her voice cutting through the mounting noise. "Thirty... Thirty-five... Forty..."

As the Accelerator approaches fifty percent, the once singular horn transforms into a symphony of sound—an amalgamation of horns, their resonance eerily akin to the trumpets prophesied in ancient texts. The sheer volume forces Ty'mmie' to shout, "Forty-five... Fifty!"

The Accelerator now roars, a cacophony of sound so intense it could rival the thunderous approach of an oncoming train or the deafening blast of a jet at takeoff.

The noise envelops the tent, and Ty'mmie' instinctively raises her hand to signal the group to hold. But with their eyes closed in deep concentration, no one sees her. "Hold here! Three twenty-five on the timer!" she yells, straining to be heard over the din.

A minute later, Gig's voice commands, "Both teams, bring it up to seventy-five percent."

"We're moving to seventy-five, steady as she goes!" Ty'mmie' shouts, grabbing the mic with renewed urgency, her pacing betraying her nerves. Rev, noticing her anxiety, leans in close and reassures her, "You're doing fine. Just make sure they can hear you."

Ty'mmie' nods, her voice rising even higher. "Sixty-five... Seventy... Seventy-two... Seventy-four... Seventy-six! Hold there!" she commands, her heart pounding as the Accelerator's vibrations intensify.

The sound now reaches a fever pitch, a deafening hum coupled with the relentless blare of the trumpets. The overwhelming noise assaults Ty'mmie' and Klinchme', but the group remains unaffected, ensconced in the protective embrace of the CMB. Rev, with her AI-enhanced faculties, remains unfazed, but for Ty'mmie' and Klinchme', it's like standing on the edge of an active runway.

Gig's voice slices through the chaos, "Magnetic field is optimal. Let's push to one hundred percent."

"We're going to one hundred!" Ty'mmie' shouts back, her eyes darting to the percentage meter as it climbs. At eighty percent, both she and Rev witness a surreal transformation—a white glow materializes above the group, forming a luminous, rounded pyramid that stretches beyond the tent's confines.

Alex, now fully attuned to the group, feels a profound connection. It's akin to the CMB, yet different. Without entering a meditative state, they aren't transported to a serene beach; instead, he perceives their collective auras, their souls intertwined in a tapestry of mostly benevolent emotions. The sensation of floating overtakes him, and as the memories of the group wash over him, he gains clarity, especially with the Students and Stewards. The volunteers, however, remain somewhat distant.

Ty'mmie', her focus snapping back to the control panel, yells, "Eighty-five... Ninety percent! Sixty-one seconds on the countdown!" Her voice now a desperate scream as the sound overwhelms her.

Seconds later, she shouts, "We're at one hundred percent! Hold right there!" Turning back to the group, she's met with a sight that takes her breath away—the white glow intensifies, the trumpet-like noise now an unbearable assault on her senses. She rubs her eyes in disbelief as the entire group and the Accelerator begin to levitate, nearly a foot off the snowy ground.

A pulsating yellow glow emanates from below the Accelerator, resembling strands of energy windings spinning into the earth, creating an otherworldly spectacle. The light is so brilliant, it reveals the inner workings of this mysterious force never seen before.

"Hold it right here!" Ty'mmie' screams, her voice barely cutting through the chaos. She glances at the panel—it's holding at one hundred percent, with twenty seconds left on the clock. "Twenty seconds! You're doing great!" she encourages, her ears covered, now relying on the LED laser box from the Lab as all other systems go offline. "Bring it up a little!" she commands as the LED light flickers off. "Ten seconds! Keep it steady!" She yells.

The entire tent is bathed in blinding white light, emanating from both the Accelerator and the group within the CMB. The brilliance forces Ty'mmie', Rev, and Klinchme' to shield their eyes, the intensity too much to bear.

Dropping to her knees, Ty'mmie' counts down, "Five... Four... Three... Two... One."

The deafening roar of the Accelerator almost drowns out the sound of the shock wave as it slams into the tent, knocking down the back corner. Rev quickly signals Klinchme' to take cover, both of them curling up, hands pressed against their ears, bracing against the noise. The Pulse Reversal's wave sweeps across the planet, yet the group remains untouched. Rev, ever vigilant, ensures Ty'mmie' and Klinchme' are shielded beneath a protective blanket.

"We're holding here for a moment," Ty'mmie' yells, her voice quivering with adrenaline. Rev, an AI recording every detail, watches as the group, along with the Accelerator, hovers two feet above the frozen ground. The light from beneath the Accelerator is a near-pure white, almost blinding in its intensity.

Ty'mmie' and Klinchme' exchange a look of disbelief, their eyes wide with shock and awe. They revert to their ancient native tongue, speaking words only Rev can comprehend. As the minute draws to a close, Rev gestures for Ty'mmie' to begin the descent.

Ty'mmie', overwhelmed but resolute, rises to her feet. "Alright, we're going to bring it down to seventy-five percent, slowly," she commands, eyes fixed on the LED box. "Eighty-nine... Eighty-three... Eighty... Seventy-four."

"Hold there," she instructs, her voice firm. The LED light flickers back on, then off. "Let's drop to fifty percent now. Sixty-nine... Seventy-two... Sixty-three."

She glances at the group—they're almost back on the ground, the radiant glow above them fading. "Fifty-five... Fifty-two... Forty-nine." The LED light remains on, and she orders, "Hold here."

As the light finally dims, Ty'mmie' breathes a sigh of relief.

"Let's bring it down to twenty-five percent, nice and easy," she says, watching the group closely. The glow has completely vanished, and they stand firmly on the ground once more. "Forty... Thirty-five... Twenty-nine... Twenty-six... Twenty-three."

The light flickers on and off, and she declares, "Okay, hold here." Ty'mmie' exhales deeply, the tension slowly releasing from her shoulders.

Rev, with a reassuring hand on her shoulder, smiles. "You did an incredible job. Did you see how they lifted it?" Ty'mmie' and Klinchme' exchange smiles, still in awe. "That was insane, right? What was that?" Klinchme' asks, her voice filled with disbelief. "I've never heard of anything like that before." The light dims once more.

Ty'mmie' declares, "Alright, we're bringing it down to zero, nice and slow." Alex opens his eyes just in time to catch a tear sliding down V's cheek, accompanied by a radiant smile.

"Fifteen... now ten... five... zero. Excellent!" Ty'mmie' exclaims, her excitement bursting as she hops up and down. "We've hit zero percent!" she shouts, embracing Rev before dashing over to hug Alex and V. Declan and Swaraj release the Accelerator, which collapses onto the floor with a dull thud. The room erupts in joyous shouts and laughter, while Rev stands back, her recording complete.

After a few moments of exuberance, Alex, V, and Declan approach the control panels. Alex asks, "Any word from Gig?" Rev responds, "Nothing yet. We lost communication at the one-minute, twenty-five-second mark, just before the pulse struck the moon."

Alex pulls Ty'mmie' into another hug. "Great job. We did it." With his hands on his head, he surveys the tent and says, "It went smoothly, didn't it? No issues at all. What did you guys see? I can't believe it." Declan, arching an eyebrow, quips, "Were you expecting problems?"

Alex glances around again, slightly puzzled. "No, but we'll need to review the data to understand exactly what happened. It just felt... really smooth. Not that I'm complaining. It was a good feeling."

V fans herself dramatically. "Man, it's hot in here." "Yeah," Declan agrees, "the Accelerator at full throttle really heated the place up." Rev, Klinchme', and Ty'mmie' exchange knowing looks with the others, their expressions hinting at something more profound. It's clear they witnessed something beyond the ordinary.

Most of the group steps outside to cool down. As the energy settles, Prezzy sets up some music, and someone, possibly Prezzy or Lin, uncorks champagne, passing glasses around.

Harvey sidles up to Alex and whispers in his ear, "How are you feeling, boss?" Alex spins around, only to be swept into a bear hug. "I feel good," Alex replies, "We should hear back from Gig any minute. I'm hoping the numbers look promising."

Freida and V join them. Freida says, "I'm so proud of all of you. Everything on our end seemed to go smoothly. Once we hear from the lab, we'll know how we did, right?"

Alex nods, "Exactly. We hit a hundred percent, which was our target. Nothing bad happened, so I'd say it was a success."

Bahdubah approaches with a champagne bottle, pouring glasses for everyone. "Great job, guys." Klinchme' and Ty'mmie' join in, and they all toast to a job well done.

A moment later, Kyoryk shouts that Gig is on the radio from the lab. The room falls silent. Gig's voice crackles through the speakers, "Congratulations, everyone, it worked! I'm sending the data to your tablets, but it looks very promising. We didn't cause any discernible damage to the planet. No signs that anyone detected what we did. The Pulse Reversal appears to have had no impact on the planet. We completely neutralized it. Can you believe it?" He chuckles. "There were two small eruptions in the South Pacific, but they're in unpopulated areas—nothing unusual. The ships are on their way back. Both teams are good. The test was a success."

Harvey grabs the mic, "Thanks, Gig. That's great news. We'll see you tonight, in about seven hours."

The group continues to celebrate, Alex and V still in disbelief at the news.

Later, Rev, with Klinchme' and Ty'mmie', pulls Alex and V aside. "Did you guys realize you were floating? Almost two feet above the ground? And the Accelerator was so bright, we couldn't even look at it directly. Well, they couldn't, but I did. At its peak, it was emitting approximately 750,000 lumens. The sound... for a moment, it reached 158.352 decibels. It was like giant babies shrieking, trumpets blaring, and humming all at once."

Ty'mmie', visibly concerned, turns to Rev. "What? It started as a pleasant hum, then trumpets—thousands of them—all blaring at once, surrounding the tent. I could feel it in my body.

If this is the full Flare, we need serious protection. We might even need some kind of containment cage."

Alex nods reassuringly. "We're compiling a list of things to bring next time. Ear protection is already on it. I'll talk to Kyoryk about building a safe space for you, Ty'mmie'. As for the floating, Fem' is aware of it. She mentioned that it's something new, something connected to our CMB. She's investigating."

"How high were we?" V inquires. Klinchme' laughs, "Maybe two feet?"

V shrugs, "It's the Creator, the new Gifts, and the messages. Fem' said it might even be linked to the population growth on Amotaious. All this new stuff is happening."

Rev's expression turns thoughtful. "Interesting. I'll need to discuss that with her. Next time I go to Amotaious." She gets a distant look, as if trying to reach someone telepathically, and walks away.

Klinchme' hugs V. "That was incredible. Next time, I want to be in the circle with you guys, if that's okay."

"Yeah, I don't see why not," V replies. "We'll figure something out."

Ty'mmie' hugs Alex and grins, "I'm going to write a new tune about all this."

"Okay, great," Alex says, pointing to the camera. "We'll review the video and make any necessary adjustments."

He points to the hole left by the Accelerator. "Ty'mmie', V, look at the Accelerator. We should probably move it away from that hole before it melts down further."

Alex, V, Declan, Lev, and Kyoryk work together to lift the Accelerator, noticing a perfectly round hole plunging deep into the Earth. Alex touches the cylinder. "Yep, still hot. We need to tether this thing next time. We don't want to lose it, especially if we must push past a hundred percent."

They pack the Accelerator back into its crate and wait for the right moment to dismantle the tent before the ship arrives.

As night falls, only the bright white beams of LED flashlights cut through the darkness as they work to take down the tent.

Later, everyone lies flat as the ship touches down, scrambling to get everyone and everything back on board.

Three hours later, both groups are back at the university. Exhausted, V and Alex return to their rooms and fall into a deep sleep. Gig has scheduled a meeting for everyone at noon the next day.

XXVI

V woke up early and dove into a refreshing swim, just before 10:00. Gig had granted the group the day off, save for the meeting. When V returned to the common room, the atmosphere buzzed with excitement over the results of the test. According to Kyoryk, everything had gone exceedingly well. V, freshly cleaned from her morning routine, entered with a bright smile and a spring in her step.

"So, how did we do?" she asked eagerly.

Declan smirked. "They're all dead; we didn't make any difference."

Prezzy let out a nervous laugh.

Alex, absorbed in his virtual screen, analyzed the magnetic field's fluctuating strength, studying the Pulse Reversal. Without looking up, he said, "I can't believe the impact we made. It's truly astonishing."

V grabbed a drink and sat down beside Kyoryk. Kyoryk glanced at her, then spoke, "We anticipated triggering a few volcanoes, which, as expected, happened. As it stands, we'll need to increase the Accelerator's power by at least fifty percent compared to yesterday's results to safeguard the planet from the flare. But it works— we know that."

V opened her laptop. "Let's make a list of the changes and outline the items we'll need for next time."

At that moment, Gig, Fem', Doog, and Fair entered the room, applauding. Fem' grinned. "Outstanding work, everyone. We wanted to be the first to tell you. The footage and support on Marmutt? It's overwhelming."

They gathered around the table, and V responded, "We were just making a new list of action items for the next test."

Gig smiled approvingly. "Excellent."

Alex, still puzzled, looked up. "What footage? I haven't even seen what we recorded yet."

Fem' smiled knowingly. "No, it's what Rev filmed with her camera. She sent me a clip, and I posted a snippet on Amotaious. I hope you don't mind?"

Alex turned more in his seat, smiling. "Not at all. If it helps…"

"Oh, it helped," Gig chimed in with a broad grin.

Alex raised an eyebrow. "What's the response from our planet?"

"Rev and Mod are returning later today to work on that. But for now, we're not detecting anything significant. Some scientists claim it was a fluke, that our planet merely reacted to the sun's burst. The public remains unaware. Most believe it was just another Pulse Reversal, similar to the last time. But this time, the Earth protected itself," Gig explained, while the other three giants chuckled. "It's all quite extraordinary. We're still in disbelief that it all worked out so well."

Gig shifted his focus. "Are there any major changes that could delay the next test?"

Alex looked up at him. "No, most are just minor adjustments. The Accelerators made a nice, big hole in the ice. We need to create a tether for them. Everything went too smoothly, which is exactly what concerns me."

Gig exhaled in relief. "Good, well, everyone's okay and well-rested, then."

V nodded. "Yes, we're all fine. Just relieved the test went so well."

Fem' smiled warmly. "Great job, everyone." She placed a hand on V's shoulder. "It's truly remarkable what we've accomplished. We can't quite comprehend how it all happened." She shook her head, smiling softly. "We'll see you all at the meeting in a little bit." She and the others exited the room.

Alex chuckled. "I keep forgetting Rev's not just an AI robot. She's a massive computer— she holds all the data from the planet while we are there. It's all so wild."

V added the new items to her list: Cadge for Tiemme', headphones and ear protection for everyone, new percentage signs for the tent, extra solar radiation protection for the suits— courtesy of Kyoryk, and many other items.

Later, at the meeting, the entire North and South Teams, along with the full university staff, filled the room— plus several uninvited guests. Over a hundred people attended, their energy buzzing as food and drinks flowed. It was quickly transforming into a grand celebration— more people than V had ever seen in Teraenti Hall.

Gig opened the meeting with a resounding slam of his rock gavel. He congratulated the group warmly. V and Alex presented the changes they planned to make for the next test.

Once again, Gig slammed the rock on the table. "Another fantastic job, everyone!" The room erupted in applause. "We've made a significant impression on the other planets. The moment I received the video and test results, Fem' quickly edited the footage and sent it out to Amotaious as a public post."

"Now everyone is on board," Gig continued. "I even received a personal call from Lorness and Blain from Vindor. They're fully behind what we're doing. They were particularly interested in the elevation effect you all experienced while using the accelerator. You know, this phenomenon happens when you're in a CMB as well. I told them we're investigating it. No further follow-up Council Meeting is needed."

The room erupted in applause and cheers. Gig smiled and continued, "Everyone's asking if we could broadcast a live feed for the next test. I told them it depends on the communication lines, but we'll certainly try." Kyoryk shook his head, clearly doubtful, likely due to the communication issues during a solar event. "Once again, great job, everyone. Let's pray."

With a forceful slam, Gig dropped the rock onto the table, and Fem' stood, her smile radiating as she surveyed the room. "The future looks incredibly promising," she said, her voice filled with optimism. "We look forward to seeing you all in about a month for the next test. Let's pray and thank the Creator." She reached for the green stone resting in the box on the table, grasping it in one hand and placing her other hand gently atop it. Closing her eyes, she began to chant:

"Ooh! Raba Rashi! Naash! Ooh, Raba Rashi! Cama See La Ruh! Teraenti, Pupa, Conru, Luna! Shank, Fem'a Da Giga. See La Ruh, Neta Deta, Paru Nu, Nexta DePulsa Protecta Pat!"

The lights in the room dimmed. The stone in Fem's hand glowed, and warmth spread throughout the room.

The air began to swirl, and the tapestries fluttered as a distant, celestial thunder rumbled. Gig, still standing, slammed the rock down once more. The stone in Fem's hand blazed even brighter.

A sapphire-blue arrow shot from it, streaking across the room before splitting into five distinct arrows. They flew around the room, almost colliding with the ceiling.

The arrows then gently passed through each person. A warm, tingling sensation enveloped everyone's body, much like before. Eyes fluttered shut, and heads tilted back in bliss. V stretched her arms out on the table, a wave of warmth and joy sweeping over the group, bringing smiles to their faces.

A few seconds later, Gig cleared his throat. "If the Stewards and Students could stay for a moment, that would be great."

The group buzzed with conversation and congratulations. Within moments, everyone else filtered out of the room.

Fem' stood and addressed the remaining group. "We have fifty-three days until the next Pulse Reversal, so we'll be returning to our regular schedule during that period. Please check your tablets."

Declan grunted in response, causing a few of the Students to laugh.

Fem' continued with a smile, "Great job, everyone. I'm certain the Creator is pleased with our progress."

Declan muttered, "The Creator doesn't have to sit in class."

Alex leaned in and whispered, "We need to figure out why the Creator is orchestrating all of this."

V nodded and replied, "We'll figure that out after we save the planet."

After a lengthy meeting with the larger group and some time spent with the Elders, followed by a couple of meals, the group finally felt ready to unwind. They rose from their seats and made their way back to the common room.

Prezzy spoke up. "We're done for today. Tomorrow, we have Combat training, then more shooting."

Lev's excitement bubbled over. "Excellent!"

Lin, equally excited, turned to face the group. "I've got something to show you all. It's awesome, and you have to see it!" She hurried to grab her bag, pulled out her computer, and activated her virtual screen above it so everyone could see.

"This is a recording of Kall's band, which is going to perform at our party after the mission." She set the computer down on the table in the center of the room, where V, Miko, and Prezzy were seated, watching intently.

Lin beamed. "There will be three bands in total. Kall's band will play the first set, followed by Vindor's band, and then we'll take the stage." She paused, her eyes gleaming with excitement. "We're still working on the setlist, but all of us will perform. After the entire concert, the party begins!"

She hit the play button, and V leaned forward in anticipation.

On-screen, a small woman dressed in white appeared, playing what seemed to be a flute. The stage behind her mimicked a massive, snowy glacier. Twelve figures, also dressed in white, formed a circle behind her, performing a CMB. They were deeply immersed in their meditation, humming and singing in unison to the slow, haunting melody of her violin.

Prezzy gasped, gripping Miko's and V's arms in excitement. A cloud began to form above the stage, and then, a rainbow arced across the sky.

Declan let out a loud exclamation, "Oh, my God!"

The twelve meditating figures intensified their humming, their voices rising in volume. The tempo of the music quickened, and the cloud overhead shifted to a soft blue. Snow began to fall, collecting on the panels around the stage, creating additional sounds that harmonized with the music.

The lighting shifted as the tiny woman danced, her graceful movements adding to the energy of the performance. The drums grew louder, and the twelve participants in the CMB sang and hummed with increasing intensity. The cloud changed color once more, shifting from blue to a darker hue, and the snow transformed into rain. The panels responded to the raindrops, altering the beat and tone of the music.

As the rain fell, the song accelerated, its rhythm becoming faster and faster. The cloud darkened even further, turning ominous, and the rain turned to hail. The music grew faster still, matching the intensity of the storm. Lightning crackled from the cloud, and gongs rang out in time with the music. More musicians joined the stage, playing instruments that synchronized perfectly with the rhythm.

The Students watched in awe. Prezzy's nails dug into V's arm as the lightning struck, and she leaped to her feet, her eyes fixed on the spectacle above. V and Miko exchanged a smile, their eyes wide with astonishment.

As soon as the lightning struck across the stage, a petite woman in white danced gracefully to the center, then disappeared in a flash. Moments later, she reappeared, standing on a raised platform beside a towering, 20-foot, ten-stringed instrument. She grasped a six-foot bow, its length almost as tall as she was, and struggled to maneuver it. With determination, she began to play. The sound was hauntingly unfamiliar, evoking the sensation of meditating beneath a sky of stars, galaxies swirling, pulsars pulsing—a song that seemed to channel the vastness of the universe itself.

The melody started slow and steady. As she played, two men, hidden behind the platform, hoisted her into the air with thin ropes and pulleys, lifting her higher as she continued to strum the colossal instrument.

The music grew more magical as gongs and chimes echoed, accompanied by a mysterious glass instrument, its ethereal tones filling the space. A tall, slender man draped in a shimmering white gown added his own haunting melody to the mix. Was he on stilts, or was he truly that tall?

The room buzzed with excitement as the students whispered among themselves, commenting on the strange instruments and the unusual appearance of the performers. They marveled at the way the twelve were manipulating the weather through the Cosmic Microwave Background (CMB).

The final comment, almost in unison, was that this spectacle must be part of the grand celebration marking the mission's end. Questions flew as the Students turned to Lin, eager to learn more.

As the rainbow reappeared, the tiny woman somehow floated into the air, playing a magical flute at the center of the stage. With the final note, the song concluded, and Lin abruptly stopped the video. The room fell silent.

"Holy crap!" Prezzy suddenly shouted, startling half the group.

Lin smiled. "Isn't it incredible?"

Prezzy exclaimed again, "What the hell are we going to do? How can we top that?"

With a mischievous grin, Lin replied, "Fem and I have some pretty big ideas. We'll incorporate our own CMB work… plus a few extra surprises. She has an idea, but she's not ready to share it yet." Lin closed her computer and surveyed the room. "So, what class do we have tomorrow? Combat and Night Shooting? What's that about?"

Lev, perking up, answered, "Oh, that's where we learn how to shoot people at night. It's awesome!"

Lin, still glancing at her tablet, frowned. "What does 'Flips and Twists' mean?"

Lev stood up and approached her, giving her a playful hug from behind. "That's the technique for throwing someone to the floor or avoiding contact entirely." He wrestled with her for a moment before asking, "Hey, where's your eagle mark?"

Lin spun around, trying to catch a glimpse of it. "Wait a minute, V, did you steal my eagle mark?"

V, just catching up on the conversation, looked over at Alex. "What?" she asked.

Alex, clearly exhausted from the previous day's events, mumbled a groggy response. Maria, noticing Kyoryk's neck, teased, "Sorry, babe. Alex stole your eagle mark too."

Alex, trying to defend himself, said, "We didn't steal anything. It must've happened during the prayer."

Prezzy shouted, "Get them!" Everyone leaped to their feet, launching an all-out attack on Alex, and V. V laughed, calling for them to stop.

Unfazed, Alex laughed and pointed upward. "Blame the Creator," he said.

Lin, eyes narrowed, stared at Alex. "Tomorrow in Combat, I'm flipping your ass."

Alex grinned and pulled her into a hug. "You can try. But honestly, it all started when I met her." He pointed at V. "It's her fault! Everyone, get her!"

V attempted to flee but tripped and fell into the middle of the room, landing in a pile of floor pillows. She screamed as everyone pounced on her. Alex yelled, "Get her!"

Lin, Miko, Prezzy, and Maria piled on, laughing and tossing the pillows in every direction.

Alex, turning to Declan, said with a smirk, "Just look at them."

Declan chuckled, pointing at the pile. "They're ridiculously hot. Maybe we should join in."

Kyoryk, eyeing the scene, added, "Yeah, it does look appetizing."

Tonari, ever playful, conjured two more versions of herself, hurling pillows into the mix. The guys stood by, stunned and wide-eyed.

Lev grinned, speaking in Russian, while Candido muttered something in Spanish.

Declan, clearly enjoying the chaos, shouted, "Oh my God. Close the door!"

Kyoryk, glancing back, quipped, "There's no door."

Declan, his voice rising, cried out, "Rip her clothes off!" The boys watched, captivated, as the girls continued their pillow fight.

V, sensing an opportunity, whispered something to Tonari. She then leaned in and whispered into Maria's ear. As the other girls wrestled, Maria began to manipulate time.

"Now!" V shouted.

Maria froze time, holding the entire room still while the girls remained in motion, still wrestling in mid-air.

Lin, wide-eyed, asked, "What's going on?"

V smiled slyly. "I have an idea. The girls keep moving while all the guys are stuck in time."

Maria laughed softly. "I can hold it for about six or seven minutes. But don't stop touching me, or time will return to normal."

Tonari laughs, "We are going to play a trick on the boys, aren't we? We could just strip them naked."

Miko laughs, "Let's dress them up and put makeup on them."

Maria says, "The problem is we must get up without losing touch with one another. Or we will go back to normal time, and we only have."

Tonari laughs, "Oh my god!" Prezzy laughs hysterically while hugging Tonari. They all start laughing.

V is trying to shout everyone says, "Okay, now we have six minutes. Let's try and do it. They all try to stand up to accomplish it.

Miko says, "Let's lay them down on the pillows and try and strip them with a sheet over them. Something like that?"

V looks around the room, "Do we have blankets?"

Lin points with her nose, "There is one on the couch there."

Miko looks at a cabinet. Then motions, bobbing her head, "There is one in that drawer over there."

V says, "That's enough, let's get those."

They all stay connected and scurry around the room to get the blankets, laughing and telling each other what to do when they get back to the boys.

Tonari, trying to look up at the clock, "We have maybe around three minutes left? Let's lay them down on the pillows."

Miko unzips Declan's pants with one hand and tries to pull out some of his underwear. In contrast, she is holding on to Tonari with her other hand. V at the front is trying to knock over Alex gently. He falls over and bumps his head on the floor.

She shouts. "Oh. Crap. They all started laughing.

They lay Declan next to Alex and wrap Alex's hand over Declan with his hand on his crotch. They lay Candido down.

Tonari says, "Two minutes." The girls get into a panic and lay Swaraj on top of Candido almost sideways, and then they get to Kyoryk and lay him down at his feet, put a pillow over his head, and throw a sheet over all their bodies.

Tonari, panicking, yells, "It's almost time."

Since Lev is so big, they start to rock him back and forth almost knocking him over, but then just leaving him there standing instead. Lin wants to do something to him. So, she scrambles and, with V's help to the front and Miko to her rear. They get her bra off and quickly put it in Lev's hand, shove the rest down in his pants, and throw the remaining blanket over his head.

Tonari is yelling, "Time, Time! Time!"

The girls don't know what to do, so they all let go and run out of the room laughing. As soon as the girls let go, they scrambled for the archway.

They all go into the nearest room, which is Prezzy's room, to hide. The guys come back in time. They are not happy. Lev pulls the blanket from his head and sees the bra in his hand and pants. Sees that it is Lin's and starts yelling, "Lin!"

The other guys pull the blanket off and start yelling, Maria! V! Miko! We're going to get you."

Declan stands up. Alex stands up. They all look around at each other, laughing. Alex looks at Declan, "Your jockeys are coming out of your pants, mate.

Declan looks down and says, "What the hell! Swaraj and Candido remain on the floor laughing hysterically.

Alex's phone rings.

V says, "Put me on speaker.

Alex looks at the guys, "Okay, you are on speaker."

V laughs, "All of us girls would like you boys to meet us in our rooms for a special surprise in five minutes."

Alex and the guys chuckle, "I don't know we are all kind of busy right now. How about in ten minutes? I need to, you know, prepare. Is this a group thing?"

Declan blurts out, "Yeah. Group thing!"

All the girls laugh; V says, "No, we are not doing the group thing until after we save the planet."

Declan and Lev scoff and complain. Alex says, "Okay, we will see you in your rooms in seven minutes."

V and the girls laugh, and the phone hangs up.

Alex says, "How about a beer and a couple of shots?"

Declan says, "Cool!" The rest of the guys agree.

The guys can hear down the hallway the girls laughing and running, footsteps and doors slamming. Minutes later the guys finish up with their beers and shots and join their ladies in their rooms. Alex met V in her room for her punishment. I'm not sure what happened with the rest of the couples. The evening ends.

The group gradually returned to their routine at the university, though with a new edge to their daily lives. V and Alex now sported four Eagle Marks.

V stood in her workout tights, poised in the gym for Combat class. As usual, Hugh Hardy, Declan's steward, Kira Toda, Miko's steward, Freida Asmij, V's steward, and Roman Taktorav, Lev's steward, were leading the class. Today's focus was on weapons training and various martial arts techniques.

Hugh, a man known for his intense military background, had softened since his relationship with Kira, or so the gossip went.

"Today," Hugh began, his voice commanding, "we'll break into two groups. You six, with Kira and me, will focus on night shooting. The rest of you will work with Roman and Freida."

Declan muttered under his breath, "Crap, I'm not going to be able to flip Miko."

Roman, standing like a hulking figure with a thick mustache and goatee, his military cut thick and wavy, looked at Declan. His deep Russian accent resonated through the gym. "There will come a time when you will need this skill. Pay attention, yes? After you master it, you can flip anyone you wish." His face contorted further, making him look even more intimidating. "Understood?"

Lev smiled as Roman's stern expression didn't faze him. Declan, less willing to joke, nodded, "Yes, sir."

Hugh gave a rare smile before barking, "Alright, my team, with me to the range."

Roman turned to V. "Okay, V. You're going to flip Lev."

Lev, brimming with confidence, grinned. "Piece of cake," he thought.

V, having trained through the Intelligence Bureau, stood poised in the center of the mat. Lev, certain of his impending victory, confidently hopped onto the mat.

"No weapons this time," Roman said coolly. "Put V in a headlock to subdue her."

V smirked internally. "Alright, let's see how this goes."

Lev lunged, thinking he could overpower her with ease. In a flash, V grabbed his arm, bent her knee, and, with a fluid movement, crouched, tossing Lev over her right side and flipping him effortlessly onto the mat.

The room fell silent, stunned by her quick execution, especially Lev, whose shock was palpable.

Roman raised an eyebrow, impressed. "V has had training? Excellent!" He then turned to the group. "Lev, what was your mistake?"

Kyoryk, unable to hold back a grin, chuckled. "He definitely underestimated his opponent. He thought she had no training, and she's a woman—she's V."

Roman nodded approvingly. "Exactly. Never assume your opponent is weaker or less capable than you. Switch!"

V stood still, contemplating. Should I use my usual tactics to keep him from flipping me, or should I let him win? I don't want to embarrass him.

Lev, having some training himself, tried again, flipping V onto the mat with surprising ease.

"Good," Roman said, his tone unchanging. "This technique could be used if someone's standing in front of you or coming at you from the side. We'll practice various situations. Candido and Miko, you're up next."

Miko, with her orange belt in Karate, wasted no time, effortlessly flipping Candido. V knew Miko had received disciplined training from her parents, who thought it wise to pair her martial arts training with her gymnastics lessons.

Roman turned to Candido. "Now, it's your turn."

V observed Candido closely. A devout man who prayed at nearly every meal, Candido was deeply religious. His true passions lay in cooking and music, and he was set to attend the International Culinary Center in New York City. His interest in combat was nonexistent.

Candido awkwardly attempted the flip, his movements clumsy and ungraceful.

Lev, unable to resist, began to make a remark, but Roman swiftly cut him off. "Alright, Candido. Let's work on that a little more."

Roman positioned Candido's body, correcting his stance and guiding him with precise physical adjustments. "Try again."

Candido attempted the flip once more. It was slightly better but still lacking finesse.

V, observing the group with a discerning eye, mused, "If Alex and I ever find ourselves in battle, we'll have to keep a few of these guys out of it—or at least offer some serious assistance. Lev won't have the patience to help."

Roman cringed slightly but gave a nod of approval. "Yes, much better, Candido. V, good work."

"Now, Maria and Swaraj," Roman continued.

Swaraj, destined to become a neurosurgeon, had no physical combat background. He remained somewhat of a mystery to his peers. There were rumors circulating that a woman's dress had been found in his closet, sparking curious speculation. Alex had even mentioned noticing what seemed like makeup on his face a few times.

Roman, ever the instructor, continued, "There are many reasons to learn these skills. First and foremost, to protect yourself. Knowing how to fall from a height without causing injury could one day save your life."

Swaraj stood in the center of the mat, his hand accidentally brushing against Maria's chest. He chuckled awkwardly and muttered, "Oops." Maria, unfazed, swiftly flipped him onto the floor. As he lay there, grinning, he joked, "It was good for me. Was it good for you?"

Roman nodded in approval. "That was good, Maria." The others laughed, and Maria flashed a playful smile as she helped him up. "I bet it was," she quipped.

Over the past few months, Maria had become a loyal and dependable friend to V. Though she often seemed late to class, V had noticed that when she checked on her, Maria would frequently be lost in front of a mirror. V hadn't yet figured out why, but she remained curious. Maria had lost her mother at the tender age of four—a trauma V had never fully explored.

Swaraj quickly flipped Maria, to everyone's surprise. V's thoughts wandered, I wonder what Swaraj's past holds. I haven't delved into anyone's mind in a while…

Roman clapped his hands together. "Alright, let's practice for a few minutes. Pick someone to train with." He then left the room.

V turned to Miko. "I'm taking a break," she said, settling herself in the corner of the gym against the wall. She closed her eyes for a moment, reaching into Swaraj's memories, trying to learn more about his past.

In an instant, she found herself transported to the final years of Swaraj's college life. She saw him celebrating his graduation with his family. The joyous evening shifted to a darker night as he joined his friends at an Indian gay nightclub, dressed provocatively as a woman. V blinked, surprised—she had never known this side of him.

After the club closed, tragedy struck. As Swaraj and his friends left, they were ambushed in the parking lot by racists. Two of his friends were hospitalized, and one tragically died from the attack.

V pressed deeper into his mind, witnessing the immense trauma Swaraj endured. She saw his determination when he learned the identities of the two men responsible for his friend's death. Swaraj, with his surviving friend, meticulously planned their revenge. They carefully observed their targets, waited for months, and then devised a plan to make it look like an accident.

The plan was surgical in its execution. They disabled the security cameras at a rail platform, choosing a time when the killers worked their late-night shifts. Everything had been accounted for—their getaway, the method, and even the shopping carts they used to push the men onto the tracks before the train arrived.

V couldn't help but be awestruck by the intricacy of the plot. Swaraj and his friend had pulled it off flawlessly. The scene was ruled an accident, and no one suspected a thing.

Swaraj and his friend even returned to the gay bar to celebrate a month later. V continued to sift through the details, astonished not only by the contrast in Swaraj's secret life but also by the depth of his concealed identity. Why is this life such a secret? Is it his parents? The culture? she pondered.

As she attempted to peer deeper into the celebration at the gay bar, Miko nudged her thigh. "Hey! Space Girl. You okay?"

V blinked and returned to the present. "Yeah, I'm fine," she replied, glancing up. Roman now stood in the center of the mat, his commanding presence hard to ignore.

"Alright, everyone," Roman called, "You need to learn how to redirect your punches and position your feet correctly. You've all worked on the Wing Chun dummies, right?" He gestured toward the wooden training dummies, then glanced over, catching sight of V as she rose from her break. "V! All that swimming got to you? Or is something else going on? Please, join us."

V smiled, walking toward him. "Sorry about that," she said.

Roman grinned. "I want you to practice these techniques on your own and with each other. Who knows what the future holds with the Creator's messages? We could end up in a battle— never say never."

For the next few hours, Roman and the other Stewards focused on defensive moves, teaching the students how to fall correctly and efficiently.

When lunchtime came, the group filed into the dining area. Everyone grabbed their food and sat down together.

Declan raised an eyebrow at Miko. "Who did you flip?"

Miko smirked. "I took down Candido a few times."

Candido, finishing his prayer, looked up. "I took you down too. I just need more practice."

Prezzy sipped his soda and muttered, "Why are we learning all this? We're not soldiers."

Lev leaned in, his voice steady. "I talked to Roman about it. Over the next four years, we're trained in a lot of different areas. One of those is defending the planet and its people. We need to know these things. You won't be full combat soldiers, but you'll need to know how to protect yourselves."

He paused, his expression turning serious. "Roman explained it like this: As an Elder, you need to start thinking differently by the end of the fourth year. When you graduate, you'll be different. I assure you." He gave the trademark cringing look he always wore when discussing serious matters. "Every catastrophe presents different cultures, different types of battles, and wars. As Elders, we need to understand all these things, including combat and defense."

Kyoryk interrupts the conversation, his voice tinged with curiosity. "Hugh said something strange."

V glances at him, intrigued. "What did he say?"

Kyoryk continues, his tone thoughtful, "Alex asked if we were prepared to defend our family and friends. Hugh responded that all the students already had experience in that regard.

He suggested that might be why we were chosen—it's because we've already protected those we care about."

Alex falls silent, his gaze flickering to V. He recalls their earlier conversation about the assailant who hurt his brother—and what Alex did about it. V remains quiet as well, aware of the memories she's seen inside people's minds. Even just minutes ago, she had glimpsed Swaraj's troubled past.

Declan speaks up, his voice steady but assertive. "I've done something like that before, and I'm not ashamed to admit it."

V raises an eyebrow. "Doesn't everyone defend their family?"

Kyoryk turns to Declan, his curiosity piqued. "What happened?"

Declan hesitates for a moment before speaking. "It was two years ago, on a Sunday night. After closing hours at my mom's club, we were cleaning up when they broke in. I confronted them. We got into a fight, and one of them pulled a knife. That's how I ended up with this." He gestures to the scar on his left cheek, near his ear. "He also stabbed me in the stomach. Anyway, we ended up on the roof of a building. There was an accident. He didn't make it."

A solemn look crosses Declan's face. He adds, "I nearly went to jail over it. It was a big deal for a while, but eventually, that was it. If it happened again, I'd do the same. That's all."

Alex nods, his voice heavy with understanding. "I've heard about situations like that. You get into a fight, knock the guy out—and he dies. What are you supposed to do then? What if the guy was a scumbag, or worse, a killer? It's insane, right?"

Declan meets Alex's gaze, a knowing expression in his eyes. "Yeah, exactly. What do you do? I was just stopping him from hurting me or my mom. He came at us, and he had our money. That's what I kept telling them."

Kyoryk looks at Maria, a distant expression in his eyes. "I found myself in a similar situation with my younger brother and sister. It happened on a train in Tokyo. I still haven't gotten over it."

Maria's face softens with concern. "You had to subdue him. He could have hurt your sister. From what you told me, he was about to take her."

V reflects on the conversation, her voice calm but firm. "It's crazy, the situations we get into. We're often forced to make decisions, and you know what? I think that's okay. Whatever situations we've faced, I believe we made the right choices."

V scans the room, her eyes meeting those of her peers. They seem ready to move on from these heavy memories, so she shifts the topic. "What method did they use in the night shooting? How do you even see in those conditions?"

Alex demonstrates, his hands mimicking the action of holding a gun and flashlight. "You use a mini flashlight between your fingers, underneath the butt of the gun."

V looks around once more and notices a collective sense of relief in the group, pleased that the conversation has turned toward more practical matters.

Lin interjects her tone light but confident. "Alex and I are the most accurate of the group."

Prezzy scoffs, not easily impressed. "I don't know about that, but we're definitely improving. Tonari and I are getting better."

Tonari straightens her posture, addressing half the group with an amused expression. "I don't understand all this gun stuff. But there's a flower in my backyard that could kill a person in three seconds."

Everyone is caught off guard by Tonari's remark. Declan raises an eyebrow, placing his hands on the table. "Yeah, but you have to get pretty close to them to use it."

Tonari flutters her eyelashes, playfully tugging at her shirt to expose her cleavage. "You don't think I can get close? I can make three of me." The group erupts in laughter as Tonari grins mischievously. "Heck, I could take out an entire platoon."

Prezzy leans back in his chair, raising an eyebrow. "So, have we all done something heroic? We all share the same birthday. What else do we have in common?"

Lin shrugs. "I asked Mod about it. He said we're genetically different from the average humans on Earth. We can handle being in space longer, that kind of thing."

Declan looks intrigued. "Do you think the Gifts have anything to do with it?"

Alex chuckles, a playful grin on his face. "I think your nose is bigger."

Miko laughs heartily. "That's not the only thing that's bigger."

Declan beams, clearly proud of himself. "No, really, wasn't that in one of the sections on our tablet, under 'Who We Are'?"

Alex quickly flips through his tablet and mutters, "Yeah, I remember that being in the curriculum. It was on the first day, under 'Knowing Your Role.'"

He scans the screen, then announces, "Here it is: Who Are You? We have more genes than average—26 pairs of chromosomes and higher IQs. Our blood type is AB neutral. Birthdays are the same. There's more, but it goes into specifics if you're interested."

"We're less receptive to cosmic rays. We adapt well to low Gs, and our SpO2 level is above 110%. Whatever that means. We're also better equipped to handle stressful situations, among other things."

Everyone looks at their tablets, digesting the information. Alex suddenly grins mischievously and declares loudly, "These are only on my tablet! I'm super strong, super attractive! Women want to procreate with me, and all men admire me!"

V bursts out laughing, spitting her drink across the table. Prezzy and Lin join in, their laughter echoing through the room.

Declan slams his fist on the table, his voice filled with exaggerated indignation. "Oh, yeah, right, brother! No, that's both of us!"

Miko glances at him with a smirk. "Can you spell E. G. O.?"

Kyoryk looks across the table, coughing to punctuate his interruption. "Hack! Hack!"

Prezzy, looking utterly confused, stares blankly at them. "Looks like it's difficult to get pregnant."

Lin glances up at the ceiling and mutters, "Praise the Lord."

V spits out her drink again, caught off guard.

Prezzy erupts in laughter, his voice booming. "Does it really say that?"

Miko holds up her tablet with a triumphant grin. "Right here—Section 1, 24(b). Hah! What a trip, huh?"

Prezzy raises an eyebrow, a playful smirk forming. "What if I want to get pregnant? Do they have a pill for that?"

The entire group bursts into uncontrollable laughter once again.

Alex, barely holding back laughter, mutters, "We're all going to need some serious medication after this."

Kyoryk, who has been intently reading his tablet, looks up and speaks thoughtfully. "I read that the Common Mind slows aging, and the additional Gifts further extend it." He glances back at his tablet. "Oh, damn, we're supposed to head back to the Gym."

The laughter subsides as everyone stands and heads toward the Gym. As they enter, they find the Stewards practicing their knife-throwing skills.

Hugh looks at them, his gaze stern. "You're late. I trust you were occupied with something important?"

Prezzy grins. "We were just reading through our tablets in the 'Who Are You?' section."

Kira smiles knowingly. "So, did you figure out who you are?"

Alex and Declan laugh, sharing an inside joke.

Prezzy smirks, his voice laced with sarcasm. "We're definitely different from the people on this planet now."

V raises an eyebrow, curiosity piqued. "With these genetic changes, have we been altered in other ways? And what's this about AB-neutral blood?"

Freida smiles warmly, always the guide. "Look it up on your tablets. You can find everything you need. Let me show you." She grabs Miko's tablet, swiping through it quickly. "It's covered in a few sections. Just type in keywords like 'Elders' or 'Aging Types.' Here, try typing in 'Elders' and 'Aging' under the Keywords Search."

The group begins typing, their eyes scanning for answers. Roman, however, gives them an icy glare from across the room. Kira, sensing the tension, nudges Miko and laughs quietly. "God, that guy is angry."

They all snicker softly, walking toward the firing range. V, Lev, Candido, Miko, Swaraj, and Maria enter the room, with Kira leading the way.

Kira claps her hands together and addresses the group. "Today, we're going to teach you a few different methods for holding your lights. The first one—"

She gestures for V to step up. "Place the mini flashlight between your index and third fingers, then hold it underneath the butt of the gun. This is the preferred position because it allows you to support the gun with both hands."

Kira demonstrates a second method, holding the light with her opposite hand under the palm of the gun hand. "The second method is holding the light with your free hand, held high like this."

She pauses, explaining further. "The reason for this is that if someone is shooting at you, they'll likely aim for the light. However, holding the light up high makes it much harder to navigate through a doorway or tight space."

"The fourth method is over the shoulder, but for now, we're focusing on the first one. If you want to practice the other techniques later, feel free."

Kyoryk speaks up, raising a valid point. "Don't most guns these days come with built-in lights or lasers?"

Hugh nods. "Yes, they do. But we're starting with the basics. Once you master these, we'll get into more advanced gear. You're not ready for the planetary or space-plasma guns yet. We'll cover those later."

Kyoryk looks at Hugh in disbelief. He mutters under his breath, "Then why not just use a rubber band and a paperclip?"

Hugh shoots him a pointed look. "For today, we're sticking to this."

V takes her position, checking her magazine, loading it, and cocking the gun. Kira turns off the lights, signaling for her to begin. "Okay, now—let's practice."

Kira helps V position the flashlight, guiding her hand to steady the aim. "Identify your target, and when you're ready, shoot."

V steadies herself, feet firmly planted, light in one hand, safety off, finger poised on the trigger. She fires with precision.

"Nice job, V," Kira praises, a satisfied grin on her face.

V continues firing as Lev steps up, taking his turn. He positions himself quickly, aligning the light with the gun, and fires with impressive speed. One by one, the rest of the students take their turns.

Meanwhile, V finds herself drifting back into Swaraj's memories. She steps back, leaning against one of the nearby windows, trying to appear as though she's just observing the group. As she delves into Swaraj's mind again, she finds herself exactly where she left off—right as he walked into the gay bar to meet his friends, ready to celebrate the month following their planned act of revenge.

V was determined to uncover why Swaraj led two separate lives and why he had kept this hidden from everyone at the university. Perhaps Maria knew about his double life? She observed as Swaraj and his friends reveled in their celebration that night.

What she discovered next deepened the mystery: His parents and siblings had no inkling of his secret life. V delved further into his memories and realized that Swaraj's siblings were socially distant due to their age gap, while his parents, deeply religious and morally rigid, created a household where secrets were tightly guarded. This dual existence remained unknown to them all. As V explored more of his memories, she saw the inner turmoil that plagued him. She felt a surge of empathy and an undeniable sense of responsibility.

At that moment, she knew she had to intervene. But like Swaraj in his meticulous planning, she would have to approach the matter with great care, delicacy, and patience. Her first step would be to speak with Alex, then carefully gauge Maria's knowledge of Swaraj's hidden life.

A smile spread across her face as she emerged from her trance, only to find Lev staring intently at her.

He waved his hand in front of her face, saying, "V, hello? You in there?"

V returned his smile. "Yes, I'm here."

Lev's brow furrowed with concern. "Some of us are starting to worry about you. You've been doing this a lot lately. You look… strange. What's going on? Does this have something to do with the Creator and the messages?"

V struggled to come up with an answer. She placed a reassuring hand on his shoulder. "Yes, Lev. Something is happening. But I can't tell you everything just yet. When the time is right, I'll explain it to you and the others. Just give me a couple of days, and I promise I'll share it all. It's tied to my Gift, but I'm not ready to discuss it now. Is that okay?"

Lev smiled, his concern fading. "Okay. You just looked a bit… odd standing there. You were making expressions like you were telling a story or something."

Miko finished her turn at the range, and V nodded thoughtfully.

"I understand," V said. "I'll try to be a bit more discreet."

The group wrapped up their session at the firing range and made their way back to the gym.

Once inside, Hugh addressed the group. "Tomorrow, we'll have another training session here. Friday, we're back in the classroom. Next week, we'll be heading to the surface to review all the emergency procedures."

The last few days had passed without incident. The students were eagerly anticipating the upcoming New Year's celebration. They had attended classes, honed their Gifts, and looked forward to the challenges ahead. The next month promised new trials, including the next Pulse Reversal and another round of Accelerator testing.

XXVII

As Alex blinked away the remnants of sleep, his brother Max materialized in the chair beside him, just as he had before. Alex rubbed his eyes and sat up, the surreal encounter unfolding before him.

"Hey, brother," Max began, his voice calm yet laced with urgency. "I'm glad your test went well. I wanted to thank you again for everything you've done for our family. Today, the Creator has entrusted you with information of paramount importance. He's counting on you. What you're about to witness is yours to handle as you see fit. Even if you divulged it to everyone, in the grand scheme, it wouldn't alter much. The choice is yours—how and when to share it. But for now, the Creator asks that you keep this knowledge to yourself. There will come a time to share it with V and the others."

Max's image flickered slightly, the ethereal connection wavering. "Love you, mate," Max added, his tone softening. "Remember, I'm always with you, brother. I won't see you again until after the flare hits."

The vision of Max faded in and out, struggling to maintain its form. Finally, he got up and stood at the foot of Alex's bed, his presence more tangible. "Now, close your eyes. Lay back and relax."

Alex had come to recognize the shift in tone—it was the Creator speaking now. Obediently, Alex reclined on the bed. He felt the ghostly touch of his brother's hand on his leg, reminiscent of the night he received his first eagle mark.

A familiar burning sensation spread across his skin, intensifying as the room filled with a warm, almost suffocating air.

His thoughts raced, *"Oh, shit. What is this? What is he preparing me for?"* He looked over at the clock: 6:33. He turned back and closed his eyes.

Static electricity crackled through the air, and a low rumbling began to build. Even with his eyes closed, Alex perceived the blinding white light, followed by an astonishing image.

It was the solar system rendered in breathtaking clarity. Planets, moons, and our sun appeared before him, and the scene centered on Terraenti.

The sun's hue shifted from yellow to white, then back again, as colossal waves of plasma erupted from its surface. Pulses of energy radiated outward, resembling a series of colossal explosions, each one rippling across the cosmos. Alex watched in awe and dread as the solar superflare unfolded in excruciating slow motion. *"Has it already begun?"* he wondered, his heart pounding.

Desperately trying to remain calm, Alex took several deep breaths. But the anxiety overwhelmed him, and he snapped his eyes open. Standing before him was his brother, no, the Creator. "Alex, stay calm, just watch." The Creator intoned, his form flickering like a mirage. "I'm showing you the future. It's going to be alright. You and V will play a crucial role in what's to come. There's nothing we can do to stop this now, but you must watch. You need to prepare mentally and spiritually. Do you understand?"

Trembling, Alex tried to compose himself, sinking back into the pillow and closing his eyes once more. "Yes, I understand." *"This is insane,"* he thought, his mind racing. *"Why me? Why do I have to endure this? Someone, anyone, please knock on the door now."*

The vision resumed a stark contrast to the blackness behind his eyelids. The solar outburst expanded, engulfing the planets, the terrifying silence amplifying its power. As the sun's radiance grew unbearable, it abruptly ceased, giving way to a second wave—this one a tranquil, almost divine, blue. It cascaded through space like an angelic force, reaching out to the planets. The wave was a marvel to behold—violet and blue, reminiscent of the Creator's prayers arrow.

In the final moments, as the wave touched each celestial body, it too faded, dissipating into the far reaches of the universe.

The vision sharpened, focusing on Terraenti once more. As the remnants of the superflare drew nearer, Alex observed satellites being knocked out of orbit, some completely obliterated, while a scant few clung to life. He gripped the bed sheets tightly, his knuckles white with tension. The particles collided with the planet, sparking fires and disabling technology. On the planet's dark side, city lights flickered out, swallowed by the encroaching darkness.

Taking a deep breath, Alex glimpsed the Northern and Southern Elder Teams, their efforts visible as the sun's deadly particles were deflected by the amplified Magnetic Field, a testament to the Creator's meticulous planning.

A clock on the wall read February 18th—Alex was in the docks, preparing for the mission. *"This is the future,"* he realized, *"I'm seeing myself. I'm seeing the mission. It's like my visions."*

"Just relax, Alex," the Creator's voice cut through the chaos. "There's so much more to reveal."

Alex's eyes squinted against the intensifying light, but the image refused to let him go. *"I think he's reading my mind right now."* "Shoosh Alex, be patient." The milky white of his vision morphed once again, transporting him within the planet's atmosphere. The sound, a deafening roar, grew louder as the sky transformed from blue to a sickly yellow. The clouds had vanished, replaced by a thick, murky fog. Cyclones, hurricanes, even the regular weather patterns were no more. The once vibrant blue planet now appeared as a tarnished, yellow sphere. Alex gasped for air, struggling to breathe in the stifling vision. Time seemed to accelerate.

The skies cleared slightly, revealing cities along the Arabian Sea—possibly Muscat, Dubai, or Abu Dhabi. Alex found himself on the planet's surface, barely able to discern the sun through the polluted haze. Below, chaos reigned as people fought desperately for food and water. Fires raged, explosions echoed through the streets—it was pandemonium.

At first, Alex thought a tsunami was approaching, but the sound was all wrong. It was a storm, yet unlike any he had ever encountered—more like an electrical tempest. He saw the wave then, not of water, but of searing blue and white light.

It hung in the air, half a mile high, stretching as far as he could see. Lightning bolts arced from it, obliterating everything in its path as it swept through the city. The devastation was far worse than Alex had imagined. The wave was unstoppable, reducing buildings to rubble and leaving no survivors in its wake. As it continued its merciless advance, it became clear that only parts of the planet would be spared, protected by the enhanced magnetic field.

Alex's view shifted again. Desperation gripped him. *"I hope this is the worst-hit area. If the rest of the planet looks like this, why are we even trying? Nothing, no one will survive. Shit!"*

The vision fast-forwarded, showing him governments deploying their militaries in a futile attempt to restore order.

But months later, chaos still reigned, with humanity tearing itself apart. *"Governments, military—come on, people! Get it together! There's still hope, damn it. There must be."* Alex thought, clinging to the last vestiges of optimism.

Alex inhales deeply, observing clusters of people establishing communities on the fringes of cities. He muses, *"Great. People. Communities. They're building them outside the cities. That's great! But why is He showing it to me so fast? Slow down."*

The vision accelerates—years seem to pass in an instant—and he witnesses the atmosphere slowly returning to normal. Communities have sprung up beyond the major urban centers, with people farming and coming together, initiating trade within the different countries. More years pass, and the planet stabilizes; the storms, the atmosphere, and the seasonal rains and snows all resume their natural cycles.

He notices, however, that regions above and below the forty-fifth parallel remain frozen, reminiscent of a time millennia ago. Yet, even these frozen expanses begin to thaw. Suddenly, he finds himself in a room, staring at a piece of paper displaying a staggering statistic: a 50% population loss. The scene shifts again. Alex breathes deeply, trying to process it all. "Fifty percent," he murmurs in disbelief. The vision fast-forwards once more, now revealing global communication and trade networks.

It speeds forward perhaps twenty to thirty years into the future, he sees the reconstruction of some major cities, air travel resuming, a few planes and helicopters crisscrossing the skies. He senses international trade reemerging, though power is unevenly distributed—present in the countryside and around airports but still absent in the urban cores.

Then, the perspective zooms out, revealing a planet bathed in blue. A sense of resolution washes over him; it feels as though the worst is behind them, and a semblance of normalcy is returning.

Suddenly, Alex is on a balcony overlooking a small airport, possibly in a control tower. A distant city appears abandoned, while the airport hums with life, surrounded by a crowd of 5,000 to 10,000 people near a burgeoning community. He watches as a plane lands and the passengers disembark to enthusiastic cheers.

Twelve young people, perhaps his age, emerge from the aircraft and ascend a stage. The crowd erupts in applause as they form a circle, levitating and rotating counterclockwise in mid-air. A pure white aura envelops them, shooting skyward like a beacon.

At the last moment, Alex notices a sign to his right: "New Veracruz 2058." His eyes shift back to the ship they arrived on; it resembles the ones they currently use. In the final second, he sees himself and V descending the steps of the ship, hand in hand, heading toward the stage.

An older version of Alex gazes up at the tower balcony and smiles before stepping onto the stage. Lying in bed, the present-day Alex smiles and thinks, *"This is it. The Creator is restoring the Gifts to humanity. This is the vision He's showing me. But why is He not telling V all this yet? I saw myself... part of the Creator's new plan, at least."*

The vision shifts again, revealing world leaders uniting, forging alliances. Lights begin to illuminate the darkened portions of the planet. Alex pleads internally, *"When is this? Please, tell me."* He strains to see further but is thwarted. *"Damn it, it's going to happen during the next Pulse Reversal. At least power is restored in under... what, sixty years? We'll save 50% of the population."*

"That's far better than losing 95% or more like before. And we preserved our technology too." A shiver runs down his spine as he opens his eyes.

His brother is back, sitting in the chair, watching him. Alex turns and sits up in bed, speechless, as a tear slips down his cheek. His brother breaks the silence, "This is some crazy shit, isn't it brother? The Creator wanted you to glimpse the next hundred years. I know it's a lot to absorb." Alex, still reeling, sits up further, striving to maintain his composure. He looks at his brother and asks, "What's next?" His brother responds, "Now you know."

The image shimmers, and now it's the Creator speaking directly to Alex. "What you're about to do, Alex, will save millions upon millions of lives, along with most of the current technologies."

"This isn't a full reset like in previous CATs, and it's not always a full reset anyway. It merely sets back technology, preventing it from spiraling out of control. This planet always advances so rapidly; that's why your clock is set to 4,400 years. Terraenti and Vindor, Chimps and Eagles."

He chuckles, "This time, however, I'm extending it, your people have changed this time, that's what I'm hoping anyways. Never before have I seen such a growth in consciousness, with such a peace between minds."

"Moreover, future events may necessitate their assistance. That's why I'm allowing you all to present your Gifts to the public in the future."

The Creator continues, "I know you wanted to protect the planet more, but this plan, Alex, unfolds over a century, not millennia. I couldn't do much more than that. Be patient. Stay the course. You and V will be the Master Elders. It's up to you two to lead the way."

"Assure the others that this is the correct path. Stay the course! We have much more to come. Keep this to yourself for now, Alex. V is crucial. She is the key. " The image shimmers once more, and his brother reappears, saying, "I won't see you again until after the CAT. Raba Rashi is pretty fun, but that One guy is very impressed with the two of you. Stay the course, Alex. Love you, brother." With a final deep breath, Alex watches as his brother's image dissipates like a wisp of smoke in a fog.

Alex sits up on the edge of his bed, wiping tears from his face. He sits in silence for a few minutes, absorbing the gravity of the message he has just received. *"It's the end of the world. How much of a difference can we truly make?"* he ponders. *"I need to see my family before the next Pulse Reversal. Will they even survive?"*

"I have to do something. What difference are we really making? Alright, calm down. If I tell everyone, they'll freak out. Gig and Fem' had it much worse. I should be grateful. But who should I tell? V, only? Should I reveal the entire vision to her? Damn it! This is too much. Shit!"

As Alex hears Students walking by in the hallway, he forces himself to think, *"Get your act together. It's far better than if we had never received the Creator's plans. They predicted a 95% loss of life—75%, 80%, or even 50% is much better, right? And electricity will return to the entire planet in less than sixty years. Damn."* Alex stands and begins pacing around the room. *"I need to cool off. A cold shower should help. Damn it, why is the Creator revealing all this to me now?"*

He opens his door slightly to check the hallway. Finding it empty, pauses, and gathers his courage before grabbing his robe and making his way to the shower. The bathroom is empty as well. As water splashes over his face, he can't shake the memory of the vision. He wants to punch the wall but restrains himself, letting the water cascade over him for several minutes. Still, no one enters.

Finally, he steps out and dries off, thinking, *"I'm not telling anyone. It's too insane. Many of the Students believe we're going to completely save the planet. Shit! I need to put it out of my mind and stop dwelling on it."*

Just then, Declan walks in. "Hey, bro, happy New Year." Alex thinks, *"Damn, it's New Year's. Focus on that."* He smiles as he puts on his robe. "Same to you, mate. Big party tonight. Tonight, I'm forgetting everything! You're my friend, right? You're with me?" Declan steps under the shower, "Right, I'm with you." He pokes his head out of the water, asking, "You okay, brother?" Alex replies, "Yeah, I'm okay!" and leaves the room.

For the rest of the day, Alex keeps his distance, concealing his frustration. He knows what's coming but, for now, decides to keep it to himself.

Hours before midnight, Alex and V sat together on a bench overlooking the cascading falls and tranquil small lake.

Behind them, the rest of the Students, Stewards, and Elders commenced their New Year's celebration on the deck.

It was the same serene spot where Alex and V had first met nearly one hundred and twenty days ago when he had felt the Common Mind with his group. When V had first read his mind. Alex turned to V, a smile playing on his lips. "Are you ready for the new year? The year that will alter everything as we know it?"

V returned his smile, her gaze drifting to the view before them. "I'm looking forward to it. As far as we can tell, it's going to work. We'll save countless lives on the planet. And if not, we'll adapt to whatever comes."

Alex chuckled, masking the turmoil within him—his secret meeting with the Creator still fresh in his mind. He met V's eyes again. "What if the Creator hadn't given us the plans? We would have watched civilization crumble, thrown back thousands of years."

V grasped his hand, her grip firm and reassuring. "Even if we're successful, the world will be plunged into darkness, devoid of electricity for who knows how long. Society will become unstable, and wars over food and resources will be inevitable."

Alex frowned, his thoughts racing. *Did V receive the same message? Stay calm, don't let emotions take over.* He spoke, his voice measured, "You've been thinking about this a lot, haven't you? Talking to Kyoryk?" V's gaze lingered on the distant glacier. "Everyone's been talking about it."

"Saturday morning," Alex began, "I met with Harvey and Kyoryk. We discussed what the world might look like after the Flare. The only way to prevent a catastrophe would have been to warn the governments and amass enough food for fifteen years, which would violate the Directives and Laws. Even then, it would have taken years to grow enough food for the current population. We just don't have that kind of time. The Super Flare is coming in four months, without a doubt."

V's expression grew serious as she tightened her hold on Alex's hand. "I wish we could have prevented it entirely. Maybe we're here so that next time, we can. Have you seen anything of the future? Any messages?"

Alex released her hand and pulled her into an embrace, his voice a soft murmur. "No, nothing. The last message was 'Stay the Course.' Remember? So, that's what we're doing. I just hope we save as many people as possible. Before we came here, the only time I ever thought about this was when I saw a prepper video online. The guy said, 'When a VEI 7 or bigger erupts, max out your credit cards on canned and freeze-dried food because the planet will have years of barely any sunlight.' That was the only thought I'd ever had before coming here. Can you believe what's about to happen? I can't dwell on it. I'm just grateful you're here with me now. It's so much pressure."

V wrapped her arms around Alex, kissed him, and whispered, "Let's enjoy tonight."

She glanced at the group, reveling in the festivities, and added, "Let's join them. We can forget for a few hours and pick it back up on Tuesday. Remember, we get to go to the surface. You can take me on a moon buggy ride."

Alex stood, taking her hand. "You're right. Let's do this New Year's thing."

Together, they approached Declan, Miko, Swaraj, and Prezzy. Prezzy leaped onto Alex, enveloping him in a hug. "Here's the Northern Team Leader, everyone!"

Alex returned her hug, then gently set her down, planting a kiss on her cheek. "Happy New Year, you wild one. What's on the drink menu?"

Miko grinned. "Kyoryk and Bahdubah concocted some crazy multi-colored drinks that you have to set on fire."

Determined to shake off his funk, Alex exclaimed, "Let's get completely blinded!"

The group made their way to the bar, where Declan called out to Kyoryk and Bahdubah, "Pour the drinks! Alex wants to get 'Blinded.'"

Kyoryk poured their drinks and raised his glass. "To getting blinded!"

After a few rounds, Fem' and Fair took the stage, serenading the crowd with a tune from a bygone era. When they finished, Gig and Fem' led a prayer for the upcoming year—a prayer no one would remember.

As they spoke of the mission and the years ahead, the lights flickered, and the stone in Fem's hand glowed. She completed the prayer, and blue-violet arrows of light swirled through the room, passing through everyone present.

At 11:55, the group gathered for the countdown. Harvey and Freida joined Alex and V at the table, discussing all they had learned at the university over the past year. As Alex and V observed, they noticed that some of the Stewards—Hugh and Kira, Harvey and Freida, Roman and Keira—seemed to have something brewing between them, relationships perhaps. The status of the others remained uncertain. With that, Harvey and Freida began passionately kissing right in front of them.

Alex and V exchanged smiles. Alex remarked, "It's all part of the Creator's plan—me and you," he said, gesturing to Harvey and Freida, "and them. All of this is part of the plan."

V kissed him and whispered, "Happy New Year, my love. I couldn't have asked for anyone else to go through this with."

Alex kissed her back, murmuring into her ear, "I couldn't agree more, Vibrean Aboli. Of all seven planets, you're the one for me. I love you too."

The countdown began: 5... 4... 3... 2... 1... "Happy New Year!"

The glacier deck area erupted in simulated fireworks and special effects, the walls echoing with explosions and a cacophony of sounds. Declan, completely out of control, jumped onto Alex's back, slurring his words. "Happy New Year, brother! I love you! Look at this place—it's the best party ever!"

Miko followed suit, exclaiming, "He's out of control! I think it's those flaming drinks."

V laughed, hugging Miko and giving her a kiss. "Happy New Year, sister." Miko, equally inebriated, attempted a full-on kiss with V. Declan looking over, amused. "This is getting interesting." Miko, still clinging to V, slurred, "I love you; V. I love you." V laughed. "How many of those flaming drinks did you guys have?" Declan, jumping up and down to the music, shouted, "Not enough! More drinks!"

V took Alex's hand and led him to the dance floor. They danced for a while before she pulled him up the ramp to end the evening.

As Alex ascended, he glanced back, his thoughts a whirlwind. *Well, I made it through today without telling anyone.* He surveyed the crowd. *This is a great group of people to face the almost-end of the world with, I suppose.* He looked at V, his thoughts turning inward. *And a remarkable woman to go through it with. But wait—who were those people in New Veracruz in 2058? They were conducting a CMB, but they weren't us. They resembled us, but they weren't us. Who were they?*

A puzzled expression crossed his face. V noticed and asked, "Something wrong?"

Alex quickly shook off the thought. "What? No, nothing." *But who were they? Only we can float. Only we can spin and emit the white aura, and they did it so quickly, we can't even do it that fast What's up with that? This is the second time he mentioned the One. Who is that? My brother said He was very impressed with V and me. What's up with that? I need another drink."*

Alex's face twisted into an odd expression as he tried to pull V back to the party, both teetering on the edge of inebriation.

"No," V insisted, her tone firm despite her drunkenness. "No, you've had enough. Let's go to bed. I don't think I've ever seen you drink this much before."

Slurring his words, Alex responded with a grin, "I'mmm okay! Yourr okay. We're all okay! Everybrodies is rokay!"

V shook her head, her patience wavering. "Okay? Let's get you to bed."

Despite the chaotic festivities, Alex had managed to keep his secrets to himself. They stumbled into one of their rooms, where the remnants of New Year's Eve still clung to them like the lingering haze of alcohol.

XXVIII

The shrill ring of Alex's tablet pierced through his pounding headache, barely audible over the relentless thudding in his ears. Groaning, he reached over, grasping the device with sluggish hands. "Hello," he mumbled, his voice a mere rasp.

"Alex, it's Gig. Is V with you?" Gig's voice crackled through the speaker, sharp and urgent.

Still disoriented, Alex replied, "Hold on." He rubbed one bleary eye, scanning the room with the other. V lay sprawled across his bed, her hair a wild tangle obscuring her face, her body barely covered by her disheveled underwear. The sheets lay discarded on the floor, a testament to the previous night's debauchery.

A smirk tugged at Alex's lips. "Yeah, she's here. What's up? What can we do for you? And... what time is it?"

Gig began to answer, but Fem' interrupted him, her voice more authoritative. "Alex, could you and V join us at the Master Elders' Residence for breakfast? Let's say in an hour?" V groaned beside him, clutching her head. "Shut up, my head."

Alex shushed her gently, placing a pillow over her face. "Of course, we'll be there. See you in an hour."

Turning to V, he asked, "Hey, do you know where the Master Elders' Residence is? Gig and Fem' want us to meet them there." V's hand waved weakly in the air as she mumbled, "Water. Headache."

Alex fetched a bottle of water from the side table and placed it in her hand. "Here, drink this." V attempted to sip, but most of the water spilled onto the bed, further dampening the sheets.

"So," Alex began, "do you know where the Master Elders' Residence is?" "It's at the very top of the university," V mumbled, her voice muffled by the pillow now on her head, hair still a mess, and only in her bra and panties she squirmed on the bed.

Alex looked around the room, confusion etched on his face. "What happened last night?" V groaned, "My head hurts. Why? Why?" She guzzled more water, pushing the pillow aside.

"Gig and Fem' want us to meet them at the Master Elders' Residence," Alex repeated. "What's that?" V blurted out, spitting her water in shock. "What!" She popped her head out from under the pillow, her hair still a wild mess. "Did you say they want us to come to the Master Elders' Residence?"

Alex gently brushed her hair from her face. "Yes, that's what Fem' said. They just called. They want us there for breakfast."

V's panic surged. She threw the water bottle onto the floor, pushing Alex off the bed. He landed with a thud, the water spreading across the floor. "You're spilling the water," Alex protested.

"Shit." V jumped to her knees, her eyes wide with fear. "No one is allowed at the Master Elders' Residence for any reason. Klinchmay said it's where Gig and Fem' sleep." She leaped to her feet, standing on the bed, her panic palpable. "The only people allowed there are Master Elders, you idiot!"

She jumped out of bed, frantically searching for her clothes, throwing them on haphazardly—shirt backward, pants backward, socks nowhere to be found. Alex grabbed her, trying to calm her down. "We need to shower and stuff. Relax, we have time."

She pushed him back into a cabinet, her voice frantic, switching to Hindi as she scrambled to undress again, struggling with her clothes. "Are you going to be okay?" Alex asked, his concern deepening.

V clutched her head, "My god, I have a huge headache. What happened last night?"

Alex, now doing push-ups to clear his head, responded, "We drank a lot; it was New Year's. We just woke up and got a call from Gig—that's all I remember."

V's eyes narrowed. "The last thing I remember was talking to you by the falls. Oh, and Declan saying you wanted to get 'Blinded.'" She grabbed his hands, her expression intense. "What does this mean? What the hell is going on?" Alex smiled, trying to reassure her. "I have no idea. Does it have to mean anything? Let's just get ready and go. It might be nothing. You're freaking me out."

V darted out of the room, heading for the shower, shouting over her shoulder, "Freaking you out? You're the one who got me into all this!"

Alone, Alex muttered to himself, "I didn't do anything. It's fucking Harvey's fault. Fuck, my head hurts."

Forty minutes later, they found themselves in an unknown archway. "This must be it." Alex admitted, "The University only has eight stories, pretty sure it's on the top. He looked at V and smiled. "These go up."

V took off up the stairs, her anxiety palpable. Alex, struggling to keep up, called out, "Would you slow down?"

"Klinchmay told me the last time a Student was invited to the Master Elders' Residence; it was after their third year. Fuck!" V's voice trembled with urgency. Nearly out of breath, Alex asked, "Who were the Students then?"

V stopped, her gaze piercing as she replied, "Gig and Fem'."

A worried look crossed Alex's face. Without another word, he quickened his pace, now leading the way up the stairs. He looked back, "Why the hell didn't you tell me that earlier…?"

Finally, they reached an open area that overlooked the entire university. They stood before the entrance to the Master Elders' Residence, the weight of what lay ahead heavy in the air.

Alex looked to his left, an ominous giant Short-Faced Bear standing, leaning against the rockface of the crater.

Below it was a Scimitar Cat lying on the floor, looking up smiling, that led to a grand patio sprawled out while to the right, an elegant archway beckoned the way to the Residence. Alex walked towards the patio, he could see all the way down to the deck area.

The patio, adorned with hand-carved wooden chairs and tables, exuded an air of timeless craftsmanship. Alex had long wondered where the university's majestic waterfalls originated, and now, he had discovered the source. He grabbed the rail and followed it all the way around speechless.

Coming out of one, a Giant Beaver, as it looked up to the rock above staring down was a Dire Wolf mounted to the side of the rock waterfalls.

From the ceiling, water cascaded from the ice and rock above, flowing down the walls, enveloping the structure, and gracing the carved patio—a sight that was truly breathtaking. Below, the entirety of the university is stretched out in panoramic splendor.

As Alex and V marveled at their surroundings, Bahdubah emerged with a tray of drinks, his presence as comforting as the morning sun. "Hello there…. How are we faring?" he inquired with a warm smile.

Alex, his worry masked by a grin, replied, "I can't recall a thing from last night. How are you?" Almost stumbling on a chair walking away from the railing, Alex pointed back, "It's____ like the view from up here is incredible."

Bahdubah chuckled, offering them each a glass. "Take this—my special hangover remedy. It'll have you feeling brand new in under five minutes."

V, looking as though she was about to collapse, leaned in and whispered, "What happened? Are we in trouble?"

With a reassuring pat on her hand, Bahdubah replied, "No, you're not in trouble. Relax. Everything is fine. Gig and Fem' will explain why you're here—it's not for me to say."

Just then, Klinchmay waltzed out with a tray of food, humming a cheerful tune. "Good morning, everyone! Happy 2034!" she sang as she set the tray down beside them, then retrieved a couple of boxes from another table.

"These are for you," she announced, unveiling two exquisite silk kimono-style robes. "It's a very special day for the two of you. Gig and Fem' will be out shortly. You missed some fun last night when you left early." V, her curiosity piqued, asked, "What's that?"

Bahdubah and Klinchmay exchanged amused glances. "When you see Declan and Prezzy, ask them," Klinchmay said, laughing. "It's pretty funny—if they remember. Miko and Swaraj had to fish them out of the lake. Something about Prezzy teaching Declan how to surf—naked."

V's face twisted in bewilderment, while Alex couldn't help but smile. Bahdubah and Klinchmay poured them another drink, then busied themselves preparing breakfast before departing. Left alone, Alex and V continued to take in the awe-inspiring view of the entire university, nestled within the glacier's cavernous embrace.

"So, this is the view from up here," V mused, her eyes tracing the vast expanse of ice and rock formations. He said, "The entire glacier. Cavern it's all within the moon."

Alex, captivated by the surroundings, wondered aloud, "How did they find this place?"

He turned to V, who was watching him with a peculiar expression. "What?" he asked, puzzled. "Always trying to figure things out," she teased. "Just enjoy the moment."

He smiled warmly. "When I look at you, that's when I truly enjoy the moment. You are my 'Enjoy.'" V's face lit up with a radiant smile. "That's so sweet—I'm your 'Enjoy.' Wow, that was so special." She leaned in and kissed him softly.

Alex, suddenly contemplative, asked, "Are we going to live here after CAT 6? Then teach the kids for CAT 7? Carry on the history? Are you ready for all of this?"

V, her gaze sweeping over the immense cavern, "So much will happen between now and then. Let's promise each other something."

"What's that?" Alex asked, intrigued. "Let's live our lives and have as much fun as possible along the way. Can we do that?"

With a solemn nod, Alex raised his hand as if taking an oath. "I, Alexander Cooper Katz, swear to Vibrean Padame' Aboli that whatever happens, I will have as much fun as possible and live life to the fullest. Now, your turn."

V mirrored his gesture, lifting her hand. "I, Vibrean Padame' Aboli, swear to Alexander Cooper Katz that whatever happens, I will have fun and live life to the fullest."

As they embraced, Gig and Fem' appeared on the patio, both wearing matching silk robes. With warm smiles, they approached. "Morning," Fem' greeted. "How are we feeling?"

V and Alex moved toward them, V answering, "We're okay—we survived the night."

Gig shook Alex's hand. "Morning, Gig," Alex said.

Gig gestured expansively at the breathtaking surroundings. "What do you think?"

As they all settled into their seats, Gig continued, "When we received our fifth eagle marks, we were invited here, just as you are today."

Alex and V exchanged surprised glances, suddenly realizing the significance of the previous night's events. Alex glanced at the back of V's neck just to make sure. There it was, a fifth Eagle Mark. *"Holy crap,"* Alex thought, *"We have five eagle marks now? Breathe."*

Gig, noticing their shock, chuckled. "We were three years into our schooling when we got ours. And how long have you been here—barely a hundred days?" "One hundred and twenty," Alex responded without hesitation.

Raising his glass, Gig said, "Well, congratulations. No one has ever earned five eagle marks and not become Master Elders. So, it's safe to say—you two will be the next Master Elders. Congratulations."

In stunned silence, Alex and V barely managed to breathe. They raised their glasses in a toast, and Fem' added, "It's incredible to witness this—how the Creator has accelerated your progress so swiftly."

As they sat back, absorbing the news, V admitted, "We had no idea we received the marks last night. The whole evening is a blur."

Alex took a deep breath, his heart pounding as he tried to steady his thoughts. "Thank you so much—it's truly an honor."

V echoed his sentiments, "Yes, thank you. It's an honor."

Fem', holding up two fingers, said, "For now, everything will remain the same. But eventually, your training will diverge from the others. Your time and classes will change because of who you are. That won't happen until your third year."

Alex and V nodded, managing faint smiles. Alex, overwhelmed by the events of the past day and the enormity of what was unfolding, focused on his plate of food. The sounds around the table faded as he stared at his eggs benedict, his vision blurring.

Lost in thought, he recalled his first day at the airport with Harvey, the initial talk about attending this extraordinary university with a unique purpose. Memories of his first meeting with Gig at Teraenti Hall, of V, and of making love to her in the hot tub flooded his mind. He remembered seeing the angel rise from the pool, receiving messages from the Creator, and thinking of his brother. He thought of the Students and their Gifts, the progress they had made, and the harrowing events of the previous day—the Super Flare and the loss of half the population. Who would be the next twelve to undergo the CMB? And now, the staggering realization that he was becoming a Master Elder.

A rush of blood surged to his head, his heart pounded in his chest, and his ears rang. His legs went numb as he reached for the water glass, his mind repeating, *"Take a cool drink of water. Everything will be okay. Just take a cool drink, close your eyes, breathe—slowly. Breathe."*

His vision wavered between clarity and darkness as he tried to steady himself.

Alex strained with all his might, yet his arm refused to obey, locked in a paralyzing grip as he attempted to grasp the glass before him.

His body betrayed him, immobile and unyielding. Gig glanced at them, a smile curling on his lips. "You guys okay?" he asked, his tone light.

Alex, struggling to find his voice, reached across the table and grasped V's hand. He looked at her, then shifted his gaze to Gig and Fem'. A smile flickered across his face though uncertainty gnawed at him. Words eluded him.

Barely managing to open his eyes, Alex turned back to V. "From the day we arrived, we've been driven by a desire to aid the people of this planet and preserve its technology. We comprehend the importance of safeguarding our world's history, as well as the histories of the other five planets. We simply want to become the best Master Elders we can be," he declared, squeezing V's hand with newfound resolve. "What I'm trying to say is, we'll get through the next year and see where it takes us."

V shot him a sharp, almost perplexed look, pulling her hand away. "Be the best Master Elders we can be? Really?"

Alex hesitated, unsure of what had gone awry. "Well…"

V's gaze darted between him, Fem', and Gig. "It's all overwhelming. Do we even have a choice in this?"

Without waiting for a response, V pushed her chair back and walked away.

Alex, feeling a pang of concern, murmured, "Let me talk to her." Gig and Fem' exchanged knowing smiles, gesturing for him to follow.

He approached V cautiously. "Are you okay?" he asked, his voice laced with concern.

V remained silent, her eyes distant. Alex turned his gaze to the sprawling view of the cavern, his thoughts in disarray. "It all hit me at once," he admitted.

"I couldn't think straight. I felt like I was going to pass out. My ears were ringing, and all the chaos we've faced here rushed through my mind at the same time. My entire body went numb. I couldn't even reach for a glass of water."

V looked at him, placing a hand on his shoulder. "No, I'm not okay," she confessed, her voice steady. "But I will be. Just give me some space." She gave him a look—one that carried a weight he could hardly decipher. "Be the best Master Elder you can be? That's something... I don't know."

Alex shrugged helplessly, and V offered a faint smile. "Just give me a minute. Okay?" She gave him a look that spoke volumes, one he'd seen her reserve only for her parents. Taking the hint, Alex returned to the table, finally taking that long-desired sip of water. He looked up at Gig and Fem' with a weary smile.

Gig smiled back, his curiosity piqued. "Is she okay?"

Alex returned the smile but subtly shook his head. "Yeah, I think so," he said, though his eyes betrayed doubt. "She just needs... She's like a tiger with a thorn."

Gig chuckled softly while Fem' rose from her seat. "I'll go check on her," she said, walking over to where V stood.

Gig leaned back, reminiscing. "I remember that day. It was a long time ago—four thousand, four hundred years ago."

Alex let out a weary sigh. "Pffff. Just hearing that makes everything seem off-kilter."

Gig's smile broadened. "Let's change the subject to something that might pique your interest. There's something I've been meaning to share with you. Let's take a walk."

Alex hesitated. "Can I bring my water?"

Gig chuckled again, nodding as they both stood. They began to walk towards the main entrance of the Residence. As they passed through the grand archway, Alex's eyes fell upon two stone models of magnificent cities. Gig gestured to the one on the right. "This," he said, "is Atlantica, or as you know it, Atlantis. My great-great-grandmother's sisters designed the sewage system. The one on the left is Mammotaious, a city that once thrived in North America, near the Atlantic Ocean and the Gulf of America. These were the most populous cities of our time. What I wanted to discuss with you is the nature of our society back then. We had a monetary system, much like today."

"But after hearing what I'm about to say, you might ask how we can return to such a state. I'll tell you now: I have no idea. No one does, but I hope to hear your thoughts on the matter someday."

Gig's tone grew thoughtful as he continued. "Our society was driven by a pursuit of greatness, not power or profit. Men and women are created out of a desire for excellence, not for possession. Theft and murder were virtually nonexistent due to the shame associated with such acts. Wars were unheard of. If one committed such a transgression, they were shunned from the community, losing everything they had. There was no return from such disgrace. These values were instilled from birth and taught by parents from the earliest age. Many in my family were creators of great things, entrusted with responsibilities like building and engineering grand structures. Others ran small businesses. Education focused on trades, while family life centered around bettering the family's standing."

"In today's world, however, I see very little in the way of true mind and body development. Schools are lost or misleading, and parents struggle to nurture their children's minds. I believe that's why the suns are all on a timely reset."

"The Creator has designed it this way," Gig mused. "Has he set our clock on a 4,400-year cycle? Perhaps. It's just a theory of mine. The moment your people discovered gunpowder—the bullet, the machine gun, the bomb—everything changed. Consider how nuclear weapons altered this civilization. I just wanted you to understand the importance of studying and investigating past cultures. Mine, I believe, was better in many ways. Some were far worse than today."

Alex, curious, asked, "But your society had the intervention of the Common Mind in public life, right?"

Gig nodded. "Yes, we did have some who were connected to the Common Mind, but they were few—only a handful across the entire planet. I wasn't even aware of them until I attended university. They were revered as god-like beings."

"They didn't interact with the public in the way you might think. It was more of a spiritual connection, akin to what your group experiences in a CMB. That's how they interacted."

Alex pondered this. "Are there others out there? Not from the six planets, but different from us?"

Gig smiled, a hint of mystery in his eyes. "Real aliens? Different dimensions? That's a whole other discussion. There's a group that meets on Amotaious—you could meet with them after you graduate if you're interested. As for myself, I don't get too involved in such matters unless they directly impact us. When I can shake the hand of one of them, then I'll start paying attention. Until then, it's not worth my time."

Fem' and V entered the room, their eyes meeting Alex's with a shared smile. Fem', her voice laced with gravity, was saying, "You and the other Students must start thinking in terms of centuries, not decades. Now that you possess the Common Mind and your Gifts, your lifespan will extend far beyond the ordinary, whether you desire it or not. You must come to terms with this reality; it will take time, but it's essential."

With a tender gesture, Fem' kissed Gig before continuing, "I must confess how arduous our journey was."

"Witnessing the downfall of our civilization, enduring endless years on Amotaious without returning home—it was grueling. Without the support of those on Amotaious, we could not have survived. I still marvel at how they managed before us. Their culture was even more fractured than ours and certainly worse than the world today."

Gig interjected gently, "Alright, that's enough, Fem'. We don't want to overwhelm them. Today is meant to be a celebration. Let's show them the rest of the residence."

As they stepped into the grand entranceway, V's gaze was drawn to two colossal models, each towering over ten feet and spanning thirty feet in diameter. "How long have you been here before us or before the Stewards arrived?" V inquired, curiosity piqued.

"Our primary residence is on Amotaious," Fem' replied. "Before the Stewards came, we visited three or four times a year to maintain records and update the staff. You'll learn all about your responsibilities in your third year."

Alex, captivated by the array of artwork and sculptures surrounding him, murmured, "I had no idea this was here. These must be the finest rooms in the university."

Gig and Fem' exchanged knowing smiles as they led them further into the main chamber, which suddenly opened up to a vast, ceilingless expanse. The room was a marvel—one half gleamed with the smooth, white clamshell walls, while the other was a masterpiece of hand-carved wood, with intricate cabinets and paneled walls.

It appeared to be the main gathering space. As Alex looked upward, he could see areas of the cavern that had been skillfully carved into bookcases and storage spaces, interspersed with untouched sections of natural rock.

Passing through another archway, they entered a library—a room entirely crafted from wood, from the floor to the ceiling, including the bookcases. The warmth of the wood contrasted with the cool, tiled floors of the master bedroom and bath, where plush rugs softened the stone. Fem' and Gig had decorated the space with fur bed coverings, portraits of relatives, and a conspicuous absence of modern items—save for the metal fixtures on the toilets and showers.

"We brought you here to show you this," Gig said, his tone both proud and serious. "It's a tradition, and it's crucial that you begin to anticipate it as part of your future."

Fem' added, her voice tinged with empathy, "It's a lot to absorb. We had more time, more preparation, more understanding, more training."

"So, we can't fully comprehend what you're going through. But remember this—we're here to help. If you have questions or concerns, don't hesitate to reach out. We aren't going anywhere, and there are many here to support you. Klinchmay and Bahdubah are already aware, so that you can talk to them anytime, and you're welcome to start planning your space whenever you're ready."

V, with a mix of gratitude and defiance, responded, "We won't be doing that just yet, but this place is truly extraordinary. We're incredibly grateful and honored. Thank you."

V embraced Gig and Fem', while Alex followed suit, hugging Fem' and shaking Gig's hand. "Thank you both so much," he echoed.

Gig smiled warmly, "Once again, congratulations."

Feeling more at ease, Alex remarked, "We'll get through the next six months, save as many as we can, along with the technology—that will be a great accomplishment. What intrigues me is what comes next. Why is the Creator orchestrating all of this? What's the purpose behind it?"

Raising his finger thoughtfully, Alex concluded, "That's the big question, at least in my opinion."

V, casting an affectionate glance at Gig and Fem', teased, "See? He can never stop. We haven't even completed the first mission, and he's already strategizing for the second and third."

Gig and Fem' chuckled, their faces alight with approval. "You two are going to make outstanding Master Elders," Gig said. "Let me know what you think about that other matter, Alex. Now, off with you."

As Alex and V departed the residence and returned to the common room, they were met with a joyful surprise. The entire group was there, waiting for them. Gig had informed Bahdubah and Klinchme' of the great news earlier, and they had rallied the Students. As Alex and V entered, the room erupted in applause, with everyone bowing in respect.

Declan approached with a congratulatory high-five, grinning. "The new Master Elders. How does it feel?"

Alex, still processing the shock, replied, "It was unexpected. Gig woke us up, and over breakfast, they just announced it. I think I nearly had a nervous breakdown or something."

The others swarmed him with congratulations, heightening his nervousness and discomfort. Turning to Declan, Alex pleaded, "Could you get me a beer or something?"

Understanding, Declan fetched him a beer and guided him away from the crowd. "You look a bit stressed, mate. Let's sit over here."

They settled on a couch by the window archway overlooking the lake, and Declan asked gently, "How are you feeling?"

Alex exhaled, "It was overwhelming. Everything hit me at once—from what Harvey told me at the airport to everything that's happened here. I couldn't breathe."

Declan nodded thoughtfully, "Sounds like a panic attack."

Alex continued, "And V freaked out too. She was like, 'What if I don't want to do this? Do I have a choice?' It was making me even more anxious."

Declan chuckled, "She was just panicking. Out of everyone here, she's the best for the job. She just didn't realize it at the moment. She's perfect for this, and so are you. You two will figure it out. It's just a lot to process, that's all."

Alex managed a smile. "I guess so."

"So, tell me," Declan prompted, "what was the residence like? Was it cool?"

Perking up, Alex described, "Of all the places we've seen, it's the best. The view is spectacular, overlooking everything, with all the waterfalls originating there. There are enormous models of Atlantis and Amotaious. The rest of the residence is incredible. Gig mentioned that their society had a Common Mind and no monetary system, at least not like ours."

"It was built on different principles, with people driven by a unique sense of morality. It's like how things are on Amotaious today, I suppose."

Declan inquires, "You mean the way governments orchestrated society?"

Alex nods, replying, "Yes, everything—from how you were raised and educated to the very fabric of family structure and lifestyle choices. He didn't delve deeply, but it's something we'll need to investigate further. He mused that perhaps that's why the sun has a clock—to reset civilizations every four thousand years."

Declan reflects, "It's intriguing to consider it that way. Our civilization has been mired in chaos for millennia, driven by power and greed. Imagine how different the world might be if, instead of conflict, all nations had united with a shared purpose. What might our world look like? We are progressing, though."

Alex, trying to remain optimistic, responds, "I suppose we'll see within the next century, won't we?"

Declan then asks, "So, which cities will you and V choose to replicate in model form? That's something you should start considering."

Alex grins, "That's a good point. I should have Rev, and Mod captured detailed images of all the major cities. Then the twelve of us could decide which two to model." He chuckles, "Speaking of which, what's this I hear about you and Prezzy? Something about surfing in the pond last night—without clothes?"

Declan, smirking, replies, "I only recall fragments. Prezzy wanted to teach me how to surf, and the next thing I knew, Miko was dragging me out of the pond, both of us stark naked. I woke up in Swaraj's room with the three of them. So, it was quite an eventful night. We somehow managed to relocate Prezzy's bed into Swaraj's room. A very productive evening, indeed."

Alex laughs, "Wow, sounds like New Year's Eve tends to spiral out of control, no matter where we are. Haven't you been hoping for something like this to happen?"

Declan frowns slightly, "Yes, I just wish I could remember more of it." The two laugh heartily.

Bahdubah then commands the room's attention, raising a glass, "Let's toast to our new Master Elders of CAT 6! Congratulations, Alex and V, on a job well done. We stand with you every step of the way. Whatever you need, we're here for you. Cheers!" The room erupts in toasts and celebration.

After some time, Alex and V retreat to their quarters, seeking rest and solace amidst the excitement.

For the next forty-eight days, the Students immerse themselves in classes. They find joy on the moon's surface, riding buggies and exploring. They also complete their emergency security training. Despite being only about fifteen percent through their university curriculum, nothing noteworthy occurs. However, Alex and V grow closer, their bond deepening as they navigate their journey together.

Now, fast-forwarding to the day of the next Pulse Reversal, Alex has more than an inkling of what lies ahead. The Students and Elders brace themselves, hoping it's not the dreaded Super Flare. But Alex's vision, as revealed by the Creator, suggests otherwise.

Meanwhile, Fem' collaborates with Lin, Maria, and Prezzy to plan a grand event.

XXIX

To their astonishment, Max Jr. stood beside V's grandmother, Saanvi, both occupying Alex's chair. The figures flickered, phasing in and out, their voices overlapping in a chaotic, unintelligible cadence.

V and Alex exchanged bewildered glances, their expressions mirroring a shared confusion. They quickly sat up in bed, and V, exasperated, raised her voice. "Hey! Hello?"

At her outburst, Max Jr. and Saanvi halted their speech, their forms stabilizing. V, now accustomed to these surreal encounters, smiled. "Did you want to tell us something?"

The apparitions returned her smile. Saanvi spoke first, her tone gentle yet solemn. "We came to wish you good luck, to ensure you're prepared, and to deliver a message from the Creator. Congratulations on becoming the new Master Elders."

V's smile broadened, her anxiety easing. "Thank you. We feel much more confident now. We're ready for the next test. It's wonderful to see you both after so long. What's the message?"

Max Jr. stepped forward, his grin widening as he began to speak. "The Creator is deeply impressed with both of you, which is why you've received your fifth eagle marks. He's arranged something special just for you."

Their smiles grew unnervingly wide as they simultaneously declared, "You will now be able to contact the Creator whenever you wish!"

Alex and V shared a concerned look, their earlier relief now tinged with unease. Saanvi's gaze settled on V. "You must keep this stone, here on the table, with you at all times."

They both glanced down at the table, where a small crystal stone streaked with violet rested. It was compact, fitting snugly into the palm of a hand. Saanvi continued, "When you wish to make contact, follow these instructions. Please stand."

Nervously, Alex and V rose from the bed, standing together in the center of the room.

"Alex," Saanvi instructed, "place your left hand over V's left hand, holding the stone. V, place your other hand on top of Alex's, and Alex, place your remaining hand on top of V's."

As they complied, the images of Max and Saanvi began to waver, flickering in and out. Max's voice resonated, "Now, V, recite these words: 'Ooh! Raba Rashi! De-Vibrean, De-Alex! Cama See La Ruh! Taraenti! Ooh! Raba Rashi! Que! Pertenti! Ooh, Yahyeah! Raba Rashi! Tanka! Pat!' Shortly after, one or both of us will appear."

V, trying to keep her composure, reached for her tablet. "I need to write this down," she said, smiling nervously at Alex. Internally, she marveled at the absurdity of the situation. *"I can't believe this. It's insane."*

Alex, still processing, asked, "What do you mean by 'short time'?"

Max's form shimmered as he replied, "When the Creator wishes to respond. Remember, He knows your thoughts."

Alex lowered his hands, searching Max's eyes. "Is there anything else we need to know about today?"

Max's voice softened as his image faded slightly. "Ensure that Gig and Fem' say a prayer before you depart. This will guarantee the additional Gift when you need to make contact."

They both shimmered in and out once more. Max's final words echoed, "Today is the day. Stay the course, Alex. Love you, mate."

Saanvi's voice followed, her tone warm and reassuring. "V, you are more than capable. You are the key to the future. You will get it done. Love you, sister."

With those words, their images dissipated, vanishing in a misty puff of smoke.

V and Alex stared at each other, the gravity of their new abilities weighing heavily on them. Alex broke the silence. "So, we can now communicate directly with the Creator. Should we tell anyone about this?"

V, busy moving her backpack onto the bed, shook her head. "I don't know, but for now, I'd say no. Let's just get through today and see what lies on the other side."

As Alex helped her prepare, he muttered, "It's probably a good thing, I suppose."

V smiled, her expression tinged with apprehension. "Sure, now we can talk to God. Who wouldn't want that?"

Alex remained silent, lost in thought, while V's mind raced. *"What did she mean by 'I'm the key?' Damn! I'm losing it. I need to focus on the test, not on talking to God. Jeez! What's happening in my life?"* She laughed aloud, her voice tinged with hysteria. *"I'm going to lose my mind!"*

Alex, noticing her outburst, asked, "Something funny?" V glanced at him as she finished packing, a strained smile on her lips. "No, just thinking about everything."

Alex, now standing in the doorway, nodded. "I get it. I'll grab my bags. Be right back."

V looked up, "Okay."

As they continued to get ready, they eventually joined the rest of the team down at the docks. Most of the group had already gathered. V approached Fem', "Are we going to say a prayer before we leave?"

Fem' smiled warmly, "That's a great idea. I'll let Gig know."

V returned to Alex, who was looking slightly nervous. "Okay, the prayer is all set."

Alex nodded, "Good." He glanced at her, his tension palpable. "I think we've covered everything."

V, her expression resolute, replied, "We've gone over it a hundred times. We're ready."

Mod and Rev approached with purposeful strides. Mod spoke first, "We've secured all the additional supplies you requested, along with a few extras, just in case. Alex, as per our discussion, I've briefed everyone involved. All preparations are confirmed, and all personnel have checked in. Those specific ones you mentioned? They were as difficult as you predicted."

V's brow furrowed in confusion. "What's that about?"

Alex shot Mod a stern look before turning back to V with a reassuring smile. "It's nothing, really. I'll explain later today. Just put it out of your mind for now."

V's thoughts churned. *What is he hiding from me? I know he's keeping secrets—probably getting messages from the Creator without telling me. Or maybe he's seen something in the future and isn't sharing it. What could he be up to? And now, we can speak directly to God. What's next? This is all madness. Am I going insane? No, we're all going insane.*

V managed a smile. "Fine, but you'd better tell me later. It doesn't sound like 'nothing.'" She turned on her heel, heading off to find Fem' for the prayer.

A few minutes later, the entire group stood ready to board the ships. Declan's sharp whistle cut through the morning air, capturing everyone's attention as Gig stepped forward to address the group. "Alright, everyone. The CAT has never occurred on the fourth Pulse Reversal. If it happens today, we must be fully prepared. Is everyone ready? Team North?"

V raised her clipboard and tablet, her voice steady but subdued. "Team North, ready."

Gig's expression soured slightly. "Look, I know it's 6 a.m., but could we muster a bit more enthusiasm?"

Prezzy started bouncing on her toes, clapping her hands as others joined in. "Team North, ready!" she shouted, grinning widely.

Laughter rippled through the group, and Gig cleared his throat, his voice rising with renewed energy. "Okay, once again, our mission today is nothing short of monumental. We're here to save an entire planet—its people, its technology, its creatures—all of it. When Fem' and I last faced this, we watched our entire world regress by thousands of years. Today, our goal, with the Creator's guidance, is to limit that setback to just a couple of centuries. So, I ask you—CAN WE DO IT?"

The group roared back, "YES, WE CAN! YES WE CAN!"

Gig pressed on, his voice booming, "TEAM NORTH, ARE YOU READY?"

V, Alex, the other ten Students, their twelve Stewards, and the selected Elders from Team North responded in unison, "TEAM NORTH READY! WE ARE READY, YES WE CAN!"

Gig's gaze swept over the crowd. "TEAM SOUTH, ARE YOU READY?"

Team South's response was just as fervent, "TEAM SOUTH IS READY! YES, WE CAN!"

Gig and Fem' exchanged a look, smiling and laughing with a level of emotion they rarely displayed. The sight was inspiring. Gig turned to the smaller group. "Team Lab, are you ready?"

The six members of Team Lab responded with a more subdued but still determined, "TEAM LAB READY!"

Chuckles spread through the crowd. Gig's voice softened as he delivered the final part of his speech. "I just want to say how proud I am to be part of this incredible team. Today, we remake history. Today, humanity won't have to start over from scratch. Today, a young group of Students has dared to defy the inevitable, to say, 'No! We won't allow it.' Today, we will execute the Creator's plan to avert disaster and save humanity. Today is the day!"

His voice dropped to a near whisper, "Of course, today is just the test—we hope."

Prezzy, unable to contain his excitement, yelled out, "Today is the day!" Others echoed his enthusiasm as anticipation electrified the air.

Fem' steps forward, her voice resolute as she declares, "Now it's time for a prayer. Let us seek His wisdom, strength, and compassion, and ask for the grace to accept the outcomes of today and the days that follow." Her gaze shifts to Gig, and she whispers with a hint of trepidation, "Let's hope this remains just another test."

Gig, with a deliberate motion, slams the rock onto the floor. Immediately, the stone in Fem's hand begins to glow with an ethereal light.

"Ooh! Raba Rashi! Naash! Ooh, Raba Rashi! Cama See La Ruh!" Fem' chants with fervor, the ancient words resonating through the room. "Teraenti, Prepa, Comensi Cata! Terraenti Technolosua Ooh! Pupa, Stu, Eldas, All Eldas! Norda, Souda! Shanka, Fem'a Da Giga! Handa, Putta Keepa, Kashanka! Pat!"

As the prayer unfolds, the room responds in kind. The lights dim, casting elongated shadows, while the stone in Fem's grasp brightens, radiating warmth.

The air stirs, swirling around the room with a gentle yet noticeable force, causing the papers on V's clipboard to rustle. A sound reminiscent of heavenly thunder reverberates through the docks. Gig slams the rock once more, and the stone's glow intensifies. Suddenly, a blue-violet arrow of light shoots upward, nearing the ceiling before snapping with a crack, sending countless luminous arrows cascading down, passing gently through each person in the docks before retreating back into the stone.

For V, the sensation was almost familiar—an electrifying jolt coursed through her, followed by a lingering euphoria. But this time, something was different. Her right hand throbbed with a new, searing sensation reminiscent of that first night when she felt the burn on her neck. She glanced down at her palm and gasped. There it was—the infinity symbol, now indelibly tattooed into her flesh. She looked up, catching sight of Alex approaching her.

"Did you feel that?" Alex asked concern etched on his face. V instinctively grabbed his right hand; she felt the cold of his three mechanical fingers. No symbol. Then she took his left hand, and there it was—the same infinity mark.

"Yes, I felt it," V replied, her fingers gently tracing the symbol. She looked around cautiously before whispering, "That's why they had Fem lead the prayer. The infinity symbol—it must be necessary, along with the stone." She pulled Alex aside, seeking more privacy. "You realize they never told us whether we're supposed to reveal that we can communicate with the Creator. What the hell is going on?"

Alex sighed his brow furrowing in thought. "Let's keep it to ourselves for now. We have too much on our plate today. Why would they spring this on us now? What's He trying to do to us? Or… what if it's a She?"

V muttered something in Hindi, her frustration evident. "We have enough to worry about right now. Let's just survive today. We can deal with contacting the Creator tomorrow. If we make it to tomorrow."

Alex, taken aback by her ominous tone, grabbed her by the shoulders. "What do you mean? Of course, we'll make it to tomorrow. I'm certain of it."

She fixed him with a disapproving look. "I know you're hiding things from me, from everyone."

Alex, bewildered, defended himself. "I'm not hiding anything. Everything I've seen or seen by, or been told by my brother."

"I've always been outright in things all the time. You and the others know that I'm a truthful guy. You know, if the Creator told me something to tell you all, I would have told you and Gig. I love you so much." Alex is trying to hug her.

V's frustration deepened. "See, that didn't even make sense. What are you trying to say?"

Alex chuckled, attempting to diffuse the tension. "Let's just focus on today, alright? You're being silly." He playfully nudged her shoulder. "You're a silly person. I don't even remember the last time they contacted me except for this morning. Like Gig said, let's concentrate on today." He looked away, then back to her. "I need to tell Rev something before we go."

V shot him a glare as she walked away, muttering, "You're an asshole. Asshole."

The group boarded the ships, and after a three-hour journey, their vessel touched down on the northern magnetic pole. They quickly set about unloading the equipment, their breath visible in the freezing air. The early departure had been necessary—they only had a few hours of daylight left, and the sheer volume of equipment demanded swift and efficient work. This time, Alex, V, and the others had ensured they were well-prepared, with Mod and Rev supplying them with days' worth of provisions rather than mere hours. Alex had been adamant about it.

As the ship departed, leaving them isolated in the stark wilderness, the crates were stacked against the tent walls, forming a makeshift barrier.

Four countdown clocks and four percent meters were mounted on each wall, their numbers ticking down with an unsettling finality. Two large heaters roared in the tent's center, providing some respite from the biting cold.

Finally, with the interior set up, V, Miko, Lev, Kyoryk, and Alex stood outside the tent, the night now fully descended. The wind had calmed, leaving a tense silence in its wake. Despite the familiarity of the task, the group remained on edge.

Kyoryk broke the silence, "We have about an hour until the *Utbrott Av Eos* hits."

Lev looked at him, confused. "What?"

Miko quickly clarified, "The Pulse Reversal. The Super Flare—that's what he calls it."

Declan emerged from the tent, eyeing the stacks of supplies. "Dude, do you think we have enough? Looks like we're prepped for a month or two. And why all the extra tent poles?"

Alex, maintaining his calm demeanor, replied, "Better to be over-prepared than caught off guard. The ship might have to wait a day or two before returning."

Lev, with a hint of apprehension, asked, "So, you think this time it could be the real thing?"

Kyoryk, ever the pragmatist, shrugged. "The odds are one in ninety, according to past history. So probably not."

Alex, growing agitated, snapped, "We need to be ready, no matter what. If we're not mentally prepared, we could lose focus at the last minute. Once the lab calls us, we'll have eight minutes. They'll make the call, and we'll know."

V gently wrapped her arm around him; her touch meant to calm. "You're right, Alex. We must be prepared for the worst."

Kyoryk interjected, "We actually have a little more time. But you're right; once the lab sees what happens in the sun, they'll alert us, and we'll have a couple more minutes than them. If it's the Super Flare, it'll take days for the planet to stabilize enough for our ships to re-enter the atmosphere. The electric storms alone will be severe. Luckily, we're in a spot that shouldn't be too bad. The Southern Team will be hit harder, and the middle of the planet will take the worst of it."

Miko's face turned pale. "So, the CAT could hit today?"

V nodded, her expression serious. "That's exactly what Alex is saying. We've prepared for this. That's why we added all the extra supplies. If it happens, we're ready. No need to worry." Miko, still unsettled, retreated into the tent.

Declan offered a reassuring smile. "She'll be fine. I've been trying to tell her anything could happen. Look at the planet's history—thousands of years, so many disasters."

Kyoryk added, "We're supposed to think in centuries now, not just years, right? Our lives have changed, but we'll be okay. In a few days, we'll be talking about this over a couple of beers. One way or another, we'll make it through."

Lev, now visibly discouraged, muttered, "Can we talk about something else? What's the temperature out here?" "Twenty," Kyoryk replied.

"Twenty?" V echoed. "Negative twenty," Kyoryk clarified.

V sighed. "At least it's not as windy as last time."

"True, wind chill is brutal. I need to run some tests," Kyoryk said, turning to head back inside. V offered a final reassurance. "We'll be fine. See you in there."

As Kyoryk and Lev reentered the tent, Prezzy and Lin joined Alex, V, and Declan outside.

Prezzy squinted into the darkness. "What's going on out here?"

V asked, "How's everyone doing in there?"

Lin smiled. "Better than last time. Everyone knows what to do."

V, her eyes lighting up, inquired, "I haven't asked lately—how's the big event planning going? Have you been working with Fem' and Fair on the party?"

Lin and Prezzy exchanged grins. "Yes," Lin replied, drawing out the word. "It's all hush-hush for now. I showed you guys the Kall band. Now, I've got the Vindor's video—I can show it to you later. We need to start working on our part soon. If things are happening now, the event will be on the first Friday of March."

V raised an excited brow. "Wow, sounds like it's going to be fun."

Lin's eyes twinkled with excitement. "It's going to be huge. All of Amotaious will attend, and all the Elders from all six planets—close to 100,000 people. We've been coordinating with them over the last few weeks. It's interesting to see how the other planets like to party. Vindor and Kall are all set with their opening tunes."

Alex, lost in thought, mused aloud, "I was thinking in the library the other night—what if the Creator gave consciousness to different animals on each of the six planets? Like, on our planet, it's apes or chimps, and on Vindor, it's eagles, or on Vattan, maybe fish or dolphins. What do you think?"

Declan's jaw dropped in astonishment while V pulled Alex aside and whispered excitedly, "I know what we're going to ask the Creator—that could be one of our first questions. You're a genius!" She hugged him tightly, kissed him, and then led him back to the group.

V addressed the group, "What do you think? Is Alex onto something?"

Lev, his mind racing, speculated, "Do you think Gig and Fem' know about this? Wouldn't it be wild if consciousness was given to different species just to kickstart technology? That's insane."

Declan chimed in, "Maybe it's all a game to the Creator. And who is the Creator, anyway? An alien? A single entity or a collective? Maybe the Creator made all the animals and planets too. It's all too perfect."

Lin, with a mischievous grin, suggested, "We should take some psychedelics and figure it out."

Prezzy, bouncing with excitement, exclaimed, "I don't think mushrooms do that, but I'm willing to try! I saw some in the pantry. I'm sure they used them in the past to figure some things out. Maybe?"

Laughter erupted among the group. Harvey poked his head out of the tent, smirking. "You all need to come in soon."

Alex called out, "Hey, Harvey, did the Creator give different mammals consciousness on six different planets to procreate and build technology?"

Harvey shook his head with a smile. "You're thinking about this now? Let's discuss it tomorrow. Good question, but save it for later. Now, get your butts in here." The group, still chuckling, headed back into the tent.

As they walked, Declan asked Prezzy, "Where exactly did you see the magic mushrooms in the pantry?"

Meanwhile, V approached Kyoryk. "How's everything?"

Kyoryk, ever diligent, replied, "We need to get ready now. I'm set—all communication lines are active, and the monitors are working."

V turned to Ty'mmie' and Klinchme'. "You two ready?"

Klinchme' nodded, and Ty'mmie' responded, "Ready to go. Why isn't Rev here this time?"

"Rev and Mod are on Amotaious, just like the Master Elders," V explained. "Just in case."

V's tone grew serious as she addressed them both. "If this is the real thing, we have to keep going, no matter what. Whatever you hear, whatever you see, whatever happens—you keep going. Understood?" They both nodded solemnly.

V gave Ty'mmie' a final look, placing a firm hand on her shoulder. "It could get rough. You have an enclosure now. I want you in there as soon as we hit 75%. Got it?" Ty'mmie' nodded again, resolute. "Yes, got it."

Alex strides over to V, locking eyes with her. "So, who's giving the speech this time? You or me?"

V grins, "I handled it last time. The honor's all yours now."

With a smirk, Alex leans in and plants a kiss on her lips. "Alright then, I'll take a shot at it. Love you." "Love you too," she replies, her smile radiating warmth.

Turning to Kyoryk, Alex asks, "Kyoryk, are we set? Ready to go?" Kyoryk, his gaze fixed on the monitor, gives a thumbs up. "Yes, we're good to go. We should join the group soon."

Alex signals to Declan, who promptly whistles to gather everyone's attention. "Ladies and gentlemen," Alex announces, his voice carrying authority, "In just a moment, we'll form up like last time. Swaraj, Declan, V, and I will take our positions around the Accelerator. The rest of you align yourselves in the infinity symbol. This might actually be the CAT, so if that happens, listen only to Ty'mmie'. Her voice will guide us. After Ty'mmie', the next voices should be the four of us at the Accelerator, followed by the lab on the radio. As we approach one hundred percent or beyond, trust your instincts within the CMB. If this is indeed the CAT, it could shake the tent, create unnerving noises, and rattle all of us. Stay calm, stay bonded, and focus on the group. In the worst case, concentrate on V—she'll guide us if necessary, and she'll signal what needs to be done. You might not even notice it, but stay focused, and we'll get through this."

"Today, we're pushing the Accelerator to its limit. Regarding your protective gear—under no circumstances should you remove it until V or I give the all-clear."

"Cosmic rays will persist long after the event, so keep your gear on until instructed otherwise. That includes glasses and ear protection. Does everyone understand?" Alex scans the tent, ensuring everyone's attention is locked on him. "If you can't hear Ty'mmie', keep an eye on the monitors around the room. Pay attention to the percentage indicators: if the LEDs are off, increase power; if they're on, decrease it. The timer is set for startup and ramp-down. Expect it to get very loud and very hot. If this is the CAT, it could stir up a storm outside. Whatever happens, stay focused— think about all the lives we're saving."

"Consider the years of technology we're safeguarding. Take a deep breath," Alex pauses, a smile touching his lips, "If this is it, Lin, Maria, Prezzy, Fem', Fair and the others have a big celebration planned for us back on Amotaious. So, let's nail this, head back, and enjoy the fruits of our labor. The Creator is with us—let's do this."

With a glance at the countdown clock, Alex announces, "Two minutes. Let's hold hands." The group quietly begins to assemble, Kyoryk breaking free from his conversation with Ty'mmie' and the Lab to join them. Gig, Fem', and others had already departed for Amotaious, as planned.

Doog and Fair are in the lab, coordinating with the North and South Teams. Ty'mmie' increases the volume for everyone to hear Doog's voice over the radio. "One minute to go for the pre-test," Doog announces. Both groups fall silent; the only sound is the crackling static of the radio. "We have about 2-3 minutes before we know. Let's ramp up to 50% and run tests with both groups. Everyone okay with that?"

Ty'mmie' glances at Alex, who nods in approval. She relays, "Okay!" The Southern Team echoes, "Okay!"

"Let's start," Ty'mmie' commands.

"Swaraj," Alex instructs, "center the core. Miko, once it's centered, Declan, begin the spin."

Swaraj and Declan focus intensely while Miko watches the Accelerator's core. After a few tense seconds, Miko confirms, "Babe, it's centered. Go ahead."

Alex flashes Miko a reassuring smile. "Nothing yet," Ty'mmie' reports, her tone steady.

"Give it a second," Declan advises, his voice calm. The group collectively concentrates, their energy converging on the task.

"Alright, everyone," Alex guides, "slowly focus on the four of us here at the Accelerator. Align your minds with ours—our thoughts, our emotions, our focus. Follow our energy."

"5%," Ty'mmie' suddenly shouts, jolting everyone.

Alex opens his eyes, glancing at the meter on the wall before locking eyes with Ty'mmie'. He smiles, the hum of the Accelerator growing louder. "15%," Ty'mmie' announces a minute later.

"Great progress, everyone. Let's push it up to 50%," Alex encourages.

The Accelerator's hum deepens, escalating to a sharp whistle reminiscent of a horn. "40%. The countdown clock reads 2 minutes till P.R.," Ty'mmie' updates.

"Let's bring it up to 50% and hold," Alex commands.

Over the radio, Doog's voice crackles through, "Northern Team, increase by 10 and hold, please."

"Roger that, Mr. Doog," Ty'mmie' responds, her tone crisp.

A few seconds later, Doog instructs, "Both teams, hold there. Take a breath. We'll maintain this level for a minute. Ninety seconds till P.R."

The group relaxes momentarily, opening their eyes and glancing around. The percentage drops slightly but stays above 45%. The Accelerator hums steadily, its whistle constant.

"50 seconds, hold," Doog orders. Everyone seems calm. Alex catches V's eye and winks, offering a small gesture of reassurance.

But as the seconds tick by, "Alarms" suddenly blare in the lab—sounds unfamiliar to most. V's thoughts, briefly soothed by Alex's wink, are abruptly washed away by concern. Her expression shifts to worry as she silently mouths, "What is it?" Alex mouths back, "It's going to be okay."

The concentration of both teams falters, causing the percentage meter to plummet to 30%.

"Alright, everyone, focus," Alex urges. "Let's bring it back up to 50%—we're at 30%." The group, in their haste, overshoots to 70%, forcing Alex to calm them quickly. "Listen up, everyone. We don't know what's happening yet. Let's stay calm and hold here until we hear back from Doog. Ty'mmie', ask Doog for a status report, please."

Ty'mmie' relays the request, her voice steady. "Mr. Doog, Alex would like a status report."

Doog's voice comes through the radio, tinged with nerves. "To both teams, we have a Super Flare. I repeat, we have a Super Flare. We're calculating time and strength. Sorry, give me a second. Turn off that damn alarm!"

Alex, striving to maintain composure, addresses the group. "Everyone, stay calm. We'll hold at 60% until further notice. Follow my lead—take a few deep breaths, in through your nose, out through your mouth. Ready? Now, in through your nose, out through your mouth. Slowly... continue."

Doog's voice crackles over the radio, "Alright, I've reset the clocks and recalculated the percentages. Based on our new calculations and what we believe the Accelerators can endure, we need to push them beyond 175% in precisely 520 seconds. Ty'mmie', Merl, confirm that the countdown clocks are now reflecting the adjustments."

Ty'mmie' promptly responds, looking up, her voice steady, "Yes, it's displayed."

Kyoryk exchanges a glance with Alex, both seeking and offering reassurance. They had meticulously reviewed the numbers countless times, and Alex was certain that the Accelerators could, in theory, reach anywhere between 250 to 300% if needed.

What they couldn't predict was the impact on the planet or the fate of the 37 individuals huddled inside the tent.

The alarms abruptly silence on the radio, and Doog's voice cuts through, "Did everyone hear that?"

Ty'mmie', her expression tight with worry, turns to Alex. "Did you catch that, Alex?"

Alex nods, maintaining a calm exterior. "Yes, inform Doog that we're set and ready to proceed."

Ty'mmie' clicks the mic, her tone professional, "Mr. Doog, Roger that. We've received your message, and we're ready to go."

Alex takes a deep breath, surveying the tense faces around him. "Alright, everyone, let's dial it down to 30% so we can hear each other clearly. Ty'mmie', let Doog know." As Ty'mmie' relays the message, Alex notices her safety glasses are missing. "Ty'mmie', please put your glasses on."

He exhales slowly, his gaze shifting to the LED displays: 480 seconds, 35%. "This is it, everyone. We can do this. Stay in formation and focus within the CMB. The Accelerators are robust; they can handle it, and so can we."

He locks eyes with Kyoryk, almost as if seeking validation, then adds, "It's going to get very loud and very hot in here. Is everyone alright?"

Ty'mmie' interjects, "Alex, Doog wants to make an announcement."

"Go ahead," Alex replies.

The radio clicks a few times as voices murmur in the background. Fair's voice comes through, "Doog is okay with holding at 30% until 200 seconds, then ramping up by 10% every 10 seconds.

That way, if we lose radio contact, both teams can stay on the same page. Does everyone understand?"

Alex, hearing every word, affirms, "Yes. Ty'mmie', tell Gig we understand and will follow the plan."

Ty'mmie' clicks the mic, "Roger, Mr. Doog. We understand. We'll commence at 200 seconds." Alex glances around at the Students and Stewards; they look composed, though some seem apprehensive. His eyes then shift to the 12 Elder volunteers from Amotaious, who appear more visibly terrified.

Fair's voice returns over the radio, "We'd like to test the laser LED now, just in case. Is that alright?"

Ty'mmie' answers, "Go ahead."

Fair's voice confirms, "Okay, testing now." The LED next to the monitor flares to life, and Alex sees the corresponding lights on the walls next to the other monitors illuminate. Ty'mmie' clicks the mic, "Mrs. Fair, everything checks out here. All systems are go."

Alex watches the timer—360 seconds, 38%. "Ty'mmie', check in with them now for any last-minute instructions before we potentially lose contact."

Ty'mmie' queries, "Mr. Doog, any further instructions?"

Doog's voice replies over the airwaves, "That's all for now. Good luck to you all; we're locked in on our end and will reestablish contact as soon as we can. Our prayers are with you. Over and out."

Ty'mmie', her voice cracking with emotion, responds, "Same here, Mr. Doog. Our prayers are with you, over and out."

Kyoryk turns to Ty'mmie', "Ty'mmie', go ahead and pull the levers we discussed earlier. First, the red one, then the blue on the adjacent panel. That will switch the lights to battery power."

Ty'mmie' pulls up on the red lever, shutting down the generator, then pulls down the blue lever. She secures herself in the spot designed for her protection, and Kyoryk ensures she's safe before checking the clock—289 seconds, 32%.

V, trying to reassure everyone, speaks up, "Just over a minute left before we start ramping up. Take a few deep breaths and center yourselves. Try to relax."

Loved ones exchange glances around the room, though communication is limited. Hand gestures are impossible, as everyone's hands are interlocked, and the protective earphones and glasses obscure much of their expressions. The 12 Students and 12 Stewards are joined by 12 Elder volunteers from Amotaious. Among them are familiar faces like Bahdubah and Klinchme', while others are strangers to the Students. All are solemnly aware that this is the moment—the time of the Super Flare, the 4,400-year cycle of the sun's destructive power upon the planet.

V's eyes drift to the clock—240 seconds, 37%. She turns her gaze to Alex, thinking back to their first encounter at the university's grand table.

Even now, he wears that same silly yet assuring grin. Memories of the past six months flood her mind—endless preparations, sleepless nights, the planning, the intimacy, and the ominous visit from the Creator's Messenger. Questions of where, who, why, and what the future holds for them race through her thoughts.

"V, V, are you with us?" Alex's voice snaps her back to reality. He speaks more loudly this time, "Hey, are you with us?"

She looks up, smiles softly, and whispers, "I'm here with you."

She glanced at the clock—210 seconds, 33%. Suddenly, one of the women volunteers collapsed behind Alex, unconscious. Declan's voice sliced through the air, "Holy shit!"

"What is it?" Alex snapped, his gaze darting toward the commotion.

Another woman dropped to the floor, likely triggered by witnessing the first fainting spell. V noticed the chaos unfolding behind Declan. The room erupted into panic as the line broke, and the percentage meter plummeted to zero.

Amidst the turmoil, Alex, Harvey, Declan, and Lev rushed to assist the fallen women. Both remained unconscious. V, Roman, Miko, Maria, and Prezzy hurried to aid the second woman. The room buzzed with anxiety, as they moved the women to where Ty'mmie' stood, hastily covering them with protective blankets.

Alex locked eyes with V, desperation lacing his voice, "What do we do?" Alex thinking. *"This can't be right. We are supposed to succeed. What the hell is happening?"*

Attempts to revive the women ensued, but panic continued to spread like wildfire. Alex turned to Declan and ordered, "Whistle, now!"

He whistled, but it didn't work, then shouted, "Silence, please! We need two people, immediately!" His eyes searched for answers first looking towards the ceiling, then in the faces of Harvey, Roman, and V, but found no one answering him.

"I can do it!" Tonari shouted, uncertainty in her tone. "I think?"

V's gaze flickered from Alex to the unconscious women, then back to the group. Alex will that work?" Alex, trying to bring back some control to the chaos, "We don't have a choice. We must try—now!" he commanded, his voice firm. All eyes turned to Tonari as she summoned two more versions of herself.

"Okay, it better work," V said, steeling herself. "Can you hold them long enough?"

Tonari swallowed hard. "We'll see. I've only managed to hold two for about ten minutes before." She started to shake. Candido held her tight. "You can do it."

"We have to try," Alex urged, a hint of a smile tugging at his lips as he met V's eyes. She gave him a look that said he knew something more. *"He knows something that Bastard."* Alex thought. *"It's going to work, this is it…"*

Kyoryk grabbed two additional cosmic blankets, further cocooning the women. He cast a worried glance at Ty'mmie', who was in the cage, trembling. "Don't let them come out of the blankets," he warned.

"Let's get back into formation," Alex urged V, who glanced at the clock—it now read 140 seconds at 0%.

V inhaled deeply, steadying herself. "Alright, let's go." Shaking her head. Ty'mmie' sealed the door of her cage as the group repositioned themselves. The additional Tonaris took over the spots vacated by the fainted women. All at the same time, all the Tonari's spoke, "Okay, let's do this." They all smiled in unison.

"Alright, let's ramp up quickly. We need to catch up," Alex said, winking at V.

V thought to herself, *"He knows something. He must. He's too confident, even in this chaos. Meanwhile, I'm about to lose it, and he's acting like he just stubbed his toe. What an ass!"*

"I hate him..." She stole a glance at Ty'mmie', who looked petrified, her body shaking uncontrollably.

"It's okay, Ty'mmie', you can do this," V encouraged. She heard Alex's voice cut through the tension, "Okay, let's stabilize it and bring it back to 50%. Swaraj, center the core. Miko, once it's centered, Declan, you start the spin." Swaraj and Declan focused intensely as Miko fixed her gaze on the core. The group concentrated on the Accelerator, channeling their energy, thoughts, and emotions into the task.

"We're at 15%," Ty'mmie' announced, her voice trembling.

"Great, let's push back to 50," Alex responded.

V's eyes flicked to the timer—100 seconds, 50%. She glanced back at Alex, who now had his eyes closed, focusing deeply. Then, she looked at Ty'mmie', who was curled up, shouting, "50% at 100 seconds!" The Accelerator hummed louder, and the room's temperature began to rise.

V shut her eyes, reaching out mentally to the group. *"We can do this. This is one of the most crucial moments of our lives. Right now, we're saving the planet. For my sister, for my grandmother, for the Creator, for everyone on Earth, for our families, for the technology, and for that crazy man across from me—Alex, can you hear me?"*

V opened her eyes and met Alex's gaze as the Accelerator hit 100%, and the room was engulfed in silence.

"110% at 80 seconds," Alex announced, though V could no longer hear him. *"We are going to do it,"* He thought as the Accelerator's hum transformed into a multi-tonal roar, its amber-yellow glow intensified into a blinding white light. *"I think V is on to me. She looks pissed off. I need to concentrate. I do love her. She probably hates me right now."*

V felt the warmth in the room seep through her well-lined parka. She glanced at the wall, where the LED light had flickered back on. She focused, driving her energy to spin the Accelerator's core faster. It now read 180%, with only 40 seconds left on the clock.

"The CMB is even stronger now," she thought, concentrating harder. In her mind, she urged the group, *"We're close to 200%, and the countdown is almost at zero. Breathe—slowly in, slowly out."*

"We're almost there. Think about all our loved ones, the technology we're preserving, the celebration that awaits us. I love you all. Believe in the Creator."

The ground began to tremble as V realized she was floating about a foot above it. Her hand gripped the Accelerator, but she couldn't feel it. The machine was now a solid white beacon, vibrating with an intensity that drowned out all sound, replaced by a blizzard-like wind roar.

"Everyone, we need 195% at 0 seconds. Then it's over. We can do this. Breathe in and out. Just relax. We're doing great," V communicated mentally.

Alex's voice pierced through the mental noise, *"I can hear you, babe. Great job! Do you hate me?"*

V and the rest of the group focused with renewed vigor as the room pulsed with the Accelerator's white glow. Outside, the camera Kyoryk had set up captured the white light shooting from the tent, soaring into the atmosphere. Heat radiated from the tent, visible even in the surrounding snow and ice.

A massive shockwave struck the planet at zero seconds, as the Accelerator surged to 202%. The southern side of the tent was ripped away from its tethers by the force. Outside, the wind howled at over 100 knots, whipping the snow and ice into a blinding whiteout. Inside, the group was at their peak, the Accelerator teetering on the brink of destruction, its base glowing red and blue. Crates toppled from the tent walls, narrowly missing Ty'mmie', who had curled into a ball, paralyzed with fear. The women remained unconscious, oblivious to the chaos around them.

Inside the CMB, the group is utterly oblivious to their surroundings, their consciousness fused within the Common Mind Bond. Suddenly, they find themselves transported to a serene beach, the same one Fem' guides them to during their usual journeys. The Students, enveloped in the warmth of the sun and the caress of the sea breeze, begin to forget their previous tasks. The sand beneath their feet feels almost tangible, the air soothing, as the ocean mist kisses their skin. They are no longer individuals but a single entity, unified in mind and body.

At this moment, it seems the Creator has taken control, enveloping everyone and everything in a sense of tranquility. V floats in a state of weightlessness, her anxiety dissolved, her entire being utterly relaxed, as if in a deep meditative trance. *"Yes, I can hear you. Yes, I hate you..."*

Outside the CMB, a kilometer high, white aura swirling beyond the ceiling of the wind-blown tent.

The thirty-four individuals now fully synchronized—except for Tonari, who exists in three forms—share this extraordinary experience. V, however, remains slightly detached, observing the scene with a clarity that allows her to sense the situation's surreal nature. The Students have never experienced a Bond this vast, this intense; it is a spectacle that defies reality.

V tries to open her eyes, but they remain firmly shut. She is locked in the CMB with the others, unable to see the tent, the two feet of air beneath them, or the white light radiating from the Accelerator. Desperately, she reaches out to communicate, her thoughts echoing through the bond. *"This is incredible. How is this happening? Why are we on this beach?"*

"I don't know, but I like it," Alex responds, his voice laced with contentment. The others murmur in agreement, marveling at the beauty around them. V looks around, seeing the group arranged in an infinity symbol on the beach, basking in the sun's warmth.

But as the minutes pass, V's awareness sharpens. She begins to remember where they were and what they were doing. A sense of urgency grips her. *"Alex, something's wrong. We shouldn't be here. We need to leave,"* she insists.

"But it feels so good," Alex protests, his voice heavy with reluctance, looking at her within the group, smiling.

V pushes forward, trying to shake everyone from their stupor. *"Alex, you shit, we need to get out, we need to leave the beach. I'm going to count down from five. When I clap, we will come out of the CMB. Does everyone understand?"* The group grumbles in protest, but eventually, they acquiesce. Alex looking around at the group says, *"Okay everyone listen to V. follow the countdown, we are going to go back."*

"Five. We're coming out of the CMB. The calm you feel will stay with you. Four. We accomplished our mission, I think. We will return to our bodies and our minds. Three. Focus on

your own thoughts, your own bodies. Two. When we reach one, you will return to yourself, remembering the bond we shared. Your body, your mind. One."

With all her strength, V breaks free first. She opens her eyes to find the tent shrouded in darkness, the others lying scattered on the ground. She takes a deep breath and claps loudly, pulling the rest from the CMB. Slowly, the thirty-four begin to stir, their faces reflecting confusion and disorientation.

The darkness inside the tent is almost suffocating, and with their ear protection on, they can barely hear each other. Alex, blinking rapidly, turns to V. "What happened?"

"I think we almost got stuck in the CMB," V replies, her voice tinged with concern.

Alex, struggling to his feet, pulls out a flashlight and clicks it on, the beam slicing through the darkness. "Are you okay?" he asks, shining it directly into V's eyes.

"Get it out of my face," she grumbles, shielding her eyes with her hand.

"Watch out for that!" Alex suddenly warns, his voice sharp.

"For what?" V asks, squinting against the light.

He points with the flashlight, illuminating a massive hole in the snow where the Accelerator had been. Just then, Ty'mmie' comes rushing over, nearly knocking V over in her haste. "Did we do it?" she asks, her excitement evident.

She inadvertently shines her flashlight in V's face, blinding her momentarily. V mutters something in Hindi, annoyed. "I think so," she replies, blinking away the afterimage. Around the tent, more flashlights flicker on, casting eerie shadows.

"Holy cow! What happened to the tent?" Harvey exclaims, surveying the damage.

"It was crazy," Ty'mmie' responds, shaking her head in disbelief.

"Lev, bring that crate lid over here," Alex instructs, his tone steady despite the chaos.

Lev does as he's told, peering into the gaping hole. "Wow, how deep does it go?"

"Why don't you go down there and find out?" Alex quips with a half-smile.

Lev shoots him a skeptical look, holding the lid tightly. "Yeah, right, buddy. I'm guessing the Accelerator is at the bottom."

"Man, I hope we don't need it anymore," Harvey mutters, his voice laced with dread.

Kyoryk steps forward, his eyes wide. "Oh shit! I hope we did it."

The group starts to talk, their voices overlapping as they try to piece together what happened. Ty'mmie' gathers them around, her words spilling out in a rush. "When we hit zero on the timer, we were over 200%. Then the tent exploded. You all were floating, and the percentage started to drop slowly. I thought you were controlling it, but you couldn't hear me. It lasted two or three minutes, maybe four. I don't know, it was so dark. Then I heard someone clap, and Alex asked V if she was okay. That's all I remember."

Alex turns to her, his expression serious. "What about the ladies? Did they wake up?"

Ty'mmie' glances back toward the cage where the women had been. "They woke up right after the clap. It was the weirdest thing. I think they're okay." She looks around, frowning. "Where are they?"

Kyoryk interjects, "What was the shockwave like?"

Ty'mmie's face darkens, her voice dropping. "Oh, that was terrifying. All the crates fell. One almost hit me. The wind and snow blasted into the tent. The noise from the Accelerator—I think I'm scarred for life." She pauses, then grins. "I'm going to write a tune about this. It was insane. The light was blinding." She continues speaking rapidly, her excitement bubbling over.

Harvey, sensing the need for calm, suggests they take a break and reconvene later. "We need to get the main lights up, the heaters going, and start fixing the tent," he advises.

V turns to Alex, Harvey, and Kyoryk, her expression serious. "What's next?"

Kyoryk, looking slightly nervous, responds, "We need to fix the tent to protect ourselves. We have about twelve hours before the electromagnetic shockwave hits, bringing with it a powerful wave of lightning. After that, we'll have to wait another twenty to forty-eight hours before the ships can return to pick up both our teams. We need to be prepared—sleeping, eating, whatever. Has anyone checked outside?"

V, Alex, Ty'mmie', Lev, and Kyoryk move toward the tent's entrance. As they step outside, they are greeted by an unusual sight—the sky, though dark, is painted with strange, vibrant colors, a sight unlike anything they've ever seen.

As they turn southward, the sight is mesmerizing. The wave is illuminated in a spectacular display, a haunting beauty that captures their attention. Kyoryk points to the light and remarks, "See that?"

V squints at the phenomenon. "What is that?" Kyoryk's voice is grave. "The entire planet is being torn apart by an immense electrical discharge. A massive lightning storm is ravaging the surface. Imagine the Thread we travel on between planets, but now magnified a million times— it's all transformed into lightning and plasma. We have about twelve and a half hours before it hopefully dissipates."

Alex, eyes wide with concern, asks, "Jesus, mate. Will the tent protect us?" V, echoing his anxiety, adds, "Right? Will it?"

Kyoryk nods, though his expression remains serious. "We need to keep our protective gear on and fix the tent as quickly as possible. But yes, that's what it was designed for."

They hurry back inside, where Ty'mmie' is animatedly explaining the recent events to Harvey, Freida, and a few others who listen with rapt attention. "It was the loudest noise I've ever heard," Ty'mmie' recounts, her voice filled with awe. "You all were floating two feet above the ground. The percentage clock hit 202 percent just as we reached zero seconds. The room felt like it was over a hundred and thirty degrees. The Accelerator—it was blinding, a pure white light that lit up the entire tent. I had to close and cover my eyes. And the sound... it was like a horn, mixed with the roar you'd hear if you were standing next to one of Vindor's rocket ships at takeoff."

Ty'mmie' takes a deep breath, her excitement palpable. "Then the shock wave hit. I shut my eyes and felt it slam into my body, like being pushed by an invisible force. It wasn't just wind— there was another pressure, something that felt like it was trying to shove me over."

V interrupts gently, "Ty'mmie', make sure to remember all of this so we can document it later. You did a great job. Harvey, we need to organize a team to fix the tent."

Harvey, holding up his tablet, indicates he's already recording her account. Lev steps forward, offering, "I can help."

Alex takes charge, "Alright, let's get to it. Where's your list of what's in the crates?"

As Ty'mmie' continues her recount with Harvey, V moves over to the area where they store the radios and computers. She digs around, saying, "Here's my clipboard. I've got a hard copy somewhere of what's in the crates."

Alex follows, his mind on the task. "Look for a Tent Repair Kit."

V quickly scans the list. "C-2. I'll have Lin, Miko, and Tonari handle the meals and sleeping setups. Everyone, prepare to fix the tent and set up the sleeping arrangements."

Miko, struggling with her faulty flashlight, asks, "When can we turn on the lights?"

V replies, "Kyoryk is checking on that. Our first priority is to fix the tent and get the heaters on; then, we can worry about the lights." Miko grumbles as she bangs her flashlight, "Figures, I got a crap light." As it goes back on, it shines right into V's eyes. "That's three times now…" Miko frowns, "Sorry."

V glances up, seeing the men working on the south side of the tent. The beams from their headlamps flicker as they reinforce the tent poles.

"Let's see if the guys need anything before we start," V suggests.

She leads Miko, Lin, Prezzy, and Tonari outside to the south side of the tent. The darkness is deep, the sky an eerie shade of gray. They find Alex, Harvey, Lev, Maria, Declan, Roman, Hugh, and a few others working tirelessly to secure the tent. Flashlights in hand or strapped to their foreheads, they illuminate the task.

V approaches Alex. "Is there anything we can help with?"

Alex looks up from his work. His flashlight on his head shines right in her eyes, "I think we have enough hands out here. How's it going inside?" V starts cursing in Hindi. That's four times now." She pulls him aside and starts pounding on his chest. "You lied to me. I know you knew something."

Alex laughs. "It's okay. I'll tell you everything when we get back. But I need to sit down and talk to you about it; it's much more than you think." She starts shaking and tearing at his coat. "You are an ass." She hugs him. "I do love you though." Miko runs up. "I hope we don't need the Accelerator anymore. Have you seen the hole it made? It's gone."

Harvey overhears and nods grimly. "Yeah, we know. It's gone. We noticed when we came out of the CMB."

Prezzy runs up and chimes in, "I hope everything worked."

Alex chuckles, "Ty'mmie' said we gradually brought the percentages down while we were on the beach. We didn't even realize it."

Harvey laughs, "That's crazy. Well, we hit two hundred percent, so we did what we came here to do. I just hope it made a difference." In the background, Lev can be heard directing, "Lift, lift. Steady. Good," as they maneuver one of the tent poles back into place.

V asks, "The heaters run on propane, right? We can start them without any electronics, is that correct?" Alex nods. "Yes, it should be fine. Double-check with Kyoryk, but it should be okay."

Miko, her gaze fixed on the sky to the south, murmurs, "What's happening over there?"

V, following her line of sight, explains, "Kyoryk says it's a magnetic shockwave headed our way. It'll be here in about ten hours. That's why we need to get everything set up. Once that's done, we can have the ships return."

Miko, captivated by the sight, whispers, "It's strangely beautiful."

V shakes her head, the weight of the situation heavy in her voice. "That right there is going to circle the entire planet and wipe out everything."

"If you're not underground, it could kill you. It's like lightning—we can't afford to get struck by it. Let's hope it dissipates a lot more before it reaches us." Miko's eyes widen. "Oh, shit, that's messed up." V nods. "Without this tent and our protective gear, we'd be toast."

The group turns back toward the tent, Miko suggesting, "We should start working on the cots and food."

V gives Alex a small smile. "Alright, see you back in the tent. We'll get the other preparations underway." Alex waves a hand in acknowledgment. "Okay." Harvey, still focused on the task, reminds V, "Keep everyone on the northern side of the tent for now, and make sure they keep their protective clothing on." V nods. "Will do, thanks, Harvey."

A couple of hours later, the tent is nearly repaired. V and the others have set up the cots, and everyone has had a chance to sit down and enjoy a hot meal. The heaters are running, and most of the team is sleeping. V and Alex manage to get some rest as well, though when the sun finally rises, it's hidden behind a thick, gray atmosphere.

Eight hours later, Alex gently wakes V. His voice is tense. "Hey, you need to get up—we might have a problem." V rubbed her eyes, her expression etched with concern. "What's happening?"

Kyoryk's brow furrowed. "The magnetic wave hasn't dissipated as much as it should have." V turned to Alex, her eyes widening. "What does that mean?" Alex's face was grim. "Our protective gear and the tent might not offer sufficient protection. We need to either be a couple of feet isolated from the ground or buried six feet underground."

V sprang to her feet, stretching in frustration. "Shit, does this ever end? It's one goddamn problem after another." She scanned the room for Kyoryk, shouting, "Kyoryk!"

Alex hissed, "People are still sleeping."

V shot him a scowl. Kyoryk approached, his demeanor tense. "What should we do? What's the solution?" Kyoryk replied, "I'm not certain. We only have two hours. We must either be isolated from the ground or at least six feet below it." Declan interjected, "We could all get into the Accelerator hole."

V glared at him. "All thirty-seven of us? That's not going to work." She demanded, "How badly will we be hurt?"

Kyoryk grimaced. "I believe we'll face electrocution. Like you said, struck by lightning." Leaning closer, he whispered, "Some could die."

V stomped her foot in frustration and muttered curses in Hindi. Harvey and Freida approached; Freida, V's Steward, smiled at her. "I haven't heard those words since we were en route to the university. What's going on, V?" V glanced at everyone. "We need to discuss this outside." The group moved outside the tent: Harvey, Alex, V, Freida, Kyoryk, and Declan.

As they headed towards the back of the tent, the wind began to pick up. Freida rubbed her hands together. "So, what's the situation?"

V shot a furious glance at Kyoryk, who began to explain, looking as though he might be on the verge of a physical confrontation.

"In less than two hours, the magnetic shockwave will sweep over us. It's akin to a violent lightning storm, discharging plasma as it encircles the planet. We designed the tent and our gear to shield us from it. This wave was expected to dissipate by about sixty percent by the time it reached the poles. It's only dissipated by forty percent so far. I'm unsure how much twenty percent will affect us. We need to either isolate ourselves from the ground or be underground by six feet, or underwater by ten."

Alex shook his head. "We can't go underwater. Declan's idea of us all crowding into the Accelerator hole—no way. Maybe ten or fifteen people, but not thirty-seven."

Harvey suggested, "What if we floated the cots in the air using nonconductive material, like rope? We could all sit on them."

Kyoryk responded, "I don't think we have enough rope for everyone."

V's gaze drifted to Freida, who was staring anxiously at the massive electrical storm approaching them. The storm resembled a colossal, rolling wall of blue and white plasma, slowly engulfing the sky. The ominous glow illuminated the atmosphere.

V asked Freida, "Are you okay?" Freida turned, her face a mask of worry. "That doesn't look good." Alex, sensing the fear, embraced V reassuringly. "Hey, we'll figure this out. We always do." He released her and turned to Harvey. "We will, right Harvey? We'll figure it out."

Alex stepped away from the group, moving closer to the wave. He paused, taking in the storm's daunting scale. The others continued to discuss options for another minute.

V, exasperated, said, "Why does this always happen?" She looked around at the group, all with flashlights. "Where's Alex?"

The flashlights converged on Alex, who stood ten to fifteen feet away, directly in front of the blue wave. V shouted, "Alex!" He didn't respond.

They hurried over to him. His expression was vacant. Harvey shook him gently. "Alex. Son, are you okay?"

Alex turned with a serene smile. Facing V, he declared, "CMB!"

V frowned. "What?"

Kyoryk's eyes lit up. "That could work! We'd be eighteen inches off the ground. We just need one person to guide us." Freida, her determination evident, shouted, "I'll do it!"

Harvey protested, "No, Freida. Why you?" Freida explained, "I've been training with Fem'. I've completed the first few books. V got them out of it without even reading them."

Kyoryk nodded thoughtfully. "This might work. Alex continues to stare at the vast wave of plasma, "Look at it. How many people is it destroying right now?"

V pulled Harvey aside, her voice tense. "What's happening to Alex?" Harvey shrugged. "I don't know. Fem' and Gig don't know either. We're all unsure." V, illuminated by the flashlights, said, "Well, it's freaking me out." Harvey nodded somberly. "Let's get back inside and prepare. Alex must be seeing something that can guide us through these things. We need to trust him. The Creator has a special bond with him." He smiled at her, "With you as well." He placed his hands on her shoulders. "You see that right?" V frowned, "I guess so." She smiled mildly, "It still freaking me out." Harvey and V laughed.

V, her frustration still mounting, muttered curses in Hindi. She, Harvey, Alex, and the others returned to the tent.

They briefed the group on Alex's idea. V was uneasy about Alex's condition but focused on ensuring everyone's safety.

Just before the wave struck, they rearranged and secured everything. A cot was floated in the air using nonconductive material, with Freida seated on it. The group formed a tight circle, all in their protective gear, with the tent sealed. The atmosphere grew increasingly tense as the sound of the storm intensified, a relentless cacophony of electrical discharges and low-toned thunder that began to shake the ground. The southern end of the tent blazed with a light that rivaled daylight.

The tent poles quivered, rattling ominously. Water bottles and various items left atop crates tumbled to the ground.

All electronics had been turned off, leaving only two small tripod lights flickering. Freida's headlamp provided additional illumination. Alex glanced at V, his own light extinguished. "Okay, we're ready," he said, turning off his light.

V met Freida's gaze and switched off her own light. "Alright, everyone, let's stay calm."

"Listen to Freida. We'll get through this. In thirty minutes, we won't even remember what happened. We'll be fine. Freida, go ahead."

Freida instructed, "Close your eyes. Focus on your breathing—inhale and exhale slowly. Today, we will imagine ourselves relaxing on a warm beach near the coast of Tunimbria on the planet Amotaious, the seven-mooned world. Breathe in deeply... and out."

V closed her eyes, steadying her breathing.

"We'll start by walking down a grassy meadow, counting down from ten. Feel the grass beneath your toes. Breathe in slowly and out. Nine. We're growing more relaxed. Look around and see the path leading toward the swaying trees. Eight. We are even more at ease."

V visualized the path through the grass, the cool sensation on her feet. Freida guided them further into the meditation, into the Common Mind Bond.

Freida, striving to maintain her composure, briefly opened her eyes as a massive bolt of lightning struck just outside the tent, jolting the ground. The wind intensified, causing the fabric to billow in waves. She closed her eyes and continued. "Join hands in a circle and connect within the Common Mind. Experience joy, a sense of community, and wholeness. Our hands are joined— thirty-six bodies, thirty-six minds, and thirty-six souls united as one. One Common Mind, one Common Bond. We'll start another countdown from five. We are completely relaxed, weightless. Our minds are free of all other thoughts. Our souls are one."

Kyoryk had set a timer for her, with four minutes remaining. When it reached zero, they were to be at full height and remain there for three minutes.

"You are entirely relaxed, floating on air. Steady your breathing. As you gaze at everyone, begin to see their auras. From a bottom blue, transitioning to orange in the middle, and finally to pure white at the top."

V focused on her breathing, observing the auras of others emerging, some more vivid than others.

"As the auras intensify at the top, they will merge into a brilliant white. Feel the collective joy and love. Breathe and relax. Three."

V now felt weightless. Freida continued in the same manner as Fem' had done before. Opening her eyes, Freida saw the entire group floating more than a foot above the ground. She glanced at the clock—thirty seconds remained until the electromagnetic wave would hit. The ground below trembled, and the tent's fabric appeared on the verge of ripping apart. Freida gripped the cot's edges, her nails digging into the fabric. The sound had shifted from intermittent lightning crashes to a continuous, deafening roar.

She pressed on, "One. You no longer feel yourself, only the group. You are free weightless. Merge all thoughts into one, all as one—one body, one mind, one soul. We'll count down again from three. You will become a single light, moving and feeling as one. Two."

V could no longer distinguish individual forms, only a unified light. The sensation was extraordinary, far surpassing previous experiences. She felt no connection to her body, only the warmth and kindness within. "One. You are now one light, one person, one soul, one creation. The Creator guides you. As one, you travel down the beach. Your mind is clear."

Freida checked the timer—fifteen seconds remaining. She saw that the group had ascended not just a foot but perhaps two feet. They were now rotating counterclockwise, an adjustment Alex had made for an oval configuration rather than a figure-eight.

Overwhelmed by the ferocious sound and blinding light, Freida held onto the cot for dear life. She no longer needed to monitor the timer and focused on guiding the group through the CMB. After a minute, she reopened her eyes to find the timer had reset and was counting down from three minutes, currently at 2:02.

Freida was relieved to discover that the worst of the wave had passed. She guided the group out of the meditation, and all was well. V emerged from the CMB feeling elated. Experiencing the bond with thirty-six people again was extraordinary. The tent sustained some damage but was repairable. The group, though relieved, was disheartened to learn that the ship would not return for another 48 to 72 hours. As the storm faded, the atmosphere grew less intimidating. The group spent the following days waiting for the skies to clear. Fortunately, Lin, Prezzy, and Maria had the foresight to pack more champagne than the others thought. Also, speakers and party decorations make the wait more bearable.

V and the women gathered around.

Lin was very excited about setting up her computer and projected a virtual screen. She had mentioned earlier that the whole group would participate in the party afterward. She was involved with the people on Amotaious. "This is the second band performing at our concert. They're from Vindor. Our performance will be the third tune. We'll delve into that when we return."

V watched the video displayed above the computer. The Vindorians, with their avian features—hunched shoulders, longer arms, shorter legs, rounder red eyes—were performing on a stage resembling a giant tree with nests in its limbs. The stage wasn't fully completed, but it was impressive.

V recalled their religious tradition, the Trinop, where families battled atop a tower or tree to claim victory. The stage might be related to this tradition.

As the girls watched, their interest attracted others in the tent. With the champagne's effects making everyone more relaxed, Lin enlarged the screen, drawing more viewers.

A well-built man emerged on stage, drumming rhythmically. Twelve Elders performed a CMB in the background. Instruments joined in—a symphony of drums, gongs, and large percussion tubes, all in perfect harmony. Then, a woman with large, feathered adornments signaled her avian nature and began to sing.

The music soared with a high-pitched, exhilarating quality. The unfinished stage left much to the imagination, especially when shrouded in darkness and illuminated by lights. As the band continued to play, the group in the Common Mind Bond (CMB) began to hum and sing an eerie melody. Figures adorned with feathers, resembling birds, floated gracefully in the air around the amphitheater, alighting gently in the makeshift nests nestled within the colossal stage tree. Their movements were likely orchestrated by those in the CMB.

As the tune intensified, so did the pace, transforming from serene to chaotic. The avian performers clashed violently, vying for dominance atop the tree. Some plummeted to the stage floor, bloodied and lifeless. The performance grew increasingly thunderous and aggressive yet captivating.

Prezzy gasped, "Oh my God!"

"Wow! That's insane! Cool!" Declan exclaimed.

As the tune reached its climax, Harvey chuckled, and others remarked on its brutal intensity. Lin closed her computer with a satisfied smile.

Alex inquired, "So, what's next after them?"

Lin addressed everyone. "Fem'—" She paused, exchanging a smile with Maria. "Maria, some others, and I from Amotaious have been brainstorming. We plan to perform our CMB, featuring our full band with a fresh rendition of 'It's a New Galaxy.'"

"We'll incorporate some of our Gifts, though we're still refining the details. Fem' has some intriguing ideas. We'll follow with a tune by Ty'mmie'."

"After Ty'mmie's performance, all the teams will take the stage for an award ceremony. Then, the concert will proceed with a couple of extra tunes from all three bands from the three stages."

Harvey surveyed the group with a serious yet enigmatic expression. "This is the beginning. All of you are the harbingers of change."

Prezzy leaped up and embraced him. "Love you, Harvey."

Freida, with a contemplative expression, added, "He's right. You've been here only a short while, yet there's so much to learn—about civilizations, the planet's history, and the struggles faced. This truly marks the dawn of a New Galaxy."

An elderly couple, previously unnoticed, rose from the back. They appeared wise and graceful, part of the original thirty-six, yet had seldom interacted with Alex, V, Harvey, or Freida. Removing the hoods of their cloaks, they resembled wizards. Hand in hand, they stood before the group.

The man smiled enigmatically. "Sorry to interrupt." Alex and Harvey looked at him to proceed. "You have no idea what you've achieved today. You've altered the galaxy's course forever. We are Elders prior to CAT 1."

Their appearance was ancient yet radiant. The woman's smile was equally profound. "We may be the oldest Elders here, and it's an honor to be with you on this momentous day—the most significant in over 24,000 years or of all time."

Alex, V, Declan, Miko, Harvey, and Freida stared in awe, speechless.

The wise couple bowed in reverence. The man introduced himself, "I am Jesut. This is Mara. We have witnessed countless epochs and are deeply grateful."

Declan muttered, "Holy shit!" Prezzy hopped on her toes in excitement. V, unsure of her actions, instinctively reached out and embraced Mara.

After nineteen years of abstaining from hugs, V felt an overwhelming sense of joy. She then glanced at Alex, who promptly embraced Jesut. It was a pivotal moment for V.

Mara and Jesut engaged in a private conversation with V and Alex that night. They revealed their desire for anonymity, preferring not to disclose their involvement to others. They also shared that they were the original Master Elders preceding CAT 1 and would reach out to V and Alex in the future.

Another secret to ponder, another surprise to unravel in the years to come.

The group celebrated with drinks. It took an additional fifty hours to reestablish communication with the lab, followed by another four hours before the ships could return to retrieve the teams.

V remained puzzled about the Creator's intervention during the Super Flare. Upon resuming communication, she learned that the mission had achieved partial success. The Accelerator had indeed amplified the Magnetic Field, but the precise impact remained unknown. It would take days and weeks of analysis to understand the effects—how people reacted, where the wave struck the planet, and how it dissipated.

They packed up the tent and crates and boarded the ship late that night. V knew only that she was safely en route back to the university.

XXX

As the ship glides over the final feet of track, Alex and V lean forward in their seats, their eyes locked on the solitary window that frames the eager faces of those awaiting them on the docks. The anticipation is evident.

Descending the steps from the ship to the dock's floor, they are greeted by the warm smiles of Fem and Gig. Fem envelops them each in a tight embrace, exclaiming, "You did it! Our initial estimates suggest that a third of the population will survive—an extraordinary achievement. Congratulations!"

Applause and cheers ripple through the crowd of over a hundred well-wishers, all eager to celebrate the victory. Yet, a shadow of somberness falls as the Southern Team disembarks; the jubilation fades when four individuals emerge on stretchers—one in a coma, the others gravely injured.

V discreetly pulls Fem aside, her voice tinged with concern. "What happened?"

Fem's expression turns serious. "The Southern Team neglected to execute the CMB during the Electromagnetic Wave. Ten were injured, and one remains in a coma. Tragically, we lost one."

V's heart sinks, the weight of the news overwhelming her. Fem studies V's troubled face and asks, "How did you know to perform the CMB?" V, struggling to muster a smile, replies, "Kyoryk calculated the numbers, realizing the peril we were in. Then Alex—he did that thing again, staring into the void, and suddenly he said, 'Why don't we do a CMB?' I'm beginning to think he has a direct line to the Creator or something."

Fem scoffs lightly but concedes, "Well, it worked. The Creator's design prevailed, and the reaction from the other Master Elders has been nothing short of ecstatic. 'It's going to be one hell of a party!'"

V laughs, though a look of worry soon clouds her features. "Any news about our families?"

Fem's expression shifts as she begins, "That's another thing—Alex instructed Rev and Mod to..." But before she can finish, Gig interrupts with a jubilant hug. "Congratulations, V! You did it. It's incredible."

Everyone is overjoyed, except for a few from the Southern Team. And what Alex directed Rev and Mod to do—without our knowledge—was unbelievable. We're going to have to give him some kind of award."

V, her frustration mounting, demands, "What did he do? What happened to our families?"

Gig recounts, "Just after the Super Flare, while we were on Amotaious, we received a call from Rev and Mod. On the orders of the new Master Elder, Alexander Katz, they had been instructed before the Flare to relocate all the Students' and Stewards' families to underground shelters off the coast of Chile. Alva Global has safe locations there."

V's relief is immediate and overwhelming as she embraces and kisses Gig, then Fem'. "So, my sister is safe?"

Fem smiles, a chuckle escaping her lips. "Yes, your sister, your parents—everyone's families are fine."

V murmurs something in Hindi, then adds with a smirk, "That rascal, Alex. I'd like to personally reach out to the family of the person who lost their life, if I may. I'll do it with Alex." "Of course," Fem replies.

As Alex approaches, V springs up and wraps herself around him completely, planting a passionate kiss on his lips. "Thank you. I love you!" Alex, taken aback, stammers, "What did I do?"

V slides down from him with a grin. "Just for being you." She whispers in his ear, "I'm going to give you something special later." Alex laughs, casting a knowing glance at Declan as he joins them. "Okay?"

Gig steps forward, raising both Alex's and V's hands high in the air, tears glistening in his eyes as he bellows, "WE DID IT! HOOYAAHHAAHH!!! ALEX AND V, THE CONQUERORS!" The sight of Gig, Doog, Fem, and Fair—the giants of the group—so overwhelmed with joy, especially to see a tear in Gig's eye, is something to behold.

After the revelry subsides, Fem turns to V with a warm smile. "V, the Master Elders Council wishes to express our gratitude to all the Students."

"In a few days, we plan to host you at the Sky Suites, overlooking the bay of Alloo." V, exhausted yet exhilarated, inquires, "Sky Suites? What's that?"

Fem's smile broadens. "It's the finest place to stay in Amotaious. All twelve of you for a week, with full amenities—six-star treatment."

V, overwhelmed, laughs and smiles, "Okay, I'll let everyone know."

Later that evening, Alex and V finally retreat to V's room. After resting briefly on the bed, V takes a deep breath, rises, and faces Alex. "I've been working on this for a while. You've been so creative in the past; I thought it was my turn. Here, you need to put these on."

She pulls out a cowboy hat and sexy leather chaps that leave little to the imagination. For herself, she dons a garment of six silk scarves, barely covering her most delicate areas. As she puts on a romantic mix of Babayaga, Indian, and Zill music, she attaches some Zills to her fingers and begins to dance around the room.

Then, turning down the music, she sits on the bed with a serious expression. "I need to tell you how incredible it was what you did for everyone and their families."

Alex, standing there in his cowboy attire, smiles. "I couldn't tell you. The Creator told me not to tell anyone. He instructed me to protect everyone, so I kept my word. It was on New Year's Day. It was tough. I think that's why I got so drunk."

V, sitting in her six scarves outfit, nearly in tears, replies, "Just knowing I'll see my sister again someday is a tremendous gift."

Alex smirks, hands on his hips. "I also had Rev and Mod spread a rumor on the internet that the sun would do another Pulse Reversal around February 18th, advising people to go underground by six feet. Who knows, maybe it saved some lives. Plus, from Raba's message, it looks like there will soon be Elders living knowingly on the planet; I'll tell you more about that later."

V reclines on the bed, a mischievous smile playing on her lips. "Okay. Wait," she teases, "you broke a rule by telling the public to get into the caves."

Alex shakes his head, grinning. "No, I didn't. It was presented as the vacation of a lifetime—all expenses paid. I made it irresistible. And the internet thing? Just a rumor."

V's brow furrows. "But my parents... I know they didn't agree to that."

Alex's smile widens as he explains, "I instructed Mod to tell them there was a notorious Indian spy they needed to investigate—and they had to bring your sister along. Mod said he and Rev would handle the rest. Your aunt wasn't an issue."

She embraces him tightly. "So, no one knows?"

Alex rises to his feet. "They probably do now."

V shakes her arms and legs, a sigh of contentment escaping her. "It's so nice to be back in my room finally. I don't know why but I feel safe here," she looks up at him, "with you now."

Alex adopts a playful cowboy drawl, his eyes twinkling. "I've come a long way through the prairie, haven't had water for days... nor a woman. Are you gonna dance for this lonely, thirsty cowboy or what? It's been five years since I've felt a woman's touch, two weeks since I've had a sip of water."

V's smile becomes precious as she turns up the music on her tablet, pushing Alex down into a chair. She cracks open a warm beer she had stashed in her drawer, spins around, turns the music up louder, and begins dancing around the room, tapping her Zills.

Alex can't help but burst into laughter, the hat perched on his head slightly too small. As he settles down, he starts to enjoy the show. V removes a scarf, wrapping it around his neck, then leaps onto the bed, continuing her dance.

She returns to him, wraps another scarf around his right leg, and then another around his right arm, all while teasing him with tender touches, revealing only tantalizing glimpses of her body.

Alex attempts to reach out, but she playfully slaps his hand away with a toy whip. "No touching," she commands, her voice firm but playful. She resumes dancing, the Zills on her fingers clinking rhythmically before she wraps another scarf around his left leg. "Two more left," she announces, "where do they go?"

Alex tries to respond, but she places a finger to his lips, silencing him. "No talking either. Shush." She moves her body seductively around him, intensifying the teasing as she wraps the penultimate scarf around his left arm. "Only one scarf left," she declares, her voice dripping with anticipation. "STAND UP!"

Alex rises, the cowboy hat and chaps clinging to him as he smirks, trying once more to speak. She hushes him again, "Shush." As she dances closer, she asks, "Where do you think this one goes? All soft, cold, and silky."

Alex, visibly aroused after minutes of teasing, chuckles and looks down. "I think I have a guess. Is this another form of meditation you learned from a book passed down by the Intelligence Bureau?"

"This is where the sixth scarf goes—my scarf, and only my scarf." She skillfully lassos his manhood, maintaining a slight distance. "Until we say otherwise, do you understand? Now speak."

With a submissive tone, Alex replies, "Yes, ma'am."

"Good," V says, stepping forward to wrap the lasso around Alex's once-concealed gun firmly. She pulls him onto the bed with a swift motion, declaring, "Now I'm going to ride you like only a cowgirl knows how."

Alex, speechless, thinks *I'm not interested in anyone else; she has nothing to worry about. No one's scarf is getting near my Happy Fella. She has such a vivid imagination. Even after five months, she's still as aggressive as ever.*

She cranks up the music and begins to ride him, the scarves strewn across his body as she yells, "Go, cowboy, go!"

A passerby laughs from outside the room. Both Alex and V burst into laughter, stopping their play to lie back on the bed, giggling uncontrollably. Alex grabs the sheets, covering them both as they lie on their backs, staring up at the ceiling, each lost in their own thoughts about the whirlwind of the past days, weeks, and beyond.

V's mind races. *Well, we did it. What's next for me? I'm relieved my sister is safe. But what's next for the group?* She glances at Alex, who is also staring at the ceiling. *What's next for me, Alex?* she wonders. *This guy has a direct line to the Creator. What's coming next? Something big, no doubt. Good thing I have Alex. He'll help me figure it out. I do love him. I can't believe I'm in love with someone. This is all so crazy. What the hell just happened? Six months... crap, I've got sex on my brain. What's wrong with me? Meeting Jesut and Mara was incredible. I can't believe they joined our group—the oldest living, unofficial Master Elders. What a trip. From what they said, we still have so much to learn about past civilizations. The people today have no idea. I can't wait to talk to them again. To think they are the ones that started it all. The ones that created the Creator's Plans. They must have a direct line with the Creator, like Alex and I.*

Alex's thoughts echo hers. *Well, we did it. I can't believe it. I hope I helped. The other Elders were amazing. Mara and Jesut... I still can't believe they were there. I need to learn more from them when I go to Amotaious—all the pre-civilizations... so much to learn. I can't believe they are the ones from the beginning. I need to meet with them again."*

"They are just like me and V. We almost lost it when those two women fainted, but I knew we'd make it, thanks to the Creator's vision. What's next with the Creator? Some big challenge must be coming?"

What am I going to do? Fuck! I have V and the others. He looks over at V, seeing her gazing up at the ceiling. *She's so beautiful. How did I get so lucky? Will she stay with me? She's going to leave me. She'll find someone else, someone smarter, better than me. Shit. Stop thinking like that. I'm okay; I just saved the world. Kind of. She's right next to me. What am I talking about? I can do this. Just tell her you love her."*

"I'll be okay. I can do this. She's incredible. I need to rest. What a week. What a crazy few months. I'm surprised I'm not insane yet. Oh, just have sex now.

V turns to Alex, her eyes blazing with desire, and begins to kiss him fervently, her touch growing more insistent with each passing moment. "Make passionate love to me," she commands, her voice husky with longing.

Snapped out of his thoughts, Alex meets her gaze, a smile curving his lips. "I love you," he murmurs, his voice filled with sincerity.

Her eyes widen slightly. "You do?" she asks, searching his face for confirmation.

"Yes," he replies without hesitation.

V glances down, her voice softening. "Then prove it."

Alex chuckles, the sound deep and warm. "Okay, you wild woman," he teases, his hands moving with purpose.

She sighs in satisfaction. "There, that's better."

Alex laughs again, his confidence unwavering. "Don't worry, I've got this."

V moans in response, her voice thick with pleasure. "Yes, you do!"

They make love, their passion overflowing, before finally succumbing to the embrace of sleep, the evening drawing to a close.

Meanwhile, the Elder Students prepare for their third journey to Amotaious. Given that several Students were involved in organizing the upcoming celebration concert, it was decided they would stay at the Sky Suites overlooking the Bay of Alloo for two weeks instead of one. They would head directly to the concert on March 10th, the day before their scheduled departure.

During their time on Amotaious, the Students indulged in various activities, including skinny dipping on the pristine beach and fishing in the Nallawalla Ocean, located opposite the Bay of Alloo and the Two Dunes Harbor. Alex finally found a moment to unwind amidst the serene surroundings.

Alex also took the opportunity to take the whole group to explore Millapillar Valley, where they witnessed the impressive use of a CMB in cutting stone and timber—a fascinating process that also demonstrated how large materials are transported. The entire group reveled in the experience.

Lin was particularly engaged with the concert production, while Maria and Prezzy contributed in the final days leading up to the event.

The entire population of Amotaious was set to attend the celebration, an unprecedented gathering in the newly completed amphitheater. This marked the last weekend before the Students had to return to school, to classes, and to combat training, though such concerns were far from their minds at the moment.

A week before the concert, Fem' and Freida sent Alex, V, Declan, and Miko into town to shop for new outfits for the event. On the day of the concert, Fem' had also arranged for a professional hairdresser to style their hair in preparation for the night's festivities. With all tasks completed, the Students and Stewards were ready to join in the celebration with the people from all the planets.

XXXI

From the furthest balcony, V and Alex stood, gazing over the vast expanse of the Seven Moons Amphitheater. It was Friday night, and the brand-new venue, carved into the side of a mountain composed of multi-colored boulders and volcanic colonnades, overlooked the tranquil Two Dunes Harbor. The amphitheater, capable of seating nearly the entire population of Amotaious—a hundred thousand strong—sat proudly on the southern coast of the Sea of Tunimbria, adjacent to the Bay of Alloo. The wind-blown sand from the towering Two Dunes, visible in the distance, mingled with the old, towering trees and rugged grey shrubs that dotted the landscape.

The harbor, shaped like a horseshoe, cradled a thousand yachts from various planets. Across the water, the massive dunes loomed fifty to sixty miles away, their silhouette stark against the sky. The skies of Amotaious, unlike the soft blue and white clouds of Teraenti, presented a darker blue canvas with clouds tinged in yellow—an atmospheric quirk Kyoryk had tried to explain, though it remained elusive to many of the Students. It was as if one viewed the world through perpetual sunglasses, though no lenses were in sight.

Alex surveyed the colossal theater and then turned to the stage, puzzled. "Where is everyone?" he asked.

V, her gaze sweeping the scene, replied, "Lin and Kyoryk are on the stage. We're supposed to join them soon, but Fem' wanted me to bring you up here first to take in the view. We'll head to the stage shortly, and later, we're to meet them in a VIP box." She pointed to the corner of the amphitheater.

Alex took in the grandeur of the place, nodding in appreciation. "This place is incredible," he said, turning to her. "And you—you are incredible. You've really outdone yourself with that outfit."

V leaned in to kiss him, her lips curving into a smile. "Is it just my outfit you find incredible?" she teased.

Alex's eyes roved over her, admiring the intricate details the hairdresser had crafted. "No, it's everything—the feathers, the beads, your lipstick," he continues further down, "the way your green dress turns, shimmers red at the bottom in flames as the sun hits it. Oh, my goodness," he said, his voice filled with genuine admiration.

"Stop it," she laughed, her eyes twinkling.

Alex pulled her into a hug, his voice dropping to a tender whisper. "If I could, I'd crawl inside you. Always being with you…. You complete me, V. Without you, I'm just a fraction of myself. You make me whole."

V tried to kiss him again, careful not to smudge her lipstick. "That's the sweetest thing you've ever said," she murmured.

"You look like a queen," Alex said, bowing theatrically. "Queen V. My lady, would you accompany me down to the stage?"

Alex himself had taken fashion advice from Gig and Harvey, blending styles from different ages over the past seven thousand years. He wore soft sage suede pants, hand-sewn from deerskin, and handmade loafers adorned with tassels. His pure white silk shirt, with its billowing cuffs and black stained bone buttons, added a touch of elegance, while his full-back suede jacket, high-collared and long in the back, gave him a commanding presence. His tie, a subtle blend of cowboy and bowtie, completed the ensemble. Both Alex and V were adorned with rings, earrings, and beads; their hairstyles and outfits were truly works of art.

As they continued to survey the amphitheater, people began to trickle in. The sound checks echoed across the space, and unusual yachts drifted in and out of the harbor. One flew out of the water and flew, making the two of them think it was probably from Vattan, the water planet.

It was a perfect day on Amotaious; four of the seven moons hung visible in the sky. The amphitheater, situated eighty-five miles south of Tunimbria, basked in the late afternoon warmth. The sun would set in two hours, and the concert and celebration would soon begin.

Declan rounded the corner, his expression one of mock exasperation. "Jesus, Fem' said you were up here. Took me forever to find you." Dressed in a full-length black leather raincoat, polished boots, and a dark blood-red silk shirt, he cut an imposing figure.

Miko followed closely behind, panting slightly. "What the hell are you doing way up here?" she asked, then paused, taking in the view. "Oh, wow, now I get why they call it the 'Two Dunes Amphitheater.' Look at that harbor! We need to go sailing."

Miko's elaborate feathered hat and bright red dress, fading to black at the hem, matched her flamed boots, making her and Declan a striking, albeit intimidating, pair. She spun playfully as she approached. "You two look amazing!"

Declan, ever the joker, asked, "Where's the bar? Is there one up here?" He pulled out a blunt, looking around. "Anyone got a lighter?"

V and Alex laughed as Miko took V's hands, admiring her dress. "You look stunning! I knew you'd pick the green one, but I wasn't sure which dress you'd choose tonight."

V beamed, "Yes, I always seem to gravitate towards green." She nudged Miko towards Declan. "You two look fantastic together. We need to get a picture of all of us."

Alex eyed Miko and asked, "Why is Declan talking so fast? Did he already take something?"

Declan laughed, "Just started with some coffee drinks hours ago." He dashed over to one of the amphitheater workers and quickly returned. "Got a lighter! And he's going to take our picture." The four of them struck a pose, capturing the moment.

The attendant, curious, asked, "Are you from Teraenti?"

Declan, ever the showman, boomed, "Yes, this is Alexander Katz and Vibrean Aboli!" The young man muttered something in a foreign language before scurrying off, prompting the group to burst into laughter.

"He'll be back," Declan said with a grin.

V sighed, "Yeah, well, maybe we should get going before he does."

Alex raised an eyebrow, "Why did you do that?"

Declan lights the blunt, exhaling a cloud of smoke. "Let's enjoy this first," he says, passing it around. The four of them take turns, savoring the moment.

"So, the mission's done. What now?" Alex asks, his voice carrying a note of curiosity. Declan shakes his head with a chuckle. "Jesus, Alex, now we celebrate! After that, it's back to school, and the Creator will decide our next move. For now, just smoke and relax." V, thoughtful, adds, "Our families are safe. How long do you think it'll take to restore power to the major cities? A hundred years?"

Alex exhales a thick plume of smoke, his expression serious. "Harvey and I went over everything the last few days."

"If they don't all end up killing each other, it could take less than a hundred years to reestablish some semblance of normalcy for the big governments. We're keeping our families out of the mess for at least six months until we can properly assess the situation."

Miko, concerned, asks, "So we really have no idea what's happening down there yet?" V shakes her head slightly. "No, not entirely. Rev and Mod are preparing a full report, which should be ready in about a week. Fem' mentioned they'll start doing monthly updates. But from what we've done—both teams, with the Accelerators and enhancing the magnetic fields—we've saved millions if not a billion lives. The real game-changer, though, is the technology. Fem' said that's the key."

Declan grins, blowing out a long stream of smoke. "See? We made a difference. Now, let's find that bar." Now bouncing, pushing himself off the rail, "Look at this place, just incredible. We are on another planet."

He cups his mouth, starts to shout. "Start the show!" V and Alex laugh.

Suddenly, Miko spots something and groans. "Oh, no…"

Alex follows her gaze and sees two females and a male approaching, all from different planets, their excitement palpable. "We should get moving," Alex mutters, but Declan, ever the thrill-seeker, replies, "No, this could be fun." Alex rolls his eyes, a smile tugging at his lips. "Great," he says sarcastically while V suppresses a laugh.

The two girls, practically bouncing on their toes, ask breathlessly, "Are you from Teraenti?" Declan, seizing the moment, announces, "This is none other than Alex Katz and Vibrean Aboli."

The girls squeal in delight. "Can we get your autographs?" V, ever gracious, smiles warmly. "Of course, we'd be happy to." She and Alex quickly sign their papers.

Declan, eyeing the young man who looks Vattan by appearance, says, "Hey, how about taking a couple of pictures for us?" The young man nods eagerly, and they pose for a few more shots from their various tablets. Declan, always thinking ahead, asks, "What's the quickest way to get to the stage? We're supposed to be there now." The kid grins, "I can take you down there. I know a shortcut." Declan claps his hands. "Great, let's go!"

The four of them follow the young man down to the stage, where they reunite with Lin, Kyoryk, Prezzy, Swaraj, Gig, and Fem'. The atmosphere quickly becomes a flurry of activity as the crowd begins to fill the amphitheater.

Alex, looking around at the bustling scene, asks, "Lin, what's the plan? Do we need to do anything?" Lin, smiling calmly, replies, "No, you're free until after the first and second bands perform. Then, we'll take the stage to do the CMB with our group while the band sings *A New Galaxy*. After that, Ty'mmie' and J.T. will perform their tune, and then you and V will join them, followed by the North and South Teams and the rest of the volunteers. After that, the concert officially kicks off, and we can head up to the VIP area to relax. It'll be quick—less than an hour, really, just three tunes. There's a spot down front where we can watch the first bands before it's our turn."

"Sounds good," Alex says, nodding. Lin then rushes off, clearly feeling the pressure of the event.

V, noticing Lin's anxiety, asks Kyoryk, "Is she going to be okay?" Kyoryk nods reassuringly. "Yeah, she'll be fine. She just feels like she's carrying the weight of the whole event, but she'll manage. Let's grab a drink at the bar, and then we can head to our seats."

After a round of drinks, they move to their seats, set aside in an orchestra-like area. Before sitting down, Alex takes a moment to observe the diverse faces in the crowd and the breathtaking beauty of the amphitheater. The first fifty rows are filled with young people, mostly girls, all buzzing with anticipation.

The first band begins to play, showcasing the spectacle Lin had shown them—the mesmerizing sounds of snow, rain, and hail from Kall. By the time the second band from Vindor takes the stage, with their birds of prey and intense percussion, Alex and the group are backstage, preparing for the CMB.

As soon as the Vindor performance ends, the stage shifts to a different atmosphere. A soft wind-like sound emanates from the stringed instruments, followed by the deep rumble of expertly crafted percussion. A young violinist walks out, playing softly, drawing all eyes to the main stage.

A new **"Song"** begins. *The Sky And The Dawn And The Sun*

When Alex, V, and the other Students step onto the circular platform at the center of the stage, the amphitheater erupts with cheers. The audience stands, their excitement unmistakable, this is the main event. The new Elder Students are performing.

The Students form a circle, holding hands as they begin their CMB. Fem' and Fair enter, singing, "La, la. Di da da Di da Di da. La la di da. Dahhhhhh," with Fem' leading and Fair harmonizing in chorus. Four other, very tall ladies from CAT 5 join in, singing the chorus as they walk out. The crowd's cheers grow even louder as images of the countryside and clouds appear on the virtual screens behind the stage.

She sang with a voice that soared, "High are the stars tonight," followed by, "We will not give up the fight."

"La, La, La. La, La, La, Lahhhhhh," her voice resonated, "From our sun to your sun, from our moon to your moons." As all the women gathered on stage, the tune swelled, building in intensity. Alex and the Elder Students, deeply connected through their CMB, began to hum, their synchrony perfected over time.

Behind the stage, vivid images of solar systems emerged, displaying the intricate dance of six planets within their galaxy. The girl with the violin took flight, her melodies filling the air as she played, "La, La, La. La, La, La, Lahhhhhh." Her voice intertwined with the celestial vision, "In the light of the Galaxy. We are the planets; He is the Galaxy." The tune continued, beckoning, "Come with us, and you will see—it's a New Galaxy."

The chorus joined in, all twelve ladies from CAT 5, all standing three meters tall dressed in fantastic attire, "La, la. Di da da Di da Di da. La la di da. Dahhhhhh." The stage pulsated with energy as the women sang, "Follow us, and you will see—to build our New Galaxy." The tempo quickened, the anticipation building as V, Alex, and the others began to rise, a foot off the platform, spinning in unison. Fem' and the chorus echoed the refrain, "We are the Stars. We are the Suns." The orchestra joined its instruments, blending into a symphonic crescendo.

The violinist reached a fever pitch, her notes piercing the air as Gig and eleven other giant men from CAT 5 stormed the stage, their footsteps thundering in time with the beat. They chanted, "Come Join With Me!" over and over as twelve women of equal stature to Fem' and Fair joined them, their powerful presence commanding the stage.

The entire ensemble, now including all members of CAT 5, sang in unison, "We are the Stars. We are the Suns." The audience, caught in the moment, sang along. Alex and the Students spun higher, now two feet above the platform, as lights flashed wildly around them.

Above them, an aura began to form, radiating and shooting thousands of feet into the sky. The crowd erupted into wild applause. On the virtual screen behind the stage, Fem, Lin, and Maria projected images of giant Woolly Mammoths and creatures from Teraenti's ancient past. These long-lost animals appeared to charge toward the crowd—Sabretooth Cats, Sloths, Wild Black Bears, and Dire Wolves—stirring awe and fear as they seemed to burst from the screen into the audience of thousands.

The crowd recoiled as the drums pounded and the gongs clanged. The chorus beside them sang in harmony as the orchestra played at full force. The tiny violinist floated midair, her bow dancing across the strings in perfect rhythm with the grand finale.

Gig and Fem' stepped forward, hands clasped, and began to ascend, floating three to four feet above the stage. The entire stage blazed with light, every instrument at its peak, driving the tune to its powerful conclusion. The crowd, on their feet, roared with excitement. "Come Join With Me!" "Come Join With Me!" In an instant, all the lights went out, plunging the amphitheater into darkness. Gig and Fem' shown only by the moonlight.

With a dramatic gesture, Gig raised his hands high into the air. Suddenly, "BOOM!" A lightning bolt exploded from Gig's right hand, snapping and cracking as the screen behind them darkened into storm clouds. The bolt shot into the sky, splintering into a hundred smaller bolts, seeming to strike one of the four moons above.

The sound of the lightning reverberated throughout the Seven Moons Amphitheater, the Bay of Alloo, and Two Dunes Harbor, illuminating the Isthmus between the Tunimbria Sea and the Nallawalla Ocean in a breathtaking display. As they hovered ten to fifteen feet in the air, Gig and Fem' bowed gracefully, their voices ringing out, "Thank you. We love you!"

The crowd fell silent, the thick in the air, before erupting into cheers, whistles, and thunderous applause, their feet stomping in unison.

From the balcony where Alex, V, Declan, and Miko had been just an hour before, the view was spectacular—a show for the ages.

No one had known until now what Gig and Fem's Gifts were. No Student had ever thought to ask. Fem's Gift, like Swaraj's, was the power of levitation, but Gig's—Gig's Gift was something extraordinary. He wielded the power of lightning—fantastic, awe-inspiring lightning! Who could have imagined it?

Back on stage, the Students gently descended from their CMB. Ty'mmie' and J.T., along with their band, prepared to play the next set.

Declan and Alex found a quiet spot to grab a drink. "I didn't see it, but I felt it. That was crazy," Declan exclaimed, still awestruck.

Alex laughed, shaking his head. "Yes, it was. We've got to watch the replay with Lin tomorrow. What's next?" Guzzling his drink, Declan replied, "We'll watch Ty'mmie's band, go onstage again, and then head up to the VIP box. That's it."

Alex took a deep swig of his drink. "Alright then. What's her tune about?" Declan smirked, surprised by Alex's ignorance. "You don't know this?" Alex looked at him, confused. "No, I don't." Gesturing to the bartender, Declan ordered more drinks. "It's the number one tune on the planet. She's from Teraenti, he's from Vindor—they're in a relationship, in love. You know, a forbidden relationship, given they're from different planets. And, well, they're having sex."

Alex nodded, understanding dawning. "Ah, now I get it." Declan chuckled, "Yep, that's why it's so popular. They wrote the tune, started a band, and all this hoopla started. They weren't supposed to be together because of the planetary divide, but love doesn't care about rules. She sneaks out of her window, catches a ride with the construction workers while they're finishing the amphitheater, meets Jonny on the beach, and they fall in love. Her mom finds out, forbids her from seeing him, but she dates Jonny anyway. It's a love tune—intense, raw. Klinchme' even played it at the university not too long ago."

Declan shook his head, "Can't believe you've never heard this story before."

Alex laughed, "I remember J.T. from the bar, right?" Declan nodded, "Yeah, that's him. And our Ty'mmie', Klinchme's niece. Crazy, right?"

A few minutes later, V, Lin, and Miko found Alex and Declan.

Lin, eyes narrowing in curiosity, asked, "What are you two doing here?" Declan, lifting his glass, replied, "Enjoying some drinks. This bartender here is taking good care of us."

Lin glanced at the man behind the bar, a knowing smile on her lips. "He's not a bartender. He's one of the producers. Hi, Arlo."

Arlo, from CAT 3 smiled warmly, his demeanor unruffled. Alex and Declan exchanged amused looks before Arlo grinned once more. "I just thought it would be fun to hang out with Alex and Declan for a while."

Declan, raising an eyebrow, inquired, "Why didn't you say something earlier?" Arlo simply shrugged; his nonchalance evident.

V interjected, "We should go watch Ty'mmie's band."

Alex, curious, turned to her, "Did you know what her tune was about?" V looked surprised. "Why, you didn't?" Alex rose from his seat. "No, I didn't. Nice to meet you, Arlo."

A new **"Song"** began. *Sausalito Summernight*

They all made their way to the front of the stage, settling down as Jonny and Ty'mmie' took the stage, her voice ringing out with the boys backing her up. The crowd erupted into a frenzy, particularly the girls in the front, who seemed to be smitten with Jonny, a heartthrob of sorts. As Alex started to listen to the tune, an unsettling sensation overcame him. Suddenly, he blacked out.

V, noticing the excitement among the girls, nudged Alex to share in the moment, but as she glanced at him, she saw him slumped to the side in his seat. Alex was caught in something—a Time Loop or perhaps something far stranger.

Alarmed, V turned to Declan, who sat on the other side of Alex, and exclaimed, "Declan, something's wrong with Alex!"

Declan quickly straightened Alex up in his seat, but Alex's gaze remained distant, his eyes glossy, his mouth slightly agape.

V shouted, "Is he breathing?" Declan, checking his pulse and breathing, reassured her, "Yeah, he's okay. I think he might be seeing something, maybe into the future?"

Lin, glancing at the stage where she was needed soon, asked, "Do you want me to tell Gig? He's right over there." V nodded, concern etched on her face. "Yeah, okay. How much time do we have before we need to go on stage?" Lin looked up at Ty'mmie' singing, calculating. "We go on after this tune."

V, staring at Alex with growing frustration, muttered, "What a time for him to do this." She turned to Lin, "Did you play this tune on the first Friday night at the university?"

"I think I remember it, after the whole hot tub thing." Lin shook her head, "I didn't play it, but that's Klinchme's brother's daughter up there singing right now. So maybe she played it that night." Lin then added, "I'll get Gig."

Seconds later, Gig arrived, concern in his eyes. "What's wrong with Alex?"

V gestured towards Alex. "We don't know. Look at him—he's in some kind of trance or something."

Gig placed a hand on Alex, trying to assess the situation. "I have no idea what this is."

Just then, Fem' approached her expression grave. "Should we move him? I can get a stretcher, and we can take him to one of the band rooms." Meanwhile, the crowd behind them roared with excitement, the noise overwhelming.

Fem' quickly left and returned with a couple of men carrying a stretcher. They carefully lifted Alex and moved him to a room near the stage, with V, Miko, Declan, Gig, and Fem' following closely. A minute later, a doctor arrived to check Alex's vital signs. After a thorough examination, he said, "He's okay. Everything's fine, but I can't explain what's wrong with him."

Lin entered the room, her face tense. "We have a couple minutes until we all need to be on stage."

Declan, downing his beer in frustration, muttered, "This is insane. He's never done this before. V, do you remember anything like this happening? Even when the relatives from the Creator visited?"

V, her worry deepening, shook her head. "No, no way. This is something new." She began shaking Alex, shouting his name, "Alex, Alex, wake up! Wake up, you asshole!"

Declan lifted Alex's arm, only to watch it drop limply back down. "Jesus. What are we going to do?"

Suddenly, Alex stirred. "Do about what?"

V, her relief turning to anger, snapped, "You asshole! What happened?"

Alex, still disoriented, looked around. "How did I get here?"

V's voice was edged with frustration. "No, no, what happened to you?"

Alex, still trying to piece things together, looked at Declan, then V, and finally Gig. In a dazed, almost drunken state, he slurred, "Hey guys, what's up?"

V pressed him again, "No, no. You need to tell us what happened."

Alex, slowly coming out of it, rubbed his eyes and said, "I—I was at a ceremony." He rubbed his eyes even harder. "How long was I out?"

V, still anxious, replied, "A long time, we need to go on stage. What happened?"

Gig, intrigued, asked, "This ceremony—what were we doing?"

Alex, his memory clearing, answered, "You and Fem' were putting ribbons on V and me, but the other Students and V were wearing robes. I was feeling really good. Then alarms went off, and we all rushed to the lab. We saw this huge ship coming towards our solar system."

V, her eyes wide, exclaimed, "What? A spaceship?"

Declan, incredulous, added, "Dude, that's crazy."

Gig, more focused, asked, "Were the robes yellow and blue?" Alex nodded. "Yeah."

Gig's expression darkened. "That's graduation. You were seeing the day you all graduate. What else did you see?" Alex continued, "Fem' was saying a prayer on Amotaious, then some of us were on different ships I've never seen before—it was V, me, Declan, Miko, and a few others. We were on the ships bridge., and there were other ships out there, not just one. Now there were ten. No, there was our 12 and six of the others that all looked the same." His eyes shifted to Gig, "Who's ships are they?"

Declan leaned in, "How big was the ship?" Alex, sitting back, responded, "Huge—many times bigger than our aircraft carriers."

Gig, his tone serious, stated, "We need to tell the other Master Elders about this. It gives us a timeline for the battle." Everyone stared at him, realization dawning.

Alex, confused, asked, "What battle?"

Lin hurried back, her urgency palpable. "Oh, good, you're back. We need to get on stage now."

Everyone turned to face her. She met their gazes with insistence. "Now, people! Ninety thousand eager faces are out there waiting to see you. Let's go!" She began pulling them along, spurring them into action. Alex and the others scrambled to reach the stage, the weight of the moment sinking in.

As they moved, Alex turned to Gig, his voice laced with urgency. "Gig, what's this about a battle?" Gig replied with a grave expression, "The Creator has commanded every planet to build two battleships."

Alex's eyes widened in shock. "What? And you're just telling me this now? Why? What's it for?"

They reached the stage, and the others were already beckoning Alex to join them, their impatience growing. Gig, pushing Alex forward, tried to explain, "The Creator ordered each planet to construct two Galactic Warships."

Alex demanded, "Why? Who is coming?"

The calls from the stage grew louder, urging Alex to take his place. Gig, giving Alex one final push, whispered, "The Creator's sister is coming."

Alex stepped out onto the stage, his mind reeling. He looked out over the sea of ninety thousand spectators from six different planets. "The Creator's sister?" he murmured in disbelief.

Turning to V, he repeated, "The Creator's sister?"

V, already moving into position, responded with a command, "Raise your hand and wave! Smile!"

Alex complied, raising his hand and forcing a smile. Yet, his mind raced with frantic thoughts. *We're going to war against the Creator's sister. What the hell? I need to start planning. Who will volunteer? What kind of fuel do the ships use? Who will captain them? How many soldiers will I need? How many ships does she have?*

V, noticing his distraction, nudged him sharply. "Alex, pay attention. Keep waving to the crowd."

Alex refocused, his gaze sweeping across the multitude before him—the people of Amotaious, the inhabitants of six different planets, the entire galaxy.

V, her thoughts mirroring Alex's, felt a chill of realization. *What's wrong with him? He's acting crazy. Wait, what? A war with the Creator's sister? Oh no, this is just the beginning.*

Alex's internal monologue surged with a mix of fear and determination. *Jesus! We're going to war with the Creator's sister. She must be from a different galaxy. Look at all these people— they have no idea. What about the people on the planets? V and I need to save them. This is going to happen in four years. Four years? We need to start preparing now! Now! Can you hear me, Creator? Now!*

The "Songs" End!...... *Meet Her!*

Amotaious

-

"Home Planet to the Elders of 6 planets"

Amotaious is the seventh planet in the galaxy. It is home to all the Master Elders and Elders, from all six planets. The population is just under 100,000.

Amotaious has seven moons. It is 1.9 times the size of Terraenti. It is a Terrestrial planet along with two others in its solar system. There are also three non-terrestrial, Jovian planets. A climate that could be compared to the Jurassic period. Most of the cities are located far away from the active volcanism. Tunimbria is located near a large delta. Near the sea of Tunimbria. The buildings are made of stone and timber. There is very little steel forged. The two main buildings are referred to as the Castle or what the other planets call the Master Elders Council Building, Rah Shalah! The second is Terraenti's building called the Alcazar. That's where all the housing is for people from Terraenti.

From there you work your way down the coast to the Bay of Alloo. Where Two Dunes Harbor is. And the new Seven Moons Amphitheater. It can hold almost the whole population of Amotaious. Beyond that is the Nallawalla Ocean separated by Two Dunes Isthmus. If you head towards the mountains you will find the resort at Ore Gle Villa Ski Area.

Past it, up over the mountains over the Pinchers Peaks at the elevation of 79,000. Then you can travel down to a quarry, where you will find Millipillar Valley. That's where they cut all the stones and timbers using the Common Mind and the Organic Sonic Frequencies. Otherwise known as HCRD. Harmonic, Cutting, Rounding and Drilling.

Amotaious's community uses its natural resources to power the city. All the population contributes making it self-sustaining. No outside resources are necessary. Very similar to the University. It's a beautiful place to live. Even though people are from six different planets everyone gets along very well.

Until recently childbirth was limited to one per Elder couple. Not by choice or Law. It's just the way it was. In the last couple centuries, things have changed. Some think the Creator has gotten involved. Influencing procreation through the Common Mind. Newly married couples are now having three to four kids.

In recent years there has also been a rise in youth from different planets dating and having sexual relationships. Although no children have been born yet? The Master Elders have been up in arms about this and there have been several Master Elder Council Meetings about the subject. This could be a problem since there is a slight difference in their biology.

Stewards

-

The Elder Stewards were brought and initiated on September 5, 2032. A year before the Elder Students were brought and initiated into the university. They went to classes, just like the Students. Gig, Fem, and others taught them the ways of the Elders. Received the Common Mind. Learned about the six planets. About the Master Elders. About all of it. As you read you know that they too have become a family. Some are very close to one another. The Stewards are only Gifted with the Common Mind. They spent a lot of time studying the Students before they arrived at the university. All the Stewards do not have many family ties. Most do not have children, if they do, they are raised now. If they were married, they would be divorced now. Or have never been married. The Stewards are very attached to their Students and would do pretty much anything for them. All Stewards have Eagle marks, right below their necks. Signifying that they are Elder Stewards of CAT 6. If you look closely the Eagle marks on V's neck are different than the one on Freida's neck.

Alex Steward, Harvey Goldmen. He is an American that lived in Australia for the last twenty years. He is a retired lawyer and businessman who used to work in the entertainment business for the Australian Communications Network. He's been married twice. And doesn't have any children. Everyone is pretty sure he has been in love with V's Steward Freida, since before the Students arrived. Harvey is originally from New York but moved to California after college and then to Australia in his early thirties. He is 63 now. 5' 8". He is white. Has dark brown wavy hair. Likes to wear casual 80's 90's mild not flashy plaid-type suits. He is the kind of guy you would want to sit and have a drink with. Super smart, one to get advice from. And he loves Alex.

V's Steward, Freida Azmij. Is from India. She is very intelligent. Has had many jobs. Her last one was as a personal assistant to a politician in the Indian Government. The guy was an ass. But she did a fantastic job for him. She ran around and managed all his tasks. She is organized and keeps her life well-maintained as well. She is very pretty. Strong-willed, and speaks very good English. She has light skin for an Indian woman. Dark hair. Light brown eyes. 5' 6" tall. She likes to wear very flashy apparel when she is out on the town. She is in her late 50's. Has a great personality, likes to drink martinis, and is a joy to be with. She became close to Kira where she learned to throw knives and learned some combat skills. V has several times called her, her wise sister. Evidently, she has a big collection of porcelain Beatles figurines. Her favorite tune is Paperback Writer so?

Declan's Steward, Hugh Hardy. Hugh is an ex-military man from England. He is very well-built. Very well disciplined. Has many skills in Combat Techniques. And Firearms. Carries himself very well. He has an okay personality. Maybe not one you would want to be confined within a small space for too long. He has tanned skin. Crew cut, brown hair. 6', 4" tall. With his English accent, I guess he is attractive in a certain kind of way. Kira thinks so anyway. They have become quite the item, lately. He likes to wear jeans and a T-shirt when relaxing. When going out, we've seen him in a nice, blue silk suit with alligator boots, and a Skinny Tie. Some say he is like Roman, but Alex doesn't think that.

Miko's Steward, Kira Toda. Has been trained in several disciplines of martial arts, from Japan. She is 5', 5" tall, with black hair. When in class she dresses very casually. Jeans, with a flavored T-shirt. Hoody and tennis shoes. The few times that she has been out at night she shines. Very attractive. She doesn't skimp on the costs of her dresses, let's just say that. She worked in America for the last 15 years at the Japanese Consulate in Washington DC. At one point she was in charge of all travel and part of the diplomats' security. Miko is really glad she is here. She has a relaxed personality. A mellow, quiet person. She has a law degree. And is often seen swimming with V in the pool in the mornings. She became good friends with Freida and is seeing Hugh. Never been married, no children.

Prezzy Steward, Beauta Fowler. Beauta has lived in Australia all her life. She is from Canberra. She was a political investigative reporter. Who, once in a while would appear on the Telly. She has a law degree. Is 5', 9" tall. Blonde, with blue eyes. Her name was coined The Beautiful Flower. Built very well. She has a strong personality. Great fun to be with. She likes to party. Drinks Expresso Martini's. And Vodka shots. She does surf, but not as much as Prezzy. On the second day of the interview with Prezzy, it was on a surfboard. She is in her mid-50s and loves to dance. She dresses in colorful casual dresses in classes and business-type attire at night when out to dinner.

Lin's Steward, Keira Clarke. She has a thin face, a long nose. Full British accent. Attractive. Tall, 6 feet. Blonde hair, green eyes. Dresses in business attire in class. Very nice gown-type outfits. When out on the town. She has the full British thing going on. She's lived in the south of England her whole life. She has had a private education and full credits from Oxford. She is strict and to the point with the Students. There is a rumor that Keira and Roman have something going on, which is a very remarkable combination. V and Alex think it's great.

Lev's Steward, Roman Taktarov. Roman is a TANK! If there is a battle. Thank God Roman will be there to lead them. He is a brutal teacher. He is impatient. Not subtle at all. But he gets it done. He has had his military training in Russia. Lived his life in Russia. He's retired from the military. Can kill you in 2 seconds, like in three or four different ways. 6', 4". Has a red face. Crew cut. Built like the Terminator. Dresses still like he is in the military. When he goes out, he looks awkward in a polyester suit. For some reason, Keira and him have something going on which most people think is unusual. He has a collection of knives that he polishes in his cabin on the ship, or room.

Maria's Steward, Darya Shutova. Surprisingly, the opposite of Roman and Maria and Lev. Darya is very Petite. A small, little nice Russian woman. She is a professor from Saint Petersburg. She taught Microbiology. Maria was in her class for a day early on in college. But never came back after one day. She helped in the design of the A3MB Cannon Bolide. That goes in the Cannons on the Tithon and the Mantis that are the Galactic Battleships being prepared on Amotaious. That Bolide shell melts and destroys any material made out of anything. Even a ship that is biological. At 5', 3". She is the quietest Steward out of all of them. Has a great personality. Has a deep passion for the planet and is devoted to helping to get all the missions completed. Alex and V love to sit, drink with her and chat. Everyone was surprised when she helped develop the weapons.

Swaraj Steward, Sanjay Babu. Sanjay was so intrigued when he arrived at the university with the Elders and the Common Mind because he had been studying Meditation and Hypnotherapy for 30 years. Sanjay is a very mellow guy. He is very intelligent. Grew up in India. Studied in America and India. Single. No children. Tall, looks like he could be V's father's brother. He's balding, in his late fifties, wearing a pleasure suit most of the time, 6 foot tall. Beard and mustache. Smart looking. Speaks very good English. Has an affinity for young girl rock bands. From times past. Loves Martinis like Freida. He is the nicest person. Alex and V think so. Everyone adored him after he helped and handle Swaraj through his troubles. Especially when Kyoryk and Swaraj got together after the kids were born.

Kyoryk's Steward, Hiro Oguri. Hiro was in the Japanese military and has been flying commercial airliners for the last 10 years. He is a very sexy-looking man. He had been involved in their space program. Or at least tried to get into it. He had a mild case of Limb Girdle, Muscular Dystrophy, before he got to the university. The Creator fixed that once he received the Common Mind. Hiro is the guy who organizes all the board games and the nights on the town. Along with Tonari's Steward Amand. Or could it be Vitor? The two or three of them seem to be an item as well. Everyone is still trying to figure it all out.

Candido's Steward, Vitor Aldo. He is a mystery. Keeps to himself. Very intelligent. Speaks many different languages. Some say he is a CIA-type guy but from Latin America. He keeps his I on Candido and takes care of him. Vito is very Spanish-looking. Very attractive. 5', 9", wavy dark hair. Beard, and mustache. Always dressed to impress. Rico Suave-type guy. Candido once said he had a concealed weapon on him. You know, one of those leather things that wraps around your body under your suit jacket to hold a gun. Declan was drilling him about it. But Candido didn't want to talk about it anymore. He has a collection of old spiritual Spanish art in his room. He seems like a nice guy. Alex and V thought. Once, someone saw him going into Hiro's room late one night.

Tonari's Steward, Amand Vanzantg. Like Tonari. She is the most attractive of all the Stewards. Super intelligent. She has several master's in psychology. She has one in Applied Behavior Analysis (ABA) and one in Master of Arts in Psychology. (MAP) Believe it or not, she also, in her younger years was Miss Brazil. At the same time, she keeps her eye on Tonari. She helps Rev and Mod with the Analysis of the group on their mental health. She has auburn hair. Beautiful brown skin. Brown eyes. 5', 7". Dresses in colorful attire. In her room and once in a while at breakfast will wear sweats. As I said, she is very attractive and seems to have a relationship going on with Hiro, Kyoryk's Steward.

Like I said Hiro is a mystery. The last three have something going on. Something may be revealed after we meet the Creator's Sister.

Alexander Cooper Katz

- DOB: December 12, 2012

- Height: 6.2

- Weight: 187

- Hair Color: Brown, Short

- Eye Color: Blue

- Distinguishing Marks: Missing three right hand, pinky, ring, middle, and tip of his index of fingers. Has a scar above his left eye

- Address: Darwin, Coolalinga, Australia

- Selected University: MIT, Massachusetts, USA

- Major: Design Engineering and Business

- Gifts: Common Mind. See into the Future. Contacting the Creator.

- Job Description: Student. Machinist. Welder. Auto Mechanic. Inventor.

- Strengths and Weaknesses: Self-driven. Wants the best for everyone and everything. Constantly second-guessing himself. Cares too much maybe?

- Passions: Dreams of a free world, a peaceful world. Loves music. Listens to it constantly. Uses is as a form of meditation. To getting his jobs done. Has tried to play Guitar and Piano but not successfully.

- Interests: Desert Racing in the Northern Territory. Building engines. Working with 3D printing machines. Finds the human past fascinating. Has been investigating the pyramids and Puma Punku for many years.

- Parents: Father, Max Katz. Mother, Ella Katz. Skip Kats, his uncle. His name is Cooper. They called him the "Cooper" originally. Then it switched to "Cap" or the "Captain". Then or now, it's just "Skip". Alex's middle name is Cooper. That name goes way back. His, Alex's great. Great grandfather, his name was Cooper. He apparently escaped prison and lived off the land, met a woman and brought her back out to his camp, and lived out the rest of his life in 1860's,

- Parent Occupations: Own and Operate WNM Engineering and Design Firm

- Siblings: Audry, 15, Blonde/brown hair, blue eyes, loves music too. Brother Max Jr. died at the age of 25 from a guy who assaulted him and Mellisa when they were in the outback camping. By the time Mellisa was able to get help, Max Jr. his brother was dead. 2 years later Alex found the guy camping near the area where his brother was camping and got into it with the guy. Alex and the man fought by the river.

When it was over the man lost his life and Alex left with his fingers missing. His father found out and told him about it the day he left for university. Mellisa, Max Jr.'s fiancé, returned to the family almost three years later with a little surprise.

- Accomplishments: Speed Record in the flats of NT 220 mph, 4-cylinder division, 3 patents for General Motors - Cadillac division. Made modifications to 3D printers to accept multi-color base materials, Made and designed a three-finger mechanical prosthetic for himself that one him an award and also a patent with a company in France and the U.S.A. Alex worked with a prosthetics company and has won an award for excellence in a 3D design on his finger prosthetic design of his metallic fingers, they are used worldwide with people who have lost finger do to machine shop accidents.

- Additional Notes: Alex lost his three right-hand fingers while fighting the guy with a knife, not to a gator. He left his brother's killer in an old half-submerged hand-made canoe to die by the gators in a revenge move. Alex then went back to his father's machine shop business and claimed that his hand was damaged by one of the machines. Alex took it upon himself to find and kill his brother's killer. He just didn't explain the whole thing to V. Luckily he is left-handed.

Vibrean Padame Aboli, AKA V

- DOB: December 12, 2012, 12:12am

- Height: 5.7

- Weight: 120

- Hair Color: Brown, reddish when the sun hits it.

- Eye Color: Light Crystal Green

- Distinguishing Marks: Mole above her right eye

- Address: Bhubaneswar, India

- Selected University: Master's degree at the Institute of Science, India

- Major: already has a bachelor's degree from a local college, Biological, Chemical, Biological Sciences, and project lead

- Gifts: Common Mind. Mind Reading. Contacting the Creator

- Job Description: Student. Side work for the Intelligence Bureau over the previous six years before the EU.

- Strengths and Weaknesses: Physically fit, a swimmer, a runner, thinker, she curses in Hindi when she gets mad. Once she is set on a goal, she is very confident and true. Doesn't waver like an Oak Arrow. Once she is set on a goal she is set, so, get out of her way. She doesn't worry about the little things like cleaning her room, being completely orginized like that.

- Personality Traits: kind of a loner, and keeps things to herself until she knows it's true and 100%. Her parents think she is a psychological mess, but that's furthest from the truth, it's because she is strong-willed, set in her ways. She knows what she wants. She can be outgoing and aggressive. With no nuts on her Ice cream or fudge...

- Passions: Succeeding in all she does. Taking care of her sister.

- Interests: Playing board games with friends, likes Velvet mint chocolate chip, Root Beer. She likes the beach. Hasn't really spent that much time out until the university.

- Parents: Grandmother - Saanvi died two years ago; V was very close to her; she was the role model, not her parents. Dad is Anil Aboli. Mom is Aishwarya Aboli

- Parent Occupations: Dad is a Criminal psychologist for the Intelligence Bureau. Mom is a Psychotherapist for the Intelligence Bureau.

- Siblings: Sister, Saanvi, 16. She is Bipolar, with some speech problems,

- Accomplishments: Previous training at the Intelligence Bureau, her parents wanted her to be an Undercover Operative for a High School or a community-type college. She won an award at the I.B. for the youngest person to pass the I.B. of India intelligence integration test when she was 20.

- Notes: V was trained starting at the age of fifteen to work at the Intelligence Bureau. She attended two years of summer classes only offered to preferred students through her parents at the Bureau, which included; weapons training, combat, driving, interrogation, deception, and false identities. Of which she was top of her class. After her B.S. degree, her parents were sure she would join but V had other plans. She wanted to get away from them and seek other opportunities. She had a big interest in saving other parts of the world mainly the environment.

V took it upon herself to find and kill her grandmother. Her grandmother was in an altercation at a jewelry store and was injured and later died. V later found the killer, locked him in a room, and tortured him to death. Out of everyone in the group V is the most vicious of all of them, as of yet. No one knows but the Creator. The Stewards and the Master Elders know that the killer is dead, they just don't know how. They found seveal pieces of his body burnt to a crisp, in the trunk of his car, weeks later. She has yet to tell anyone.

Declan Kyle Koile

- DOB: December 12, 2012
- Height: 6' 1"
- Weight: 190
- Hair Color: Reddish/brown
- Eye Color: blue
- Distinguishing Marks: Scar above his left cheek, near to his ear. Scar at his waistline.
- Address: Bristol, England; originally from Edinburgh, he moved when he was 4.
- Selected University: Cal Arts, Valencia, CA. USA
- Major: Acting, and the Arts, Comedy
- Job Description: Bouncer / Bodyguard for underground and regular gambling establishments in Bristol. Student.
- Gifts: Common Mind. Can move objects, a form of attraction and detraction.
- Strengths and Weaknesses: Physically fit, Funny personality. A Joker. Uses humor to hide his emotions. Very outgoing. Self-driven. Can't focus.

  Has trouble focusing on one thing at a time. He is getting better. Loves Movies. Around the time his dad died, he would have high fevers and hallucinate. Declan is a free spirit. Known to tell white lies.
- Passions: Loves movies and music. Boxing, Making friends with everyone. Loves women.
- Interests: Mother, physical fitness. Has practiced self-meditation. Smokes Marijana and vapes. Loves to party. Been in many situations, has many stories to tell.
- Parents: Mother is Rose, Father David passed at the age of 12, Ewan.
- Parent Occupations: Father was a boxer and gym owner from Scotland. Mother was also from Scotland. She is a professional gambler and owns and runs some legal and illegal gambling places. They all lived in Scotland up until the death of his father then his mother and he moved to Bristol.
- Siblings: None.
- Accomplishments: B.S. Degree Local College did some plumbing work.
- Notes: Declan and his mother came into her office one Sunday morning at her club when a guy was breaking into the safe. Declan chased the guy to the adjacent building, and he fell to his death. It was ruled an accident by the police. Declan was stabbed twice once in

the waist and once by his left cheek below his ear. Declan is one of the within the group that doesn't feel bad at all about what happened in his situation. He has much to tell about his father. Someday he might just say.

Miko Machenyu Jonetsu

- DOB: December 12, 2012

- Height: 5.4

- Weight: 107

- Hair Color: Black

- Eye Color: Brown

- Distinguishing Marks: Red birthmark in a disclosed area.

- Address: Tosa, Kochi, Japan

- Selected University: Cambridge U.K.

- Major: Environmental Sciences

- Job Description: Student

- Strengths and Weaknesses: Somewhat shy, tries not to stand out, self-conscious, had a boyfriend, but once she feels comfortable she is no longer shy. Bi-Sexual, leaning towards the male. Physically fit, she has some training in Martial Arts. Miko trained up to an orange belt in Karate. She also excelled in her gymnast classes tremendously.

- Gifts: Common Mind. Can see through matter, walls up to two meters and more.

- Passions: Gymnast, parallel bars, Floor Routine.

- Interests: Understanding Weather, Volcanoes.

- Parents: Dad - Takashi, Mom - Anna

- Parent Occupations: Dad is a Specialist in the stock trade. Mom is a retired nurse from the U.S.

- Siblings: Yuki - 10, Hiro 13, Devon she's 16

- Accomplishments: She almost qualified for the Olympics, as a gymnast, but her parents wanted her to go to University. Her parents were all about school.

- Notes: In Miko's early years she lost her best friend. She was kidnapped and never found. This had a terrible impact on Miko's life for years. Some say still to this day.

- Just months before Eternal University Miko got to know some of the younger gymnasts found out that one of the older coaches was praying on some of the children. Rapping them. So, she took a hose out of the trunk of a car, stuck it in a tailpipe, put it in the back window, sealed up the rest of the windows, and started the car. This is after knocking the man unconscious. She left a suicide note on the dash of the car said some choice words to the man and walked away. And that was it for the man. It was that simple for Miko. She cared deeply for the kids that were going to take over for her when she left, and she didn't want that dirty man all over them. She took it upon herself to do something about it. Even though V and her were already friends V was really impressed by her actions and her bond with Miko became even stronger after she learned this.

Kyoryk Sho' Dragoon

- DOB: December 12, 2012
- Height:5.7
- Weight: 140
- Hair Color: dark
- Eye Color: Brown
- Distinguishing Marks: Scar under chin from Aikido practice
- Address: Kesennuma, Miyagi, Japan
- Selected University: Harvard
- Major: Law, Business
- Gifts: Common Mind. Gift of Knowledge.
- Job Description: Student. Pet Store Manager. Commercial Fisherman
- Strengths and Weaknesses: Shy, until he knows you then he's very open. Physically fit, Consider it Done kind of guy. Stuff from his past bugs him. Living up to his parent's expectations bothers him.
- Passions: Clean Ocean. Fishing. Farm Fishing from one side of his family.
- Interests: Martial Arts, living on the ocean.
- Parents: Dad - Toshiro, Mom - Rinko
- Parent Occupations: Dad - Neurosurgeon, Mom - Corporate Attorney
- Siblings: Sessue is 16, Miyoshi is 14,
- Accomplishments: Black belt in Aikido.
- Notes: Kyoryk had an altercation when he was on a train with his younger siblings. An addict, possible mentally ill guy was on the train with them. The guy got out of control, grabbed, picked up his younger sister, and started to take her down the car. To actually kidnap her. Kyoryk had to subdue him, and he passed out from the drugs, experience who knows. The police came. The ambulance gave him something, the man died and Kyoryk still feels somewhat responsible.

The police said that Kyoryk was not responsible yet; he still feels responsible. So, he is dealing with it.

Maria Anna Kalita

- DOB: December 12, 2012
- Height: 5'10"
- Weight: 130
- Hair Color: Black with Blonde streaks. Slight blue/purple at the bottom, barely visible.
- Eye Color: Blue
- Distinguishing Marks: Tattoos
- Address: Volkovskoye near Saint Petersburg
- Selected University: Technical University of Denmark
- Major: Design Engineering
- Gifts: Common Mind. Maria can stop time.
- Job Description: Student. Welder. Machinist.
- Weaknesses and Strengths: Outgoing, know how to program and work various fabricating machines. Bi-Sexual. Temperamental but very friendly, can be quick to make large decisions, Loyal. Can be quick to be judgmental.
- Passions: Keeping physically fit,
- Interests: Works with weights. Has been involved in various groups. Liberal-type things. While at university, she was very involved and got in trouble, almost violently, a couple of times. During demonstrations.
- Parents: Anna - Mom died when she was four. Her mother was said to be very educated and of Royal blood, possibly in the government. She died of Cancer. There is a whole history behind her. Maria talks very little about her but has opened up to V once. Dmitriy Kalita - Dad is a compassionate man who raised her by himself, consumed with his work, speaking Russian; her dad looks to be around 60, with graying thinning hair, a slight mustache, and a goatee, over 6 feet, dressed nicely. He appears to be a very relaxed, layback kind of man.
- Parent Occupations: Machinist, Inventor, Space Station parts for water purifiers. Toilet vacuum parts.
- Siblings: None
- Accomplishments: Awards when younger for science and applications, mainly with electricity

- Notes: Maria was mostly involved with her dad's work, but when she was in college, she was involved in many liberal movements. Some of her friends were into drugs, and one was a drug dealer. She was very close and in love with her. She sold ecstasy and died from one of the pills she got from a certain drug dealer. One night, Maria took him out and gave him a high dose of amphetamines. Maria can be quite vindictive and smart. The guy was wired beyond belief. She took the guy out for the night on the town and a meal, then told him to come and look at the stars, then injected him with an animal tranquilizer so he could not move. Then proceeded to show him what her girlfriend's death might have looked like. He sat there dying in his car. Maria figures the case is closed, and all is square with the world. Maria followed the case; police found the body in the car and ruled it a drug or gang case. No further response from anyone has ever followed Maria up on it. Maria was not really into drugs. She has always been a lover until she is betrayed. She takes care of people. She never knew her mother, but she knows all about her through her father and reading about her through their extensive library. On her mother's side of the family, there are politicians and royalty.

Swaraj Aran Priyanka

- DOB: December 12, 2012
- Height: 6' 1"
- Weight: 195
- Hair Color: Black
- Eye Color: Brown
- Distinguishing Marks: Birthmark on his right butt cheek in the shape of a heart.
- Address: Lives near the Forest of Andaman, India
- Selected University: University of California, San Fransisco,
- Major: Neurosurgery.
- Gifts: Common Mind. Antigravity.
- Job Description: Student. Forest Management Trainee
- Strengths and Weaknesses: Quiet, well-balanced, likes to correct others when he was getting his B.S. degree, but has gotten past it now.
- Personality Traits: He likes to wear make-up and dress like a woman.
- Passions: Very passionate. Loves everyone. Loves people and the planet. Wants everyone to be happy. Bisexual. More towards gay. Cares deeply about the planet.
- Interests: Loves the forests. Loves animals and how things grow to fruition. A mature guy...
- Parents: Mother is Deepika. Father is Kanul, and they are very religious.
- Parent Occupations: Mom is an Attorney, and Father is a Cardiothoracic Surgeon.
- Siblings: All younger. Karan, she is 4. Ajay he is 7, Shabana she is 10. Nina is 13.
- Accomplishments: He won an award for planting the most trees in his year during his college years with Forest Management at the Forest of Andaman.
- Notes: During his first years at the Eternal University, he hid the fact that he was Bisexual. And that he liked to dress up in women's clothing. Maria, V, and eventually Alex and then Kyoryk helped him transition into his true self.

- When he was just graduating from his first years of college, Swaraj, along with a friend, took it upon themselves to track down and kill two murderers. What happened was, after a party one night at a gay bar, two of Swaraj's friends were assaulted severely by two racists. One later died. Swaraj and his friend found out who did it, made a plan, and waited patiently. Months and months went by. Waiting for the right opportunity. Swaraj and his friend had planned it out perfectly so as not to get caught and to make sure it looked like an accident. V thought it was the best-planned assault out of all that she had seen so far. She also wanted to help Swaraj with his dilemma of coming out to people about his sexuality. She thought that Swaraj was a very thoughtful and delicate man.

Prezzy Elizabeth Bondi

- DOB: December 12, 2012
- Height: 5.8
- Weight: 126
- Hair Color: Bleach Blonde
- Eye Color: Blue
- Distinguishing Marks: Scar on the forehead from surfing.
- Address: Barrack Heights. New South Wales, Australia
- Selected University: Masters at University Santa Barbara, USA
- Major: Environmental Sciences.
- Gifts: Common Mind. Invisibility.
- Job Description: Student. Waitress.
- Strengths and Weaknesses: Professional Surfer. Physical Fit. Self-Driven. Very outgoing. She could be a little too lively. Too bubbly, possibly annoying at times?
- Passions: Surfing. The environment. Helping others. Helping her parents run the business.
- Parents: Dad - Benjamin, Mom - Naomi
- Parent Occupations: Own and Operate a chain of restaurants called Sangers and Grog between Melbourne and Brisbane.
- Siblings: Older brothers Owen, 27, and James, 24.
- Accomplishments: She won two years of the Yeti Young Surfers Competition."
- Notes: Prezzy took it upon herself to kill a man. After learning that this man she had known all her life had been molesting and raping young girls and boys through a surfing program. She knew the man and had previously taken many trips with him out on the ocean before. So, she used the opportunity to inject a syringe full of Box Jellyfish into the man and then wait for him to have a heart attack before bringing him into the harbor.

She had all the proof and was one hundred percent sure that this man was guilty of his crimes. He was high up in the community, and she was sure that he would never stand trial if he ever got close to it.

Lev Viktor Yaroslav

- DOB: December 12, 2012

- Height: 6' 5"

- Weight: 239

- Hair Color: Brown,

- Eye Color: Brown

- Distinguishing Marks: Mole off the center of the face just above his eyebrows

- Address: Rostov, near Saint Petersburg, Russia

- Selected University: Harvard

- Major: Business Law

- Gifts: Common Mind. Electricity Control, not sure yet.

- Job Description: Student. Tailor shop manager.

- Strengths and Weaknesses: Slightly Social, Outgoing. Daily fitness program. A little shy, possibly. Ready to fight.

- Passions: Dressing well, clean cut, well-mannered

- Interests: Father and Grandfather business, being a professional Tailor. Running a business. Wasn't sure, really. He liked guns, went shooting with his brothers a couple of times, and watched historical videos on Russian History. Just went out drinking with them a couple of times.

- Parents: Dad - Viktor. Grandfather - Igor. Mother - Katerina

- Parent Occupations: Fourth Generation, Own and operate 5 Tailor shops around Saint Petersburg, Russia

- Siblings: 2 younger brothers, Aleksandr 12. Eduard 14. He had an older brother Boris. He was killed when Lev was 18.

- Accomplishments: Men's Fashion Design Award. An Award for Excellence in Military school in the summer, when he wasn't in college.

- Notes: Unfortunately, when Lev was 16, his grandfather confronted him with a family tradition that goes back many, many generations. To keep the peace with another family he has to kill a kid from another family. He refuses. Then he finds out that this kid killed his brother and Lev takes a knife and kills the kid.

Lev is 21 now. Pretty sure this has had an impact on his life. To keep the peace this happens every sixty to seventy years. Before this happened in 1451 out of the 82 members of both families. 31 were left. So, I guess it's worth it. Or is it?

Linnea Adoline Adder

- DOB: December 12, 2012, 12:12am

- Height: 5' 7'

- Weight: 128

- Hair Color: Reddish Blondish

- Eye Color: Blue

- Distinguishing Marks: None

- Address: Southern Aberdeen, UK, Parents Homestead, near a kid's park. Selected University: The only Student that wasn't officially going to college for a master's degree

- Major: Lin had been invited to sing at a college and was considering going; she was interviewed by Keira Clarke, who got her to accept an invitation to see and possibly go to the University of Westminster; she accepted Keira's invitation and was on the way to University.

- Gifts: Common Mind. Gift of understanding languages.

- Job Description: Works on her parent's homestead. Entertainer, YourScreen income.

- Strengths and Weaknesses: In her top year, she made $100,000 on her YourScreen channel. She is Outgoing. Her Gift is speaking and understanding all languages. Lin is a little goofy, but not as much as Prezzy. Open to many things, smoke a little pot, magic mushrooms, kind of hippie-like thing going on if you can call them weaknesses.

- Passions: Singing, writing music, playing instruments, is the main party organizer of the group, very passionate about others and the world.

- Interests: Loves her parents. They built a self-sustainable homestead after the U.S. Black out of 2026. And she admires what and how they did it.

- Parents: Father, late 60s Sean Adder, family owned and operated barges and freighters up and down the coast of Scotland U.K. Mother 60 Yoa, Joanna, studied to be an actor, became interested in raising animals and working a farm.

- Parent Occupations: Owners of the Homestead raise their food and sell beef, chicken, pork, and eggs; quite a few other people live on the homestead as well.

- Siblings: Katie, age 26, lives and works on the homestead. Karen, age 30, works for her grandfather's business in shipping. Ewan, age 24, works on the homestead and goes to college. James 18, works on a homestead, just graduated from grade school.

- Accomplishments: Makes money off of YourScreen and sings at weddings and events. Lin is more accomplished than she makes people believe. She is very talented.

- Notes: In 2031 the family as it does sometimes take on people to help on the homestead. That summer her family had gotten itself into a bad situation with one of the people that they let stay there. The man had tried to take advantage of Katie and Lin. He was really, infatuated with her music and made several attempts to physically seduce her. This didn't sit well with her father so he had a friend of theirs look into the guy's past anonymously and found out that he was wanted for questioning for rape and other things. Ewan, Lin's brother ended up getting into it with the guy he pulled a knife and Lin hit him on the head with a steel hammer and he died. It was all sudden and Lin just reacted. It was after her brother was already severely hurt. She saved his life. They ended up shipping his body to another country. Her father did not want his body on the property. And told his other daughter Karen to ship his body to Africa to a steel recycling plant. Lin's mother to this day still does not know. V did not have to use her mind-reading to find this out. Lin confided in her prior to the concert celebration in 2034. Although Lin thinks about this once in a while. She doesn't feel guilty about it.

Candido Alonzo Vargas

- DOB: December 12, 2012
- Height: 5' 9"
- Weight: 145
- Hair Color: Dark Brown
- Eye Color: Brown
- Distinguishing Marks: None
- Address: Sao Paulo, Brazil
- Selected University: International Culinary Center, New York, N.Y.
- Major: Food Prep and Services.
- Job Description: Student
- Strengths and Weaknesses: Polite and courteous, dressed casually. Very religious.
- Personality Traits: Stubborn. He is a bull. Once he is locked in, look out.
- Gifts: Common Mind. Put his hands through matter. Eventually, he will be able to walk through walls.
- Passions: Poetry, Cooking.
- Interests: School. Singing. Playing the guitar.
- Parents: Morena, mother; Bruno, father
- Parent Occupations: Mother is a well-known Artist in Brazil; Father is an Actor.
- Siblings: Sister Giselle, age 16.
- Accomplishments:
- Notes: Candido is the opposite of his parents. They would have parties and be celebrating life. Candido, on the other hand, would be trying to figure out what life was about. At the same time, he played guitar and sang. He would read and study. So, there was a different dynamic between them. His little sister was more like his parents. It was good that he stayed with Tonari. They work well together. Later in the story, they become a force to recon with.

Tonari Blair Fermes

- DOB: December, 12, 2012
- Height: 5' 6"
- Weight: 106
- Hair Color: Brown
- Eye Color: Brown
- Distinguishing Marks: Tattoo of a ballerina on her left ankle. On her other ankle, she has a tattoo of a flower of Deadly Nightshade.
- Address: Natal, Brazil
- Selected University: Faculdade Santa Marcelina, Sao Paulo, Brazil, but was transferred to the USC Medical in California, USA
- Major: Medical, Biological
- Gifts: Common Mind. Multiplication of her body. Up to three.
- Job Description: Student, Actor
- Strengths and Weaknesses: Shy. She is okay once she feels familiar with people. Quiet and keeps to herself. She spends many days meditating in her garden. She is a mystery so far to the Stewards and Elders.
- Personality Traits: Involved in arts and arts in regular college.
- Passions: Acting, singing, dancing. She is not much of an actor because of her shyness. She can dance well.
- Interests: She has an awesome garden in her backyard, mostly flowers but some veggies.
- Parents: Mom is Marina. Dad is Rodrigo.
- Parent Occupations: Both work in government in Natal Brazil
- Siblings: All sisters, older, Alice is 32, Fernanda is 35, and Adriana is 37
- Accomplishments: B.S. Degree, majoring in acting, arts, and drama. She changed her direction and is now interested in medical and biological sciences.
- Notes: Tonari was a latecomer to her family's lives. Her sisters are all older and didn't pay much attention to her. Her parents had her by accident. They were already planning their retirement. So, she didn't get the attention that she deserved. She spent most of her time in school. And in her garden. She was closed in the first several months at the Eternal University. really take the reality of all that has happened to her here at the university until

just before graduation. Then, she explodes with excitement and joy. She finds a new life and joy with Candido.

All the amazing tunes are integral parts of the story. They also were instrumental in writing many parts of it.

"I dedicate this novel to the unwavering courage of those who face the daily trials of Muscular Dystrophy. Their indomitable spirit, enduring both physical and emotional pain, is a testament to human resilience. To my sister GG and to all who walk this path, your strength leaves an indelible mark upon this world. May your struggle and your endurance never be forgotten."

R. H. Burton

For rights and permissions, please contact:

R. H. Burton
Cotopaxi, Colorado USA

rhburton@eldersofedens.com

Even though it is a fascinating story about the planet and its past, planets, and the galaxy, it's fictional.

V, Alex, and the other Students have so much to look forward to in the continuation of Elders of Edens.

www.ingramcontent.com/pod-product-compliance
Lightning Source LLC
Chambersburg PA
CBHW081526120626
46550CB00009B/2633